Practicing Financial Planning
A Complete Guide for Professionals

SID MITTRA

Professor of Finance, Oakland University
and
Academic Director, Institute for Financial Education

Prentice Hall
Englewood Cliffs, New Jersey 07632

Library of Congress Cataloging-in-Publication Data

Mittra, Sid
    Practicing financial planning : a complete guide for professionals
    Sid Mittra.
        p.   cm.
    Includes bibliographical references.
    ISBN 0-13-491580-1
    1. Finance, Personal.   2. Investments.   I. Title.
HG179.M55   1990
332.024'0622--dc20   89-48294
                                                                  CIP

Editorial/production supervision
  and interior design: *Jacqueline A. Jeglinski*
Cover design: *Ben Santora*
Manufacturing buyer: *Kelly Behr*

 © 1990 by Prentice-Hall, Inc.
A division of Simon & Schuster
Englewood Cliffs, New Jersey 07632

The publisher offers discounts on this book when ordered
in bulk quantities. For more information, write:

> Special Sales/College Marketing
> Prentice-Hall, Inc.
> College Technical and Reference Division
> Englewood Cliffs, NJ 07632

This publication is designed to provide accurate and authoritative information in
regard to the subject matter covered. It is sold with the understanding that the
publisher is not engaged in rendering legal, accounting, or other professional
service. If legal advice or other expert assistance is required, the services of a
competent professional person should be sought.

Printed in the United States of America
10 9 8 7 6 5 4 3 2 1

ISBN 0-13-491580-1

Prentice-Hall International (UK) Limited, *London*
Prentice-Hall of Australia Pty. Limited, *Sydney*
Prentice-Hall Canada Inc., *Toronto*
Prentice-Hall Hispanoamericana, S.A., *Mexico*
Prentice-Hall of India Private Limited, *New Delhi*
Prentice-Hall of Japan, Inc., *Tokyo*
Simon & Schuster Asia Pte. Ltd., *Singapore*
Editora Prentice-Hall do Brasil, Ltda., *Rio de Janeiro*

For
Bani

Contents

PART II   Key Financial Planning Areas: R-E-T-I-R-E

LIFE INSURANCE PLANNING 92

CHAPTER 4 Health, Homeowner's, Automobile, and Liability Insurance: Structure, Concepts, and Planning   113

GENERAL PRINCIPLES 113

HEALTH INSURANCE 116

PROBLEM SOLVING WITH THE HP-12C CALCULATOR **178**

CHAPTER   6   Budgetary, Savings, Credit, and Debt Planning   **194**

NET WORTH AND CASH MANAGEMENT PLANNING **195**

SYSTEMATIC SAVINGS PLANNING **202**

PART III Putting It All Together

A Personal Message

Dear Reader:

The millennium is almost here. As we embark upon the decade of the 1990s, incredible events unfold, inviting reflection, warning, hope, fear, and both optimistic and ominous predictions. Observed and analyzed ceaselessly, the current events provide compelling reasons to believe that the new decade will be *different* from the one before.

Americans are evolving into a different people: older, more diverse, insecure due to foreign domination, and worried about living too long with inadequate financial support. We are also realizing that, in the 1990s, most baby boomers will approach their 40s. For the first time in history, three-quarters of all Americans will be of prime working age—24 to 55. And as the median age rises to 36 for the first time, reassessments and creations at a rapid pace will become the order of the day.

Of all the different types of revolutions we are likely to experience in the 1990s, perhaps none is of greater interest to Americans than the financial and economic revolution. Even more importantly, economic prospects for the 1990s remain highly controversial at best, and totally confusing at worst. At one extreme is the view that America is fast becoming a third-rate world power and is doomed to permanently become a mediocre nation. We owe the world $600 billion—and the amount keeps rising. The rate of growth of productivity is down to 1 percent, which ensures a stagnant gross national product. Superimpose on this bleak situation a massive budgetary problem, inadequate domestic savings, a decaying infrastructure, a failing educational system, a turbulent financial market, and a strained economic system, and we have a picture of doom and gloom.

At the other extreme are the optimists who reject the doomsayer's analysis. According to this group, by the year 2000, America's debt of $1 trillion will be less than 1 percent of the country's GNP of $12 trillion. The budget deficit, which in 1986 accounted for 5.2 percent of GNP, is likely to fall to less than 1 percent. A global *perestroika* and technological advancement will boost America's exports, thereby wiping out massive deficits in her balance of payments. The baby-boom generation, highly educated, sensitive to the global economic challenges, and with two decades of work experience, will reach peak productivity, which will help push the nation's productivity growth to the 3 percent level. In short, the next ten years will bring unparalleled prosperity for the U.S.

And that brings us to the main point: This massive confusion is the backdrop against which all Americans must make decisions regarding their financial future. Even without this confusing state of affairs, establishing and reaching a variety of financial goals is at best an onerous task. With so much uncertainty looming on the horizon, the majority of Americans believe they need external help and guidance in articulating and achieving their financial goals. However, because of the complex world in which we live, and also because of the multi-faceted needs of the American people, only the highly trained and experienced financial planners, who are committed to serve the public with dedication while maintaining the highest level of ethics and professionalism, can serve the financial planning needs of a changing nation.

This, then, is the backdrop against which *Practicing Financial Planning: A Complete Guide for Professionals* has been developed. It is not merely a collection of facts or a collage of practice-related ideas. Rather, my objective in writing this book is to educate the aspirants so they may take the *first* important step toward becoming a professional financial planner. Throughout the book important financial planning theories and concepts have been interwoven with practically-oriented planning strategies to emphasize the practice of comprehensive financial planning in a real world. I have also taken great care to ensure that the book encompasses the currently prevailing tax laws, theoretical developments, and state-of-the-art financial planning practices.

I should hasten to add that a book of this complexity and magnitude in an ever-changing financial world could not have been developed without the generous help of many practicing professionals associated with the financial planning industry. The names and contributions of those who have given their time so generously are presented on the following page. However, I would be remiss if I did not single out four persons for special recognition. The best way I can describe my deep gratitude to Dr. Lionel Goldstein, Ph.D., CPA, CFP, and Ms. Cynthia Forman, MA, MBA, CFP, is to state categorically that they could not have made a more valuable contribution, if they were co-authors of this book. In addition, thoughtful criticisms of Mr. Art Albin, CPA, MBA, CFP, and Dr. Dale Johnson, Ph.D., CFP, were responsible for both extensive revisions and a major expansion of the scope of the book. In fact, in a real sense, all are responsible for raising the book to a much higher professional and practical level, improving its clarity, expanding its coverage, and helping remove inaccuracies that slipped into the first draft.

Incidentally, publishing a book of this complexity can be a harrowing experience. Fortunately, that was not true in my case. The credit goes to John Willig, the Executive Editor at Prentice Hall. The frequent assurance by John that this book was "developing to be a winner" provided me with the impetus to do my best to live up to his expectations. My special thanks go to Jacqueline Jeglinski, Production Editor at Prentice Hall, who should get most of the credit for the outstanding "production quality" of this book.

I would like to conclude with a personal note. On October 14, 1989, I attended the Parents & Partners Program at the University of Pennsylvania Medical School in Philadelphia where my son, Robert, is a second year medical student. In his opening remark to the attending parents of medical students, Dean Frederic D. Burg, M.D. challenged every potential medical professional to embrace the following philosophy:

> This is not a time of mediocrity
> It is a time for greatness
> This is not a time for timidness
> It is a time for courage
> This is not a time for dullness
> It is a time for imagination
> This is not a time for greed
> It is a time for charity
> This is not a time for followers
> It is a time for leaders . . .

For a long time it has been my dream to help raise the level of the financial planning profession so one day it would be perceived as venerable as the medical profession. I do believe that in the foreseeable future we will achieve that goal and financial planners will be able to embrace Dr. Burg's philosophy meant for the medical professional. And, if *Practicing Financial Planning* helps you become a more sophisticated, better educated, and prepared professional financial planner, thereby moving us a little closer to the goal of achieving a universally-accepted true profession, I will have achieved my objective.

Sid Mittra, *Oakland University*

ACKNOWLEDGMENTS

In a very real sense, a book of this complexity and uniqueness must be recognized as a *joint product*. In fact, the significance of the contributions made by a large group of excellent reviewers can be judged only by comparing the final version with the original draft. I appreciate their many suggestions and criticisms, which have had a strong influence on various aspects of this book.

Given this myriad of assistance one might conclude that there is no scope for improvement. Nothing could be further from the truth. In fact, since I am convinced that, over time, this book will radically change, I urge you to be generous with your suggestions for improvement. I would also be grateful to you if you would take the time to point out the remaining errors of omission or commission. My special thanks go to the following people for reviewing all or part of the manuscript.

ACADEMIC REVIEW

Name	Affiliation	Reviewed
Arthur E. Albin, CPA, CFP	Plante & Moran, CPAs	Entire Manuscript
Peter Bacon, D.B.A., CFP	Professor, Wright State University	Investment Planning, Chapters 9–11
Patricia Barnett, MBA	Senior Business Planner, General Motors Corporation	Investment Planning, Chapters 9–11
David G. Bommarito	Agency Director/CEO Health Care Benefits, Inc.	Health Insurance, Chapter 4
Daniel H. Boyce, CFP	Financial Planner, Center for Financial Planning, Inc.	Time Value of Money, Chapter 5
Theodore K. Bugenski, B.S.	Comerica, Inc.	Entire Manuscript
Richard Burgeon	President, Retirement Services Corp.	Retirement Planning, Chapters 12–13
Sherman T. Folland, Ph.D.	Associate Profesor of Economics, Oakland University	Investment Planning, Chapter 10
Cynthia E. Forman, MA, MBA, CFP	Academic Associate, College for Financial Planning	Entire Manuscript
Chris M. Gassen, CFA, MBA	Investment Officer, National Bank of Detroit	Investment Planning, Chapters 9–11

Name	Affiliation	Reviewed
Lionel A. Goldstein, CPA, CFP, Ph.D.	President, Goldstein & Associates, A Financial Consulting Firm	Entire Manuscript
Larry D. Hayden, CFP	President, International Board of Standards and Practices for Certified Financial Planners, Inc.	Entire Manuscript
Tahira K. Hira, Ph.D., CFP	Professor, Iowa State University	Entire Manuscript
Richard Huttenlocher	Insurance Counsellor, Huttenlochers Kerns Norvell, Inc.	Casualty/Property Insurance Planning, Chapter 4
James A. Jacobs, CLU, ChFC, LTC , MBA.	President, James A. Jacobs Co., Inc.	Life Insurance Planning, Chapter 4
Dale S. Johnson, Ph.D., CFP	Financial Planning Consultant and Writer	Entire Manuscript
Robert Kleiman	Assistant Professor of Finance, Oakland University	Investment Planning, Chapters 9–11
Jerald W. Mason, Ph.D., MBA, CFP, ChFC, CLU	Director of Education, International Association for Financial Planning	Entire Manuscript
Robert Martel, CFP, ChFC, CLU	President, Financial Planning and Management, Inc. Assistant Professor of Finance, Bentley College	Business Planning, Chapter 17
Dale McClelland	President, Financial and Tax Planning, Inc. Board of Directors, IAFP	Investment Planning, Chapters 9–11
James W. McPherson, MBA	MIS Manager, Wayne State University	Savings Planning, Chapter 6
Sheena M. Mill, B.S.	Pension Consultant, Advance Benefits Systems Corporation	Retirement Planning, Chapters 12–13
Samuel R. Palise	Insurance Agent, State Farm Insurance Co.	Casualty/Property Insurance Planning, Chapter 4
Edward J. Phillips, CPA	Managing Partner, Perrin, Fordree & Company P.C., Certified Public Accountants	Tax Planning, Chapters 7–8
W. James Piercey, CPA	Partner, Piercey & Toepel, P.C. Certified Public Accountants, Advisor, Institute for Financial Education	Tax Planning, Chapters 7–8
William H. Rector	President, Great Lakes Pension Administrators, Inc.	Retirement Planning, Chapters 12–13
John Rogers, Esqr.	Googasin, Hopkins, Rogers, Hohauser, Forhan, P.C.	Estate Planning, Chapters 14–15
John A. Roselli, CFP, MSF	President, Financial Planning Perspectives, Inc.	Entire Manuscript
John M. Savio, MBA	Vice President, Michigan State University Federal Credit Union	Savings Planning, Chapter 6

Name	Affiliation	Reviewed
Jerry Schatzman, J.D.	Principal, Schatzman & Associates, P.C.	Estate Planning, Chapters 14–15
Eileen M. Sharkey, CFP	President, E. M. Sharkey & Associates, President, ICFP	Entire Manuscript
Jay L. Smith, CFP	President, JLS Financial Planning	Entire Manuscript
John Sweet	Owner, John C. Sweet & Assoc.	Business Planning, Chapter 17
Barbara A. Theisen MST, CPA	Assistant Professor, Oakland University	Tax Planning, Chapters 7–8
Fred Tillman, J.D., CFP	Professor, Georgia State University	Estate Planning, Chapters 14–15
Anton T. Vanek, Jr., MBA, CLU, CFP, ChFC., LIC	President, Anton T. Vanek Associates	Life Insurance Planning, Chapter 3
Wade J. Webster	President, PlanFirst Company, Registry of Financial Planning Practitioners	Comprehensive Financial Planning, Chapter 16

EDITORIAL ASSISTANCE

Name	Affiliation
John Willig	Acquisition Editor, Prentice Hall
Jacqueline Jeglinski	Production Editor, Prentice Hall

ADMINISTRATIVE ASSISTANCE

Name	Affiliation	Activity
Ted Bugensky	Comerica	Proofreading and Computation Checking
Lisa M. Emrich	University of Michigan, Flint	Manuscript Typing
Maria Emrich	Coordinated Financial Planning	Project Coordinator
Shanti Kandaswami	University of Pennsylvania	Index Preparation
Bani Mittra		Project Supervisor
Alicia Myers	Visual Services, Inc.	Research Assistance

PART I

The General Setting

"An era can be said to end," observed playwright Arthur Miller, "when its basic illusions are exhausted." By that standard, the era of casual or substandard personal financial planning is over. We have already begun the new era of professional financial planning. The overriding consideration of this new era will be to ensure that every financial planner maintains the highest level of professionalism in every phase of the planning process. In short, personal financial planning has just passed the adolescent stage and is now becoming a mature profession.

Before attempting to approach financial planning in a systematic manner, a thorough understanding is needed of the respective roles financial planners and financially concerned Americans must play to assure success in the 1990s. The purpose of Part I is to provide the general setting necessary before undertaking a comprehensive analysis of financial planning concepts and practice.

Part I consists of two chapters. Chapter 1 describes the emerging role of the professional financial planner in an uncertain and highly complex economic and financial environment. Chapter 2 discusses how the financial planner begins the planning process by selecting and interacting with the client.

CHAPTER 1

The Emerging Role of the Financial Planner

DEMANDS OF THE FINANCIAL FUTURE

Many things have been achieved in the twentieth century that were once thought impossible. This century has also given us a vision of the awesome and astonishing possibilities of the future: technological marvels, sophisticated communications, artificial intelligence, reaching the moon and the other planets, and, most amazing, cloning life itself. But in this, the last decade of the century, a far different scenario emerges: fears of the negative aspects of living too long, catastrophic illness, another major depression leading to a collapse of the world economy, widespread poverty among retirees, and a continued deterioration of the United States as a world economic power.

As the year 2000 approaches, in contrast to the bleak picture just painted, Americans also realize that they are enjoying a better quality of life than previous generations: longer life spans, better health, more leisure time, and more varied choices about lifestyles. But they also recognize that in order to take full advantage of these benefits they need financial security and thus must surmount complicated financial hurdles. In short, both unprecedented opportunities and extremely difficult challenges have become the order of the day.

THE EMERGING TRENDS[1]

Changing Family Patterns

Recent U.S. census figures suggest that by the year 2000 less than 23 percent of all U.S. households will consist of married couples with children— a monumental decline from the 70 percent that made this unit typical in 1950. Single-person households, on the other hand, have risen from 11 percent in 1950 to an amazing 25 to 26 percent of American families.

Where traditional families do continue, they are becoming less able to financially assist their aging parents and their children as much as they would like. The implications are clear. In contrast to a society that traditionally buttressed each individual with a network of family support, the twenty-first century will be marked by an increasing need for each individual to take responsibility for meeting his or her own financial expectations.

The Rising Cost of the American Dream

The cost of achieving the lifetime goals once taken for granted continues to mount. Mortgage payments on a home eat up 44 percent of the average 30-year-old's salary today, compared to just 14 percent in 1949. The expenses associated with having a family are escalating as well. In 1980, it cost less than $80,000 to raise a child to age 18; just nine years later, it cost well over $200,000. With education costs rising at more than seven percent per year— faster than wages or inflation—the pressures put on tomorrow's parents can only increase.

The Realities of Retirement

Based on current trends, the average individual of the future will enjoy at least the potential for a longer retirement. One reason is that the average life span is lengthening. Biotechnological advances are expected to stretch life expectancy more between now and the year 2000 than in any other comparable period in history. As a result, some futurists predict that the grandchildren of the current generation could live to be 100 to 120 years old.

Concurrently, Americans are retiring earlier. A recent U.S. Department of Labor study showed that early retirement is increasingly popular today, with approximately 60 percent of all private sector employees now retiring

---

[1] This section is adapted from "Meeting the Demands of the Financial Future," special advertising supplement, sponsored by Oppenheimer Fund Management, Inc., *Changing Times* Magazine, 1986.

before the age of 65. But does the lengthening of retirement guarantee that these will be "the golden years" that Americans hope they will be? For many individuals, the answer is, "not necessarily."

The Bureau of Labor Statistics estimates that 70 to 75 percent of preretirement income is needed to continue at a comparable lifestyle during retirement. Where will this money come from? The Social Security system currently provides a maximum annual benefit of around $9,200—no matter how high the preretirement earnings. In short, the gap between retirement dreams and reality can be bridged only by the savings and investments of individuals themselves. The combination of a shorter working life (perhaps just 40 years) and a longer retirement (possibly more than 25 years) makes this challenge increasingly tough to meet.

A Summary View

Current trends suggest that the future will offer Americans unparalleled possibilities in all areas of life. Yet, it is also clear that in order to enjoy them, individuals will have to assume increasing responsibility for their own financial well-being rather than relying on traditional sources of assistance. The process of making the most of one's money is a long-term endeavor; in this instance, it can be said that the future, however distant it seems, is now. Fortunately, Americans do not have to face the challenges alone. The professional financial planners, who only a decade ago were unknown even to most financial institutions, are now recognized by the general public as invaluable partners in the financial planning. In short, personal financial planning has finally come of age.

CONCEPT OF PERSONAL FINANCIAL PLANNING

The term "personal financial planning" has been loosely and broadly applied to a wide range of advisory services and financial products sales efforts. Several financial planning professional organizations have attempted to define the term in order to foster a unified financial planning profession. For instance, the International Association for Financial Planning (IAFP) has defined financial planning as follows:

> Financial planning is providing to a person, for compensation, a plan recommending strategies and actions designed to help achieve the financial goals of that person on the basis of an evaluation of the personal and financial conditions and capabilities of that person.

This definition emphasizes the personal conditions and capabilities of the client. In contrast, in defining financial planning, the Institute of Certified Financial Planners (ICFP) has stressed the importance of monitoring and periodic review. In its position paper entitled "What is personal financial planning? Who is a financial planner?" the ICFP states:

> Personal financial planning is the organization of an individual's financial and personal data for the purpose of developing a strategic plan to constructively manage income, assets, and liabilities to meet near- and long-term goals and objectives. Important to the success of the personal financial planning process is the monitoring and periodic review of the plan to ensure that it continues to meet individual needs.

The most comprehensive definition of financial planning has been developed by the International Board of Standards and Practices for Certified Financial Planners (IBCFP). Note this:

> Financial planning is the process of determining whether and how an individual can meet his or her life goals through proper management of financial sources. The management of financial sources can be seen as the technical side of the process; and in today's fast-changing financial world, this side of the process demands a willingness to stay abreast of new financial strategies and instruments. The other side of the process requires that all the planner's knowledge of financial strategies and instruments be brought to the surface of the client's *goals*. Perhaps the most distinctive skill a financial planner [needs] is that of helping clients to articulate their life goals so that together ... [they] can begin to determine, first of all, whether these goals are achievable through financial resources, and then how. Working with clients in this state of the financial process requires sensitivity because ... [financial planners] discuss issues that may be difficult for many people to address. ... [Financial planners] may find that the planning process itself brings deeper values and unrealized conflicts to the surface, and from time to time it may be appropriate to refer clients to other counsellors to resolve these conflicts before they can proceed with a financial plan.[2]

KEY AREAS OF FINANCIAL PLANNING

Financial planners must be informed in all aspects affecting their clients' lifetime financial decisions, especially in the following key planning areas:

R   Risk management planning
E   Essentials of budgeting, savings, and credit planning
T   Tax planning

---

[2] *Financial Planning: A Career Profile*, International Board of Standards and Practices for Certified Financial Planners, Inc., 1989, pp. 2–3.

I   Investment planning

R   Retirement planning

E   Estate planning

The six key financial planning areas are presented in Figure 1-1. Financial planners may be experts in just one or two of these areas. But they must have a clear understanding of all areas so they can work with other professionals while servicing their clients.

In order to provide valuable services as a true professional, a financial planner must possess the five Cs of financial planning:

Client:	Client interests must always come first.
Communication:	Communication is the key to motivating clients to implement plan recommendations.
Coordination:	Coordination among various professionals provides the highest quality of overall planning service.

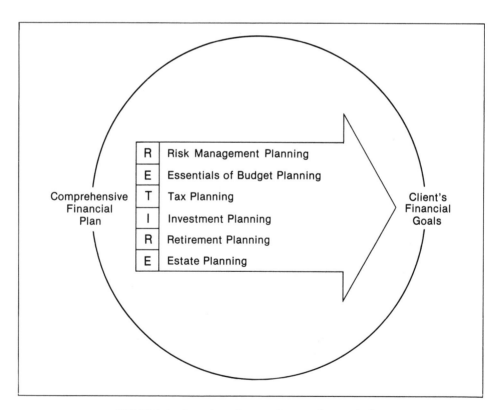

FIGURE 1-1 Overview of comprehensive financial plan

Competence:	Competence firmly based on both education and experience is essential for professional performance.
Commitment to Ethics:	Commitment to ethics and professionalism is the basis for providing quality service.

THE CLIENT

Barbara Streisand recorded a very popular song about people who need people and how they are the luckiest people in the world. A similar theme applies to financial planning. People need financial planners, and the only commitment financial planners need make is to fulfill the needs of these people—or clients—with utmost competence, care, and professionalism.

The Emerging Client

From the end of World War II until the beginning of the 1970s, financial planning was simple. Starting in the mid-1970's, with the advent of a double-digit inflation, stagflation, high unemployment, massive budget and trade deficits, and constant tax law changes, financial planning became more complicated. A new breed of consumers emerged who demanded a different norm. During the final decade of the twentieth century, we discover that Americans stay single a lot longer. If two wage earners marry, often their financial plan does not include children. And even where children are included in the plan, each parent may have a prenuptial agreement, thereby making financial planning more complicated. Finally, even average families faithfully following the recommendations of their comprehensive financial plans often find their lives disrupted as aging—and often ailing—parents move in with them. It is little wonder that today the *average client* is nonexistent and there is no one ideal financial plan that fits all situations.

The trend toward an endlessly diverse individual and family configuration is clear from the following expression: "The evolving icons of pop culture tell it all: The Cleavers' solid certitude has yielded prime time to the Huxtables' dual income dilemmas. The Bumsteads now share the comics with Cathy, a perennial single. *Ad infinitum.* 'People look at modern families and think they are seeing departures from the norm. . . . In fact, departures *now* are the norm,' says Peter A. Morrison, director of Rand Corporation's Population Research Center."[3]

Notwithstanding the major changes that are taking place in the lifestyles of the American consumers, certain basic financial needs of these consumers

---

[3] Author, "The New Gospel of Financial Planning," *Money*, March 1989, p. 55.

remain intact. Identification of these needs can provide a basic foundation on which the financial planning process can be built.

The Common Denominators

Some people dread heights, others fear crowded rooms. But in the financial arena most Americans have three distinct fears: the fear of living out old age with a vastly reduced income, dying too young, or becoming disabled. Each fear is distinct and requires elaboration.

Living too long.   Many Americans have "pensionphobia": the fear of not having enough money to retire in peace and dignity. The reasons are not hard to find. The average life expectancy for women has already reached 78 (72 for men) and by the year 2000 is expected to be around 85. The potential bankruptcy of the Social Security system distinctly looms on the horizon. Catastrophic health care costs threaten to cripple the Medicare system. Housing costs continue to skyrocket. Finally, the horror of double-digit inflation and the possibility of the collapse of the world economic system frequently turn the retirement dream into a nightmare.

There is a trend that is lengthening the period of retirement. More and more Americans are retiring well before age 65. Today, the average retirement age is 61; in 1970 it was 65. Many Americans these days are declaring their independence in their 50s and even in their 40s. For some, this might mean taking up volunteer work at social service agencies, taking hobbies seriously, roaming the world, or simply running part-time businesses. For the vast majority, however, early retirement still remains a fantasy.

Nearly everyone looks forward to retirement as a time of doing exactly as one pleases, be it early retirement or retirement at the "normal" age of 65. Whatever lifestyle a person envisions, the best way to ensure that the retirement goal is met is to plan as far ahead as possible. Two primary duties of financial planners are (1) to emphasize to clients that the choices they make when younger will determine how well they reach retirement goals, and (2) to articulate the steps they should take to effectively plan for retirement.

Broadly defined, retirement planning encompasses a variety of financial planning areas. The first step in planning for the future is to determine retirement goals. How one wants to live after retirement is the basis for estimating how much money is needed to achieve the retirement goals.

The second step in this process is to determine the current financial status, called net worth. This is calculated by adding up all the assets and subtracting the liabilities. Once it is determined how much income is needed after retirement and the amount of net worth available to generate that income, planning for the future can begin to take shape.

Savings planning constitutes the third step of retirement planning. It begins with a determination of what the annual expenses are likely to be during retirement. Then this amount can be inserted into the retirement plan to estimate how much must be saved each year during the working life to maintain the desired lifestyle after retirement. In this context, financial planners can help their clients recognize that (1) both the desired lifestyle and the amount of savings they wish to generate are their personal decisions, and (2) there is a trade-off between the sacrifice of present income necessary to generate current savings and future income.

Completion of savings planning naturally leads to the fourth step of retirement planning. It relates to the starting of investment planning, the main objective of which is to channel the savings into a number of investment products selected to achieve various financial goals. Where to put the money to work depends upon the answers to the following questions: (1) How much should the investment earn? (2) How much risk is involved? (3) How long will it be before the investment pays off? (4) Can the investment be easily converted into cash? (5) What are the tax ramifications of the investment?

An investment plan cannot be developed in a vacuum. In order for it to be effective, as the fifth step of retirement planning, it must be integrated with tax planning. Tax-advantaged investments completely avoid or postpone tax payment. This can result in substantial savings, thereby significantly contributing to the growth of net worth. Of course, risks and lower investment returns of tax-advantaged investments must be weighed against the benefit of tax savings; these decisions form an integral part of tax planning.

An ever-present desire on the part of Americans is to accumulate a large estate to be passed on to beneficiaries: This is the essence of estate planning. Investment techniques employed to accumulate a large estate are different from those developed for achieving educational, retirement, and other living goals. In addition, a sophisticated estate plan tends to eliminate, or significantly reduce, the federal estate and state inheritance taxes that must be paid before the estate can be distributed to the beneficiaries.

Dying too young. We live in a turbulent society in which the threat of an early death is ever-present. In the absence of proper risk management planning, an untimely death of the breadwinner can be catastrophic, and the surviving family may never be able to financially recover from it. In this case, risk management planning involves the transfer of risk to an insurance company by buying adequate life insurance. This presents a major challenge for financial planners for two reasons. First, the determination of adequate life insurance coverage is not an exact science, since the quantification of several variables requires making value judgments. For instance, a husband whose spouse with small children is willing and able to join the labor force (at an adequate salary level) immediately after his death needs far less life insurance than the person whose wife wants to stay home until the children are graduated from college. Second, for psychological reasons many people refuse to buy life insurance regardless of the consequences, and it is difficult to help them appreciate life insurance as a valuable tool. Despite these difficulties, however, risk management planning remains one of the major tasks of a financial planner.

Becoming disabled. An integral part of risk management planning is disability planning. Perhaps the greatest challenge faced by financial planners is to convince their clients that they should have a good disability plan. Several reasons account for the universal apathy consumers have toward buying a comprehensive disability policy. First, most people do not recognize that long-term disability poses a real threat in their lives. Second, unlike death, where all expenses related to the deceased cease, a long-term disability is likely to put enormous financial burdens on the family. Third, most people naively compare disability insurance premiums with life insurance premiums and inevitably come to the wrong conclusion that a disability policy is too expensive. For instance, a $5,000 annual premium may buy a $500,000 life insurance policy for a 55-year-old male, but the same premium would buy *only* a $4,000 a month disability income policy for the same individual. The correct way to compare the two policies, of course, is to calculate the present value of the two income benefits, a task better performed by a competent financial planner.

Summing up. Most Americans have the fears of living a poverty-stricken old age, dying too early, or becoming disabled. It is the duty of financial planners to help their clients gain the necessary financial security. This can be achieved only if the clients are treated with patience, utmost care, and professionalism. More specifically, the success financial planners can achieve inevitably depends on their making a commitment to help their clients articulate their short- and long-range objectives and develop comprehensive financial plans designed to help them achieve these objectives in the most professional manner.

COMMUNICATION

Even the best-laid financial plan falls by the wayside if the advantages of implementing the plan are not effectively communicated to the client. It is little wonder that financial planners are expected to be professional communicators.

Over the years many articles and books have been written on the development of communication skills by financial planners. Some deal with general, scientific techniques of communication, while others tailor their discussions to communicating with financial planning clients. We will approach the subject from the perspective of communicating with potential clients as well as with financial planning clients at different levels of the planning process.

The Potential Client

The following is a famous saying in the financial planning industry: People don't care how much a financial planner knows until they know how much the planner cares. It is also frequently asserted that people do not want to learn about financial planning. They just want to find someone they can trust so they can dump their financial problems in this person's lap. This often is the potential client's mindset to which a financial planner needs to respond.

A financial planner interacting with a potential client needs to use a set of communicative skills different from the skills required to deal with a client who has already entered the planning process. At this juncture the financial planner needs to convince the individual that he or she is trustworthy. This involves communicating with the person that the planner is:

A   Accountable for all planning-related actions.

B   Both caring and committed for the long term.

C   Competent, both academically and experientially.

This is achieved as the planner carefully recognizes and spells out the needs, fears, and dreams of the potential client and unveils a broad program designed to meet these objectives. Additionally, the potential client should be made aware of the fact that financial planning is not an exact science: Quick fixes will likely fail and unrealistic expectations will not be met. Put differently, through proper communication the potential client would learn that financial planning is a long-term process, and complete cooperation and continuous monitoring are essential for the achievement of both the short- and long-term goals.

The Planning Client

Once the individual has engaged the financial planner and the planning process has begun, the technique of communicating with the client is different. To appreciate this technique it is necessary to specify the six key stages of financial planning: (1) gathering quantitative and qualitative data, (2) establishing client objectives, (3) analyzing the planning data, (4) producing a written comprehensive financial plan with specific recommendations for action, (5) implementing the plan, and (6) conducting periodic reviews. Each stage requires a different communication strategy, as we shall shortly observe.

Gathering data. Data gathering is a mechanical process. It is tedious, time-consuming, laborious, and, above all, onerous. Yet, it is a vital function, since the data gathered here is used exclusively to develop the client's comprehensive financial plan.

At first it might appear that the only task the financial planner needs to perform here is to supply a personal financial questionnaire and collect it after its completion. That is simply not true. The planner must not only convince the client that the data gathering is of utmost importance but also provide assistance in completing the questionnaire. This is especially true for answering such loaded questions as those dealing with the desired age of financial independence, future expected inflation rate, and the income desired at retirement.

Establishing client objectives. Financial planners face their greatest challenge as professional communicators in this area. There are two reasons for this. First, most clients are not too sure about their objectives and face even greater difficulties in articulating what they believe they know. Second, since establishing client objectives is at the heart of financial planning, financial planners must develop widely diverse communication skills to effectively perform this function. These skills include nonverbal and verbal forms of communicating. The former may take the form of supplying reading materials that emphasize the importance of articulating short- and long-term objectives in financial planning. In the case of verbal communication, a financial planner can use a variety of skills such as probing, restating, paraphrasing, and summarizing clients' views.

Since the task of establishing client objectives is extremely important, it is necessary to develop a special communication model, which we will call the goals and objectives interview. The salient features of this model are described next.

We have specified earlier that the six major areas of financial planning are risk management, cash management, tax, investment, retirement, and estate planning. After a close examination of the financial planning questionnaire, the financial planner may conduct an in-depth goals and objectives interview by covering each of the financial planning areas just specified. In addition, the interview may cover other matters of importance to the client. At the conclusion of the interview, the planner can take a test by summarizing the results of the interview and inviting the client to be the grader. If the financial planner passes the test, the summary of the goals and objectives interview would be committed to paper and transmitted to the client. This is the most effective way of establishing client objectives and laying the foundation for providing a valuable planning service to the client.

Financial plan analysis. This aspect of the process requires the least amount of communication with the client. In fact, contact with the client can be limited to clarification of unclear data and setting up parameters for some key planning variables, such as expected inflation, desired investment returns, and so on.

Plan submission with recommendations. A critical step in the communication process is the transmission of a comprehensive financial plan to the client. While the level of technical analysis, length of explanations, and style of presentation may vary—sometimes considerably—among financial planners, the success of the comprehensive plan is assured only if the planner is able to effectively communicate the recommendations to the client and set the stage for their timely implementation.

Ideally, a comprehensive financial plan should contain the following distinct elements:

Results of the Goals and Objectives Interview: This section articulates the client's short- and long-term objectives and establishes the basis for the planner's recommendations.

Basic Observations: The body of the comprehensive financial plan can often be voluminous, and the client may find it burdensome to go through the entire plan. To obviate such a problem, a special section entitled Basic Observations can be added to the plan. This section summarizes the plan's key elements and presents its six major areas (R-E-T-I-R-E) in capsule form.

Key Recommendations: This section presents all the recommendations in minute detail. The recommendations are first presented in generic form. Specific investment, insurance, and legal products are then selected to supplement the generic recommendations.

Trip Tick: This section sets out in order of priority specific steps the client can take to implement the plan.

Comprehensive Plan: The last section should contain the financial plan supported by a detailed analysis of the financial data pertaining to each of the major planning areas.

Plan transmission constitutes the biggest test of the financial planner as a professional communicator. The client is likely to accept the recommendations and quickly act on them only if the planner is able to convince the client that by implementing these recommendations the client would achieve the majority of his or her stated objectives. This is a tall order, and it may be necessary to use both verbal and nonverbal forms of communication to achieve this goal. Of course, in the final analysis, action on the plan recommendations is assured only when the planner is able to meet the client in his or her comfort zone.

COORDINATION

The discipline of financial planning is relatively new and has developed as a way of dealing with our modern complex society. Even as late as the 1960s, there was no demand for financial planners. Most people were content with dealing with their traditional advisors, such as attorneys, accountants, bank-

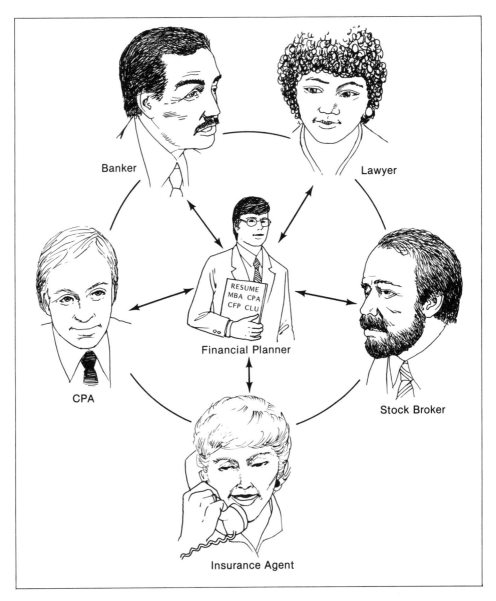

ers, insurance agents, and stockbrokers. However, as we entered the 1970s, society grew more complex. As observed, with the advent of the most severe recession since the 1930s, the oil embargo, double-digit inflation, an unacceptable level of unemployment, and the infamous bracket creep in personal and corporate taxes, no one field was equipped to handle all of a client's financial planning needs. The idea of the financial planner, as we know today, was thus born to deal with this complex situation.

As is generally the case with the birth of a new discipline, initially most people believed that the financial planner could be "all things to all people." That dream, however, was short-lived. It was quickly recognized by most financial planning professionals that consumers' interests would be truly served only if the financial planner acted as a quarterback or orchestra leader and coordinated other traditional advisors for support in planning for the client. For instance, if a client needed a sophisticated estate plan, an attorney would be needed. The tax return could be prepared by a CPA. Additional life insurance could be purchased from an insurance counselor. Similarly, the investment portfolio could be reorganized with the help of a portfolio manager.

Let there be no misunderstanding, however. To suggest that a financial planner should closely work with other professionals is not to imply that the planner cannot—or should not—perform one or more of the tasks just listed. In fact, frequently a financial planner is a licensed member of one or more of these professions and hence can successfully perform the associated tasks. For instance, most practicing financial planners are registered investment advisors and many are also licensed to sell securities and insurance. Several planners are also CPAs, while others are JDs and are licensed to practice law. Nevertheless, most sophisticated financial planners understand that even though it is best to know about all the components that go into a comprehensive financial plan, they must recognize their limitations and know when to contact other advisors for additional support. The following is a brief description of the approach usually taken by each type of professional and the importance of including such a person on the planning team.

Attorney

In recent years a great deal has been written on the client-attorney relationship and on the legal community's indifferent behavior toward the financial planning community. These writings generally suggest that at least some of the dissension appears to stem from turf battles. The thinking behind such behavior is not only misplaced but if allowed to continue can be counterproductive and ultimately damaging to the client.

In the context of financial planning, an attorney's key function is to pass on the legality of any proposal that the financial planner may develop and to help implement it by preparing the associated legal documents. For instance, if charitable giving is recommended, the financial planner would ask for the attorney's opinion on whether a charitable trust is the most appropriate instrument to use to satisfy the client's needs. The attorney would either suggest a better instrument or confirm that the one suggested is best. The attorney would then prepare the associated legal document to implement the recommendation. The same approach would be used for recommendations relating to estate, education, life insurance, joint ownership, and other types of planning. It should be clear that in the scenario just described, there is no room for turf battles and acrimonious debates, for in this role the attorney becomes an integral part of the team of professionals.

Accountant

Traditionally, accountants and CPAs have performed two principal functions: maintaining financial records and preparing taxes. As accountants they also have performed certain financial planning functions. Whatever the role, CPAs have commanded the respect and admiration of their clients partly because of their independence. Until recently they were not allowed to receive a commission on the sale of products.

Now that the financial world has become more complex and financial planners have clearly established themselves as chief coordinators of the professional team, the role of accountants has significantly changed. Today, accountants still perform the tasks of financial record keeping and compliance services such as audits and tax preparation. But as team players they also play a major role in analyzing the overall tax consequences that flow from a particular investment vehicle or legal instrument. In addition, accountants also provide invaluable assistance to the financial planners by (1) interpreting and evaluating the ever-changing tax laws, (2) recommending ways of taking advantage of these changes in the law, and (3) occasionally computing and monitoring investment results by acting as investment advisors.

Portfolio Manager

The two most important components of financial planning are the creation and preservation of a client's estate. While the attorney and accountant help preserve the estate, the portfolio manager helps create or build it. Specifically, a financial planner first creates a target investment portfolio structure by taking into account the client's short- and long-term objectives. A portfolio manager then helps the planner identify the appropriate investment vehicles—stocks, bonds, mutual funds, annuities, limited partnerships, and so on—thereby helping the planner complete the investment planning process.

Insurance Counselor

An important dimension of estate protection is the purchase of life, disability, property, casualty, professional liability, and other forms of insurance. In addition, it must be recognized that in the event of an untimely death, the client's estate should have adequate liquidity so the taxes and administrative expenses can be paid without undue financial hardship on the surviving family. The financial planner is responsible for developing a comprehensive and coordinated risk management plan covering various types of insurance. The task of the insurance counselor is to select from a wide variety of insurance products those that are particularly suited for the client.

Other Professionals

The financial planner works with other professionals as well, depending upon the client's needs. These include trust officers, real estate brokers, securities brokers, and professional estate planners. In each instance, the planner's objective is to seek external assistance where such assistance would enhance the value of the overall plan developed for the client.

Summing Up

Establishing harmonious and professional relationships with traditional advisors generally provides the best service to the client. If these advisors are handled properly, it is usually possible to engage in productive working relationships with them that benefit all parties: the client, the financial planner, and the other advisors.

In an effort to promote the greatest possible cooperation between the financial planner and the traditional advisors, the financial planner should be attuned to the need for establishing an excellent rapport with the client and the existing advisors. This can be achieved only if the planner makes a firm commitment to the client and offers to conduct the financial planning process by coordinating the efforts of the traditional advisors.

COMPETENCE

Financial planning is an emerging profession. Consequently, what constitutes a well-qualified, objective financial planner is often debated. In this section we will discuss this issue in terms of academic degrees, required credentials, and professional experience.

Academic Degrees

The most significant step in establishing financial planners' minimum standards of competence took place in June 1986 when the International Board for Standards and Practices of Certified Financial Planners (IBCFP) was formed. It will be some time before the IBCFP succeeds in firmly establishing universally acceptable model curriculum guidelines for financial planning degree-granting institutions. Still, it is worth reviewing the current status of the model curriculum developed by the IBCFP.

The IBCFP recognizes that in the practice of personal financial planning, the professional planner helps achieve the client's short- and long-range goals. To assume these responsibilities, the professional should have a broad understanding of human experience, cultural values in American society, business and finance, planning techniques, counseling issues and skills, and fiduciary obligations. Educational institutions should provide the necessary education to develop financial planners' understanding of such matters.

In order to guide educational institutions in their efforts to develop degree and certificate programs in financial planning, the IBCFP has developed the model curriculum guidelines. These guidelines are broad; they include studies in economics, finance, accounting, communication skills, business ethics, legal environment of business, taxation, investments, computer sciences, and financial analysis. Subject matter and required competencies derive from a study of the practice of financial planners.[4] At present, completion of this, or a similar, curriculum would lead to a granting of an undergraduate or a graduate degree in financial planning. Any person seriously considering financial planning as a career would be well advised to obtain a degree in financial planning.

The Credentials

In 1986, when the IBCFP was formed, the CFP certification mark was transferred to the IBCFP from the Denver-based College for Financial Planning which since the 1970s had owned and granted the CFP certification marks. Initially the IBCFP endorsed the passing of the six-part examination as a prerequisite to granting the CFP certification. However, as of 1991, the IBCFP will replace it with a single comprehensive examination comparable to the bar and CPA examinations.

CFP is not the only valid certification mark for practicing financial planning. Instead, there are several credentials, all of which ensure that whoever gains any one of them can perform financial planning services. In fact, in addition to CFP (Certified Financial Planner), ChFC (Chartered Financial Consultant), and RFP (Registered Financial Planner), other financial services credentials include CLU (Chartered Life Underwriter), CPA (Certified Public Accountant), and JD (Doctor of Jurisprudence).

The Experience

The academic degree and the credentials are not substitutes for experience as a financial planner. Consequently, the IBCFP has made three years of experience a prerequisite for gaining the CFP certification mark. For purposes of this requirement, experience is defined as full-time (or equivalent part-time) employment in situations in which the candidate actively uses the knowledge, skills, and abilities required for the certification examination. Under this definition, experience gained in corporate settings (as an accountant, attorney, banker, stockbroker, financial planner, insurance salesman, tax preparer, and so on) are accepted.

---

[4] L. Skurnik, *Job Analysis of the Professional Requirements of the Certified Financial Planner* (Denver: College for Financial Planning, 1987).

Continuing Education

All CFP registrants are required to report continuing education credits to the IBCFP. The IBCFP has established 60 hours every two years of continuing education as one of the standards for continued use of the certification marks, CFP and Certified Financial Planner. Although a firm set of rules has not yet been developed that automatically qualifies continuing education seminars, the IBCFP has established that the standards of continuing education must be (1) consistent with the standards for certification and marks usages (that is, quality controlled); (2) meaningful and not financially burdensome or discriminatory; (3) protective of the public interest; and (4) effective as a means of helping ensure continued competency as a financial planner.

Summing Up

A qualified practicing financial planner should: (1) have earned an appropriate academic degree in financial planning; (2) possess the appropriate professional certification; and (3) meet continuing education requirements. Of course, these are necessary, but not sufficient, conditions for acting as a qualified financial planner. It is also apropos to add here that, depending upon the activities performed, the planner is also required to possess the necessary securities, insurance, and registered investment advisor licenses.

In the final analysis, competent financial planners are entrusted with detailed knowledge of their clients' finances and assets as well as their personal financial goals and values. Ideally the financial planner is far more sophisticated and informed about financial, tax, economic, and legal considerations than the client; thus the client is almost always *very dependent* on the skill, judgment and guidance of the planner. Only a competent financial planner deserves to earn a client's complete trust.

COMMITMENT TO ETHICS

A "standard" definition of ethics is not very useful in defining the ethical standards by which financial planning professionals should do business. The reason is that there are well over 400 national associations, including medicine, law, and public accounting, all of which have published written codes. To this, one would have to add countless numbers of ethics codes among individual business firms, government bodies, and labor organizations in order to obtain a complete list of ethical standards from which to choose those for financial planners.

Let there be no misunderstanding, however. To say that financial planners must maintain the highest levels of ethical standards is not to deny the fact that they are also entrepreneurs, engaging in a business to make a profit.

So the key point is this: A less-than-ethical financial planner concentrates on making money by engaging in activities that may harm the client, whereas an ethical financial planner always serves the client's interest and his or her income is generated as a by-product of that service.

We have observed earlier that financial planning is an emerging profession. As the profession matures, a great deal is being written about financial planners' unethical practices, conflicts of interest, and self-serving activities. The water is muddied even further by the prevailing practices among most financial planners of both offering planning services and selling investment and insurance products. The establishment of the Board of Ethics as an intregal part of the IBCFP is a response to the deep concerns society has towards such practices. However, it is also argued that guarding the sanctity of the CFP marks and policing the ethical conduct of those who hold the marks are not enough to protect the consumer.

It is obvious that the task of policing unethical, self-designated, financial planners is complicated and should be left in the hands of regulatory agencies. However, we will present the basic framework for establishing an ethical practice.

We firmly believe that financial planners should organize their practices along these lines:

E	Efficient
T	Trustworthy
H	Honest
I	Ingenious
C	Completely loyal to client
S	Sincere

That is, if financial planners make a firm commitment to be efficient, trustworthy, honest, ingenious, completely loyal to the client, and sincere, they will automatically maintain the highest levels of ethical standards and financial planning will emerge as a venerable profession in the foreseeable future.

APPENDIX TO CHAPTER 1

PROFESSIONALISM AND THE CERTIFIED FINANCIAL PLANNER*

Some people have said that the old concept of a professional is no longer suited to our times. The disciplined, highly educated, voluntary, and deeply ethical practitioner dealing with clients one by one probably has been more of an idea than an established reality. However, this image seems to be replaced by collective group enterprise that is shared by many people that represent layers of specialism. Some might allege that this approach is flawed by the lack of concern for comprehensive and dedicated service and is probably marked by self-interest, and in some cases perhaps by incompetent performance. But regardless of what may have been the case in the past, it is evident that there needs to be an assurance of quality in meeting the complex, changing, and interactive requirements of a modern financial planning practice which addresses the most pressing and most comprehensive of financial situations.

It is readily apparent that a wide range of financial knowledge is imperative, regardless of whether a financial planner serves a specialized group or a particular segment of our society. While there has been a general emphasis on organized and structural activities, many financial planning professionals are growing irritated by what seems to be a mindless proliferation of courses and conferences, each of which may be valuable but which are not collectively supported by any unifying conception of how education can be used in a mature and continuing way to achieve excellence. Financial planners can advance the process by which greater conceptual understanding and competence will be brought about by educational endeavors of practicing professionals.

The key ingredient for those who are either entering or already engaged in the practice of financial planning in the 1990's and beyond is the idea of a dynamic professionalization that will grow in prominence as we enter the 21st century. It is important for the financial planning professional to understand the difference between the words learning and education. We, all too frequently, hear and read about students who have graduated from high school, and yes, even college, who have apparently achieved the educational requirements for graduation but have actually learned or retained very little. As a professional, the importance must be on continued learning because that is the process by which people gain the knowledge and the sensitivity and the mastery of skills to serve the public in a safe and prudent manner.

The prosperity of our nation depends upon each of us and our individual financial prosperity in order to support the free society in which we are so

---

* Larry D. Hayden, CFP, President, International Board of Standards and Practices for Certified Financial Planners, Inc. (IBCFP), October 18, 1989.

fortunate to live. A financial planner's role is that of helping individuals make intelligent financial decisions and properly preparing for the successes that can be achieved with professional planning. A financial planner must be capable of offering to those who are seeking financial success the insight which will aid them to acquire money, to manage it effectively and efficiently, and to utilize the surpluses to earn more money. There are certain basic principles of finance that are now recognized and used the world over that are no different today than they were many years ago.

Perhaps one of the more important responsibilities of a financial planner is to impress upon the clients to appreciate the value of money. Essentially, a financial planner's role and responsibility is that of teacher, or perhaps we should say educator, motivator and advisor—to educate the public about financial matters, to motivate clients to act prudently and resourcefully, and to instill the trust and confidence of a true fiduciary. A medical doctor, no doubt, achieves a great deal of satisfaction as well as financial reward in successfully treating and curing patient ailments and disease. That same sense of professional pride and satisfaction can also be achieved by those financial professionals who are able to diagnose, prescribe, and treat financial ailments that plague our society. More importantly, a financial planner should stress that financial mismanagement can result in a terminal prognosis for a client. Until individuals understand that managing their personal finances must be conducted just like a business—for a profit—there can be no financial security for our society.

Finally, professionalism connotes public trust, a special dedication to client interest, and unfailing objectivity. Financial planning exemplifies the qualities of a true profession because it is an endeavor in which the public interest must be served. Financial planners simply cannot succeed in building long-standing client relationships unless their actions are first and foremost one of integrity and public service. Because they must integrate a rather broad spectrum of financial issues, financial planners are charged with a tremendous responsibility of unquestioned trust and faith. Therefore, it is incumbent on each financial planner to understand fully, and constantly be aware of, the fiduciary obligation to serve the public in a just and equitable manner.

CHAPTER 2

The Personal Financial Planning Process

INTRODUCTION

Financial planning as a discipline endured rapid growth in the early 1980s. Virtually unknown to the financial services industry prior to 1970, financial planning was the profession of almost half a million people by 1985. In its heyday, the lure of spectacular financial opportunities attracted into the industry the most able financial experts as well as those who nurtured their individual get-rich-quick schemes.

But time has shown that beyond glamor and mystery there is a valuable service profession that is urgently needed by many Americans on the threshold of the 21st century. Changing social, economic, and demographic forces ensure that eventually financial planning will emerge as a mature profession. Indeed, it can be said without equivocation that financial planning has already become a necessity—not only for the financial security but also for the general peace of mind it affords. In the face of today's ever-changing economy along with individual changeable circumstances, careful planning is essential.

In a very real sense, the process of financial planning begins when an individual recognizes a very simple fact: Every person or family is in a unique financial position. Therefore, any course of financial action must also be unique—carefully planned to meet specific needs and goals. Obviously, what is right for one person may not be right for another person with a different set of circumstances.

Recognition of the need for appropriate action, of course, does not automatically answer the question: What *is* the best course of action for an individual or a family? Furthermore, when we consider that the average family will make over $1 million before retirement—and many, much more than that—it becomes an important question for everyone. To put it succinctly, only when people understand (1) their current financial position, (2) their financial goals for the future, and (3) what effects a particular action will have on their financial situation, can they begin to appreciate what actions are appropriate for them. However, since many people are hard pressed to comprehend these difficult—and often confusing—issues, a financial planner can maximize their welfare by helping them achieve their goals in the most efficient manner.

In this chapter we will discuss in detail how the financial planning process is initiated, what constitutes the intermediate steps in this process, and how the process is successfully completed. In our discussion we will cover issues that arise both before and after one recognizes the need for engaging the services of a financial planner. More specifically, first we will describe the personal financial planning process beginning with the initial interview, followed by contract signing, data gathering, preliminary analysis, data and goal refinement, plan development and presentation, plan implementation, plan monitoring, and plan review and update.

THE FINANCIAL PLANNING PROCESS

There is no standardized process for performing personal financial planning activities. Even the six-step process developed by the Registry of the International Association for Financial Planning (IAFP) is not as comprehensive as one would like. A comprehensive financial planning process, contrasted with the Registry's six-step process is presented in Table 2-1. It should be pointed out that a comprehensive process is different from the Registry's process in that it adds several steps of qualifying the client and defining the scope of the engagement.

An important caveat should be added here. While every financial plan should complete steps A to J as presented in Table 2-1, not all plans have to achieve the same level of comprehensiveness or sophistication. In fact, in practice financial planners offer more than one level of service in order to accommodate clients with different needs and goals. A variety of terms has been applied to the many levels of services that exist. For instance, the American Institute of Certified Public Accountants (AICPA) has identified three levels

TABLE 2-1 Steps in Financial Planning Process

Step	Comprehensive process	IAFP registry steps
A	*A*ccept the client on the basis of the preliminary interview.	
B	*B*ase the complexity of the data gathering process on the basis of client goals, needs, and resources.	II, III
C	*C*ollect relevant data and conduct goals and objectives interview.	I
D	*D*evelop a comprehensive financial plan on the basis of a detailed analysis of the quantitative and qualitative data.	IV
E	*E*stablish recommendations consistent with client goals, needs, and resources.	
F	*F*urnish the client with a written comprehensive plan, detailed recommendations, and an action trip tick.	
G	*G*o over the plan recommendations, make suitable modifications, and finalize the recommendations.	
H	*H*ave the action trip tick reviewed and modified, and develop the final trip tick acceptable to the client.	
I	*I*mplement or coordinate implementation of recommendations.	V
J	*J*ustify the need for continuous monitoring and annual updating of the comprehensive financial plan.	VI

Registry Steps:
 I. Collect and access all relevant data
 II. Identify goals and objectives
 III. Identify financial problems
 IV. Develop a written financial plan
 V. Implement or coordinate the implementation of recommendations
 VI. Periodic review and revision of the plan and recommendations

of service: consultant engagements; segment planning engagements, and comprehensive personal financial engagements. Individual planners across the country refer to various levels and types of service by such names as retirement planning, investment planning, tax planning, and comprehensive planning. Regardless of the level or the type of service performed, however, there is no substitute for a sophisticated, professional approach to financial planning.

SUBJECT AREAS OF PERSONAL FINANCIAL PLANNING

In practice, the comprehensive financial planning process, and the resulting comprehensive financial plan developed for a client, should address six elements of the client's financial situation. These elements, and their respective

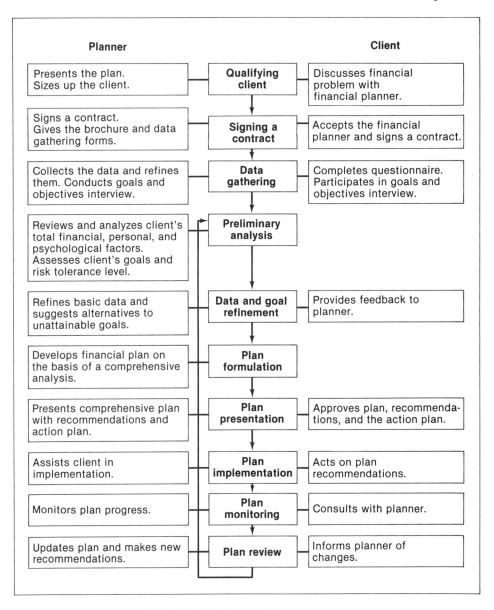

Planner		Client
Presents the plan. Sizes up the client.	**Qualifying client**	Discusses financial problem with financial planner.
Signs a contract. Gives the brochure and data gathering forms.	**Signing a contract**	Accepts the financial planner and signs a contract.
Collects the data and refines them. Conducts goals and objectives interview.	**Data gathering**	Completes questionnaire. Participates in goals and objectives interview.
Reviews and analyzes client's total financial, personal, and psychological factors. Assesses client's goals and risk tolerance level.	**Preliminary analysis**	
Refines basic data and suggests alternatives to unattainable goals.	**Data and goal refinement**	Provides feedback to planner.
Develops financial plan on the basis of a comprehensive analysis.	**Plan formulation**	
Presents comprehensive plan with recommendations and action plan.	**Plan presentation**	Approves plan, recommendations, and the action plan.
Assists client in implementation.	**Plan implementation**	Acts on plan recommendations.
Monitors plan progress.	**Plan monitoring**	Consults with planner.
Updates plan and makes new recommendations.	**Plan review**	Informs planner of changes.

FIGURE 2-1   The financial planning process

chapter references, are presented below:

	Elements	Chapters
R	Risk management planning	3 and 4
E	Essentials of budgeting, savings, and credit planning	5 and 6
T	Tax planning	7 and 8
I	Investment planning	9, 10, and 11
R	Retirement planning	12 and 13
E	Estate planning	14 and 15
	Comprehensive Plan (R-E-T-I-R-E)	16

Of course, a comprehensive plan should also have as an integral part a list of specific recommendations, an action plan, and a timetable which can be followed by the client on a systematic basis.

Now that we have presented an overview of the financial planning process, it might be interesting to elaborate on the essential steps associated with this process, an overview of which is presented in Figure 2-1.

QUALIFYING A POTENTIAL CLIENT

Every financial planner-client relationship has a built-in life span. Unless great care is taken to nurture it, some relationships are destined to die early or last only a few years, while a rare few are likely to ripen to old age. Clearly, long-term success depends on client relationships that stand the test of time.

Perhaps the most important factor contributing to a lasting relationship is a carefully orchestrated, all-important initial interview. During this interview the financial planner sizes up a potential client by determining if there is a firm basis for establishing a long-term relationship with the individual or the family.

To be sure, the initial interview is not an end in itself. It is designed to help the financial planner recognize the potential client's *true* desires and determine if the chemistry is right for establishing a long-lasting relationship. Sometimes, the former element will not surface quickly, and the planner may have to probe "behind the scenes" in order to discover these desires. Here are three real-life examples designed to demonstrate the complexity of the task at hand.

Case 1

Bob Smith, and his fiancee Jane Coy, have engaged Karl Dixon to develop a comprehensive financial plan for them. Bob was a registered pharmacist in

Cleveland for 20 years but has recently been forced to move to Arizona for health reasons. He sold his pharmaceutical business in Cleveland and is contemplating buying a suitable business in Arizona. Jane is a tenured school teacher in Cleveland and earns an annual salary of $48,000. She participates in the school's retirement benefit plan and enjoys the usual (health, disability, eye care, and so on) fringe benefits. Bob and Jane are planning to get married in a few months and settle down in Arizona. This is a second marriage for both and there appears to be a great deal of understanding, open communication, and flexibility on the part of both. Karl Dixon's responsibility is to develop a comprehensive financial plan by assuming that Bob and Jane are already married, even though they will not be officially married for several months.

Bob and Jane's situation is straightforward, or so it seems on the surface. But after the initial interview, planner Karl Dixon discovered that the task is far different from merely developing a comprehensive financial plan for the couple. Bob Smith loves Jane and has no problem accepting the fact that Jane will quit her teaching job, lose her $48,000 teaching salary plus the associated fringe benefits, and be content with playing the role of an unemployed housewife. In contrast, Jane Coy is unwilling to take such a situation lightly. She fears that after marriage she will lose (1) an annual salary of $48,000 plus future increments, (2) her school's retirement contribution, (3) her fringe benefits, (4) her financial independence, (5) money on the forced sale of her home, and (6) her option to retire at age 59 with full retirement benefits, currently offered by her school system to all employees with at least 25 years of service. In addition, her daughter has been admitted to an Ivy League school, but Bob is totally opposed to financing such an expensive education. Given all of these concerns, Jane wants Bob to pay her $400,000 before marriage as compensation for the losses she would suffer, but Bob is willing to only take financial responsibility for her, and is totally opposed to making any cash payments to Jane. Karl Dixon's task is much more complicated than he was led to believe, and he may not wish to handle this case loaded with psychological problems. This case illustrates the importance of the use of qualitative data in financial planning.

Case 2

Robert Powers, 52, and Janet Powers, 49, are a happily married couple. They have three children, ages 28, 25, and 23. Robert feels that their financial situation is in shambles, and he needs a financial planner to bring order to this chaotic situation. Janet feels the same way, and is willing to pay a handsome planning fee ($4,000) to have a comprehensive plan developed for them. The Powers have just engaged Bill Kifer to develop a financial plan for them. Before making his final decision to engage Bill Kifer, however, Robert made the unusual request that his mother's net worth (in excess of $2 million) should be included in their plan. A quick review of the Powers' initial data suggests that, with the exception of Bob's unusual request, the Powers' case is straight-forward.

During the initial interview Bill Kifer discovered some very interesting facts. Robert, now 52, is currently unemployed and has no intentions of going back to work. He is an only child and will inherit his mother's estate of over $2 million. Furthermore, the mother is 85 years old and Robert argues that since he would have all of her money "very soon" it makes no sense for him to go to work. This is a source of great friction between Janet and Robert. Janet strongly believes that Robert should not count on this money at all because the mother could still live for a long time and could lose most of her wealth through bad investments. That creates a special problem: Robert wants Bill Kifer to include his mother's net worth in their plan, whereas Janet wants Kifer to ignore the mother's estate altogether.

There is another family matter that is creating enormous friction between Robert and Janet. All three of their children are adults and should be firmly established in life. Unfortunately, that is not the case. None of them has more than a high school education, a job, or any means of support. The oldest one has a serious health problem, but physically the other two are normal. All the children live at home and are totally dependent on their parents for full financial support. Robert is very upset about the current situation and believes that the only way to resolve this problem is to "throw the children out of the house and force them to become responsible human beings." Janet, however, feels that since it is the parents who have failed, they should set up separate trusts and adequately fund them to take care of the children for the rest of their lives.

Finally, there is the emotional problem. Since Janet is compelled to work because Robert refuses to, Janet wants her salary to be spent solely for her own use and does not want to support the family. Robert disagrees with that approach, since in his judgment family finances should never be split in that fashion. Here again, Bill Kifer must decide if he is comfortable accepting the Powers as his clients.

Case 3

John and Nancy Well are an affluent couple. The Wells live in the exclusive suburb of Bloomfield Hills in Detroit. John owns two businesses and has an annual income of $400,000. The Wells have two children both of whom are well settled in life. The Wells have had the benefit of counsel and professional help from a CPA, an attorney, an insurance counselor, a banker, a casualty/property insurance agent, and a retirement benefit specialist. However, John firmly believes that a financial planner would be able to "put it all together" and develop an exclusive road map for the family to follow.

The case of John and Nancy Well is not too different from the cases financial planner Cindy Rawlins routinely handles. Consequently, she is delighted to consider the Wells as valued potential clients. However, the initial interview raised great doubts in her mind about the advisability of handling this case.

The facts discovered by Cindy Rawlins are as follows. Despite their apparent affluence, both John and Nancy feel that taxes and inflation are going to eventually "kill them." Yet, they insist on maintaining an extravagant lifestyle which puts enormous strains on their spendable income. This leads the Wells to insist on receiving unreasonably high rates of return on their investable funds. However, what really complicates the matter is the fact that both John and Nancy are risk averse and would never entertain the thought of losing a part of their principal. So, Cindy Rawlins wonders if there is any true benefit to developing a comprehensive financial plan until the Wells have reoriented their thinking.

On the basis of the three cases just presented, it is possible to make some general observations. Regardless of their orientation and expectations, what clients really need is an *objective* rather than a *subjective* perspective in the area of personal financial planning. Of course, a financial planner must understand the mechanics of plan development and implementation. However, the planning process also requires that the planner must successfully blend mechanical expertise with human understanding and develop acceptable solutions which will best serve the clients. Consequently, to a large degree, the success of a planning process is assured only if the financial planner succeeds in identifying and establishing a professional relationship with the right type of clients.

SIGNING A FORMAL CONTRACT

After the financial planner and the individual have agreed to establish a professional relationship, a formal contract or agreement must be signed. This contract should specify: (1) the range of services to be performed by the planner; (2) the method of compensation; and (3) the client's responsibility in the planning process. Also, the contract should clearly state that: (1) the client agrees to participate in the planning process on a voluntary basis; (2) the financial planner is not authorized to perform any legal functions; and (3) the client is responsible for compensating other professionals (for instance, CPA or attorney) if they are consulted by the financial planner on behalf of the client. Of course, to help achieve the third objective, the client should be asked to sign an Authorization for Information form. A standard contract is presented in Appendix A, which can be suitably modified to fit the needs of a financial planner.

At this time, if licensed as a registered investment advisor with the Securities and Exchange Commission (SEC), the financial planner is obliged to provide the client with a planning brochure in compliance with SEC Rule 204-3, commonly known as the "Brochure Rule." The brochure must describe the financial planning services offered by the financial planner. Furthermore, if the planner performs both planning and implementation services, it should also clearly state that if the client implements through the planner any of the plan recommendations which generate commissions, then the planner will earn these commissions in addition to the planning fee (conflict of interest rule). A sample brochure is presented in Appendix B. This rule can also be satisfied by providing the client with ADV (Part II) of the registered investment advisor. A summary of Investment Advisers Act of 1940 is presented in Appendix C to Chapter 2.

Before leaving this topic it is important to mention that the contract should include a provision permitting the client to cancel it within five business days and have the advance planning fee, if any, fully refunded. This provision makes it possible for the client to go over the contract and the brochure carefully and, if desired, have them reviewed by an attorney. Such a provision also helps to emphasize that, by signing the contract, both parties agree to establish a long and fruitful relationship.

GATHERING THE DATA

It is often said that a plan, irrespective of its complexity, is only as good as the data and assumptions on which it is based. There is a great deal of truth in that statement. Unless the data are accurate and reflective of the client's goals, aspirations, and fears, no matter how "sophisticated," the plan will not have much value for the client. Consequently, a standard rule of thumb is that the data must be sufficiently comprehensive to enable the planner to: (1) evaluate the client's financial condition; (2) determine the client's personality, dreams, and fears; (3) articulate the client's short- and long-range goals; and (4) formulate a set of strategies for helping the client achieve his or her stated goals. It is therefore imperative that the financial planner collect both quantitative and qualitative data as the basis for developing a comprehensive plan.

At this point it is necessary to add an important caveat. Before starting the data collection process it is desirable for the financial planner to make the client comfortable by explaining why such a detailed personal, financial, and psychological set of data is needed to develop the plan. Few people appreciate the complexity of the planning process. Consequently, an informed and enlightened client might be expected to supply a far more complete and accurate set of data than the client who has little appreciation for the value of collecting massive sets of accurate data and hence might find such an exercise overpowering and distressful.

Quantitative Data

Clearly, the extent of data collection will depend upon the type of plan developed and the level of sophistication desired by the client. For instance,

Investment Portfolio Statement

NAME: _____   DATE: _____

Investments	Purchase date	Cost	Market value	Qualified plans*	Maturity date /interest rate
Liquid:					
_____	_____	_____	_____	_____	_____
_____	_____	_____	_____	_____	_____
_____	_____	_____	_____	_____	_____
_____	_____	_____	_____	_____	_____
_____	_____	_____	_____	_____	_____
_____	_____	_____	_____	_____	_____
_____	_____	_____	_____	_____	_____
_____	_____	_____	_____	_____	_____
_____	_____	_____	_____	_____	_____
_____	_____	_____	_____	_____	_____
Liquid Total:			[_____]		
Fixed:					
_____	_____	_____	_____	_____	_____
_____	_____	_____	_____	_____	_____
_____	_____	_____	_____	_____	_____
_____	_____	_____	_____	_____	_____
_____	_____	_____	_____	_____	_____
_____	_____	_____	_____	_____	_____
_____	_____	_____	_____	_____	_____
_____	_____	_____	_____	_____	_____
Total:			[_____]		

* IRA, KEOGH, PENSION, PROFIT SHARING, AND 401(K)
ADDITIONAL INFORMATION:

Continued

Investment	Purchase date	Cost	Market value	Qualified plans*	Maturity date /interest rate
Growth:					
___	___	___	___	___	___
___	___	___	___	___	___
___	___	___	___	___	___
___	___	___	___	___	___
___	___	___	___	___	___
___	___	___	___	___	___
___	___	___	___	___	___
___	___	___	___	___	___
___	___	___	___	___	___
___	___	___	___	___	___
Growth Total:			☐		
Nonliquid:					
___	___	___	___	___	___
___	___	___	___	___	___
___	___	___	___	___	___
___	___	___	___	___	___
___	___	___	___	___	___
___	___	___	___	___	___
___	___	___	___	___	___
___	___	___	___	___	___
Nonliquid Total:			☐		
Grand Total:			☐		

* IRA, KEOGH, PENSION, PROFIT SHARING, AND 401(K)
ADDITIONAL INFORMATION:

MORE IN-DEPTH INVESTMENT DATA

STOCKS

NAME _____

IMPLEMENTATION: (　) 　B = BEFORE, C = CURRENT
TYPE: (　) 　2 = STOCK, 3 = MUTUAL FUND (　)
REAL ESTATE: 　YES 　NO 　TYPE OF STOCK _____

OBJECTIVE: _____
OWNERSHIP: (　) 　C = CLIENT, S = SPOUSE, J = JOINT, CP = COMMUNITY
PROPERTY

ASSET TYPE: (　) 　F = FIXED, V = VARIABLE, N = NONWORKING
LIQUIDITY: (　) 　1 = LIQUID, 2 = CONVERTIBLE, 3 = NONLIQUID

CLASSIFICATION: (　) 　1 = PERSONAL, 2 = PENSION, 3 = PROFIT SHARING,
4 = KEOGH, 5 = IRA, 6 = CUSTODIAN,
7 = OTHER RETIREMENT

VALUE AT DEATH: $_____ S = SAME AS CURRENT VALUE
TAXED IN ESTATE: (　) 　1 = TAXABLE/PROBATABLE, 2 = TAXABLE/NONPRO-
BATABLE, 3 = NOT TAXED (　)
EXCHANGE: _____ SYMBOL: _____ (STOCKS ONLY)

CURRENT PRICE/SHARE: $_____ CURRENT YIELD: _____%

Cost Data:

Date purchased	Number of shares	Total cost	Cash flow (Y or N)
__/__/__	_____	$_____	Y　N
__/__/__	_____	$_____	Y　N
__/__/__	_____	$_____	Y　N
__/__/__	_____	$_____	Y　N
__/__/__	_____	$_____	Y　N

Income Distributions:

Date received	Amount	Long-term capital gain (Y or N)	Percent taxable Federal	State
__/__/__	$_____	Y　N	_____%	_____%
__/__/__	$_____	Y　N	_____%	_____%
__/__/__	$_____	Y　N	_____%	_____%
__/__/__	$_____	Y　N	_____%	_____%
__/__/__	$_____	Y　N	_____%	_____%

BONDS

NAME _____

IMPLEMENTATION: ( )   B = BEFORE, C = CURRENT
MUNICIPAL BOND?   YES   NO

TYPE: (1)   1 = BOND
REAL ESTATE: YES   NO   TYPE OF BOND _____

OBJECTIVE: _____
OWNERSHIP: ( )   C = CLIENT, S = SPOUSE, J = JOINT, CP = COMMUNITY
PROPERTY

ASSET TYPE: ( )   F = FIXED, V = VARIABLE, N = NONWORKING
LIQUIDITY: ( )   1 = LIQUID, 2 = CONVERTIBLE, 3 = NONLIQUID

CLASSIFICATION: ( )   1 = PERSONAL, 2 = PENSION, 3 = PROFIT SHARING,
4 = KEOGH, 5 = IRA, 6 = CUSTODIAN,
7 = OTHER RETIREMENT

VALUE AT DEATH: $_____S = SAME AS CURRENT VALUE
TAXED IN ESTATE: ( )   1 = TAXABLE/PROBATABLE, 2 = TAXABLE/NONPRO-
BATABLE, 3 = NOT TAXED ( )

YEAR OF MATURITY: _____   COUPON RATE: _____%

Cost Data:

Purchase date	Face amount	Total cost	Market value	Cash flow (Y or N)
/ /	$	$	$	Y N
/ /	$	$	$	Y N
/ /	$	$	$	Y N
/ /	$	$	$	Y N
/ /	$	$	$	Y N

Income Distributions:

Date received	Interest income	Long-term capital gain (Y or N)	Percent taxable Federal	State
/ /	$	Y N	%	%
/ /	$	Y N	%	%
/ /	$	Y N	%	%
/ /	$	Y N	%	%
/ /	$	Y N	%	%

MUTUAL FUNDS

NAME _____

IMPLEMENTATION: (   )   B = BEFORE, C = CURRENT
TYPE: (   )   2 = STOCK, 3 = MUTUAL FUND
REAL ESTATE: YES   NO   TYPE OF MUTUAL FUND _____

OBJECTIVE: _____
OWNERSHIP: (   )   C = CLIENT, S = SPOUSE, J = JOINT, CP = COMMUNITY
                   PROPERTY

ASSET TYPE: (   )   F = FIXED, V = VARIABLE, N = NONWORKING
LIQUIDITY: (   )   1 = LIQUID, 2 = CONVERTIBLE, 3 = NONLIQUID

CLASSIFICATION: (   )   1 = PERSONAL, 2 = PENSION, 3 = PROFIT SHARING,
                        4 = KEOGH, 5 = IRA, 6 = CUSTODIAN,
                        7 = OTHER RETIREMENT

VALUE AT DEATH: $_____ S = SAME AS CURRENT VALUE
TAXED IN ESTATE: (   )   1 = TAXABLE/PROBATABLE, 2 = TAXABLE/NONPRO-
                        BATABLE, 3 = NOT TAXED (   )
EXCHANGE: _____   SYMBOL: _____   (STOCKS ONLY)

CURRENT PRICE/SHARE: $_____   CURRENT YIELD: _____%
REINVEST DIVIDENDS: YES   NO

Cost Data:

Date purchased	Number of shares	Total cost	Cash flow (Y or N)
/ /	_____	$_____	Y N
/ /	_____	$_____	Y N
/ /	_____	$_____	Y N
/ /	_____	$_____	Y N
/ /	_____	$_____	Y N

Income Distributions:

Date received	Amount	Long-term capital gain (Y or N)	Percent taxable Federal	State
/ /	$_____	Y N	_____%	_____%
/ /	$_____	Y N	_____%	_____%
/ /	$_____	Y N	_____%	_____%
/ /	$_____	Y N	_____%	_____%
/ /	$_____	Y N	_____%	_____%

Note: Boxed information will be collected by planner at data gathering session

---

STOCK INVESTMENT GUIDELINES

PURCHASE SPECIFICATIONS

Amount $_____

Beta Range

Below 0.75
0.75–1.00
1.00–1.25
Over 1.25

Minimum Dividend Yield

2–4%
4–6%
Over 6%

Maximum Price/Earnings Ratio

 5
10
15
20
Other _____

Maximum Price Per Share

$10
$20
$30
$40
$50
$60
Other _____

SELL SPECIFICATIONS

If Price Drops

_____% Below Purchase Price
$_____ per Share Below Purchase Price

If Price Rises

_____% Above Purchase Price
$_____ per Share Above Purchase Price

---

for a simple investment plan, investment data can be collected on the form presented in the box entitled Investment Portfolio Statement. In contrast, development of a far more comprehensive plan requires a *more sophisticated set of investment data*, as can be obtained from the box entitled More In-Depth Investment Data: stocks, bonds, mutual funds. In any event, as a general rule, any meaningful economic profile will have to contain information on the following:

- Personal Profile
- Cash
- Bank, Savings, and Money Market
- Notes and Loans
- Mortgages
- Stocks, Bonds, and Mutual Funds
- Real Estate/Oil and Gas/Other Limited Partnerships
- Income Data
- Employee Benefits

- Insurance Coverage
- Educational Funding
- Tax-related Data
- Wills/Trusts/Estate-related Data

INSTRUCTIONS FOR FILLING OUT INVESTMENT PORTFOLIO STATEMENT*

RELAX. It's going to be simple. Classify your investments under four categories:

1. *Liquid:* Include balances in checking and savings accounts, savings and loan associations, money market and other liquid funds.
2. *Fixed:* Include investments in bonds, bond mutual funds, single premium whole life, immediate annuity, CDs, and other fixed income instruments. Give interest rates and maturing dates.
3. *Growth:* Include investments in stock mutual funds, stocks, limited partnerships, and other securities with growth potential. Give original cost and number of shares.
4. *Nonliquid:* Include investments in various tax shelters and other investments which cannot be liquidated for some time.
5. Make sure you give the current market value of each investment.
6. In the column entitled "Qualified Plan," appropriately mark investments in: IRA, Keogh, pension, profit sharing, and 401(K).

In addition, key documents should also be collected as a source of obtaining additional quantitative data. A list of several important business and personal documents is given next:

Personal documents.
Wills: Clients and Spouse
Trust Agreements
Deeds or Contracts
Tax Returns
Divorce Decree
Nuptial Agreements
Separation Agreements
Children's Assets

---

* The Investment Portfolio Statement can be found on pp. 31–32.

Insurance Policies:
  Life
  Health
  Property/Casualty
  Liability

Business documents
Corporation or Partnership Papers
Income Tax Returns
Financial Statements
Stock Purchase Agreements
Employment Agreements
Employee Benefit Programs
Pension/Profit Sharing Plan
Leases

Perhaps the most efficient means of collecting quantitative data is to use a fact finding questionnaire and an explanation sheet commenting on various questions which might be difficult to answer. The data gathering questionnaire could be relatively simple, or it could be highly complex if conditions warrant the use of such a complex questionnaire. A simple fact finding questionnaire with an explanation sheet is presented in Appendix D.

Qualitative Data

The quality of a comprehensive plan is also intimately related to the collection of the qualitative data. A practical yet effective means of collecting this type of data is to conduct an extensive goals and objectives interview during which this type of data can be collected. Examples of qualitative data include: (1) priorities of various objectives; (2) risk tolerance level; (3) good and bad experiences with various types of investment products; (4) feelings toward life insurance; (5) difficulty with generating savings; (6) need for obtaining financial independence before retirement; (7) desire to find a public or private college education for children; and (8) general feeling toward money. As a general rule, open-ended questions can be used to obtain qualitative data.

PRELIMINARY ANALYSIS

The primary use of financial information in personal financial planning is in the analysis, planning, and control of ongoing personal financial decisions directed by the financial planner. It is difficult, if not impossible, to identify financial objectives and formulate strategies for their achievement without knowing a client's current financial situation and resources.

A preliminary analysis immediately following initial data gathering should be performed with three objectives in mind: (1) identifying gaps, inconsistencies, and inaccuracies in the data already collected; (2) developing highlights of the client's current financial condition; and (3) carefully documenting client's goals which appear unrealistic. These objectives are achieved through the preparation of a number of personal financial statements on a *tentative* basis, a partial list of which follows:

- life insurance needs analysis
- budget analysis
- tax analysis
- investment analysis
- retirement analysis

Each analysis or computation should be carefully reviewed by the financial planner with the objective of preparing a list of questions to be presented to the client at the beginning of the next meeting.

DATA AND GOAL REFINEMENT

This step begins with the presentation to the client of a list of questions generated in the previous meeting. The client should be encouraged to spend the necessary time and resources to provide the missing data and clarify the confusion surrounding some of the data already collected. For instance, if the purchase price and dividend distribution of ABC stock are missing, it would be impossible to calculate the tax liability resulting from the sale of this stock. Another example of incomplete data relates to the pension plan balance which is not subdivided between fully vested and nonvested contributions. A third example of confusing data is a single premium deferred annuity (SPDA) investment purchased five years ago for which the surrender charges have not been clearly specified. If this SPDA does not impose any surrender charges after four years, it could be sold now without incurring these charges. If, however, the company imposes a six-year surrender charge in addition to an interest penalty, the financial planner will have to take this factor into account if a liquidation of this investment is contemplated.

The modification of unrealistic client goals constitutes an even bigger challenge for the financial planner. This is because complicated psychological, emotional and social factors may have to be handled by the planner to solve this type of problem. As a general rule, the financial planner can attempt to solve the unrealistic goals problems by suggesting a variety of alternatives to convert the unattainable goals, as specified below:

Unattainable goal	Alternative suggestion
Become financially independent at a given age	1. Increase the time frame 2. Reduce the financial independence income 3. Increase investment return by assuming more risk 4. Reduce expenditures
Saving goal of a specified amount	1. Cut flexible expenses 2. Cut fixed expenses 3. Increase income (e.g., unemployed spouse may seek employment) 4. Employ forced savings techniques
Finance a college education involving a specified amount	1. Apply for student loan 2. Child find employment 3. Participate in an educational trust offered by the State

PLAN FORMULATION

Once the data have been refined and perfected, a detailed analysis can be undertaken. This analysis can be divided into two convenient groups. First, an analysis of the data can be completed with the help of a financial planning computer software program. The selection of a software program would of course depend upon the degree of sophistication desired. Some software programs are quite basic while others are highly complicated and require a great deal of technical knowledge on the part of the paraplanner.

Once the basic analysis is completed, the financial planner can then run "what if" simulations to address client's concerns and determine the most efficient ways of achieving client's goals. This type of analysis brings "life" to the plan and makes the planning process truly meaningful.

An important feature of the comprehensive plan is the recommendations designed to help the client achieve the predetermined goals. Of course, one of the unpleasant, albeit necessary, tasks of a financial planner is to identify those goals which appear unrealistic and help the client modify them.

Assuming that the goals are realistic, plan recommendations should be directed towards helping the client achieve goals in each of the six major areas: namely, risk management, cash management, taxes, investments, retirement, and estate planning. These recommendations should first be made in generic terms. For instance, the planner may suggest that the client purchase $500,000 worth of additional life insurance, invest $50,000 in a single premium deferred annuity, reduce taxes by investing in a tax shelter, and create an irrevocable trust. Subsequently, the planner should recommend specific steps which the client could take to implement these recommendations. As an example, the planner may recommend that the client purchase $500,000 worth of universal life insurance from ABC Company and invest $50,000 in XYZ Company which markets one of the best single premium deferred annuity products. The planner should also assist the client in implementing these recommendations, if such assistance is desired.

PLAN PRESENTATION

The highlight of the financial planning process is the presentation of the comprehensive financial plan to the client. Ideally, the plan should be subdivided into the following sections:

Section	Contents
Goals and Objectives Interview	A summary of the initial interview with the client during which short- and long-term goals were articulated, and the client's fears, dreams, and major concerns were recognized.
Basic Observations	Highlights of the major components of the comprehensive financial plan.
Key Recommendations	Recommendations for achieving the specified objectives in each of the six planning areas covered by R-E-T-I-R-E.
Action Plan	"Trip tick," specifying the actions required on the part of the client, and the priorities of these action plans.

In addition to the written comprehensive financial plan, if financially and administratively feasible, the financial planner may also provide the client with a video and an audio cassette as supplements to the written plan. These ancillary products can go a long way toward motivating the client to study the plan and implement its recommendations without delay.

During the plan presentation session, the planner should explain to the client the key recommendations and impress upon the client that the value of the plan cannot be fully realized until its recommendations are systematically implemented.

PLAN IMPLEMENTATION

An effective financial planner is able to motivate the client to closely follow the plan articulated in the "Action Plan" section of the comprehensive financial plan. While both parties explicitly recognize that the client is under no obligation to implement the recommendations through the planner who developed the plan, the client should realize that to derive full benefits the plan recommendations must be implemented in a timely fashion. The financial planner of course has the moral and professional obligation to assist the client in implementing the plan. In addition, if the client purchases insurance and investment products from the financial planner, the planner must (1) clearly specify that any sales commissions generated by these sales are in addition to, and not in lieu of, the planning fees already collected, (2) provide in writing to the client the advantages, disadvantages and risks associated with each product, and (3) make sure that the client clearly understands their attendant risks and is comfortable with them.

PLAN MONITORING AND REVIEW

Personal financial planning is a never-ending process. The reason for this is not hard to find. Over time, a client's personal situation, financial conditions, economic conditions, and tax environment—all of these can and do change. Consequently, the client's progress vis-à-vis the short- and long-range goals set in the plan should be monitored on a continual basis and the client should be advised about factors which could affect the plan's progress. In addition, a periodic review and revision of the plan's recommendations are not only desirable but are essential if the financial planner wishes to participate in the financial planning process on a long-term basis. There is, of course, no universal definition of how frequently this periodic review should be conducted. A typical time cycle is comprised of an annual update with provision for a more frequent review whenever personal, financial, or economic conditions change.

In this chapter we have presented an overview of the personal financial planning process. Next, we will undertake a detailed analysis of each of the six major financial planning areas covered by the acronym R-E-T-I-R-E. A real-world comprehensive financial plan using the financial planning process developed here will be presented in Chapter 16.

APPENDIX A TO CHAPTER 2

FINANCIAL PLANNING PARTICIPATION AGREEMENT

Part I

I understand and agree to the following provisions:

1. This program is strictly voluntary and I am participating at my own discretion.
2. I agree to assist Financial Planners, Inc. (FP) by furnishing it with all current data, copies of documents, and such other information relevant to my financial situation as may be reasonably requested.
3. All information given to FP and all recommendations and advice furnished to me shall be regarded by both parties as confidential. It is also understood that FP will not furnish to any individual or firm, including my employer, any information about me or my financial position without my explicit permission in writing.
4. I hereby grant full authority to FP to discuss, impart, disclose, or communicate any or all information given by me with Straford Company, FP's broker-dealer. I further understand that in compliance with the law, the financial plan developed by FP may be submitted to Straford Company for its review.
5. The recommendations with supportive data will be submitted to me by FP in a written form (or orally if I so choose) for my consideration and acceptance.
6. I shall at all times be at liberty either to follow or disregard, wholly or partially, any information, recommendation, or advice given by FP. Also, I will be fully responsible for all decisions relating to the advice given.
7. FP will take the necessary steps to implement on my behalf the recommendations made by them, if I request them to do so.
8. I understand that FP is not qualified to render any legal advice or to prepare any legal documents for the implementation of my financial plan and that my personal attorney shall be solely responsible for such advice and opinions.
9. I understand that if I direct FP to obtain on my behalf legal and accounting counsel, then all fees of independent legal counsel and accountants for document preparation and advisory services will be paid directly by me to the attorney or the CPA.
10. Since the services rendered under this Agreement are advisory in nature, I expressly agree that FP shall not be held responsible for the consequences of its recommendations, as long as those services are rendered by it in good faith, and provided that FP is not in violation of applicable Federal and State Securities laws, rules, and regulations.
11. I acknowledge that I have received and reviewed the brochure provided by FP in accordance with Rule 204-3 (Brochure Rule) under the Investment Advisor's Act of 1940, and understand that certain officers and employees may maintain various business relationships through which may result in FP receiving compensation other than the fees outlined in this contract. The receipt of such fees may be considered to represent a conflict of interest. I am under no obligation to execute any investment, insurance, or other transactions with or through such employees or officers.
12. Miscellaneous Provisions:
    a. This Agreement shall be governed by and constructed according to the laws of the State of Michigan.
    b. FP shall not assign this Agreement without my written consent.
    c. No modification or amendment to this agreement shall be effective unless made in writing and signed by me and FP.
    d. *This Agreement may be terminated by me without penalty upon delivery to FP of written notice of termination within five (5) business days from the date of my acceptance of this Agreement.*
    e. FP reserves the right to determine the appropriateness of a particular financial plan to a particular client.

I have read the attached Agreement and understand the provisions set forth therein. IN WITNESS WHEREOF, I have this date executed this Agreement in duplicate.

Client: _____ Date _____
          name

_____
          address

_____

Home: _____ Office: _____
      phone   phone

Client: _____ Date _____
(Spouse)

Accepted by: FINANCIAL PLANNERS, INC.

_____   _____
Financial Planner   Date

Exhibit A
Fee Schedule
Hourly Rate Schedule

Person responsible	Document modification	Data gathering	Analysis	Planning	Presentation
Clerical	$ 25.00	N/A	N/A	N/A	N/A
Paraplanner	$ 45.00	$ 45.00	N/A	N/A	N/A
Certified Financial Planner	$ 75.00	$ 75.00	$ 75.00	$ 75.00	$ 75.00
CFP and Member of Registry	$100.00	$100.00	$100.00	$100.00	$100.00

Additional Fees:
    All financial services are subject to our increase of fees as to the procurement of outside professional advice and services. The client retains the right to be informed in advance and reject those costs.
Subsequent Reviews:
    The hourly rate schedule just presented will apply.
Note: Financial Planners, Inc. reserves the right to determine in advance the estimated number of hours required to complete a plan or a review. The client has the right to accept or reject the offer.

APPENDIX B TO CHAPTER 2

DESCRIPTION OF FINANCIAL PLANNING SERVICES

Financial Planners, Inc. (hereafter called FP) provides financial planning services to its clients. In conjunction with the financial planning services it renders, FP does provide advice regarding investments. Therefore, it is registered with the Securities and Exchange Commission as an Investment Advisor. This Description of Financial Planning Services ("Brochure") is provided in accordance with Rule 204-3 ("Brochure Rule") under the Investment Advisor's Act of 1940, and should be reviewed prior to entering into a financial planning agreement with FP.

THE INFORMATION PROVIDED IN THIS BROCHURE HAS NOT BEEN PASSED UPON OR APPROVED BY THE SECURITIES AND EXCHANGE COMMISSION, NOR HAS THE COMMISSION PASSED UPON OR APPROVED THE BUSINESS PRACTICES OF FINANCIAL PLANNERS, INC.

INTRODUCTION

Financial Planners, Inc. believes that most individuals, partnerships, and corporations need assistance in managing their financial affairs in a knowledgeable, effective manner. This is frequently evidenced by the lack of coordination of the various aspects of financial planning. Most successful individuals have accountants, attorneys, stockbrokers, life insurance consultants, and other advisors. However, although well founded, the efforts of these advisors may not necessarily result in a sound financial plan.

FP accepts the responsibility of becoming a working partner with its clients and their other advisors, undertaking a thorough review of the clients' financial affairs, and creating written financial plans. Furthermore, if requested, FP may partic-ipate in the implementation of recommendations made in the financial plans of its clients.

FINANCIAL PLANNING PROCESS

FP provides several types of financial plans and its financial planning process normally includes the following steps:

1. The Financial Planning Participation Agreement is prepared and executed.
2. A detailed questionnaire is completed and the client's present position is analyzed in light of his/her circumstances and objectives.
3. A written financial plan is prepared, including a profile of the client, a statement of estimated net worth, an analysis of cash flow and tax position, a description of current investments and insurance programs, statement of estimated estate tax computations, and other relevant statements.
4. The financial plan is presented, which includes recommendations for meeting short- and long-term living goals, postmortem goals, and objectives relating to the reduction of tax liability and maximization of personal savings.
5. A detailed program for implementation of recommendations is provided which can be used by client as an "action plan."
6. An offer to provide an ongoing consultation is made to every client.

FEES AND OTHER COMPENSATION

FP establishes fees for financial planning services based upon the type of financial plan selected by the client and upon its prior assessment of the relative complexity of the services to be rendered for a prospective client.

Financial Planning Services for Individuals

FP charges a fee for the creation of a personal financial plan for its individual clients. The fee is payable in two install-ments: 50 percent of the amount is charged in advance of services rendered, and the balance is payable upon presentation of the client's final plan.

FP's minimum fee is set out in Exhibit A (Fee Schedules). However, as just stated, a higher fee may be quoted based upon the relative complexity of a case. For instance, if a client has complex trusts, manages one or more closely held corporations, owns complicated tax shelters, and so on, the planning fee may have to be negotiated.

Exhibit A
Fee Schedule
Hourly Rate Schedule

Person responsible	Document modification	Data gathering	Analysis	Planning	Presentation
Clerical	$ 25.00	N/A	N/A	N/A	N/A
Paraplanner	$ 45.00	$ 45.00	N/A	N/A	N/A
Certified Financial Planner	$ 75.00	$ 75.00	$ 75.00	$ 75.00	$ 75.00
CFP and Member of Registry	$100.00	$100.00	$100.00	$100.00	$100.00

Additional Fees:
     All financial services are subject to our increase of fees as to the procurement of outside professional advice and services. The client retains the right to be informed in advance and reject those costs.
Subsequent Reviews:
     The hourly rate schedule just presented will apply.
Note: FP reserves the right to determine in advance the estimated number of hours required to complete a plan or a review. The client has the right to accept or reject the offer.

Financial planning is an ongoing process. Changes occur in tax laws, the economic environment, investments, and in the personal circumstances of the clients. Consequently, FP encourages its clients to establish a long-term consulting relationship with FP. However, in most cases, the work involved with the annual review is less intensive than with the initial services just described. Hence, FP charges a review fee based on an hourly rate, as illustrated in Exhibit A.

FP realizes that not all clients need a comprehensive financial plan or long-range forecasting plan. Some clients may only need the restructuring of their investment portfolio. FP performs this service and charges a fee in accordance with the schedule illustrated in Exhibit A.

Financial Implementation for Individuals

This is a natural extension of the planning phase whereby FP initiates the plan of action, frequently with the assistance of the clients' advisors, to accomplish their investment objectives. A very important part of the implementation phase is the selection of investments and the monitoring of their progress. This is accomplished through FP's extensive network of specialists who assist in such technical areas as insurance, marketable securities, real estate, private investments, gift giving, and tax planning.

Consistent with FP's philosophy of financial implementation, its owner, John Planner, registered representative of Straford Company, a registered securities Broker-Dealer, may sell securities, tax shelters, commodities, real estate, and insurance, and may be involved in the formation of partnerships, venture capital companies, and other investment vehicles in connection with implementation of financial plans. FP believes that accessibility to a wide range of products is most advantageous to its clients, but wishes to make clear that clients are under no obligation whatsoever to purchase any products through John Planner and Straford Company. However, if products are purchased by a client from Planning Company, then in addition to the FP's receiving a fee for developing a financial plan, John Planner will also receive commissions or other remuneration. This may be considered to represent a conflict of interest. Straford Company is not responsible for the recommendations made by FP.

In the area of financial implementation, FP does not create legal documents, provide legal or accounting advice, or create tax documents.

Financial Services for Business Clients

FP also provides financial services to partnerships and corporations. Such services, generally provided in cooperation with other professional advisors, include analysis and recommendations regarding fringe benefits, compensation planning, investment management, buy/sell and stock redemption agreements, qualified and non-qualified retirement programs, recapitalization, long-range forecasting, budgeting, risk management, and so on. Fees for partnerships and corporate financial services are charged on an hourly basis, as specified in Exhibit A.

In addition, many partnerships and corporations recognize that the personal financial well-being of key officers and employees can have a positive effect upon their performance. Consequently, a corporation may ask FP to provide, as a fringe benefit, personal planning consultation services for its key officers and employees. FP will offer such a service for a fee negotiated between FP and the corporation.

Education and Business Standards

John Planner is the president and chief planner of Financial Planners, Inc. He holds an M.B.A. and a CFP. Mr. Planner also serves on the local chapter of the board of directors of the IAFP. Mr. Planner is assisted by three paraplanners and other employees trained in handling financial planning clients.

All financial planning clients receive a written comprehensive plan, supplemented by a video and an audio cassette. Clients are also encouraged to participate in an annual review.

APPENDIX C TO CHAPTER 2 *

I. BACKGROUND

Financial planning typically involves providing a variety of services, principally advisory in nature, to individuals or families regarding the management of their financial resources based upon an analysis of individual client needs. Generally, financial planning services involve preparing a financial program for a client based on the client's financial circumstances and objectives. This information normally would cover present and anticipated assets and liabilities, including insurance, savings, investments, and anticipated retirement or other employee benefits. The program developed for the client usually includes general recommendations for a course of activity, or specific actions, to be taken by the client. For example, recommendations may be made that the client obtain insurance or revise existing coverage, establish an individual retirement account, increase or decrease funds held in savings accounts, or invest funds in securities. A financial planner may develop tax or estate plans for clients or refer clients to an accountant or attorney for these services.

The provider of such financial planning services in most cases assists the client in implementing the recommended program by, among other things, making specific recommendations to carry out the general recommendations of the program, or by selling the client insurance products, securities, or other investments. The financial planner may also review the client's program periodically and recommend revisions. Persons providing such financial planning services use various compensation arrangements. Some financial planners charge clients an overall fee for developing an individual client program while others charge clients an hourly fee. In some instances financial planners are compensated, in whole or in part, by commissions on the sale to the client of insurance products, interest in real estate, securities (such as common stocks, bonds, limited partnership interests, and mutual funds), or other investments.

A second common form of service relating to financial matters is provided by "pensions consultants" who typically offer, in addition to administrative services, a variety of advisory services to employee benefit plans and their fiduciaries based upon an analysis of the needs of the plan. These advisory services may include advice as to the types of funding media available to provide plan benefits, general recommendations as to what portion of plan assets should be invested in various investment media, including securities, and, in some cases, recommendations regarding investment in specific securities or other investments. Pension consultants may also assist plan fiduciaries in determining plan investment objectives and policies and in designing funding media for the plan. They may also provide general or

* Courtesy of John R. Clay, et al., Guide to Personal Financial Planning, Practitioners Publishing Company; May 1989, pp. 15-53–15-60.

specific advice to plan fiduciaries as to the selection or retention of persons to manage the assets of the plan.[1] Persons providing these services to plans are customarily compensated for their services through fees paid by the plan, its sponsor, or other persons; by means of sales commissions on the sale of insurance products or investments to the plan; or through a combination of fees and commissions.

Another form of financial advisory service is that provided by persons offering a variety of financially related services to entertainers or athletes based upon the needs of the individual client. Such persons, who often use the designation "sports representative" or "entertainment representative," offer a number of services to clients, including the negotiation of employment contracts and development of promotional opportunities for the client, as well as advisory services related to investments, tax planning, or budget and money management. Some persons providing these services to clients may assume discretion overall or a portion of a client's funds by collecting income, paying bills, and making investments for the client. Sports or entertainment representatives are customarily compensated for their services primarily through fees charged for negotiation of employment contracts but may also receive compensation in the form of fixed charges or hourly fees for other services provided, including investment advisory services.

There are other persons who, while not falling precisely into one of the foregoing categories, provide financial advisory services. As discussed below, financial planners, pension consultants, sports or entertainment representatives or other persons providing financial advisory services, may be investment advisers within the meaning of the Advisers Act, state adviser laws, or both.

II. STATUS AS AN INVESTMENT ADVISER

A. Definition of Investment Adviser

Section 202(a)(11) of the Advisers Act defines the term "Investment adviser" to mean:

. . . any person who, for compensation, engages in the business of advising others, either directly or through publications or writings, as to the value of securities or as to the advisability of investing in, purchasing, or selling securities, or who, for compensation and as part of a regular business, issues or promulgates analyses or reports concerning securities . . .

Whether a person providing financially related services of the type discussed in this release is an investment adviser within the meaning of the Advisers Act depends upon all the relevant facts and circumstances. As a general matter, if the activities of any person providing integrated advisory services satisfy the elements of the definition, the person would be an investment adviser within the meaning of the Advisers Act, unless entitled to rely on one of the exclusions from the definition of investment adviser in clauses (A) to (F) of section 202(a)(11).[2] A determination as to whether a person providing financial planning, pension consulting, or other integrated advisory services is an investment adviser will depend upon whether such person: (1) Provides advice, or issues reports or analyses, regarding securities; (2) is in the business of providing such services; and (3) provides such services for compensation. These three elements are discussed below.

1. ADVICE OR ANALYSES CONCERNING SECURITIES

It would seem apparent that a person who gives advice or makes recommendations or issues reports or analyses with respect to specific securities is an investment adviser under section 202(a)(11), assuming the other elements of the definition of investment adviser are met, i.e., that such services are performed as a part of a business and for compensation. However, it has been asked on a number of occasions whether advice, recommendations, or reports that do not pertain to specific securities satisfy this element of the definition. The staff believes that a person who provides advice, or issues or promulgates reports or analyses, which concern securities, but which do not relate to specific securities, generally is an investment adviser under section 202(a)(11), assuming the services are performed as part of a business[3] and for compensation. The staff has interpreted the definition of investment adviser to include persons who advise clients concerning the relative advantages and disadvantages of investing in securities in general as compared to other investments.[4] A person who, in the course of developing a financial program for a client, advises a client as to the desirability of investing in, purchasing or selling securities, as opposed to, or in relation to, any non-securities, investment or financial vehicle would also be "advising" others within the meaning of section 202(a)(11).[5] Similarly, a person who advises employee benefit plans on funding plan benefits by investing in, purchasing, or selling securities, as opposed to, or in addition to, insurance products, real estate not involving securities, or other funding media, would be "advising" others within the meaning of section 202(a)(11). A person providing advice to a client as to the selection or retention of an investment manager or managers also, under certain circumstances, would be deemed to be "advising" others within the meaning of section 202(a)(11).[6]

2. THE "BUSINESS" STANDARD

Under section 202(a)(11), an investment adviser is one who, for compensation, (1) engages in the business of advising others as to the value of securities or as to the advisability of investing in, purchasing, or selling securities, or, alternatively, (2) issues or promulgates reports or analyses concerning securities as part of a regular business. Each of these two alternatives in the statutory definition of investment adviser contains a business test — one involves "engaging in the business" of advising others while the other involves issuing reports about securities as "part of a regular business." While the "business" standards established under section 202(a)(11) are phrased somewhat differently, it is the staff's opinion that they should be interpreted in the same manner. In both cases, the determination to be made is whether the degree of the person's advisory activities constitutes being "in the business" of an investment adviser. The giving of advice need not constitute the principal business activity or any particular portion of the business activities of a person in order for the person to be an investment adviser under section 202(a)(11). The giving of advice need only be done on such a basis that it constitutes a business activity occurring with some regularity. The frequency of the activity is a factor, but is not determinative.

Whether a person giving advice about securities for compensation would be "in the business" of doing so, depends upon all relevant facts and circumstances. The staff considers a person to be "in the business" of providing advice if the person: (i) Holds himself out as an investment adviser or as one who provides investment advice, (ii) receives any separate or additional compensation that represents a clearly definable charge for providing advice about securities, regardless of whether the compensation is separate from or included within any overall compensation, or receives transaction-based compensation if the client implements the investment advice, or (iii) on anything other than rare, isolated and non-periodic instances, provides specific investment advice.[7] For the purposes of (iii) above, "specific investment advice" includes a recommendation, analysis or report about specific securities or specific categories of securities (e.g., industrial development bonds, mutual funds, or medical technology stocks). It includes a recommendation that a client allocate certain percentages of his assets to life insurance, high yielding bonds, and mutual funds or particular types of mutual funds such as growth stock funds or money market funds. However, specific investment advice does not include advice limited to a general recommendation to allocate assets in securities, life insurance, and tangible assets.

In applying the foregoing tests, the staff may consider other financial services activities offered to clients. For example, if a financial planner structures his planning so as to give only generic, non-specific investment advice as a financial planner, but then gives specific securities advice in his capacity as a registered representative of a dealer or as agent of an insurance company, the person would not be able to assert that he was not "in the business" of giving investment advice. See discussion of the broker-dealer exception set forth in section 202(a)(11)(C) of the Advisers Act, *infra*. In the staff's view, it is necessary to consider these other financial services activities. Section 208(d) of the Advisers Act makes it illegal for someone to do indirectly under the Advisers Act what cannot be done directly.

3. COMPENSATION The definition of investment adviser applies to persons *who* give investment advice for compensation. This compensation element is satisfied by the receipt of any economic benefit, whether in the form of an advisory fee or some other fee relating to the total services rendered, commissions, or some combination of the foregoing. It is not necessary that a person who provides investment advisory and other services to a client charge a separate fee for the investment advisory portion of the total service. The compensation element is satisfied if a single fee is charged for a number of different services, including investment advice or the issuing of reports or analyses concerning securities within the meaning of the Advisers Act.[8] As discussed above, however, the fact that no separate fee is charged for the investment advisory portion of the service could be relevant to whether the person is "in the business" of giving investment advice.

It is not necessary that an adviser's compensation be paid directly by the person receiving investment advisory services, but only that the investment adviser receive compensation from some source for his services.[9] Accordingly, a person providing a variety of services to a client, including investment advisory services, for which the person receives any economic benefit, for example, by receipt of a single fee or commissions upon the sale to the client of insurance products or investments, would be performing such advisory service "for compensation" within the meaning of section 202(a)(11) of the Advisers Act.[10]

B. Exclusions From Definition of Investment Adviser

Clauses (A) to (E) of section 202(a)(11) of the Advisers Act set forth limited exclusions from the definition of investment adviser available to certain persons.[11] Whether an exclusion from the definition of investment adviser is available to any financial planner, pension consultant or other person providing investment advisory services within the meaning of section 202(a)(11), depends upon the relevant facts and circumstances.

A person relying on an exclusion from the definition of investment adviser must meet all of the requirements of the exclusion. The staff's view is that the exclusion contained in section 202(a)(11)(B) is not available, for example, to a lawyer or accountant who holds himself out to the public as providing financial planning, pension consulting, or other financial advisory services. In such a case it would appear that the performance of investment advisory services by the person would not be incidental to his practice as a lawyer or accountant.[12] Similarly, the exclusion for brokers or dealers contained in section 202(a)(11)(C) would not be available to a broker or dealer, or associated person of a broker or dealer, acting within the scope of the business of a broker or dealer, if the person receives any special compensation for providing investment advisory services.[13] Moreover, the exclusion from the definition of investment adviser contained in section 202(a)(11)(C) is only available to an associated person of a broker or dealer or "registered representative" who provides investment advisory services to clients within the scope of the person's employment with the broker or dealer.[14] For example, if a registered representative provides advice independent of, or separate from, his broker or dealer employer such as by establishing a separate financial planning practice, then he could not rely on the exclusion because his investment advisory activities would not be subject to control by his broker or dealer employer.[15] Similarly, the exclusion would be unavailable if he provides advice without the knowledge and approval of his employer because in that capacity his advisory activities would, by definition, be outside the control of his employer.[16]

III. REGISTRATION AS AN INVESTMENT ADVISER

Any person who is an investment adviser within the meaning of section 202(a)(11) of the Advisers Act, who is not excluded from the definition of investment adviser by virtue of one of the exclusions in section 202(a)(11), and who makes use of the mails or any instrumentality of interstate commerce in connection with the person's business as an investment adviser, is required by section 203(a) of the Advisers Act to register with the Commission as an investment adviser unless specifically exempted from registration by section 203(b) of the Advisers Act.[17] Also, any person who is an investment adviser within the meaning of any state investment adviser definition, and who is not excluded from that definition, may be required to register with that State. The materials necessary for registering with the Commission as an investment adviser can be obtained by writing the Publications Unit, Securities and Exchange Commission, Washington, DC 20549. As to the various States, persons should contact the office of the State securities administrator in the State in which they must register to obtain the necessary materials.

IV. APPLICATION OF ANTIFRAUD PROVISIONS

The antifraud provisions of section 206 of the Advisers Act [15 U.S.C. 80b-6], and the rules adopted by the Commission thereunder, apply to any person who is an investment adviser as defined in the Advisers Act, whether or not the person is required to be registered with the Commission as an investment adviser. [18] Sections 206(1) and (2) of the Advisers Act, upon which many State antifraud provisions are patterned, make it unlawful for an investment adviser, directly or indirectly, to "employ and device, scheme, or artifice to defraud client or prospective client" or to "engage in any transaction, practice, or course of business which operates as a fraud or deceit upon any client or prospective client." [19] An investment adviser is a fiduciary who owes his clients "an affirmative duty of 'utmost good faith, and full and fair' disclosure of all material facts." [20] The Supreme Court has stated that a "failure to disclose material facts must be deemed fraud or deceit within its intended meaning, for, as the experience of the 1920's and 1930's amply reveals, the darkness and ignorance of commercial secrecy are the conditions under which predatory practices best thrive." [21] Accordingly, the duty of an investment adviser to refrain from fraudulent conduct includes an obligation to disclose material facts to his clients whenever the failure to do so would defraud or operate as a fraud or deceit upon any client or prospective client. In this connection the adviser's duty to disclose material facts is particularly pertinent whenever the adviser is in a situation involving a conflict, or potential conflict, of interest with a client.

The type of disclosure required by an investment adviser who has a potential conflict of interest with a client will depend upon all the facts and circumstances. As a general matter, an adviser must disclose to clients all material facts regarding the potential conflict of interest so that the client can make an informed decision as to whether to enter into or continue an advisory relationship with the adviser or whether to take some action to protect himself against the specific conflict of interest involved. The following examples, which have been selected from cases and staff interpretive and no-action letters, illustrate the scope of the duty to disclose material information to clients in certain common situations involving conflicts of interests.

The adviser's duty to disclose material facts includes the duty to disclose the various capacities in which he might act when dealing with any particular client. For example, an adviser who intends to implement the financial plans he prepares for clients, in whole or part, through the broker or dealer or insurance company with whom the adviser is associated, should inform a client that in implementing the plan the adviser will also act as agent for the broker or dealer or the insurance company. [22]

An investment adviser who is also a registered representative of a broker or dealer and provides investment advisory services outside the scope of his employment with the broker or dealer must disclose to his advisory clients that his advisory activities are independent from his employment with the broker or dealer. [23] Additional disclosures would be required, depending on the circumstances, if the investment adviser recommends that his clients execute securities transactions through the broker or dealer with which the investment adviser is associated. For example, the investment adviser would be required to disclose fully the nature and extent of any interest the investment adviser has in such recommendation, including any compensation the investment adviser would receive from his employer in connection with the transaction. [24] In addition, the investment adviser would be required to inform his clients of their ability to execute recommended transactions through other brokers or dealers. [25] A financial planner who will recommend or use only the financial products offered by his broker or dealer employer when implementing financial plans for clients should disclose this practice to clients [26] and inform clients that the plan may be limited by the products offered by the broker or dealer. Finally, the Commission has stated that "an investment adviser must not effect transactions in which he has a personal interest in a manner that could result in preferring his own interest to that of his advisory clients." [27]

An investment adviser who structures his personal securities transactions to trade on the market caused by his recommendations to clients must disclose this practice to clients. [28] An investment adviser generally also must disclose if his personal securities transactions are inconsistent with the advice given to clients. [29] Finally, an investment adviser must disclose compensation received from the issuer of a security being recommended. [30]

Unlike other general antifraud provisions in the Federal securities laws which apply to conduct "in the offer or sale of any securities" [31] or "in connection with the purchase or sale of any security," [32] the pertinent provisions of Section 206 do not refer to dealings in securities but are stated in terms of the effect or potential effect of prohibited conduct on the client. Specifically, section 206(1) prohibits "any device, scheme, or artifice to defraud any client or prospective client," and section 206(2) prohibits "any transaction, practice, or course of business which operates as a fraud or deceit upon any client or prospective client." In this regard, the Commission has applied sections 206(1) and (2) in circumstances in which the fraudulent conduct arose out of the investment advisory relationship between an investment adviser and its clients, even though the conduct does not involve a securities transaction. For example, in an administrative proceeding brought by the Commission against an investment adviser, the respondent consented to a finding by the Commission that the respondent had violated sections 206(1) and (2) by persuading its clients to guarantee its bank loans and ultimately to post their securities as collateral for its loans without disclosing the adviser's deteriorating financial condition, negative net worth, and other outstanding loans. [33] Moreover, the staff has taken the position that an investment adviser who sells non-securities investments to clients must, under sections 206(1) and (2), disclose to clients and prospective clients all its interest in the sale to them of such non-securities investments. [34]

1 The authority to manage all or a portion of a plan's assets often is delegated to a person who qualifies as an "investment manager" under the Employee Retirement Income Security Act of 1974 [29 U.S.C. 1001 et seq.]. Under that statute, which is applicable to private sector pension and welfare benefit plans, an "investment manager" must be a registered investment adviser under the Advisers Act, a bank as defined in the Advisers Act, or an Insurance company that is qualified to perform services as an investment manager under the laws of more than one State.

2 See discussion of section 202(a)(11)(A) to (F) in section IIB, infra.

3 In this regard, as discussed in detail below, it is the staff's view that a person who gives advice or prepares analyses concerning securities generally may, nevertheless, not be "in the business" of doing so and, therefore, will not be considered an "investment adviser" as that term is used in section 202(a)(11).

4 See, e.g., Richard K. May (pub. avail. Dec. 11, 1979).

5 See, e.g., Thomas Beard (pub. avail. May 8, 1975): Sinclair-deMarinis Inc. (pub. avail. May 1, 1981).

6 See, e.g., FPC Securities Corp. (pub. avail. Dec. 1, 1974) (program to assist client in selection and retention of investment manager by, among other things, recommending investment managers to clients, monitoring and evaluating the performance of a client's investment manager, and advising client as to the retention of such manager); William Bye Co. (pub. avail. Apr. 26, 1973) (program involving recommendations to client as to selection and retention of investment manager based upon client's investment objectives and periodic monitoring and evaluation of investment manager's performance). On occasion in the past the staff has taken no-action positions with respect to certain situations involving persons providing advice to clients as to the selection or retention of investment managers. See e.g., Sebastian Associates, Ltd., (pub. avail. Aug. 7, 1975) (provision of assistance to clients in obtaining and coordinating the services of various professionals such as tax attorneys and investment advisers, including referring clients to such professionals, in connection with business as agent for clients with respect to negotiation of employment and promotional contracts); Hudson Valley Planning Inc. (pub. avail. Feb. 25, 1978) (provision of names of several investment managers to client upon request, without recommendation, in connection with business of providing administrative services to employee benefit plans.)

7 See Zinn v. Parish, 644 F.2d 360 (7th Cir 1981).

8 See, e.g., FINESCO (pub. avail. Dec. 11, 1979).

9 See, e.g., Warren H. Livingston (pub. avail. Mar. 8, 1980).

10 Section 202(a)(11)(C) of the Advisers Act excludes from the definition of investment adviser a broker or dealer who performs investment advisory services that are incidental to the conduct of its broker or dealer business and who receives no special compensation therefor. See discussion of section 202(a)(11)(C), infra.

11 Section 202(a)(11) provides that the definition of investment adviser does not include:
(A) A bank, or any bank holding company as defined in the Bank Holding Company Act of 1956, which is not an investment company;
(B) Any lawyer, accountant, engineer or teacher whose performance of such [advisory] services is solely incidental to the practice of his profession;

(C) Any broker or dealer whose performance of such [advisory] services is solely incidental to the conduct of his business as a broker or dealer and who receives no special compensation therefor;

(D) The publisher of any bona fide newspaper, news magazine or business or financial publication of general and regular circulation;

(E) Any person whose advice, analyses, or reports related to no securities other than securities which are direct obligations of or obligations guaranteed as to principal or interest by the United States, or securities issued or guaranteed by corporations in which the United States has a direct or indirect interest which shall be designated by the Secretary of the Treasury, pursuant to section 3(a)(12) of the Securities Exchange Act of 1934, as exempted securities for the purpose of that Act***

Section 202(a)(11)(F) excludes from the definition of investment adviser "such other persons not within the intent of this paragraph, as the Commission may designate by rules and regulations or order."

[12] *See, e.g., Mortimer M. Lerner* (pub. avail. Feb. 15, 1980); *David R. Markley* (pub. avail. Feb. 8, 1985); *Hauk Soule & Fasani, P.C.* (pub. avail. May 1, 1986). The "professional" exclusion provided in section 202(a)(11)(B) by its terms is only available to lawyers, accountants, engineers, and teachers. A person engaged in a profession other than one of those enumerated in section 202(a)(11)(B) who performs investment advisory services would be an investment adviser within the meaning of section 202(a)(11) whether or not the performance of investment advisory services is incidental to the practice of such profession. Unless another basis for excluding the person from the definition of investment adviser is available, the person would be subject to the Advisers Act.

[13] *See, e.g., FINESCO, supra* note 8. For a general statement of the views of the staff regarding special compensation under section 202(a)(11)(C), see Investment Advisers Act Release No. 640 (October 5, 1978), and *Robert S. Strevell* (pub. avail. April 29, 1985). See discussion of the "business" standard, *supra.*

[14] *See, e.g., Corinne E. Wood* (pub. avail. April 17, 1986); *George E. Bates* (pub. avail. April 26, 1979).

[15] *See, e.g., Robert S. Strevell, supra* note 13; *Elmer D. Robinson* (pub. avail. Jan. 6, 1986); *Brent A. Neiser* (pub. avail. Jan. 21, 1986).

[16] *Id.*

[17] Section 203(b) exempts from registration:
(1) Any investment adviser all of whose clients are residents of the state within which such investment adviser maintains his or its principal office and place of business, and who does not furnish advice or issue analyses or reports with respect to securities listed or admitted to unlisted trading privileges on any national securities exchange;
(2) Any investment adviser whose only clients are insurance companies; or
(3) Any investment adviser who during the course of the preceding twelve months has had fewer than fifteen clients and who neither holds himself out generally to the public as an investment adviser nor acts as an investment adviser to any investment company registered under the [Investment Company Act]***

[18] The antifraud provisions of some State statutes may apply to any person receiving consideration from another person for rendering the investment advice even if the person rendering the investment advice is technically excluded from the State definition of investment adviser.

19 In addition, section 206(3) of the Advisers Act generally makes it unlawful for an investment adviser acting as principal for his own account knowingly to sell any security to or purchase any security from a client, or, acting as broker for a person other than such client, knowingly to effect any sale or purchase of any security for the account of such client, without disclosing to such client in writing before the completion of such transaction the capacity in which he is acting and obtaining the consent of the client to such transaction. The responsibilities of an investment adviser dealing with a client as principal or as agent for another person are discussed in Advisers Act Rel. Nos. 40 and 470 (February 5, 1945 and August 20, 1975 respectively).

20 SEC v. Capital Gains Research Bureau, 375 U.S. 180, 184 (1963) quoting Prosser, Law of Torts (1955), 534-535.

21 Id. at 200.

22 See Elmer D. Robinson, supra note 15. See also In the Matter of Haight & Co. Inc., (Securities Exchange Act Rel. No. 9082. Feb. 19, 1971), where the commission held that a broker or dealer and its associated persons defrauded its customers in the offer and sale of securities by holding themselves out as financial planners who would, as financial planners, give comprehensive and expert planning advice and choose the best investments for their clients from all available securities; when in fact they were not expert in planning and made their decisions based on the receipt of commissions and upon their inventory of securities. Accord Institutional Trading Corporation (pub. avail. Nov. 27, 1972).

23 David P. Atkinson (pub. avail. Aug. 1, 1977). See also Corrine E. Wood, supra note 14.

24 Id.

25 Don P. Matheson (pub. avail. Sept. 1, 1976).

26 Elmer D. Robinson, supra note 15.

27 Kidder, Peabody & Co. Inc., 43 S.E.C. 911, 916 (1968).

28 SEC v. Capital Gains Research Bureau, supra, note 19, at 197.

29 In the Matter of Dow Theory Letters et.al., Advisers Act Release No. 571 (Feb. 22, 1977).

30 In the Matter of Investment Controlled Research et. al., Advisers Act Release No. 701, (Sept. 17, 1979).

31 Section 17(a) [15 U.S.C. 787 q(a)] of the Securities Act of 1933 [15 U.S.C. 77a et. seq.].

32 Rule 10b-5 [17 CFR 240.10b-5] under the Securities Exchange Act of 1934 [15 U.S.C. 78a et seq.]. See also section 15(c) [15 U.S.C. 78o(c)] of the Securities Exchange Act of 1934.

33 In the Matter of Ronald B. Donati, Inc. et al. Advisers Act Rel. Nos. 666 and 683 (February 8, 1979 and July 2, 1979 respectively). See also Intersearch Technology, Inc. [1974-1975 Transfer Binder] Fed. Sec. L. Rep. (CCH) Paragraph 80.139 at 85.189.

34 See Boston Advisory Group (pub. avail. Dec. 5, 1976).

Questionnaire

(print please)

1. Your Name _____
First   Middle Initial   Last

2. (Check)   Mr. ☐   Mrs. ☐   Miss ☐   Ms. ☐   Dr. ☐   Male ☐   Female ☐

3. Home Address _____
                                              Street

City   Zip

4. a. Home Phone (   ) _____   **b.** Your Business Phone (   ) _____

5. Marital Status   (Check)   Married ☐   Unmarried ☐   Separated ☐   **6. Your Social Security Number** _____ – ____ – _____

7. Spouse's Name (If Applicable) _____
                          First   Middle Initial   Last

8. (Check)   Mr. ☐   Mrs. ☐   Ms. ☐   Dr. ☐

9. Spouse's Social Security Number _____ – ____ – _____   Spouse's Business Phone (   ) _____

10. Your Date of Birth _____ / _____ / _____   **Spouse's Date of Birth** _____ / _____ / _____

11. a. Your Employer _____   **b. Spouse's Employer** _____

     Address _____   Address _____

12. Length of Current Employment   You _____   Spouse _____

13. College Education For Children (If Applicable).   (Please list oldest child first, youngest last)

Child's First Name	(must be completed) Date of Birth	Current Grade	Total Projected Number of Years in College	*Monthly* Savings for This Child	Existing Assets Intended for Child's Education	% Total College Bills You Will Pay	Other Income Available Per Year
1							
2							
3							
4							
5							

14. College Choice For Children (If Applicable).

   a. Do you know which college or university each of your children will attend? If yes, please answer questions A, B, and C below.

   b. If you don't know which institution they will attend, would you prefer we assume a more expensive private college, less expensive public college, or an average of the two? (Check either question D, E, or F below)

Child's First Name	(A) Name of Institution	(B) City and State	(C) Current College Costs	(D) Private Institution	(E) Public Institution	(F) Average
1						
2						
3						
4						
5						

Page 1 of 5

15. Existing Assets of You (and Your Spouse)
(Please do not include assets intended for child's education.)

Category	Current Value		Current Savings Per Month Excluding Dividends and Interest Income
Cash			
Checking Account(s)	$	$	
Passbook/Credit Union Accounts	$	$	
Certificates of Deposit	$	$	
Money Market Accounts (Banks/Credit Unions)	$	$	
Money Markets (Mutual Funds)	$	$	
Stocks (Common, Preferred and Stock Mutual Funds)	$	$	
Bonds			
U.S. Savings Bonds	$	$	
Gov't Bonds/Treasury Issues	$	$	
Corporate Bonds	$	$	
Taxable Bond Mutual Funds	$	$	
Tax Free Municipal Bonds and Mutual Funds	$	$	
Pension Accounts			
Employer Contribution (Vested Portion)	$		N/A
Voluntary Contribution	$	$	
Profit Sharing Accounts			
Employer Contribution (Vested Portion)	$		N/A
Voluntary Contribution	$	$	
IRA Accounts (Husband & Wife)	$	$	
Keogh Account(s)	$	$	
Other Corp. Plans (401K, Stock Purchase, Thrift Savings, Etc.)	$	$	
Home and Personal Possessions (Market Value)	$		N/A
Other Privately Owned Real Estate (Market Value)	$		N/A
Real Estate Limited Partnerships	$	$	
All Other Limited Partnerships	$	$	
Gold, Silver, Rare Coins, or Precious Metal Mutual Funds	$	$	
Gems, Jewelry, Art, Antiques, Other Collectibles (Market Value)	$		N/A
Automobiles and Other Vehicles	$		N/A
Cash Value Life Insurance	$	$	N/A
Other Assets (List)	$	$	
	$	$	

16. Existing Liabilities of You (and Your Spouse)

Estimated *Current* Balance

Home Mortgage _____ $ _____

Other Mortgages _____ $ _____

Auto Loan(s) _____ $ _____

Credit Cards _____ $ _____

Bank (Personal) Loans _____ $ _____

Credit Union Loans _____ $ _____

Educational Loans _____ $ _____

Other Liabilities (List) _____ $ _____

_____ $ _____

_____ $ _____

_____ $ _____

_____ $ _____

_____ $ _____

17. What is your **tax filing status**? (Front page of tax return immediately below name).
(Check one)

☐ Single   ☐ Married, filing jointly   ☐ Married, filing separately   ☐ Head of Household   ☐ Qualifying Widow

18. What is your total **annual earned income** from employment before taxes?

You $ _____   Spouse $ _____   Exact Figure ☐   Approximate ☐   (Check)

19. What is your **take home pay**? (Round up to the nearest dollar)

a. You $ _____ Each Paycheck   Exact Figure ☐   Approximate ☐   (Check)
Pay Schedule: (check one) Weekly ☐   15th & 30th ☐   Every 2 Weeks ☐   Once a Month ☐

b. Spouse $ _____ Each Paycheck   Exact Figure ☐   Approximate ☐   (Check)
Pay Schedule: (check one) Weekly ☐   15th & 30th ☐   Every 2 Weeks ☐   Once a Month ☐

20. a. Do you have **sources of income other than salary**? Yes ☐ No ☐ (Example: Rental Income, Bonuses, Commissions, Alimony, Child Support, Etc.)
If yes, approximately how much **per month** do you receive? $ _____

b. Does your spouse have **sources of income other than salary**? Yes ☐   No ☐
If yes, approximately how much **per month** does he/she receive? $ _____

21. What is your **taxable income**? (Please refer to your most recent tax return)

You $ _____ Spouse $ _____ or Joint $ _____ Exact Figure ☐   Approximate ☐   (Check)

22. a. Do you expect to receive a substantial **gift, inheritance, or lump sum distribution** from any source? Yes ☐   No ☐

b. If yes, what is the approximate amount? $ _____   In what approximate year will these funds be received? _____

23. Personal budget — How much do you (and your family) spend monthly or annually on the following?
(Please <u>do</u> <u>not</u> include any expenses that may be automatically deducted from your paycheck. Also, do not list any savings noted in Question #15)

Type of Expense	Monthly Expenditure	OR	Annual Expenditure
Housing (mortgage or rent payment)	$		$
Food	$		$
Utilities (telephone, gas, electric, oil, water, sewer)	$		$
Auto maintenance, gas, parking, tolls, public transportation	$		$
Medical expenses (other than insurance premiums)	$		$
Clothing	$		$
Club and professional dues	$		$
Yard maintenance, property repairs	$		$
Domestic (cleaning) help	$		$
Property taxes (if not included in mortgage or rent payment)	$		$
Entertainment and vacations	$		$
Donations — church, charitable	$		$
Child care / babysitters	$		$
Alimony/child support	$		$
Books, magazines, periodicals, newspapers	$		$
Home furnishings and appliances	$		$
Gifts, birthdays, etc.	$		$
Unreimbursed business expenses	$		$
Insurance premiums:			
Homeowners	$		$
Automobile	$		$
Life & Disability	$		$
Laundry and dry cleaning	$		$
Pet care	$		$
Loan payments	$		$
Credit card payments	$		$
Other expenses (Explain):			
_____	$		$
_____	$		$
TOTAL	$		$

24. At what age would you like the choice of retiring with **financial independence**? _____ You _____ Spouse

25. Look at your total monthly expenses in Question 23.
How much would you (and your spouse) spend **per month** in **today's** dollars to live the lifestyle you expect at retirement? $ _____

26. a. Approximately how much **per month** do you expect your employer's retirement plan to pay you when you retire? $ _____
At what age is it available to you? _____

    b. Approximately how much **per month** does your spouse expect his/her employer's retirement plan to pay when he/she retires? $ _____
At what age is it available to you? _____

(Continued on next page)

27. a. Are you covered by Social Security? ☐ Yes ☐ No

   b. Is your spouse covered by Social Security? ☐ Yes ☐ No

28. a. Do you (and your spouse) expect any sources of income **other than** Social Security employer retirement benefits or income from assets at retirement?
   ☐ Yes ☐ No
   b. If yes, how much will be available monthly? $ _____ Exact Figure ☐ Approximate ☐ (Check)

29. If you died tomorrow, how much money would your life insurance coverage provide your family? $ _____

30. If your spouse died tomorrow, how much money would his/her life insurance coverage provide your family? $ _____

31. If you became disabled today, how much money **per month** would your disability insurance coverage provide your family? $ _____
                                                                                                                  (Please list dollar amount)

32. If your spouse became disabled today, how much money **per month** would his/her disability insurance coverage provide your family? $ _____
                                                                                                                  (Please list dollar amount)

33. How would you describe your financial attitude? (Choose One Letter) _____

Ultra Conservative	Conservative	Middle of the Road	Moderately Aggressive	Ultra Aggressive
A	**B**	**C**	**D**	**E**

34. What do you think the average inflation rate will be for the next five years? _____ % Don't Know ☐ (Check)

35. a. Do you have a will? ☐ Yes ☐ No **b.** If yes, in what approximate year did you sign your will? _____

   c. Does your spouse have a will? ☐ Yes ☐ No **d.** If yes, in what approximate year did your spouse sign his/her will? _____

36. Please rank your financial objectives below from 1 (most important) through 8 (the last area of importance to you).
   _____ minimize income tax liability _____ provide income at retirement _____ provide additional income now
   _____ fund my children's education _____ maximize my return on investments _____ provide wealth growth
   _____ review my current use of debt _____ other _____

37. Do you, your spouse, or children have any medical, personal, legal or financial problems to be considered in this profile?
   Yes ☐ No ☐ Explain _____

I authorize the use of the information I have provided here to have my financial evaluation prepared. I recognize that the quality and usefulness of my evaluation will depend on this information being complete and accurate. I request that this evaluation be released to and presented by my financial advisor if applicable. In addition, my financial information will not be disclosed to others without my prior written consent, unless such disclosure is required by law.

_____
         Signature   Date

NOTES TO QUESTIONNAIRE

We know that completing the questionnaire can be a demanding process; however, you must fill it in fully and accurately so that our analysis of your financial situation may include all of your personal variables.

Question 6

Social security number. This is *extremely* important information. Please be sure you have included your Social Security number.

Question 11

Your employer. This question is straightforward with one exception. If you are retired and continue to work part-time, please give us the name of your part-time employer—and include your retirement pension income as "Other Income" in Question 20.

If "retiree" is entered in place of a company name, you will be treated as a retired person. If you are retired and working, enter company name here and place retirement income in Annual Earned Income (Question 18) and Take Home Pay (Question 19).

Question 13

Monthly savings for this child. If you save regularly for your child's education, calculate the monthly savings amount and place this figure under the column heading "Monthly Savings for This Child." Many families, however, do not save on a regular basis. If this is your situation, please leave this column blank.

Current assets in child's name. This sum is used in determining whether your child will have a positive or a negative Educational Dollar status when ready to enter college. The key to remember when filling out this section is whether or not assets are set aside *specifically* for your child's education. For example, opening a savings account in your name *which is strictly intended for your child's education* should be included in this column. Please be sure NOT to include these same assets in YOUR asset section (Question 15).

Percent of total college bills you will pay. Some parents intend to finance all of their child's college bills. If this is your plan, write 100% in this column. However, if you expect that your child will work and/or take out student loans while attending college, write the percentage of the bills you will pay. (For example, if you expect to pay three-quarters of your child's educational bills, write 75%.)

Other income available per year. Most people will leave this column blank. In some cases, your child may be scheduled to receive income from a trust fund. If your child has other income he/she will begin to receive at college age, write the amount that will be available to help pay for their college education in the space provided.

Current grade. Grade is not required if the child is not yet in school.

Projected number of years in college. The total projected number of years in college is to *reflect the full length of time the child is expected to be in college:* four, six, eight years. Do not enter the amount of years *left* to complete the education.

Example: Grade 13 Freshman
          Grade 14 Sophomore
          Grade 15 Junior
          Grade 16 Senior

If Joe is a sophomore, he is in Grade 14 with two years left in order to complete his education. Do not enter "2" for years left, instead enter "4" for total number of years in college.

Other income available per year.
Other available income per year means
scholarships, student earnings, or any other
nonparental source of income. Do not include your savings or income here.

Question 14

College choice for children. Do you
know which college or university your child
will attend? If you do, complete columns A
and B of the question. Unless you have the
total tuition cost at this institution available, do not fill in column C. We will complete this information for you.

If you do not know the specific college
or university your child will attend, then
you should mark "Public," "Private," or
"Average" college. A predetermined set of
tuition amounts is then used to determine
the educational fund needs. These tuition
figures are taken from the *College Cost
Book* and are updated annually.

If you know the name of the college
but do not know the exact tuition cost, leave
tuition cost blank. We will enter the most
recent tuition figures as taken from the *College Cost Book*.

Question 15

*Existing assets of you (and your
spouse).* Question 15 is a long one. Be sure
to *exclude* any assets that are intended for
your children's education.

The section which asks you to list
your contribution to pension and profit
sharing plans will most likely require that
you ask your employer's personnel department for the data. PLEASE DO NOT
LEAVE THESE SPACES BLANK. *We are
not able to calculate your retirement status
without information on pension and (if appropriate) profit sharing contributions.*
Also, if your company sponsors a 401(k),
stock purchase, or other plans, be sure to
ask your personnel department for this
data.

Current savings per month
A. Do *not* forget the monthly savings column entries. These are extremely important data.

B. Please *do not* include any dividends and
   interest that may be received from your
   investments here. Our evaluation automatically includes those figures for
   you.
C. The following items are *not* included in
   projecting income at retirement: home
   and personal possessions, gems, jewelry,
   automobiles, and checking accounts.

   The current pension value (and future *pension* savings) toward your pension are eliminated if Question 26 dealing with retirement income distribution
   is answered.
D. "Other privately owned real estate" and
   "real estate limited partnerships" are
   reduced by the amount of "other mortgages" in the Liabilities section.

Example:

Total Other Private Real Estate	$100,000
Total Real Estate Partnerships	100,000
Total Real Estate	$200,000
Other Mortgages	50,000
	$150,000

$150,000 is used for retirement calcu-
lation purposes.

E. The monthly savings recorded in the
   asset section are considered to be made
   after you receive your paycheck (take
   home pay) with the exception of savings
   into corporate accounts (pensions, profit
   sharing, other corporate plans)—these
   corporate savings are assumed to go directly into these (pre-take home) accounts. All other savings are recorded in
   after-tax dollars.

   If your savings are taken from a
   payroll deduction program, the amount
   of the payroll deduction savings will be
   added back to the take home pay in
   Question 19 (take home pay). This is
   necessary for the budget calculation
   (which subtracts budget and savings
   from the take home pay) to reflect a
   budget surplus or deficit.

Example:

Savings:

Other Corporate Plans*	$100
Children	50
Passbook	100
Stocks	100
	$250

Budget:

Budget		$2,000
Savings		250
	Total:	$2,250

Take Home Pay:

Take Home Pay		$2,500
Budget/Savings		−2,250
	Surplus/Deficit	$ 250

Question 17

What is your tax filing status? You will find this information on the front page of your tax return immediately below your name.

Question 18

Annual earned income. This question asks for your gross annual earnings (before tax) from *employment only.*

Question 19

Take home pay. This is the amount of income which actually appears on your pay stub (after taxes) and any other deductions which have been withheld. All unstructured payments should be estimated (suggested monthly) and included in this answer, such as if you receive payment on commission only. For example, last year you made $30,000 and this year you will make approximately $36,000. $36,000 divided by 12 = $3,000 a month.

Question 20

Sources of income other than salary. Do you have rental income, alimony payments, commissions, or bonuses? If so, please include these *monthly* amounts here.

* Not included

The amount recorded here is added to *gross income* and as a monthly amount to your *take home pay.* Do not include monthly dividends or interest here. These are assumed to be reinvested each month and are accounted for in the "Asset" section when we calculate projected income for retirement.

Question 21

Taxable income. Taxable income is the amount of your annual income remaining after all deductions have been made. As the name implies, this is the amount of money on which you pay income taxes. This should be the approximate *taxable income* as reported on your most recent tax return.

Question 22

Gift, inheritance, or lump sum distribution. Do not enter unless both the amount of the gift or the inheritance *and* the year it is expected are known.

Question 23

Personal budget
A. Most of these expenses can be identified by reviewing canceled checks and/or careful estimation. Unreimbursed business expenses are on your Federal Tax Form 1040.
B. The budget contains two columns: *monthly* and *yearly.* You only need to make entries in the *monthly* column. We will calculate the yearly amount in the plan.
C. Be sure that the total monthly budget plus the total monthly savings do not exceed the monthly take home pay and other sources of income reported in Questions 19 and 20 unless that is actually the case. Remember, do not include any *pre-take home* savings listed in "Other Corporate Savings Plans" when checking these entries.

Question 24

Financial independence. This question requires that you understand what we mean by "financial independence." We define financial independence as having enough income generated each month from investments and pensions (if appropriate) to live the lifestyle you expect without ever touching the principal. A true financial independence age goal asks when you would like to have the choice of going to work or not on Monday morning—please be reasonable!

Question 25

Desired income at retirement. Enter this figure in *today's dollars—not* dollars adjusted for inflation. We will do this automatically.

Question 26

How much will your employer's retirement plan pay? Remember that an entry here will eliminate any calculated pension monies reported in the Asset section.

Question 28

Other income available. We have already included your investments, IRA, possible Keogh, and possible inheritance in your retirement dollar calculation. PLEASE DO NOT USE THIS BLANK TO LIST THESE SOURCES OF RETIREMENT INCOME. Rather, we have provided you with this question in the event that you will receive income from sources other than those already noted. What sources? Perhaps you will receive royalty income from a published work, or receive the proceeds from the sale of a business or idea over the course of time. You may expect to receive proceeds from a life insurance policy at retirement. This type of income should be reported in Question 28.

Question 33

Financial attitude. We have our own ideas about how much risk we are willing to take when we invest our money. As investors, it is important to understand that the higher the potential gain, the higher the risk. How comfortable are you with taking a risk with your money?

This information is important to us as we analyze your data. Generally, it is best to invest heavily in risky investments *only* if you have an emergency fund to fall back on.

If you mark "Ultra Aggressive," we will assume that you are willing to "risk it all."

"Moderately Aggressive" means that you are willing to take a good bit of risk, but fall short of being an all-out gambler.

"Middle of the Road" is where most of us fall. We know that we must accept some risk to make a return better than so-called "risk-free" investments, but we do not accept the possibility of losing all of our invested dollars.

The "Conservative" investor has preservation of investment dollars foremost in mind. The idea of losing any of that money is out of the question. This investor will gladly give up the promise of "big bucks" so as to be able to sleep well. However, the conservative investor does want to invest—after all, no one can get anywhere with all of the money in the cookie jar. This investor is interested in safe investments with returns that can be counted on.

Lastly, the "Ultra Conservative" investor wants safety above all else. This person will tolerate no risk with investments. Therefore, U.S. Treasury issues and bank investments are this investor's idea of total investing.

Question 34

Inflation rate. Do you have an idea of what the inflation rate will be for the next five years? Perhaps you have done some reading on the question and have a firm opinion. If so, fill in the blank. If you really don't have any educated idea, simply mark "Don't Know" and we will use the appropriate rate.

PART II

Key Financial Planning Areas: R-E-T-I-R-E

Part II is devoted to six key financial planning areas. These areas are best described by the acronym, R-E-T-I-R-E:

R: Risk Management Planning
E: Essentials of Budgeting, Savings, and Credit Planning
T: Tax Planning
I: Investment Planning
R: Retirement Planning
E: Estate Planning

In Sections I through VI which follow, we will undertake a detailed discussion of each of the six planning areas. In each case, we will present the basic structure of the area followed by the key planning strategies applicable to that area.

CHAPTER 3

Life Insurance: Structure, Concepts, and Planning Strategies

LIFE INSURANCE: AN OVERVIEW

INTRODUCTION

No one ever knows for sure exactly when, where, and how our lives, and thus our ability to generate income, will end. The primary objective of purchasing life insurance is to convert uncertainty that a person will be able to meet all financial obligations in the event of a possible misfortune into the certainty that these obligations will be gracefully fulfilled. More specifically, the main purpose of buying life insurance is to create an estate, preserve an estate, or transfer an estate.

As revealed by Figure 3-1, the financial obligations may include the following:

1. Provide for spouse, children, and other financial dependents
2. Pay off final expenses and estate taxes
3. Pay off all debts and mortgages

4. Provide funds for education
5. Pass money to heirs
6. Transfer ownership of a business
7. Provide for retirement income

In purchasing life insurance, the main concerns should be to determine, as accurately as possible, who in the family needs protection, how much insurance should be purchased to achieve the primary objective, and which company offers the best buy for the money.

A secondary objective of buying life insurance is to treat it as a form of savings. Life insurance can offer a plan that forces a person to save, allowing the savings to grow in a life insurance company income tax-free at a predetermined rate. If insurance is used for this purpose, the objective should be to insure that, after taking into consideration income tax and forced savings,

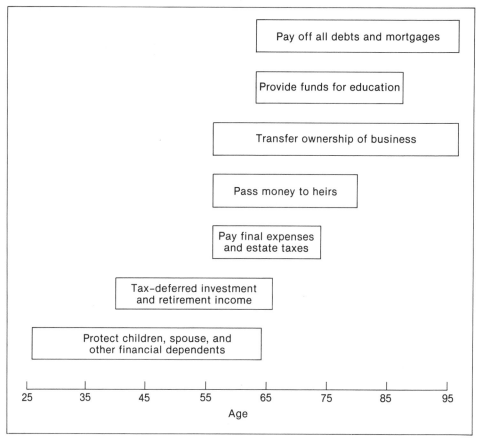

FIGURE 3-1   Key reasons for purchasing life insurance

investment in a life insurance company does provide the policyholder with the best long-term savings opportunity. Of course, it should always be recognized that since money spent on buying insurance is diverted from investment, it is rarely desirable to buy as much insurance as one can afford. Also, in buying insurance, no one should get carried away by emotion.

THEORY OF RISK TRANSFER

Risk is a way of life. If managed properly, risk can be handled with relative ease. The five strategies of risk management are risk avoidance, risk reduction, risk retention, risk sharing, and risk transfer. As Figure 3-2 reveals, risk

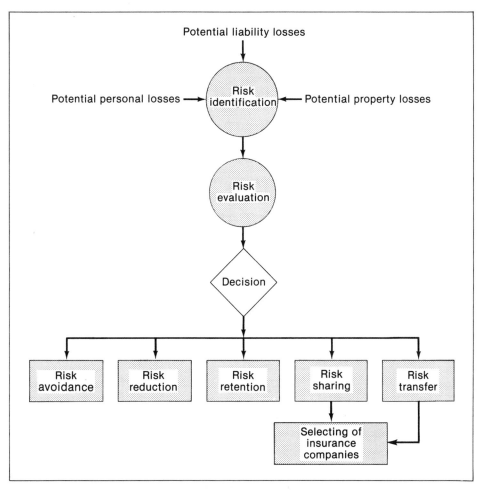

FIGURE 3-2   Personal risk management: an overview

TABLE 3-1 Risks and Risk Management Strategies

Risks		Strategies for reducing financial impact		
Personal events	Financial impact	Personal resources	Private sector	Public sector
Disability	Loss of one income Loss of services Increased expenses Other losses	Savings, investments Family observing safety precautions Other resources	Disability insurance Other strategies Worker's compensation	Disability insurance Social Security
Illness	Loss of one income Catastrophic hospital expenses Other losses	Health-enhancing behavior	Health insurance Health maintenance organizations Other strategies	Military health Medicare, Medicaid
Death	Loss of one income Loss of services Final expenses Other expenses	Estate planning Risk reduction Other resources	Life insurance Other strategies	Veteran's life insurance Social Security survivor's benefits
Retirement	Decreased income Other expenses	Savings Investments Hobbies, skills Other resources	Retirement and/or pensions Other strategies	Social Security Pension plan for government employees
Property loss	Catastrophic storm damage to property Repair or replacement cost of theft	Property repair and upkeep Security plans Other resources	Automobile insurance Homeowners insurance Flood insurance (joint program with government)	Flood insurance (joint program with business)
Liability	Claims and settlement costs Lawsuits and legal expenses Loss of personal assets and income Other expenses	Observing safety precautions Maintaining property Other resources	Homeowners insurance Automobile insurance Malpractice insurance Other strategies	

Source: Adapted from *Personal and Family Financial Planning: A Staff Development Workshop for Secondary School Trainers and Teachers* (Washington, D.C.: American Council of Life Insurance, 1983, p. vi/13d.

sharing and risk transfer are strategies that lead to the selection of appropriate insurance companies.

Examples of risks and risk management strategies are presented in Table 3-1. Clearly, buying insurance is only one of many ways of reducing risk. For instance, personal savings, security plans, and health-enhancing behavior—all are methods of avoiding or reducing risk. However, not all risks can be avoided or reduced to manageable levels through the use of personal resources. Consequently, transferring risk by purchasing life insurance is an integral part of risk management strategy. The various types of insurance available for different types of risk we routinely face are illustrated in Figure 3-3. In this chapter we will discuss risk management planning through the purchase

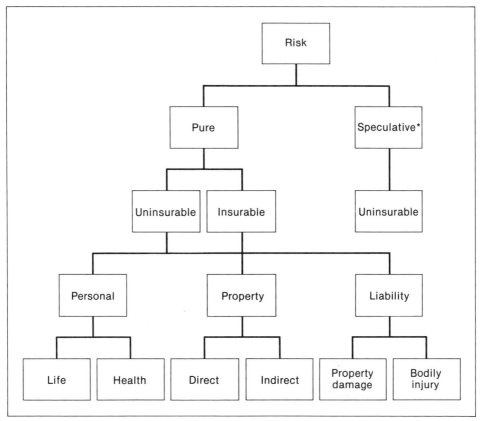

*A speculative risk is one in which there is a chance of either loss or gain. Starting a business and gambling are examples of speculative risk.

FIGURE 3-3 Types of insurance available for certain risks. Adapted from David L. Bickelhanpt, *General Insurance*, 11th ed. (Homewood, Ill.: Richard D. Irwin, 1979), p. 11, copyright 1983, Richard D. Irwin, Inc.

TABLE 3-2   Overview of Life Insurance Policies

Type	General description	Investment products	Flexibility of investment	Safety of cash value	Potential rate of return
Term: Annual Renewable and Convertible	Quality Term. After-tax life insurance.	None	N/A	N/A	N/A
Whole Life	Basic Coverage. Dividends add flexibility.	Long-term bonds and mortgages.	None Alternative is to borrow from policy and invest.	High	Low to Moderate
Single-Premium Whole Life	Basic coverage plus cash value build-up. Lump-sum premium.	Long-term bonds and mortgages.	None Insured may borrow from policy and invest, or withdraw dividends.	High	Moderate to High
Universal Life	Flexible premium payments.	Interest-sensitive investments	None Insured may *borrow* from cash value or *withdraw* capital.	High	Moderate to High
Variable Life	Investment selected by insured.	Stock, bonds, mutual funds, zero coupons, money market, instruments, etc.	Excellent Insured directs movement of funds.	Low to Moderate	High

Source: Adapted from Don Johnson and Cheryl Toman-Cubbage, "Have Your Cake . . .," *Financial Planning*, January 1986, p. 191.

of life insurance. Casualty, property, disability, and liability insurance plans will be discussed in the next chapter.

BASIC TYPES OF LIFE INSURANCE POLICIES

An overview of various types of life insurance policies, their relative advantages and disadvantages, and their appropriateness for different groups of peo-

TABLE 3-2 (continued)

Flexibility of premium	Alteration of death benefit	Advantages	Disadvantages	Appropriate buyer
None Increases annually/ periodically.	None	Lower initial cost. Dollars can be invested elsewhere. Pure death protection.	No savings element. Expires after specified period. Cost increases.	Young couples who need a large amount of insurance. People who do not want to invest in an insurance vehicle. People whose insurance needs will decrease over time. People who have temporary needs.
None Premium fixed. Dividends can lower or eliminate payments. Loans available.	None	Lifetime coverage. Savings element. Loan privileges. Variety of premium payment plans.	Higher cost of death protection. Low rate of return. Lack of flexibility. Does not keep pace with inflation.	People who need forced savings. People who want lifetime coverage.
N/A	None	Lifetime coverage. Tax-deferred savings. Loan privileges. Higher rate of return.	Need up-front lump-sum payment. Does not keep pace with inflation. Restrictions on withdrawals under current law.	Higher income people who want to shelter money.
Excellent Maximum: Allowed by law. Minimum: To cover mortality and expenses.	Excellent. Amount can be increased or decreased as desired.	Flexibility. Higher rate of return. Full disclosure of fees, loads, proportion invested.	No forced savings. Potential drop in rate of return. Not the most competitive investment vehicle.	People who want choice and flexibility. People who want a cash value fund with a higher rate of return.
None	None	Potentially high rate of return. Control of investments. Full disclosure required by law.	No guaranteed cash value. Element of risk. Need for familiarity with investments. Generally high expense ratio.	People who are investment-oriented and want a higher rate of return.

ple are presented in Table 3-2. In this section we will elaborate on each type of life insurance policy.

Term Insurance

The essential features. To be sure, "death" insurance has an unpleasant connotation. Thus the life insurance industry came up with a synonym for death insurance: term insurance. A term policy is a policy *rented* for a specified time, the time period varying from one to 20 years. At the end of the term, if the policy is renewable, the insured can renew the protection generally by paying a higher premium. These policies can be purchased in blocks of $1,000 or more, and a medical examination may be required to establish the insurability of the buyer. Term insurance premiums are lower in a person's early years than any other type of policy, but they increase dramatically in later years, and at age 65 or 70 become prohibitively expensive.

The best way to understand the importance of term insurance is to ask why a family is likely to buy such insurance. The lifestyle of a family is almost always related to its income. Since the possibility always exists that the flow of income could be greatly diminished or even eliminated by the death of a breadwinner, each income earner should make certain that the flow of income will continue in the event of his or her death. For a price—a premium—an insurance company will guarantee to pay a specified amount, either as a lump sum or in the form of monthly income, to the beneficiaries named in the policy should the policyholder die during the period the contract is in force. However, if the person outlives the expiration period of the policy, the family does not receive any money from the insurance company in return for the premium dollars paid.

In a real sense, term life insurance is very similar to automobile or home insurance: The insurance pays *only* when there is damage to "property." There are, however, two important differences between term life insurance and property (automobile or home) insurance. First, in the former case one's life is insured, whereas in the latter case one's physical property is insured. Second, in the case of term life insurance it is the beneficiaries of the deceased who receive the money, whereas in the latter case, the person carrying the insurance receives the benefits.

A term policy, like a cash value policy (discussed in the next section) can be either *participating* or *nonparticipating*. In a par (short for participating) policy, the insurance company initially charges a higher premium rate than would be necessary to provide the coverage. Later it returns the overcollection of premiums in the form of *dividends*, unless it has grossly miscalculated its expenses and income. In a par policy, therefore, dividends are never guaranteed, and the insured must make a judgment about dividends on the basis of the company's history of dividend payments. In contrast, in a nonpar (short for nonparticipating) policy, the company fixes the premium at a level necessary to meet the insurer's expenses. Consequently, premium rates in a nonpar policy are generally lower than a par policy, but no dividends are returned. If a company has a good history of dividend payments, however, it is possible that dividends will bring the true cost of a par policy below that of a nonpar policy if the policy is held for an extended period of time.

Types of term insurance. Since no two families of the same size and having the same income are likely to *feel* they need the same amount of term life insurance, insurance companies have devised numerous schemes to fit individual needs. The three schemes that have gained considerable popularity are discussed next.

Annual (Renewable) Term. This type of policy insures the life of a person for a period of one year. Since protection lasts for only a relatively short period, this policy is inexpensive. Also, if the policy is issued as renewable, the insured may continue the protection at the termination of the original policy date for one or more equal periods without having a physical examination. However, the premium on this type of policy increases with age, and as already stated, by the time a person reaches 65 or 70, the rate becomes prohibitively expensive.

Annual renewable term insurance is popular among young people, not only because they like the idea of reviewing their insurance needs frequently but also because they can get low-cost protection at a time when they may not be able to afford more costly coverage. In addition, this type of policy provides young people with the opportunity to shop around for insurance with lower premiums if they are insurable and in good health.

Level Term. Persons who dislike paying progressively higher premiums can buy level term policies. In this type of policy, the premium and the protection level remain fixed for the life of the policy, which covers 5-, 10-, or 20-year periods. Thus, the policyholder pays the insurance company more than is necessary to meet claims in the early years and less in later years. A level term policy is generally terminated at age 65 because at that age the probability of death is very high, and consequently the premium rate is prohibitive.

Decreasing Term. This policy requires the payment of a level premium during the tenure of the policy, but the face value of the policy declines progressively to zero at the expiration of the policy period. Decreasing term insurance is widely used in cases in which protection is temporarily desired to meet a specific credit need, such as to cover a mortgage or satisfy a similar debt obligation.

Cash Value Insurance

The essential features

Death Protection. Cash value insurance provides income protection for the family in case of the breadwinner's premature death. As mentioned earlier, this is one of the primary reasons for buying life insurance today.

Permanence. Cash value insurance keeps the coverage in force until the insured dies or stops paying the premium and cancels the policy. Also, the level of premium paid by the insured remains fixed regardless of the drop in the life expectancy as the insured grows older.

Cash Value. In addition to providing death protection, cash value life insurance policies accumulate a savings element called cash value. When all the premiums required by the contract have been made—or in technical jargon, the policy is paid up—this cash value is generally made available to the insured by the insurance company either in the form of a lump sum or in installments.

The role played by cash value in a cash value insurance policy is clearly demonstrated in Figure 3-4. This figure shows that a reducing term (amount of risk) plus the increasing savings (cash value) are so calculated that they add up to the face amount of the policy. It is worth noting that only the reducing-term portion, not the face value, truly represents insurance. Consequently, every cash value insurance is term plus a long-range savings plan called cash value.

Flexibility. Cash value life insurance accumulates a cash value against which a loan may be made. For instance, if the policyholder lacks the cash to meet a premium payment, the insurance company can make a premium loan to continue the protection, and the loan may be repaid later. If the policyholder wishes to discontinue paying premiums on the policy but wants the policy to remain in force, the accumulated cash value may be used either for extended term insurance or for reduced paid-up

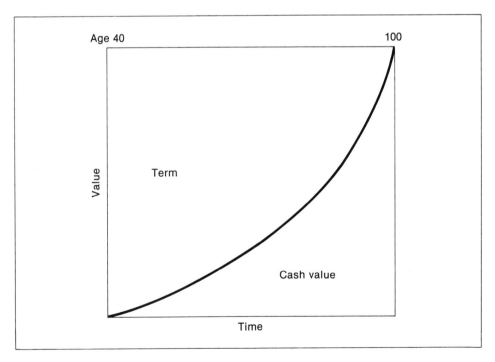

FIGURE 3-4   Cash value insurance

insurance. In the former case the insured would continue to be covered for the original face value, but only for a limited time. In contrast, the reduced paid-up insurance calls for a reduction in the face value of the insurance (which becomes permanent and is explained later in this chapter), but no further premiums are due on the policy.

Equal-Payment Plan (Level Premiums). The rate at which the insured is charged premiums is determined on the basis of life expectancy. And since life expectancy declines with age, premium rates are generally lower in earlier years and higher in later years. This arrangement does not suit most people buying permanent life insurance. They would rather pay a little more in earlier years to avoid the burden of higher premium rates in later years. Consequently, insurance companies have devised level premiums which provide a way of paying more in the earlier years and less in the later years than the cost of protection at those ages. The additional money paid in the earlier years helps to equalize the greater cost of life insurance protection in later years so that there is no need for the company to increase premium payments at that time. A comparison of level premium, which remains fixed for life, with step-rate premium, which increases with age, is shown in Figure 3-5.

Dividend Option. All cash value insurance policies offer the option of buying them on a participating (par) or nonparticipating (nonpar) basis. In a nonpar policy the company fixes the premium at a rate barely sufficient to provide both death protection and cash savings. Consequently,

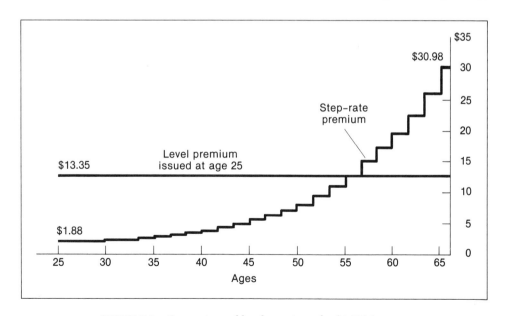

FIGURE 3-5 Comparison of level premiums for $1,000 insurance

there is no provision in these policies to return the overcollection of premiums in the form of dividends. In the case of a par policy, the insurance company initially charges a higher premium rate but *hopes* to return the overpayment of premiums in the form of dividends. The policyholder of a par policy may elect to use the dividends in five ways: (1) receive dividends in cash; (2) invest dividends with the insurance company at a specified interest rate; (3) purchase additional paid-up insurance; (4) reduce future premiums; or (5) buy additional one-year term insurance.

Emergency Fund. The cash value may be tapped for a financial emergency when the traditional emergency fund runs out. For instance, after 20 years the cash value of a $50,000 whole life policy issued at age 45 would be about $25,000. The policyholder may borrow from the insurance company against this cash value at a low rate of interest. However, the face amount is reduced by the amount of the outstanding loan.

Lifetime (permanent) protection. A lifetime policy provides permanent insurance protection; that is, it is kept in force as long as the policyholder pays premiums on it. Upon the death of the insured, the face value of the policy is paid to the beneficiary. In taking out a permanent policy, it is possible to select one that calls for the payment of premiums (1) for a lifetime, (2) for a predetermined number of years, (3) to a certain age, or (4) only once as a lump sum. The choice of a premium payment plan should depend upon the current conditions of the beneficiary. There are two major types of permanent life insurance policies, as described next.

Whole Life. A whole life policy, which is also known as straight life or ordinary life policy, has the lowest premium rate of any lifetime policy because it involves the payment of premiums over the longest period of time. It is the most widely purchased type of permanent policy because, to most families, it offers a fine balance between protection and cash accumulation. While this policy calls for premium payments for as long as the insured lives, the premium payments may be stopped after a stipulated period of time and a choice may be made among the following options: (1) leave the cash value with the insurance company for reduced protection; (2) cancel the policy and take a cash settlement; (3) buy an extended term insurance; or (4) discontinue the policy and receive an income from the accrued cash value for a selected period of time or for life.

Limited-Payment Life. This policy differs from a whole life policy in three respects. First, although it provides lifetime protection, the payment of premiums ceases after a period of ten, 20, or 30 years, or at a certain age (usually 60 or 65), depending upon the insurance contract selected. Second, since the premium-paying period is limited, the premium rate is

LIFE INSURANCE CONTRACT

Title	Explanation
Incontestability Clause	The company cannot dispute the validity of a life insurance contract if the policy has been in effect for two years, even if there were material misstatements in the application.
Grace Period	Automatic extension for premium payment, usually to 31 days after due date.
Extended Insurance Coverage	Upon expiration of a permanent policy due to nonpayment of premium, the policy is continued as term insurance until cash value is exhausted. This is also called a nonforfeiture option.
Cash Values	The policy contains a table showing the cash value available to the policyholder upon policy cancellation.
Loan Values	Cash value policies permit borrowing on the policy up to a specified percentage of cash value, usually at guaranteed interest rates.
Reduced Paid-Up Insurance	Insurance which can be purchased with policy cash value. This is another nonforfeiture option that ensures the cash value is not lost upon nonpayment of premiums.
Dividend Option	Participating policies return excess premium as dividend in various forms: cash, reduced premium, paid-up additions, accumulations at a specified interest, and additional one-year term.
Beneficiary Provision	The insured can name first, second, third, or more beneficiaries and arrange distribution of death benefit through settlement options. Beneficiary can be an individual, a business entity, or a trust.
Ownership Clause	This clause names the person who owns the policy. The policy proceeds are generally included in the owner's estate. Change of policy ownership is permitted by all insurance companies.
Policy Change	This clause describes the options the owner has in converting the existing policy into other types of policies.
Offer and Acceptance	If a person makes the first premium payment along with the application, the company generally agrees to insure the applicant if the applicant meets the insurability requirements. If a policy other than that applied for is issued, then the new policy becomes a counter-offer and the applicant accepts it by paying the first premium.

Consideration	The consideration given by the insurance company comprises its promises as defined in the contract. The consideration given by the insured comprises his or her statements made in the application and payment of the first premium.
Settlement Option Upon Death	Besides lump-sum, cash payment settlement options include the following: (1) Interest only: The policy proceeds are left on deposit with the insurance company for which the company makes interest payments. (2) Payments for stated period: The face amount of the policy together with earned interest are fully distributed over a fixed number of years. (3) Payment of stated amount: Fixed amount is distributed until the face amount and interest are fully liquidated. (4) Life Income: The insurer guarantees a fixed amount for life of the insured or for joint life of both spouses.
Nonforfeiture Clause	Cash value policies offer three nonforfeiture options: (1) Withdraw the cash value (called cash surrender value) of the policy. (2) Trade the policy's cash surrender value for a fully paid-up policy of the same duration as the old policy, but with a reduced face amount. (3) Trade the policy's cash surrender value for a fully paid-up term policy with the same face amount, but with a shorter duration than the previous policy.
Spendthrift Clause	Some states have laws that automatically exempt proceeds of insurance from the claims of the beneficiary's creditors. Many states also allow the insured to add a "spendthrift clause" to the policy to protect the proceeds. These clauses, which state that proceeds are not assignable and are exempt from claims of creditors, are applicable only in cases of installment settlement options.
Simultaneous Death Clause	If the insured and the beneficiary die simultaneously, it will be presumed that the beneficiary died first. The proceeds will then be paid to the secondary beneficiary or to the estate of the insured, if no secondary beneficiary has been named.

higher than for a whole life policy. Third, the policy builds cash values faster than a whole life policy because of the higher premium rate and shorter payment period.

The limited-payment life policy is generally preferred by persons who anticipate enjoying high earnings over the early periods of their lives and who wish to build a nest egg should their earnings drop in later life, as in retirement.

SINGLE-PREMIUM WHOLE LIFE

As the name clearly suggests, single-premium whole life (SPWL) is a whole life insurance policy where the lifetime premium is paid up front as a lump sum. However, the difference between traditional whole life and a SPWL is more than that implied by the method of premium payment. The most compelling reason for buying a SPWL comes from the desire to use a life insurance policy as a tax-deferred investment. However, the Technical and Miscellaneous Revenue Act (TAMRA) of 1988 made significant changes in the way SPWL policies are treated, as we shall now observe.

TAMRA of 1988

The TAMRA of 1988 made several important changes in the method of taxation of certain life insurance contracts. The legislation did not end the treatment of SPWL insurance contracts as life insurance contracts for federal income tax purposes, but it did change the treatment of distributions from a new class of contracts called modified endowment contracts (MECs). Distributions include partial withdrawals, all policy loans, including those to pay premiums, loans or loan interest, and partial surrenders. If a contract is considered an MEC, distributions received from it are treated first as taxable income and then as a nontaxable return of principal. In addition, if a distribution is taken prior to age $59\frac{1}{2}$, an additional ten percent penalty tax is imposed by the IRS. The income and estate taxation of death benefits, whether the plan is a traditional life or an MEC, remains unchanged under TAMRA of 1988.

All policies that were issued after June 20, 1988, are affected by TAMRA. In order to *avoid* being considered an MEC, policies issued after this date must meet several criteria, as described next.

Seven-pay test. If the cumulative premium paid into a contract during the first seven years exceeds a specified rate per thousand, the policy will be considered an MEC. This test is applied each year with each premium payment. Each insurance contract may have different limits because the calculation is based on the individual contract's guaranteed interest rate and the 1980 Commissioner's Standard Ordinary (CSO) Mortality Table. For instance, contracts that are unisex will have different maximum premiums than those that distinguish between male and female or smoker and nonsmoker.

Material changes test. The second test to determine if a policy may be classified as an MEC relates to material changes in the contract. Such changes include any increase in the future benefits provided under a life insurance contract. A material change also includes the exchange of one life insurance contract for another and the conversion of term to whole life.

The Penalty Tax

The 1988 legislation also provides that any payment received from a life insurance company and declared as taxable income is subject to a ten percent penalty tax. There are three exceptions to this penalty tax: (1) distributions made on or after the taxpayer attains age 59½; (2) distributions attributable to the taxpayer becoming disabled; and (3) substantially equal distributions made for the life of the taxpayer or joint lives of the taxpayer and the beneficiary.

Additional Advantages

Besides being a vehicle for tax-advantaged investment, the SPWL policy provides three additional advantages.

1. Unlike a corporate bond or a savings account where interest must be declared as ordinary income whether or not it is actually received, cash value can be left in an SPWL policy where it continues to compound tax-deferred.
2. Under the present tax law, tax-free municipal bond interest is added to other taxable income in order to determine whether or not Social Security income would be taxed. In contrast, interest earned on an SPWL policy is not added to other taxable incomes for the calculation of taxes on Social Security income.
3. When a policyholder is ready to receive distribution from an SPWL policy, the insurance company generally offers a variety of distribution choices to suit the special income needs of the policyholder.

UNIVERSAL LIFE

Universal life (UL) insurance differs from whole life in three key respects: (1) the premium payments are flexible; (2) the death benefit is adjustable; and (3) the investment risk is shifted from the insurance company to the policyholder. This permits policyholders to tailor their life insurance policy to their changing needs—a privilege whole life policyholders never enjoy.

In the case of a nonpar UL policy, the insured buys what amounts to a renewable term policy, the cost of which rises with the age of the insured. The other part of the premium goes into a cash accumulation fund. However, unlike a whole life policy, interest above the guaranteed four percent interest is deposited into the cash accumulation fund. In effect, the insured invests the money with the insurance company which invests the money in fixed rate debt instrument and pays competitive interest rates on this investment.

As mentioned, in a UL policy the death benefit is variable. The insured can select a fixed amount when buying the policy and, with medical evidence, this amount can be adjusted up or down annually. More specifically, the insured can choose between two options: (1) Constant face value with an increasing cash value. In this case, upon death the beneficiary receives *only* the face value. (2) Face value and cash value. In this option, upon death the beneficiary receives both the face value *and* the accumulated cash value. Similarly, a variable or fixed premium is paid at regular intervals and the insured can occasionally skip, reduce, or increase premium payments.

As in the case of SPWL, in a UL policy loans are permitted against accumulated cash value, although there is an interest cost associated with such borrowing. In addition, although it can vary between policies, UL policies also permit the withdrawal of up to 90 percent of the capital. However, as in the case of an SPWL, if a UL policy is classified as a modified endowment contract (MEC), all loans and assignments to the extent of the gain in the contract are treated as taxable distributions from the contract. Furthermore, each policy should be frequently reviewed to ensure that the accumulated cash value remaining with the company is sufficient to cover the monthly deductions for increasing mortality cost and policy expenses.

SURVIVORSHIP LIFE

A relatively new concept relates to survivorship life insurance policies which are used for estate planning purposes, since the financial burden of death primarily rests on the beneficiaries upon the second death. These policies provide coverage for two lives, with death benefits paid after the second death. The premiums, cash values, and dividends are based on the joint equal concept. That is, premium payments are made until the death of both parties. Life insurance proceeds are received by the beneficiaries upon the second death.

In the case of a survivorship policy, since an insurer has to set aside reserves for only one death-benefit payment, rather than two separate ones, the premium cost is substantially lower than what two people would pay to purchase the same amount of whole life coverage.

VARIABLE LIFE

Variable life is whole life insurance in which death benefits and accumulated cash values vary with the value of equity and fixed income securities constituting the main investment of the insurance reserves. A variable life policy shifts the investment risk to the insured and lets the insured direct some or all of the cash value into the securities markets, primarily through mutual funds. Variable life thus provides the insured with an opportunity to keep up with inflation. The face amount of the policy—known as death benefit—and the cash value will rise and fall, depending upon the performance of the investment portfolio. However, in almost all instances, the insurance company guarantees that death benefits will never be less than the face amount of the policy. Thus, in a variable life what is fluctuating is the cash value. Because the insured continually pays a level premium, the cash value will increase, but it may increase slowly if poor investments are made. As Indiana University insurance professor Joseph Belth points out: "If you invest in a variable life policy, your beneficiary's best hope is that you will die on an uptick."

An interesting variant of variable life is single-premium variable life. This policy is suitable for someone in search of a tax-deferred investment but who is willing to purchase a minimum amount of life insurance in the hope that a lump sum earns a highly competitive rate of return and grows tax-deferred.

Variable life policies issued before June 20, 1988, are not subject to the TAMRA rules and therefore permit tax-free loans which need not be repaid. However, outstanding loans are deducted from the face value upon death. For policies issued after that date, the usual restrictions discussed in the previous section apply.

VARIABLE UNIVERSAL LIFE

Variable universal life, also known by such names as flexible-premium variable life and universal life II, makes both the premium payment and the death benefit variable. The initial death benefit, which is chosen by the insured, can be made flexible, depending upon the family's need and investment performance. Also, like the traditional universal life, the cash values can be paid to a beneficiary in addition to, *or* as a part of, the death benefit, tax-free.

Essentially, a variable universal life policy, which is a tax-deferred mutual fund with management and administration fees, permits a variety of investment choices. These include stock, bond, mutual funds, fixed income accounts, and money market portfolios; switching between these products is permitted. The advantages of variable universal life are flexible family protection as well as premium and investment flexibility. However, the buyer of such a policy should also be a knowledgeable investor in order to maximize the gains from buying such a policy.

LIFE INSURANCE FOR INDIVIDUAL FAMILY MEMBERS

Life insurance agents are often profit maximizers; hence, it is reasonable to expect that at times some unprofessional, uninformed and short-sighted agents might sell policies that are not in their customers' best interests. Two important conclusions can be drawn from this observation. One is that prospective customers may be sold a more expensive policy when they really need a cheaper one. The other conclusion is that sometimes overzealous agents might sell policies to those members of the family who do not need insurance protection. It is therefore appropriate to ask: Who in the family *really* needs life insurance?

Wife Insurance

If the wife is the family's sole breadwinner, the same rules apply as for insurance on a husband breadwinner. Additionally, it is often argued that a wife's economic value—particularly when she is also the mother of small children—is extremely high. To replace her with maids, baby sitters, and other persons to provide even the minimum of essential services would cost a staggering sum. In this case, the strategy for wife insurance should be to buy an annual renewable term or a level term policy in order to help the family financially in the event of a sudden death of the wife and mother of minor children.

Insurance for Children

Two extreme views exist in the area of life insurance for children. At the one extreme is the view that there is little reason for buying this type of insurance because no one is dependent on children. At the other extreme is the view that the benefits of children's insurance far outweigh their costs. For instance, one of the advantages of child insurance is that without proof of insurability a child's policy might be convertible into a $10,000 whole life policy. Also, in the event of the death of the father, the child's insurance policy can be considered paid up until the end of the conversion date. Finally, without proof of insurability, the policy might offer additional insurance equal to five times the face value of the original policy.

A careful consideration of the arguments just presented reveals that both views are extremes. People should no more reject the idea of buying children's insurance because they feel it is useless than they should purchase it because it is cheap or convenient. In this case, as elsewhere, the philosophy of insurance buying remains the same: One should purchase children's insurance if the benefits of such a policy exceed its cost. While the cost of a children's policy is usually easily handled, only parents can determine the benefits they expect to derive from this insurance.

GROUP LIFE INSURANCE

This form of insurance provides a means for insuring a group of people under one policy. The most usual group is made up of the employees or members of an organization who are insured without medical examination under a master contract issued to the organization. Each insured employee receives a certificate stating the amount of insurance, the name of the beneficiary selected, and a summary of the rights and benefits. The amount of insurance is often one to two times the annual salary or earnings.

Group life insurance is usually issued on the term insurance basis. That is, the premium collected for the entire group buys protection only from one year to the next and does not buy permanent protection. Employer and employees may share the cost of group insurance: The employees' portion may be deducted (with their consent) from their salaries or wages, with the balance of the premium being paid by the employer. The employer may, however, pay the entire cost, provided the coverage does not exceed $50,000. Coverage of this type of policy expires or drops substantially at an advanced age.

If an employee leaves the employer, the group insurance coverage is lost; but the employee may buy an individual policy for the same coverage, even though he or she may be uninsurable at that time. This conversion privilege must be exercised within one month of the termination of employment. However, as a general rule, the group insurance coverage purchased by an individual is more expensive than an individual term policy if the policyholder is young, a nonsmoker, and in good health (unless the group policy is subsidized).

LIFE INSURANCE RIDERS

Title	*Explanation*
Multiple Indemnity	This clause provides a doubling or tripling of the face amount if death results from certain specified causes, such as an accident.
Waiver of Premium Benefit	If the policyholder becomes totally or permanently disabled, the insurance will remain in force without further premium payments. There is usually a six-month waiting or elimination period before this benefit becomes applicable. In a permanent policy, the cash value grows just as if the premiums are still being paid, and the insured is allowed to borrow against the cash value in the policy. Furthermore, in the case of a universal life policy, only the mortality costs are covered.
Guaranteed Insurability Rider	This rider guarantees that, up to the specified age, additional life insurance can be bought on certain "option dates" without proving insurability.
Accidental Death and Dismemberment	This rider provides benefits for loss of limb, eye, or death by accident.
Disability Income Rider	This rider provides a monthly income to the insured upon becoming disabled.

Incidentally, a large part of a person's life insurance coverage may be through group protection. Consequently, the financial planner must be alert for clients who plan to leave their job and start a new business. The planner should encourage these people to start building individual insurance protection long before losing the group insurance protection.

TAXATION OF LIFE INSURANCE

One of the most overrated and misinterpreted statements in the life insurance industry is that life insurance proceeds are tax-free. This statement is not only misleading but, in certain instances, could be devastating.

A summary of the rules governing the taxability of life insurance proceeds is presented in Table 3-3. Clearly, there are significantly different tax consequences between distribution upon death and during lifetime.

TABLE 3-3   Taxability of Life Insurance Proceeds

Type of insurance	Policy owner	Upon death			During life		
		Federal income tax	State inheritance tax[1]	Estate tax	Loan Income tax	Annuity distribution Income tax	Total surrender Income tax
Term	Insured	None	Yes	Yes			
	Other than insured	None	None	None			
	Irrevocable life insurance trust	None	None	None			
Cash value	Insured	None	Yes	Yes	Taxed[2]	Tax on gain	On excess of cash over premium
	Other than insured	None	None	None	Taxed[2]	Tax on gain	On excess of cash over premium
	Life insurance trust	None	None	None		Tax on gain	On excess of cash over premium
Deferred annuity	Insured	Tax on gain	Yes	Yes		Only on interest	On excess of cash over premium
	Other than insured	Tax on gain	No	No		Only on interest	On excess of cash over premium
	Life insurance trust	Not applicable	No	No		Only on interest	On excess of cash over premium

[1] In some states, death benefits are not exempt from state inheritance tax.

[2] Loans are not taxed if seven-pay test is met.

Distribution upon Death

Table 3-3 reveals that all life insurance policy death benefit distributions are exempt from federal income tax and, with few exceptions, from state inheritance taxes. In addition, whether a policy's death benefit is subject to federal estate taxes depends on who owns the policy. Life insurance proceeds are included in the gross estate of the insured only if the insured owns the policy. If someone other than the insured, for instance, a life insurance trust or an irrevocable trust, owns the policy, the proceeds will not be included in the gross estate of the insured for purposes of figuring federal estate taxes. The only exception to this rule is that if an insurance policy is transferred to an irrevocable life insurance trust within three years of death, the insurance proceeds will be included in the gross estate of the original owner before the transfer.

Distribution during Life

Policy loan. The law permits the tax-deferred accumulation of interest as long as the growth takes place inside an insurance policy. However, for policies which are issued after June 20, 1988, and do not meet the seven-pay test, if the accumulated interest is withdrawn in the form of a loan, it is taxed as ordinary income.

Annuity distribution. Both fixed and variable annuity contracts assume that periodic payments represent a combination of return of principal and distribution of interest. Consequently, when a life insurance company makes an annuity payment, the return of principal portion escapes federal income taxes and the interest portion is taxed as ordinary income.

Total surrender. When a policy is surrendered and life insurance coverage is canceled, the cash value, or the surrender value, is returned to the policyholder. In this case, the difference between the total amount of money received (cash value plus loans outstanding) and the cost basis (which includes insurance costs) is taxed as ordinary income.

LIFE INSURANCE AND ESTATE TAXES

As a general rule, if the life insurance proceeds are not received by or for the benefit of the estate and the decedent had no "incidence of ownership" in the policy, the insurance proceeds (with one exception) are not included in the gross estate for estate tax purposes. The one exception relates to the gifts of insurance policies made within three years of the decedent's death in which case the proceeds are included in the gross estate of the decedent. It should be mentioned that because life insurance is a contract, death benefits bypass the probate process, unless the beneficiary is the estate. This subject will be discussed in detail in Chapter 15.

SWITCHING OF POLICIES

A well-planned life insurance program requires much thought before the actual policy purchase. Consequently, insurance policies should be treated as long-term purchases and held on a permanent basis. While this statement is generally true, there are circumstances which might call for switching of policies.

The most compelling reasons for a reexamination of the existing policies is the steady decline in the cost of life insurance. Overall, as compared to 1958, the new mortality table reflects an average 15 percent drop in the number of deaths per 1,000 people. As a consequence, the premium rates have dropped for many types of insurance contracts. For this reason, it pays to investigate switching old policies for new ones.

The explosion of whole life policies being replaced by universal life and other kinds of policies is the second reason for switching life insurance policies. The old, traditional whole life policies are complex, inflexible, and costly. In 1979 a Federal Trade Commission study, which was controversial, concluded that in 1977 the rates of return on these policies averaged 1.3 percent. Also, in whole life policies the premium payments, death benefits, and the number of payments all remain fixed as long as the policy remains in force. The newer universal life policies are not only flexible with respect to both the death benefit and premium payments, but also offer competitive rates of return.

Changing family conditions may be the third reason for switching policies. A policy covering a spouse's life may no longer be necessary if the children are grown up and gone. Some of the old riders which made sense earlier may not be appropriate. Even the amount of coverage may have to be modified to suit the family's changing needs.

The switching of policies may have several drawbacks as well. Most policies provide for a two-year period of contestability after which the insurer cannot refuse to pay the benefit for any reason. The old policies may have superior settlement options, disability provisions, suicide provisions, and other terms. Furthermore because the new policy will be bought at an older age, and also because it will include commissions or sales costs, the premium payments for the new policy will most likely be higher. Also, the old policy may have a contingent deferred sales load which would become payable if it is switched for a new policy.

Finally, it is important to reiterate the modified endowment contract (MEC) problem which might be created by switching a policy. As mentioned, if the new policy is considered an MEC, distributions received from this policy are treated first as taxable income and fully taxed. Only distributions in excess of the accumulations in the policy are treated as a nontaxable return of principal. In addition, unless a policy is directly exchanged for another policy—which is known as a 1035 exchange—if a distribution is taken prior to age $59\frac{1}{2}$, an additional ten percent tax is imposed. Consequently, extreme caution is advised before giving up an old policy which is not affected by the 1988 tax law and which might have other advantages just discussed.

LIFE INSURANCE PLANNING

DETERMINATION OF LIFE INSURANCE NEEDS

Traditionally, many simple rules have been applied to determine the *true* insurance needs of a family. Today families receive much simple advice on how to allocate their insurance nest-egg dollars. For example, one insurance counselor suggests spending each year a sum equal to six percent of a breadwinner's gross income, plus one percent for each dependent—a total of $900 a year for a sales clerk who earns $10,000 a year and has a spouse and two children. Another counselor argues the rule of thumb for coverage is four to six times annual income. A third counselor maintains that the breadwinner should have three or four times the annual income in insurance, while a fourth asserts that five percent of one's take-home pay should go for life insurance premiums. But such guidelines are at best of limited value because individual needs vary tremendously. More important, insurance professionals applying standard rules of thumb also disagree sharply on how much insurance a given family with certain basic responsibilities should carry.

Before attempting to determine the adequacy of life insurance for any given family, one point should be made clear. Regardless of financial status, practically every head of a family dreams that, in the event of a premature death, even if the surviving spouse is unwilling or unable to work, the financial lifestyle of the family will not be affected adversely. This dream can be realized only if the flow of income to the family continues unabated. While a breadwinner may want the family to receive the same income should he or she die prematurely, it is unwise to determine the family's life insurance *needs* on this basis. A more logical objective would be to plan for providing family income (including Social Security survivorship benefits, investment, and other income sources) in the range of, say, 60 to 75 percent of the insured's gross pay at the time of death, after allowing for final expenses, debt payments, and financing for children's education.

As stated earlier, two key objectives of buying cash value life insurance are to achieve financial security for the family and receive retirement income. In order to meet these objectives, the following questions should be answered: (1) In the event of death, how much money would the family need for living purposes? (2) How long would this amount of income be needed? (It should at least last until the children are out of high school, and preferably until they finish college.) (3) How much Social Security income can be expected until the children are no longer covered? (4) How much income will the spouse need after the children are on their own? Answers to these questions will provide the basis for the determination of life insurance needs. One popular technique of determining how much life insurance is needed is known as Capital Needs Analysis.

Capital Needs Analysis

Basic considerations. It is an axiom of risk management planning that the insurance amount should be sufficiently large to cover the family's economic needs if a breadwinner were to die tomorrow. Consequently, the starting point in capital needs analysis is a valuation of income needs against the estimated income to be received upon the death of the breadwinner.

The typical income needs of a family and the various sources of income expected to be received by the surviving spouse are listed in Table 3-4. The excess of income needs over the expected income must be covered by income from a lump sum investment to be made by the surviving spouse with the life insurance money.

The lump sum required to generate a predetermined monthly income would vary greatly depending upon whether the surviving spouse wishes to preserve or deplete the capital. The monthly income generated in the former case would be far less than in the latter case, since part of the monthly income in the latter case would represent a return of the principal. For instance, if a surviving wife wishes to preserve the capital and invests $100,000 in a ten-year bond at nine percent, she will receive $750 a month from this investment for ten years and a return of the principal in ten years. If, however, $100,000 is annuitized over a ten-year period, this person might receive, say, $1,270 per month but would exhaust the principal in ten years.

TABLE 3-4   Expense Needs Versus Sources of Income

Expense needs	Sources of income
A. Single-Period Needs	A. Social Security: Survivor's Income
i. Administrative/Final Expenses*	B. Group Life Insurance
ii. Estate Settlement Costs*	C. Spouse's Earnings
iii. Debt Liquidation*	D. Investment Income
iv. Emergency Fund*	
B. Multiple-Period Needs	
i. Educational Cost	
ii. Surviving Spouse's Income Needs	
iii. Children's Income Needs	
iv. Retirement Needs	

* Life insurance does not necessarily need to cover these expenses. These items should be considered optional in determining the life insurance needs of a family.

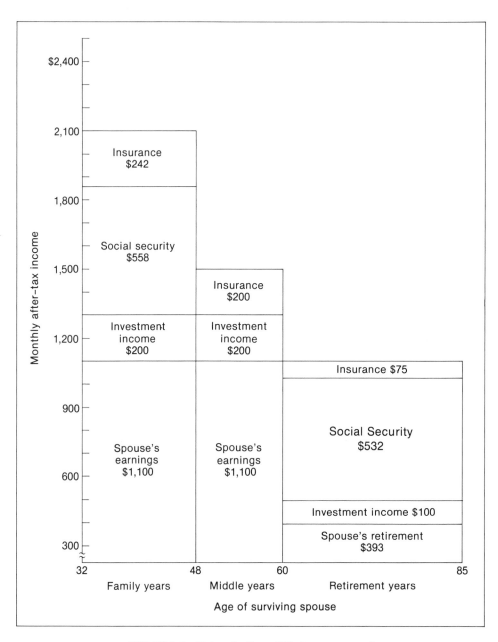

FIGURE 3-6. Determination of life insurance need

An important consideration in purchasing life insurance relates to the fact that the needs of a family change over time. For instance, group health insurance may expire some time after retirement. Social security no longer pays benefits to the surviving spouse when the youngest child reaches age 16. The surviving spouse may not be able to work while the children are at home. Also, if the spouse joins the work force on a full-time basis after the children are gone, the Social Security income will be reduced. Finally, real investment returns (that is, returns adjusted for inflation) will vary from year to year depending upon the types of investments made and prevailing market conditions. The concept of varying life insurance needs to accommodate changing conditions of a hypothetical family is depicted in Figure 3-6. For example, in the illustration, in the middle years, $1,500 of after-tax monthly income is required, with only $200 supplied by insurance, whereas during family years $2,100 of monthly income is required, with only $242 supplied by insurance.

A simplified illustration. Capital needs analysis, which is designed to accurately calculate a family's life insurance needs, is based on the application of the present value concept presented in detail in Chapter 5. Here is a simple illustration to estimate the life insurance needs of a family with two children.

John Smith, 30, and Mary Smith, 29, have two children. Jeff is four and Nancy is two years old. The Smiths' family and financial data are presented in Table 3-5, while the technique for arriving at the new capital needed for John Smith is demonstrated in Table 3-6. This technique is discussed next.

Step 1: Final Expenses. The final expenses are estimated to be $27,000. Since the Smiths have $2,500 in liquid assets and an additional $255 is

TABLE 3-5 Family and Financial Data of John Smith

Family data			
	John Smith	Age 30	
	Mary Smith	Age 29	
	Jeff Smith	Age 4	
	Nancy Smith	Age 2	

Financial data			
Assets		*Liabilities and net worth*	
Cash/Liquid Assets	$ 2,500	Home Mortgage	$ 70,000
Invested Assets	0	Other Liabilities	12,000
Other Assets	20,000	Net Worth	30,500
Home	90,000		
	$112,500		$112,500
Life Insurance Coverage = $50,000			

TABLE 3-6 Capital Needs Analysis of John Smith

Line	Income needed	Years income needed	Amount needed	Available sources Social Security	Available sources Employ- ment	Available sources Other sources	Additional needed	Capital required
A.	Final Expenses		$27,000*	$ 255	0	$2,500	$24,245	$ 24,245
B.	Housing		70,000*	0	0	0	70,000	70,000
C.	Education		32,000*	0	0	0	32,000	24,252

Monthly income for Mary Smith

Line	Income needed	Years income needed	Amount needed	Social Security	Employ- ment	Other sources	Additional needed	Capital required
D.	Until Jeff is 18	14	2,200	1,043	$1,067	0	90	13,200
E.	Nancy between 16 and 18	2	2,200	522	1,067	0	611	14,387
F.	Alone, age 45 to 65	20	1,550	0	1,067	0	483	95,636
G.	Alone, age 65 to 80	15	1,550	695	0	0	855	133,087

Assumptions:
1. Capital amounts needed for monthly expenses are assuming that the capital will be exhausted when Mary Smith is 80 years old.
2. Capital funds are assumed to earn interest at an after-tax, inflation adjusted rate of 2%.
3. Client is eligible for Social Security.
4. Client wishes to pay off the mortgage immediately.
5. Education fund available as lump sum when Jeff reaches the age of 18—that is, in 14 years.
6. Wife does not receive Social Security between ages 45 and 65 (20 years).
7. Wife's life expectancy is 80 (15 years since age 65).

Capital Required Calculations

Line A: Capital immediately required. No calculation necessary.
Line B: Capital immediately required. No calculation necessary.
Line C: FV(PVIF). PVIF (n = 14, i = 2%) is .757875 $24,252 = 32,000 (.757875)

	PMT (Begin Mode)	I(%/mo)	N	PV
Line D:	90	2/12	14 × 12	13,200
Line E:	611	2/12	2 × 12	14,387
Line F:	483	2/12	20 × 12	95,636
Line G:	855	2/12	15 × 12	133,087

Note: Figures are rounded off.
* Optional at the discretion of the surviving spouse.

expected to be received from Social Security, additional capital needed to meet the final expenses is $24,245 (Line A).

Step 2: Housing. The Smiths have a $70,000 mortgage loan and they would want it to be paid off in case of John's death (Line B).

Step 3: Education. The Smiths estimate that it would cost $32,000 to educate Jeff and Nancy. It is assumed that educational funds would earn interest at an after-tax rate of five percent and the rate of inflation would be three percent; that is, the real rate of return (actual rate minus the inflation rate) would be two percent. Finally, the Smiths decide that they would like to have $32,000 in approximately 14 years when Jeff will turn 18 and Nancy will be 16 years old (Line C).

Using a financial calculator (see Chapter 5 for details), we find that the present value of $1 growing at 2 percent per year for fourteen years is .757875. Multiplying the present value interest factor (PVIF) by $32,000, we determine that the capital required today to educate the two children is $24,252 ($32,000 × .757875).

Step 4: Monthly Expenses for Mary Smith. If John Smith were to die today, for the next 14 years until Jeff is 18, Mary Smith will receive $1,043 per month from Social Security and $1,067 in today's dollars from her place of employment. However, the Smiths have decided that the family needs a monthly income of $2,200 to raise the two children. The resultant short-fall of $90 per month ($2,200 − $1,043 − $1,067) can be obtained by purchasing an annuity for $13,200. The calculation method is shown at the bottom of Table 3-6, Line D.

Using the same technique, we can calculate that Mary will receive a monthly income of $611 for two years after Jeff leaves home at 18 and Nancy becomes 18 by annuitizing a lump sum of $14,387. Finally, Mary will receive $483 per month for 20 years until she is 65 by annuitizing a lump sum of $95,636; similarly, she will receive $855 per month for 15 years until age 80 (her life expectancy) from a lump sum of $133,087.

Adding all the family's needs together, the total capital need of the Smith family equals $374,807. This fact is revealed in Table 3-7.

TABLE 3-7

Needs		Particulars	Capital reqd.
Final Expenses		Immediate need	$ 24,245
Housing		Liquidation of mortgage	70,000
Education		Lump sum available when Jeff is 18—in 14 years	24,252
Monthly Income	#1	Monthly income until Jeff is 18	13,200
	#2	Monthly income when Nancy is between 16 and 18	14,387
	#3	Monthly income when Mary is between 45 and 65	95,636
	#4	Monthly income when Mary is between 65 to 80	133,087
		Total	374,807
		Less existing insurance	− 50,000
		Additional insurance need	$324,807

Note: Figures are rounded off.

HOW TO PROGRAM INSURANCE

Insurance programming is a method of anticipating and meeting family needs by determining the amount and type of insurance an individual should own and how the proceeds of this insurance should be payable. The first step in programming is calculating the individual's income needs and the needs of his or her family. The second step is valuing present assets and assets to be acquired in the foreseeable future. Next, it is necessary to see if there is a deficiency between present assets and needed income, and, if so, how great the deficiency is. Finally, it is necessary to choose and obtain insurance policies to meet the deficit.

The deficit is usually greatest early in the individual and family life cycle when the wage earner or earners are starting their careers and their children are young; debts are often high when income is lowest. Needs are high and assets are few. Life insurance provides an immediate estate to meet family needs in case of death or disability of a provider. The following table shows the amount of earnings lost before age 65 if death occurs at a given age between 25 and 60. (The table assumes a stable income to age 65, and does not reflect reductions for taxes, other payroll deductions, living expenses, etc.)

Age death occurs	Annual income				
	$ 24,000	$ 30,000	$ 36,000	$ 42,000	$ 48,000
25	$960,000	$1,200,000	$1,440,000	$1,680,000	$1,920,000
27	912,000	1,140,000	1,368,000	1,596,000	1,824,000
30	840,000	1,050,000	1,260,000	1,470,000	1,680,000
33	768,000	960,000	1,152,000	1,344,000	1,536,000
35	720,000	900,000	1,080,000	1,260,000	1,440,000
37	672,000	840,000	1,008,000	1,176,000	1,344,000
40	600,000	750,000	900,000	1,050,000	1,200,000
43	528,000	660,000	792,000	924,000	1,056,000
45	480,000	600,000	720,000	840,000	960,000
47	432,000	540,000	648,000	756,000	864,000
50	360,000	450,000	540,000	630,000	720,000
53	288,000	360,000	432,000	504,000	576,000
55	240,000	300,000	360,000	420,000	480,000
57	192,000	240,000	288,000	336,000	384,000
60	120,000	150,000	180,000	210,000	240,000

Sound planning meets a variety of needs at different times. When an insured person dies, there is a need for a "clean-up fund"—a lump sum to pay for funeral expenses, estate taxes, debts, and other postmortem expenses. If the insured person is survived by minor children, they may be eligible for Social Security benefits and/or veterans' benefits. After the dependency period (ending at age 19 for full-time students, 18 for others) ends, there may be a need for increased family income, because educational expenses will be high and income from government transfer payments unavailable. The period between the 16th birthday of the youngest child and a widow's or widower's 60th birthday is called the "Social Security gap"; widow's or widower's benefits are not available, and the benefit for the parent of a dependent child terminates. Extra income should be available to the parent at this time.

Source: Reprinted from *Financial Planning*, Prentice Hall Information Services, 1989. All rights reserved.

Further sophistication. In the preceding illustration we made several simplified assumptions which can be refined to undertake a more accurate capital needs analysis. Here are some examples of assumptions which are different from those made in the previous example:

1. The Smiths do not wish to invade the principal in generating the required income.
2. Appropriate education funds become available at the beginning of age 18 for Jeff and Nancy.
3. Capital funds earn interest at an after-tax rate of, say, eight percent.
4. The inflation rate is a more realistic five percent.
5. Spouse's employment income keeps pace with inflation.
6. The true inflation-adjusted interest rate is 2.857 percent $[(1.08/1.05 - 1) \times 100]$, instead of two percent just assumed.

If further sophistication is desired, varied assumptions can be made about different tax rates and more realistic annual rates of return depending upon the sophistication of the surviving spouse. Fortunately, these and other assumptions can be incorporated with relative ease in the capital needs analysis by using the time value of money tool developed in Chapter 5.

COST OF LIFE INSURANCE

Basic Considerations

It is a simple matter to obtain the cost of buying life insurance from various insurance companies. However, it is far more difficult to obtain the real cost—or net cost—of life insurance, as we shall now discover.

The net cost of carrying insurance in any company depends upon a variety of factors, which include the success in selecting high performing investment vehicles, selection of good mortality risks, and maintaining low costs of operations. Success in achieving these goals can significantly lower the real cost of life insurance.

The cost of an insurance policy depends not only on the efficiency of the company's management but also on the size of the company. Smaller companies often have relatively greater expenses than their more mature counterparts, due in part to the expense of running the organization, possible lack of management experience, and higher overheads. Another important expense item is the percentage of new premium dollars spent in attracting new business. Some newer companies may have the tendency to use a larger portion of premium dollars to attract new business in order to maintain their growth momentum. Finally, the death rates among a company's policyholders also affect the cost of insurance to the surviving policyholders. If mortality among the company's policyholders is excessive, the increased cost of insurance ordinarily will be met by reducing dividends on existing policies or by increasing the premium rates on future policies.

It should now be clear that an uncritical comparison of premium rates for $1,000 of coverage quoted by different companies is an inefficient method of shopping for a cost-effective insurance policy. For instance, a 21-year-old male shopping for $100,000 policy coverage might be quoted the following rates:

	Year	
Policy	1	20
5-year Renewable Term	$ 100	$ 190
5-year Renewable and Convertible Term	185	940
Whole Life	870	870
Limited Pay Life (Paid up at age 65)	920	920
Endowment (at age 65)	1,070	1,070

Obviously, these rates are not comparable, because in some cases they represent pure protection, whereas in other cases they also take cash value into account.

Essentially, four factors determine the true cost of a policy: (1) premiums, (2) dividends, (3) the cash value of the policy, and (4) the opportunity cost of investing in the policy—that is, the rate of interest the policyholder could otherwise earn on the funds. The two most popular methods frequently used for comparing costs of insurance policies are the net-cost method and the interest-adjusted cost index.

The Net-Cost Method

The net cost, which is calculated for a given point in time (say, at the end of the tenth year) during the life of the policy is given by the following:

Net Cost = Premiums Paid − (Accrued Dividends + Cash Value)

For instance, if John Jones has been paying an annual premium of $1,000 for 10 years in a participating policy, and the accrued dividend and cash value at the end of the tenth year are $5,000 and $15,000, respectively, then the net cost of the policy is −$10,000:

$$\text{Net Cost} = \$10,000 - (\$5,000 + \$15,000)$$
$$= -\$10,000$$

A negative net cost, of course, does *not* imply that the company was actually paying the insured for insuring his or her life. The reason is that the net cost method ignores the time value of money. Put differently, it does not take into account the opportunity cost of making premium payments in excess of the amount necessary to buy pure life insurance. For this reason, the interest-adjusted cost index is preferable.

Interest-Adjusted Cost Index

A more realistic method of calculating the net cost is to follow a different method, the *interest-adjusted cost index method*, shown in Table 3-8. The table shows that for a person 35 years of age the true cost of buying a $1,000 participating whole life insurance policy is $4.20 per thousand, not −$1.50, as calculated under the net cost method. While it is true that the participating policy costs are based on estimated dividends and that cash surrender values depend somewhat on the number of years a policy is kept in force, the *true* net cost method can be used as an index for measuring the cost of one policy versus another policy.

It is evident that the interest-adjusted cost method of calculating insurance costs is far superior to the traditional net cost method. However, even this method does have certain shortcomings. For one thing, the choice of a specific period for comparison, such as ten or 20 years, is arbitrary. Some companies might look better or worse when a different period is chosen. For another, this method ignores mortality rates and policy lapse rates (although these factors are taken into account in making dividend projections), factors that could be used to produce a more sophisticated index. Nevertheless, because of requirements in some states and due to voluntary actions in others, responsible associations such as the Consumers Union have been consistently publishing the interest-adjusted cost method of calculating insurance costs so that prospective insurance buyers can compare different insurance policies.

Benchmark Method

Professor Joseph M. Belth has developed a benchmark method for comparing the cost of a universal life or variable life policy against a "benchmark" which deserves special mention.[1] Under this method, the cost per $1,000 of protection each year is computed by dividing total charges under the policy by the amount of pure life insurance protection. The annual charges are determined by analyzing changes in the cash value. Since, at any point in time, the cash value of a policy is equal to the accumulated premiums plus interest less any charges, the cost of a policy can be calculated by analyzing changes

---

[1] Joseph M. Belth, "Universal Life and Variable Life—How to Evaluate the New Wave of Products," *Insurance Forum*, Vol. 11, No. 6, June 1984, pp. 21–24.

TABLE 3-8 Net Costs Versus Interest-Adjusted Cost Method

(A) Net Cost Method

1. Total premiums for 20 years ($240/year)	$4,800
2. Less dividends for 20 years ($75/year)	− 1,500
3. Net premiums for 20 years (1–2)	$3,300
4. Less cash value at end of 20 years (given)	− 3,600
5. Insurance cost (3–4)	− $ 300
6. Average cost per year (1/20)	− $ 15
7. Cost per year per $1,000 of insurance divided by number of thousands of face amount of policy (10 in this case)	− $ 1.50

(B) Interest-Adjusted Cost Method

1. Total premiums for 20 years, each accumulated at 4%	$7,147[1]
2. Less dividends for 20 years, each accumulated at 4%	− $2,233[2]
3. Net premiums for 20 years (1–2)	$4,914
4. Less cash value at the end of 20 years (given)	− $3,600
5. Insurance cost (3–4)	$1,314
6. Amount to which $1 deposited annually will accumulate in 20 years at 4%	$ 31[3]
7. Interest-adjusted cost per year: divide $1,314 by $31	$ 42
8. Cost per year per $1,000 (1/10): divide $42 by 10	$ 4.20[4]

Note: The illustration is based on a $10,000 policy bought at 35 years of age. The policy is assumed to have been cashed in after 20 years. Cash value at the end of 20 years equals $3,600.
(1) PMT = $240, n = 20, i = 4, cv = 7,147
(2) PMT = $75, n = 20, i = 4, cv = 2,233
(3) PMT = $1 (beginning of year, or annuity due), n = 20, i = 4, cv = 31
(4) This figure is rounded off. The exact cost is $4.24 as shown here:

Line	Amount (2 decimals)
1	$7,146.74
2	2,233.36
3	4,913.38
4	3,600.00
5	1,313.38
6	30.97
7	42.41
8	4.24

in the cash value during a given year. Belth's formula for computing the cost per $1,000 of protection is given by:

$$YPT = \frac{(P + CVP)(1 + i) - (CV + D)}{(DB - CV)(0.001)}$$

where

YPT = Yearly price per $1,000 of protection

P = Annual premium

CVP = Cash value at the end of the preceding year

i = Assumed interest rate expressed as a decimal

CV = Cash value at the end of the year

D = Dividend for the year

DB = Death benefit at the end of the year

For instance, assume the following information:

Annual premium = $370
Cash value at the end of previous year = $675
Cash value at the end of current policy year = $915
Annual dividend = none
Interest rate = 6 percent
Death benefit at the end of the year = $50,000

The cost of this whole life policy per $1,000 of coverage is $3.93:

$$\frac{(\$370 + \$675)(1 + .06) - (\$915 + 0)}{(\$50,000 - \$915)(.001)}$$

$$= \$3.93$$

The $3.93 cost of protection per $1,000 can now be compared with "benchmark" costs that are computed with "normal" assumptions to determine if the cost of this policy is reasonable. In general, as compared to the benchmark price:

If the policy cost is	*Then the mortality and loading charges are*
Same or lower	Small
Higher but less than 200 percent of the benchmark cost	Medium
Higher than 200 percent of the benchmark cost	Large

LOANS FROM A LIFE INSURANCE POLICY

We have observed earlier that the cash value grows tax-deferred inside an insurance policy, which can make it an attractive tax shelter. But what really makes cash value life insurance an attractive savings vehicle is that accumulated interest in a policy can be withdrawn as a loan, often at a "net borrowing cost" of around two percent. When compared to the current average 15 percent rate on unsecured personal loans or the ten percent on popular home equity loans, the insurance policy loan appears to be very attractive. Equally important is the fact that obtaining a policy loan is easy and the loan need never be repaid. Of course, any unpaid loan is deducted from the face amount of the policy upon death.

Of the many advantages of an insurance policy loan just cited, the low net cost of borrowing is utterly misleading. The reason is that in the net cost method the opportunity cost of borrowing money is ignored. This point requires elaboration.

Let us assume that a policyholder wishes to borrow $10,000 from a cash value policy which is currently earning 11 percent. The cost of the policy loan is eight percent. However, the company will simultaneously reduce the interest on the cash value from 11 percent to 5.5 percent as long as the loan remains unpaid. Thus, the true cost of borrowing from a policy works out to 13.5 percent:

Pre-loan return (1)	Post-loan return (2)	Loan rate (3)	True cost of loan $(1 - 2 + 3)$ (4)
11.0%	5.5%	8.0%	13.5%

The true cost of a loan from a variable life policy may be even more costly. For instance, the Lipper Analytical reported that during the year ending February 1, 1989, the Monarch Variable CAPTN variable life policy earned 32.8 percent. If a loan against this policy lowers the post-loan return to 4.3 percent and the policy loan costs eight percent, the true cost of borrowing would be a whopping 36.5 percent:

Pre-loan return (1)	Post-loan return (2)	Loan rate (3)	True cost of loan $(1 - 2 + 3)$ (4)
32.8%	4.3%	8.0%	36.5%

There are two additional disadvantages of taking out a policy loan. First, the raison d'être for life insurance is the death benefit. A policy loan automatically reduces the death benefit by the amount of the loan, thereby partially defeating the purpose of carrying the insurance protection. Second, policy loans from all insurance contracts issued after June 20, 1988, that violate the seven-pay test are taxed as ordinary income, a new feature which significantly reduces the attractiveness of policy loans. Despite the high cost and associated disadvantages, however, policy loans may prove to be desirable in those cases where an urgent need for a loan exists and alternative sources of a loan at a reasonable cost are not available.

LIFE INSURANCE SETTLEMENT OPTIONS

Basic Considerations

The main purpose of purchasing life insurance is to create an estate, preserve an estate, or transfer an estate. More specifically, life insurance can be used to provide funds to cover: (1) the insured's death expenses; (2) unpaid debts; (3) taxes; (4) an emergency fund; (5) a life income sufficiently large to enable the members of the family to maintain the desired lifestyle; (6) an income for the children until they are independent; and (7) a fund for financing college expenses. All of these needs are not necessarily present in every case. For instance, the surviving spouse may be a career person who would not need life income from life insurance. The family may not have any children. In certain instances, if grandparents have taken the responsibility for educating their grandchildren, there might not be a need to provide for children's education.

Regardless of how many needs just listed are present in any given situation, the manner in which the life insurance proceeds are distributed makes a difference between complete protection and partial achievement of one's stated goals. For example, if the insured has chosen a lump-sum payment option, it might impose an unreasonable burden on the beneficiary who must invest the proceeds wisely in order to obtain an adequate income. In contrast, an annuity option, which locks in a fixed interest rate, may be unwise if the surviving spouse is an astute investor and can realize a significant growth by investing the lump sum in growth securities. For these reasons, every policyholder should select the settlement options most appropriate for the prevailing economic conditions, tax benefits desired, and most consistent with the abilities of the beneficiaries to manage their funds. In the following pages, we will discuss the key settlement options available to life insurance policyholders.

Lump-Sum Payment

Lump-sum payment is by far the most popular life insurance settlement option. A cash settlement may enable the beneficiary to retire outstanding debts, pay off administrative and funeral costs, meet federal estate and state inheritance tax liabilities, and provide emergency funds. In addition, the lump-sum payment provides funds for creating a diversified investment portfolio especially designed to achieve the multiple objectives of growth, current income, liquidity, and diversification. Of course, a policyholder opting for this type of settlement must make sure that the beneficiary or the associated advisor is sufficiently sophisticated to construct and manage such an investment portfolio.

Fixed Annuity

For those who do not wish to put an unreasonable burden of investment management on their beneficiaries, the fixed annuity settlement option is desirable. This option offers three distinct choices.

Fixed period option. Under this option, the period of payment is selected, and the amount of each payment is so calculated that both the principal and interest will have been paid by the end of the period. This form is effective for providing income for such purposes as raising children or buying time before the surviving spouse can join the labor force.

Fixed income option. Under this form, the installment amount is first selected, and then payments are made until the principal and interest are exhausted. This option is more appropriate in situations where the main objective is to provide temporary readjustment income for the surviving spouse.

Life-income option. Both the options listed above suffer from a basic deficiency: The income may cease before the need for it ends. Under the life-income option, the beneficiary cannot outlive the income, since the payments are made as long as the beneficiary may live. The amount of each installment is determined on the basis of the age and sex of the beneficiary at the time the option is selected. It should also be noted that the life income option generates a monthly income lower than any other type of option available to the insured.

The life-income option is an excellent means of assuring that the beneficiary totally dependent upon this source would never outlive this income. This would particularly be attractive where the beneficiary lives an exceptionally long life. However, there are at least three problems associated with this option. (1) If the beneficiary dies at an early age, a substantial portion of the principal would be forfeited. (2) Over time, inflation would certainly erode the value of the monthly income. (3) The recipient can never invade the principal. For those who are concerned with these potential problems, a variant known as *life-income-with-installment-certain* option is available. This option guarantees that payments will continue for at least a specified period (usually ten, 15, or 20 years) if the principal beneficiary dies early. Of course, the insurance company would still continue to make payments after the expiration of the minimum guaranteed period for as long as the primary (or secondary in the case of joint life) beneficiary lives. An overview of the fixed-annuity option as well as the variable-annuity option (discussed next) is presented in Table 3-9.

Variable Annuity Option

One of the major limitations of the fixed annuity option is that it is, in effect, a savings account that earns a fixed interest rate for a specified period. Consequently, it does not provide a satisfactory hedge against inflation. An alternative to the fixed annuity is the variable annuity option, which provides an individual with two options: accumulation and distribution. In the first case the value of units increases with positive investment results, whereas in the second case the units remain fixed and the additional income is periodically distributed. Simply stated, a variable annuity is a family of mutual funds within an annuity contract. Under this option, the insurance company offers an assortment of stock, bond, and money market funds and puts the responsibility of choosing between them squarely on the shoulders of the policyholder. Variable annuity contract values fluctuate with the fund's value. When annuitized, the annual payouts also vary with the portfolio's performance. For a mortality and risk fee of 0.8–1.4 percent of assets, most variable annuities provide a guaranteed death benefit (if death precedes annuitization) of the greater of the total purchase payments, less any withdrawals, or the value of the account. The fee also guarantees that annuity payments will not be decreased should the insurance company incur adverse mortality experiences or increases in administrative costs. A summary of variable annuity options is presented in Table 3-9.

Funds Left with Insurance Company

The final option for the beneficiary is to leave the funds at a stipulated rate of interest with the insurance company which acts as a trustee. The interest rate offered by the company may vary, depending upon prevailing market conditions; however, the *guaranteed* minimum interest rate paid is always around four percent. This option is the least attractive and is generally not preferred by most policyholders.

Life Insurance in Irrevocable Trust

One of the key insurance planning ideas is to create an irrevocable life insurance trust. Such a trust transfers the ownership of the insurance to the

TABLE 3-9 Fixed and Variable Annuity Options

Basic considerations	Fixed annuity	Variable annuity
Investment Products	Long-term bonds, mortgages.	Stocks, bonds, mutual funds, zero coupons, money-market investments).
Flexibility of Investment	None.	Excellent. Insured directs movements of funds.
Safety of Cash Value	High.	Low to moderate.
Potential Rate of Return	Moderate.	High, over long periods.
Advantages	Guaranteed interest and principal.	Potentially high rate of return. Control of investments. Flexibility.
Disadvantages	Limited inflation hedge. Potential drop in rate of return. Earns below competitive rates of return.	No guaranteed cash value. Amount of monthly payment not guaranteed. Requires familiarity with investments. Elements of risk are always present.
Appropriate Buyer	People who (i) want to follow a conservative policy, (ii) need guaranteed monthly income, (iii) want a tax-deferred cash value fund and can tie up funds until annuitizing.	People who (i) need a monthly income, (ii) are investment-oriented, (iii) want flexibility, (iv) want a tax-deferred fund and can tie up funds until annuitizing, and (v) are well diversified in other areas (e.g. carry fixed-income-type investments).

trust, and the current owner, who could also be the insured, gives up all rights to change the beneficiary and other terms of the policy. If properly set up, the irrevocable trust can help reduce estate taxes by removing the insurance proceeds from the estate of the policy owner. In the case of large estates this could ultimately result in significant tax savings for the beneficiaries.

While the irrevocable life insurance trust is a valuable planning tool, it does have several drawbacks which should be explicitly recognized. For one thing, creating such a trust is an irreversible decision, and it may prove to be a very costly decision if conditions dramatically change in the future. For another, possible gift taxes might be involved in transferring a policy to a trust. It should also be noted that if life insurance is transferred by gift to a trust within three years of the transferor's death, the gift of life insurance will be included in the owner's gross estate. Furthermore, an individual who wishes to make a tax-free gift of up to $10,000 can do so directly, thereby avoiding the problem of paying premiums for a policy placed in an irrevocable trust. Despite these negatives, however, the irrevocable life insurance trust remains a valuable planning tool.

ADDITIONAL LIFE INSURANCE PLANNING TECHNIQUES

There are many creative ways in which life insurance can be used to accomplish a variety of objectives. While it is beyond the scope of this book to undertake an in-depth analysis of these planning techniques, it is appropriate to briefly discuss some of the more important techniques.

Buy-Sell Agreement

The death of a principal owner of a business can create serious financial problems for the business and for the estate and survivors of the deceased individual. Usually, the deceased's interest in the business is a dominant portion of the total estate. The estate tax payable can place a substantial burden on the estate and the business. To meet expenses, the estate may be forced to liquidate the interest in the business. And, if it is sold under adverse conditions, substantial losses may be suffered as a result of a forced sale. Even more important, if corporate stock is sold to outsiders, the surviving shareholders' interests may be jeopardized.

All of these problems can be handled with buy-sell agreements, which provide for the orderly transfer of the deceased's business interest to surviving partners, stockholders, or key employees at fair values determined in advance. Life insurance is used to assure that the funds will be available either to the business or to an individual when the business interests are to be transferred. The death of the owner whose interest is to be purchased triggers the mechanism that produces the necessary funds—the life insurance policies on the owner's life. The proceeds from these policies give the buyers the needed funds to pay the estate the agreed price.

Insurance in Qualified Plans

People make financial plans for their retirement in various ways: investments in equities, mutual funds, real estate, hard assets, and so on. An important facet of retirement plans is a contribution to qualified (pension and profit sharing) plans, which appreciates on a tax-deferred basis. Life insurance plays an important role in the operation of many qualified plans.

There are four principal ways in which qualified plans can be funded with insurance: (1) individual policies; (2) group permanent insurance; (3) group annuities; and (4) deposit administration contracts. Of these, the first two are self-explanatory. The group annuity contract is a method of pension funding in which units of individual annuity contracts are accumulated each year and are fully paid for on a regular basis. In contrast, a deposit administration contract is a form of *group* annuity in which the employer makes the contribution into a deposit administration fund, which is a single fund for all employees in the group. When an employee reaches the retirement age, sufficient funds are withdrawn to provide the retiring employee with the annuity.

An important aspect of life insurance in a qualified plan is that death benefits provided in these plans are required by law to be "incidental." In a defined benefit plan, which prespecifies the monthly income to be received upon retirement, the incidental test is satisfied if the benefit does not exceed 100 times the expected monthly pension benefits. In a defined contribution plan, which specifies the annual contribution, the insurance premiums are limited to a certain portion of the contributions.

One of the advantages of having insurance in a pension plan is to provide a large benefit for the beneficiaries of those relatively young employees who die before their money in the qualified plan has a chance to grow. Another advantage of this strategy is to offer insurance protection for the key employees who are "rated" and can only obtain insurance by paying significantly higher premiums. It should also be added here that premium payments are treated as tax deductible contributions. Furthermore, the distribution of cash value is taxable, but the difference between the face value and the cash value is treated as a tax-free distribution.

Key Man Insurance

No one would try to run a business without adequate insurance to cover possible loss of assets, operating facilities, and profits in the event of fire, theft, or other disaster. Similarly, businesses frequently protect themselves against the loss of a partner, executive, or other key employees. This is accomplished by means of life insurance. More specifically, the company owns the insurance policy, is the sole beneficiary, and receives the full proceeds in the event of the death of the insured. In addition, by using the cash value, the company can provide a cash reserve to fund additional retirement benefits for the executive in the event that he or she does *not* die prematurely.

Deferred Compensation

As a way of providing a powerful incentive, corporations sometimes offer their executives what is known as deferred compensation. A deferred compensation plan is an arrangement whereby the company promises—but does not guaranty—to pay a predetermined compensation after retirement. This helps both parties, since the corporation does not incur salary expenditures until later, while the executive does not pay taxes until the deferred compensation is actually received. Deferred compensation payments are tax deductible at the time the payments are actually made.

A deferred compensation agreement is only as good as the financial arrangements that support it. An employer can promise benefits, but the ability to carry out the commitment depends on solvency at the time payments become due. Also, deferred compensation becomes a part of the general assets of the corporation and hence can be attached by its creditors. These problems can be solved by using life insurance as a planning tool.

More specifically, insurance on the lives of the key executives who receive deferred compensation can provide a reserve fund to make payments when they are required. The company sets up the fund on the installment plan through annual deposits to the insurance company. The funds become available when the employees involved retire or die.

Split-Dollar Life Insurance

Split-dollar life insurance is an arrangement, typically between an employer and an employee, under which the cash values, death benefits, and premiums may be split between the parties, although the employee can pay the whole premium. Under the typical arrangement, the employer pays that part of the annual premium which equals the current year's increase in the cash surrender value of the policy. The employee pays the balance of the premium. This provides an incentive to key employees on a selective basis, and a means of providing stockholder employees with substantial life insurance at a minimum cost.

An important feature of split-dollar insurance is that it is not a qualified employer benefit plan; consequently it can be used without concern for the antidiscrimination rules established by ERISA. Another advantage of this plan is that the employee is permitted to name the beneficiary, thereby providing insurance protection for the family. A further advantage of split-dollar insurance is that an employee participating in split-dollar insurance is taxed only on the cost of one-year term insurance—commonly referred to as P.S. 58 cost—less the actual premium paid by the employee. Incidentally, the IRS has also ruled that the employer will receive no deduction for premiums it pays; however, when withdrawn, cash values are nontaxable.

Insurance for the Professional

The need of life insurance coverage for professionals and small business persons is significantly different from corporate employees and owners of large businesses. The reason is that, except for the equipment and furnishings, a professional practice or a small business does not usually have much resale value. Even under the best of circumstances, the price at which the business can be sold is minuscule as compared to the income needs of the professional family.

The solution to this problem lies in the purchase of life insurance to generate a monthly income sufficient to help the family maintain a decent standard of living. In addition, the professional person may need life insurance to guarantee a secure retirement. This is because, unlike the corporate executive, the professionals cannot depend on the corporate qualified plans and must create their own retirement funds. More specifically, professionals can supplement life insurance by other qualified (e.g., Keogh) plans to create a *balanced* retirement plan.

CHAPTER 4

Health, Homeowner's, Automobile, and Liability Insurance: Structure, Concepts, and Planning

GENERAL PRINCIPLES

INTRODUCTION

Buying casualty and property insurance is a challenging undertaking. First of all, it takes skill to determine the amount of insurance one really needs. Second, as mentioned in Chapter 3, since the money spent on buying insurance is money diverted from investment, it is rarely desirable to buy as much insurance as one can afford. Third, in buying insurance, a person must not get carried away by emotion. Fourth, considerable savings in premium dollars can be achieved by shopping around and buying the least expensive insurance available for the needed coverage. For these reasons, it is desirable—in fact, imperative—that in buying insurance every individual apply the basic principle followed by business professionals; namely, get the best value for the premium dollars.

In this chapter, we will present the structure, concepts, and planning strategies for health, homeowner's, auto, and liability insurance. In our presentation, we will emphasize that in buying property and casualty insurance, people should (1) insure against significant risks while bearing the small risks themselves, (2) compare the rates before making a commitment, and (3) reduce the risks through preventive measures.

Before embarking upon a discussion of insurance against significant risks, a brief mention should be made of the principle of indemnity. In the case of all types of property, casualty, and health insurance, the objective of the insurance company is to indemnify the insured for the actual loss realized and not to create a profit for the insured. This principle of indemnity, however, does not apply to life insurance, since there is no way to determine the actual value of a human life.

INSURANCE AGAINST SIGNIFICANT RISKS

Insuring against small losses wastes valuable money that can be better spent on buying protection on larger risks. Of course, only the individual can determine which losses are big, since the amount one can afford to cover depends largely on income and the existing coverage. More specifically, the limitations of health and homeowner's insurance should be recognized in determining how much risk the insured can afford to assume. It should also be borne in mind that although casualty losses exceeding ten percent of the adjusted gross income are tax-deductible, most casualty losses rarely exceed the limit and therefore remain nondeductible.

In buying casualty/property insurance, for the most part it is possible to reduce the cost of coverage through the manipulation of insurance deductibles. For instance, the potential premium savings from increasing deductibles on an auto policy are presented in Table 4-1.

This table shows that if the deductible is raised from $100 to $200 and if an accident is the first one to occur in, say, three years, the cost savings are a negligible $13. That is, the insured must commit an additional $87 ($447 − $360) in three years for a potential net savings of only $13. This is indeed wasteful.

The money saved by increasing the deductible can be employed in expanding the coverage on larger risks. The standard homeowner's policy includes $25,000 of personal liability insurance for accidents both at home and elsewhere. The insurance company will defend the homeowner when charged with the responsibility for the accident and will pay claims up to the $25,000 limit. The company will also pay up to $500 medical expenses per person on a no-fault basis to a total of $25,000 on each accident. However, even if the injured person wins a $300,000 judgment against the homeowner—and that is a distinct possibility—the company would pay only $25,000 and the owner

TABLE 4-1 Potential Savings from Raising Deductibles

	One auto accident within			
	1 year	2 years	3 years	4 years
Cost: $200 Deductible				
Total premiums paid	$120	$240	$360	$480
Deductible payment	200	200	200	200
Total cost (A)	$320	$440	$560	$680
Cost: $100 Deductible				
Total premiums paid	$149	$298	$447	$596
Deductible payment	100	100	100	100
Total cost (B)	$249	$398	$547	$696
Added cost (savings) with $200 deductible:				
Cost (A) − Cost (B)	$ 71	$ 42	$ 13	($ 16)

would have to pay the remaining $275,000. The payment of such a large amount could be financially disastrous. For about $10 more a year, the coverage can be increased from the standard $25,000 to $300,000 liability insurance for each accident—a very worthwhile use of premium dollars.

SHOPPING FOR INSURANCE

Casualty/property insurance should be purchased with two cardinal rules in mind. First, insurance prices vary widely, and a great deal can be saved by shopping around. Second, many seemingly identical policies differ markedly on crucial points. For example, all disability policies pay an income when the insured becomes disabled, but a particular illness or injury may not qualify as a disability under every company's definition. Thus, it is imperative for the insured to select a policy which is not only reasonably priced but also provides *all the necessary coverages.*

LOSS CONTROL THROUGH PREVENTIVE MEASURES

The premium amount for any type of insurance is calculated based mainly on how many dollars are spent by insurance companies to pay claims resulting from accidents and other losses. Consequently, the higher the claims, the higher the cost of insurance. One can help reduce premium costs by reducing the hazards that cause damage. For instance, car losses can be reduced by defensive driving and by the installation of an anti-theft system in the car. Similarly, home losses can be reduced by the use of fire-resistant construction materials and furnishings, and by the installation of security devices involving police, fire departments, and hospitals. Along the same lines, health losses can be reduced by periodic physical checkups, by dietary control, by regular exercise, and by taking prompt care of illnesses.

ORGANIZATION OF PERSONAL RECORDS

For most of us, record-keeping is an onerous chore we would prefer to ignore. And yet, in the areas of health and property/casualty insurance, it is extremely important to maintain up-to-date, accurate, and detailed records. This is especially important when submitting a claim, because the extent of reimbursement by the insurance company would largely depend upon the ability of the policyholder to produce documents supporting the claims.

More specifically, every homeowner should keep an up-to-date inventory of all the personal possessions. This would involve (1) maintaining an inventory book, (2) recording the purchase price and the date of purchase of every household item of value, and (3) taking a color video or photograph of every room in the house. The insured should also maintain an accurate record of the purchase price and the cost of all improvements made to the house since the purchase of the home.

Record-keeping is also important for auto insurance. This becomes especially important if a claim is submitted to the insurance company after a car is totally destroyed in an accident. The adjuster bases the replacement value of a car not only on the *market value* but also on optional equipment and how well the car was maintained. Consequently, good maintenance of service records can add significant value to the car.

As in the case of homeowner's and auto insurance, accurate record-keeping helps expedite a health insurance claim. This is because the reimbursement of a health-related expense is directly related to the actual cost of sickness or injury covered by the policy.

HEALTH INSURANCE

INTRODUCTION

Even though we live in a health-conscious society, every day millions of people are afflicted with injuries and illnesses. By 1991, the annual expenses paid for health care in the U.S. will have increased to more than $750 billion.

Fortunately, for many people health insurance has become a popular way of easing the financial burdens resulting from medical problems. Approximately 85 percent of the American population now has some form of health coverage. Health insurance provides protection against financial losses caused by illness, injury, and disability. Interestingly, the concept of health insurance was not established until the 1930s. The first health maintenance organization (HMO) and the first Blue Cross plan were both introduced in 1929. Subsequently, in 1935, with the passage of the Social Security Act, the federal government became part of the health insurance system.

Primarily because of the numerous kinds of injuries and illnesses that can affect people, health insurance has become the most complicated form of insurance. Today, health insurance policies offered to the public come in various sizes and forms. Consequently, before selecting a health insurance company, individuals must know what type of protection will best satisfy their personal and financial needs.

NEED FOR HEALTH INSURANCE

Individuals must consider a variety of financial and economic factors as the basis for deciding if they need to purchase health insurance. With rare exceptions, it is essential to have appropriate health insurance coverage, because the risk of suffering severe financial losses due to health-related incidents is sufficiently high.

TYPES OF HEALTH INSURANCE

Hospital Insurance

Hospital insurance covers the cost incurred during a hospital stay. Examples of expenses covered under this plan are room and board charges, operating room charges, nursing services, and drugs. The majority of Americans have some sort of hospital protection, even though many have insufficient coverage.

Hospital insurance is divided into three categories: hospitalization insurance, hospital indemnity insurance, and hospital-service-incurred plans.

Hospitalization insurance gives policyholders a cash payment for specific hospital charges. Expenses covered under this protection are per diem hospital room fees, operating room fees, and costs of medical supplies. The reimbursement amount equals the total expenses of the hospital stay less any deductibles and coinsurance expenses. Frequently, restrictions are placed on hospital expense insurance; examples of these restrictions are a daily maximum reimbursement, an overall per-stay maximum, and a maximum number of days for which expenses will be paid.

Hospital indemnity insurance offers a specific amount of cash payment for each day of hospitalization. If the stated reimbursement does not cover the daily expenses, then the policyholder must make up the difference. Of course, the policyholder can keep the excess if the reverse is true.

Hospital-service-incurred plans pay the hospital directly for services provided and the policyholder does not get involved in the payment process, but will make up any shortages. Except for this difference, these plans are very similar to the hospitalization insurance plans.

While all hospital insurance policies cover the expenses associated with hospitalization, the total coverage, deductibility, or method of payment varies, depending on the types of coverage offered by various groups. For instance, Health Maintenance Organizations (HMOs) offer medical services on a prepaid basis. In contrast, Preferred Provider Organizations (PPOs) provide complete coverage if participating providers are used, and a partial coverage when nonparticipating doctors are used. HMOs and PPOs are explained more fully in a subsequent section.

Surgical Insurance

Surgical insurance protects people from the financial burden of surgical procedures. One type of this coverage, known as *surgical expense insurance*, reimburses patients directly (less deductibles) for up to 50 listed operations. A maximum amount is set up for each procedure. In addition, specific methods are used for figuring out the amount of reimbursement to be paid for procedures that are not listed. Another type of surgical insurance, called the *surgical-service-incurred* plan, pays the operation service providers directly for their service. The reimbursement amount is calculated on the basis of the fees charged by most service providers for similar services in that geographic area.

Medical Expense Insurance

Medical expense insurance pays for doctors' services, excluding their surgical charges. These plans (excluding HMOs and PPOs) usually include a maximum limit, a coinsurance clause, and a deductible. In most cases, the deductible clause is written on an item basis. This means that the insured is required to pay the charges incurred during the first few office visits, the number varying by different companies. Medical expense insurance is another coverage that may be written on a service-incurred basis.

Major Medical Expense Insurance

Major medical expense insurance provides reimbursements for all-encompassing medical treatments. In general, this type of coverage is used as a supplement to hospital, surgical, and medical expense insurance and pays only those charges that are not covered by the other basic forms.

Major medical insurance provides for quality medical care that is appropriate for individual needs, diagnosed and approved by qualified physicians.

In addition, many policies provide for second surgical opinions, pre-admission testing, extended hospital care, home health care, and hospice care.

Major medical expense insurance normally has $1–2 million lifetime benefit for each covered person. The deductible amount of $100 to $2,500 applies to each covered person during each calendar year. Deductibles may be waived after three deductibles have been claimed for a family during a given calendar year.

The annual reimbursement for each covered person after the deductible is generally 80 percent of the first $5,000 of all covered expenses and then 100 percent thereafter. Furthermore, certain types of covered expenses may not be subject to the deductible or the 80 percent rate of payment. The basic concept of coinsurance is demonstrated in Figure 4-1.

Comprehensive Health Insurance

Although no longer popular, a comprehensive health insurance plan combines hospital insurance, surgical insurance, medical expense insurance, and major medical expense insurance into one single package. This type of insurance coverage has deductibles ranging from $100 to $200 and coinsurance requirements of around 20 percent. Comprehensive health insurance plans are usually offered on a group basis by businesses which want to give their employees or members complete health insurance protection.

Dental Expense Insurance

Dental expense insurance makes cash payments for dental care expenses. It is similar to other health insurance policies in that it includes deductibles,

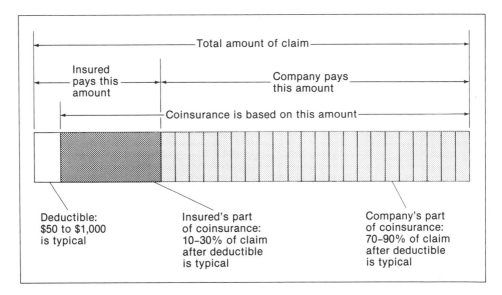

FIGURE 4-1 Summary of health insurance deductibles and coinsurance

coinsurance requirements, and maximum limits. In most instances, dental expense insurance is offered by employers only on a group basis and provides for preventive dental care.

Eye Care Insurance

Eye care insurance provides protection from expenses connected with the purchase of prescription glasses and contact lenses. The coverage given to policyholders includes various eye examinations, the fitting, and the cost of lenses and frames. Eye care insurance, too, is usually offered only on a group basis by employers.

Supplemental Health Insurance

Supplemental health insurance plans fill the void left by the basic insurance plans. Most supplemental plans are usually advertised through the mail or on television. These plans offer to pay for surgery, hospital stay, treatment for accident, etc. regardless of the existence of other medical coverages. In most instances, supplemental plans are not as attractive as they first appear. Premiums for these plans are usually very high and many restrictions are imposed on the coverages they provide. Consequently, there is very little demand in the marketplace for these plans.

DISABILITY INCOME INSURANCE

The Basic Need

Not all illnesses or injuries are curable or arrestable. Some may result in permanent or long-term disability. Once disabled, the breadwinner may not be able to work again for a long time. To cope with such situations, besides medical coverage one needs coverage for loss of income.

There is no regular medical health program that offers income during periods of loss of income. All conventional protections have limitations. Social Security has a waiting period. Workers' compensation handles only work-related injuries. Company sickness or accident plans also have waiting periods. Finally, disability income riders on life insurance do not cover catastrophic illness or injury. The only safe way to be assured of adequate protection against a loss of income due to long or permanent illness is to purchase a disability income policy.

Types of Insurance

There are two types of disability coverage. A short-term disability policy provides for a relatively short disability benefit period, such as 13 weeks, 26 weeks, or one year. A long-term disability policy provides for longer disability periods, such as five years, ending at age 65, or for life. Of the two, the long-term disability type is the more important and the most often neglected.

Waiting Period

Waiting period, or elimination period, is the amount of time the insured must be disabled before benefits begin. Short-term disability insurance usually has a waiting period of zero to thirty days. Long-term disability coverage has a waiting period of one, three, or six months, but most typically three months. As a general rule, the three-month waiting period buys the best value for the premium dollars.

Definition of Disability

Most definitions of disability fall into two categories. The company will pay disability benefits only if the insured cannot perform "any job"; or the benefits will be paid if the insured is unable to perform the occupation for which he or she has been trained. The latter definition, called "own occupation," is most preferred by consumers.

Some companies market disability policies which use a combination of both definitions. Typically, these policies provide the "own occupation" type benefits for two or three years. Any disability claims made thereafter switch to the "any job" definition.

An important aspect of disability insurance relates to partial disability. Most companies pay total disability income even after the disabled person returns to work but makes less than 50 percent of normal income. If the income earned is between 50 percent and 85 percent of the previous income, however, a proportionately reduced disability income is paid by the company.

In passing, it should be mentioned that if the policyholder pays the premium, it is not deductible from income tax, but the disability income is treated as a tax-free income. However, disability income is taxed as ordinary income to the disabled employee if premiums are paid by the employer.

Integration with Social Security

Some disability policies coordinate their total benefits with Social Security. Integration with Social Security means that the policy will pay a set benefit *minus* any payments which are received from Social Security. For instance, suppose John Kline has a disability policy which provides $3,000 in monthly benefits. John might expect to receive $4,500 per month in disability benefits if his Social Security pays him $1,500 a month. This will, however, not be the case if the policy is integrated with Social Security. That is because each dollar of Social Security payments will be a direct offset to the insurer's obligation to pay. Incidentally, disability policies coordinated with Social Security could offer the best value for the money, if the insured could count on receiving Social Security benefits. Unfortunately, conditions for receiving disability payments under Social Security are so restrictive that it is advisable not to depend on these payments.

Determining the Income Need

A simplified method for determining the disability income need is presented in Table 4-2. Assume John Kline earns a net, after-tax, income of $2,000 a month and is not covered by disability insurance. If he were to become disabled today, his family would need $2,850 per month to maintain the current standard of living. If his wife continues to earn a net, after-tax, income of $1,000 a month and his after-tax investments generate $500 a month, he would need to purchase a disability income policy for $1,350 ($2,850 − $1,000 − $500). However, since John earns $2,000 net per month and disability companies typically offer 60 percent of earned income, John would most probably be able to purchase only a $1,200 (60 percent of $2,000) disability coverage.

Features of a Good Policy

It is not always easy to select the best disability income policy because of the difficulties in determining what disability income coverage is, what it costs, and how to buy it. Before selecting this kind of insurance, every person should at least check the vital points listed in Table 4-3 to ensure that the policy fills the gaps in the regular health insurance plan. Of these, the noncancelable and guaranteed renewable clause is perhaps one of the most important features of a disability policy.

Cost of a Disability Policy

The typical long-term disability policy provides for payment of a stated percentage of a specified monthly salary or a specified amount per month. The

---

TABLE 4-2 Disability Insurance Need

Current Expenses per Month		$2,850
Sources of Income upon Disability:		
Social Security	$ 0	
Spouse's Earned Income	$1,000	
Income from Investment	$ 500	($1,500)
Monthly Shortfall for the Family		$1,350

Disability Coverage Available

Salaried Income	$2,000
Maximum Disability Income Allowed:	
60% ($2,000)	$1,200

TABLE 4-3   Features of a Good Disability Policy

Key questions	Suggested recommendations
1. How does the policy define disability?	Select the policy that covers partial disability, not the one that specifies benefits only for total disability.
2. What job definition does the company use?	Select the company which uses the "your occupation" definition, not the "any job" definition.
3. Is the policy noncancelable and guaranteed renewable?	Choose a policy that guarantees that the policy will be renewed at the rates guaranteed in the policy up to the age specified (usually 65).
4. Does this policy cover disability resulting from both accident and illness?	Select the company that covers both forms of disability.
5. For what period of time will the policy pay?	Select the policy that covers at least through age 65.
6. How much will the policy pay?	Select the company which pays at least 60% of take-home pay at the time of accident or illness.
7. How long is the waiting period?	A three-month waiting period is preferable.
8. Does the company offer cost-of-living adjustments?	The basic benefit should rise automatically by a set percentage or in step with inflation.
9. Does the policy offer standard-of-living adjustments?	After a policy has been in force, the insured should be able to boost the monthly benefit by a certain amount at standard rates without a medical exam.

cost of a policy depends upon the amount of coverage, the duration of payment, and the additional riders selected. For instance, a standard "own occupation" type of disability policy for a 45-year-old male may cost $1,800 per year. This policy will (1) pay a disability income of $2,300 per month, (2) cover the insured until age 65, (3) have a five percent annual inflation adjustment factor, and (4) be noncancelable and guaranteed renewable.

It is appropriate to mention here that disability insurance policies purchased on an individual basis are fairly expensive. By comparison, larger groups get much better terms, as revealed by Table 4-4. Consequently, whenever possible, disability insurance should be purchased on a group basis.

	Maximum benefit period		Maximum monthly benefit
Number insured	Accident	Sickness	
25–49	10 years	10 years*	$ 500
50–99	To age 65	10 years*	750
100 and over	To age 65	To age 65	1,000

TABLE 4-4   Disability Insurance for Large Groups

* Payment stops when the insured reaches age 65.

Coordination of Benefits

Persons who are either currently employed or have been previously employed are entitled to a variety of health benefits. This section describes the most important feature of these benefits.

Social Security benefits.   Social Security insurance includes Medicare, which provides medical insurance benefits to persons age 65 or older, or to those who are disabled for 24 months before age 65. Medicare benefits come in two major parts: Part A—Hospital Insurance, and Part B—Supplementary Medical Insurance. Benefits under Part A are automatic and free. Benefits under Part B are optional and must be applied for within three months before or after the 65th birthday or during the first three months of any calendar year thereafter. Most insurance companies offer packages that coordinate their benefits with Social Security benefits.

Workers' Compensation benefits.   Workers' Compensation covers accidental injuries and illness caused by one's employment. These programs are controlled by individual states and funds are provided by states through employee contributions. Most states—though not all—allow full coverage of any job-related accident or illness.

GROUP HEALTH INSURANCE

Most employers offer one or more types of group health insurance plans. If an employee is relatively young, a nonsmoker, and has no prior history of major sickness, an individual health insurance policy may be cheaper than a group policy. This is because in a group policy the risk of insuring older employees and employees with a medical history is spread across the board so the younger employees in good health have to bear the additional burden. Nevertheless, a group policy might be cheaper than an individual policy for a number of reasons. For one thing, a company issuing a group policy substantially cuts its expenses by writing one policy covering a larger number of people. For another, by spreading the risks over a large number of diverse people, it might enjoy substantial cost savings, thereby enabling it to offer cheaper rates to its policyholders.

Another advantage of group coverage is that it is usually more comprehensive. There are generally fewer exclusions and limitations in group than in individual policies. Preexisting conditions, exclusions, and waiting periods are less frequent in a group policy, although there might be waiting periods for maternity coverage. Also, the insured is rarely required to take a physical or provide a detailed statement on existing physical condition. Nearly all accidents or illnesses, including heart conditions, are covered. Generally, the only eligibility requirement is that a person be actively at work when coverage begins.

INSIDE TOP DISABILITY POLICIES

The rates shown here for two top-quality, noncancelable policies are for a 40-year-old nonsmoker, man or woman, doing professional or managerial work. There's a big difference in premiums for the basic benefit of $2,500 per month after 90 days of disability until age 65. But the policies cost about the same when the most desirable options are added.

Features	Annual Premiums	
	Paul Revere Life	Connecticut Mutual Life
Monthly benefits to age 65	$1,032.25	$810.00
Lifetime benefits	257.28	175.50
Adequate residual (partial) benefits	0	121.50
"Disabled" means you can't perform the main duties of your regular occupation	61.50	151.20
$500 extra per month until your Social Security disability benefits begin	100.80	210.60
Automatic cost-of-living increases each year while you are totally or partially disabled	266.34	249.30
Total premium	$1,718.17	$1,718.10*

* Dividends, at the current rate, would reduce this premium by ten percent in the third year.

Source: Robert J. Klein, "The Right Way to Buy Disability Income Insurance," *Money*, August 1988, p. 121.

Group health insurance has one major disadvantage: Leaving the place of employment also means the loss of the group coverage. Usually, however, the employee is able to convert the health coverage to an individual policy with the same company within 30 days, but the coverage may not be as good as the group coverage and the price will be higher. Generally, insurance companies point out the gaps between private and group coverage and offer recommendations most suited to the applicant's needs.

Incidentally, not all group plans are alike and not all group plans are bargains. For instance, many group plans provide a major medical plan along with more basic coverage, while others do not. Also, many plans exclude maternity coverage, cover maternity costs inadequately, or provide for problem pregnancies only. Even the flat maximum payments for maternity found in group coverage sold by many commercial companies are often less than the full cost of pregnancy and childbirth. If the coverage is inadequate under a group plan, it is important to supplement that coverage to fill the gaps.

SOURCES OF HEALTH INSURANCE

There are six types of organizations from which one may obtain health insurance. These are: Blue Cross and Blue Shield, Health Maintenance Organizations (HMOs), hybrid companies like Preferred Provider Organizations (PPOs), self-funded employee health benefits private commercial insurance companies, and Government Health Care Insurance. These sources are presented in Table 4-5.

Blue Cross and Blue Shield

Blue Cross and Blue Shield is the largest single health insurance plan existing today. In many states Blue Cross primarily offers hospitalization, whereas Blue Shield provides surgical and general medical insurance. Organized as a nonprofit corporation, Blue Cross and Blue Shield cooperates in issuing joint plans for comprehensive medical care.

Health Maintenance Organizations (HMOs)

HMOs operate on a prepaid basis. In most instances, the insured individuals pay a certain amount a month in advance and then they can use the HMO for whatever medical services they need. In some cases, patients pay a minimal ($1–$5 per visit) fee and are also required to make small co-payments.

The organization of HMOs has several attractive features. Patients save time because physicians, labs, and pharmacies have been organized within a system, often under one roof. Clients choose a physician within a system, and most HMOs have evening hours with at least one doctor on 24-hour duty. The fixed-price contract overcomes the patient's reluctance to seek medical advice for minor ailments or preventive medical check-ups. HMOs also permit those

TABLE 4-5 Sources of Health Insurance*

Type	Particulars
Blue Cross/Blue Shield	Producer cooperatives that provide health care protection on a service-incurred basis. These are nonprofit organizations, providing both individual and group health coverage.
Health Maintenance Organizations (HMOs)	HMOs provide health care on a prepaid basis. A monthly fee is charged for services. There are no deductibles or coinsurance costs.
Preferred Provider Organizations (PPOs)	PPOs are a group of medical care professionals who contract with health insurance companies for providing services at a discount. Premiums are generally lower than comparable policies.
Commercial Insurance Companies	These are companies (such as Travelers and Aetna) providing health protection for half the U.S. population. They get most of their business through advertising on television and radio.
Government Health Care	This source provides health care for people at the local, state, and federal levels. Services include Social Security, disability income, Medicaid, and Medicare.

* The self-funded employee health benefit, another source of health insurance, is explained on p. 128.

doctors to spend more time with their patients who are not also engaged in private practice, because these doctors are not paid on the basis of the number of patients per day.

Preferred Provider Organizations (PPOs)

A mention should now be made of the health care providers known as Preferred Provider Organizations (PPOs). The plan features a network of physicians, hospitals, and other providers of health care services who agree to provide medical care at discounted rates. These are the participating providers. An insured has the complete freedom to use any providers of his or her choice. However, the plan encourages the use of participating providers by paying a higher level of benefits when these designated providers are used. For instance, when non-participating providers are used, and the basic PPO requirements are met, calendar year deductible applies, a copayment ratio of 20 percent is used (that is, the insured pays 20 percent of the charges), and the insured is required to obtain a pre-treatment review and certification. None of these restrictions applies if the participating provider network is used.

When the insured uses the participating providers in the network, the plan directly pays 100 percent of all covered charges, although the insured may be required to pay a small service fee. The PPO covers both hospitalization and outpatient care.

It should be mentioned here that a careful blending of a PPO plan with major medical insurance can provide outstanding value for the employees of an organization. In fact, there appears to be a growing trend among many employers toward providing a comprehensive health care plan using the combination just cited.

Self-Funded Employee Health Benefits

A relatively new arrival on the health insurance scene is known as self-funded employee health benefits (SEHB). Traditionally, protection and cost control in health care services have meant providing conventionally insured group health care plans to employees as part of fringe benefits. Today, a novel approach to group health care comprises unique plan design, claims management, and the ability to monitor utilization and provider performance.

In a partially SEHB plan, the employer assumes the amount of risk (claims) which can be anticipated. Stop loss insurance is then obtained to cover claims which exceed the actuary predetermined level. Specific stop loss protects the plan against an individual catastrophic claim. Aggregate stop loss provides coverage for claims exceeding a given amount on the entire covered group, thus limiting overall claim costs.

Because claim reserves are managed by the employer, greater financial control results. Funds may be contributed to an employer-established account and transferred when needed to pay claims. Excess funds remain in the account to collect investment earnings. In addition, cost savings are realized because (1) premium tax, usually two to six percent, does not apply to self-funded claim funds in most states, (2) the cost of operating the plan is generally lower, and (3) insurance carrier profits and risk charges are reduced. It is little wonder that many large corporations are moving toward SEHB plans.

Commercial Insurance Companies

These companies provide health insurance coverage for a large segment of the U.S. population. These companies, which include such household names as Travelers and Aetna, obtain most of their participants through advertisement on TV and radio. Under this arrangement, a policyholder can receive medical care from any place of his or her choice and does not have to be treated by a preassigned hospital or doctor.

Government Health Care Insurance

This insurance refers to the services provided under Medicare, which is a federal health insurance program for people age 65 or older and certain disabled people. It has two parts: hospital insurance provided by Medicare, and medical insurance offered under Medicaid. In view of its importance as a provider of comprehensive medical coverage, it is appropriate to discuss Medicare in some detail. It should, however, be noted at the outset that rapid changes are taking place in this area, and the details provided here are likely to change in the near future.

At the heart of Medicare is the "allowable charge." Medicare scrutinizes each bill to determine the allowable portion that the government approves for coverage under the program. For hospital services, Medicare pays the entire bill less a deductible. For most physician's services, it pays 80 percent of an allowable charge and the beneficiaries pay the remaining 20 percent and any excess of each bill plus any physician's fee. The 20 percent of the allowable charge beneficiaries pay is called *coinsurance*. Beneficiaries must also pay deductibles, which are subtracted from the allowable charge before Medicare determines its 80 percent payment.

The particular deductibles, coinsurance, and excess charges depend on the type of service Medicare covers. Part A benefits pay for hospital and related services and are the most comprehensive. Part B benefits cover doctors' fees, various outpatient services, and outpatient psychiatric care.

The various types of coverages under Medicare and the gaps in these coverages are summarized in Table 4-6. This table reveals that medical hospital insurance helps pay for four kinds of care: (1) inpatient hospital care; (2) medically necessary inpatient care in a skilled nursing facility after a hospital stay; (3) private duty nursing care; and (4) hospice (doctor and medical services) care. Medicare covers all necessary hospitalization, except deductibles. It also covers up to 150 days (except deductible) in a skilled nursing facility, and 80 percent of approved medical services. In addition, it covers (not shown in Table 4-6) doctors' bills that exceed $1,870 cap, and in and after 1991 it will cover the cost of prescription drugs after a $500 deductible. The table also reveals that Medicare does not cover the biggest catastrophic cost of all—long-term nursing home care—which averages about $22,000 a year. Nor does it cover the following: (1) private-duty nursing; (2) skilled nursing care beyond 150 days; (3) treatment outside the U.S.; (4) dental work; (5) most immunizations; (6) cosmetic surgery; (7) routine foot care; (8) eye and hearing exams; and (9) prescription glasses and hearing aids.

Medicare's hospital benefits (Part A) are financed solely out of Social Security payroll taxes. The Medicare portion of Social Security taxes flows into a separate trust fund which is used to pay the hospital costs. Medicare's medical benefits (Part B) are financed from general tax revenues and by the beneficiaries themselves. Part B coverage is optional. Those who wish to buy this coverage pay a specified monthly premium. The monthly premium, which was $27.90 in 1989, is scheduled to rise every year.

In 1988, Congress passed the Catastrophic Coverage Act. This Act required Medicare (Part B) beneficiaries to pay an additional amount on top of the basic premium. In 1989, that amount was $4.00 per month. In 1990 and 1991, this additional amount was scheduled to increase to $4.90 and $7.40,

TABLE 4-6 Medicare—and the Gaps

Service	Medicare pays	You owe	Required minimum benefits	Comprehensive coverage pays
Hospitalization	Everything except deductible	$560	All or none of $560	$560
Post-hospital care in skilled nursing facility	Up to 150 days in skilled nursing facility, except deductible of first 8 days	$25.50 for first 8 days	$25.50 for first 8 days	215 days of skilled nursing care at $140 or more per day
Private duty nursing	Nothing	All costs	Nothing	80% of usual and customary charges; no limit on number of shifts*
Custodial nursing care	Nothing	All costs	Nothing	Nothing
Blood deductible	All but first 3 pints under Part A; 80% of approved amount after $75 deductible under Part B	Under Part A; first 3 pints (unless replaced); under Part B: approved amount (after $75 deductible)	Payment for first 3 pints (under A or B) unless blood is replaced	Same as in column 4
Doctor and medical services	80% of approved charges after $75 deductible	20% of approved charges, plus $75 deductible	20% of approved charges up to $5,000 with deductible and copayment up	100% of fees in excess of approved charges, with no cap on bills

* Most patients never exceed the Medicare-allotted skilled nursing care days, which is a consideration if you want to pare back benefits to save on premiums.

Source: Reprinted with permission from *Changing Times* Magazine, © Kiplinger Washington Editors, Inc., April 1989. This reprint is not to be altered in any way, except with permission from *Changing Times.*

respectively. However, in 1989 Congress repealed the Catastrophic Coverage Act.

The Catastrophic Act had imposed an additional tax called a *supplementary premium* on everyone who is eligible for Medicare (Part A). This premium was a surcharge on a beneficiary's federal income taxes. In 1989, the surtax was $22.50 for each $150 of federal taxes due, up to a maximum of $800 per individual. With the repeal of the Catastrophic Coverage Act the supplementary premium is no longer payable.

A majority of the Medicare gaps listed are sought to be covered by a new private insurance called Medigap. All Medigap policies sold as "supplements" to Medicare must cover the benefits listed under "Required Minimum Benefits" in Table 4-6. However, most comprehensive policies provide the additional coverage listed in the last column. The minimum coverage policies cost around $21.50 per month. By comparison, the comprehensive plans cost about $90 per month.

Long-Term Health Care

A number of insurance plans are emerging to help cushion the devastating, previously uninsurable costs of care for patients who have had a stroke, Alzheimer's disease, or other chronic illnesses. Many companies, including Aetna, CNA, and Fireman's Fund, offer policies that pay as much as $120 a day toward the cost of a skilled or custodial-care nursing home or nursing home care.

A comparison of several long-term health care policies is presented in Table 4-7. All policies listed in this table (1) permit the beneficiaries to receive custodial care in a nursing home without prior hospitalization, either with a rider or as a benefit in the basic premium; (2) cover Alzheimer's disease and

TABLE 4-7 Long-term Health Care Policies

Company & policy	Annual premium for $80 a day	Inflation protection*	Home health care	Remarks
AETNA Long-Term Care Plan B (call local Aetna rep) States: 50	Age 60: $524 Age 70: $1,751 Benefit period: 4 years Waiting period: 20 days	5% per year increase for 15 years	50% of daily nursing home rate; 30-day stay qualifies for 30 home-care days; 60 to 90 days qualify for 60; 91 or more days qualify for 365. Covers all care levels.	Coverage also available up to $120 a day through age 84; includes custodial care facility at same rate as home health care for combined maximum of 2 years.
AIG LIFE Nursing Home Insurance Plan 46041 (800-521-2773) States: 42	Age 60: $529 Age 70: $1,459 Benefit period: 3 years Waiting period: 20 days	7% per year increase for 10 years	Maximum 90 days; requires 30 days in nursing home for 30 home-care days at 100% of rate. Remainder covered at 50%. Rider ($93) provides 2 more years of benefits at $60 a day. Covers all care levels.	Coverage also available up to $120 a day through age 79 (age 81 if both spouses are covered).

TABLE 4-7 (continued)

Company & policy	Annual premium for $80 a day	Inflation protection*	Home health care	Remarks
AMEX Long Term Care (800-736-3660) States: 46	Age 60: $392 Age 70: $1,098 Benefit period: 4 years Waiting period: 20 days	5% per year increase up to age 85	Benefit days equal the number of paid days in nursing home, reimbursed at 70% of daily rate for first 30 days; 60% for days 31 to 60; and 50% afterward. Covers all care levels.	Coverage also available up to $100 a day through age 79, limited version through age 84.
CNA Convalescent Care Plan (800-262-1919 or, in Illinois, 800-325-1843) States: 46	Age 60: $491† Age 70: $1,166† Benefit period: 3-plus years Waiting period: 30 days	5% per year increase until policy expires	2-year maximum at up to 50% of daily rate after a 15-day nursing home stay. Covers all care levels.	Coverage also available up to $100 a day through age 79; limited version up to age 84.
JOHN HANCOCK Protect Care (800-543-6415) States: 44	Age 60: $651 Age 70: $1,768 Benefit period: 3 years Waiting period: 20 days	Increase offered every 3 years based on the medical consumer price index.	50% of daily nursing home rate through policy life. No prior nursing home stay required. Covers all care levels but requires skilled.	Coverage available up to $200 through age 79.
MUTUAL OF OMAHA Long Term Care Plus; #NH23 (call local Mutual of Omaha rep) States: 50	Age 60: $718** Age 70: $1,544** Benefit period: 5 years Waiting period: 30 days	Built into policy: After one year in nursing home, daily rate increases 5% each year. Up to age 66, can raise rate every 4 years until it doubles.	50% of daily nursing home rate for 1 year after 30 days' waiting. No prior nursing home stay needed. Covers all care levels but requires skilled.	Coverage available up to $80 through age 75. Becomes a 6-year plan if no claims are filed within the first 2 years of purchase. Inpatient hospice facility covered at 100% of daily rate.
NEW YORK LIFE Group Long Term Care (call local New York Life offices) States: 39	Age 60: $879† Age 70: $2,120† Benefit period: 5 years Waiting period: 20 days	5% per year increase for 20 years	Combined charges cannot exceed daily rate. Lifetime benefit: $50,000 of the policy's $150,000 maximum. Requires no prior nursing home stay. Covers all care levels.	Coverage also available up to $150 a day through age 80.
NORTH AMERICAN LIFE & CASUALTY CO. Assured Care plus Plan B (415-472-1010) States: 17	Age 60: $756 Age 70: $1,676 Benefit period: 3-plus years Waiting period: 20 days	5% per year increase for 10 years up to 50% of policy lifetime maximum	80% of charges up to daily nursing home rate. Covers all care levels up to one-third of policy lifetime maximum of $168,000.	Coverage also available up to $100 a day through age 79, limited version through age 84. Case manager oversees home health care.
SENTRY LIFE Nursing Home & Home Health Care (800-328-4827, ext. 1069) States: 38	Age 60: $608 Age 70: $1,608 Benefit period: 4-plus years Waiting period: 90 days	None, but policy may be upgraded.	$25 a day until dollar amount of policy expires, or 12 years. Requires no prior nursing home stay. Covers all care levels.	Coverage also available up to $100 a day through age 79.
THE TRAVELERS Independent Care (800-736-3660) States: 46	Age 57: $545†† Age 67: $1,737†† Benefit period: 3 years Waiting period: 20 days	Annual increase tied to the consumer price index.	80% of costs for at-home care, up to daily benefit maximum or 5 years. Requires no prior nursing home stay. Covers all care levels.	Coverage available up to $150 a day through age 79.

* Optional feature. Except for Mutual of Omaha policy, cost is not reflected in the premium.

† Home health care is an option and is reflected in these rates. (CNA bases premium on health; those cited refer to generally healthy person.)

** Assumes rate for someone living in a two-person household.

†† Rate based on $75 a day per person charge at ages 57 and 67, so will be higher at ages 60 and 70.

Source: Reprinted with permission from *Changing Times* Magazine, © Kiplinger Washington Editors, Inc., July 1989. This reprint is not to be altered in any way, except with permission from *Changing Times.*

TABLE 4-8 Cost of Insurance Packages

Items	Normal cost range	High-cost range
Medicare Part B basic premium	$ 383	$ 383
Medicare supplemental premium	$280-$300	$750-$850
Supplemental insurance policy	$600-$650	$900-$1,000
Long-term care insurance policy	$600-$650	$900-$950
TOTAL	$1,863-$1,983	$2,933-$3,183

Source: Various companies offering health care coverage.

other organic brain disorders; (3) allow for at least three-years stay; (4) are guaranteed renewable; and (5) include some coverage for home health care. Annual premiums can run from approximately $400 to $1,000 at age 60 and from $1,100 to $2,100 at age 70. In selecting the best long-term health care policy, it is better to shop around and select the policy which offers the coverages needed at the most competitive price.

For those suffering from incurable diseases such as AIDS, nearly half of all Blue Cross/Blue Shield organizations offer plans during open enrollment periods. However, the cost and coverage vary by locality. Open enrollment usually occurs one month a year.

To recap, a comprehensive long-term health care plan should cover (1) Medicare Part B basic insurance; (2) Medicare supplemental insurance; (3) supplemental insurance; and (4) long-term-care insurance. Table 4-8 reveals that a 65-year-old retiree may have to set aside between $1,850 and $3,200 a year for all health insurance coverages, depending on the supplemental premium tax and the price of both the Medicare supplement and long-term-care policies.

THE IDEAL HEALTH INSURANCE COMPANY

There is no magic formula by which one can determine the best health insurance company that is also the least expensive. Often, the strongest companies financially offer large premiums, good policies, and the best service. But some of the small companies also meet these same criteria, so that it is not possible to select a good company merely on the basis of size.

In selecting an insurance company it is best to avoid those companies that have a poor financial record and have a history of fighting their customers' claims rather than paying them. Also, it is best not to buy insurance from a company that would not be able to withstand losses higher than expected or has investment income consistently lower than anticipated. What is needed is a company that is financially strong, with liberal benefits and reasonable premiums. It should also be fair, efficient, and courteous in handling its claims.

An indication of the financial strength of insurance companies is the rating they receive in *Best's Insurance Report*, the leading authority on the subject. A high rating from *Best's* may mean that the company is less likely to go broke. One should try to avoid companies that do not receive either the "most substantial" or the "very substantial" rating from *Best's*; namely, A + or A. This report is available in most public libraries.

To conclude, in making the final selection of a health insurance company, it is desirable to obtain an affirmative answer to each of the following questions:

1. Is the company's loss ratio high? The loss ratio is the percentage of premiums that a company pays back in benefits to its policyholders. A loss ratio of over 50 percent may be satisfactory.
2. Does the company receive one of the two highest ratings for financial stability from *Best's Insurance Report*?
3. Does the company offer efficient, fair, and courteous claim service?
4. Is the company prevented from canceling a policy?
5. Does the company raise premiums based on claims?

THE IDEAL HEALTH INSURANCE POLICY

It is difficult to identify an *ideal* health insurance policy because the total coverage of such a policy should reflect both the general and specific needs of a given family. Nevertheless, a good policy should have all the universally acceptable features. Simply stated, a good health insurance policy should not have important exclusions and limitations, should have a reasonably short waiting period for disability coverage, and should offer both noncancelable and guaranteed renewability options. In addition, a good policy should offer reasonable maximum benefits and coverages in terms of both medical expenses and disability income loss.

To recapitulate, a time-tested approach to selecting a good health insurance company relates to the identification of a company which has been stable in the health care market for a long time. Once such a company is selected, the limitations and exclusions in its policy should be carefully analyzed vis-à-vis the cost of buying the policy. If the company also passes the five key questions test presented above, it would be a prime candidate for ultimate selection.

A PLANNING STRATEGY

Self-Analysis

For financial planning purposes, the best strategy is to make sure that the family has adequate coverage for medical and hospital expenses as well as for the loss of income caused by disability. Even more important, young families should buy adequate medical and disability coverage even if it means a sacrifice of the life insurance coverage. This is because a long-term disability is likely to be more devastating to such a family than death. A convenient worksheet is provided in Table 4-9 which can be used to determine if individual levels of coverage match the desired levels of coverage.

TABLE 4-9   Health Insurance Worksheet

	Current coverage	*Desirable coverage*
Hospital Expense:		
Amount per day	_____	100% of semi-private room
Maximum number of days	_____	365 days; thereafter 80%
Additional expenses	_____	Reasonable
Diagnostic X-ray and lab work	_____	
Deductible	_____	
Surgical Expense		
Highest surgical fee	_____	100%
Regular Medical		
Dollars per day	_____	100%
Number of days	_____	30 days
Major Medical Coverage		
Major medical (deductible)	_____	$300 per illness
Maximum	_____	$1 million lifetime per family
Coinsurance Percentage	_____	80% up to breakpoint, after which insurer pays 100%.
Disability Income Benefit:		
Short-term disability	_____	60 to 75% of earned income
Long-term disability	_____	60 to 75% of earned income
Disability Benefit Period:		
Short-term disability	_____	1 year
Long-term disability	_____	Until age 65
Waiting Period		
Short-term disability	_____	7 days, unless company provides sick pay for a week
Long-term disability	_____	90 days

THE HOMEOWNER'S POLICY

INTRODUCTION

A homeowner or renter is exposed to many types of risk. Damages may occur to the property and its structures due to fire or storm. Losses may be generated by injuries suffered on or off the premises. Personal property may also be lost because of theft or fire.

The main elements of a homeowner's policy are coverage (1) on the house, (2) for personal property, and (3) against the homeowner's liability for bodily injury or property damage caused to other people or property. The standard homeowner's policy is a "package deal" containing all three types of coverage. The standard renter's or condominium policy offers only the last two types of coverage.

THE POLICY FORMS

As revealed by Table 4-10, the package policy, known as the homeowner's policy, comes in three forms: basic, broad, and special. The *basic* policy is the least expensive. It covers the homeowner against personal liability and damage or loss due to the most common risks. The *broad* policy includes the basic coverage but adds damage from snow, sleet, and ice, and accidental discharges of the plumbing system, and so on. Finally, the *special* policy, which is the most expensive, includes most perils except those risks that are specifically excluded such as damage due to earthquake or flood.

There are seven types of homeowner's policies: HO-1, the basic form; HO-2, the broad form; HO-3, the special form; HO-4, the contents broad form; HO-5, the special form which is HO-3 plus all risk on contents; HO-6, coverage for condominium owners; and HO-8, for older homes. HO-1, HO-2, HO-3, HO-5, and HO-8 are for people who own their homes; HO-4 is for people renting homes or apartments; and HO-6 is for condominium owners. The salient features of these forms are shown in Table 4-11.

The key elements of the seven different types of policies just mentioned can now be discussed. First, in most forms of homeowner's policies the insured is entitled to compensation for a loss if it is caused by a specifically named peril. HO-3 provides all-risk coverage for the dwelling but not contents or personal property. HO-5, however, is an "all-risk" type that covers all losses except those that are specifically excluded. Second, overall protection broadens as the insured moves up the scale to HO-5 (building and contents), both in the number of perils covered and in the interpretation of the peril. For example, the theft insurance of HO-1 does not apply, as it does in all the other policies,

TABLE 4-10 Forms of Homeowner's Policies

	Basic Form**	Broad Form	Special Form
COVERAGE FOR:			
Dwelling	Yes	Yes	Yes
Replacement cost of dwelling	No	Yes	Yes
Related private structures	Yes	Yes*	Yes*
Personal property on premises	Yes	Yes	Yes
Personal property away from premises	Yes	Yes	Yes
Improvements made by tenant	Yes	Yes	Yes
Lawns, plants, shrubs, trees	By endorsement	Yes–limited perils	Yes–limited perils
Rental value	Yes	Yes–either rental value or additional living expense*	Yes–either rental value or additional living espense*
Additional living expense	By endorsement	Yes–either rental value or additional living expense*	Yes–either rental value or additional living expense*
Contents removed to new principal residence	30 days coverage at both locations	30 days coverage at both locations	30 days coverage at both locations
Jewelry and furs	Yes	Yes	Yes
PERILS COVERED:			
Fire and lightning	Yes	Yes	Yes
Windstorm	Yes	Yes	Yes
Outside antenna windstorm damage	Only by endorsement	Only by endorsement	Only by endorsement
Hail	Yes	Yes	Yes
Riot and civil commotion	Yes	Yes	Yes
Explosion other than steam boiler	Yes	Yes	Yes
Explosion of steam boiler	No	Yes	Yes

TABLE 4-10 (continued)

	Basic Form**	Broad Form	Special Form
Bursting of steam or hot water appliances and heating systems	No	Yes	Yes
Smoke—sudden and accidental damage:			
From industrial operations	No	No	Contents only
From fireplaces	No	No	Yes
From heating or cooking unit	Yes	Yes	Yes
Aircraft	Yes	Yes	Yes
Sonic boom	Yes	Yes	Yes
Vehicle damage by other than occupant of property to:			
Building	Yes	Yes	Yes
Personal property	Yes	Yes	Yes
Fences	No	Yes	Yes
Driveways	No	Yes	Yes
Walks	No	Yes	Yes
Lawns	No	Yes	Yes
Trees, shrubs, and plants	No	Yes	Yes
Vehicle damage to house or garage by dwelling occupant	No	Yes	Yes
Vandalism and malicious mischief	Optional	Yes	Yes
Water:			
Surface water or flood	No	No	No
Backing up of sewers or drains	No	No	No
Leakage from plumbing or heating systems	No	Yes	Yes
Rain through doors, windows, bad roof	No	No	Yes—building only
Freezing of plumbing, heating systems	No	Yes	Yes

TABLE 4-10 (continued)

	Basic Form**	Broad Form	Special Form
Falling objects (from outside)	No, except aircraft	Yes	Yes
Weight of ice, snow, sleet	No	Yes	Yes
Collapse of building	No	Yes	Yes
Landslide	No	No	No
Earthquake	No, except by endorsement	No, except by endorsement	No, except by endorsement
Residence glass breakage	By named perils	Yes	Yes
Sudden and accidental damage from artificially generated electrical current	No	Yes	Yes
Burglary damage	Building only	Yes	Yes—including theft of part of completed and occupied structure
Unspecified perils	No	No	Yes ("all risk" coverage)

* This is an additional amount of insurance.
** Extended Coverage perils and Vandalism and Malicious Mischief are optional under DP-1.
Source: Compiled from homeowner's policies of various insurance companies.

to "disappearance" situations in which there is a presumption but no concrete evidence that a missing article was stolen. It should be mentioned, however, that most policies do not cover *mysterious disappearance* for theft. Loss of diamonds out of a ring provides an example of such a theft.

Third, to get full coverage, the insured cannot buy *less* than the amounts of minimally specified insurance. If the coverage for a particular category of claims is calculated as a percentage of the insurance on the house, usually that coverage can be increased for an additional premium without raising the amount for the house. Fourth, in the event the home is damaged by fire or other disaster and the owner has to rent living quarters while it is being repaired, the company pays extra living expenses.

TABLE 4-11 Homeowner Coverages

Coverage	HO-1 (basic form)	HO-2 (broad form)	HO-3 (special form)	HO-4 (contents broad form)	HO-6 (unit owner's form)	HO-8 (modified coverage form)
			Section I Coverages			*Section I Coverages*
A. Dwelling	$15,000 minimum	$15,000 minimum	$20,000 minimum	Not applicable	Not applicable	Same as HO-1 except losses are paid based on the amount required to repair or replace the property using common construction materials and methods
B. Other structures	10% of A	10% of A	10% of A	Not applicable	Not applicable	
C. Personal property	50% of A	50% of A	50% of A	$6,000 min.	$6,000 min.	
D. Loss of use	10% of A	20% of A	20% of A	20% of C	40% of C	
Covered perils	Fire or lightning Windstorm or hail Explosion Riot or civil commotion Aircraft Vehicles Smoke Vandalism or malicious mischief Theft Breakage of glass or safety glazing material (limit of $100) Volcanic eruption	Fire or lightning Windstorm or hail Explosion Riot or civil commotion Aircraft Vehicles Smoke Vandalism or malicious mischief Theft Breakage of glass or safety glazing material Falling objects Weight of ice, snow, or sleet Accidental discharge or overflow of water or stream Sudden and accidental tearing, cracking, burning, or bulging of a steam, hot water, air conditioning, or automatic fire protective sprinkler system, or appliance for heating water Freezing Sudden and accidental damage from artificially generated electrical current Volcanic eruption	Dwelling and other structures covered against risks of direct physical loss to property except losses specifically excluded Personal property covered by same perils as HO-2 plus damage by glass or safety glazing material, which is part of a building, storm door, or storm window	Same perils as HO-2 for personal property	Same perils as HO-2 for personal property	Same perils as HO-1 except theft coverage applies only to losses on the residence premises up to a maximum of $1,000; certain other coverage restrictions also apply
		Section II Coverages				*Section II Coverages*
E. Personal liability	$100,000	$100,000	$100,000	$100,000	$100,000	$100,000
F. Medical payments to others	$1,000 per person	$1,000 per person	$1,000 per person	$1,000 per person	$1,000 per person	$1,000 per person

Source: Reprinted with permission from *Changing Times* Magazine, © Kiplinger Washington Editors, Inc., February 1975. This reprint is not to be altered in any way, except with permission from *Changing Times*.

MAJOR PROVISIONS

The Home

The coinsurance clause. In order to be assured full payment for any partial damage to the house, the "Rule of 80" should be applied; that is, the house must be insured for at least 80 percent of its full replacement value, not including the cost of the lot. For instance, if the $150,000 home is insured for at least $120,000 and fire destroys the recreation room, causing $20,000 in damage, the entire $20,000 less the deductible would be reimbursed. However, if the home was insured for, say, $100,000, then only a percentage of the $20,000 would be paid.

If separate building structures exist on the residential property—such as a detached garage—then annexed private structures coverage should be purchased, assuming that the value exceeds the coverage provided in the policy. Such coverage will provide insurance in the amount equal to ten percent of the dwelling amount on separate building structures. Of course, this percentage can be increased to a higher amount by paying an additional premium.

Inflation guard policies. In view of the ever-increasing cost of replacing a home, it is advisable to purchase coverage for the replacement value of the house (excluding the lot). This is accomplished by keeping the insurance updated—an inflation-guard endorsement as it is called—so that the home will be adequately insured. This policy increases the amount of the coverage by eight to ten percent every year. The cost of the endorsement would vary, depending on the type of coverage and variations in the cost-of-living index.

Unscheduled Personal Property

Market value. This refers to those personal household contents which are not specifically listed by name and value in the policy. The homeowner's policy provides insurance on these items equal to 50 percent of the amount of insurance on the house. However, when a property is destroyed, the company asks for some type of proof of ownership and an estimate of the depreciated value of such property. For this reason, a complete video, or if that is not possible, an updated itemized inventory of personal property, should always be maintained.

It is important to mention here that certain types of property are excluded from coverage under homeowner's insurance, and special limits of liability exist on other types of property. Excluded property includes motorized vehicles, sound equipment in an automobile, property rented to others, and so on. In addition, the following dollar limits of coverage generally apply: $100 on money, bank notes, and coins; $1,000 on securities; $500 on watercraft; $2,500 (varies by states) on theft of jewelry and furs (aggregate); $2,500 on theft of silverware and goldware; $2,000 on firearms; $10,000 on oriental rugs (aggregate); and $3,000 on home computers and equipment.

A standard homeowner's policy covers personal property away from the home up to an amount equal to ten percent of the amount specified in the policy or $1,000, whichever is greater. However, if the property is stolen from a car, one must show proof of forced entry into the car, unless the person has the extended theft endorsement.

Replacement cost.   The actual cash value, that is, the replacement cost less depreciation leaves a great deal to be desired. For one thing, such a method requires the owner to maintain detailed records of date of purchase, the purchase price, the estimated percentage depreciation on the date of loss, and other related bookkeeping records. For another, the reimbursement amount is likely to cover only a fraction of the replacement cost of the article. For these reasons, most insurance companies now offer replacement cost coverage. For instance, for an additional premium representing five to 15 percent of the policy's total premium, the homeowner can receive the actual replacement cost versus fair market value of a destroyed or stolen item. Nevertheless it is wise to maintain a detailed inventory of personal effects and supplement it with videos or still pictures of personal articles.

Floater policies.   In situations where personal properties are valued in excess of the coverage or limitations offered by a typical homeowner's policy, two types of floater policies are available. The *personal articles floater* provides all-risk protection for each article specified on the face of the policy. In contrast, *personal property floater* offers protection on *all* articles on a worldwide basis. Because these policies can be expensive, it is best to include in these policies only those articles which warrant special coverage, such as jewelry, furs, and boats. Incidentally, an insurance company may require the homeowner to have these items appraised before insuring them.

Personal Liability

Personal liability protection means that if someone outside of the family is injured in an accident on the property, or in an accident (but not an auto accident) off the premises that is caused by a member of the family, the homeowner's policy covers the insured against a lawsuit. This involves two kinds of protection. The company will pay medical expenses of people hurt by a member of the owner's family, or the pets, on or away from the home, even when they are not legally responsible for the injury. The company will also pay for damage to the property of others, even if the owner is not legally at fault. However, the insured does not personally receive any money from policy sections covering personal liability as well as damage to property of others and medical payments. The compensation is for injury to people other than family members living with the homeowner, and the money is paid directly to the injured person.

In the average homeowner's policy the minimum personal liability coverage is $25,000. This amount should be increased to at least $100,000, especially since the cost of raising it to $100,000 is modest.

The Cost Issue

Of all the proven strategies for reducing the cost of a homeowner's policy, selecting the most economical policy from a group of alternative quotations for identical coverage tops the list. Another strategy of cost reduction is to increase the deductible from $250 to, say, $500 which can significantly cut premiums. In general, because small losses of less than $500 can dramatically increase administrative costs, thereby jeopardizing the renewal of a policy, this amount of deductibility should generally be considered. The reason is that the ideal philosophy of buying protection against risk is to cover that which one cannot afford to assume.

Special Insurance

Replacement cost. As mentioned, as a general rule the contents of a home are insured for no more than 50 percent of the dwelling's coverage, although the coverage can be raised to 70 percent. Consequently, without additional coverage, the most one could collect on the contents if the home were insured for $100,000 would be $50,000. But that is only one type of limitation of a homeowner's policy. As mentioned, in most states there is a $2,500 limit on furs and jewelry lost in a single theft. Furthermore, for certain losses companies will pay only a fixed sum: $100 for any and all coins and money, $500 for stamps, $2,000 for firearms, $2,500 for jewelry and furs, and $1,000 for manuscripts. Moreover, collectible coins are grouped with regular money, bullion, and bank notes. Stamps are classified with securities, evidence of debts, deeds, and tickets. Other valuables and collectors' items, such as fine art, antiques, cameras, and musical instruments, can be claimed up to their insured cash value, provided a sales receipt can be produced.

After taking an inventory of the valuables, a homeowner may feel the need for additional coverage; in that case, there are two basic possibilities. The basic homeowner's coverage may be raised, which would automatically raise the unscheduled personal-property protection. Additionally, the owner may have valuables—furs, jewelry, fine art, silverware, cameras, stamps, coins, and sports and hobby gear—listed individually in special endorsements or "floaters." When buying floaters it is advisable to get the inflation-guard endorsement assuming rising replacement values. Although it may vary by company, generally for five percent of the regular premium, the amount of coverage is adjusted upward on a regular basis.

Crime insurance. Burglary and robbery insurance for up to $10,000 is available to homeowner's and tenants in certain states such as Florida and New York. The premium for $10,000 of insurance ranges from $60 a year in low-crime areas to $80 in the highest-crime area.

Flood and earthquake insurance. In 1969 the federal government and the private insurance industry introduced a joint program to make flood insurance available at rates subsidized by the government, since it is not available through homeowner's policies. To qualify, the property must be located in a community that has declared its intentions to carry out land-use control measures to reduce future flooding.

In contrast to the way flood insurance is written, earthquake insurance is usually written as an addition to a fire or homeowner's policy, with minimum payments of as low as $.03 per $100 for dwellings. That is, the coverage for a $100,000 dwelling would be $300.

TABLE 4-12   Homeowner's/Renter's Insurance Worksheet

	Current coverage	*Desirable coverage*
Home Replacement Value	$_____	80% of Replacement Cost
Type of Coverage	HO-1, HO-2, HO-3, HO-5	HO-3 or HO-5
Renter's/Condo Insurance	HO-4, HO-6	HO-4, HO-6
Personal Property:	$_____	50% of face amount
Cash	$_____ Limit	Increase limits to suit personal needs
Financial Documents	$_____ Limit	Increase limits to suit personal needs
Boats	$_____ Limit	Increase limits to suit personal needs
Jewelry and Furs	$_____ Limit	Increase limits to suit personal needs
Silverware and Gold	$_____ Limit	Increase limits to suit personal needs
Musical Instruments	$_____	Increase limits to suit personal needs
Fine Art	$_____	Increase limits to suit personal needs
Other	$_____	Increase limits to suit personal needs
Liability Insurance	$_____	$100,000 plus $1 million under umbrella policy

THE PLANNING STRATEGY

Self-Analysis

For financial planning purposes, the best strategy for carrying a satisfactory homeowner's policy is to make sure that the family has adequate coverage against all major risks associated with owning a home. A convenient worksheet is presented in Table 4-12 which can be used to determine if individual coverages match the desired levels of coverage.

Annual Check-up

In addition to self-analysis, it is desirable to have an annual check-up of the homeowner's policy by an insurance professional. We will briefly review here the annual check-up process for the family of John and Betty Smith. Recently the Smiths received the following letter from John Sipe, their insurance agent. We will review only the homeowner's policy here. Auto and umbrella liability policies will be examined in subsequent sections.

February 1, 1990

John and Betty Smith
151 George Street
Detroit, Michigan 48602

Dear Mr. and Mrs. Smith,

As part of my continuing service to you, I review your file from time to time. Presently you have the following policies with me:

AUTO   1984 LASER, 1985 DEVILLE, 1987 TOWN CAR
FIRE   HOMEOWNERS (HO-5), PERSONAL LIABILITY
          UMBRELLA
LIFE   NONE
HEALTH   NONE

I feel a thorough review of all your present policies would be very beneficial at this time. We call this free service the Family Insurance Check-up. To set up a convenient time for us to get together, give me a call at 643-1234, or stop by to set up an appointment soon.

Remember, our company offers economical protection for all your insurance needs . . . car, home, health, life, boat, and even your business. I am attaching the following for your review:

Form A: Family Insurance Check-up Check List

     B: HO Policy Status

     C: Auto Policy Status

     D: Umbrella Policy Status

Thank you for allowing me to serve you.

Sincerely,

Jim Sipe
Friendly Insurance Agent

Form A: Fire

You should consider	
Replacement cost on dwelling:	Watercraft:
Replacement cost on contents:	Oriental rugs/personal computer:
Higher liability limits:	Jewelry/furs/fine arts/silverware:
Higher deductibles:	Sports equipment/musical instruments:
Mortgage disability/life:	Tools/equipment/goods for sale:
Umbrella coverage:	Pets:

You should consider

Replacement cost on dwelling:
Replacement cost on contents:
Higher liability limits:
Higher deductibles:
Mortgage disability/life:
Umbrella coverage:

Do you have?

Other buildings on premises:
Improvements since insured:
Photo inventory:
Coins/gold/silver:
Cameras:
Stamp collections/collectibles:
Trailer (not boat):

Watercraft:
Oriental rugs/personal computer:
Jewelry/furs/fine arts/silverware:
Sports equipment/musical instruments:
Tools/equipment/goods for sale:
Pets:
Smoke alarms/extinguishers:
Dead bolts/security systems:
Firearms:
Woodburning stove/kerosene heater:
Roomers/resident employees:
A need for professional liability:
Office/business:
Childcare in the home:
Sewer/drain/sump pump problems:
Earthquake/flood:
Other homes/rental property/farms:

Form B: Homeowner's
Policy Status

February 1, 1990	Policy No: 000-000	Yr. issued: 86
Type: Homeowners EX (HO-5)	Term: Annual	Amount paid: $498.00
Premium: $498.00	Renewal date: 7-02-90	Date paid: 6-29-90
Deductible applies: $500		Bill to: MTG. Co.

Coverage information

Dwelling	$205,200	Mortgagee:
Dwelling extension	20,520	Interfirst Fed Sav.
Personal property	153,900	2250 W. Michigan Ave.
Loss of use	Actual loss	Detroit, MI 48197-0922
		Loan No: 12345
Personal liability	300,000	
Damage to property	500	
Medical	1,000	

Insurance to value

Replacement cost: $177,800   Current coverage amount: $205,200
Square footage: 1700   Local adjustment factor: 11.16
Replacement cost criteria:
   Masonry, one family, wet bar
   1980, standard plus
   2 story, basement

Additional building features

Post 1980	Central air
1 Deck	1 Fireplace hearth
1 Masonry chimney	3 Car attached garage
Kitchen package	

The Smiths met with Jim Sipe to review their homeowner's policy. After some discussion the Smiths agreed to make the following changes in their policy which would bring the coverage to the level with which they were most comfortable.

1. Personal property coverage was increased to $200,000
2. Optional coverages were extended to:
   a. Jewelry and Furs
   b. Silverware/Goldware
   c. Home Computers and Equipment
   d. Property used in business

AUTOMOBILE INSURANCE

INTRODUCTION

Practically every year Americans set a new record for the number of automobile accidents, as well as the number of injuries and deaths, they cause. In 1989 there were millions of injuries causing economic losses amounting to billions of dollars. These statistics should be kept in mind as we discuss the need for having basic automobile insurance coverage. Additional coverages—such as collision, comprehensive, uninsured motorists, and medical payments—are also important. As a matter of public policy, many states encourage the purchase of automobile insurance by imposing financial responsibility laws, and a few states make the purchase of auto insurance mandatory through compulsory liability insurance laws.

Determining the *basic* coverages of an automobile insurance policy, known as personal auto policy (PAP), is not easy, for there is more to choosing the right one than meets the eye. As can be seen from Table 4-13, there are two basic types of damages that could result from an auto accident: (1) property damage (including damage to the automobile); and (2) bodily injury (including death). These damages could be the result of the driver's negligence or that of "the other guy." Accidents also happen due to circumstances completely beyond the control of the drivers involved. Add to these complications others such as: The "other guy" happens to be an uninsured motorist, or the motorist

TABLE 4-13   Summary of Basic Automobile Insurance Coverages

Coverages	Principal applications	
	Policyholder	Other persons
Bodily Injury		
Bodily injury liability	No	Yes
Medical payments	Yes	Yes
Protection against uninsured motorists	Yes	Yes
	Policyholder's Automobile	Property of Others
Property Damage		
Property damage liability	No	Yes
Comprehensive physical damage	Yes	No
Collision	Yes	No

is encouraged by a lawyer to build up a claim because he or she perceives the driver to be wealthy. That gives a fairly good idea of what is involved in selecting a good automobile insurance policy.

It is appropriate to begin with the *minimum* coverage. Thereafter, this coverage should be expanded in various directions, subject of course to the family's budget constraints.

BASIC COVERAGES OF PERSONAL AUTO POLICY

There are six major parts to a personal auto policy (PAP). These are discussed next.

Liability Coverage (Part A)

Under the PAP, the following persons are covered:

1. The named insured.
2. The spouse living in the principal household.
3. The relatives of the first person named in the declaration.
4. Any other person who obtained the consent of the insured or the spouse.
5. Any other person or organization liable for the use of such a car by one of the previously mentioned insureds.

The coverage is not extended to automobiles used in any other business or occupation, or to persons working in any car business.

One of the most significant factors in PAP is the *single limit* coverage for both bodily injury and property damage. The limit of liability shown in the policy is the maximum limit of liability for all damages resulting from any one accident. Each of the two liabilities is discussed next.

Bodily injury liability. In buying auto insurance the major concern should be to protect against others' claims arising from bodily injury or death caused by the members or employees of the family. When a policy is purchased that includes liability, the insurance company promises to honor the claims of the aggrieved party or parties up to the financial limits stipulated in the policy. These limits are often expressed as 25/50 which means that the insurance company is liable for up to $25,000 for any one person injured, and up to $50,000 for all persons injured in the same accident. While most states now prescribe the minimum amount of liability insurance that residents must carry, as a bare minimum one should carry at least a 100/300 coverage, which means $100,000 coverage for one person and up to $300,000 for all persons. As a general rule, an insurance agent should analyze the net worth and annual income of an individual in order to determine the satisfactory level of liability insurance for that person.

Property damage liability. This coverage applies when a car damages the property of others. The property may be the car of the other person or it may be other properties such as lamp posts, buildings, or telephone poles. Property damage liability coverage provides protection in the form of legal defense and indemnification through the payment of damages for which the driver is legally liable. This coverage can be purchased in amounts ranging from $10,000 to $50,000 or more. Here again, a minimum $50,000 coverage is desirable.

Medical Payments (Part B)

If medical payments coverage is included in the policy, it would cover the cost of medical services for the insured, relatives, and anyone else in the insured's car. It does not apply to pedestrians or to occupants of the other vehicle. The advantage of having automobile medical payments coverage in addition to liability insurance is that payment is prompt, since there is no wait to determine liability.

Uninsured Motorists (Part C)

This coverage implies that the insurance company will protect the driver against losses inflicted by someone who has no insurance, or an insurance carrier that is insolvent. However, in order to collect on a claim, it is necessary to show that the other driver was at fault. This type of policy applies only to bodily injuries, and the payment for injury by the insurance company under this coverage is limited to the state's liability minimum. A variation of this protects against underinsured motorists, where the other driver is at fault and does not have sufficient insurance to pay for all of the losses.

Coverage for Damage to Insured's Auto (Part D)

Comprehensive physical damage. Comprehensive insurance protects the car against theft, vandalism, falling objects, fire, lightning, and so on. However, it does not apply when the car is damaged in a collision with another car or object, nor does it cover normal wear and tear on the car. The extent of the coverage depends upon the amount specified in the policy. The presence or amount of deductible varies from policy to policy. Some comprehensive fire and theft policies also reimburse the policyholder for rental of a substitute car during repair or until a new car can be purchased.

Collision/overturn. Generally speaking, if the car is damaged by the person who struck it, the driver should be able to get it repaired or replaced at the cost of the person at fault, provided he or she has coverage. If liability insurance is nonexistent, the person may refuse to pay for the damages. It is also possible that the insurance company representing the driver at fault may delay paying for the damages, in which case the driver would have to get the car fixed. For these reasons, and also because the driver may be responsible for damages to the car, it is desirable to purchase collision insurance. Essentially, collision insurance is a pledge by an insurance company to pay for any damage to a car should it collide with another vehicle or object, regardless of who is responsible for the accident.

Collision insurance normally has a deductible amount, often $100 or more. One of the most efficient ways to reduce the auto premium is to take a higher deductible, such as $250 or $500. The insured risks losing the amount of the deductible if the car is damaged, but the premium savings are substantial. Another sensible strategy is to buy no collision coverage if the car is, say, six years old. This decision can easily be made by comparing the market value of the car with the premium charged.

Duties after Accident or Loss (Part E)

In case of a claim, a policyholder must:

1. Send the insurance company accident-related paperwork, duly filled out
2. Authorize the insurance company to obtain medical and other pertinent records
3. Submit proof of loss
4. Cooperate with the insurance company in every way

General Provisions (Part F)

Several important provisions form an integral part of a PAP. Some of the important ones are listed here:

1. The terms of a policy may be changed or waived only by an endorsement signed by the company.
2. The policyholder does not have a right of action against the company until all the terms of the policy have been met, and under the liability coverage, until the damage amount an insured is legally liable to pay has been finally determined.
3. The policyholder may cancel the policy by notifying the company in writing of the date to cancel, signing a lost policy release, or returning the policy.

NO-FAULT INSURANCE

In those states which do not have no-fault insurance, an insurance company is obligated to reimburse the policyholder for damages only if the insured is at fault. However, determination of fault is not always easy. It may require legal negotiations, and may even lead to costly lawsuits. Furthermore, the liability system becomes onerous in a situation where neither motorist is at fault, or perhaps both parties are at fault. For this reason, and also to reduce the number of cases which plague our court system, there has been a trend for states to adopt no-fault insurance laws.

There are four essential elements in the basic no-fault plan: (1) An accident victim's losses should be paid for by his or her insurance company; this makes court action unnecessary to determine liability; (2) the right to sue for additional compensation is significantly limited; (3) no-fault insurance is mandatory, thus insuring payment to all accident victims without recourse to courts; and (4) insurance companies must provide safeguards against cancellation or nonrenewal so that all drivers can possess the required insurance.

The idea of pure no-fault insurance was to eliminate lawsuits and have victims reimbursed by their own insurance companies for their medical expenses, without any reimbursement for "pain and suffering." This would eliminate the "fault" concept and allow immediate reimbursement for bodily injuries. However, no state has adopted this version of no-fault. Every state allows lawsuits if there are severe injuries, prolonged disability, or large expenses accumulated for a given accident. States that have adopted such no-fault laws include Colorado, Connecticut, Florida, Georgia, Hawaii, Kansas, Kentucky, Massachusetts, Michigan, Minnesota, New Jersey, New York, North Dakota, Pennsylvania, Puerto Rico, and Utah. In these states, no-fault insurance is compulsory and has proved to be an effective way to compensate auto accident victims.

Coverage limits and deductibles vary from state to state. Deductibles range from $50 to $2,000. This represents the amount the injured person must assume before making a no-fault claim. Coverage for personal injuries may range from $10,000 to $25,000 for an individual and $20,000 to $50,000 for injuries to two or more persons.

Incidentally, some states have adopted a more liberal no-fault insurance known as "add-on no-fault." This type of no-fault insurance gives the injured party the right to sue the party at fault. These states, together with the states already mentioned, account for over half of the states having some form of no-fault insurance.

THE PLANNING STRATEGY

Self-Analysis

As in the case of homeowner's insurance, planning for adequate auto insurance coverage involves making sure that the existing coverages compare favorably with the desired limits. A convenient worksheet is presented in Table 4-14 for completing the task.

TABLE 4-14 Automobile Insurance Worksheet

	Current Coverage	Desirable Coverage
Liability Insurance:		
Bodily injury	_____	100/300
Property damage	_____	$50,000
Umbrella policy*	_____	$1 million
Collision	_____	$250 deductible
Comprehensive	_____	$100 deductible
Uninsured Motorists' Coverage	_____	Same as liability coverage limits
Underinsured Motorists' Coverage	_____	Same as liability coverage limits
Medical Payment Coverage	_____	$10,000 per person
No-Fault Insurance:		
Medical expense	_____	Reasonable amount
Other coverage	_____	Reasonable amount

* Insurance companies generally require higher limits (e.g., 250/500) in order to provide an umbrella policy.

Annual Check-up

It is highly desirable to subject the auto policy to an annual check-up by an insurance professional. We refer to John Sipe's letter to the Smiths (see pages 145–46) to which he attached the Family Insurance Check-Up list (Form A) and the Automobile Policy Status (Form C).

Form A: Auto

How many cars are in the household:	Uninsured/underinsured:
Are cars driven to work/used for business:	Death, dismemberment, loss of sight:
	Loss of earnings:
Which children drive/which cars:	Other coverages:
Other regular drivers:	Nonowned auto coverage:
Annual mileage:	

You should consider	*Do you have?*
High liability limits:	Motorcycle/scooters:
Higher medical/no-fault coverage:	Trucks/RVs/motorhomes/campers:
Higher deductibles comp./collision:	Other vehicles/trailers:
Emergency road service:	Cellular phone/CB/cassette radios:
Rental/travel expense coverage:	Plans to purchase new car:

Form C: Auto Policy Status February 1, 1990

	Lincoln Town Car, 1987	Cadillac DeVille, 1985	Chrysler Laser, 1984*
Policy Number	000-00-001	000-00-002	000-00-003
Class	1A 3011	1A 3011	8V 3011
Total Premium	$380.58	$302.04	$484.29
Status	Paid	Paid	Paid
Covered Date	4-15-90	4-15-90	4-15-90
Birthdate	5-13-30	2-14-35	4-23-66
Bodily Injury Liability (A)	100/300/50	100/300/100	100/300/100
Property Damage Liability (out of state) (B)	100/300/50	100/300/100	100/300/100
Cost of Coverage of (A) and (B)	$ 33.40	$ 38.52	$ 70.23
Personal Injury Protection	$ 24.13	$ 26.61	$ 84.53
Property Protection Insurance (in state) (N)	$ 4.35	$ 4.91	$ 8.96
Uninsured Motorists: 100/300	$ 7.60	$ 7.60	$ 7.60
Limited Property Damage: Mini-Tort (Y): $400	—	$ 2.55	$ 4.65
Comprehensive (D 100)	$ 76.33	$ 51.51	$ 79.98
Broadened Collision	$214.71	$150.28	$244.28

* The driver of this car is John Smith, Jr., who is 19 years old.

The Smith family met with Jim Sipe to discuss their auto policy. Following the meeting, a number of changes were made, as listed next:

1. The bodily injury liability and the property damage liability on the 1987 Lincoln Town Car were increased from 100/300/50 to 100/300/100 to make them consistent with the coverage on the other cars.
2. Limited property damage coverage (Y) was extended to the Lincoln which did not have this coverage.
3. Comprehensive coverage on the 1984 Chrysler car was dropped, because its cost was too great relative to the value of this old car.

The Smiths also discussed the advisability of purchasing a 1985 Mercedes 380 SE. However, when they discovered that it would cost $990 a year to insure this car, the idea was quickly dropped.

UMBRELLA LIABILITY INSURANCE

INTRODUCTION

Under the property-casualty type of insurance policies explained in pages 143 and 149, there are recommended liability and property damage coverage limits to provide adequate protection for claims made against a policyholder resulting from loss of property or personal injury. However, coverages provided by these policies may still be insufficient for reimbursing the aggrieved parties. An umbrella policy supplements, but does not replace, an insured's homeowner's, auto, boat, aircraft, and other nonbusiness coverages.

BASIC UMBRELLA COVERAGE

Typically, umbrella coverage limits are $1 million to $5 million. The cost of this policy depends on the insured's risk exposure and is relatively inexpensive. Basic coverage under an umbrella policy generally extends to bodily injury, mental anguish, shock, sickness, disease, disability, false arrest, false imprisonment, wrongful eviction, detention, libel, defamation of character, and invasion of privacy. A typical umbrella policy excludes the insured's obligation for worker's compensation and disability benefits, damage to property of the insured, or product failure.

The umbrella policy fits over a homeowner's policy like an umbrella of added coverage payable after the coverage under the homeowner's policy has been exhausted. For instance, suppose an insured is sued for $1 million and is carrying both a $100,000 personal liability coverage under the homeowner's policy and a $1 million umbrella policy. The insurance company will pay $100,000 under the homeowner's policy and $900,000 under the umbrella policy. It should be added here that an insurance company will not sell an umbrella policy to a policyholder whose homeowner's policy does not have a minimum of $100,000 personal liability coverage.

As in the case of the homeowner's policy, an umbrella policy will supplement the coverage provided by an auto policy. For instance, if an insured person carrying a 100/300 auto policy and a $1 million umbrella policy is sued for $750,000 in an auto accident, the insurance company will cover $100,000 per person under the auto policy and $650,000 under the umbrella policy. Without this umbrella coverage, the driver would become financially crippled.

DIRECTOR'S LIABILITY INSURANCE

This type of insurance is used to protect officers and directors from claims of wrongful acts such as error, neglect, or omission while performing their duties. In today's litigative society, this insurance coverage is almost routinely provided by corporations, banks, and other institutions for their directors. Board members of Condo Associations, Subdivision Associations, and Charitable Organizations should also be able to be covered by this type of insurance. As a general rule, a large deductible is the only way to keep the premium at an affordable level.

PROFESSIONAL LIABILITY INSURANCE

Today, many professionals, like doctors, lawyers, and financial planners, are exposed to malpractice suits and other comparable risks, and need protection from these risks. Incorporating a professional business does not provide the necessary protection because the corporate status does not shelter the corporate officer from malpractice suits. Most professional liability policies are written on a claims-made basis, which means that the insurance company is only responsible for claims made during the policy period. Costs of professional liability insurance policies are fairly high. Consequently, professionals shopping around for these policies should thoroughly investigate various options, including those offered by their respective professional associations.

THE PLANNING STRATEGY

Self-Analysis

The adequacy of the personal liability umbrella coverage should be checked at the time of the annual review of homeowner's and auto policy. A $1 million policy is an absolute minimum; however, depending on circumstances, the possibility of increasing the coverage should also be explored. Individuals should also make sure that they carry Worker's Compensation for household help, outdoor help, and babysitters.

Annual Check-up

John and Betty Smith received the accompanying personal liability umbrella policy details (Form D) from Jim Sipe, their insurance agent. After a brief discussion, John Smith decided to increase the policy coverage to $1.5 million, since this amount of insurance could be purchased at an additional cost of only $26 per year.

Form D: Personal Liability Umbrella

Term:	Continuous		
Renewal date:	2-26-90	Date paid:	1-26-90
Premium:	$103.00	Amount paid:	$103.00
Bill to:	Insured		
Present liability:	$1,000,000		
Self-insurance:	$500		
Rate class:	II		
CL:	Y		

CHAPTER 5

Time Value of Money: The Universal Tool

THE BASIC CONCEPT

INTRODUCTION

We have observed that the financial planner's primary goal is to maximize the client's financial welfare by analyzing at least the following six areas:

R: Risk Management Planning
E: Essentials of Budgeting, Savings, and Credit Planning
T: Tax Planning
I: Investment Planning
R: Retirement Planning
E: Estate Planning

A central part of all these areas is the planner's ability to analyze the cash flow values over various time periods. In fact, of all the techniques used in financial planning, none is more important than the time value of money (TVM) concept. In this chapter we will discuss in detail the conceptual framework of the TVM and its applications.

SIMPLE INTEREST

Simple interest is the dollar return from investing, or dollar cost of borrowing, money. This interest, which is always stated on an annual basis, is calculated by

$$I = P \times R \times N \qquad\qquad \text{Eq. 5-1}$$

where

I = Simple Interest

P = Principal

R = Rate of Interest

N = Time period for which the principal is invested or lent

Thus, the simple interest on $1,000.00 for 35 days at 11 percent is $10.55:

$$I = [\$1,000.00 \times .11] \times 35/365$$
$$= \$10.55$$

COMPOUND VALUE: FIXED SUM

Multiple Year Annual Compounding

A dollar invested today would earn interest and end up next year worth more than one dollar. During the second year, the original dollar will earn interest, *and* the interest earned during the first year will also earn interest. To illustrate this process, called *compounding*, suppose Marcia Simon deposited $1,000 in a bank certificate of deposit that paid ten percent interest compounded annually. How much money would she have at the end of two years?

The future value of a fixed sum is calculated by:

$$FV = PV (1 + r)^n \qquad\qquad \text{Eq. 5-2}$$

where

FV = Future value of the investment at the end of n years

PV = Value of the investment today, or present value

r = Interest rate during each compounding period

n = Number of years, or compounding periods

We can use Eq. 5-2 to determine the value of $1,000 at the end of two years, compounded annually at ten percent:

$$FV = \$1,000 \, (1 + .10)^2$$
$$= \$1,000 \times 1.21$$
$$= \$1,210.00$$

If the CD had a maturity of ten years, the original investment of $1,000 would grow to $2,593,74:

$$FV = \$1,000 \, (1 + .10)^{10}$$
$$= \$1,000 \times 2.59374$$
$$= \$2,593.74$$

Fortunately, future value interest tables are available which present the future value interest factors in a convenient form. Consequently, Eq. 5-2 can be rewritten as:

$$FV = PV \times FVFF \qquad \text{Eq. 5-2A}$$

where

$$FVFF = \text{Future value fixed sum factor}$$

For instance, Table A3-1 in Appendix 3 (p. 640) shows that the future value fixed sum factor (FVFF) for $1, invested at ten percent for ten years, is 2.5937. Multiplying $1,000 by FVFF of 2.5937 produces the following result:

$$\$1,000 \times 2.5937$$
$$= \$2,593.70$$

This is approximately the same result we obtained by using the long method.

Figure 5-1 shows how a fixed sum of money grows over time at various interest rates. As expected, the higher the interest rate or the longer the compounding period, the larger the future value at the end of the investment period.

At this point it is appropriate to introduce the use of the HP-12C calculator which can be used to answer many questions in personal finance. Among them: How much must one save for future goals, such as college costs and retirement? How big a mortgage can one afford? How would interest rate changes affect monthly payment, on an adjustable loan? Should one buy or lease a car? Should tax-exempt investment be preferable to taxable investment?

Let us start by introducing the keyboard of the HP-12C calculator, which is reproduced in Figure 5-2. The calculator keyboard shows (though not in this

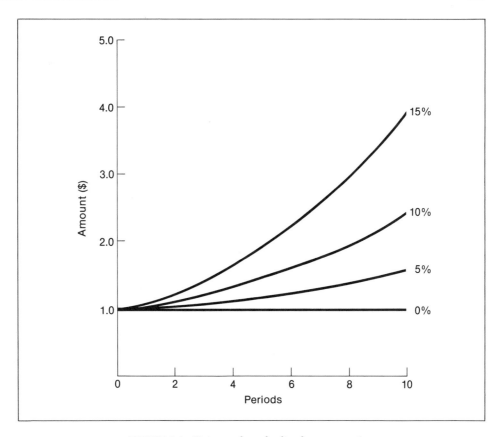

FIGURE 5-1   Future value of a fixed sum over time

figure) three colors: white, gold, and blue. Two keys, one labeled "f" (gold) and the other "g" (blue), match the colors of the keyboard. These keys, shown above the key or the face of a key in the appropriate color code, access specific operation modes of the calculator. The power key is labeled "ON." When the [ON] key is pressed, several zeros and a decimal point (0.00) appear on the window. The calculator can be cleared by pressing [f] followed by [CLX]. The gold lettering above CLX reads REG. Above this a gold bar appears with the word CLEAR. Knowing that the gold [f] accesses the gold operation mode, it is possible to tell that [f] [CLX] "clears the register (display)."

To set the number of decimal places one should press [f] and the number of decimal places desired. For example, [f] [4] results in 0.0000.

The problem relating to the $1,000 CD earning ten percent and maturing in ten years can be easily solved by using the HP-12C calculator. The use of the calculator in solving this problem is demonstrated in Table 5-1.

HP-12C CALCULATOR

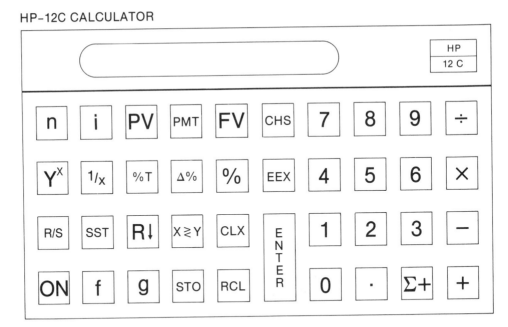

FIGURE 5-2 HP-12C calculator

It might be helpful to mention here that in a present/future value problem, four variables are involved; namely, (1) present value, (2) future value, (3) interest, and (4) number of years (period). If any three variables are known, the value of the fourth variable can be easily calculated.

TABLE 5-1	
Step 1:	Identify known variables:
	Present value: $1,000
	Interest: 10%
	Number of periods: 10 years
Step 2:	Clear calculator [f] [CLX]
Step 3:	Enter data
	Press [1] [0] [0] [0] [CHS] [PV]
	[10] [i]
	[10] [n]
	[FV]
	Answer: $2,593.74

Note: [CHS] key is used when money is paid out. It is *not* used when money is received.

Rule of 72

The "rule of 72" provides a speedy method for determining the time or the interest rate required for an investment (or any index) to double in value. This "rule," which really is only an estimate, is explained next.

In order to determine the number of years for an investment to double in value, 72 is divided by the annual interest rate. For example, if the annual interest rate is eight percent, the time required for an investment to double in value is 72/8, or nine years.

Looking at it another way, the interest rate required for an investment to double in value over a specified number of years is determined by dividing 72 by the number of years. For instance, if Betty Johnson wishes to double her investment in ten years, she must invest the principal to earn an interest rate of 7.2 percent (72/10), compounded annually.

Multiple Compound Periods Per Year

The preceding section presented the case of annual compounding, where each year consisted of one compound period. Often, financial institutions use more frequent compounding periods. For example, compounding semiannually means there are two compound periods per year; compounding monthly means

---

TABLE 5-2

Step 1:	Identify known variables:	
	Present value:	$1000
	Interest:	10%/quarterly (4)
	Number of periods:	2 years × quarterly (4)
Step 2:	Clear calculator [f] [CLX]	
Step 3:	Enter data	

Press   [1]   [0]   [0]   [0] [CHS] [PV]

[10] [ENTER] [4] [÷]   [i]

[2] [ENTER] [4] [X] [n]

[FV]

Answer: $1,218.40

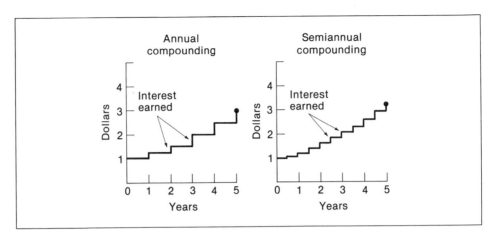

FIGURE 5-3 Future value of a fixed sum using multiple compound periods per year

12 compound periods per year; and compounding daily indicates there are 365 compound periods per year.

Equation 5-2 can be modified to calculate the compound value of $1,000 after n years if invested at r percent, and the amount is compounded over multiple periods per year:

$$FV = PV (1 + r_{nom/m})^{mn} \qquad \text{Eq. 5-3}$$

where

r_{nom} = Declared interest rate, or nominal interest rate

m = Number of compounding periods per year

n = Total number of time periods

Using Eq. 5-3 we calculate the FV for $1,000 after two years, which is invested at ten percent and is compounded quarterly:

$$FV = \$1,000 (1 + .10/4)^{4 \times 2}$$

$$= \$1,218.40$$

The same answer could be obtained by using the HP-12C calculator, as demonstrated in Table 5-2.

Incidentally, note that the quarterly compounding resulted in a value of $1,218.40, as compared to the annual compounding value of $1,210.00. Values of other compounding periods ($PV = \$1,000$, $r = 10$ percent, $n = 2$ years) are given next:

Type of compounding	Future value
Annual	$1,210.00
Semiannual	1,215.51
Quarterly	1,218.40
Daily	1,221.37

These relationships are illustrated in Figure 5-3. It should be obvious that the more frequent the compounding period, the larger is the final compound amount, because interest is earned on interest more often.

PRESENT VALUE: FIXED SUM

A dollar in hand today could be worth more than a dollar to be received next year because, if an investor has it now, she could invest it, earn interest, and end up next year with more than one dollar. For instance, if $100 is invested at five percent for one year, the amount will grow to $105. Put differently, the *present value* of $105 expected to be received next year, *discounted* for one year at five percent, is $100. In general, the present value of a sum due n periods in the future is the amount which, if it were on hand today, would grow to equal the future sum. The concept of discounting a future value to arrive at the present value of a fixed sum is presented in Figure 5-4.

Finding the present value—or *discounting*, as it is generally known—is merely the reverse of compounding. For instance, the compound value equation is:

$$FV = PV (1 + r)^n \qquad \text{(Eq. 5-2 restated)}$$

Solving for PV we obtain

$$PV = FV/(1 + r)^n$$
$$= FV (1 + r)^{-n}$$
$$= FV [1/(1 + r)^n]$$

where

PV = Value of the investment today, or present value

FV = Future value of amount expected to be received in n time periods

r = Interest rate with which the amount is discounted

n = Number of periods over which discounting is performed

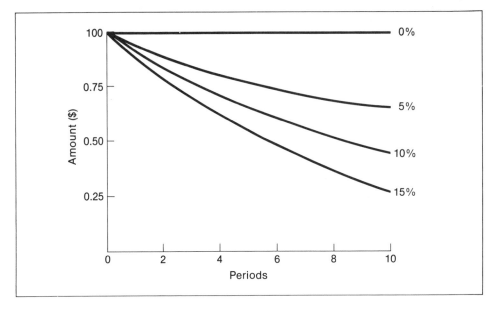

FIGURE 5-4   Present value of a fixed sum over time

For instance, an investor expects to receive $10,000 from a limited partnership seven years from today. Using a discount rate of ten percent, the present value of this investment is $5,132:

$$PV = \$10,000\ [1/(1\ +\ .10)^7]$$

$$= 10,000\ \times\ .5132$$

$$= \$5,132$$

TABLE 5-3

Step 1:	Identify known variables:
	Future value: $10,000
	Interest: 10%
	Number of periods: 7 years
Step 2:	Clear calculator [f] [CLX]
Step 3:	Enter data
	Press [1] [0] [0] [0] [0] [FV]
	[1] [0] [i]
	[7] [n]
	[PV]
	Answer: $5,131.58

Note: [CHS] key is *not* used when money is being received.

As expected, by using the calculator we obtain the same result, as can be seen from Table 5-3. The PV concept is also useful in determining how much must be invested today at, say, eight percent in order to accumulate $15,000 five years from today to fund a child's education:

$$PV = \$15,000 \, [1/(1 + .08)^5]$$

$$= 15,000 \times .6806$$

$$= \$10,209$$

As in this case of FV, the present value table reproduces values of fixed sum factors (PVFF) which can be directly used to calculate present values. For instance, Table A3-2 (on p. 641) shows that the PVFF for eight percent for five years is .6806. Therefore, using the previous example, an investor requiring $15,000 in five years from today at eight percent would invest:

$$PV = \$15,000 \times PVFF$$

$$= 15,000 \times .6806$$

$$= \$10,209$$

This is the same value we arrived at in our long calculation.

Since PV is a mirror reflection of FV, $10,209 invested at eight percent should grow to $15,000 in five years:

$$FV = \$10,209 \, (1 + .08)^5$$

$$= 10,209 \times 1.4693$$

$$= \$15,000$$

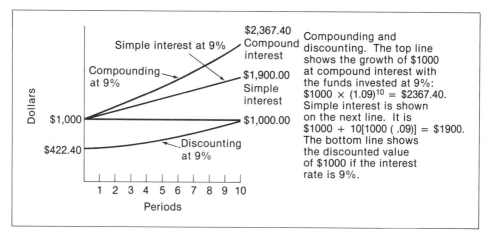

FIGURE 5-5 Relationship between simple interest, compounding, and discounting

---

TABLE 5-4

Step 1:   Identify known variables:
            Future value: $15,000
            Interest: 8%/quarterly (4)
            Number of periods: 5 years × quarterly (4)

Step 2:   Clear calculator [f] [CLX]

Step 3:   Enter data
            Press   [1] [5] [0] [0] [0] [FV]

                           [8] $\begin{bmatrix} E \\ N \\ T \\ E \\ R \end{bmatrix}$ [4][÷] [i]

                           [5] $\begin{bmatrix} E \\ N \\ T \\ E \\ R \end{bmatrix}$ [4] [X] [n]

                           [PV]
            Answer: $10,094.57

Interestingly, if interest were compounded *quarterly* and the investor wanted to find out how much must be invested today at 8 percent to accumulate $15,000 five years from today, the PV calculation would be as follows:

$$PV = \$15,000\ [1/(1 + .08/4)^{5 \times 4}]$$

$$= 15,000 \times .6729713$$

$$= \$10,094.57$$

The same calculation performed on a calculator is shown in Table 5-4. As expected, since more frequent compounding produces a larger terminal value, the investor needs to invest a smaller amount ($10,094.57) when quarterly compounding is involved as compared with annual compounding ($10,209).

The relationship between simple interest, FV, and PV is presented in Figure 5-5. An understanding of these relationship are essential for their effective use as financial planning tools.

FUTURE VALUE: ANNUITY

Frequently, individuals accumulate funds on an *annual basis*. For instance, a person may invest $2,000 at the end of the year into an IRA for five years and

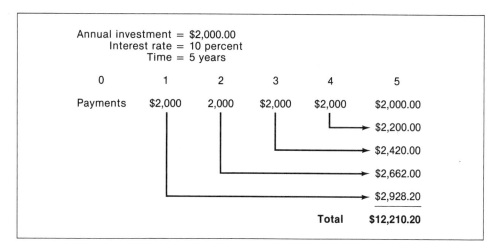

Annual investment = $2,000.00
Interest rate = 10 percent
Time = 5 years

| 0 | 1 | 2 | 3 | 4 | 5 |

Payments $2,000   2,000 $2,000 $2,000 $2,000.00

$2,200.00

$2,420.00

$2,662.00

$2,928.20

Total   **$12,210.20**

FIGURE 5-6   Future value of an ordinary annuity

then wish to determine the total accumulated value of this fund at the end of that period. As revealed by Figure 5-6, if the investment earns ten percent per year, the fund would grow to $12,210.20. The future value of an annuity can be calculated by:

$$FVA = PMT \sum_{n=1}^{N} (1 + r)^{N-n}$$ Eq. 5-4

where

$$FVA = \text{Future value of an annuity}$$

$$PMT = \text{Payment per compound period}$$

$$n = \text{Number of compound periods}$$

$$N = \text{Total number of years}$$

Equation 5-5 can be used to solve the IRA problem:

$$FVA = \$2,000 (1 + .10)^{5-1} + \$2,000 (1 + .10)^{5-2}$$

$$+ \$2,000 (1 + .10)^{5-3} + \$2,000 (1 + .10)^{5-4}$$

$$+ \$2,000 (1 + .10)^{5-5}$$

$$= \$2,000 (1.4641) + \$2,000 (1.331)$$

$$+ \$2,000 (1.21) + \$2,000 (1.10) + \$2,000 (1)$$

$$+ \$2,928.20 + \$2,662.00 + \$2,420.00 + \$2,200.00 + \$2,000.00$$

$$= \$12,210.20$$

TABLE 5-5	
Step 1:	Identify known variables: Payment: $2000 Interest: 10% Number of periods: 5 years
Step 2:	Clear calculator [f] [CLX]

Step 3:	Enter data
	Press [2] [0] [0] [0] [CHS] [PMT]
	       [1] [0] [i]
	       [5] [n]
	     [FV]
	Answer: $12,210.20

As in previous cases, convenient tables are available for making future value annuity calculations. More specifically,

$$FVA = PMT \times FVAF \qquad \text{Eq. 5-4A}$$

where

$$FVAF = \text{Future value annuity factor}$$

For the previous problem, from Table A3-3 (on p. 642) we see that the FVAF for ten percent for five years is 6.1051. Thus

$$FVA = \$2,000 \ (6.1051)$$

$$= \$12,210.20$$

As expected, the use of a calculator yields the same result, as revealed by Table 5-5.

PRESENT VALUE: ANNUITY

Perhaps the most important tool in the financial planner's kit is the present value of an annuity (PVA) concept. Identification of an undervalued stock, evaluation of an income-producing limited partnership, or a lump sum versus a pension for life retirement settlement—all of these problems can be solved by using the PVA concept.

Here is an interesting problem which requires the use of the PVA concept. A client has just won a lottery. He is offered the following alternatives: (1) a four-year annuity with payments of $1,000 at the end of each year, or (2) a lump sum payment of $3,170 today. Which one should he choose? At first blush, either the four-year payment or the lump sum *may* appear more attractive.

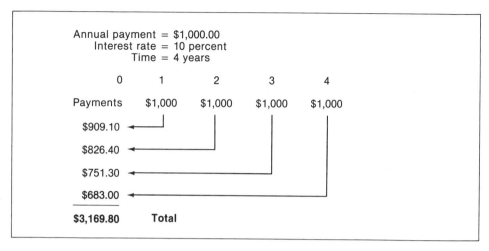

FIGURE 5-7   Present value of an ordinary annuity

However, as revealed by Figure 5-7, if the money is expected to earn ten percent per year, *both alternatives are of equal value.* The algebraic equation for calculating the PVA is as follows:

$$PVA = PMT \sum_{n=1}^{N} (1/1+r)^n \qquad \text{Eq. 5-5}$$

In the preceding example, PVA equals

PVA = $1,000 (1/1 + .10)^1 + \$1,000 (1/1 + .10)^2$

     + $1,000 (1/1 + .10)^3 + \$1,000 (1/1 + .10)^4$

     = $1,000 \times .90909 + \$1,000 \times .82644$

     + $1,000 \times .75131 + \$1,000 \times .68301$

     = $909.09 + \$826.44 + \$751.31 + \$683.01$

     = $3,169.85

By now it should be clear that the present value annuity tables provide the present value annuity factor (PVAF) which can be directly used to arrive at the present value. Consequently, Equation 5-6 can be modified as

$$PVA = PMT \times PVAF \qquad \text{Eq. 5-5A}$$

where

$$PVAF = \text{Present value annuity factor}$$

TABLE 5-6

Step 1:   Identify known variables:
               Payment: $1,000
               Interest: 10%
               Number of periods: 4 years

Step 2:   Clear calculator [f] [CLX]

Step 3:   Enter data
               Press [1]   [0] [0] [0] [PMT]
                     [1]   [0] [i]
                     [4]   [n]
                     [PV]
               Answer: $3,169.87

Note: If the payments were received at the beginning of each period,
step 3 would have been modified as follows:
               Press [g]   [7]
                     [1]   [0] [0] [0] [PMT]
                     [1]   [0] [i]
                     [4]   [n]
                     [PV]
               Answer: $3,486.85

Note:
1. [CHS] is *not* used since this is money being received, not paid out.
2. [g] [7] is pressed to initiate the "beginning" mode.

Using Equation 5-5A, the PVA of $1,000 a year for four years, discounted at ten percent is $3,169.90:

$$PVA = PMT \times PVAF$$

$$= \$1,000 \times 3.1699$$

$$= \$3,169.90$$

By using the calculator, we obtain the same result as shown by Table 5-6.

ANNUITY DUE: A REFINEMENT

In our previous discussions we assumed that all payments were either received or made at the *end* of the year. That is not always the case. For instance, all insurance premiums are paid at the *beginning* of the period; the same is true of lease payments. The former type of payments, received at the end of the period, are called *ordinary* annuities. Payments due at the beginning of the period are called *annuity due*.

Annuity Due: Compound Value

Let us refer to the IRA problem where the individual has put in $2,000 at the end of each year for five years. The *ordinary* annuity value was calculated as $12,210.20. Now let us assume the IRA payments were invested at the beginning of each year. Equation 5-6 can be developed to accommodate this change:

$$FVA \text{ (Annuity Due)} = PMT \ (FVAF)(1 + r)$$

$$\$2,000 \ (6.1051)(1.10) \qquad \text{Eq. 5-6}$$

$$= \$13,431.22$$

Clearly, since the payments are made earlier, the annuity due is more valuable than the ordinary annuity.

Annuity Due: Present Value

Equation 5-7 for an ordinary present value annuity can be developed in the following manner to calculate the present value of an annuity due:

$$PVA \text{ (Annuity Due)} = PMT \ (PVAF) \ (1 + r) \qquad \text{Eq. 5-7}$$

Referring to the lottery example, had the $1,000 annual payments occurred at the beginning of each year, the present value of the annuity due would have been $3,486.99 as demonstrated here:

$$PVA \text{ (Annuity Due)} = \$1,000 \times 3.1699 \times (1 + .10)$$

$$= \$3,486.89$$

As revealed in Table 5-6, this was also the result we obtained by using the calculator.

PRESENT VALUE OF A PERPETUITY

What is the present value of a preferred stock which has no maturity and makes annuity (dividend) payments indefinitely? Here the payments resemble an infinite series, and the series is defined as a *perpetuity*. The present value of a perpetuity is given by:

$$PV \text{ (Perpetuity)} = PMT/r \qquad \text{Eq. 5-8}$$

Let us assume that IBM Preferred pays an annual dividend of $5.00. If the rate of discount is eight percent, the present value of IBM Preferred is $62.50:

$$PV \text{ (Perpetuity)} = \$5.00/.08$$

$$= \$62.50$$

PRESENT VALUE OF AN UNEVEN PAYMENT SERIES

In our previous value discussions it was assumed that the periodic payments were even. This would not be a valid assumption for a common stock, which can realistically be expected to declare dividends on an uneven basis. What, then, is the present value of ABC Common Stock which declares uneven dividend payments?

The present value calculation of ABC Common is demonstrated in Figure 5-8. An arbitrary discount rate of 8 percent is selected for this calculation. Two observations are apropos here. First, the PV of an uneven stream of expected future dividends is merely the sum of the PVs of the individual components of the stream. The PV of each individual dividend payment can be calculated by referring to Table A3-2 (on p. 641). Second, if within the series dividend payments for two years or more remain constant, as is the case here during years 3 through 7, the Present Value Annuity Factor (Table A3-4, on p. 643)

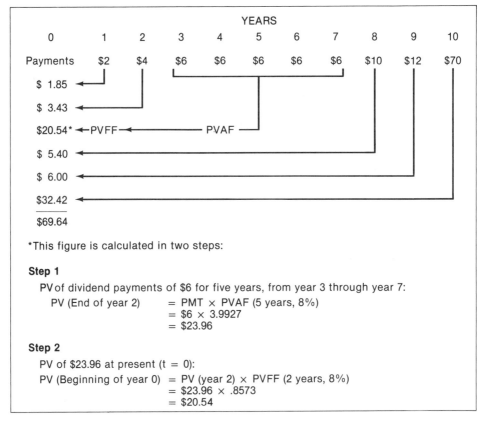

FIGURE 5-8 Present value of ABC common stock

can be used to calculate the present value of the dividend payments for these years. Assuming that the ABC Common is sold for $70 in the tenth year and the future expected dividend payments and the sale price of ABC are discounted by a nine percent discount rate, the PV of ABC Common works out to $69.64.

NOMINAL VERSUS EFFECTIVE INTEREST RATE

As mentioned, not all payments are received and compounded annually. For instance, bonds make interest payments semiannually, stock dividends are paid quarterly, and banks tend to charge loan interest on a daily basis. As previously demonstrated, quarterly versus annual compounding produces the following results:

	Annual compounding	Quarterly compounding
Amount	$1,000.00	$1,000.00
Interest Rate	10%	10%
Number of Years	2	2
Compound Value	$1,210.00	$1,218.40

Since the compound values are higher for more frequent compounding, it is appropriate to differentiate between the two by contrasting the *nominal*, or stated, interest rate with the *effective* annual rate (EAR). The EAR can be determined by:

$$EAR = (1 + Ynom/m)^m - 1.0 \qquad \text{Eq. 5-9}$$

where

$$EAR = \text{Effective annual rate}$$

$$Ynom = \text{Nominal, or stated, interest rate}$$

$$m = \text{Number of compounding periods per year}$$

Using the preceding example,

$$EAR = (1 + .10/4)^4 - 1.0$$

$$= (1.025)^4 - 1.0$$

$$= 1.1038 - 1.0$$

$$= .1038 = 10.38\%$$

In this case, the *nominal* interest rate is ten percent. However, if the amount is compounded quarterly, the *effective* annual rate, or the rate actually being

TABLE 5-7

Step 1:	Clear calculator [f] [CLX]
Step 2:	[f] [5]
Step 3:	Effective annual rate

PRESS

[.] [1] [0] $\begin{bmatrix} E \\ N \\ T \\ E \\ R \end{bmatrix}$ [4] ÷

[4] [Yˣ]]

Answer: .10380 or 10.38%

Note: [f] [5 will change the key function to 0.00000

earned, is 10.38 percent. The solution to this problem with the use of a calculator is presented in Table 5-7.

ROLE OF INFLATION IN FINANCIAL CALCULATIONS

Frequently, it is important to take into consideration the effect of inflation in making decisions about future income needs. For instance, suppose Bob Smith wishes to receive $36,000 a year ($3,000 a month) in today's dollars at the beginning of each year for the next five years. Bob assumes that the rate of inflation over this period will be five percent a year and that he will be able to generate an after-tax return of eight percent on his investments. He wants to know from his financial planner how much money he should invest *now* to meet with his objective.

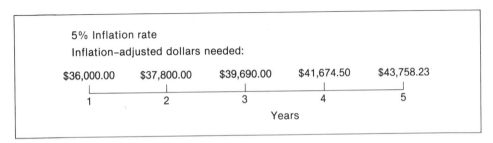

FIGURE 5-9   Impact of inflation on future income needs

TABLE 5-8

Step 1:   Identify key variables:
          Payment: $36,000
          Interest: 8% after-tax return
          Number of period: 5 years
          Inflation rate (r):   5%

Step 2:   Clear calculator [f] [CLX]

Step 3:   Enter data
          Press   [g]   [7]
                    [3]   [6]   [0]   [0]   [0] [PMT]
          Note*   [1]   [.]   [0]   [8]   [ENTER] [1]   [.]   [0]   [5]   [÷]

                    [1]   [-]   [1]   [0]   [0]   [X]   [i]
                    [5]   [n]
                    [PV]
          Answer: $170,273.94

Note: The following equation is used:

$$d = \frac{1 + i}{1 + r} - 1 \times 100$$

where d = inflation-adjusted interest rate
      i = after-tax interest rate
      r = inflation rate

Bob Smith's problem is graphically presented in Figure 5-9. The financial planner feeds this data into a HP-12C calculator and determines that Bob needs to invest $170,273.94 today in order to meet his objective. This calculation is presented in Table 5-8.

INTERNAL RATE OF RETURN

One of the most frequent questions asked by individuals relates to the internal rate of return on an investment. For instance, suppose Judy Kelly wishes to purchase 10, ten-year zero-coupon bonds for $250 each. Upon maturity, each bond will pay her $1,000, or a total of $10,000. She wants to know what would be the internal rate of return (IRR) on this investment, assuming that the tax consequences and cost of this investment are ignored.

The calculation of the IRR on this investment, presented in Table 5-9, shows that Judy Kelly will receive an annual return of 14.35 percent.

TABLE 5-9
_____

Step 1:   Identify known variables:
            Present values: $250 × 10 = $2,500
            Future: $1,000 × 10 = $10,000
            Number of periods: 10 years × semiannual (2)

Step 2:   Clear calculator [f] [CLX]

Step 3:   Enter data
            Press [2] [5] [0] [0] [CHS] [PV]
                        [1] [0] [0] [0]   [0]   [FV]
                        [2] [0] [n]
                        [i] [2] [x]
            Answer: 14.35%

PROBLEM SOLVING WITH THE HP-12C CALCULATOR

In this section we will demonstrate the use of a HP-12C calculator in solving different types of financial problems. For convenience, we will select problems from each of the six key areas of financial planning:

R: Risk Management Planning
E: Essentials of Budgeting, Savings, and Credit Planning
T: Tax Planning
I: Investment Planning
R: Retirement Planning
E: Estate Planning

RISK MANAGEMENT PLANNING

Problem I

John and Betty Storer came to you for risk management planning. An analysis of their finances produced the following result:

John Storer	
Amount of Current Life Insurance	$150,000
At John's Death	
Betty's Earned Income Per Month Available	$ 800
Income Per Month if Insurance Proceeds ($150,000) are invested at 8%	+$ 1,000
Total Dollars Per Month Available to Betty	$ 1,800
Monthly Income Betty Needs After John's Death	−$ 2,500
Monthly Shortfall for Betty	−$ 700

Betty is 55 years old and her life expectancy is 80. She wishes to ignore her Social Security payments. How much additional life insurance does John Storer need to purchase in order to provide Betty the additional $700 of monthly income if he were to die today?

Solution I

The problem should be stated as follows: What is the present value of an ordinary annuity (at the end of each month) which invested at, say, eight percent, will produce a monthly income of $700 for 25 years (Betty's life expectancy of 80 less her current age of 55)?

$$PVA = PMT \times PVAF$$
$$= \$700 \times 129.56453$$
$$= \$90,695.17$$

Thus, John should purchase $91,000 (rounded off to nearest $1,000) worth of additional life insurance.

The solution to this problem by the use of a HP-12C calculator is presented in Table 5-10.

Problem II

As a financial planner you have recommended that your client purchase a $3,500 a month disability insurance policy, which costs $3,000. The client, Rita Harris, who is 45 years old, is shocked to learn that a $3,500 policy would cost her $3,000, and has summarily rejected your recommendation. Your task is to explain to Rita the *true* value of the policy you have recommended for purchase.

TABLE 5-10

Step 1:	Identify known variables:
	Payment: $700/monthly
	Interest: 8%
	Number of periods: 25 years
Step 2:	Clear calculator [f] [CLX]
Step 3:	Enter data
	Press [7] [0] [0] [PMT]
	[8] [.] [g] [i]
	[2] [5] [g] [n]
	[PV]
	Answer: $90,695.17

Note: [g] [i] makes adjustment for monthly interest calculations.
          [g] [n] makes adjustment for number of periods (not number of years) calculations.

Solution II

The problem should be stated as follows: What is the present value of an annuity which, invested at, say, seven percent, will produce a monthly income of $3,500 for 20 years? You should explain to Rita that (1) the disability income is paid monthly, while the premium is paid annually; (2) if disabled today, the company will make *monthly* payments for 20 years until Rita reaches age 65; and (3) disability payments are completely tax-free. The present value of the disability policy is $451,438.77 as shown by Table 5-11. You can now point out that, by paying $3,500 today, Rita would purchase a *potential* value of $451,438.77.

TABLE 5-11

Step 1:	Identify known variables:
	Payment: $3,500/monthly
	Interest: 7%
	Number of payments: 20 years
Step 2:	Clear calculator [f] [CLX]
Step 3:	Enter data
	Press [3] [5] [0] [0] [PMT]
	[7] [.] [g] [i]
	[2] [0] [g] [n]
	[PV]
	Answer: $451,438.77

ESSENTIALS OF BUDGETING, SAVINGS, AND CREDIT PLANNING

Problem III

John Jones has approached you with a budgetary problem. He is financing the purchase of a new car with a three-year loan at 10.5 percent annual interest, compounded monthly. The purchase price of the car is $7,250. His down payment is $1,500. What are his monthly payments to be made at the end of every month?

Solution III

It is best to set this problem up as such:

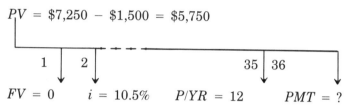

$$PV = \$7,250 - \$1,500 = \$5,750$$

$$FV = 0 \qquad i = 10.5\% \qquad P/YR = 12 \qquad PMT = ?$$

Using Eq. 5-5A we have

$$PVA = PMT \times PVAF$$

$$\text{or } PMT = PVA/PVAF$$

$$= \$5,750/30.767$$

$$= \$186.89$$

The use of the calculator in solving this problem is demonstrated in Table 5-12.

TABLE 5-12

Step 1:	Identify known variables:	
	Present value:	$5,750
	Interest:	10.5%
	Number of periods:	3 years
Step 2:	Clear calculator [f] [CLX]	
Step 3:	Enter data	
	Press [5]	[7] [5] [0] [CHS] [PV]
	[1]	[0] [.] [5] [g] [i]
	[3]	[g] [n]
	[PMT]	
	Answer: $186.89	

Problem IV

Let us assume that in Problem III John Jones informs you that he cannot pay more than $177 per month. What is the interest rate he can afford to pay if he wishes to purchase this car?

Solution IV

You could ask John Jones to shop around for a specific interest rate which would reduce his monthly payment to, say, $176.89 (i.e., $10 less than the current monthly payment).

Using Eq. 5-5A,

$$PVA = PMT \times PVAF$$

$$\$5,750 = \$176.89 \times PVAF$$

$$PVAF = 32.51$$

The interest rate associated with the PVAF of 32.51 is 6.75 percent. Therefore, John can purchase this car for $7,250 provided he can find a bank which offers him an interest rate of 6.75 percent. Of course, if such a low interest rate cannot be found, John would have to find a cheaper car or make a larger down payment.

The solution to this problem with the use of a HP-12C calculator is presented in Table 5-13.

TABLE 5-13

Step 1:	Identify known variables
	Present value: $5,750
	Future value: $0
	Payments: $176.89/month
	Number of periods: 3 years
Step 2:	Clear calculator [f] [CLX]
Step 3:	Enter data
	[5] [7] [5] [0] [PV]
	[1] [7] [6] [.] [8] [9] [CHS] [PMT]
	[3] [g] [n]
	[i]
	$\left.\begin{matrix} E \\ N \\ T \\ E \\ R \end{matrix}\right]$ [12] [x]
	Answer: 6.75%

Problem V

Dick Shaft has just joined the brokerage firm of A. M. Merrill. They have offered Dick two different salary arrangements. He can have $50,000 per year for the next three years, or $25,000 per year for the next three years, along with a $50,000 initial bonus today. Dick wants to know which alternative is best for him. He wants to use an interest rate of 16 percent, compounded quarterly.

Solution V

Step 1. First, we need to calculate the effective annual rate so the rate will be on the same basis as the payments. The effective annual rate is 16.986 percent, as shown below:

$$EAR = (1 + r_{nom/m})^m - 1.0$$
$$= (1 + .16/4)^4 - 1.0 \qquad \text{Eq. 5-10 restated}$$
$$= .16986 = 16.986\%$$

Step 2. The *PV* of $50,000 for three years with $r = 16.986$ percent is $110,504.31.

$$PVA = PMT \times PVAF$$
$$= \$50,000 \times 2.2100862$$
$$= \$110,504.31$$

Step 3. The *PV* of $25,000 for 3 years is $55,252.16.

Step 4. The total value of option 2, which includes an immediate bonus of $50,000, is only $105,252.16 ($55,252.16 + $50,000.00). Consequently, the first option of $50,000 per year for 3 years is more desirable.

The solution to this problem with the use of a HP-12C calculator is presented in Table 5-14.

Problem VI

Sam Johnson, your valued client, wants to purchase a home. He can make a down payment of $12,000 and can afford a monthly payment of $630. The interest rate on a 30-year fixed mortgage is 11.5 percent. How much mortgage on this house can Sam afford?

TABLE 5-14

Step 1:	Clear calculator [f] [CLX]
Step 2:	[f] [5]
Step 3:	Effective annual rate

Press [.] [1] [6] $\left[\begin{array}{c} E \\ N \\ T \\ E \\ R \end{array}\right]$ [4] [÷]

[4] [Yˣ]

Answer = .16986 or 16.986%

Step 4:	Press [5] [0] [0] [0] [0] [PMT]
	[1] [6] [.] [9] [8] [6] [i]
	[3] [n]
	[PV]

Answer: $110,504.31

Step 5:	Press [2] [5] [0] [0] [0] [PMT]
	[1] [6] [.] [9] [8] [6] [i]
	[3] [n]
	[PV]
	[5] [0] [0] [0] [0] [+]

Answer: $105,252.16

Step 6:	Option I (Step 4) = $110,504.32
	Option II (Step 5) = $105,252.16
	Option I is better.

Note: [f] [5] will change the key function to 0.00000

Solution VI

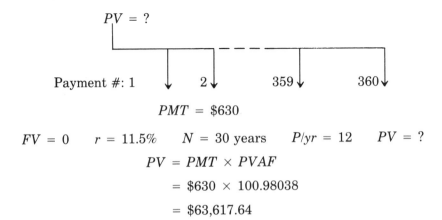

$$PV = ?$$

Payment #: 1   2   359   360

$$PMT = \$630$$

$$FV = 0 \quad r = 11.5\% \quad N = 30 \text{ years} \quad P/yr = 12 \quad PV = ?$$

$$PV = PMT \times PVAF$$

$$= \$630 \times 100.98038$$

$$= \$63{,}617.64$$

TABLE 5-15

Step 1:	Identify known variables	
	Payment:	$630/monthly
	Interest:	11.5%
	Number of payments:	30 years
Step 2:	Clear calculator [f] [CLX]	
Step 3:	Enter data	
	Press	
	[6] [3] [0] [CHS] [PMT]	
	[1] [1] [.] [5] [g] [i]	
	[3] [0] [g] [n]	
	[PV]	
	[Add $12,000 down payment] [1] [2] [0] [0] [0] [+]	
	Answer: $75,617.64	

Clearly, a monthly payment of $630 for 30 years will be sufficient to purchase a home valued at $63,617.64. However, since Sam can make a down payment of $12,000, he can afford a home valued at $75,617.64 ($63,617.64 + $12,000.00).

The solution to this problem with the use of the calculator is presented in Table 5-15.

TAX PLANNING

Problem VII

Joan Pace, one of your valued clients in the 28 percent tax bracket, is excited about investing $100,000 in a tax shelter. Basically, she is a risk averse person; however she wants to purchase this tax shelter because of the 90 percent write-off she will receive from it for the next five years. She has asked you to calculate how much money she will have accumulated at the end of five years as a result of these write-offs.

Solution VII

Assuming that Betty is correct in her assumption about the write-off, the key facts are listed here:

| Total investment: | $100,000 |
| Write-off (90%): | $90,000/year for 5 years |

TABLE 5-16

Step 1:	Identify known variables	
	Payment:	$25,200/year
	Interest:	9%
	Number of periods:	5 years
Step 2:	Clear calculator [f] [CLX]	
Step 3:	Enter data	
	Press [2] [5] [2] [0] [0] [PMT]	
	[9] [i]	
	[5] [n]	
	[FV]	
	Answer: $150,814.71	

At her marginal tax bracket of 28 percent, Betty's tax savings are $25,200 at the end of each year (28% of $90,000) for five years. So the question is this: What is the future value of a $25,200 annuity for five years? Let us assume the interest rate to be used in this case is nine percent:

$$FV = PMT \times FVAF$$

$$= \$25,200 \times 5.9847107$$

$$= \$150,814.71$$

The solution is also presented in Table 5-16. Incidentally, as her financial planner you should explain to Joan that the tax write-offs are not guaranteed and that these tax savings are merely deferred taxes which become due when the tax shelter is liquidated.

INVESTMENT PLANNING

Problem VIII

Sheldon Blair learned from his broker that the AAA-rated, XYZ bond, which has a coupon of ten percent and a ten-year maturity, is completely risk-free. However, he became totally confused when he attended one of your seminars in which you pointed out that even AAA bonds are subject to market interest rate risks. Sheldon is visiting with you and is anxious to find out if you are correct in your assertion.

Solution VIII

First, you should assure Sheldon that the interest-rate risk is totally different from the possibility that the company would miss a coupon payment

---

TABLE 5-17

Step 1:	Identify known variables	
	Future value:	$1,000
	Payment:	$100/year
	Interest:	12 percent × semiannual (0.5)
	Number of periods:	10 years × semiannual (2)
Step 2:	Clear calculator [f] [CLX]	
Step 3:	Enter data	
	Press [1] [0] [0] [0] [FV]	
	[5] [0] [PMT]	
	[6] [i]	
	[2] [0] [n]	
	[PV]	
	Answer: $883.30	

---

or would not pay the face value upon maturity. Next, you present the information given in Table 5-17. In this table, you demonstrate that if the market interest rate immediately rises to 12 percent, the price of the AAA-bond would drop to $883.30—a loss of $116.70. That is, if the interest rate rises to 12 percent today and Sheldon is forced to sell the bond, assuming the bond market to be efficient he would incur a loss of $116.70 despite the fact that the bond represents a *safe* investment.

Problem IX

One of the commonly asked investment planning questions of financial planners relates to educational planning. Let us assume that Linda Garrison's son just turned five today, and she plans to save for his college education by making equal semiannual deposits in an investment account which pays a stated rate equal to 9.1 percent compounded semiannually, with the first deposit to be made immediately. Linda wants to provide $24,000 per year for four years after he turns 18. Linda wants to know how much money she should deposit twice a year until her son is 18 (13 years, or 26 deposits).

Solution IX

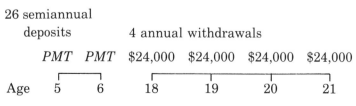

This problem needs to be solved in three steps.

Step 1. The effective rate is:

$$EAR = (1 + 9.1/2)^2 - 1$$

$$= 9.31\%$$

Step 2. At age 18, the value of four withdrawals at 9.31 percent is:

$$PV = PMT \times PVAF$$

$$= \$24,000 \times 3.2178$$

$$= \$77,227.14$$

Table 5-18

Step 1:	Clear calculator [f] [CLX]
Step 2:	Enter data
	Press [·] [0] [9] [·] [1] [ENTER] [2] [÷]
	[1] [+]
	[1] [·] [0] [4] [5] [5] [X]
	[1] [−]
	Answer: 9.31%
Step 3:	Enter data
	Press [2] [4] [0] [0] [0] [CHS] [PMT]
	[9] [·] [3] [1] [i]
	[4] [n]
	[PV]
	Answer: $77,227.14
Step 4:	Enter data
	Press
	[7] [7] [2] [2] [7] [·] [1] [4] [FV]
	[9] [·] [1] [ENTER] [2] [÷] [i]
	[1] [3] [ENTER] [2] [X] [n]
	[PMT]
	Answer: $1,611.86

Note: Since semiannual deposits are made, 9.1%/2 is used rather than the effective annual rate of 9.31%.

Step 3. To achieve the educational funding goal, the future value of the deposits at age 18 must equal $77,227.14. Therefore, the semiannual deposits required are:

$$FV = PMT \times FVAF$$

$$\$77,227.14 = PMT \times 47.911816$$

$$PMT = \$1,611.86$$

In this case, Linda would have to make a semiannual deposit of $1,611.86 earning 9.1 percent interest so she would be able to provide $24,000 per year for four years to finance her son's education when he turns 18.

The calculator-generated solution is presented in Table 5-18.

Problem X

Bob Sweet is ecstatic about an investment he bought three years ago for $5,000. Since he claims that in this short period his gain is almost 100 percent, Bob wants to buy more of this investment. As a financial planner, your task is to demonstrate to him the *true* annual return on this investment, given the fact that the current market value of this investment is $8,000.

Solution X

The compounded annual return of this investment can be calculated by

$$FV = PV \times FVFF$$

$$\$8,000 = 5,000 \times 1.6$$

The interest rate associated with 1.6 for three years is 16.96 percent. The calculator-generated solution is presented in Table 5-19.

TABLE 5-19

Step 1:	Identify known variables
	Present value: $5,000
	Future value: $8,000
	Number of periods: 3 years
Step 2:	Clear calculator [f] [CLX]
Step 3:	Enter data
	[5] [0] [0] [0] [CHS] [PV]
	[8] [0] [0] [0] [FV]
	[3] [n]
	[i]
	Answer: 16.96%

RETIREMENT PLANNING

Problem XI

You have recently been introduced to a young executive named Sam Dunn who wants you to engage in retirement planning. He wants to invest $5,000 per year at an effective annual rate of return (EAR) of nine percent for the next 30 years, with the first deposit beginning on his thirtieth birthday. Beginning at age 60 he will tour around the world for five years, and he will need a large sum each year to accomplish that objective. After Sam completes this tour, he would like to receive an annual income of $30,000 per year for the next 15 years. Assuming an EAR of nine percent for the entire time period, what is the maximum amount of capital Sam can spend on his world tour?

Solution XI

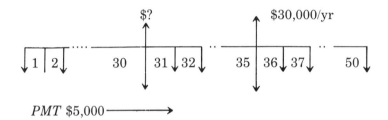

This problem should be broken down into four steps.

Step 1. Value of annual investments of age 60:

$$FVA = PMT \times FVAF$$
$$= \$5,000 \times 136.3075$$
$$= \$681,537.69$$

Sam will have accumulated $681,537.69 by age 60.

Step 2. The PV of $30,000 in annual payments for 15 years, starting with year 36 (age 65) is:

$$PVA = PMT \times PVAF$$
$$= \$30,000 \times 8.0606883$$
$$= \$241,820.65$$

Step 3. The PV of $241,820.65 at age 60, discounted for five years at nine percent, is:

$$PV = FV \times PVAF$$

$$= \$241,820.65 \times .6499313$$

$$= \$157,166.83$$

Step 4. Therefore, Sam should be able to spend the difference between what he would have at age 60 and the amount he would need to generate current income starting at age 65. Specifically,

Amount accumulated by age 60 = $681,537.69

Amount needed to generate income at age 65 = $157,166.83

Amount available for world trip = $524,370.86

The calculator-based solution is presented in Table 5-20.

TABLE 5-20

Step 1:	Clear calculator [f] [CLX]
Step 2: Press	[5] [0] [0] [0] [CHS] [PMT]
	[9] [i]
	[3] [0] [n]
	[FV]
Answer:	$681,537.69
Step 3:	[0] [FV]
Step 4: Press	[3] [0] [0] [0] [0] [PMT]
	[9] [i]
	[1] [5] [n]
	[PV]
Answer:	$241,820.65
Step 5: Press	[2] [4] [1] [8] [2] [0] [·] [6] [5] [FV]
	[9] [i]
	[5] [n]
	[PV]
Answer:	$157,166.83
Step 6:	Sam should be able to spend
	$681,537.69
	−$157,166.83
	$524,370.86

Problem XII

John VanZandt, one of your valued clients, has been asked by his company to choose between a retirement payout of $500,000 and a lifetime annuity of $5,000 a month. He is impressed by the half-a-million-dollar lump sum payment, but his wife wants him to go for the annuity offer. John trusts you completely, and will accept your recommendation. What is your recommendation?

Solution XII

It is important to explain to John at the outset that the solution to this problem can be found only if certain specific assumptions are made. After much discussion, you make the following assumptions:

1. John's life expectancy is 82. That is, since he is 65 years old, you will assume that the annuity will pay him for 17 years, or a total payment for 204 (17 × 12) months.

2. If John receives a lump sum, he will be able to obtain a compounded annual return of eight percent, which translates into a monthly return of 0.6667 percent (8/12).

3. You will ignore the tax consequences of these payments.

The solution to this problem is presented in Table 5-21. Based on your findings, you recommend that John choose the lifetime annuity payment option.

TABLE 5-21

Step 1:		Clear calculator [f] [CLX]				
Step 2:	Press	[g]	[8]			
		[5]	[0]	[0]	[0]	[PMT]
		[8]	[g]	[i]		
		[1]	[7]	[g]	[n]	
		[PV]				
	Answer:	$556,633.67				

Step 3: The present value of the annuity payments exceeds the lump sum distribution by:

$$\begin{array}{r} \$556,633.67 \\ -\$500,000.00 \\ \hline \$\ 56,633.67 \end{array}$$

Consequently, given the specified assumptions, the annuity payments are better. Of course, the situation could be reversed under a different set of assumptions.

ESTATE PLANNING

Problem XIII

Your client, Shirley Jones, is 40 years old and is in excellent health. Her husband, Jim, is also 40 and is paralyzed for life. Shirley holds a good position and believes that she will be able to take care of Jim until she retires at age 70. However, she fears that she might die soon thereafter and no one else would look after Jim.

Shirley wants to create a revocable trust for the benefit of Jim. She will start putting money into this trust right away and hopes that it will have a value of $1 million when she reaches age 70. Upon her death, the entire amount will be transferred to Jim, and because of a marital deduction, no estate taxes will be due on this transfer. Shirley believes that she can obtain a compounded annual return of eight percent (after-tax) and wants to know how much she should invest at the beginning of each month to achieve her objective.

Solution XIII

The solution to this problem is presented in Table 5-22. Shirley should invest $666.54 at the beginning of each month for 30 years to accomplish her goal.

In this chapter we have demonstrated the use of the concept of the time value of money and the HP-12C financial calculator in solving different types of financial problems. In the next chapter we will undertake a comprehensive analysis of the issues involving budgetary, savings, and credit planning.

TABLE 5-22

Step 1:	Identify known variables	
	Future value:	$1,000,000
	Interest rate:	8%
	Number of periods:	30 years
Step 2:	Clear calculator [f] [CLX]	
Step 3:	Enter data	
	Press [g] [7]	
	[1] [0][0][0][0][0][0] [FV]	
	[8] [g] [i]	
	[3] [0][g][n]	
	[PMT]	
	Answer: $666.54/month	

CHAPTER 6

Budgetary, Savings, Credit, and Debt Planning

INTRODUCTION

In the last few years, financial planning has come of age. And yet, most people have only a vague idea of how they stack up financially. The reason is not hard to find. Given the constant barrage of bad financial news in the media, most Americans worry about inflation, rising health care costs, college tuition, safety of savings, and complexities of the ever-changing tax laws. A national survey conducted in 1987 by the International Association for Financial Planning discovered that by 2 to 1, consumers say their net worth is not what they would like it to be. The sluggish economy is making it hard for them to save, now and in the future. And two out of five people fear, above all else, that they would outlive the funds earmarked for retirement. To put it succinctly, most people are making more money than ever before but claim they are not making much progress in getting ahead.

This pervasive sense of financial unease reflects the haphazard approach the average person takes where money matters are concerned. Some find even filing income tax returns overwhelming, let alone the construction of net worth statements over a period of time which would document their financial progress on a systematic basis. Others confuse documentation of each little expense with budget planning. Clearly, the problem is that most people do not run their personal affairs like a business which routinely draws up at least an annual income statement and a balance sheet.

In this chapter we will discuss issues relating to budgetary, savings, credit, and debt planning. More specifically, in the first part we will analyze the techniques of net worth and cash management planning. Systematic savings planning techniques will be presented in the next part. Finally, in the last part we will discuss the issues relating to credit and debt planning. Also, various methods for calculating different types of interest rates will be presented in the appendix to this chapter.

NET WORTH AND CASH MANAGEMENT PLANNING

NET WORTH PLANNING

The Basic Concept

The objective of net worth planning is far more ambitious than merely constructing a net worth statement. Net worth planning involves the calculation of current net worth, setting a net worth goal for next year, and developing specific strategies for meeting that goal. The main reasons for undertaking net worth planning are to: (1) establish financial discipline; (2) organize a financial life around a future target; (3) measure financial progress on a regular basis; and (4) feel financially secure about the future. Clearly, the starting point of net worth planning is the calculation of net worth.

Calculation of Net Worth

For an individual or family, net worth is the basic measure of financial health. It is the total fair market value of all assets owned, such as a house, stocks, bonds, and other securities, minus all outstanding liabilities owed, such as mortgage and revolving-credit loans. Simply stated, net worth is the amount by which assets exceed liabilities at a specific point in time.

The process of calculating net worth begins with pulling together the relevant financial records. These include the latest tax records, bank statements, cancelled checks, credit card information, other itemized living expenses, brokerage account and mutual fund records, mortgage payments, real estate closing records, insurance policies indicating free market value of personal property, pension account records, and loan repayment schedules for automobile and other articles purchased on credit. Coming up with all of this

TABLE 6-1 Statement of Net Worth

Assets			Liabilities		
Items	Current value	%	Items	Current value	%
I. LIQUID ASSETS			I. SHORT-TERM		
1. Cash and Checking Accounts	———		1. Current Bills	———	
2. Savings Accounts	———		2. Credit Cards	———	
3. Credit Union	———		3. Installment Loans	———	
4. Money Market Funds	———		4. Other	———	
5. TOTAL (1-4)	———		5. TOTAL (1-4)	———	
II. INVESTMENT ASSETS			II. LONG-TERM		
A. SHORT-TERM			1. Mortgage	———	
1. CDs	———		2. Life Insurance Loans	———	
2. Treasury Bills	———		3. Borrowing from Qualified Plans	———	
3. Cash Value-Life Insurance	———		4. Loans to Purchase Investment	———	
4. Other	———		5. Other	———	
5. TOTAL (A1-4)	———		6. TOTAL (1-5)	———	
B. LONG-TERM			III. NET WORTH (Total Assets minus Total Liabilities)	———	
(i) *Equity*					
1. Common/Preferred Stock	———				
2. Mutual Funds—Stock	———				
3. IRA-Stock	———				
4. Pension/Profit Sharing-Stock	———				
5. Other	———				
6. TOTAL (B-i-1-5)	———				

(ii) *Debt*
1. CDs-Long-Term
2. Corporate/Government/ Muni. Bonds
3. IRA-Bonds
4. Pension/Profit Sharing- Bonds
5. Other
6. TOTAL (B-ii-1-5)

(iii) *Miscellaneous*
1. Limited Partnerships
2. Tangible Assets
3. Business Ownership
4. Real Estate (ex. Residence)
5. Other
6. TOTAL (B-iii-1-5)

III. PERSONAL ASSETS
1. Residence/Vacation Home
2. Automobiles
3. Personal Property
4. Other
5. TOTAL (1-4)

Total Assets   100

Total Liabilities & Net Worth   100

documentation may seem daunting, but is essential for net worth planning. We will shortly learn that these records not only help us calculate net worth but also lay the foundation for risk management savings, credit, debt, investment, tax, retirement, and estate planning.

The statement of net worth, presented in Table 6-1, has several important features. First, assets are categorized as liquid, investment, or personal assets. Second, investment assets are further classified as short-term and long-term. Third, long-term assets are termed equity, debt, or miscellaneous assets. Fourth, liabilities are categorized as short-term or long-term. Once the statement has been completed, subtracting total liabilities from total assets would provide the net worth figure for the family as of a given date.

The Planning Strategy

The net worth figure just derived provides the basis for developing an appropriate net worth planning strategy. If the net worth figure is negative, which is not only possible but in some cases quite likely, it does not necessarily mean that the family is on the verge of declaring bankruptcy. It does mean, however, that particular attention should be paid to developing more aggressive strategies for debt reduction, higher investment return, and revised goal setting.

Simply having a positive net worth does not mean financial planning ends; it represents a unique planning opportunity. More specifically, a positive net worth figure at the end of a given year (or at any other given time period) should be compared with that of the previous year. If the annual rate of growth in net worth meets the prespecified target, consideration should be given either to maintain the existing rate of growth or to devise improved strategies for accelerating the rate of growth to a higher level. If, however, the current rate of growth in net worth falls short of the target set by the family, a conscious effort should be made either to develop new strategies for correcting the situation or to set a more realistic net worth goal.

Before leaving this topic it should be mentioned that there is little benefit to calculating net worth unless it is done on at least an *annual* basis. For only then can one tell if the savings, credit, investment, and other related programs measure up to the short- and long-term financial objectives set by the family.

CASH MANAGEMENT PLANNING

The Basic Concept

The net worth statement determines the value of assets and liabilities taken at one point in time, whereas a cash flow statement paints a picture of the cash flow over a period of time not exceeding one year. It should now be clear that the only way net worth can grow is to have a positive net cash flow or savings. Savings are positive when the annual cash inflow exceeds the annual cash outflow. And that is precisely the basis for using cash management planning as a dynamic financial planning tool. If total savings during a given year do not measure up to the level necessary to achieve the targeted growth in net worth, then positive actions are called for to correct the situation. Such actions can take the form of reduction of expenses, increase in income, or a combination of both. If, however, these strategies fail to generate sufficient income, the family may have to reevaluate the net worth goal. Furthermore, even in those cases where adequate savings are being generated, cash management planning can help a family set a higher net worth target and then meet that target by generating larger savings.

Essentially, for families with inadequate savings, the techniques for improving the prevailing cash flow situation consist of (1) cash outflow control; (2) debt restructuring; and (3) asset repositioning. The first technique requires the development of some restraints in consumption with the ultimate objective of instituting a workable, long-term plan of expenditure control. Debt restructuring techniques may take the form of (1) paying off all outstanding credit card balances by consolidating all such debt into one low-interest, personal line of credit; (2) refinancing the personal residence; (3) discontinuation of credit cards; and (4) deferring the purchase of big ticket items. Finally, the strategy of repositioning assets could mean the improvement of cash flow through postponing the purchase of (1) *nonessential* consumer items (such as a boat or fur coat); (2) non-income-producing investments like gold and coins; and (3) negative cash flow properties, such as leveraged real estate and other limited partnerships requiring long-term periodic payments. The three cash management techniques—namely, cash outflow control, debt restructuring, and asset repositioning—will be discussed in detail later in this chapter.

Preparation of Cash Flow Statement

As in the case of net worth planning, the starting point of cash management planning is the preparation of a cash flow statement, which is presented in Table 6-2. For those who maintain a regular budget, or who currently budget cash flow, filling out the statement should present little problem. For others who do not maintain a budget, checkbook, savings, and money market account registers can provide a record of historical cash receipts and expenditures. Using this as a starting point, annual cash inflow and outflow figures can be estimated by *guessing* at monthly amounts. Although not quite accurate, these "guesstimates" are adequate for providing the necessary data for undertaking cash flow planning.

Analysis of Cash Flow Statement

As mentioned, the primary motivation for undertaking cash management planning is to determine the adequacy of savings to meet the desired growth

TABLE 6-2   Statement of Cash Flow

Inflow		*Outflow*	
	Amount		*Amount*
I. SOURCES, BEFORE TAX		I. FIXED EXPENSES	
1. Salary-Husband	_____	A. FAMILY NEEDS	
2. Salary-Wife	_____	1. Food	_____
3. Self Employment	_____	2. Clothing	_____
4. Divided/Interest	_____	3. Auto	_____
5. Capital Gains/	_____	4. Other	_____
Losses		5. TOTAL (1-4)	_____
6. Rents/Annuities/	_____		
Pension		B. HOME	
7. Bonus/Gift/Misc.	_____	1. Mortgage	_____
Income		2. Insurance	_____
8. Alimony/Child	_____	3. Utilities	_____
Support		4. Tax	_____
9. TOTAL (1-8)	_____	5. TOTAL (1-4)	_____
II. TAXES		C. INSURANCE PREMIUMS	
1. Federal	_____	1. Life	_____
2. State	_____	2. Disability	_____
3. Local	_____	3. Health	_____
4. Social Sec./	_____	4. Auto	_____
Disability		5. Liability	_____
5. TOTAL (1-4)	_____	6. TOTAL (1-5)	_____
III. INFLOW, AFTER		D. OTHER DEBTS	
TAX (I minus II)	_____	1. Installment	_____
		Loans	
		2. Charge	_____
		Accounts	
		3. Other	_____
		4. TOTAL (1-3)	_____
		II. FLEXIBLE EXPENSES	
		A. FAMILY NEEDS	
		1. Vacation	_____
		2. Entertainment	_____
		3. Gifts	_____
		4. Other	_____
		5. TOTAL (1-4)	_____
		B. EDUCATION	
		1. Tuition	_____
		2. Other Expenses	_____
		3. TOTAL (1-2)	_____

TABLE 6-2 (continued)

Inflow		Outflow	
	Amount		Amount
		C. MAJOR APPLIANCES & EXPENDITURES	
		1. Appliances	_____
		2. Other	_____
		3. TOTAL (1-2)	_____
		D. MISCELLANEOUS	
		1. Charity	_____
		2. Other	_____
		3. TOTAL (1-2)	_____
		III. TOTAL SAVINGS (Total Inflow minus Total Outflow)	_____
TOTAL INFLOW	_____	TOTAL OUTFLOW & SAVINGS	_____

in net worth. For better results, the net worth growth target can be further refined by setting up investment, educational funding, and retirement goals. An integral part of achieving financial goals is to have adequate funds which can be earmarked for achieving these goals. Cash management planning can help one achieve these goals in a systematic and efficient manner.

Cash management planning can also be used to develop an important diagnostic tool. For instance, if currently negative savings are being generated, a close scrutiny of flexible and fixed expenses can be undertaken to determine how the current situation can be reversed. The cash flow diagnostic tool can also be used to identify areas of *excess* spending so the spending patterns can be restructured to bring down the cash outflow to a more desirable level.

Systematic Savings Planning

As a general rule, the majority of people who maintain a monthly budget consider it to be their primary target. We have clearly demonstrated that preparing a monthly budget is only a means toward achieving a much broader, and a far more valuable, objective. The key to long-range financial success is the development of a systematic savings planning strategy. This strategy refers to the development of specific plans which can: (1) generate the required savings; and (2) systematically direct these savings toward the targeted areas so the specific financial goals can be achieved.

SYSTEMATIC SAVINGS PLANNING

INTRODUCTION

The construction of a net worth statement together with a cash flow statement is not an end in itself. These statements provide the basis for undertaking effective financial analysis. Most Americans dream of owning a home and a cottage on the lake, sending their children to private universities, enjoying vacations in exotic places, accumulating a large estate, and achieving financial independence before the age of 50. However, a number of national surveys show that these are vague aspirations rather than clearly articulated objectives. Planning in the areas of net worth, savings, cash management, and credit converts these aspirations into well-thought-out objectives. In this section we will discuss the essentials of systematic savings planning.

THE STARTING POINT

As mentioned, systematic savings planning begins with net worth planning. This is because the annual rate of growth of net worth determines the rate at which savings should be generated. This point requires elaboration.

Let us assume John Client has a net worth of $750,000 and he wishes it to grow annually by a predetermined rate. John can achieve his objective only if savings increase at an accelerated pace. This fact is clearly revealed by Table 6-3. For instance, starting with a base of $750,000, if John wants his net worth to grow by ten percent a year, he would have to generate a positive savings of $75,000 during the first year—a formidable target indeed. Even more serious is the fact that during the fifth year savings must equal $109,000 if the ten percent growth rate in net worth is to continue. By comparison, a base of

TABLE 6-3 John Client: Net Worth Planning

	Current	Year 1	Year 2	Year 3	Year 4	Year 5
Target: Annual Growth: 5% ('000) Projected						
Net Worth	$750	$787.5	$826.9	$868.2	$911.6	$957.2
Additional Savings Required	—	+37.5	+39.4	+41.3	+43.4	+45.6
Target: Annual Growth: 10%						
Net Worth	$750	$825	$907	$998	$1,098	$1,207
Additional Savings Required	—	+75	+82	+91	+100	+109

$400,000 would require additional savings of $40,000 during the first year and larger amounts in subsequent years if the net worth is expected to grow by ten percent, still a big challenge for most Americans. It is therefore desirable to set a *realistic* target for the growth of the net worth, so the family does not despair and give up savings planning altogether.

GOAL SETTING

Setting the overall savings target begins the systematic savings planning process at the macro level. However, it is the micro-level strategies which are at the heart of systematic savings planning.

Positive savings increases net worth in one of three ways: an increase in assets, a decrease in liabilities, or a combination of both. It is therefore important for the family to give due consideration to setting its goals in both areas. A goal-setting worksheet is presented in Table 6-4. This worksheet not only specifies the amount of savings needed to finance each of the stated objectives but also commits future savings to these objectives.

TABLE 6-4   Goal-Setting Worksheet

Goal	Amount needed $	Savings period: months	Expected after-tax return %	Monthly savings required $
I. Home				
II. Appliance				
III. Major Purchases				
1.				
2.				
3.				
4.				
IV. Vacation				
V. Education				
1.				
2.				
3.				
VI. Retirement				
VII. Charity				
VIII. Other _____				
Other _____				
Other _____				
TOTAL:	$ _____			$ _____

The next step in the goal-setting process is to calculate the amount of savings required to achieve each of the specific goals and record them in the last column. This task can be accomplished by using the future value annuity factor (FVAF) concept developed in Chapter 5. For instance, let us assume that the objective is to save $50,000 by the end of ten years to finance a child's education. If three percent compound interest can be earned on monthly savings net of inflation and taxes, and if money is saved at the end of every month, then by using HP-12C calculator we can determine that the monthly savings required to achieve this objective is $357.80, as shown in Table 6-5. The same technique can be used to determine the savings required for meeting other financial goals listed in Table 6-4.

The total *annual* savings required to meet all the stated objectives (Total Monthly Savings Required × 12 in Table 6-4) should now be compared with the total *annual* savings available (Item III of Outflow column in Table 6-2). If the available savings are greater than or equal to the savings required, consideration might be given to further improve the savings situation. If total available savings fall short of savings needs, however, specific steps must be taken to correct the problem.

Adequate Savings Scenario

Even when current savings are sufficient for meeting both short- and long-term financial goals and net worth growth targets, refinements in savings plans are still possible. That is because we have never been taught to treat savings as a fixed expense. Most of us do not recognize the idea that we must pay ourselves first in the form of savings in order to ensure our own financial security. The result is that normally we live up to our means and go into debt whenever we need replacement of big ticket items or have to meet a major financial crisis. Thus, a practical strategy in this case is to treat savings as a

---

TABLE 6-5

Step 1: Identify known variables
        Future value: $50,000
        Interest rate: 3%/12 months
        Number of periods: 10 years × 12 months

Step 2: Clear calculator [f] [CLX]

Step 3: Enter data
        Press
        [5] [0] [0] [0] [0] [FV]
        [3] [g] [i]
        [1] [0] [g] [n]
        [PMT]
        Answer: $357.80

fixed expense and not a residual amount after all other needs have been met. This strategy can help generate additional savings which, if properly channeled, could accelerate the rate of growth of net worth.

Inadequate Savings Scenario

If savings are inadequate to meet desired goals, drastic steps must be taken to bring savings up to the desired level. For convenience, these steps are divided into several broad categories.

Expense reduction. The first order of business is to carefully analyze current expenses. The main emphasis should be placed on those flexible expenses which can be successfully reduced without seriously affecting the desired lifestyle. These generally include personal expenses like clothing, personal care, and entertainment, but may also include the purchase of big ticket items, home remodeling, and expensive vacations. In addition to flexible expenses, it also pays to look for additional savings in the area of fixed expenses. With some effort, even some of the fixed expense items can be reduced without affecting basic comfort or lifestyle, although such a reduction in fixed expenses may require moving to a different location or into a smaller home.

A practical expense reduction strategy is to make a monthly estimate for each major expense category and then compare the estimate with the actual expense. If the *actual* expense for a given category consistently exceeds the *estimated* expense, then a conscious effort should be made to either reduce the actual expense or, if justifiable, increase the level of estimated expense. A convenient worksheet is presented in Table 6-6 which can be used to develop a meaningful expense reduction strategy.

Increase in income. There is a natural tendency for most people to assume that there will be only a certain amount of income flowing in, especially if the breadwinners earn salaried income. This is a mistake. In the following section we will discuss several ways in which nonsalaried income can be augmented even by those people who are employed by others.

Interest bearing investment. Returns on investments can be improved by selecting those investments which offer the highest consistent returns but have a risk level acceptable to the family. The income situation can also be improved by reducing the checking account balance to the minimum and shifting the rest of the liquid funds into higher-yielding money market funds and short-term certificates of deposit.

Enhanced investment return. The level of income can also be raised by reorganizing the investment portfolio, a detailed discussion of which will be undertaken in Chapter 11. At this time it would suffice merely to state some

TABLE 6-6 Expense Reduction Worksheet

Expenses	Jan.		Feb.		Mar.		Apr.		May		June		July		Aug.		Sept.		Oct.		Nov.		Dec.		ANNUAL		
	B	A	B	A	B	A	B	A	B	A	B	A	B	A	B	A	B	A	B	A	B	A	B	A	B	A	S/D
I. FIXED EXPENSES																											
A. FAMILY NEEDS																											
1. Food																											
2. Clothing																											
3. Auto																											
4. Other																											
5. TOTAL (1-4)																											
B. HOME																											
1. Mortgage																											
2. Insurance																											
3. Utilities																											
4. Tax																											
5. TOTAL (1-4)																											
C. INSURANCE PREMIUMS																											
1. Life																											
2. Disability																											
3. Health																											
4. Auto																											
5. Liability																											
6. TOTAL (1-5)																											
D. OTHER DEBTS																											
1. Installment Loans																											
2. Charge Accounts																											
3. Other																											
4. TOTAL (1-3)																											
II. FLEXIBLE EXPENSES																											
A. FAMILY NEEDS																											
1. Vacation																											
2. Entertainment																											
3. Gifts																											
4. Other																											
5. TOTAL (1-4)																											
B. EDUCATION																											
1. Tuition																											
2. Other Expenses																											
3. TOTAL (1-2)																											
C. MAJOR APPLIANCES & EXP																											
1. Appliances																											
2. Other																											
3. TOTAL (1-2)																											
D. MISCELLANEOUS																											
1. Charity																											
2. Other																											
3. TOTAL (1-2)																											

B: Budget   A: Annual   S/D: Surplus or Deficit

of the strategies which might assist a financial planner in accelerating the growth of investible funds or increasing the cash flow generated by these funds.

It is generally accepted that risk and reward are positively related. This means that an investor can obtain higher returns by moving the funds from low-risk to higher-risk investments. The success of this strategy, of course, depends on an accurate determination of the investor's risk tolerance level. The best strategy is to move the funds into those investments that are in the highest risk categories acceptable to the investor.

The second strategy is to become yield conscious. For instance, the annual return on a five-year, nine percent, certificate of deposit with quarterly compounding is 9.31 percent, but the same CD with daily compounding could yield as much as 9.42 percent. Similarly, yields on brokered CDs (discussed later) could be much higher than those offered by local banks.

The third strategy is to concentrate on tax savings. For instance, assume that an AAA-rated, ten-year corporate bond is currently yielding nine percent. Switching the money to a municipal bond of similar quality and maturity and yielding seven percent would increase the yield from nine percent to 9.7 percent, assuming a 28 percent tax bracket. Tax savings can also be realized by investing part of the money into limited partnerships which generate tax-sheltered cash flow, although the attendant risks of these investments should never be overlooked.

The fourth strategy is to convert a growth-oriented stock portfolio into an income-oriented stock portfolio or a bond portfolio. Typically, growth-oriented stock portfolios have low dividend yields. By moving such a portfolio into an income-oriented portfolio, the investor can increase current cash flow.

The final strategy relates to the switching of nonincome-producing investments, such as gold, coins, and antiques, into income-producing assets. These nonincome-producing investments are inappropriate for persons with cash flow problems, and substitution of income-producing assets like bonds and utility stocks can generate much-needed additional income.

EFFECTIVE SAVINGS STRATEGIES

There are several "common sense" types of strategies that help people save more. These are outlined next.

Goal Setting

Unrealistic goal setting is perhaps the most important reason for the failure of savings strategies. Imposition of a 20 percent a year savings goal on a family that is experiencing difficulty in making both ends meet is bound to fail. The best rule is to set a savings goal which the family does not consider onerous.

Self-Rewarding Plan

Saving for college education, retirement, vacation, or purchasing a big ticket item is a long and difficult undertaking. Consequently, if the family exceeds the targeted savings goal, it should reward itself by spending the extra savings. This will provide an added incentive for the family to meet the savings goal.

Savings-First Approach

We live in a consumption-oriented society where it is extremely easy to buy on credit. Few of us realize that our savings rate would dramatically increase if we avoided buying items on credit. The reason is that we would not only save the interest charges, but could also benefit from investing these savings.

Automatic Savings Plans

One of the painless ways of saving is to automatically deduct money right from the paycheck and invest it in an appropriate vehicle. Money saved this way has a tendency to grow to impressively large amounts to the surprise of everyone.

There are several vehicles available for implementing automatic savings plans. One of these is the Series EE savings bonds. If these bonds are held for five years or longer, the return will be based on the average yield of five-year treasury notes (9.0 percent in November, 1989). The yield cannot dip below a minimum rate—at the time of writing, six percent. Also, the interest is exempt from state and local taxes. Contribution to company qualified plans is the second method of instituting an automatic savings plan. A qualified plan can take the form of a pension, profit sharing, thrift, or 401(K) plan. Many plans allow participants to choose among various investments, including stock and fixed-income funds, company shares, and guaranteed investment contracts. Earnings in qualified investments grow tax-deferred until the money is withdrawn.

A third technique for instituting an automatic savings plan is to instruct the bank to automatically switch a fixed amount every month into one or more specified mutual funds in order to benefit from using the technique of dollar cost averaging. This will not only make the net worth grow faster, but will also help the saver achieve with greater ease the longer-term financial goals like educational funding and retirement.

EMERGENCY FUNDING STRATEGIES

Occasionally, even the best structured budgetary plans face temporary difficulties due to circumstances beyond our control. In these situations it might be necessary to tap liquid fund reserves which might have been saved for "a rainy day." Once these reserves are exhausted, however, it would be important to quickly raise some more liquid funds. While one should use extreme caution in tapping them, it is important to know some of the better known sources of emergency funds.

One of the best known sources of emergency funds is a home equity line of credit which is available in many states. Once the loan is approved, the homeowner can draw an amount equal to 70 or 80 percent of the home's market value. Such a loan, which cost around 12 percent in November 1989, is much cheaper than a personal loan. In addition, interest is fully tax-deductible on loans of up to $100,000. Of course, the homeowner should have the ability to make higher monthly payments. Another major source of cash is the accumulated cash value in a life insurance policy. Loans from life insurance policies issued prior to June 20, 1988, are completely tax-free and most insurance companies charge low interest rates on these loans.

A third source of funds is company savings plans. Many companies allow their employees to borrow against any vested profit sharing or company stock plan assets up to $10,000 and half of the rest, with a total limit of $50,000. Finally, money can be withdrawn from an IRA investment to meet a short-term emergency, as long as it is returned within the allowable 60 days.

CRITERIA FOR SAVINGS MEDIA SELECTION

Essentially, there are three reasons for savings: (1) to accumulate funds for meeting emergencies; (2) to have funds available for purchasing consumer items in the short run; and (3) for increasing net worth, which is often referred to as capital formation. As might be expected, savings strategies for the first two reasons are significantly different from those for capital formation. The reason is that the major emphasis for saving for the first two reasons is on popular liquid assets, whereas the main criterion for capital formation savings is long-term growth, for which the more traditional long-term investment vehicles are used.

We will now discuss the key issues relating to the selection of popular liquid assets. The more traditional, long-term investment vehicles will be discussed in Chapter 9.

There are six major criteria for determining where money should be saved: safety, liquidity, return on savings, simplicity and minimum balance requirements, special service features, and tax considerations.

Safety

At the present time, all national banks and many state banks are members of the Federal Deposit Insurance Corporation (FDIC). This means that the checking, savings, and certificate of deposit accounts maintained at these banks are insured against bank failure for up to $100,000 on *each* account. Similarly, savings and loan associations are insured for the same amount by the Federal Savings and Loan Insurance Corporation (FSLIC). Interestingly, by using various combinations of accounts (individual, joint, trust, revocable, and so on) in banks, and savings and loan associations, a typical family of four can insure up to $1.4 million. In addition to the deposits insured by various government agencies, savings put into various types of government bonds are completely safe. However, money market accounts at various brokerage firms and other financial institutions are neither insured nor completely safe.

Safety concerns were foremost on the minds of the American public when in 1988 widespread savings and loans association and bank failures were reported by the media. The Bush Administration quickly moved to institute a plan to bail out the failing institutions to ensure that no one lost their savings. However, this incident, labeled the "Savings and Loan Mess," has created deep concerns among the public, and it will be some time before confidence in savings institutions is fully restored.

Liquidity

If one desires to convert savings into cash quickly without losing the principal, checking and savings accounts in banks and credit unions as well as money market accounts provide a high degree of liquidity. In contrast, certificates of deposit provide higher interest rates but restrict withdrawal privileges. Similarly, the various types of U.S. government bonds lack complete liquidity in that an early conversion results in a partial loss of return.

Return on Savings

An important criterion in selecting a savings institution is the return it offers. Actually, the true return on savings depends not only upon the advertised rate, but also upon other considerations, including the type of account used for accumulating savings. This point requires elaboration.

Bank savings accounts. The most traditional of all bank savings accounts, which were previously called passbook accounts, form the backbone of bank savings. Until the interest rate ceiling was removed in April 1986, the maximum legally allowable rate on regular savings in federally insured institutions was 5.5 percent. However, even with the legal ceiling removed, most banks still pay only 5.5 percent on savings accounts.

Bank checking accounts. Contrary to commonly held belief, interest can be earned on checking accounts, but only if certain stated criteria are met. Generally, a *regular checking* account pays no interest and usually costs about $5.00 per month. This cost is generally waived by the bank if a minimum balance of $400 to $500 is maintained. In contrast, *NOW* (Negotiated Order of Withdrawal) accounts pay interest and also allow check withdrawals. Often they waive maintenance fees if a minimum balance of $1,000 is maintained. Another variety, popularly known as *MMDAs* (money market deposit accounts) are not full-fledged checking accounts because they limit the depositors not only to three checks and three preauthorized transfers per month, but also require a minimum balance of $300 to $500. However, these accounts pay the highest rates of any bank account on which checks can be written.

For those with $5,000 to $20,000 in cash and securities, *AIOAs* (All-In-One Accounts) provide the best alternative. These accounts consist of a package of automated cash management, preferential personal treatment, and certain investment services provided by the bank or an outside firm that offers such services for the bank. On the cash management side, the bank covers the check written by the depositor by transferring exactly the right amount from the money-market balance to the checking account. On the investment side, the depositor can use the bank facilities not only for trading securities but also for financial planning, managing real estate investments, and trust and estate planning. Even more important, dividends, interest, and proceeds from the sale of securities are deposited directly into the interest-bearing money market account.

The real yield.   One of the most difficult tasks savers face is to figure out the real yield on their savings. The reason is not hard to find. Fierce competition for available savings often prompts financial institutions to make exaggerated claims which must be decoded to identify the real yields.

Simple versus compound interest.   A common practice among financial institutions is to advertise a high interest rate on multi-year accounts; but it is only simple interest, not compound. This practice can be utterly misleading to the neophyte and the unsuspecting saver. For instance, if ABC bank pays $10\frac{3}{4}$ percent simple interest on its five-year CD, and XYZ bank pays only 9 percent interest on its CD compounded annually over the same period, to the uninitiated the former bank looks more attractive. But based on what we learned in Chapter 5, in reality it is the XYZ bank which offers a better deal.

Delayed deposit credit.   The real yield on a deposit also depends upon the number of days the money is allowed to earn interest. Some banks wait several days before crediting the account with the new deposit. This practice could significantly cut the yield on the deposit.

Minimum monthly balance requirement.   Basically, there are six methods for paying interest: (1) low quarterly balance, (2) low monthly balance, (3) pro rata balance—FIFO, (4) pro rata balance—LIFO, (5) day-of-deposit to day-of-withdrawal balance, and (6) average daily balance. For instance, assume a $10,000 deposit is made on January 1 at $5\frac{1}{4}$ percent, and no additional deposits or withdrawals are made for a year. If interest is compounded and paid quarterly, under each of the preceding six methods the annual interest would be $535.42. Differences among these methods result from deposits or withdrawals of funds during the interest period and their effect on the final amount of interest paid, depending on which method of calculation is used.

The best savings method for depositors is the average daily balance method, in which the bank calculates the ending balance for each day, and then computes the average balance for the period to get the amount for which it is paying interest. The worst of course is the low balance method, in which the bank pays interest based on the lowest daily balance on deposit each day.

Grace period allowance. Grace days are also important in determining how much interest an account will earn. A grace period for deposits allows savings institutions to pay the interest from the first calendar day of the month and also on deposits withdrawn during the month's last three business days (called dead days). When a bank allows a grace period, it automatically boosts the real yield.

Other factors. Other factors that affect real yield include charges for excess withdrawals, penalties for premature closing of accounts, and other assorted charges. The impact of these charges and penalties on the real yield can vary greatly depending upon individual policies adopted by various financial institutions.

Money market mutual funds. A money market fund is a mutual fund that invests only in short-term money market instruments. Investors purchase and redeem these shares without paying a sales charge. Minimum initial investments for most funds vary from $500 to $5,000. Generally, these funds have a check writing option that enables individuals to write checks of $300 or more. Shares can also be redeemed from most money market funds by telephone or wire request, in which case the fund either mails the payment to the investor or remits it by wire to the investor's bank account.

Incidentally, money market fund rates are generally higher than those offered by banks on their savings accounts. However, unlike bank accounts, money market accounts are not insured by the Federal Deposit Insurance Corporation (FDIC).

Certificates of deposit. Certificates of deposit (CDs) significantly differ from savings accounts in one respect: They must remain on deposit for a specified period of time. Consequently, investors earn a higher return on CDs than on savings. The difference in the rates depends on a CD's amount and the length of maturity. However, a substantial interest penalty is imposed on a CD's early withdrawal, and in certain instances early withdrawal may even result in partial loss of the principal.

In this connection, mention may be made of brokered CDs which have gained considerable popularity in recent years. Brokered CDs are simply CDs issued by a bank or a savings and loan association through a middleman—a broker—who gets paid a commission by the issuing institution. As long as the issuing bank is covered by the FDIC, brokered CDs are also fully insured by the FDIC up to the usual $100,000 limit.

The incentive for investing in a brokered CD does not come from a superior return, for generally the returns on these CDs are not appreciably higher than those on ordinary CDs. Their main attraction is that investors can liquidate them at any time without incurring the usual early withdrawal penalty associated with ordinary CDs.

Treasury bills. U.S. treasury bills are the shortest-term marketable U.S. obligations offered and, by law, cannot exceed one year to maturity. The most frequent and most popular treasury bill issues are three-month and six-month maturities which are offered on a weekly basis. Bids (tenders) for both issues are usually invited approximately one week prior to the auction. At that time, the amount offered and the terms of the offering are announced, with the terms for the two issues being similar. Treasury bills are sold on a discount basis. This means that investors pay a discount price for a bill but receive the face value upon maturity. The difference between the discount and maturity prices, or the additional cash received, as a ratio of that investment is the return on the treasury bill. Incidentally, the minimum denomination of a treasury bill is $10,000, followed by increments of $5,000. It should also be noted that although treasury bills are perfectly liquid and absolutely safe, an investor compelled to sell them before maturity could incur a loss.

Simplicity and Minimum Balance Requirements

It is simple to deal with all of the various institutions under consideration. In most instances, in order to transact business with them, the depositor need only present the passbook, have the account number put on a withdrawal/deposit slip, call the broker to deal in U.S. treasury bills, or fill out a simple application to open a money market account with check writing privileges.

Regarding minimum-balance requirements, banks and credit unions require a small minimum balance to open an account and a reasonable balance to maintain it. Savings bonds and U.S. bonds can be purchased for amounts ranging from a low of $25 (Series EE bonds) to $10,000 (treasury bills). Finally, money market accounts generally require a minimum balance of $500, although the minimum may be as high as $5,000 with some funds.

Special Service Features

For providing special services, no other institution can match those offered by commercial banks, or what are frequently called full-service banks.

In addition to the traditional banking services, most banks offer special services that add to their quality. These include twenty-four-hour banking through automatic teller machines (ATMs), good deals on loans, travellers checks, income tax preparation services, investment management services, and even travel advice and airline tickets. Of course, many non-bank institutions provide similar types of services as well.

Tax Considerations

Of all the savings alternatives just discussed, only interest income received on a *tax-exempt* money market fund is exempt from federal income taxes. The simplest way to decide the relative attractiveness of a tax-exempt money market fund is to convert it into a fully taxable equivalent. This can be easily done by using the following equation:

$$\text{Equivalent Fully Taxable Yield} = \frac{\text{Tax-Exempt Yield}}{1\text{-Marginal Federal Tax Rate}}$$

Thus, if the yield on a tax-exempt money market fund is five percent and the investor is in the 28 percent tax bracket, the equivalent fully taxable yield is 6.94 percent: $[5/(1-.28)]$.

TABLE 6-7   Selection of Savings Media

	Safety	Liquidity	Simplicity	Special Services	Rate of Return	Minimum Required	Federal Tax Advantage
Commercial Bank	A	A	A	A	C	A	C
Mutual Savings Bank	A	A	A	B	A	A	C
Savings and Loan Association	A	A	A	B	A	A	C
Credit Union	A	A	A	B	A	A	C
Series EE Bonds	A	C	B	C	C	B	B
Series HH Bonds*	A	C	B	C	C	C	C
Treasury Bonds*	A	C	C	C	C	C	C
Municipal Bonds*	A	C	C	C	C	C	A

Differences have been ranked on an A, B, or C scale, with A denoting the highest and C the lowest degree of characteristic.
* These investments are not discussed in the text, and are included here merely for comparison.

It is equally simple to calculate the after-tax equivalent yield from a fully taxable investment. For instance, suppose the taxable yield on a money market fund is nine percent. For an investor in the 28 percent tax bracket, the after-tax yield is 6.48 percent: $[9(1 - .28)]$.

Summing Up

Deregulation of financial institutions has brought about widespread changes in the financial services industry. Today's financial institutions provide a wide variety of choices and their services are superior to what they were even a few years ago. An overview of the popular liquid assets available today is presented in Table 6-7.

CREDIT AND DEBT PLANNING

INTRODUCTION

Shakespeare's Polonius was adamant on the subject of credit. "Neither a borrower nor a lender be," he cautioned his son. And many parents today believe that is good advice to give to both their sons and daughters.

Unfortunately, such advice on credit is no longer sound. In our society, credit provides us with a valuable money management tool that should be used judiciously to maximize our welfare.

Credit—whether it is buying now and paying later or borrowing money—lets us have *what* we want *when* we want it. In addition, credit also gives us time to pay gradually for the things that we want now. Our primary objective, then, should be to weigh the cost of borrowing money against the benefit to be derived from it (in terms of consuming goods and services now rather than later) and obtain credit when the benefits exceed the cost. Our secondary objective should be to protect our credit rating so that we may maintain the highest level of creditworthiness at all times.

A DEBT OR A CREDIT?

A desirable and often necessary method of stretching income is to borrow—commonly known as indulging in consumer credit or debt. Since there exists a great deal of confusion about the real distinction between debt and credit, we shall begin by defining both terms.

Formerly, debt was taboo. No one liked to be in debt if it could be helped. Today, old attitudes have changed. Most people now believe that debt allows families to raise their living standards and increase their productive capacities. In fact, debt has become such an integral part of our lives that it is not even considered cynical to ask: Remember when people worried about how much it took to buy something instead of how long?

While debt has generally contributed to growth and prosperity, it has its bad side, too. Everyone at some time has seen the disastrous consequences of excessive debt accumulation by a person or business. Most families filing bankruptcy proceedings of various kinds in this country are generally overextended. Their debts accumulate to the point where they cannot be paid back without resort to the court system. Thus, debt appears both good and bad—a paradox that must be resolved before debt can be used as a financial planning tool.

In our society, people who borrow are often looked upon as lacking thrift and a sense of responsibility, while those who are creditworthy are viewed with respect. Yet such perceptions are really two sides of the same coin—to incur credit is to incur debt. It is now easy to see why debt is inherently neither good nor bad. What is important is the relationship between debt and one's ability to adequately service it and ultimately liquidate it with assets.

Incidentally, of all the different types of debts which exist today, consumer debt—or consumer credit, as it is popularly called—is of special interest. The term "consumer credit" refers to the use of credit by individuals and families for personal needs, in contrast to credit used by business or government. We will now undertake a discussion of consumer credit.

SOURCES OF CREDIT

Commercial Banks

The term *bank* refers to commercial banks and mutual savings banks. These are full service institutions offering a variety of loans—secured, unsecured, installment, and noninstallment—to consumers and businesses. Many banks allow their depositors to use passbook savings accounts as collateral for loans and will consequently charge a lower interest rate. Most banks also make automatic overdraft loans, which permit depositors to write checks in amounts larger than the funds in their accounts. Typically, banks tend to make loans to their own customers, although loans are also made to others who are good financial risks.

Consumer Finance Companies

These lending institutions specialize in small loans and are therefore popularly known as small loan companies. They make secured and unsecured loans on an installment basis. There are limits on the maximum amount that can be lent ($2,000 to $5,000) and on the maximum interest that can be charged (48 percent on loans of less than $500).

Credit Unions

Another important source of credit for many customers is credit unions. Credit unions are cooperative thrift and loan associations which limit their loans to their own members. The annual percentage rate charged by these unions is nine to 18 percent, although federal credit unions are legally permitted to charge up to 21 percent. In general, charges by credit unions are generally lower than those charged by commercial banks and finance companies.

Savings and Loan Associations

Savings and loan associations generally make mortgage loans, although they are permitted to make other types of loans as well. Furthermore, these institutions also make certain types of home improvement and mobile home loans, as well as some personal and education loans using passbook savings as collateral. Typically, savings and loans charge ten to 18 percent on consumer loans, depending upon the borrower's creditworthiness as well as the terms of repayment.

Life Insurance Companies

Whole life insurance policies can serve as excellent collateral for loans at the cheapest possible rate. Most insurance companies let their whole life policyholders borrow most or all of the accumulated cash value at five or six percent. These loans are easy to obtain, and technically they do not even have to be repaid. However, financial protection is reduced by the loan amount the policyholder obtains, and that reduces the attractiveness of loans against insurance policies.

Auto Dealers

Loans from auto dealers are easily obtainable for financing automobiles. The formalities for obtaining these loans are kept at a bare minimum. However, auto loans are frequently expensive, and they may run as much as two percentage points above a typical bank installment loan used to finance new cars. It should be mentioned here, however, that frequently new car dealerships advertise low financing rates (2.9 to 4.9 percent) for certain dealer-selected models. In these cases the finance charges could be significantly lower than those charged on loans granted by the institutions just discussed.

Summing Up

On the basis of a discussion of the major sources of consumer credit just presented, it is possible to argue that no one source of credit is best for everyone.

Individual family situations vary considerably, and each of the sources listed previously satisfies a specific family situation. For instance, credit unions lend to their members only, while banks grant loans only to those who qualify. Persons with poor credit ratings and a desperate need for money are left with little choice but to borrow from pawnbrokers or loan sharks, and families with limited payment capacity in need of small loans often find it more convenient to borrow from small loan companies.

CREDIT HISTORY

Its Importance

Sooner or later just about everybody wants to buy on credit. Even the few consumers who usually pay cash eventually need to make installment purchases. If these credit-conscious consumers have not already established a credit rating, it may be difficult for them to borrow money.

Opening that first charge account, or getting that first charge card, is not always simple. Factors such as age, income, address, and employment stability, are important to credit managers. Traditionally, there have been noticeable biases against young, single or married adults of either sex, against divorced women, against ADC (aid to dependent children) mothers, and against persons with legal problems, although existing laws relating to credit prohibit these biases. However, some of these biases still prevail, and in our credit-oriented society, in spite of these difficulties, establishing a good credit rating is a must for everyone.

Factors Influencing Credit History

In its broadest sense, consumer credit is based on faith in the consumer's good intentions to repay. In this sense, each prospective debtor is judged in terms of "the four Cs of credit." These are:

> *Character* as judged by honesty, reliability, responsibility, and record of financial responsibility.
>
> *Capacity* as measured by the financial ability to meet obligations; that is, it is based on the present and future earning power.
>
> *Capital* as judged by the financial resources that can serve as collateral or security for the loan.
>
> *Credit rating* as judged by the overall capacity to repay the loans.

The credit rating standards (recommended for the use of bankers) published in a manual prepared by the American Bankers Association are presented in Table 6-8.

TABLE 6-8 Credit Rating Standards

	Favorable	Unfavorable
Employment	With good firm two years or more. Job involves skill, education.	Shifts jobs frequently. Employed in seasonal industry such as construction work. Unskilled labor.
Income	Steady; meets all normal needs.	Earnings fluctuate, depend on commissions, tips, one-shot deals. Amount barely covers requirements.
Residence	Owns own home or rents for long periods in good neighborhoods.	Lives in furnished rooms in poor neighborhoods. Changes address frequently.
Financial structure	Has savings account and checking account that requires minimum balance. Owns property, investments, life insurance.	No bank accounts. Few, if any, assets.
Debt record	Pays bills promptly. Usually makes large down payment. Borrows infrequently and for constructive purposes.	Slow payer. Tries to put as much on credit as possible. Frequent loans for increasing amounts.
Litigation	No suits by creditors.	Record of suits and other legal action for nonpayment. Bankruptcy.
Personal characteristics	Family man. Not many dependents relative to income. Mature.	Large number of dependents. Marital difficulties. Young, impulsive.
Application behavior	Seeks loan from bank with which he regularly deals. Answers all questions fully and truthfully.	Applies for loan at banking office far removed from his residence or place of business. Makes misstatements on application. In great hurry to obtain cash.

Source: Constructed from various banking and credit union publications.

Protection of Credit History

Denial of credit by a finance company may hurt a consumer badly, especially if it is based upon an incorrect credit report. Until the spring of 1971, the law permitted credit companies to treat credit reports as a secret dossier, and there was no way of checking the accuracy of the "confidential" financial information it contained. The Federal Fair Credit Reporting Act of 1971, which covers the rights of those providing and receiving credit or insurance to be used primarily for personal purposes, brought new hope to millions of American consumers. The law directs any credit company denying a loan to inform the consumer that the loan application was rejected on the basis of information contained in a credit report. The applicant is then free to contact the local credit bureau for further details. The bureau, in turn, must disclose all the information (excluding medical) in the file. If the file contains incorrect or incomplete information, the applicant has the right to ask the bureau to check the facts and, if warranted, make suitable adjustments in the record. If the bureau's information cannot be verified, these items must be dropped.

TYPES OF CREDIT

The Basic Issue

In our credit-oriented society, it is safe to assume that, from time to time, most of us would find it desirable—and often necessary—to borrow; hence it is important to understand the nature of credit and learn the art of using it judiciously. This involves an appreciation of the *true* cost of credit and the knack of discovering the source of credit that is not only the cheapest but also right for the type of credit being sought.

Let us begin by recognizing that there is no such thing as the *single cost of credit*. Costs vary according to a host of factors, such as types and sources of credit, the prevailing prime interest rate, duration of loans, credit rating of the borrower, and even the value and type of collateral offered. In fact, depending upon certain factors, credit may even be practically costless. In the following paragraphs we shall discuss the various categories of credit and the principal ways in which costs are calculated and expressed.

Categories of Credit

All consumer credit transactions fall into two broad categories: *sales credit* and *cash credit*. Sales credit is granted by department stores, automobile dealerships, repair shops, and other types of businesses in connection with the purchase of goods or services. In contrast, cash credit is extended to individuals by lending agencies in the form of cash.

Cross-dimensionally, sales and cash credits could be classified as *non-installment credit* and *installment credit*. The former is single-payment credit and is used for charge accounts, utility bills, bills for professional services, and single-payment cash loans. On the other hand, installment credit is used for paying off loans over time, granted for the purchase of durable goods, and for paying off major expenditures. A variant of installment credit is the *check-credit plan*, under which the credit user is authorized to write checks against the credit limit as long as the amount for which checks are written does not exceed the approved limit.

Within these major categories, depending upon borrowers' preferences, credit-granting institutions offer one of the following three types of sales credit.

Thirty-day or regular charge accounts. Most Americans use credit generously as a convenience, especially when they are not charged for the use of such credit. A universal built-in feature of all regular charge accounts is that the seller of goods or services promises to deliver these products on credit without charge, provided their customers pay for them within a stated grace period. This arrangement obviates the need for carrying cash and also helps consumers consolidate their payments at regular intervals. This credit for convenience is an excellent idea, although one must never lose sight of the fact that the credit user will be charged a high rate of interest on the unpaid balance of the loan if payments are not made by the due date.

Revolving and optional charge accounts. Revolving accounts revolutionized the business enterprises of our major stores. They not only boosted overall sales enormously but also changed the budget styles of consumers. Under this arrangement, businesses allow their customers to make repeated purchases as long as the total does not exceed the limit established when the account was opened. Furthermore, there is no finance charge if the payment is made within a stated grace period. But if a customer chooses not to pay for the purchases either partly or in full within the grace period, then a finance charge is imposed on the unpaid balance. Charges computed at 1, $1\frac{1}{2}$, or 2 percent monthly are equivalent to annual rates of 12, 18, or 24 percent, respectively.

Installment purchases or time-payment plans. The most popular demand for credit, of course, stems from the use of installment credit for buying durable goods. A sharp rise in personal expectations and demands for durable consumer goods, coupled with the inability of most buyers to pay cash for them, has been instrumental in the phenomenal growth of installment credit. In all cases installment credit—or buying on time, as it is popularly called—is payable in several predetermined installments, hopefully, but not necessarily, spread out over the useful life of the durable goods in question.

As mentioned, there are two methods of financing installment credit. One is buying on time directly from the seller; the other is borrowing money from a credit institution. In either case there is a *cost* involved in incurring a debt. This cost, which has several names—simple interest, add-on interest, interest discounted, monthly interest, finance charges, and points—is not a uniform charge. Methods for calculating various types of interest are presented in the appendix to this chapter.

Regardless of which payment method is selected, the consumer will probably have to go through sales finance agencies to take the credit card route. A large number of retailers and other businesses find it uneconomical to extend their customers credit by tying down their working capital, and hence they transfer their loan business to sales finance agencies. If an account is transferred to a finance company, the consumer will become responsible to that company for the repayment of the loan.

An important alternative to paying directly to sales finance companies is the credit card, the issuer of which honors the customer's creditworthiness. There are several advantages of using credit cards, chief among them being convenience, creation of instant credit, flexibility, ease of payment, and emergency use. Not all credit cards are cost-free, however. Travel and entertainment cards charge an annual fee—usually $15 to $75—but no interest on the loan. There is also a fee for cards issued by banks; in addition, there is an interest charge if payment is not made within a specified time. Typically, this ranges from one to $1\frac{1}{2}$ percent per month—a 12 to 18 percent annual rate. The same is true of most retail store cards.

EFFECTIVE INTEREST RATE

John and Janet Client recently shopped around for a quality stereo system. The information they gathered about the cost of credit is summarized in Table 6-9. If they took out a two-year simple interest loan from a credit union at a 12 percent interest rate, the $1,000 stereo would cost them $1,125. The same stereo would cost them $1,131.15 at an interest rate of 12.59 percent, $1,190.63 at 18.3 percent, and $1,256.25 at 24.6 percent. The Clients also discovered that the longer the repayment period, the higher the cost. The finance charge on a 12 percent $1,000 loan for one year was $65; if the time period was extended to three years, the finance charges almost tripled. Understandably, the Clients were confused by all of these numbers and had difficulty in deciding which method of financing the stereo was best for them.

Like the Clients, millions of American consumers when confronted with such decisions are unable to cope. However, for an intelligent buying decision there is no substitute for recognizing *effective* or *real* rates of interest under various types of loan provisions.

TABLE 6-9 Cost of Borrowing $1,000

I: High interest rates raise total cost of credit

Total amount borrowed	$1,000	$1,000	$1,000	$1,000	$1,000
Interest rate (annual)	12%	12.59%	18.3%	24.6%	40%
Finance charge	$ 125.00	$ 131.15	$ 190.63	$ 256.25	$ 416.67
Total payment (principal and interest)	$1,125.00	$1,131.15	$1,190.63	$1,256.25	$1,416.67

II: Longer time payments raise total cost of credit

Total amount borrowed		$1,000	$1,000	$1,000
Interest rate (annual)		12%	12%	12%
Financed over		1 year	2 years	3 years
Finance charges		$ 65.00	$ 125.00	$ 185.00
Total payment (principal and interest)		$1,065.00	$1,125.00	$1,185.00

Note: Finance charges are calculated by using a complex system consisting of: (1) declining balance method; (2) a point system; and (3) a varied loan payment method.

Interest represents the price borrowers pay to lenders for credit over specified periods of time. The amount of interest paid depends on a number of factors: the dollar amount lent or borrowed, the length of time involved in the transaction, the stated or nominal annual rate of interest, the repayment schedule, and the method used to calculate interest. A discussion of various methods of interest calculations is presented in the appendix to this chapter.

THE NEW TAX RULES

The *true* cost of credit is arrived at by taking into account the tax deductibility of the interest charged on a loan. Unfortunately, current tax laws have all but eliminated this break. Only ten percent of interest costs are deductible in 1990 and, in 1991, the write-off will be gone.

Consumer debt includes personal loans, charge cards, auto loans, student loans, and life insurance loans. The tax law change applies to old and new debt, as the deduction phaseout covers interest currently paid, regardless of the rules that initially governed them. The only exception to this rule is that the law still allows consumers to fully deduct, subject to certain restrictions, interest paid on mortgage debt secured by the primary and one secondary residence.

THE BURDEN OF DEBT

An Overview

We have learned that consumer credit is a powerful financial planning tool. However, used unwisely, it can create a nightmare for the family. It is therefore of extreme importance for every family to determine how much debt it can handle and then keep its consumer debt within that limit at all times. Unfortunately, no simple formula or all-purpose table is available that can neatly determine how much debt is safe for an individual or a family. Given individual psychological make-up, financial resources, values, goals, and willingness to accept discipline, each person must establish his or her credit capacity. With the preceding basic ideas in mind, we shall develop two distinct guidelines, hopefully one of which will be applicable in every case.

TABLE 6-10   Debt Limit Calculation Worksheet

	Part A	Part B*
Types of loans/ charge accounts	*Average monthly payments*	*Total expected payments*
1.		
2.		
3.		
4.		
5.		
6.		
7.		
8.		
9.		
10.		

Total: $_____

Part B

I. Total monthly payments.	$_____
II. Total net monthly income.	$_____
III. Debt limit: Divide II by appropriate percentage desired (e.g., 10 for 10% limit, 6.7 for 15% limit, 5 for 20% limit).	$_____
IV. Surplus (+) or Deficit (−). Subtract III from I.	$_____

* This column is included for reference purposes only.

Guidance from the Business World

One way to determine how much debt one can afford is to borrow from business experience. As a general rule, a business reaches its debt limit when its debt reaches the level of its equity. In other words, financial lenders consider businesses with a debt/equity ratio equal to or greater than one noncreditworthy and will not grant them additional loans. Consumers may regard their personal debt/equity ratio, calculated from their net worth statement, as a yardstick for determining their credit capacity. Note, however, that in calculating the debt/equity ratio the value of the home (an asset) and its mortgage (a liability) should be excluded, since financing a home falls into a category separate from borrowing for acquiring other assets.

The Rule of Thumb Approach

Another approach, based upon personal experiences of financial planners, involves setting the consumer installment debt limit as a fixed percentage of monthly income. Experts say the debt payment should be no more than ten to 15 percent of total monthly income. Debt payments should include all items purchased on credit except home mortgages. Net monthly income can be calculated by subtracting all taxes, Social Security, IRA contributions, and contributions to pension and profit sharing plans. A debt limit calculation worksheet is presented in Table 6-10 which can be used to determine the maximum debt limit permissible for a given family. If debt payment exceeds the permissible limit—that is, if Item IV in Part B is a negative number—then immediate action should be taken to correct the situation.

BANKRUPTCY

The Modern Interpretation

Formerly, a debt was supposed to be honored by all means and bankruptcy was taboo. Thus it seemed to Mark Twain, who, to his disbelief, was forced into bankruptcy in 1894. His creditors were happy to come to a compromise with him, but he promised to return "100 cents on the dollar," and at the age of 59, despite uncertain health, he embarked on a 13-month foreign lecture tour to earn the necessary money. He did not return to the United States until after he had fulfilled his vow to return "100 cents on the dollar," not even when he learned of the illness and subsequent death of his beloved daughter.

Today, the honorable man who wrote *Huckleberry Finn* would probably be regarded as a nut. The stigma once attached to taking a financial bath no longer seems to be an important consideration for many modern-day debtors. Bankruptcy courts are filled with petitions from real estate agents, contractors,

BREAKING THE DEBT HABIT

If you are already addicted to credit cards, have a long line of loans from the bank and are burdened by a hefty mortgage, cutting your debt won't be easy. But there are methods you can use that should help you to curb your free-spending ways:

- Figure out just how much of your take-home pay each month is earmarked to paying off debt. If more than 30% goes toward a mortgage and more than 20% goes to installment loans, you should cut back on your use of credit.
- Try to curb your current credit purchases while you pay down your old debts. Drive your car a little longer, avoid shopping sprees and pay cash whenever possible.
- If you have a hard time kicking your habit after three months, be ruthless with yourself: cut up your credit cards; close your charge accounts; force yourself to pay cash for everything.
- If all else fails, you may need to see a credit counselor. The experience might be less traumatic than you think.

Around the country, some 240 non-profit credit counseling organizations can help you get a grip on your finances. Find the one nearest you by getting in touch with the National Foundation for Consumer Credit, 8701 Georgia Ave., Silver Spring, Md. 20910 (phone: 301-589-5600). Almost without exception, these organizations are preferable by far to for-profit credit counseling groups that advertise their services and charge as much as $1,500. They include debt-consolidation firms, which merely refinance your debt at a higher rate, and so-called credit repair shops, which promise to restore your credit rating and obtain new credit cards for you. Extending credit to a heavy spender can be as dangerous as offering a drink to an alcoholic.

Founded in 1951, the National Foundation for Consumer Credit is supported financially by banks, department stores, the AFL-CIO, Family Services of America, the Legal Aid Society, the American Bar Association and other organizations and businesses with an interest in helping people handle their debts. Last year counseling centers affiliated with the NFCC arranged the payment of bills totaling $117 million, up from $108 million in 1983.

At a credit counseling agency, you'll be asked to fill out a confidential application outlining your after-tax income and total indebtedness. Then you'll see a credit counselor. The expertise of the counselors varies; they may have passed two days of tests administered by the NFCC or just held a job that offers comparable experience, such as a bank lending officer. The counselor will review your cash flow, help set up a budget and advise whether you can handle your own bills or need a debt-repayment plan in which you'll typically turn over to the agency a monthly amount equal to 1/30 of your total indebtedness. He may even recommend that you take a part-time job or sell some assets, depending on how severe your shortfall is. The agency will also get in touch with your creditors; in turn, many of them may halt additional interest charges while you work out a reorganization plan. In any event a good counselor will try to protect your interests by saving your car from repossession or shielding your wages from garnishment.

For the initial consultation, an NFCC agency will charge you up to $50, though $10 to $20 is more usual, and no one is ever turned down because he can't pay. If you go into a debt-payment plan, you also will pay a fee of $10 to $20 a month.

Half of credit counseling clients don't return after the initial consultation, many because they decide that they can solve their own financial problems. About 10% are counseled to seek a lawyer's help. Bankruptcy may be recommended in cases where clients would face garnishment and other hardships. But it's the last resort: your credit record can be tarnished for up to 10 years, and you can find it difficult to land a job. The spender who manages to pay off all his debt, however, can emerge with a feeling of accomplishment and begin his life anew debt-free.

Source: Money, December 1985, p. 190.

schoolteachers, journalists, stockbrokers, architects, engineers, and financial planners. In fact, even wealthy movie stars, professional athletes, and prominent business people have declared—and others like them continue to declare—bankruptcy.

While bankruptcy is no longer taboo, it still remains an outcome which should be avoided. In the following section we will address this issue.

Avoiding Bankruptcy

Obviously, not all financial difficulties result in bankruptcies. Financial problems may arise when expenses and obligations consistently exceed income and the ability to make payments. Such a situation may be created by either a mismanagement of finances or a set of circumstances totally beyond one's control. Whatever the reason, an individual can avoid a lot of grief by knowing some basic facts about the alternatives available to a person with serious financial difficulties.

The objective approach. It is impossible to solve a financial crisis by juggling books or by making random payments to only some of the creditors. These creditors are professional people who can easily outwit debtors when it comes to confronting such delinquent payers with legal claims. The best thing to do is to make a simple statement showing the money that can be spared for loan payments and the total monthly payments that must be made. This statement will clearly reveal where the consumer stands with respect to outstanding debts.

Informal arrangements with creditors. When financial difficulties occur that can no longer be handled in the usual manner, an informal arrangement should be made with the creditors that can be settled out of court. If the necessary goodwill is shown by working with creditors rather than avoiding them, they may be willing to defer payments or refinance the debt to reduce the size of monthly payments. To reduce the debt, these creditors may also permit the return of some of the merchandise bought on credit.

If the informal arrangements fail to resolve the overextended debt problem, it may be possible to find a lending agency that could arrange for lower monthly payments extended over a longer period of time.

Credit counseling. If the first two steps fail, the next recourse should be to seek the help of a community credit counseling service. Such a service provides expert, confidential guidance for little or no charge. It can be located through a banker or a lawyer, or the National Foundation for Consumer Credit—8701 Georgia Avenue, Suite 507, Silver Spring, MD 20910—can be contacted for a copy of their clinic directory.

Credit counseling services operate at two levels. First, through recasting the budget at a more modest level, the service may be able to help one keep the spending plan at a realistic level, thereby enhancing one's ability to meet financial obligations. Second, if expenses far exceed income and there is no way to bring the two together, the counseling service will try to arrange new repayment schedules with the creditors. If this is possible, the debtor may be asked to give the service a predetermined amount every month. According to an established plan acceptable to the creditors, the service will then distribute the amount to creditors.

Wage-earner plan.   The last step before filing for bankruptcy is the wage-earner plan, a form of debt consolidation allowed under Chapter XIII of the Federal Bankruptcy Act. Under this plan, under the guidance and protection of the Bankruptcy Court, and with the assistance of an attorney, the debtor draws up a budget for paying all the debts, along with meeting the normal living expenses for a period of three years. If this plan meets with the approval of the court and the creditors, interest and late charges on the debts are suspended, and each month the debtor turns over to a court trustee the predetermined installment payments for distribution to the creditors. The important feature of this plan is that the consumer does not give up any assets and a bankruptcy is not declared.

APPENDIX TO CHAPTER 6

INTEREST CALCULATION METHODS

Simple interest

All the methods used to calculate interest are basically variations of the simple interest calculation method, which was introduced in Chapter 5. Under this method, interest is paid only on the original amount borrowed for the length of time the borrower has use of the credit. The amount borrowed is referred to as the principal. The interest is computed only on that portion of the original principal still owed. Suppose $1,000 is borrowed at ten percent and repaid in one payment at the end of one year. Using the simple interest calculation, the interest amount would be ten percent of $1,000 for one year, or $100, since the borrower had use of $1,000 for the entire year.

When more than one payment is made on a simple interest loan, the method of computing interest is referred to as *interest on the declining balance*. Since the borrower only pays interest on that amount of original principal that has not yet been repaid, interest paid will be smaller the more frequent the payments. At the same time, of course, the *amount of credit the borrower uses is also smaller*. The amounts of actual monthly payments required to retire a $1,000 declining balance loan at different interest rates and for various maturities is presented in Table A6-1. For instance, in the case of a typical auto loan, a monthly payment of $33.22 is required to retire a 36-month loan granted at 12 percent interest. Incidentally, a $15,000 loan would require monthly payments of $498.30 ($33.22 × 15).

Table A6-1 conceals an important fact which should be explicitly recognized. Since the loan is fully retired by the maturity date, each payment must represent both principal and interest. This information is contained in Table A6-2. It may be noted that since the monthly payment remains fixed at $33.22 throughout the life of the loan, interest payments decline while prin-

TABLE A6-1 Monthly Repayment of a $1,000 Simple Interest Loan

Rate of interest	*Loan payable in*					
	12 Months	18 Months	24 Months	36 Months	48 Months	60 Months
10	87.92	60.06	46.15	32.27	25.37	21.25
11	88.50	60.64	46.73	32.86	25.97	21.87
12	88.85	60.99	47.08	33.22	26.34	22.25
13	89.32	61.45	47.55	33.70	26.83	22.76
14	89.79	61.92	48.02	34.18	27.33	23.27
18	91.68	63.81	49.93	36.16	29.38	25.40

TABLE A6-2   Repayment of a $1,000, 12 Percent, 36-Month Loan

Month	Outstanding loan balance (1)	Monthly payment (2)	Interest (3)	Principal (4)
1	$ 976.97	$ 33.22	$ 10.19	$ 23.03
2	953.52	$ 33.22	9.77	23.45
3	929.84	$ 33.22	9.54	23.68
4	905.92	$ 33.22	9.30	23.92
5	881.76	$ 33.22	9.06	24.16
6	857.36	$ 33.22	8.82	24.40
7	832.71	$ 33.22	8.57	24.65
8	807.82	$ 33.22	8.33	24.89
9	782.68	$ 33.22	8.08	25.14
10	757.29	$ 33.22	7.83	25.39
11	731.64	$ 33.22	7.57	25.65
12	705.74	$ 33.22	7.32	25.90
18	544.79	$ 33.22	5.72	27.50
24	373.94	$ 33.22	4.03	29.19
30	192.58	$ 33.22	2.24	30.89
36	0.00	$ 33.22	0.33	32.89
TOTAL		1,195.92	195.92	1,000.00

cipal payments rise proportionately to keep the monthly payment at the predetermined level. Incidentally, this equal-payment variation is commonly used with mortgage payment schedules. Each payment over the duration of the loan is split into two parts. Part one is the interest due at the time the payment is made, and part two—the remainder—is applied to the balance or amount still owed. In addition to mortgage lenders, credit unions typically use the simple interest/declining balance calculation method for computing interest on loans. Consumer installment loans are normally set up on this method and many banks also offer personal loans using this method.

Add-on interest, bank discount, and compound interest methods differ from the simple interest method as to when, how, and on what balance interest is paid. The annual percentage rate (APR) for these methods is that annual rate of interest which, when used in the simple interest rate formula, equals the amount of interest payable in these other calculation methods. For the declining balance method, the APR is the stated or nominal annual rate of interest. We will now explain the methods of calculating other types of interest.[1]

---

[1] The following discussion borrows from Ann Marie Laport "ABC of Figuring Interest," *Business Conditions*, Federal Reserve Bank of Chicago, September 1973, pp. 3–11.

MATHEMATICS OF INTEREST CALCULATION

Before discussing the various methods of calculating interest it might be desirable to review briefly the mathematics behind the calculation of interest cost. The mathematics of finance dealing with the cost of credit can be complex. However, the following formula gives an acceptable approximation of the cost of borrowing:

$$d = \frac{2 \times m \times I}{R \times n(n + 1)}$$

where

d = the percentage rate of simple discount

m = the number of payments in one year (12 if paying monthly; 52 if paying weekly)

I = interest charge or carrying charge (in dollars)

R = the payment per payment period

n = the number of payments, excluding the down payment

Suppose a stereo is listed for $349.95 cash. It may be bought for $49.95 down and ten monthly installments of $35 each. The cost of purchasing this set on time can be calculated as follows:

m = 12

I = $50 (The unpaid balance on the date of purchase is $349.95 − $49.95 = $300, and the carrying charge is 35(10) − 300 = $50. Although the carrying charge includes the cost of items such as bookkeeping and the investigation of the purchaser as a credit risk, it is the usual practice to treat the entire carrying charge as an interest charge.)

R = $35

n = 10

$$d = \frac{2(12)(50)}{35(10)(11)} = \frac{27}{77} = 0.312, \text{ or } 31.2 \text{ percent}$$

Add-On Interest

When the add-on interest method is used, interest is calculated on the full amount of the original principal. The interest amount is immediately added to the original principal and payments are determined by dividing principal plus interest by the number of payments to be made. When only one payment is involved, this method produces the same effective interest rate as the simple interest method. When two or more payments are to be made, however, use of the add-on interest method results in an *effective* rate of interest that is greater than the *nominal* rate. True, the interest amount is calculated by applying the nominal rate to the total amount borrowed, but the borrower does not have use of the total amount for the entire time period if two or more payments are made. Table A6-3 clearly shows that the APR under the add-on interest method is significantly higher than under the simple interest method on a $1,000, one-year loan charging 12 percent interest.

Bank Discount

When the bank discount rate method is used, interest is calculated on the amount to be paid back and the borrower receives the difference between

TABLE A6-3   Simple Versus Add-on Interest

	Simple interest	Add-on interest
Stated rate on loan	12%	12%
Finance charges	$ 66.20	$ 120.00
Monthly payments (12)	$ 88.85	$ 93.33
Total payments made	$1,066.20	$1,120.00
APR	12%	21.4%

the amount of the original principal and the interest amount (that is, prepaid interest). If a 12 percent $1,000 loan is to be paid back at the end of one year, two approaches are possible using the method of bank discount rate. The first approach would be to deduct the interest amount of $120 from the $1,000, leaving the borrower with $880 to use over the year. The $1,000 loan is paid back at the end of the year. The interest amount in this case is $120. The borrower in the case of simple interest, however, has the use of $1,000 over the year. Thus the APR using the method of bank discount rate is greater than that for the simple-interest rate calculation. The APR here would be 13.64 percent—that is [($120/$880) × 100]—compared with 12 percent in the case where simple interest is calculated.

The second approach to calculating interest by using the method of bank discount rate would be to determine the amount that would have to be paid back so that, once the interest amount was deducted, the borrower would have the use of $1,000 over the year. This amount is $1,136.36, and this becomes the face value of the note on which interest is calculated. The interest amount (12 percent of $1,136.36 for one year) is $136.36, and this is deducted, leaving the borrower with $1,000 to use over the year. The effective rate of interest, again, is 13.64 percent. The bank discount method is commonly used with short-term business loans. Generally, there are no intermediate payments and the duration of the loan is one year or less.

Compound Interest

When the compound interest calculation is used, interest is calculated on the original principal plus all interest accrued to that point in time. Since interest is paid on interest as well as on the amount borrowed, the APR is greater than the nominal interest rate. The compound interest rate method is often used by banks and savings institutions in determining interest they pay on savings deposits "loaned" to the institutions by the depositors.

Suppose $1,000 is deposited in a bank that pays a five percent nominal annual rate of interest, compounded semiannually (that is, twice a year). At the end of the first six months, $25 in interest (five percent of $1,000 for one-half year) is payable. At the end of the year, the interest amount is calculated on the $1,000 plus the $25 in interest already paid, so that the second interest payment is $25.63 (5 percent of $1,025 for one-half year). The interest amount payable for the year, then, is $25 plus $25.63, or $50.63. The APR is 5.063 percent, which is greater than the nominal five percent rate.

The more often interest is compounded within a particular time period, the greater will be the effective rate of interest. In one year, a five percent nominal annual rate of interest compounded four times (quarterly) results in an effective annual rate of 5.0945 percent; compounded 12 times (monthly), 5.1162 percent; and compounded 365 times (daily), 5.1267 percent. When the interval of time between compoundings approaches zero (even shorter than a second), then the method is known as continuous compounding. Five percent continuously compounded for one year will result in an effective annual rate of 5.1271 percent.

Rule of 78

In the foregoing examples, it was assumed that periodic loan payments were always made exactly when due. Often, however, a loan may be completely repaid before it is due. When the declining balance method for calculating interest is used, the borrower is not penalized for prepayment, since interest is paid only on the balance outstanding for the length of time that amount is owed. When the add-on interest calculation is used, however, prepayment implies that the lender obtains some interest that is unearned. The borrower then is actually paying an even higher effective rate, since the funds were not used for the length of time of the original loan contract.

Some loan contracts make provisions for an interest rebate if the loan is prepaid. One of the common methods used in determining the amount of the interest rebate is referred to as the *Rule of 78*, or *Sum of the Years' Digits*. Application of the Rule of 78 yields the percentage of the total interest amount that is to be refunded to the borrower in the event of prepayment. The percentage figure is arrived at by dividing the sum of the integer numbers (digits) from one to the number of payments remaining by the sum of the digits from

---

FIVE WAYS TO LOWER YOUR COST OF CREDIT

If you've been borrowing more than you did a few years ago, consider yourself one of the crowd. After postponing major purchases during the high interest days of the recession, consumers have been buying more on credit. But many people are playing the borrowing game without knowing all the rules and may be making mistakes that could translate into hundreds or thousands of dol- lars. Below are five such errors—and tips on how to avoid making them yourself.

- *Choosing a long-term loan.* Shortening the length of your loan will increase your monthly payments, but it will also decrease your total finance charge. Say your bank is offering automobile loans at 15% and you're borrowing $10,000. You can choose between loans with payments of about $485 for 24 months, $347 for 36 months, or $278 for 48 months. The 48-month loan will cost $1,722 more than the 24-month loan and $879 more than the 36-month loan. Many people unwittingly run the risk of stretching out their payments by choosing variable-rate installment loans, a new borrowing option. Interest might be pegged to indexes such as certificates of deposit or three-month Treasury bills. Instead of altering your monthly payments, however, [some banks stretch] out the loan term if rates go up and [shorten] it if rates drop. Banks are pushing variable rates because they protect them against getting stuck with low-interest loans on their books. They can be a good deal for customers, too—but only if rates drop or hold steady. Some banks are offering variable-rate loans at 1% or $1\frac{1}{2}$% less than comparable fixed-rate loans to attract customers.

- *Not building a credit history.* This is a special concern to women, who only ten or 15 years ago faced a maze of obstacles when they tried to obtain credit based on their own income. A good first step toward building a credit rating is to apply for a retail store card. If you're a married woman and want to build a credit history that is unquestionably your own, get an "authorized user" card for your husband instead of opening a joint account. That way, the account will be in your name and based solely on your income.

- *Using higher-cost loans.* Obviously, you want to check the market for the lowest rate. But the rate depends to a large extent on the *kind* of loan you obtain. Borrowing against assets you already have is probably your cheapest source of financing. There are several ways to go about doing it.

  Home equity loans. Many banks and other financial institutions will offer you a line

of credit at favorable interest rates if you're willing to pledge the equity in your home as collateral. Since you stand to lose the roof over your head, you should consider such a loan only if you're in stable financial shape and can keep a tight rein on your borrowing.

Securities. You can arrange a margin loan through a brokerage house, but you'll have to place stocks and bonds in a special account as collateral. Under Federal Reserve Board regulations, you can generally borrow up to 50% of the market value of common and preferred stocks in your margin account, up to 70% of the market value of corporate bonds and up to 90% on government securities. There are no loan applications to fill out and no fixed repayment schedules.

Life insurance. On older policies the interest on a loan against the cash value could be as little as 5%, on new ones often 8%. You are under no obligation to repay the principal, and the interest can be added to the loan. However, your insurance protection will be reduced by the amount you owe. Any interest you pay when due may be deductible if you itemize.

- *Not challenging errors.* Errors sometimes creep into the credit files that loan officers rely on for rating loan applicants' creditworthiness. If your loan application is rejected, ask which credit bureau the lender used and request a summary of your file to make sure it's accurate.

- *Skipping the fine print.* The federal truth-in-lending law governing consumer borrowing requires lenders to provide a clear explanation of the charges involved. Your yearly borrowing cost must be quoted as the annual percentage rate. That APR takes into account loan fees, finders fees and interest and is the most accurate way to compare lending rates. But bear this in mind: Some costs, such as applications and late payment fees, are not included in the APR, although they must be itemized in the loan documents. Despite legal safeguards, you still have to be on the alert.

Source: Reprinted with permission from "Five Ways to Lose When You Borrow," in *Changing Times* Magazine, © Kiplinger Washington Editors, Inc., April 1985. This reprint is not to be altered in any way, except with permission from *Changing Times.*

one to the total number of payments specified in the original loan contract. For example, if a five-month loan is paid off by the end of the second month (that is, there are three payments remaining), the percentage of the interest that the lender would rebate is as follows:

$$\frac{1 + 2 + 3}{1 + 2 + 3 + 4 + 5} = \frac{6}{15} = 0.4 = 40 \text{ percent}$$

The name derives from the fact that 78 is the sum of the digits from 1 to 12 and, therefore, is the denominator in calculating interest rebate percentages for all 12-period loans.

Application of the Rule of 78 results in the borrower's paying somewhat more interest than would be paid with a comparable declining-balance loan. How much more depends on the effective rate of interest charged and the total number of payments specified in the original loan contract. The higher the APR charged and the greater the specified total number of payments, the greater the amount of interest figured under the Rule of 78 exceeds that under the declining balance method as shown in Figure A6-1.

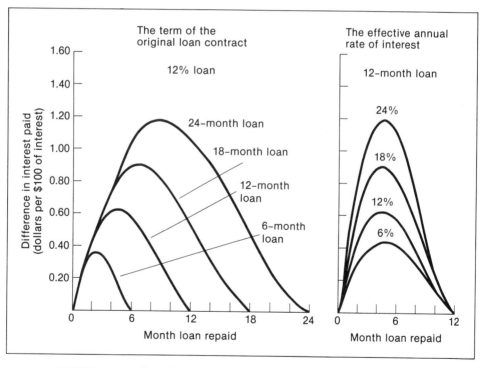

FIGURE A6-1 "The Rule of 78's Graph," Anne Marie Laporte, ABC's of Figuring Interest, *Business Conditions*, Federal Reserve Bank of Chicago, September 1973, p. 8.

The difference between the Rule of 78 interest and the declining-balance interest also varies depending upon when the prepayment occurs. This difference over the term of the loan tends to increase up to about the one-third point of the term and then decrease after this point. For example, with a 12-month term the difference with prepayment occurring in the second month would be greater than the difference that would occur with prepayment in the first month; the third-month difference would be greater than the second-month difference; and the fourth month (being the one-third point) would be greater than both the third-month difference and the fifth-month difference. After the fifth month, each succeeding month's difference would be less than the previous month's difference.

CHAPTER 7

The Basic Federal Income Tax Structure

THE BASIC TAX STRUCTURE

INTRODUCTION

The sweeping changes contained in the Tax Reform Act of 1986 and the Revenue Act of 1987 have successfully reduced for many taxpayers the income tax rate, but not necessarily total tax liability. Yet, people still work from January through May each year just to pay their taxes. In fact, even though the highest income tax bracket is only 33 percent, the federal, state, and city income taxes and the Social Security tax may combine to take nearly half of one's annual income. Since problems facing federal and municipal governments today are increasing, and since taxes are the major source of income for these governments, tax rates are likely to increase in the future, taking an ever-increasing bite out of individual income. A basic understanding of tax law and the method of tax computation can help each taxpayer (1) identify all allowable deductions to minimize tax liability; (2) develop tax planning strategies to minimize long-term tax liability; (3) avoid violating tax limits or rules that could result in sizable tax penalties; and (4) make improved financial decisions, with full consideration of tax implications.

Clearly, there are many types of taxes paid by individuals: federal, state, city, Social Security, and so on. However, in this chapter we will concentrate on federal income taxes because, for most individuals, this is the largest and most complex component of their tax liability.

THE FEDERAL INCOME TAX SYSTEM

The Purpose of Income Tax

The primary purpose of income taxes is to provide the government with the income necessary to meet the needs of its people. The government must not only provide for defense, but also address many of the social problems facing the nation. Pollution, decay of the inner cities, drug-related problems, inadequate educational facilities, and conservation of scarce resources are but a few of the major social problems facing governments today. Income tax is a primary source of revenue to meet these and other related needs.

A simple, fair, and equitable levy of income taxes against all citizens is certainly a worthwhile goal of the federal government. However, this goal is hard to achieve because tax rules, laws, and regulations are extremely complex and inevitable. There are three primary reasons for this: (1) The sources of personal income are diverse, and any attempt to tax all sources of income is bound to be onerous; (2) income tax is used not only to provide revenue to the government but also to encourage certain forms of economic and social activity, such as home ownership, savings, capital gains, job credit, and earned income credit; and (3) large special interest groups lobby to receive preferential tax treatment. The current tax laws have evolved within this complex environment.

Income Tax History

The Sixteenth Amendment to the U.S. Constitution, passed in 1913, authorized the U.S. government to collect income taxes, and the first permanent income tax in the U.S. became effective on March 1, 1913. With that the U.S. Congress became the tax policymaker and the Internal Revenue Service was charged with the responsibility for enforcing the prevailing tax law. While the initial rates were modest, maximum federal income tax rates increased dramatically from 1930 to 1945 as shown in Figure 7-1. These income tax rates remained quite high (around 90 percent) until 1963 when Congress markedly lowered them to the 70 percent level. It can also be claimed that the Economic Recovery Tax Act of 1981, the Tax Equity and Fiscal Responsibility Act of 1982, the Tax Reform Act of 1986, the subsequent tax legislations—all have significantly reduced individual and corporate tax rates to levels not seen since the Hoover Administration.

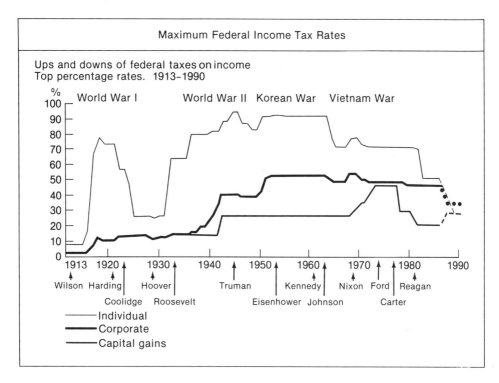

FIGURE 7-1 Maximum federal income tax rates. Reprinted by permission of *The Wall Street Journal* © Dow Jones & Company, Inc., August 18, 1986. All Rights Reserved Worldwide.

ERTA and TEFRA. The Economic Recovery Tax Act (ERTA) of 1981 was designed to stimulate savings and investments. It reduced the maximum tax rates on dividends, interest, and capital gains, provided new tax incentives for Individual Retirement Accounts (IRAs) and Keogh plans, as well as reduced the gift and estate tax rates. Furthermore, a reduction in the highest marginal tax bracket from 70 to 50 percent effectively reduced the maximum long-term capital gains tax rate from 28 percent (40 percent of capital gains tax times 70 percent highest tax rate) to 20 percent (40 percent capital gains tax times 50 percent highest tax rate).

The Tax Equity and Fiscal Responsibility Act (TEFRA) of 1982 was designed to reduce the highest U.S. deficit in history by raising additional revenues for the federal government. While it did not raise tax rates, it did contain provisions that affected individual taxpayers. These provisions included new tax withholding and reporting procedures, depreciation allowances, and tax preferences. Partial rollovers of IRA investments into new IRAs were authorized and self-employed individuals were allowed to make tax-deductible contributions on an expanded scale to enable them to have nearly the same benefits as corporate employees.

TRA. The Tax Reform Act (TRA) of 1986 reduced individual income taxes by an average of six percent. This decline varied from about one percent for those in the $75,000 to $100,000 income bracket to over 65 percent for persons with incomes of $10,000 or less. The TRA also significantly reduced the number of tax brackets from 15 to three and increased the allowable standard deductions. Furthermore, TRA eliminated the preferential tax treatment of long-term capital gains and provided for taxation of these gains at the lower overall rates applicable to ordinary income. A summary of the major provisions of TRA and subsequent tax laws is presented in Table 7-1. We will discuss each of these changes later in this chapter.

Of the many sweeping changes brought about by TRA, the separation of earned, portfolio, and passive incomes and losses deserves special mention. With few exceptions, TRA ended the long-standing strategy of reducing earned income with passive losses. Under the current law, earned income, portfolio income, and passive income are all taxed as ordinary income. However, unlike the pre-TRA era, net passive losses cannot be used to reduce earned income; instead, they must be carried forward to future tax years. Portfolio losses are also similarly treated under the new tax law, except that each year up to $3,000 of net capital losses are allowed to be deducted from ordinary income.

RA. The Revenue Act (RA) of 1987 contained approximately 200 amendments to the Internal Revenue Code, with primary focus on business tax rules. Changes affecting individuals included the effective repeal of the estate freeze technique and a five-year deferral of the reduction from 55 to 50 percent in the maximum estate and gift tax rates. A host of pension provisions, primarily affecting minimum funding requirements, constituted another major component of this Act. It also placed new limits on the deduction for qualified residence interest.

TAMRA. In the early morning hours of October 22, 1988, the Technical and Miscellaneous Revenue Act (TAMRA) of 1988, almost given up for dead earlier, came to life and passed as one of the last actions of the 100th Congress.

TAMRA made the long-awaited technical corrections to TRA of 1986 as well as the Reform Act of 1984. It also contained a number of substantive revisions. An important addition to TAMRA was the Taxpayer Bill of Rights, which entitled taxpayers to (1) a pre-audit written explanation of their rights and the IRS's obligations; (2) required abatement of penalties resulting from reliance on erroneous written IRS advice; and (3) authorized recovery of damages for failure of the IRS to remove a lawful lien. Changes in the income tax provisions for individuals included rules concerning married taxpayers filing

TABLE 7-1 Major Provisions of TRA and Subsequent Tax Laws

Tax brackets	Three: 15%, 28%, 33%. Surcharge of 5% on upper income levels	Keogh deduction	Annual deduction up to $30,000 or 20% for owner-employee income
Standard deduction	$3,100 Single return $4,550 Head of household $5,200 Joint return $2,600 Married, filing separately	Mortgage interest	Deductible for principal residence and second home, within limits
Personal exemption	$2,000	Other consumer personal interest	Deductible up to 10% in 1990; none thereafter
Inflation adjustments	Tax brackets and standard deduction indexed beginning in 1989, personal exemption in 1990	Charitable contributions	Deductible (up to 50% of AGI) for those who itemize
		State, local income, and property tax	Totally deductible
Long-term capital gains and losses	Taxable with ordinary income; losses offset gains; entire loss up to $3,000 offsets ordinary income during current year. Excess losses are carried forward	State and local sales tax	Not deductible
		Medical expenses	Deductible if over 7.5% of adjusted gross income
Dividend exclusion	No exclusion	Misc. deductions	Deductible above 2% of adjusted gross income
Losses from passive activities	Only deductible against passive income, after five-year phaseout	Business meals	80% deductible
IRAs	Maximum deduction of $2,000 for each wage earner but limited to certain income levels	Employee business	Deductible only when combined with other misc. deductions
		Income averaging	None
401(k) plans	Annual tax-deferred employee contribution up to $7,313 (indexed to inflation)	Two-earner income	No deduction
		Alternative minimum tax	21% rate, tighter rules

separately, divorced taxpayers, sale of principal residence, and capital losses. These changes, along with others, have been incorporated in the discussion of the current tax laws presented in the following sections.

COMPUTATION OF FEDERAL TAXABLE INCOME

Before embarking upon a discussion of the calculation of taxable income, it is useful to quickly review the basic income tax structure, presented in Figure 7-2. The figure reveals that first the *gross income* is calculated. Next, adjustments to gross income are made to arrive at the *adjusted gross income*. From this figure, standard or itemized deductions and exemptions are subtracted to arrive at the *taxable income*. This income is the basis for computing the tentative federal income tax. From this tentative figure, *tax credits* allowed by law for certain conditions (e.g., age 65 or over, disability, and so on) are deducted to arrive at the *net tax liability*, or the total tax due figure.

Having briefly reviewed the basic income tax structure, we now proceed to a discussion of the procedures for calculating gross income.

Calculation of Gross Income

Calculation of tax liability begins with the computation of total gross income. Unless specifically excluded in the law, this income comprises all income received in the form of money, property, and services. For joint returns, incomes of both spouses must be reported. Also, based upon the source, income must be divided into several major categories. Each of these categories is discussed in detail in the following section.

Earned income. Earned income of employees, which is sometimes called active income, is reported annually on a W-2 form entitled "Wages and Tax Statement," or on Form 1099 for self-employed individuals. While salary, commissions, fees, and business profits are the most common forms of earned income, there are additional types of income directly related to gainful employment. An example of this type of income is self-employment income which is reported on Form 1099. Because earned or active income depends on some form of personal activity and remuneration for that activity, losses generally cannot be deducted against this form of income. The only exception is that ordinary and necessary business expenses may be deducted even if a loss results.

Portfolio income. Portfolio income is generated directly from investment activity. More specifically, portfolio income consists of interest, dividend income, and capital gains. The current tax law has very specific rules governing the reporting of portfolio income and deduction of losses against this income.

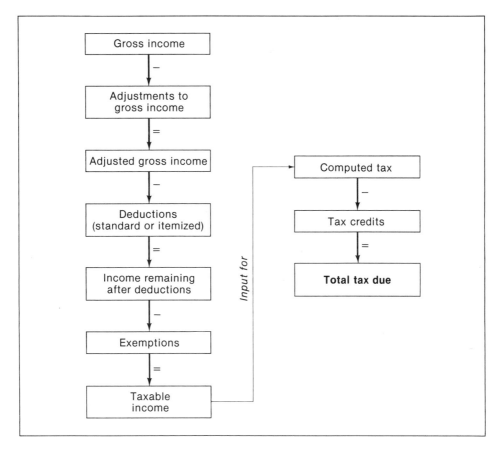

FIGURE 7-2 Basic income tax structure

Interest. Interest income includes interest from accounts with banks, credit unions, savings and loan associations, money market funds, and mutual funds. Interest from the following sources must also be reported as income: (1) personal notes; (2) loans and mortgages; (3) corporate bonds and debentures; (4) U.S. treasury bills; (5) certain taxable municipal bonds; and (6) maturing or annual liquidation of U.S. savings bonds. Generally the payor sends each income recipient a Form 1099-INT for this interest. If the total interest reported exceeds $400, the sources of interest must be detailed on the tax return (Schedule B).

Dividends. Dividend income results from distribution of earnings and profits which corporations or mutual funds pay to shareholders. Generally, the payor sends the income recipient a Form 1099-DIV reporting dividend income.

As with interest income, if the total dividend income exceeds $400, the sources of income must be detailed on the tax return (Schedule B).

One of the major changes in the current tax law was the repeal of the $200 exclusion ($100 on single returns) applicable to qualifying dividends. TRA made all dividend income subject to ordinary income tax. However, one notable exception is the dividend received from a mutual insurance company which is treated as a nontaxable return of excess premium payment to the extent it does not exceed accumulated premiums paid.

Capital gains and losses: an overview.   A capital gain is the profit realized from the sale of a capital asset, which is property owned by an individual for investment purposes or for personal use. For example, stocks and bonds, real estate, furniture, automobiles, and household furnishings are all capital assets. Gains on property held for personal use must be reported as capital gains, but losses on these assets are not deductible. Gains on investment property, such as stocks and bonds, real estate, and so on, must also be reported as capital gains. However, capital losses on investments can be offset in full against capital gains. Capital losses in excess of gains can be used to offset up to $3,000 of ordinary income on a dollar-for-dollar basis. Any excess losses can be carried forward to offset capital gains and income in later tax years.

Incidentally, gains on capital assets held over one year are considered long-term capital gains, whereas profits generated by assets held for twelve months or less are considered short-term capital gains. Currently both short-term and long-term capital gains are taxed as ordinary income.

Computation of capital gains and losses.   The current tax rules on capital gains and losses can best be understood by examining the following steps required for reporting gains and losses:

Step 1. Calculate the cost or tax *basis* of the capital asset. The basis is the sum of (1) the purchase price of the asset, (2) expenses incurred in improving the asset, and (3) depreciation (if applicable).

Step 2. Determine whether each transaction qualifies as a short- or long-term capital gain or loss by subtracting the cost basis from the final exchange value or sale price.

Step 3. Calculate the net short-term capital gain or loss by subtracting short-term losses from short-term gains.

Step 4. Calculate the net long-term capital gain or loss by subtracting long-term losses from long-term gains.

Step 5. Determine the net long-term or short-term capital gain or loss. The formula is:

$$\text{Net Gain/Loss} = \text{Amount Realized} - \text{Adjusted Basis}$$

The results of these computations are used to calculate the taxable income. The capital gain or loss reporting rules are summarized in Figure 7-3.

Wash sales. The wash sale provision applies to the sale of stocks and securities. This provision denies the deduction of a loss on the sale or exchange of securities if substantially identical securities are acquired within 30 days prior to, or subsequent to, the sale or exchange. The wash sale rules apply regardless of whether the individual voluntarily sells the stock to realize a loss for income tax purposes, is forced to sell, or sells to prevent an even greater loss. A repurchase of substantially identical securities within 30 days before or after the sale at a loss prohibits the deduction. These provisions also apply when the individual enters into an option to acquire substantially similar stocks or securities. The wash sale rules apply only to loss transactions and do not include transactions involving gains. The nondeductible loss is deferred and added to the purchase price of the reacquired shares.

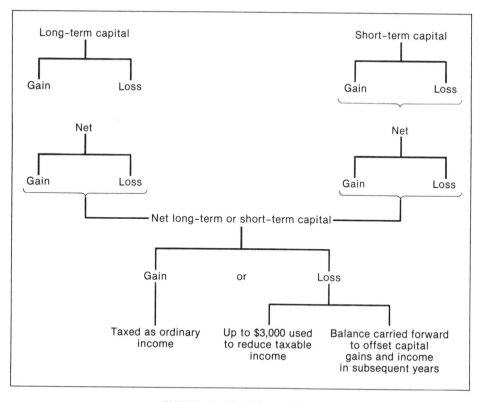

FIGURE 7-3 Capital gains tax calculation

Capital gains and sale of residence.   Capital gains realized on the sale of the principal residence receive special consideration. If an individual's principal place of residence is sold at a profit, capital gains taxes are deferred as long as another home of at least the same or greater value is purchased, or construction of a new home is completed within two years before or after the sale of the old home. Incidentally, the equity (cash) received from the sale of the principal residence can be spent on expenses other than purchasing a new home to qualify for deferment of taxes on capital gains. That is, if an old home is sold for $190,000 and a new home is purchased with a down-payment of $50,000 and a $150,000 mortgage, it would still qualify for special tax treatment under the law.

It should be mentioned here that not all homeowners purchase or construct another home after the sale of the principal residence. If another principal residence is not purchased, capital gains are computed by subtracting from the sale price any selling expenses, the original purchase price of the residence, and all costs incurred to improve the property. These costs may be for landscaping, home remodeling, and purchases of appliances included in the sale of the residence. The net capital gain on the sale of the residence is then taxed as ordinary income. However, a one-time lifetime exclusion of up to $125,000 of gain on the sale of a principal residence is allowed if the homeowner is 55 years or older.

Passive income.   The tax law generally provides that losses from passive activities, such as tax shelters, in which an individual does not materially participate, may be used only to offset income from such activities. In general, the *passive activity losses* may not be used to offset the income from compensation, interest, dividends, royalties, nonbusiness capital gains, or active business income.

TABLE 7-2   Allowable Deduction of Real Estate Losses

Assume Carl has annual wages of $70,000 and income from an equipment leasing limited partnership of $3,000.

Carl owns and operates a real estate investment property which generates the following tax loss.

Income	$35,000
Out-of-pocket operating expense	−$30,000
Net operating income	$ 5,000
Less depreciation expense	−$10,000
Net tax loss	−$ 5,000

Carl can use the $5,000 loss to offset his $3,000 income from a passive activity, and the remaining $2,000 to offset his ordinary income.

An exception applies to losses from those passive activities acquired on or before October 22, 1986. The ability to currently use losses from those older passive activities to offset non-passive income is limited to 10 percent of the losses in 1990 and none thereafter. Disallowed passive activity losses are carried forward and applied against income from passive activities in future years. These losses may also be deducted in the year in which the passive activity is entirely disposed of.

Another exception to the passive loss rules applies to certain real estate activities with material participation. Individuals who own rental property and whose adjusted gross income is less than $100,000 have the right to offset regular income with up to $25,000 of rental related losses. The maximum deduction is reduced by $1 for every $2 of adjusted gross income that taxpayers earn between $100,000 and $150,000. Application of this exception to the passive income rule is demonstrated in Table 7-2.

THE COMING OF THE PIG

If you bought a tax shelter that will produce losses, you need to know how tax reform affects you. Your losses from limited partnerships are now defined as passive activity losses ("PALs"). Tax reform also defines "passive activity income" as the only type of income you can shelter with PALs.

As has been true since 1987, you can't fully deduct limited partnership losses from wages, salaries, dividends and interest income. But you can deduct PALs from passive activity income. Investment vehicles that create passive activity income are called "PIGs" which stands for passive income generators. (The term was coined by Alan Rachap, our good friend from Merrill Lynch, Annapolis, MD.) You net your PALs against income from your PIGs to calculate your net PAL.

Contrary to Congressional rhetoric, tax reform has not taken the Tax Code out of the investment decision making process. Instead, reform complicates the process by pigeonholing income and loss by category. There's passive activity losses and income, rental activity losses and income, and portfolio losses and income. On top of all this, you cannot deduct consumer interest expense (except for interest on your home and the bungalow in the mountains) or investment interest expense in excess of portfolio income or gain. Sure sounds like an earnest attempt to remove the Tax Code from the investment decision making process!

Your PALs can shelter PIG taxable income with one exception. "Portfolio income" within a limited partnership can only be offset by investment interest expense, not passive losses. Generally, portfolio income comes from securities held by a limited partnership, like treasury bills. A limited partnership could generate passive income and portfolio income; the former shelterable, the latter not shelterable with a PAL. (Notice how simplified the Tax Code has become?)

AVOIDING THE POKE

By the new tax law's definition, many former (pardon the expression) tax shelter investors now possess PALs from deals bought in previous years—a mixed blessing. Just like Lee Marvin's "pal," your PAL may be tougher to deal with than you think. You have to proceed carefully if you intend to buy a PIG to offset (shelter) your PAL. Here's why.

PALs from investments made before enactment of the new law have been only partially deductible since 1986—part of your PAL is "disallowed." Suppose you have $10,000 of PALs this year. Your situation looks like this:

PAL	$10,000
Allowed Loss (65%)	− 6,500
Disallowed PAL	$ 3,500

You may think a PIG with $3,500 of this year's income is all it takes to offset the disallowed PAL. But that's not the way the calculation actually works.

You must net your PIG with your PAL to find your net PAL before calculating the portion disallowed. (Got that?) Here's how the calculation works:

Example 1
INSUFFICIENT PIG "POUNDAGE"

PAL	$10,000
PIG Income	− 3,500
Net PAL	$ 6,500
Allowed Loss (65%)	− 4,225
Disallowed Loss	$ 2,275

Sixty-five percent of your net PAL, or $4,225 shelters salaries. But, you still have $2,275 of disallowed loss.

Plus, the portion of the PAL which shelters wages and salary income ($4,225 above) is treated as investment interest expense (reducing investment income) and is a tax preference for Alternative Minimum Tax ("AMT") purposes. So, you'll need to shelter all of your PALs with PIGs to avoid a poke in the eye from Uncle Sam. Ouch! (See Example 2.)

That's right sports fans—you need to match 100% of your current PALs with PIGs to avoid disallowed losses and to be free of the spillover problem PALs create with investment interest expense and the AMT. (How do you feel about political contributions to your favorite Congressmen now?) The point is you need your accountant/financial planner to estimate your tax situation for this year now. First the calculation is complicated. Second, you may need all the PIG income you can earn this year, so you'll want to buy in late this year or early next year.

Source: Adapted from *The Stanger Report*, November, 1986, a monthly newsletter on partnership investors published by Robert A. Stanger & Co., 1129 Broad Street, Shrewsburg, NJ 07702.

Example 2
PROPER PIG POUNDAGE

PAL	$10,000
PIG	− 10,000
Net PAL	$ 0

PIG OR IMPOSTOR?

What investments are PIGs? An interest in a limited partnership which owns operating assets is a PIG. And, it doesn't matter whether the operating asset is real estate, oil and gas properties, cable TV systems, equipment, etc. All the taxable income from businesses conducted in limited partnerships can be used to offset your PALs.

Most limited partnerships in the business of making loans also may be PIGs. The exception is limited partnerships that are mortgage-holding conduits (for example, partnerships which purchase and hold existing mortgage notes as opposed to writing new mortgages). The rules here are a bit uncertain. The problem is that income in a mortgage-holding conduit is portfolio income. Even inside a limited partnership, portfolio income does not offest (cannot be sheltered by) a PAL. REITs and FREITs aren't PIGs. You get no PAL offset from FREIT and REIT income.

Look for the creation of new PIGs by the score. PIGs will be bred in new investment areas for partnerships which benefit from the elimination of the distinction between capital gains and ordinary income. Here you may see partnerships converting rental apartments to condos, subdividing and selling lots, developing office condo properties, and acquiring other operating businesses such as hamburger chains or nursing homes. Before long, partnership markets will be wallowing in PIGs— prompting a critical question for the future of partnership investing: Do the boys on Capital Hill know a ham when they see one? If so, the happy union of PALs and PIGs may be destined for slaughter.

Active or passive income. Not all incomes can be neatly categorized as either active or passive income. Examples of incomes which could be either active or passive include: (1) gains received on dealings in real estate, securities, and other property; (2) interest received on securities and loans; (3) rents collected, and (4) royalties.

Miscellaneous income. Individuals are taxed on certain types of incomes which do not fall into any of the categories just listed. These include: (1) annuities and pensions, to the extent that the return exceeds the investment; (2) income from an interest in an estate or trust, excluding the principal of any gift or bequest received; (3) prizes and awards; (4) certain fringe benefits; and (5) up to one half of Social Security benefits received.

Tax-exempt income: municipal bonds. Municipal bonds are qualifying tax-free bonds issued by municipalities (such as states, cities, and school districts) to raise funds for financing local projects. Interest income from municipal bonds is completely exempt from federal income tax. The reason for this exemption is to make it easier for municipalities to sell bonds and obtain financing for community improvement by making the municipal bond interest rate more attractive than the after-tax interest rates on comparable corporate bonds.

Tax-exempt municipal bonds provide investors with an alternative to investing in taxable corporate bonds and U.S. treasury instruments. The key question therefore becomes: Which of the three types of bonds offers a higher after-tax rate of return? The answer, of course, depends on the marginal tax bracket of the investor. Consider, for example, an investor in the 28 percent income tax bracket who wishes to purchase either a municipal bond paying eight percent or a corporate bond of equal riskiness, currently yielding ten percent. The municipal bond pays eight percent after-tax, whereas the corporate bond pays only 7.2 percent on an after-tax basis, as calculated here:

$$\begin{bmatrix} \text{Before tax} \\ \text{interest rate,} \\ \text{e.g., } 10\% = .10 \end{bmatrix} \times \begin{bmatrix} 1 - \begin{bmatrix} \text{Investor's} \\ \text{income tax} \\ \text{rate, e.g.,} \\ 28\% = .28 \end{bmatrix} \end{bmatrix} = \begin{bmatrix} \text{After-tax} \\ \text{interest rate,} \\ \text{e.g.,} \\ 7.2\% = .072 \end{bmatrix}$$

In this case, the investor in the 28 percent tax bracket will find the municipal bond to be a more attractive investment than the corporate bond. A comparison of tax-exempt with taxable yields for several interest levels is presented in Table 7-3. It can be seen from this table that a taxpayer in the 28 percent tax bracket would prefer a fully taxable corporate bond over a municipal bond yielding eight percent only if the taxable bond yielded over 11.11 percent.

TABLE 7-3   Tax-Exempt Yields and Equivalent
                Taxable Yields

Tax-exempt yields (%)	Tax brackets		
	15%	28%	33%
2.00	2.35	2.78	2.99
2.50	2.94	3.47	3.73
3.00	3.53	4.17	4.48
3.50	4.12	4.86	5.22
4.00	4.71	5.56	5.97
4.50	5.29	6.25	6.72
5.00	5.88	6.94	7.46
5.50	6.47	7.64	8.21
6.00	7.06	8.33	8.96
6.50	7.65	9.03	9.70
7.00	8.24	9.72	10.45
7.50	8.82	10.42	11.19
8.00	9.41	11.11	11.94
8.50	10.00	11.81	12.69
9.00	10.59	12.50	13.43
9.50	11.17	13.19	14.18
10.00	11.76	13.89	14.93
10.50	12.35	14.58	15.67
11.00	12.94	15.28	16.42
11.50	13.53	15.97	17.16
12.00	14.12	16.67	17.91
12.50	14.71	17.36	18.66
13.00	15.29	18.06	19.40
13.50	15.88	18.75	20.15
14.00	16.47	19.44	20.89
14.50	17.06	20.14	21.64
15.00	17.65	20.83	22.39

Social Security income.   Many Social Security recipients pay higher rates than they expect because, once their incomes pass a certain level, up to half of their Social Security benefits are taxed. Unmarried recipients are hit by the extra tax when their gross incomes, which include any tax-exempt interest they have earned plus half of their Social Security benefits, exceed $25,000. For married recipients, the threshold is $32,000. Beyond the thresholds, people in the 15 percent bracket pay taxes of 22.5 percent on their income until an amount equal to half of their Social Security benefits has been taxed. Those in the 28 percent bracket pay 42 percent.

An example should make this point clear. Suppose John Smith received $8,000 in Social Security benefits in 1988. He would be liable for the tax on Social Security if he filed jointly and the Smiths have non-Social Security income of anywhere from $28,000 ($32,000 base amount *less* $\frac{1}{2}$ of $8,000) to $36,000 ($32,000 base amount *plus* $\frac{1}{2}$ of $8,000). To put it in more general terms, the income range where Social Security is taxed runs from the base amount minus half of the Social Security benefits to the base amount plus half of the benefits. Thus, above the range, increases in the non-Social Security income have no effect on how much the benefit is taxed; below the range, none of the benefit is taxed.

Nontaxable income. Several sources of income are not treated as income. These sources include the following: (1) gifts and inheritances; (2) interest on certain state and municipal bonds, and interest received from certain mutual funds that hold such bonds; (3) returns of capital; (4) reimbursements received from an employer for business expenses, if properly reported; (5) a one-time exclusion of gain from the sale of a home if the taxpayer is 55 or over; (6) half of Social Security benefits up to the exempt amount; (7) compensation for injury or sickness, including Worker's Compensation and certain disability payments; (8) amounts received under insurance if the taxpayer paid the premium and did not deduct costs (e.g., medical) on prior returns; and (9) amounts contributed by the employer to an accident or health plan on behalf of the taxpayer and the family.

Adjustments to Gross Income

Once all forms of income (and appropriate losses) are totaled, a select group of expenditures can be deducted from gross income to help reduce the individual's final tax liability to its minimum legal amount. Currently, these deductions include business expenses for self-employed individuals reported on Schedule "C," interest penalties for early withdrawal of savings certificates of deposit, alimony payments, and contributions to qualified retirement programs, such as Keogh plans for the self-employed, and certain Individual Retirement Accounts (IRAs) for persons who are not self-employed. It might be useful to briefly discuss here the tax deductibility of IRAs.

One way to reduce taxable income is to contribute the maximum allowable amount to IRAs. In the pre-TRA era, all allowable contributions were fully deductible. Under the current law, people who contribute $2,000 to IRAs but are covered by retirement plans at work generally lose $1 of their IRA deduction for each $5 of adjusted gross income over $25,000 if they are single and over $40,000 if they are married. For instance, someone who contributes the maximum $2,000 and earns $5,000 more than the cap loses $1,000 of the deduction. In the 28 percent tax bracket, that loss results in an extra tax payment of $280, added to the normal $1,400 tax on $5,000. The total ($1,400 + $280) amounts to a 33.6 percent tax on the $5,000. When working spouses both lose $1,000 of their deductions, their joint rate rises to 39.2 percent. Income above the levels at which IRA deductions are fully erased is taxed again at normal rates. Incidentally, IRA contributions are fully deductible if an individual is not covered by a retirement plan, regardless of his or her income level.

Deductions

The next step in the process of calculating tax liability is to subtract all allowable deductions from the adjusted gross income. There are two options permitted in this step: The taxpayer can either take the standard deduction, or itemize deductions.

Standard deduction. The standard deduction is the amount all taxpayers (except some dependents) may take when filing a tax return. The amount of the standard deduction is the dollar threshold for determining whether or not the individual may itemize deductions. The standard deductions for 1989 are listed in Table 7-4. Incidentally, both the standard deduction and the additional allowances for the blind and the elderly are subject to inflation adjustments.

TABLE 7-4 Standard Deductions

Filing status	1989 Standard deduction
Married, filing jointly	$5,200
Head of household	4,550
Single	3,100
Married, filing separately	2,600

In addition, the standard deduction is increased by $600 for an individual 65 years old or older or for a blind individual who is married (or $1,200 for a married individual who is both blind and 65 years old or older). An additional $750 is allowed for an unmarried individual who is 65 years old or older or blind ($1,500 if both). For a student or a dependent who may be claimed as a dependent by another person, the standard deduction is the greater of $500 or earned income, except that the deduction may not exceed the basic standard deduction.

Itemized deductions. Individuals who have tax-deductible expenses in excess of the standard deduction amount may benefit from using the itemized deductions approach. These deductions represent those specific expenses that can be subtracted from adjusted gross income. The general classifications of deductions and limitations to each category are summarized next.

Medical expenses. Medical expenses not reimbursed by insurance in excess of 7.5 percent of the adjusted gross income are deductible. These expenses include amounts paid for: (1) the diagnosis, treatment, or prevention of disease; (2) transportation primarily for and essential to medical care; (3) insurance covering medical care; (4) lodging while away from home primarily for medical care; and (5) accommodating a home to fit the needs of a physically handicapped person.

State and local taxes. State and local income taxes, real estate taxes, and personal property taxes all qualify as itemized deductions. However, state and local sales taxes are excluded from itemized deductions.

Interest expense. The new tax rules significantly affecting the deductibility of various types of interest expense are summarized in Table 7-5. A brief discussion of each of the five types of interest expense follows.

A completely new set of rules applies to the *qualified residence interest expense.* Interest paid on first and second home mortgage loans is deductible to the extent that the amount of the acquisition indebtedness does not exceed $1 million. The term "acquisition indebtedness" is defined as debt that is incurred in acquiring, constructing, or substantially improving the taxpayer's principal residence, and is secured by such residence. Interest on home equity loans is also deductible, provided the loan does not exceed the fair market value of the residence, reduced by the amount of acquisition indebtedness (that is, the mortgage) on the residence. The aggregate amount of home equity indebtedness may not exceed $100,000. Thus, the total amount of acquisition and home equity debt on a principal and second residence may not exceed $1,100,000 ($1 million plus $100,000). Interest on "points" paid to purchase a home or secure a home mortgage loan for home improvements is also deductible, but it must be pro-rated if not paid up-front but rather added to the new mortgage.

An example should make this provision clear. Suppose a homeowner paid $175,000 for a principal residence in early 1989. The original mortgage was $125,000, which was considered acquisition indebtedness. The current mortgage balance is $123,000. The homeowner takes out a second mortgage loan of $25,000 for home improvements. The acquisition indebtedness is now $148,000 ($123,000 plus $25,000). The interest on the acquisition debt, of course, will be fully deductible.

TABLE 7-5 Deductibility of Interest Expense

Interest category	Its nature	Deductibility rules
Qualified residence interest expense	Interest on indebtedness secured by any property that is a qualified residence of the taxpayer, plus one other residence.	Deductibility limited to the lesser of (1) the fair market value of the residence, or (2) taxpayer's cost basis in the home. Furthermore, the law further limits deductions of interest on loans of up to $1 million and home equity loans of up to $100,000.
Investment interest expense	Interest on debt incurred to carry property that is held for investment.	Investment interest is deductible to the extent of net investment income, which is equal to the amount of investment income over investment expenses. The phase-out rule limits the interest deduction to 1,000 over investment income in 1990, and none thereafter.
Business interest expense	Interest on loans taken to operate a business.	All interest expenses are fully deductible.
Passive activity interest expense	Interest expenses generated in carrying out passing activity in which the person does not materially participate.	Deductible only to the extent of taxpayer's activity income. Nondeductible interest expenses during a tax year can be carried forward to future tax years.
Consumer interest expense	Interest on personal loans	Limited to 10% of interest in 1990 and none after 1990.

An individual's deduction for *investment interest expense* is limited to the amount of net investment income. However, interest on loans to finance tax-exempt income, such as municipal bonds, is not deductible since the income generated is nontaxable. If an investor has a margin account with a stock-broker, in order to deduct the interest incurred by buying on margin, the investor must have credits in the margin account sufficient to evidence payment of that interest. Put differently, the investor must have enough dividends, interest income, cash payments, or proceeds from security sales credited to the account during the year to cover the amount of interest charged to the investor. If need be, the investor should make a cash deposit to the margin account on or before December 31 to cover the interest payment.

Another type of expense, namely, the *business interest expense*, incurred as a result of loans taken to operate a business, is fully deductible. However, *passive activity interest expense*, generated by carrying out a passive activity in which the taxpayer did not materially participate, is deductible only to the extent of the taxpayer's passive activity income.

Finally, the new law severely restricts the use of *consumer interest expense*. In 1989, 20 percent of the interest expense was deductible. In 1990 only ten percent of this interest is deductible; beginning in 1991 no deduction of consumer interest will be allowed.

Charitable contributions. Charitable contributions are fully deductible only for itemizing taxpayers. Deductions for charitable cash contributions to churches, schools, and other qualifying nonprofit groups are limited to no more than 50 percent of adjusted gross income. Any excess deductions during a given tax year can be carried forward to the next five tax years.

If an itemizing taxpayer gives property such as stocks or real estate to charity, the appreciation in property gifts must be added back to the income for purposes of alternative minimum tax calculations (discussed later in the chapter). Also, the appreciation in gifts of tangible personal property such as art, antiques, and collectibles is disallowed entirely unless the gift is used for the charity's tax-exempt purposes. For instance, suppose a taxpayer donates to the local museum a painting that cost him $10,000 and is now worth $300,000. If the museum auctions off the painting instead of displaying it, the taxpayer will get a deduction of only $10,000. Incidentally, the 30 percent adjusted gross income limit on charitable contribution of appreciated property is applicable.

Business use of a home. In order to deduct the expenses attributable to business use of a principal residence, it must be demonstrated that such expenses are attributable to a portion of the home that is used exclusively and on a regular basis as one of the following: (1) The principal place of business; (2) a place of business that is used by clients or customers in meeting or dealing with the taxpayer in the course of business; or (3) a separate structure detached from the residence, that is used exclusively in connection with business. A taxpayer who qualifies under these strict rules is limited further in that these deductions are limited to the taxpayer's net income from the business.

Casualty or theft losses. Casualty or theft losses not reimbursed by insurance and in excess of ten percent of the adjusted gross income plus $100 per loss are deductible. These losses may arise from fire, storm, vandalism or other sudden, unexpected, or unusual events.

Moving Expenses.   Qualifying unreimbursed moving expenses to a new job location are deductible only if the taxpayer claims itemized deductions. Moving expenses are not reduced by the two percent adjusted gross income floor.

To deduct moving expenses, the taxpayer must move at least 35 miles from the former home and must work full time for at least 78 weeks during the 24 months immediately following the arrival, of which at least 39 weeks occur in the first 12 months.

Only certain types of expenses are fully deductible, such as the cost of moving household goods and related travel costs. Other expenses, such as the costs of pre-move house hunting trips, or temporary quarters at the new job location, are deductible only within limits.

Miscellaneous expenses.   Two general categories of miscellaneous expenses are deductible against adjusted gross income. The first category includes personal expenses incurred to generate employee business or investment income, or to preserve or protect income-producing assets. These expenses include: (1) union or professional association dues and membership fees; (2) a safe deposit box used to store papers related to income-producing investments; (3) purchase and maintenance of specialized clothing for on-the-job use; (4) 80 percent of unreimbursed employee business meals, and entertainment expense; (5) tax counsel, tax preparation fees, and financial planning fees; and (6) tools used in a profession. These expenses are deductible only to the extent that they exceed two percent of the adjusted gross income.

The second general category of miscellaneous expenses includes: (1) gambling losses which offset reported gambling income; and (2) business expenses for handicapped workers and performing artists. Expenses in this category are not subject to the 2 percent floor.

Summing up.   Once the amounts of standard deductions and itemized deductions have been determined, the greater of the two is subtracted from the adjusted gross income to arrive at the penultimate step in the process of taxable income calculations.

Exemptions

The final step necessary to determine taxable income is to compute exemptions, which represent the legally permitted deduction from the taxpayer's taxable income based on the number of persons supported by that income. TRA permits a personal exemption of $2,000 (in 1989) with annual adjustments for inflation. The total value of exemptions is computed by multiplying each deduction by $2,000, that is, one for the taxpayer and each dependent. Once the value of exemptions is computed, the taxable income is determined by subtracting the exemptions from income remaining after deductions.

Number of Dependents

In order to meet the basic requirements, a dependent must: (1) have received less than $2,000 of gross income (tied to exemption amount); (2) have received from the taxpayer over half of the support in the tax year; (3) not have filed a joint return; (4) have been a citizen or resident of the U.S., a resident of Canada or Mexico, or an alien child adopted by and living the entire year with a U.S. citizen in a foreign country; and (5) have been related to the taxpayer or lived with the taxpayer the whole year. Incidentally, a person under 19 who is enrolled as a full-time student is exempted from complying with the first condition just listed, although the other four tests must be satisfied.

The tax law requires that a Social Security number be reported for all dependents who are at least two years old by the end of the tax year. The law also requires that children (limit age 24) who can be claimed as dependents on parents' returns may not claim themselves on their own returns. Further changes in TRA governing tax rates on the income of children under 14 will be discussed in Chapter 8 as they relate to the use of gifts as a form of tax planning.

COMPUTATION OF INCOME TAX

TAX COMPUTATION

Basic Computation

For 1989, there were two tax rates—15 percent and 28 percent. However, for certain higher income individuals, a five percent additional tax is used to phase out the benefit of the 15 percent tax rate. Thus, the marginal rate becomes 33 percent for taxable income in this phaseout range (that is, $74,850 to $155,320) for married persons filing a joint return. For a single taxpayer the phase out range is $44,900 to $93,130.

For example, suppose in 1989 a couple filing a joint return had a taxable income of $100,000. Using the tax rates presented in Table 7-6 we find that the tax will be $25,233:

For income of	The rate is	And the tax is
$0– $30,950 = $30,950	15%	$ 4,642
$30,950– $74,850 = $43,900	28%	12,292
$74,850–$100,000 = $25,150	33%	8,299
	Total:	$25,233

TABLE 7-6

1989 Tax Rate Schedules

Caution: *Do not use these Tax Rate Schedules to figure your 1988 taxes. Use only to figure your 1989 estimated taxes.*

Schedule X—Single

If line 5 is: Over—	But not over—	The tax is:	of the amount over—
$0	$18,550	........15%	$0
18,550	44,900	$2,782.50 + 28%	18,550
44,900	93,130	10,160.50 + 33%	44,900
93,130	....	Use **Worksheet** below to figure your tax.	

Schedule Z— Head of household

If line 5 is: Over—	But not over—	The tax is:	of the amount over—
$0	$24,850	........15%	$0
24,850	64,200	$3,727.50+ 28%	24,850
64,200	128,810	14,745.50 + 33%	64,200
128,810	....	Use **Worksheet** below to figure your tax.	

Schedule Y-1—Married filing jointly or Qualifying widow(er)

If line 5 is: Over—	But not over—	The tax is:	of the amount over—
$0	$30,950	........15%	$0
30,950	74,850	$4,642.50 + 28%	30,950
74,850	155,320	16,934.50 + 33%	74,850
155,320	....	Use **Worksheet** below to figure your tax.	

Schedule Y-2— Married filing separately

If line 5 is: Over—	But not over—	The tax is:	of the amount over—
$0	$15,475	........15%	$0
15,475	37,425	$2,321.25 + 28%	15,475
37,425	117,895	8,467.25 + 33%	37,425
117,895	....	Use **Worksheet** below to figure your tax.	

Worksheet (Keep for your records)

1. If your filing status is: { Single, enter $26,076.40 / Head of household, enter $36,066.80 / Married filing jointly or Qualifying widow(er), enter $43,489.60 / Married filing separately, enter $35,022.35 } . . . . **1.** _____

2. Enter your taxable income from line 5 of the Form 1040-ES worksheet . . . . . . **2.** _____

3. If your filing status is: { Single, enter $93,130 / Head of household, enter $128,810 / Married filing jointly or Qualifying widow(er), enter $155,320 / Married filing separately, enter $117,895 } . . . . **3.** _____

4. Subtract line 3 from line 2. Enter the result. (If the result is zero or less, use the schedule above for your filing status to figure your tax. DON'T use this worksheet.) . . . . . . **4.** _____

5. Multiply the amount on line 4 by 28% (.28). Enter the result . . . . **5.** _____

6. Multiply the amount on line 4 by 5% (.05). Enter the result . . . . **6.** _____

7. Multiply $560 by the number of exemptions claimed. (If married filing separately, see Note below.) Enter the result . . . . **7.** _____

8. Compare the amounts on lines 6 and 7. Enter the **smaller** of the two amounts . . . . . . **8.** _____

9. **Tax.** Add lines 1, 5, and 8. Enter the total here and on line 6 of the Form 1040-ES worksheet . . . . . . **9.** _____

Note: *If married filing separately and you did **not** claim an exemption for your spouse, multiply $560 by the number of exemptions claimed. Add $560 to the result and enter the total on line 7 above.*

The Filing Status

The process of computing tax liability involves the determination of the filing status and the number of dependents to be claimed for the tax year. Filing status options, qualifications for each status, individual tax rates for tax year 1989, and the minimum income requirement for filing are presented in Table 7-7.

Marginal Tax Rate

An understanding of the difference between *marginal* and *average* tax rates is crucial to the tax planning process. The average, or effective, tax rate is merely the total tax payable divided by taxable income. For instance, suppose in 1989 a married couple filing jointly had a taxable income of $30,950. This couple would pay a tax of $4,642.00 (Table 7-6, Schedule Y-1) and the average tax rate would be 15.00 percent:

$$\frac{\text{Tax Payable}}{\text{Taxable Income}} = \frac{\$4,642.00}{\$30,950.00}$$

$$= 15.00\%$$

However, if the couple earned an additional $1,000, the marginal tax rate on this additional amount would be 28 percent.

More specifically, the marginal tax rate is used to describe the rate at which a taxpayer pays tax on the *last* dollar of income earned. Taxable income that falls within certain "brackets" or ranges is taxed at a specified percentage as set forth in the Internal Revenue Code. In past years, determining a taxpayer's marginal tax bracket was done simply by looking up the taxable income on the IRS Tax Rate Schedules. It is the same in 1989 for low and middle income taxpayers, but not for high bracket taxpayers.

If a taxpayer's income is above the 33 percent bracket, one has to compute the tax using the worksheet presented at the bottom of Table 7-6. This "worksheet bracket" is actually made up of a 33 percent bracket for the *lower* range and a 28 percent bracket for the *higher* range. This is the reverse of the normal pattern of graduated tax rates. The size of the bracket depends on the number of personal exemptions claimed by the taxpayer. This is because above a certain income level the benefit of the personal exemption is phased out. We present below an example to illustrate the technique of a marginal tax bracket calculation.

Let us assume John and Betty Smith file a joint return and have two dependents, which means that they can claim four exemptions. For 1989 John expects to have a taxable income of $200,120. Since John's income is above the $155,320 limit (see Table 7-6), he must use the worksheet to figure his tax. John Smith's tax calculation is presented in Table 7-8. In 1989, for a married taxpayer filing jointly with four exemptions, the marginal tax bracket was 33 percent for taxable income ranging between $155,320 and $200,120. The marginal tax bracket above the $200,120 taxable income dropped to 28 percent.

TABLE 7-7 Filing Status and Tax Rates Effective 1989 Tax Year

Filing status	Qualifications	Taxable income	Tax rate	Minimum income required to file	Taxable income subject to additional 5% tax if	
					More than	But not more than
Single	Unmarried or separated from spouse by divorce or separate maintenance decree and do not qualify for other filing status as of December 31	0–$18,550 Over $18,550	15% 28%	65 or older	$4,950 $5,700	$44,900	$93,130
Married Filing Jointly or Qualified Widow(er)	Married as of December 31. Combine all income, exemptions, deductions, and credits	0–$30,950 Over $74,850	15% 28%	One spouse 65 or older Both 65 or older	$8,900 $9,500 $10,100	$74,850	$155,320
	1. Could have filed joint return with your spouse for the year spouse died 2. Dependent child lived with you			65 or older	$6,950 $7,550		

3. You paid over half cost of keeping up the home for this child

   Must meet all 3 qualifications

Married Filing Separately	Married as of December 31 Each report only own income, exemptions, deductions and credits	0–$15,475 Over $15,475	15% 28%		$1,950	$37,425	$117,895
Head of Household	1. Unmarried on December 31 and 2. Paid more than half the cost of keeping up a home which was principal home of father or mother whom you claimed as a dependent or 3. Paid more than half the cost of keeping up a home in which you lived with a qualifying dependent for more than 6 months of the year.	0–$24,850 Over $24,850	15% 28%	65 or older	$6,350 $7,100	$64,200	$128,810

TABLE 7-8

Worksheet (Keep for your records)

1. If your filing status is:
   - Single, enter $26,076.40
   - Head of household, enter $36,066.80
   - Married filing jointly or Qualifying widow(er), enter $43,489.60
   - Married filing separately, enter $35,022.35
   1. *43,489.60*

2. Enter your taxable income from line 5 of the Form 1040-ES worksheet 2. *200,120.00*

3. If your filing status is:
   - Single, enter $93,130
   - Head of household, enter $128,810
   - Married filing jointly or Qualifying widow(er), enter $155,320
   - Married filing separately, enter $117,895
   3. *155,320.00*

4. Subtract line 3 from line 2. Enter the result. (If the result is zero or less, use the schedule above for your filing status to figure your tax. DON'T use this worksheet.) 4. *44,800.00*

5. Multiply the amount on line 4 by 28% (.28). Enter the result 5. *12,544.00*

6. Multiply the amount on line 4 by 5% (.05). Enter the result 6. *627.20*

7. Multiply $560 by the number of exemptions claimed. (If married filing separately, see Note below.) Enter the result 7. *2,040.00*

8. Compare the amounts on lines 6 and 7. Enter the **smaller** of the two amounts 8. *627.20*

9. **Tax.** Add lines 1, 5, and 8. Enter the total here and on line 6 of the Form 1040-ES worksheet 9. *56,660.80*

Note: *If married filing separately and you did **not** claim an exemption for your spouse, multiply $560 by the number of exemptions claimed. Add $560 to the result and enter the total on line 7 above.*

Page 4

The determination of the marginal tax bracket involves the following calculation:

Line 3: $155,320

Add Line 4:   44,800

Total $200,120

Since John's income is not above $200,120, his marginal tax bracket is 33 percent. If John's income were *above* this amount, the marginal bracket would be 28 percent.

Incidentally, the marginal tax brackets are *not* limited to 15, 28, and 33 percent. In fact, as the accompanying boxed insert reveals, depending upon individual situations, these brackets could be 39 percent, 42 percent, and even as high as 49.5 percent. Clearly, determination of the marginal tax bracket is a complex subject; however, it also provides unique tax planning opportunities for the sophisticated financial planner.

Tax Credits

After the tax liability is computed, tax credits may be used to reduce this liability dollar for dollar. Tax credits are available to businesspersons for payment of foreign taxes and employment of special targeted groups in the form of job credits. Low income elderly taxpayers may be allowed a tax credit while receiving public disability benefits. Two other forms of tax credit, applicable to many taxpayers, are explained next.

DIRTY LITTLE SECRETS ABOUT TAX BRACKETS

Now that your 1988 income tax return is safely filed, you may already be aware that our highly touted two-bracket tax system isn't exactly as advertised. In addition to the official 15% and 28% rates, the law includes a 33% bracket. And in fact, many taxpayers pay a higher *marginal* rate than their actual tax bracket suggests.

The marginal rate is the tax on your last dollar of income. If 33 cents goes to the federal government, the marginal rate is 33%. The marginal rate determines how much of any extra earnings—from investments, a raise or moonlighting—you get to keep after taxes. It also measures the saving power of deductible expenses.

We all start with the official rates, as shown in these tables.

Taxable income	Tax rate
Single	
$0–$18,550 .... 15%	
$18,551–$44,900 28	
$44,901–$93,130 33	
Over$93,130 28	
Joint	
$0–$30,950 .... 15%	
$30,951–$74,850 28	
$74,851–$155,320 33	
Over $155,320 28	

The tax rates apply only to income within each bracket. If you report $40,000 of taxable income on a joint return, for example, the first $30,950 is taxed at 15%. The 28% rate applies only to the $9,050 over $30,950.

The 33% bulge bracket is created by a 5% surcharge that takes back from higher-income taxpayers the benefit of having some of their income taxed in the 15% bracket. The income in the 33% bracket—

the $80,470 between $74,850 and $155,320 on a joint return, for example—is the amount on which a 5% surtax recoups the dollars the IRS "loses" because the first $30,950 is taxed at 15% rather than 28%.

The 33% bracket really continues beyond the limits shown in the table, covering an additional $11,200 of the income for each dependency exemption claimed on your return. On a joint return claiming four exemptions, for example, the 33% bracket extends to $200,120—$155,320 plus $44,800. The odd amount—$11,200 for each examption—is the amount on which a 5% surtax will recover the $560 tax savings produced by each $2,000 exemption in the 28% bracket. Once the benefits of the 15% bracket and all exemptions are wiped out by the 5% surtax, the rate falls back to 28%.

That's the official line. Now for the unofficial, and often painful, reality.

THE 42% BRACKET

Those receiving taxable Social Security benefits can be hit by a marginal rate of 42%. How? When income passes a certain threshold—$25,000 on single returns and $32,000 on joint returns—every extra dollar of income causes 50 cents' worth of benefits to be taxed. (For purposes of this threshold, "income" includes half of your social security benefits and all of your tax-exempt interest income.)

If you're in the 28% bracket, for example, and your income exceeds the threshold, earning an extra $100 adds $150 to taxable income—the $100 plus $50 of previously untaxed social security benefits. Taxing $150 at 28% costs you $42, or 42% of the extra $100 you earned. Regardless of how high your income, no more than half of your social security benefits can be taxed. Therefore, once your income hits the point at which 50% of the benefits are taxable, this higher rate ends.

THE 48% BRACKET

The new medicare surtax further blurs the marginal rate. That tax—which applies for the first time in 1989—adds 15% to the tax liability of each taxpayer eligible for medicare benefits. If you fall in the 15% tax bracket and owe this surtax, your marginal rate is 17.25%; if you're in the 28% bracket, the effective rate is 32.2%. Once you reach the $800 cap on the surtax this year, the surtax disappears.

If you are in the 28% bracket and are hit by the taxation of social security benefits *and* the medicare surtax, your effective marginal rate is 48.3%.

THE 49.5% BRACKET

If you own rental property and have a six-figure income, you can face a rate of 49.5%. This bulge, too, is caused by a provision that phases out the right to a deduction as income rises. Under certain circumstances, the law permits landlords to deduct up to $25,000 of rental losses against other income. As AGI rises between $100,000 and $150,000, however, that deduction disappears.

Source: Reprinted with permission of *Changing Times* Magazine, © Kiplinger Washington Editors, Inc., May 1989. This reprint is not to be altered in any way, except with permission from *Changing Times.*

Consider this example: A landlord with AGI of $110,000 is allowed to deduct up to $20,000 of rental loss. If income increases by $1,000, however, the deduction would be cut back to $19,500. That means an additional $1,500 is taxable—the extra $1,000 and the $500 no longer offset by the deduction. In the 33% bracket, that costs $495—for an effective rate of 49.5%.

WOULD YOU SETTLE FOR 39%?

If you or your spouse is covered by a retirement plan at work and your adjusted gross income on a joint return is between $40,000 and $50,000—the range in which extra income reduces the size of the IRA deduction you're allowed—your effective tax rate can be 39.2%. That assumes both you and your spouse contribute the maximum $2,000 to an IRA so that each $5 of extra income over $40,000 reduces your IRA write-off by $2. (At $50,000 your write-off is eliminated.) In other words, earning an extra $100 lets the IRS tax an extra $140—the $100 plus the $40 that is no longer protected by the IRA. In the 28% bracket, that costs $39.20—for an effective rate of 39.2%. If you file a single return and your income is in the IRA phase-out range—$25,000 to $35,000—the effective rate is 33.6% because each $5 of added income reduces the write-off by just $1.

Child and dependent care credit. A credit of up to 30 percent of child or disabled dependent care expense is permitted under the law. The taxpayer is obliged to demonstrate that this expense, which may include home upkeep, cooking, and general care, such as a nursery, was necessary because the taxpayer was working, seeking work, or attending school on a full-time basis. A maximum of $720 ($2,400 × .30) can be claimed as credit on expenses totalling $2,400. For taxpayers with two or more qualifying dependents, the credit is permitted on a maximum of $4,800 in expenses. The tax credit is 30 percent per child or dependent care expenses if the adjusted gross income is $10,000 or less. The 30 percent is reduced by one percent for each $2,000 of adjusted gross income above $10,000 until the percentage is reduced to 20 percent for income over $28,000.

Earned income credit. This tax credit is available to those individuals whose earned income and adjusted gross income are each less than a pre-specified amount. This earned income does not include Social Security payments, workmen's compensation, or unemployment compensation. To use this tax credit, the individual filing as married or a qualifying widow(er) must have a dependent child. An individual filing as head of household qualifies if there is a married child in the home even if the child is not a dependent. If qualified, an individual who might not have to file an income tax return could file for the earned income credit and receive an appropriate refund.

Alternative Minimum Tax

For some taxpayers, one final step remains in the calculation of tax liability: namely, calculation of the alternative minimum tax (AMT). This tax was conceived to prevent individuals from escaping taxation through invest-

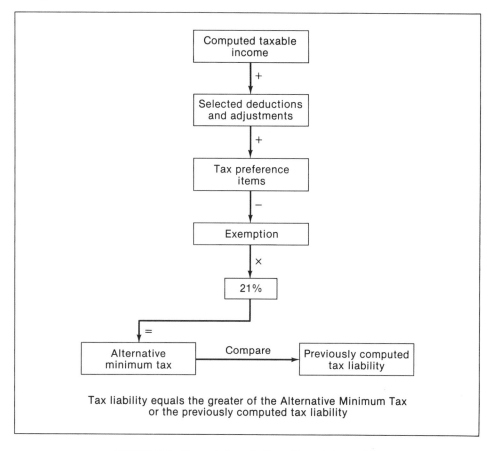

FIGURE 7-4 Computation of alternative minimum tax

ments that enjoy special tax treatment. The TRA strengthened the rules for the AMT to make it more difficult for individuals to avoid taxes.

The basic concept of the AMT provision is that the taxpayer must pay the greater amount resulting from two different methods of calculating tax: first, by the regular method already described, and second, by the AMT method. This method of AMT calculation is illustrated in Figure 7-4.

The process of AMT calculation begins by adding back certain itemized deductions to the taxable income already computed. These deductions include all state and local taxes, accelerated depreciation, the increase in market value of charitable gifts of appreciated property, and all miscellaneous expenses and personal exemptions. Then a number of "preference items" are added back. These are items that receive preferential treatment under regular tax law. Examples of preference items include unrealized appreciation on donated long-term capital gains property, incentive stock options, and accelerated depreciation on depreciable real property. Once these additions are made, the taxpayer is allowed a flat exemption: $30,000 if filing single or head of household, and $40,000 if married filing jointly (phased out at high income levels). After this exemption is subtracted from the adjusted taxable income, the final figure is multiplied by 21 percent. If this figure is greater than the tax liability computed by the regular method, the AMT becomes the individual's tax liability.

In this chapter we have presented the basic federal income tax structure and have demonstrated the technique for computing federal income tax. In the next chapter we will explore in detail various tax planning strategies.

CHAPTER 8

Tax Planning: Concepts and Strategies

INTRODUCTION

Tax planning is primarily concerned with the *timing* and *method* by which income is reported and deductions and credits are claimed. Tax law permits every taxpayer to select among various options in reporting income and claiming deductions and credits. Every taxpayer's task is to decide which of these options would minimize the tax burden. Interestingly, in 1945 the U.S. Supreme Court upheld the "legal right of a taxpayer to decrease the amount of what otherwise would have been his (or her) taxes or to avoid them altogether, by means which the law permits." Judge Learned Hand elaborated: "Nobody owes any public duty to pay more than the law demands; taxes are enforced extractions, not voluntary contributions. To demand more in the name of morals is mere cant."

In the first section we will discuss tax planning ideas for the individual taxpayer. Next we will briefly review several key tax planning ideas for the business organization. Finally, we will discuss miscellaneous tax issues relating to true marginal tax rate, amendment of tax return, and tax audit.

THE INDIVIDUAL TAXPAYER

There are many ways in which an individual taxpayer can minimize his or her tax burden. These myriad tax reduction techniques can be conveniently grouped into five major categories, which we prefer to call the *five Ds*. These categories, presented in Table 8-1, will be discussed in the following pages.

DEDUCTION

In Chapter 7 we presented in detail the deductions allowed under current tax laws. In this section we will explore some of the important planning ideas pertaining to tax deductions.

The Forgotten Deductions

Many taxpayers assume, somewhat naively, that since there are 7.5 percent and two percent floors imposed on medical and miscellaneous expenses, respectively, they cannot possibly pass the threshold at which these expenses become deductible. This is usually not a good assumption. For instance, medical expenses not only include doctor and hospital bills but also medically required home improvements, special schooling for a handicapped child, travel for medical care, eyeglasses, cosmetic surgery, and health insurance premiums. Even the difference in rental expenses if someone is forced to move to a larger home to accommodate a live-in nurse is deductible.

Another tax planning strategy is to group medical expenses to make them deductible. For instance, the taxpayer may opt to have elective surgery or braces for the kids all in one year, so health care expenses will be high. Here is a simple example to illustrate the point. Suppose John Case itemizes his deductions and has an adjusted gross income of $23,000, unreimbursed hospital and dental expenses of $600, and prescription drug expenses of $400. He also paid $600 during the year for medical insurance. The total medical expense deduction for 1989 is nil:

Hospital and dental expenses	$ 600
Payment for medical insurance	600
Medicine and drug expenses	400
Totals:	$1,600
Less 7.5% of adjusted gross income (.075 × $23,000)	1,725
Total medical expenses deduction for 1988	−$125
	= $0.

TABLE 8-1 Five Ds of Tax Planning Techniques

Category	Explanation
*D*eduction	Acceleration of deductions allowed under the current law.
*D*iversion	Steps taken by a taxpayer to channel investment return into money which will be taxed at a lower rate, will escape taxation, or will reduce taxable gain.
*D*eferral	Actions taken to defer taxes to future years.
*D*eflection	Steps taken to shift taxable income to someone who would be taxed at a lower rate.
*D*iminution	Actions which will reduce taxes by adopting various strategies.

However, if during 1989 John would have spent an additional $400 for braces (dental expenses) for his daughter, his deduction would have been $275 ($1,600 + $400 − $1,725).

Like medical deductions, miscellaneous deductions also offer valuable tax reduction strategies. For instance, cost of membership dues, financial planning and accounting fees, and unreimbursed business expenses are examples of often overlooked deductible miscellaneous expenses. Estimated savings are approximately $560 for a household grouping $3,500 worth of deductions into one year with $75,000 of adjusted gross income.

Other itemized deductions often ignored by taxpayers involve charitable contributions and state and local income taxes. For instance, people who use their car in charity work can deduct $.12 per mile plus parking and tolls. Also deductible are expenses such as a scoutmaster's uniform, and phone calls and travel expenses for charity work. A ticket to a fundraiser is deductible to the extent that its price exceeds normal admission cost. By not accepting the ticket or returning it for resale, the taxpayer can in fact deduct the entire cost.

In the area of state income taxes, the taxpayer can count not only amounts withheld from the year's paychecks and any estimated payments made but also any tax paid on the previous year's state tax return when filed. In some states, taxpayers can write off local taxes beyond income and real estate tax. Residents of California, New Jersey, New York, and Rhode Island can deduct as state income tax the mandatory contribution they make to state disability funds. Auto license fees normally are not deductible, but some states base part of the charge on the value of the car. That part of the fee as well as intangible taxes are deductible as a personal property tax. These amounts are also deductible from federal income taxes.

Flexible Spending Account

Flexible Spending Accounts (FSAs) have been available since 1978 and in recent years have become quite popular. Dollars deposited in FSAs come off the top of the salary through payroll deductions or from employer contributions or from both. These contributions completely escape taxes, including Social Security and most state income taxes as long as the funds are used within a single year for medical expenses or dependent care not covered by employee benefits. Annual limits for dependent care are $5,000; medical cost maximums are not set by law but by employers.

While FSAs provide an excellent tax reduction strategy, they do have one important drawback: The money set aside in this account during a given year must be used during that year or it will be forfeited.

Moving Expenses

The tax treatment of moving expenses is different from the treatment of most employee business expenses in that this deduction is not subject to the two percent floor that applies to other miscellaneous deductions. The moving expenses and company reimbursements must be accounted for separately on tax returns. All company reimbursements for personal moving expenses are considered taxable. However, associated expenses may be deductible, subject to limitations, as an itemized deduction if the move is related to beginning full-time employment in a new location within certain minimum distances from the previous place of residence. Deductible moving expenses include, with certain limitations (maximum $3,000), moving personal effects, traveling, house hunting, meals, lodging, and incidental expenses.

Tax-Deductible Interest

As mentioned, the deductibility of consumer interest has been practically eliminated. In 1990, only ten percent of consumer interest is deductible; starting with 1991, deduction of consumer interest reduces to zero and therefore will not be allowed.

An interesting tax planning idea is to completely pay off all outstanding consumer loans. Money for paying off the consumer debt can be raised in several ways, each of which constitutes an important tax planning idea. Here is a partial list of tax-wise borrowing methods:

1. The taxpayer can take out a home equity loan. Interest on this loan is fully tax-deductible.
2. If the taxpayer has accumulated cash value in a life insurance policy, it may typically be borrowed at five or six percent interest. Of course, only ten percent of this interest would be deductible in 1990; however, the interest cost on this loan would be much lower than the cost of a conventional consumer loan.
3. If circumstances permit, the taxpayer can sell an investment and use the proceeds to pay off a consumer debt. Later, the taxpayer could borrow to

make another investment. The interest on the second loan can be fully deducted against investment income.

A novel way to increase interest deductions is to shift debt on the vacation home (which is also used as rental property) to the principal residence, thereby moving interest out of the lineup of expenses on the vacation home. For instance, if Judy Cuddy owes $50,000 on her vacation home, she can take out a $50,000 home equity loan on the primary residence and pay off the vacation home mortgage. Judy will get a tax deduction against regular income for interest she pays on the home equity loan. And she can take deductions against rental income from the vacation home for taxes, maintenance, repairs, and depreciation provided the personal use of the home is limited to two weeks or less.

One final point: Interest on consumer and personal loans is only ten percent deductible for 1990 and not at all in following years. However, interest on loans taken out for investment purposes may be fully deductible. To take advantage of this situation, the individual must be careful when classifying the loan by tracing the proceeds so it could be demonstrated that the loan was used for making investment.

Prepayment Strategy

When a taxpayer's itemized deductions are close to the standard deductions, prepaying certain expenses can not only lower overall tax liability, but it can also be useful if the tax rates were to decrease in the future. Some deductible items can be prepaid, such as charitable contributions, miscellaneous items, property taxes, and so on. This will allow the taxpayer to claim an amount greater than the standard deduction in the current year and will minimize current tax liability. Of course, if appropriate, in the following year the standard deduction can be used to minimize the tax burden.

For example, if in 1989 Bill Jones, a single taxpayer, had itemized deductions of $2,900, he could claim the standard deduction of $3,100. However, a more profitable method of managing deductions would be to prepay in 1989 as much of the 1990 deductions as possible, raising the total itemized deductions from $2,900 to, say, $3,900. This would allow Bill Jones to claim the excess itemized deductions in the first year, and still claim the standard deduction amount in the second year which, because of indexing, will be higher. This strategy would successfully reduce the overall tax liability for both years.

Marriage Penalty

Tax rates are structured in a way which make two single people with similar incomes usually pay more tax after marriage than they would have as singles. This is known as the marriage penalty. When both taxpayers earn about the same, they might save tax by postponing marriage until the following

THE MARRIAGE PENALTY

The current tax system discourages some people from getting married and yet, at the same time, benefits married couples.

Assume Ted and Karen Kowalski have taxable incomes of $30,000 each.

1. Computed as singles, Ted's taxes are:

$$.15 \times \$18,550 = \$2,782.50$$
$$.28 \times (\$30,000 - \$18,550) = \underline{3,206.00}$$
$$\$5,988.50$$

Karen's taxes are identical   5,988.50

Total taxes for Ted and
Karen as singles $11,977.00

2. Filing jointly as a married couple:

$$.15 \times \$30,950 = \$4,642.50$$
$$.28 \times (\$60,000 - \$30,950) = \underline{8,134.00}$$

Total taxes for Ted and
Karen as a married couple $12,776.50

**Marriage Penalty = $12,776.50 −
$11,977.00 = $799.50**

However, if one partner earns all (or nearly all) the taxable income, there is a marriage benefit.

Assume Karen earns $60,000 taxable income and Ted earns nothing.

1. Karen's taxes computed as a single:

$$.15 \times \$18,550 = \$2,782.50$$
$$.28 \times (\$44,900 - \$18,550) = 7,378.00$$
$$.33 \times (\$60,000 - \$44,900) = \underline{4,983.00}$$

Taxes for Karen as a single $15,143.50

2. Filing jointly as a married couple:

$$.15 \times \$30,950 = \$4,642.50$$
$$.28 \times (\$60,000 - \$30,950) = \underline{8,134.00}$$

Taxes for Karen and Ted
as a married couple $12,776.50

**Marriage Benefit = $15,143.50 −
$12,776.50 = $2,367.00**

tax year. Conversely, a couple usually pays less combined tax after marriage when one spouse earns the bulk of the income. Such a couple could save on current taxes if they could get married during the current year. Filing separate returns might be tax-wise for another reason. Changes in the tax structure have reduced the advantages of using separate returns to get larger medical, casualty, and disaster loss deductions and virtually eliminated them for high bracket taxpayers. This is due to the phaseout of the benefit of the 15 percent bracket and of personal and dependency exemptions for high income taxpayers by the imposition of an additional five percent tax on taxable income above the following levels (1989): joint return, $74,850; separate return of a married person, $37,425; single person, $44,900; and head of household, $64,200. The 1989 rate schedules consist of a 15 percent and a 28 percent bracket for various income bracket levels depending on the filing status. Five percent is added to the 28 percent rate (combined rate of 33 percent) and applied to the taxable income in excess of the preceding levels until the phaseout is completed, at which point the rate returns to 28 percent.

An example of a tax planning idea in the context of the topic just discussed is presented in Table 8-2. Suppose that in 1989 John Smith had an adjusted gross income of $35,000 and a taxable income of $30,000 ($35,000 − $3,000 of itemized deductions other than medical deductions − a $2,000 personal

TABLE 8-2 John and Betty Smith Tax Year: 1989

	Joint Return		Single returns	
	John	Betty	John	Betty
Adjusted gross income	$35,000	$20,000	$35,000	$20,000
Less itemized deductions	−3,000	−3,000	−3,000	−3,000
Less personal exemptions	−2,000	−2,000	−2,000	−2,000
Medical expenses deductible		0*		−1,000**
Taxable income	30,000	15,000	30,000	14,000
Joint taxable income	45,000	—	—	—
Federal income tax	8,576.50	—	5,988.50	2,100

* Medical expenses not deductible because they do not exceed 7.5% of joint adjusted gross income of $45,000 ($30,000 + $15,000)

** Medical Expenses	$2,500
7.5% of Betty's AGI	1,500
Expenses deductible	$1,000

exemption). In addition, Betty Smith had $2,500 of medical expenses. If the Smiths file jointly, they get no additional deduction for medical expenses as these do not exceed 7.5 percent of their joint adjusted gross income (7.5 percent of $45,000 = $3,375). The tax on a joint taxable income of $45,000 will be $8,576.50 ($4,642.50 + 28 percent of the excess over $30,950).

If the Smiths file separately for 1989, Betty would be entitled to deduct an additional $1,000 ($2,500 medical expenses − $1,500 floor), yielding a taxable income of $14,000. The tax on this income is $2,100. The tax on John's $30,000 of taxable income is $5,988.50 (2,782.50 + 28 percent of the excess over $18,550). If filed separately, the total tax for both John and Betty is $8,088.50. This results in a total tax saving of $488 ($8,576.50 − $8,088.50) for the Smith family. Incidentally, it is important for the Smiths to recognize that if one spouse itemizes, the other spouse must also itemize.

The concept of marriage penalty applies to divorce as well. If both partners earn about the same, they may save on taxes by finalizing a divorce during the current year instead of postponing it until the following year. However, if one partner earns significantly more than the other, taxes will usually be saved if the divorce is postponed until the following year.

Other Deductions

Business expenses. As noted, miscellaneous itemized deductions are ordinarily deductible only to the extent that they exceed two percent of the taxpayer's adjusted gross income. However, if the taxpayer reports self-employment income on Schedule C, many of the same expenses, which are then treated as business expenses, become fully deductible. Examples of these ex-

---

TABLE 8-3   Deductions Allowed by Law

Fully deductible expenses:
- Charitable contributions (up to specified limits)
- Home mortgage interest (up to specified limits)
- Property taxes
- State and local income taxes

Limited deductible expenses:
- Casualty and theft losses
- Consumer interest
- Investment advisory fees
- Investment interest
- Medical expenses
- Moving expenses
- Safe deposit rental
- Tax return preparation fee
- Uniforms and protective clothing worn on the job
- Union dues
- Unreimbursed employee business expenses
- Work-related safety equipment and tools you supply
- Attorneys' fees for tax consultation

---

penses include accounting fees, interest expense, professional licenses, publications, auto expense, rent, cost of resale products, and salaries to employees.

Real estate losses.   An individual may deduct up to $25,000 for losses on rental property as long as the adjusted gross income does not exceed $100,000; between $100,001 and $150,000 of adjusted gross income, the loss deduction is gradually phased out. Furthermore, most real estate taxes and mortgage interest payments are deductible on a second personal residence.

Rental expense.   The tax law on renting a vacation home states that if the home is used 14 or fewer days per year (or 10 percent of the number of days it is rented out) and it is also rented, then it can be designated as a business. In such a situation the taxpayer will be entitled to a number of business expense deductions.

In conclusion, it should be emphasized that every taxpayer should undertake as much tax planning as is necessary to take all the tax deductions allowed by law. A list of major allowable deductions is presented in Table 8-3.

DIVERSION

The second strategy of tax reduction is diversion, which refers to the steps a taxpayer can take to channel investment returns into money that will (1) be taxed at lower rates, (2) offer higher deductions, or (3) completely avoid taxation.

Home Ownership

Perhaps the most widely used tax planning strategy of diversion is home ownership. As mentioned, both mortgage interest and interest on home equity loans are deductible and can be used to reduce the tax liability. Even mortgage interest on a vacation home that is also used for rental income is deductible as rental expense as long as the home is used for personal use not more than 14 days or ten percent of the number of days it is rented out, whichever is greater; otherwise this interest is treated as an itemized deduction. Real estate taxes are deductible, as are the points paid on securing a mortgage on a primary or secondary residence.

The most significant benefit to home ownership as a tax avoidance strategy, of course, is the ability to postpone almost indefinitely the recognition of gains on the sale of the principal residence. As long as the proceeds from the sale of the residence are used to buy or build a residence within two years, and the cost of the new residence equals or exceeds the sale proceeds from the old residence, no capital gain is recognized. Thus, in a principal residence, capital can be accumulated without tax impact, retaining the original basis of the home plus improvements. When the time comes for the taxpayer to finally sell out and not reinvest in a primary residence, if the taxpayer is 55 or older, tax on profits up to $125,000 may be completely avoided. This delaying feature has the positive effect of sheltering up to $125,000 of capital accumulation from taxation. Incidentally, this is a one-time exclusion allowed by law.

Municipal Bonds

Interest on state and local obligations is not subject to federal income tax. It is also exempt from the tax of the state in which the obligations are issued. Tax law treats bonds issued after August 7, 1986, as follows:

1. Public-purpose bonds issued to meet essential government functions are generally tax-exempt.
2. Qualified private activity bonds issued to finance housing and student loans are tax-exempt for regular income tax purposes, but are subject to alternative minimum tax.
3. Taxable municipals are issued for nonqualifying private purposes, such as building a sports stadium. They are subject to federal income tax, but may be exempt from state and local taxes in the states in which they are issued.

Taxpayers can also save on taxes by investing in municipal bond funds. Interest on these bonds is exempt from federal income taxes. Of course, they may be subject to individual state and local taxes. Also, capital gains distributions in municipal bond funds resulting from sales of municipal bonds are fully taxable.

Matching Incomes and Losses

Another strategy, matching incomes and losses, can also minimize the tax liability. As mentioned, the passive-loss limitation does not permanently disallow losses and credits from passive activities, but rather determines how and when the losses and credits can be claimed by the taxpayer. Losses from a passive activity are deductible only against income from that or another passive activity. Unused losses can be carried forward indefinitely and can be used to offset passive income realized by the taxpayer in subsequent years.

While the current law permits the postponement of current losses to future years, it is more beneficial for a taxpayer to be able to deduct the losses during the current year. For instance, if a taxpayer has significant capital gains from a passive activity in one tax year and has a potential loss on an investment, overall tax liability can be reduced by selling the losing investment and realizing the loss in the same tax year as the capital gain to offset the gain and reduce tax liability.

Tax Shelters

The change in tax law requiring that passive losses may only offset passive income has dramatically changed the use of tax shelters. Tax shelters have historically been investments designed to create accounting losses that could be used as deductions against taxable income from other sources. Investors did not materially participate in the management of these investments, hence the designation "passive activity." Most shelters were set up to generate the biggest deductions in the first few years so investors could get their money back quickly in the form of tax write-offs. If the investment went well, it eventually turned profitable. Some investments never did, partly because relatively few economic benefits were expected from them. With the change in tax law, the write-offs generated by such tax shelters are no longer deductible against any income except income from a passive activity. To soften the blow to individuals who had invested heavily in tax shelters before October 23, 1986, write-offs are being gradually phased out and will no longer be available after 1990.

The change in tax law shifted the emphasis in tax shelter investment from tax write-offs to economic profit motive. As a planning strategy, taxpayers should look to tax shelters to help them appropriately time or offset their passive gains and losses. While investors who currently have significant passive income will still seek passive losses, most investors with existing tax shelter investments and passive losses should seek to generate additional passive income.

Limited Partnerships

Most tax shelters are structured as limited partnerships, or master limited partnerships. Limited partnerships make an investor liable only for the amount of money invested in them. Many of the real estate limited partnerships intend to buy office buildings, shopping malls, apartments, or other real estate that can pay investors immediate rental income. Other major areas of limited partnerships include oil and gas, equipment leasing, and research and development. The losses from these partnerships are passed along in the form of write-offs to the individual partners in proportion to their investment. Most partnerships require a minimum of $5,000 in investment, and currently promise to yield between four percent and 12 percent annually, which is partly shielded by depreciation and other write-offs. However, investment in limited partnerships may have significant risk, and, in addition, promised income streams may not materialize. Despite these risks, however, limited partnerships frequently offer tax benefits which could reduce an individual's overall tax liability.

Master Limited Partnerships (MLPs)

Like limited partnerships, master limited partnerships (MLPs) invest in real estate or oil and gas wells and pass along to investors income from the MLPs. However, MLP units trade publicly on major exchanges and over the counter, while shares in limited partnerships are basically illiquid. An investor can buy into an MLP with a minimum investment and still receive income and losses as with a limited partnership. Many cash-flow-oriented businesses are moving into this partnership form since partnerships pay no corporate income taxes so profits are taxed only once to the partners. Investors also receive some tax deferral, since the income distributions are considered a tax-free return of capital until the original investment is returned. While many current MLPs promise an annual return in excess of ten percent, their profitability is subject to many of the same risks as limited partnerships, and their market values rise and fall in relation to their performance. Clearly, because of the nature of this investment, taxpayers may use MLPs to reduce their overall tax liability.

Personal Exemption

High-income taxpayers whose personal exemptions have been phased out might consider transferring cash or other income-producing assets to an older child or another dependent relative instead of continuing to support that person without getting any tax benefit. The former dependent would likely pay tax at the lowest rate of the income generated by the asset and will have more left to live on, after taxes, than the taxpayer might have provided.

Like-Kind Exchanges

When property that is held for productive use in a trade, business, or for investment is exchanged for property of a "like-kind" used for a similar purpose, no gain or loss is recognized upon the exchange. Whether two properties are of a "like-kind" is generally determined on a case-by-case basis. For example, a swap of one real estate property for another is considered a like-kind exchange.

The tax law allows a lot of flexibility in this maneuver. The swapped properties do not have to be equal in value. In that case, tax rules allow cash, called "boot," to be paid to make up the difference in the property values, although the "boot" is taxable to the extent of the realized gain. Furthermore, properties do not have to fall into the same category. A vacant lot can be traded for a house, an office building for an apartment building, and a condominium for a beach home, so long as each is an investment property and not a personal real estate.

Often, the best time to consider a "like-kind" trade is when a property has increased in value. A swap lets a taxpayer secure the profit and plough back a larger untaxed fund into another underdeveloped or turnaround situation.

Charitable Donations

A novel charitable donation strategy, that lets the taxpayer receive both income and tax benefits, is called the *charitable remainder trust*. These irrevocable trusts are set up to pay the donor income for a certain period, or for life; the asset then passes to the charity. There are two ways to accomplish this objective. In an *annuity trust*, the donor receives a fixed dollar amount each year, which must be at least five percent of the principal. In a *unitrust*, the donor receives a percentage of the trust's assets each year; the income fluctuates with the earnings of the trust. Between the two, the annuity trust offers a bigger tax savings up front, as explained next.

The charitable tax deduction is based on the donor's age, income, and the gift's fair market value, which is derived from an IRS valuation table. The table rates fluctuate monthly with prevailing interest rates. When setting up an annuity trust, donors can choose the rate of the current month, the preceding month, or the month before that. The higher the rate, the higher the deduction. For instance, assume Judy Clark, a 50-year-old taxpayer, set up a $100,000 annuity trust with a 6.5 percent annual return. If she chose the interest rate of 10.6 percent prevailing on July 1, 1989, she would receive a charitable deduction of $39,643. However, choosing the May 1, 1989, interest rate of 11.6 percent would give her a deduction of $43,485. Of course, the contributions are subject to the normal deductibility rules (50 percent of adjusted gross income limit).

Tax-Free Social Security Benefits

As observed in Chapter 7, under the current law, for single taxpayers, up to 50 percent of Social Security benefits are reportable as taxable income if they have other income greater than $25,000. The threshold for married taxpayers filing jointly is $32,000.

A viable tax planning strategy for individuals with taxable Social Security benefits is to reduce reportable income to the $25,000 (or $32,000) level so that all Social Security benefits are nontaxable. This is accomplished by a thorough review of currently existing investments and, if appropriate, shifting part of the investments into assets that generate nonreportable income. An example of such an asset is a single premium deferred annuity. The income from this annuity is tax-deferred and therefore is not reported as current income for purposes of Social Security tax calculation. Furthermore, when annuity payments are received, a portion of each payment is treated as a return of original principal and is not taxed. The remainder of the payment represents the prior deferred income and is fully taxed.

DEFERRAL

The third strategy of tax reduction is deferral, which refers to the action taken to defer taxes to future years. There are two main types of tax deferral: deferral with pre-tax dollars and deferral with after-tax dollars.

Deferral With Pre-Tax Dollars

Qualified pension and profit-sharing plans for business employees are essentially savings plans with two tax incentives for business contributions. First, money saved from current income and contributed to properly qualified plans is deductible from gross income as an expense and therefore reduces tax liability. Second, the interest income, dividends, and any capital gains earned in such plans are not taxable within the trust until the participant retires and actually uses the retirement fund. The money is taxed as ordinary income when received after retirement.

The second choice relates to contributions to Keogh plans. Self-employed people with Keogh retirement plans can make tax-deductible contributions to several different kinds of plans. The maximum amount the taxpayer can deposit is up to 20 percent of self-employed earnings, with a ceiling of $30,000. Self-employed people also have the right to deduct 25 percent of the cost of health insurance for themselves and their families as an adjustment to income. The adjustment, however, cannot be claimed by people who could get coverage under a subsidized plan, such as through a spouse's employer. The deduction is also limited to the taxable income from the sole proprietorship.

The third choice of tax-deferral is an IRA. An individual who is not covered by retirement plans at work as well as a married employee whose adjusted gross income on a joint return falls below $40,000 ($25,000 for single taxpayers) can deposit annually up to $2,000 in IRAs. These contributions are fully tax-deductible and related earnings are tax deferred. Furthermore, even those individuals who cannot make tax-deductible IRA contributions are allowed to treat the IRA-related earnings as tax-deferred.

Employees covered by 401(K) retirement plans at work and barred from also having a deductible IRA can contribute up to $7,627 in 1989 in this tax-deductible plan. The money can be subtracted from the salary automatically, and put in the plan to grow income tax-deferred, except that, if applicable, Social Security taxes must be fully paid. The employer frequently contributes additional money, which raises the yield even more.

Deferral with After-Tax Dollars

Insurance contracts purchased with after-tax dollars provide an excellent vehicle for after-tax accumulation of earnings as long as these earnings accumulate within the policy contract. The types of insurance contracts which qualify include single premium deferred annuity, single premium whole life, single premium universal life, and variable annuities. These investments were discussed in detail in Chapter 3. In general, at the time of withdrawal, that part of the annuity payment which is allocated to the cost of the initial investment is treated as a nontaxable return of principal; when withdrawn, the remaining balance is taxed as ordinary income.

The second choice consists of nondeductible IRAs. These contributions can be made by those taxpayers with earned income who do not qualify for a deduction. The reason to make nondeductible IRA contributions is that *earnings* on such deposits, like earnings on deductible deposits, accumulate without being immediately taxed. Incidentally, unlike deductible IRAs which cannot be withdrawn before age 59½ without a penalty, nondeductible IRA deposits (but not the related earnings) can be withdrawn at any time without incurring a tax on principal or penalty for early withdrawal. For this reason, it is a good idea to segregate non-deductible IRAs from their deductible counterpart.

DEFLECTION

The fourth tax reduction strategy is deflection, which involves shifting taxable income to someone in a lower tax bracket. There are several ways of accomplishing this objective.

Kiddie Tax

The first deflection technique of reducing taxable income is to shift part of the income to a child. However, careful planning is required to take advantage of this technique. The reason is that the Tax Reform Act introduced the so-called "kiddie tax" for children under 14 with income in the form of interest, dividends, or capital gains. The salient features of this tax are presented next.

The kiddie tax is based on a parent's top rate if the child is: (1) under 14; and (2) has net investment income after reducing gross investment income by $1,000. This tax is not levied on earned income (for example, wages). Investment income is defined as any income other than earned income and may consist of interest, dividends, royalties, rents, and profits on the sale of property.

Only net investment income is subject to tax at the parent's top rate. For purposes of this rule, net investment income equals gross investment income minus $1,000 if the child does not itemize deductions. If itemized deductions are used, net investment income equals gross investment income reduced by the larger of: (1) $1,000; or (2) $500 plus itemized deductions that are directly connected with the generation of investment income.

Notwithstanding the new kiddie tax rules, a number of strategies can be used to beat the kiddie tax. For instance, a taxpayer can take advantage of the fact that the first $1,000 of an under-age-14 child's unearned income is tax-favored. This is done by transferring assets that produce up to $1,000 of annual unearned income for the child. Another strategy is to switch the child's savings into investments that pay little or no current taxable income. These investments include U.S. Series EE bonds, municipal bonds, and tax free zero coupon bonds. Also, minor's trusts, under which assets and earnings do not have to be turned over to the child until age 21, are hopefully taxed at a lower than parent's tax rate even though the child is under 14 and has unearned income of over $1,000. However, eventually this strategy does result in double taxation.

Gifts

An attractive way to shift income is for an individual with a high marginal tax bracket to give a gift to a child in a low tax bracket. A gift of cash benefits the taxpayer to the extent that the after-tax return received by the child would presumably be higher than the after-tax return received by the taxpayer. A gift of appreciated property, such as common stock or income-producing property, can bring even higher tax benefits. For instance, the appreciated stock could be liquidated and reinvested to generate a greater after-tax return for the child than it would for the taxpayer. Although the gift is not deductible by the parent, it is not treated as income to the child.

An example can demonstrate the use of gifts as a way of reducing the tax liability. For instance, suppose John Smith wishes to create a college fund for his son Mike and has $5,000 in a money market fund earning seven percent interest. Assuming a 28 percent tax bracket, John currently pays a tax of $98 per year (28 percent of $350). If he gives the fund to Mike, who has no other sources of income, Mike immediately gains $98 because he would not owe this tax to the government.

Child Employment

A taxpayer can shelter income by putting a child on the summer payroll. A dependent child could earn as much as $3,100 from a job in 1989 without paying tax on that income. Also, if the taxpayer's business is a proprietorship or a partnership with the spouse, the earnings of the child younger than 18 escape Social Security taxes as well.

DIMINUTION

In this concluding section we will briefly mention a potpourri of tax savings ideas which were not discussed in the previous sections.

Income Shifting

Since the decline in tax rates under the 1986 Tax Reform Act is now complete, there is less reason to postpone income to lower the tax liability. Still, some tax payments can be postponed by delaying some investments or other earnings. For instance, if a taxpayer defers nonwage income, which is not subject to withholding, the money could be received early in 1991 but taxes on this income will not be due until the 1991 tax return is filed in April 1992. Furthermore, delaying income can save a taxpayer on taxes if the future income is expected to fall into a lower tax bracket. It should be mentioned, however, that the taxpayer still would have the obligation of prepaying 90 percent of all (wage and nonwage) income taxes to avoid underpayment penalties.

Expense Shifting

The reverse strategy works with respect to expenses. Since expenses reduce taxable income, accelerating deductions during the year may prove to be an attractive strategy. Prepayment of charitable contributions and professional dues, and realization of losses by selling property are examples of expense shifting.

Short Sales

If a taxpayer does not want to realize taxable gains on a security sale during a taxable year, but believes the security price may decline in the near future, the profit can be frozen by ordering a short sale of the security during the current year. Then, after year-end, the shares owned by the taxpayer can be delivered to the broker as a replacement of the borrowed shares sold as a short sale. By delivering the stock in the new year, the gain on the short sale is realized in that year.

Second Home

The government allows the taxpayer to deduct many of the costs associated with a second home as long as rental income is received from the home and it is not used for personal use for more than two weeks during a given year. Consequently, as mentioned earlier, rental income and tax deductions generated by a second home can be an important part of a tax reduction strategy.

Alternative Minimum Tax

As mentioned, there is no relief from paying alternative minimum tax (AMT) if it exceeds the regular income tax. However, several carefully planned actions can reduce this tax. For instance, since untaxed appreciation in donated property is subject to AMT, a taxpayer can reduce AMT liabilities simply by donating appreciated property to charity over several years. Another strategy is to avoid investing in those municipal bonds whose interest is subject to AMT. For instance, the interest on private-purpose bonds issued after August 7, 1986, is currently subject to AMT and should be avoided by taxpayers concerned with AMT taxes.

In passing, it should be mentioned that even though the AMT must be calculated for each individual taxpayer, the information presented in Table 8-4 can be helpful in estimating the level of preference items and adjustments that trigger these taxes.

Social Security Benefits

Social Security benefits of *over* $8,880 for taxpayers under age 70 are reduced by $1 for every $3 of "excess" earned income. Once this level is reached, additional earned income will generate a progressively smaller economic benefit due to income tax, Social Security tax, and the reduction in benefits, until the Social Security benefits are entirely eliminated. Consequently, before age 70 taxpayers planning to work after retirement should either perform largely volunteer work or work that generates substantial income.

Splitting Business Income

Tax on business income may be reduced if the taxpayer can shift part of the income to family members. This can be done by forming a family partnership or by making the family stockholders in a corporation. Generally, an

---

TABLE 8-4   Figuring the Threshold of Pain

The alternative minimum tax for individuals looms when:

	And preferences and adjustments exceed	
*Regular taxable income is**	*This amount*	*Or this percentage of regular taxable income†*
$ 50,000	$38,252	76.5%
100,000	59,288	59.3
250,000	93,733	37.5
500,000	177,067	35.4
1,000,000	343,733	34.4

---

* Married, filing joint return with four personal exemptions and $5,000 of itemized deductions.
† Reflects AMT exemption, if any, and adding back personal exemptions and deductions that aren't allowed under minimum-tax rules (such as consumer interest, state and local taxes).
Source: Reprinted by permission of *Wall Street Journal,* © Dow Jones & Company, Inc., March 8, 1989. All Right Reserved Worldwide.

S corporation in which stockholders elect to report income may be used more freely than a partnership to split income and reduce tax liability.

Mutual Fund Sales

A little-known tax savings strategy relates to the taxation of gains realized on the sale of a particular mutual fund or a stock. This strategy is best described by recounting the experience of a taxpayer named Bob Jones. To his dismay and utter disbelief, in May 1989 Bob was ordered by the Tax Court to pay $33,149 to the Internal Revenue Service. This situation was created in 1982 when Bob sold some of his shares in two mutual funds. To compute his capital gains and losses that year, Bob's CPA subtracted from the sale price the cost of the fund's shares which were most recently purchased by Bob. The newer shares were purchased at much higher prices than those purchased seven years earlier. However, Bob never specified to his fund's transfer agent the particular shares that he wanted sold. The Tax Court therefore ruled that, in accordance with IRS regulations, Bob's CPA should have assumed that the first shares purchased were those which were sold. The result was devastating. Instead of a deductible $6,708 net long-term *loss* under the original calculation, Bob Jones was actually made liable for a $168,096 long-term *gain.*

A valuable lesson can indeed be learned from the harrowing experience of Bob Jones. When placing a sell order, a taxpayer must carefully instruct the broker or the mutual fund transfer agent to send a transaction confirmation that identifies the shares that were intended to be sold. This will allow the taxpayer to minimize the taxable gains or maximize the deductible losses for that year.

Early Withdrawal Penalty

We have learned that any withdrawal from an IRA account before age 59½ is subject to an early withdrawal penalty. However, there is a little-known provision in the tax code that allows people who are younger than 59½ to draw funds from their IRAs by receiving substantially equal periodic payments, at least annually, based on life expectancy. An example should make this clear.

Let us assume Bob Bloomingdale, age 50, just rolled over $300,000 into his IRA. According to the mortality tables, Bob's life expectancy is 83.1 years. Bob could choose to annuitize his payments to avoid the early withdrawal penalty. For instance, an actuary using a standard mortality table and assuming eight percent interest would come up with an annuity factor of 11.109. Dividing the IRA balance of $300,000 by 11.109, the actuary would arrive at an annual payment value of $27,005.13. By annuitizing his distributions, Bob would be able to start drawing $27,005.13 a year starting at age 50, and he would not be subjected to the early withdrawal penalty. Of course, if Bob waits until he turns 59½ before withdrawing the funds from the IRA investment, he would not be subject to the early withdrawal penalty even if he did not annuitize the investment for life.

S Corporation Strategy

One of the major attractions of S Corporations is that, with few exceptions, these entities are taxed like partnerships, thus eliminating corporate level taxation. These corporations have become even more attractive because of the recent decline in individual tax rates. For the first time ever, corporate tax rates, which peak at 39 percent, exceed the highest individual tax bracket, currently 33 percent. In the past, when corporate rates were lower than individual rates, it made sense to retain earnings in the company. But now, depending on individual circumstances, it might lead to more tax savings if a regular corporation is restructured to an S corporation so earnings could be funneled straight through to the owner. This can be a passive activity if a shareholder is *not* an employee or officer and is therefore subject to passive loss rules. Also, note that the owner's pro rata share of earnings is taxable that year even if no cash distributions are made to the owner.

Medicare Tax

Early in 1989 a newspaper story shocked the American public by claiming that the *new* Medicare surcharge covering catastrophic illness along with reduced Social Security benefits would put many working retirees into a 102 percent tax bracket. Although this case was extreme, it was still true and underscored the complexity of the issue.

Even though the Medicare surcharge has been well publicized, few people actually realized that for the first time ever the federal income tax liability has been used as the *basis* for a new tax. Once this fact is recognized, it becomes clear that a reduction, or an elimination, of the Medicare tax can be accomplished by lowering the federal tax liability. One strategy, which had received a great deal of attention, involved tax-free municipal bonds. Since municipal bonds produce tax-free income, investment in these bonds would help a taxpayer lower the Medicare surcharge. Fortunately, such strategies are no longer needed because the Congress has repealed this tax.

THE BUSINESS ORGANIZATION

INTRODUCTION

Once a decision has been made to establish a business, the entrepreneur must decide what form of business entity it will be. There are tax considerations that will enter into this decision. Normally, a business is conducted as a sole proprietorship, partnership, or corporation.

For a sole proprietorship or partnership, the business itself does not pay any income taxes. The sole proprietor or partners include the profits or losses on their individual income tax returns. Except for an S corporation, profits of a corporation are taxed both to the corporation and to the shareholders when the profits are distributed as dividends. Also, except for an S corporation, losses sustained by the corporation usually cannot be included on shareholders' tax returns.

A sole proprietorship is the simplest form of business organization. The business has no existence apart from the owner. Its liabilities are the proprietor's personal liabilities, and the proprietary interest ends when the owner dies.

A partnership is a relationship existing between two or more persons who joined together to carry on a trade or business. Each person contributes money, property, labor, or skill and expects to share in the profits and losses of the business. A partnership is not a taxable entity, except for certain state taxes. However, it must compute its profit or loss and file a return.

Corporations include associations, joint stock companies, insurance companies, and trusts that operate as corporations. Corporate profits normally are taxed to the corporation. When the profits are distributed as dividends, the dividends are taxed to the shareholders but are not deductible to the corporation.

A qualifying corporation, known as an S corporation, may choose to be generally exempt from federal income tax. Its shareholders, commonly known as partners, will then include in their income their share of the corporation's separately stated items of income, deductions, losses (subject to passive loss rule if not active shareholders), and credit, and their share of other income or loss which is not separately stated. Although it is not generally liable for federal income tax, an S corporation may have to pay a tax on excess net passive investment income, a tax on capital gains, or the tax from recomputing a prior year's investment credit.

It is beyond the scope of this book to discuss in detail the tax considerations of the various types of business entities just presented. It may nevertheless be of some import to briefly present some tax planning ideas relating to these business entities.

SOLE PROPRIETORS

As mentioned, a sole proprietorship is the simplest form of business organization. The business has no existence apart from the owner. Its liabilities are the owner's personal liabilities, and the proprietary interest ends when the owner dies. When the taxable income is calculated for the year, the owner must add in any profit, or subtract out any loss, from the sole proprietorship.

Self-employed individuals get an important tax break which should be recognized here. In 1989 the self-employed received a two percent Social Security credit on their self-employed income up to the Social Security maximum wage base. In other words, in 1989 a sole proprietor paid self-employment tax of 13.02 percent on net self-employment earnings, while an employer together with each employee paid 15.02 percent (7.51 percent × 2) of Social Security tax on each employee. In 1989 the Social Security base was $48,000; this base increased to $50,700 in 1990.

The advantage of establishing a sole proprietorship can be appreciated with the help of the following example. Assume in 1989 John Jones' income subject to Social Security tax is $42,500. If John's business was incorporated, the Social Security tax on this income would be $6,383.50 (15.02 percent of $42,500). However, if the business was established as sole proprietorship, the Social Security tax would be only $5,533.50 (13.02 percent of $42,500—a tax saving of $850.00. It should be mentioned in this connection that, as a sole proprietor, John would not get a deduction for the Social Security taxes but will be allowed deductions for all business expenses.

EXECUTIVES

The primary tax planning objective for most corporate executives is to reduce, defer, or eliminate the tax cost of earning salary income. There are pay benefits that are not taxable, such as certain fringe benefits, disability pensions, health and accidental death benefits, and certain housing costs while working abroad. Other tax savings plans may be instituted through pension and profit sharing plans, stock options, and deferred pay plans. The objective of these plans is to defer the receipt of salary income to a future time when the income is expected to be taxed at a lower tax rate.

Topics relating to pension and profit sharing plans are discussed in Chapter 13 and need not be repeated here. A brief review of several other related topics is undertaken here.

The major objective of a deferred pay plan is to postpone the tax on pay benefits to a year in which the executive would presumably be in a lower tax bracket. Another tax-free benefit for executives is to receive not only life insurance protection, but also accident and health benefits. A third benefit is known as the Stock Appreciation Rights (SARs), which refer to a cash bonus associated with an increase in the price of employer stock. Each SAR entitles an executive to cash equal to the excess of the fair market value over the value on that date of the grant of the SAR. The executive is taxed when the cash is received. Finally, if IRS guidelines are satisfied, executives of a private foundation are not taxed on the benefits provided for their children.

PROFESSIONALS

Many professionals prefer to form a partnership or an S corporation which were covered in the previous section. For others who prefer to be sole proprietors many of the tax planning ideas have been rendered obsolete under the new tax law. There is, however, one idea still applicable to doctors, lawyers, architects, professional financial planners, and other professionals who are in the business for themselves. This idea deserves special mention.

Under the present law, passive losses can offset only passive income that is earned from passive activities. Even the transitional rule which allows a small break will be phased out by 1991. However, the law allows professionals who incorporate their practices but retain personal ownership of their offices and equipment to rent their office equipment to their corporation. The rent they receive from the corporation is passive income. Then they shelter that income from taxes by offsetting it with passive losses from investments. The rent payments may leave the firm with less cash to compensate the professionals, but they can come out ahead since the rental income is not taxed as ordinary income but compensation would be taxed as ordinary income. This advantage should, however, be weighed against the fact that professionals are taxed at a flat rate of 34 percent, which is higher than the highest individual marginal income tax bracket of 33 percent.

S CORPORATIONS

In order to qualify for S corporation status, a corporation must: (1) be a domestic corporation; (2) have only one class of stock; (3) have no more than 35 stockholders; (4) have only individuals as shareholders; and (5) have citizens or residents of the U.S. as shareholders. Basically, an S corporation is a hybrid business entity that combines the flexibility of the partnership format with the advantages of operation in the corporate form. The central fact about an S corporation is this: Unlike other corporations, S corporations generally pay no taxes. Instead, current net earnings or losses pass through to the stockholders, who will report them directly on their individual tax returns and get upward or downward adjustments in stock basis, depending upon the profit or loss realized by the corporation.

In addition to the key advantages just mentioned, S corporations enjoy the following advantages: (1) the corporate owner has limited legal liability, which sole proprietors and partnerships do not enjoy; (2) S corporation ownership can easily change hands, while sole proprietors and partnerships typically cannot; (3) interest expense on debt to acquire or carry S corporation stock is deductible by the shareholders as business interest, if there is material participation by the shareholders; and (4) nonsalary distributions by way of dividend distribution to shareholders avoid Social Security taxes.

S corporations suffer from several drawbacks as well: (1) Fringe benefits to shareholders owning greater than two percent of company stock are nondeductible. These include medical insurance and reimbursement plans, disability income plans, group term life insurance, and loans from qualified retirement plans; (2) any available investment tax credit or net operating loss carryovers under an existing C corporation are not available to the converted S corporation; and (3) passive losses are deductible inside C corporations, but only with limitations for S corporations.

An S corporation first calculates its net income or loss. It then allocates its net income or loss among its shareholders. If the S corporation has net income, each stockholder's share becomes part of his or her gross income. If the corporation has a net loss, when figuring gross income each stockholder's share is deducted, subject to the limits of basis and passive loss activity rules.

SMALL BUSINESS

Small businesses are especially attractive to financial planners because they offer unique tax planning challenges. The TRA of 1986 and subsequent tax laws significantly changed the rules applicable to small businesses. In this section we will briefly review the current tax laws governing operations of small businesses.

Favorable Changes

The most attractive change relates to the lower corporate tax rates. Beginning July 1987, the corporation tax rate dropped from 46 percent to 34 percent. This rate applies only to companies that earn more than $75,000 per year. For companies with smaller net incomes, lower, graduated rates apply: 15 percent for the first $50,000 in earnings, and 25 percent for earnings between $50,000 and $75,000. This 26 percent cut in the top rate is not quite as attractive as it seems, however. The reason is that a five percent surcharge is levied on companies with taxable incomes between $100,000 and $335,000. So companies (other than professional corporations which are taxed at a flat rate of 34 percent) whose earnings fall within that range are taxed at an effective rate of 39 percent.

The second attractive change relates to pension plans. For most employees, the vesting period drops from ten to five years. Pensions must also cover a large percentage of employees. Another piece of good news is that the new law has made Simplified Employee Pension Plans (SEPs) more attractive. In addition to the employer's contribution, employees themselves may put away as much as $7,000 of their earnings in the SEP. Taxes on their contributions are deferred, but the employer's and employee's contributions combined may not exceed $30,000. To take advantage of this new benefit, a company cannot have more than 25 employees and at least 50 percent of them must contribute to the SEP.

Unfavorable Changes

The new law completely eliminated the ten percent investment tax credit. However, as a small accommodation, the law stated that the amount of capital equipment a company can directly write off rather than depreciate over time was increased from $5,000 to $10,000, provided that not more than $210,000 of purchases are made.

The new depreciation rules are a bit more complex, since they are simultaneously more and less favorable to the small business. For instance, the depreciable lives of some assets have been increased. However, the rate at which these assets can be depreciated has been simultaneously increased by one third.

A special provision under the new law relates to real estate purchased after 1986. It must be depreciated over $31\frac{1}{2}$ (residential rental, $27\frac{1}{2}$) instead of 19 years. Businesses also get lower deductions on cars and light trucks, since they must be deducted over five instead of three years. Businesses, however, get higher write-offs on computers, since they maintain their five-year depreciable life and also get the accelerated depreciation.

Another provision under the law relates to home-office deductions, which are limited to the business's net income. Thus, if a small business grosses $30,000 this year, all other expenses total $25,000 and the home-office expense is $12,000, only $5,000 ($30,000 minus $25,000) can be deducted. However, the $7,000 ($12,000 minus $5,000) which could not be deducted this year can be carried forward indefinitely to reduce future business income. Finally, under the new law, only 80 percent of business meals and entertainment expenses is deductible. This new provision hurts almost all small businesses.

MISCELLANEOUS TAX ISSUES

Often taxpayers run into a variety of tax-related problems, some of which require expert guidance and all of which require urgent attention. In this section we will discuss some of the issues typically encountered by taxpayers.

TRUE MARGINAL TAX RATE

In an earlier section we argued that even though there are only two tax brackets, because of surcharges, exceptions, and complicated provisions, determination of the *true* marginal tax rate and the actual tax liability can be a complicated chore. This problem is compounded in the case of elderly taxpayers, as we shall now observe.

The complexity of determining the true marginal tax bracket is clearly demonstrated in Table 8-5. Let us assume that Mary Jones, age 69, has an adjusted gross income of $26,500. If she earns an additional $1,000 from part-time employment, her adjusted gross income would be raised from $26,500 to $28,000, because an additional $1,000 of either taxable or tax-exempt income will boost the taxable portion of Mary's Social Security benefits by $500.

TABLE 8-5 Tax Problems of Elderly Taxpayers

		Additional taxable income of $1,000	Additional tax-exempt income of $1,000
Income			
Taxable investment income	$4,000	$5,000	$4,000
Pension income	20,000	20,000	20,000
Taxable Social Security	2,500	3,000*	3,000*
Adjusted gross income	26,500	28,000	27,000
Deductions			
Standard deduction	−3,750	−3,750	−3,750
Personal exemption	−1,950	−1,950	−1,950
Taxable Income	20,800	22,300	21,300
Total Federal Tax	3,511	3,931	3,651
Additional tax paid because of extra $1,000 of investment income		420	140
Additional tax as percentage of extra investment income		42%	14%

* Additional $1,000 of either taxable or tax-exempt investment income boosts taxable portion of this taxpayer's Social Security benefits by $500.

Source: Reprinted by permission of *Wall Street Journal,* © Dow Jones & Company, Inc., March 17, 1989. All Rights Reserved Worldwide.

this will raise the taxable Social Security income from $2,500 to $3,000. Mary's taxes now will amount to $3,931—$420 higher than her previous tax liability. Put differently, Mary Jones paid an additional $420 because she earned an additional $1,000. Consequently, her marginal tax bracket for this additional income is 42 percent.

If Mary Jones earns additional *tax-exempt* interest on municipal bonds, the outcome again is a big surprise. Mary was led to believe that since she was buying the municipal bonds issued by her state of residence, she would receive the additional $1,000 completely tax-free. While the advice she received was correct, no one pointed out that the receipt of the additional tax-free income would boost her taxable Social Security income by $500 to $3,000, causing her taxes to go up by $140. In this case, her marginal tax bracket for the new municipal bond interest income would be 14 percent ($140/$1,000).

The elusive marginal tax bracket becomes even more confusing when the marriage tax penalty is considered. For instance, two 70-year-olds, each with taxable income of $20,800 (including $2,500 of taxable Social Security benefits) will pay federal taxes of about $3,511 each or a combined total of $7,022. But, if these same people were married, and filed a joint return, their tax bill would be about $10,112, or 44 percent higher. That is, in this example the marginal tax bracket for the married couple would be 44 percent.

The examples just presented underscore two important points. First, the tax rules are complex, even when it comes to figuring one's federal income tax. Second, these complicated tax laws provide unique planning opportunities for financial planners who are creative and committed to helping their clients in every legal way possible.

AMENDMENT OF TAX RETURN

The tax law allows taxpayers to amend their previously filed tax returns, if they discovered that an error has been made in tax calculation. Since the passage of TRA and TAMRA, however, it has become far more desirable for taxpayers to check all returns because the TRA included a number of retroactive provisions in the tax code.

Revising a tax return can boost the refund the taxpayer originally claimed or cut the taxes initially owed. It is also a way to correct an underpayment situation, thereby avoiding the payment of penalty and interest. Taxpayers should also bear in mind that amending a return will not, by itself, trigger an audit.

An overpayment of taxes can be rectified by filing a refund claim on Form 1040X. This would be the case if the taxpayer failed to take allowable deductions or credits, overstated income, or wished to take advantage of a retroactive change in the law.

Here is a list of tax breaks which have now been made retroactive under the new law: (1) alumni and others who make donations to colleges to get preference to prime football or other sports tickets can now deduct 80 percent of the donations; (2) the law now allows deferral of profit from the sale of a home if a replacement home is bought within two years, even if one spouse dies before the new home is bought; (3) authors, painters, photographers, and composers can now write off expenses yearly as they are incurred. Incidentally, if after filing a return, the taxpayer finds that an error has been made, Form 1040X may be used to correct a return.

TAX AUDIT

One of the most harrowing experiences for a taxpayer is to receive the following letter from the IRS: "Dear Taxpayer, we selected your federal income tax return for the years shown below to examine the items checked at the end of this letter. We have scheduled an appointment for you. . . ."

"Prevention is better than the cure" is the maxim that best applies to all audit situations. Tax experts across the country point out that currently there are six areas that are carefully scrutinized by the IRS: (1) interest expense deductions; (2) mortgage points; (3) home-office deductions; (4) Schedule C (self-employed income); (5) passive income/losses, and (6) alternative minimum tax.

If an audit letter is received from the IRS, it does not mean that the taxpayer must panic. It could be a routine query that is easily satisfied. In some easily resolved cases, the IRS merely conducts a mail audit. In other cases, however, a face to face meeting can be demanded.

In a personal audit, the best defense is consistency, cooperation, and confidence in handling the situation in a professional manner. In more complex cases, or in those cases where the taxpayer needs more support, it is often a good idea to take to the meeting a financial planner, a CPA, or an attorney licensed to practice before the IRS. Most issues are resolved satisfactorily by following these guidelines. If the impasse still persists, however, the taxpayer can take the IRS to court. However, the process can be complex, time-consuming, and possibly more costly than it is worth.

CHAPTER 9

Basic Investment Alternatives

INTRODUCTION

This chapter is devoted entirely to a broad review of the basic investment alternatives available in the marketplace. In the first section we will review fixed-income securities, and common and preferred stocks. A detailed discussion of mutual fund investments will be undertaken next. Other, more sophisticated, types of investments will be undertaken in the following section. Finally, we will review the salient features of tangible assets.

An overview of securities markets and the relative importance of various market indices will be presented in the appendix to this chapter.

FIXED-INCOME SECURITIES AND STOCK INVESTMENTS

FIXED-INCOME SECURITIES

Fixed-income securities are those investments that have a fixed payment schedule. The investor is promised specific payments at predetermined times, although the legal strength of the promise may vary from investment to investment.

Savings Accounts

Passbook savings accounts are the most obvious example of fixed-income investments. NOW, or SUPER NOW, accounts (NOW is an acronym for "negotiable order of withdrawal") are interest-paying checking accounts that restrict the number of permitted checks, similar to conventional savings accounts. These investments are very low risk (most are insured by the FDIC up to $100,000), convenient, and liquid, and therefore offer a generally low rate of return compared to other investment alternatives offered through commercial banks and savings and loan associations.

Certificates of Deposit

For investors with larger amounts of money who are willing to give up the use of the funds for a specified time period, certificates of deposit (CDs) are available from banks and savings and loans. CDs involve minimum amounts (usually $500, or $100,000 for jumbo CDs) and specified time periods (typically six-month increments from six months to five years). The promised rate of interest on a CD is higher than for passbook savings and the rate increases with the length of deposit of the CD. If an investor wants to cash in a CD prior to its stated expiration date, there is a sizable penalty in terms of interest received on the money. In addition, such a withdrawal may also impair the original principal if the penalty is greater than the earned interest.

At this point it is important to mention an important aspect of CDs which is becoming increasingly popular among safety-minded investors. Savers can buy CDs from issuing institutions, or they can get them through brokerage firms, popularly known as *brokered CDs*. These are simply CDs issued by a bank or a savings and loan association and sold through a middleman—a broker—who gets paid a commission by the issuing institution. As long as the issuing bank has federal deposit insurance, brokered CDs are insured, up to the usual $100,000 limit. In the last ten years, brokered CDs at savings and loan associations have grown from a total of $581 million to $55.4 billion.

Investors can sell their brokered CD before maturity without having to pay an early withdrawal penalty—though not necessarily without a loss. How much a brokered CD will bring at any given time depends on the direction of interest rates. As is the case with bonds, brokered CDs decline in value if interest rates rise and gain when interest rates decline. In general, however, the highest rates on CDs available directly from banks or savings and loan associations top those offered on brokered CDs.

Marketable Government Issues

Marketable issues, which make up about three-quarters of the federal debt, are purchased through a dealer or broker, or investors may bid for new issues through a Federal Reserve Bank. Marketable government securities differ mainly in the length of time to maturity.

Treasury bills. Treasury bills are short-term securities which mature in 13, 26, or 52 weeks from the date of issue. Bills are sold on a discount basis; the investor pays a price lower than the face value and, on maturity, receives the face value.

In both initial offerings and in secondary market trading, treasury bill yields are quoted on a true annualized yield basis. For instance, on August 8, 1989, the *Wall Street Journal* published a treasury bill quotation, which is presented in Figure 9-1. In this case the true annualized yield is 8.22 percent.

Certificates of indebtedness. Certificates of indebtedness differ from treasury bills in that the former are issued at par value and pay fixed interest, or coupon rates. The coupon rate is printed on the bond and never changes. The investor collects this interest by cashing in coupons at a bank, post office, or other federal office. These certificates are short-term investments, with ma-

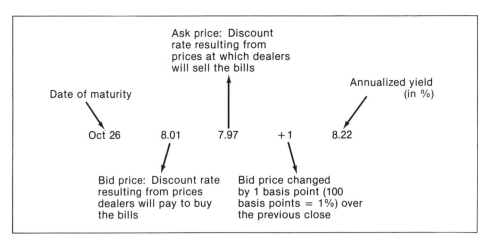

FIGURE 9-1 Reading a treasury bill quotation

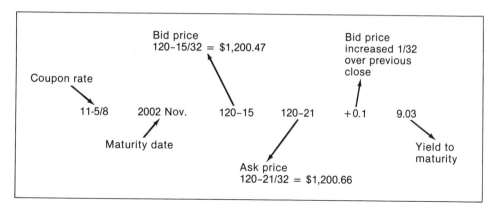

FIGURE 9-2   Reading a treasury bond quotation

turity generally set at one year. However, the Treasury can set the period of time to maturity and the coupon rate to meet current market conditions.

Treasury notes and bonds.   Treasury notes and bonds are long-term investments and are similar to certificates in that they are sold at par value. Notes are U.S. government coupon obligations with an original maturity of one to five years. Notes bear interest at a fixed rate payable semiannually. Bonds are long-term issues with an original maturity of more than five years from the date of issue until the principal amount becomes payable. Bonds may be issued with a call option, meaning that on four months' notice the Treasury can request their redemption on or after specified dates before maturity. Bonds bear interest at a fixed rate, payable semiannually. Notes and bonds are issued in registered, book-entry, or bearer (rare) form in denominations of $1,000, $5,000, $10,000, $100,000, and $1 million.

Treasury note and bond prices are quoted in percentages of $1,000 par value, and fluctuations in their prices are expressed in $\frac{1}{32}$s of a point. A typical price quotation for a treasury bond is presented in Figure 9-2.

At this point a digression may be in order. A time-related chart associated with treasury securities—popularly known as a yield curve—is widely used for predicting future economic trends. The yield curve depicts the yields associated with varying maturities, from short-term treasury bills to 30-year treasury bonds. It typically has a positive slope, meaning that 30-year treasury bonds have higher yields than shorter-term treasury securities. In theory, the higher yields compensate investors for the extra risk they are taking by tying up their money for a longer period of time. If, however, during a given period the yield curve has a negative slope—known as an inverted yield curve—this inversion is generally viewed as a sign that the economy is heading for a recession and lower interest rates.

Agency issues. Agency issues represent the bonds issued by two types of agencies. The first group, called *federal agencies*, includes a large number of agencies, all of which are fully owned by the U.S. government. This group includes, among others, the Export-Import Bank, Federal Housing Administration (FHA), and Government National Mortgage Association (GNMA). Because none has ever defaulted, these securities are assumed to carry only a small degree of default risk. Federal agencies cover a wide spectrum of activities ranging from financing agricultural industry to providing the funds necessary to satisfy America's need for homes.

The second group, called *government-guaranteed agencies*, comprised of agencies whose capital stock was originally owned by the U.S. Treasury, but has since been transferred to the general public and to organizations served by a small number of agencies. Debt securities issued by these agencies, which include Banks for Cooperatives and Federal Home Loan Banks, are not guaranteed by the U.S. government, although they raise money under the Treasury's supervision. Most of the activities of these agencies are concentrated in the area of farm credit and housing.

Summing up. The unique advantage offered to investors in federal debt is its safety. Treasury bills are generally considered perfectly safe, short-term savings instruments, whereas treasury notes, bonds, and agency issues are treated as safe, long-term savings instruments free from the risk of default. Furthermore, the government bond market is assumed to be the most efficient segment of the capital market. This implies that the market prices of government bonds are identical with, or at least close to, their intrinsic values.

Nonmarketable Government Issues

Series EE bonds. Perhaps the most widely held form of federal government debt is U.S. savings bonds, the old Series E and H bonds, and the new Series EE and HH. In 1989, over $100 billion worth of U.S. savings bonds were outstanding. These bonds cannot be traded in the securities market and have no market prices. In fact, they are nontransferable and nonnegotiable. These bonds can be purchased and redeemed only from the U.S. Treasury at the redemption prices and yield printed on them. EE bonds are zero coupon bonds, have a maturity of 11 years, and they are sold at discounts from their face values of $50 up to $10,000. Currently, these bonds guarantee a minimum yield of 6.0 percent if held to maturity, no matter how other market interest rates may fall, but yields may rise to market rates above the stated minimum yield. An important feature of these bonds is that these bonds are not subject to state income taxes, and federal income taxes on the earned interest can be postponed until maturity.

Series HH bonds. Series HH bonds pay the same interest rates as Series EE bonds. However, they have ten years to maturity and pay semiannual coupons. This income must be reported to the IRS annually. The smallest denomination Series HH bond is $500, but that bond can be purchased only in conjunction with Series EE bonds.

Municipal Bonds

Municipal bonds are issued by state or political subdivisions, such as counties, airports, school districts, cities, towns, and villages. This term also designates bonds issued by state agencies and authorities. In general, interest paid on municipal bonds is exempt from both federal taxes and local income taxes within the state of issue. There are several types of municipal bonds which can be grouped into two broad categories: *general obligation* and *revenue bonds*.

General obligation bonds.   The largest category within the municipal bond section of the bond market is *general obligation bonds*. These bonds are backed by the full faith, credit, and taxing power of the issuing government unit. An investor can buy state issues backed by the state government, school bonds backed by the school district, city bonds backed by the municipality, or various other bonds, generally backed by the county government.

Revenue bonds.   *Revenue bonds* are strictly dependent on the income from the issuing governmental unit or project to meet the interest and principal payments. These include both sewer and revenue bonds, as well as bonds used to finance bridges, tunnels, toll roads, airports, and hospitals.

In addition to these, investors can consider other types of revenue bonds. For instance, *special tax bonds* are payable from the proceeds of a special tax, such as on gasoline, liquor, or tobacco. Local school bonds are another good example. When these issues are backed by the full faith, credit, and taxing power of the issuing authority, they become general obligation bonds.

Corporate Bonds

A *corporate bond* is a debt instrument or an evidence of an obligation entered into by a company, as opposed to stock which represents ownership. Owners of bonds expect to receive no more than repayment of the bond principal and interest from the issuing firm, because they are creditors rather than owners of the company. However, bondholders must be paid interest on their principal before dividends may be paid to stockholders. Also, in the case of business failure or liquidation, bondholders must be repaid before the equity holders.

Corporate bonds on the financial pages.   Corporate bonds are traded on the NYSE, AMEX, and OTC markets. On August 8, 1989, in the *Wall Street Journal*, a bond quotation appeared, which is presented in Figure 9-3.

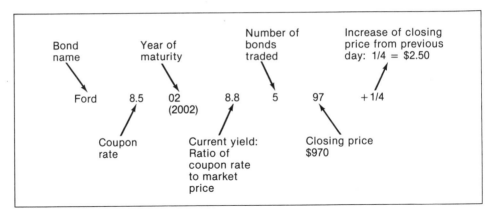

FIGURE 9-3   Reading a corporate bond quotation

Types of corporate bonds.   There are several types of corporate bonds. Some carry special features and privileges; others are distinguishable by the type of security pledged against bond repayment. Basically, bonds may be *secured or unsecured.* With a secured bond, the issuer reinforces its promise to pay the interest and principal by pledging specific property to the bondholders as collateral. In the case of an unsecured bond, the issuer merely promises to pay the stated interest and principal. There are several types of secured and unsecured bonds.

Debentures. A *debenture* is a common form of corporate bond. It is unsecured and is backed only by the faith and general credit of the issuing company, rather than secured by a mortgage or lien on any specific property. Although these IOUs have junior claim to all assets relative to all other forms of bonds outstanding, debenture claims equal those of general creditors. Incidentally, subordinated or junior debentures are the same as regular debentures, except that in case of liquidation their owners are paid after the regular debenture holders. Thus, subordinated debentures are junior to all other bonds.

Guaranteed Bonds. A *guaranteed bond* has interest or principal—or both—guaranteed by a company other than the issuer. The railroad industry uses this kind of bond when larger railroads, leasing sections of track owned by small railroads, guarantee the bonds of the smaller railroads.

Mortgage Bonds. A *mortgage bond* is a debt obligation secured by a mortgage on property. The value of the property may or may not equal the value of the mortgage bond issued against it. Because these securities are usually issued by giant utility companies, they make up a major segment of the corporate bond market.

Mortgage bonds may be either senior or junior liens, depending on the priority of the claim. Senior liens have the first claim on the property of the company under the mortgage, whereas junior liens have the secondary claim.

Convertible Bonds. These debt instruments may be exchanged by the owner for common stock or another security—usually of the same company—in accordance with the terms and exchange ratios for the issue identified in the original issue. Any of the previously listed types of bonds may be convertible, although most convertible bonds are debentures or subordinated debentures.

Callable Bonds. A *callable bond* has a set maturity date, but it can be redeemed after sufficient notice to the bondholders by the issuer at specified periods. The call feature is stated in the original offering prospectus. The callability feature of this type of bond is likely to be exercised if current market rates are less than the coupon rate.

Bond ratings. Two key agencies in the United States that rate bonds according to their risks of default are Moody's Investor Service and Standard & Poor's (S & P). The highest quality bonds are rated AAA while the lowest grade bonds have the rating of C or D (see Chapter 10 for details). In general, the higher the rating of a bond, the lower is its default risk (and the lower the default risk premium associated with it).

As a general rule, in rating bonds, the rating agencies take into consideration five major factors: (1) The level and trend of fixed charge coverage; (2) the company's long-term debt-to-equity ratio; (3) the company's liquidity position; (4) the significance of the company in the industry; and (5) the nature (secured versus unsecured, and so on) of the specific debt issue.

PREFERRED STOCK

Preferred stock may be considered a fixed income security because a yearly payment is stipulated either as a coupon (i.e., five percent of the face value) or as a stated dollar amount. However, preferred stock is junior, or subordinate, to all bonds that a company owns. Owners of preferred stock generally receive a fixed dividend when one is approved by the board of directors of the company. Preferred stock dividends must be paid before any dividends are paid to common stockholders. Furthermore, preferred stockholders have prior claims on the company's assets and, in case of liquidation, are entitled to full payment before the common stockholders receive anything. It should be noted, however, that preferred stockholders do not generally participate in company management; they have no voting rights such as the common stockholders possess.

There are different legal issues of preferred stock. If the stock is *cumulative*, the claim to dividends may be carried over from one year to the next;

if the company falls behind in dividend payments, it must make up the entire amount before paying dividends to the common stockholders. Another variety, called *convertible preferred stock*, should be of special interest. Such a stock carries a contractual clause entitling the holder to exchange it for shares of common stock of the same company within a specified period.

Another type of preferred stock is called *participating preferred stock*. As a general rule, preferred stockholders surrender any claim to the residual earnings of their company after the dividends have been distributed. However, the holder of a participating preferred stock not only receives dividends, but shares additional earnings with the common stockholder. Note also that many preferred stocks are *callable*. This means that these shares may be redeemed by the issuing company at a given "call price" within a specified number of years after issuance.

COMMON STOCK

Key Features

Common stockholders simply have equity in the corporation. Perhaps the most important privilege common stockholders enjoy is that in the event of extraordinary business success they are *usually* the only group to participate in the increased earnings via the increased dividends. They are not personally liable for debts incurred by the corporation, but in the event of business failure or liquidation, common stockholders are the last to be paid. They do, however, retain residual rights to any assets that may remain after all of the creditors are paid. Owners of common stock are entitled to participate in the management of the enterprise to the extent of voting to elect directors and approving specified changes in the company's charter. Generally, common stockholders also have the right to acquire additional stock to retain their percentage of ownership interest in the company. This feature, known as preemptive rights, refers to the purchase of any new issues of "voting stock" in proportion to their existing percentage of ownership in the company at the offering price.

Stock in the Financial Pages

On August 8, 1989, in the *Wall Street Journal*, a stock quotation appeared in the NYSE stock quotation section, which is presented in Figure 9-4. Data presented in this figure are self-explanatory.

Investment Quality

Many investors group stocks according to some of the traditional classifications used on Wall Street—for example, blue chips, growth company stocks, income stocks, and so on. The following section briefly describes the various traditional investment grades of stock.

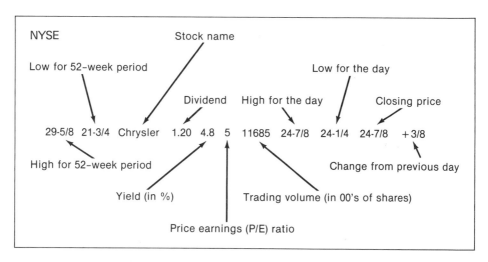

FIGURE 9-4 Reading a stock quotation

Blue chips. *Blue chip stocks* are high-grade investment quality issues from major companies which have long unbroken records of earnings and dividend payments. They are usually the largest companies in the country, and they hold important, if not leading, positions in their industries. With the advantage of size and market leadership, these corporations can weather economic downturns and post strong earnings gains during upturns, because they have the resources to capitalize on a recovery.

Secondary stocks. Secondary stocks include all stocks which are not classified as blue chips. In some cases, secondary stocks may be issued by established companies with impressive earnings records and excellent future prospects. However, the company may lack the size, corporate resources, or industry position that many consider necessary to qualify the stock as a blue chip.

Under these first two general headings that divide the thousands of stocks between "blue chips" and "secondary," stocks can be further categorized according to other important investment features. None of these categories is mutually exclusive; it is possible for some stocks to fall under one or more of the following types.

Growth company stocks. *Growth company stocks* are shares in companies in which earnings increase at a rate faster than the earnings of the average firm or the growth of the economy. These companies typically pay only a small portion of earnings in dividends, because they can maintain or accelerate their growth by reinvesting earnings in the business. Such firms are also typically aggressive in pursuing profitable ventures; they retain a substantial portion of earnings for research and development.

Cyclical company stocks. *Cyclical company stocks* are stocks of companies whose earnings fluctuate with the business cycle and are accentuated by it. When patterns in the economy are favorable to their industry, the earnings of cyclical companies peak. When the course of the economy changes direction, they suffer earnings setbacks and adversities. The most common example of a cyclical situation is that of the auto stocks, which rise in price and are a source of increasing dividends during economic booms and recoveries, but which fall during recessions when auto sales ebb.

Defensive stocks. The stocks of cyclical companies can be contrasted with those that are recession-resistant, commonly known as *defensive stocks.* Such companies sell products and services which enjoy a demand that does not greatly fluctuate with the business cycle. Familiar examples of recession-resistant industries are those involved with health care, food, and cosmetics.

Income stocks. *Income stocks* are characteristic of those firms that pay a high dividend relative to their stock prices. The dividend yields on these securities are above average for stocks and frequently are competitive with the returns on debt instruments. Income stocks, such as utility stocks, are purchased by the investors mainly for their current yield, rather than for their potential price appreciation.

Combined return stocks. Stock categories are not necessarily mutually exclusive. Some investors feel that certain stocks possess the characteristics of both income and growth company securities; that is, they offer *combined return* through dividends and price appreciation. Of course, these stocks usually do not have as high a dividend yield as a strict income stock, nor a rate of earnings growth as rapid as the growth company stock. They offer instead a dividend yield generally considered average to above average, and prospects for earnings growth which are substantial, but not spectacular.

Speculative stocks. The term *speculative stock* is usually associated with the class of stock that is frequently traded for short-term profit or one for which the purchaser is assuming an unusually large amount of risk, hoping to earn a very large return. The purchase of any stock can entail speculation; someone could buy the shares of the highest grade blue chip with the intention of selling the shares the next day for a short-term profit. However, speculative stocks generally refer to those that are considered outright gambles, such as electronics, biotech, and other types of technological entities.

MUTUAL FUNDS

INTRODUCTION

Since the end of WWII, investors have enjoyed the assurance of relatively stable domestic and international economies. As a result, they could safely rely on just a few key investments—a home, a savings account, some whole life insurance, some U.S. savings bonds, and a few blue chip stocks. Since the deep recession of 1973–74, however, which gave birth to stagflation (stagnation *and* inflation), investors have had to take widespread economic uncertainty into account when planning both for the long term and the short term. Greater investment segmentation is one direct outcome of this reality. Vehicles designed for such new and specific goals as hedging against recurring inflation, taking advantage of frequent interest rate fluctuations, minimizing the impact of taxation, and capitalizing on emerging opportunities have become part of an average investor's portfolio today.

Fortunately, the financial marketplace of the 1970s offered an unprecedented variety of investment alternatives with which to answer changing money management needs. Of these, the premier alternative is mutual funds. The accompanying box insert underscores their key attractive features. Because of their singular importance, this section is entirely devoted to a detailed discussion of investment in mutual funds.

CLOSED-END COMPANIES VERSUS MUTUAL FUNDS

An overview of investment companies, which are divided between unit investment trusts and management companies, is presented in Figure 9-5. The former consists of units or interest in an existing portfolio of long-term bonds which are deposited with a trustee. These units, known as redeemable trust certificates, are then sold to investors as unit trust shares. All interest income received by the bond portfolio and eventually the face values upon maturity, are paid by the trustee to shareholders.

Management companies, in turn, are divided into closed-end and open-end companies. The former are established by selling a fixed number of shares to investors, and their capitalization generally remains unchanged. Closed-end funds are traded on the New York Stock Exchange and the Over-the-Counter market. Just as individual stock market prices reflect changing market conditions, the net asset value (assets minus liabilities) of a closed-end company share, known as NAV, reflects the ups and downs of the securities it represents. Interestingly, while the shares of a closed-end fund can sell at a premium or discount relative to the market value of the securities it holds, experience suggests that, even over the long term, many closed-end funds continue to sell at a discount.

MUTUAL FUNDS:
THE "PROBLEM SOLVING" INVESTMENT

Investing is both a complex and time-consuming process. One reason for the booming sales of mutual funds is the comprehensive service they provide, which frees their shareholders from tasks ranging from investment evaluation to recordkeeping. Many individuals find that acquiring these services through a mutual fund also reduces both the time and the money they would otherwise spend on them. If you've ever wondered exactly what a mutual fund does "behind the scenes" for its investors, here's a quick look.

Economic, Market and Investment Research. The investment officers of a mutual fund conduct extensive research on behalf of shareholders, using sources as diverse as industry contacts and publications and government reports. Many of these sources—such as visits with company representatives—are not available to the average investor; even those that are would take hours each day to monitor and evaluate.

Securities Selection. American exchanges and over-the-counter markets encompass over 25,000 separate securities, not to mention thousands of debt and money market instruments. The management of a mutual fund monitors, analyzes and evaluates this immense investment universe with an eye to selecting those securities that not only offer the best performance potential but also reflect the fund's stated objectives most accurately.

Securities Purchase, Sale and Transfer. Once management has selected a fund's investments, it then handles the time-consuming logistics of buying and, when appropriate, selling securities on an ongoing basis at prices most advantageous to the fund.

Whether your goal is to save for a new home or manage current expenses efficiently, the odds are that one or more mutual funds can help. But how can you tell which type of fund will most effectively help you meet your specific goals? The checklist below matches typical investor concerns with the mutual funds that best answer them.

Meeting Current Expenses. The effective handling of ongoing expenses, such as mortgage payments, requires a vehicle that lets you fund expenditures at any time, ideally through checks rather than withdrawals. Consider a money market fund with checking privileges, permitting maximum flexibility, while allowing you to earn higher interest on existing balances than would be possible with a traditional checking account. (Note that most such money market mutual funds allow shareholders only to write checks in amounts above a stated minimum—normally $250—making these accounts unsuitable for small day-to-day expenses.)

Maintaining Family Cash Reserves. The necessity of having a safe financial "cushion" mandates a secure, highly liquid "fund" which can be drawn on quickly in emergencies. Low-risk, income-oriented mutual funds are therefore ideal. You might want to consider a money market fund or a government securities trust which invests in a portfolio of U.S. government issues.

Minimizing/Reducing Tax Liabilities. Individuals in high tax brackets may find that tax-exempt municipal bond funds offer them a higher return than taxable equivalents with comparable risk.

Performance Supervision. Marketable securities fluctuate in price daily, making constant supervision a necessity. As with all other aspects of investment, fund management relieves its shareholders of this burden.

Securities Custody. Mutual funds handle the physical custody of stock certificates, bonds and the like for their shareholders. Investors need not be concerned with the storage, safety or transfer of investment documents.

Performance Compilation and Reporting. The average mutual fund might hold between a few dozen and several hundred separate investments, yet investors don't have to compile and correlate information on each and every one. Instead, the mutual fund itself does so, preparing periodic statements which explain the fund's overall performance and annual statements which facilitate their tax filing.

Of course, mutual fund shareholders needn't wait for their statements to know exactly how their funds are performing. Instead, checking on current value is as easy as opening the mutual fund section of any major daily newspaper.

Share Purchase and Sale/Exchange Privileges. Shareholders can purchase, sell or exchange their fund shares as often as they like without having to worry about penalties for early withdrawal.

Dividend Distributions, Reinvestments, and Automatic Plans. Most mutual funds will either distribute or reinvest dividends depending on the shareholder's preference. Many also offer even more complex

services such as automatic withdrawal or investment plans, allowing investors to add to or liquidate their holdings over time without additional paperwork.

Funding Your Retirement. Retirement investors have a wealth of funds to choose from. Lower-risk, income-oriented vehicles (money market, government securities, taxable bonds or equity/option income funds) maximize the benefit of tax-free compounding within a retirement account such as an IRA or Keogh. Investments designed for capital appreciation, such as equity-based growth funds, may also be chosen for their potential to build retirement assets over time, particularly by those in the early phases of retirement planning.

Building Net Worth. Many individuals find it beneficial to plan for the future by allocating some of their current income to mutual funds through a disciplined periodic investment program. For this purpose, it may make sense to choose funds with exceptional long-term growth potential—even if this means accepting somewhat higher levels of risk. Aggressive growth funds may be appropriate for this purpose, as may funds which, by investing in international companies, give you the potential to benefit from worldwide economic trends.

Planning For Major Long-Term Expenditures. Buying your dream home, taking a special vacation, or funding your child's college education demands disciplined long-term savings. Choosing the right mutual fund can help make the most of your money, easing the strain of meeting future financial obligations. Growth-oriented funds offer the potential for above-average capital appreciation, while the gradual effects of compounding enhance returns from funds which focus on high current income.

Source: Adapted from "Meeting the Demands of the Financial Future," special advertising supplement sponsored by Oppenheimer Fund Management, Inc., *Changing Times* Magazine, 1986.

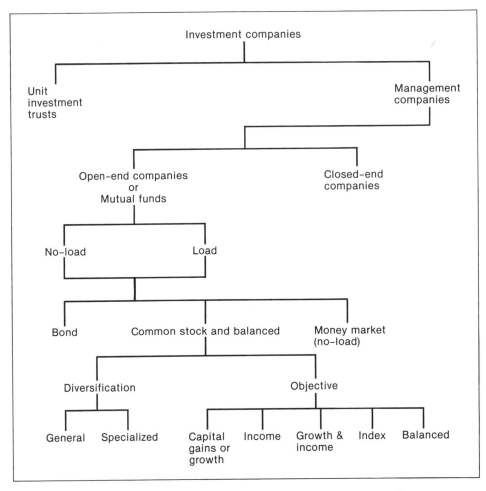

FIGURE 9-5 Major categories of investment companies. Courtesy of Sid Mittra and Chris Gassen, *Investment Analysis and Portfolio Management*, Harcourt Brace Jovanovich, Inc., 1981, p. 652.

An open-end company—popularly known as a mutual fund—continuously offers new shares. It guarantees to redeem its shares at the net asset value at any time. This value is calculated at least daily by adding the current market values of all securities in the fund's portfolio, subtracting the liabilities, and dividing the resulting figure by the number of outstanding shares of the fund's stock.

The differences between open-end and closed-end funds are summarized in Table 9-1. The rest of the discussion in this section will pertain to mutual funds.

TABLE 9-1 Comparison of Open-End and Closed-End Funds

	Open-end	*Closed-end*
Outstanding Shares	Number varies	Number fixed
New Share Offerings	Continuous	Once
Redemption Price	Net asset value (NAV); some funds require redemption fee	Not redeemed by issuer
Where Marketed	Investment dealers	Securities exchange or over the counter
From Whom Bought	Bought from an underwriter through a dealer	Bought from stockholders or from dealer inventory
To Whom Sold	Sold or redeemed in same manner as bought	Sold in same manner as common stock
Relation of Purchase to Net Asset Value	Purchase price is NAV plus any sales charges; NAV depends on value of portfolio	Purchase price is result of supply and demand, not NAV
Sales and Transfers	Public offering price usually includes sales charge, fund prospectus states sales and redemption charge, if any	Fee comparable to stock exchange commission when buying or selling through an agency; transactions on a principal basis include markups or markdowns

Adapted from *Prentice Hall Financial Planning,* 1987, pp. 3012–13.

NO-LOAD VERSUS LOAD FUNDS

Basic Concept

Mutual funds are classified as either load or no-load funds. Both types of funds charge a management fee, which in most cases ranges from .75 to 1.00 percent of the total assets managed, and are graduated based upon total dollars managed. In addition, load funds impose a maximum sales charge, or load, payable up front, of 6.5 to 8.5 percent, but it may be lower depending upon the total amount committed to that investment. This charge is often referred to as a front-end load. Therefore, assuming a load charge of 7.5 percent, a person investing $1,000 in a load fund will receive only $925 worth of shares. In contrast, no initial sales charge, or load, is involved in the purchase of shares in a no-load fund.

12b-1 Plans

Another type of charge to the investor results from the 12b-1 ruling adopted by the SEC. This ruling allows mutual funds to levy an annual percentage charge, limited to no more than 1.25 percent of the fund's net assets, to cover distribution expenses like marketing, broker's commissions, and advertising. This represents an annual drain out of the invested capital of all the fund's members. Such 12b-1 expenses are explained in the fund's prospectus and should be used in the calculation of the investor's annual yield.

Back-End Loads

Back-end loads are actually redemption fees. Some funds charge one percent whenever shares are cashed in. Other funds make a contingent deferred sales load of four to five percent if shares are redeemed in the first year and one percent less in each subsequent year until the back-load is reduced to zero. These loads and ancillary fees charged by mutual funds are presented in the accompanying boxed material. Also, the accompanying boxed insert demonstrates a method of comparing loads and fees between mutual funds.

Load: Front Versus Deferred

In November 1988 Merrill Lynch introduced a novel load choice for its mutual fund investors. Investors can choose to pay a 6.5 percent front load for stock funds (four percent for bond funds) or an annual marketing charge of one percent known as a 12b-1 fee. It might appear that the latter choice is always preferable to the former. That is not necessarily the case. For instance, on a $5,000 stock fund investment that grows ten percent annually, an investor who expects to hold the fund's shares over seven and a half years would be better off paying the front load.

READING A MUTUAL FUND QUOTE

Quotations for a family of mutual funds known as Fidelity Investments are presented in Table 9-2. It contains four important pieces of information, as detailed next.

Net Asset Value (NAV)

As mentioned, the net value of a mutual fund share is calculated each day by dividing the fund's total net assets (assets minus liabilities) by the number of shares outstanding. The NAV is the amount an investor pays for a no-load fund. On November 20, 1989, the net asset value of Fidelity Magellan was $62.99.

TABLE 9-2   Reading a Mutual Fund Quote

Family of funds

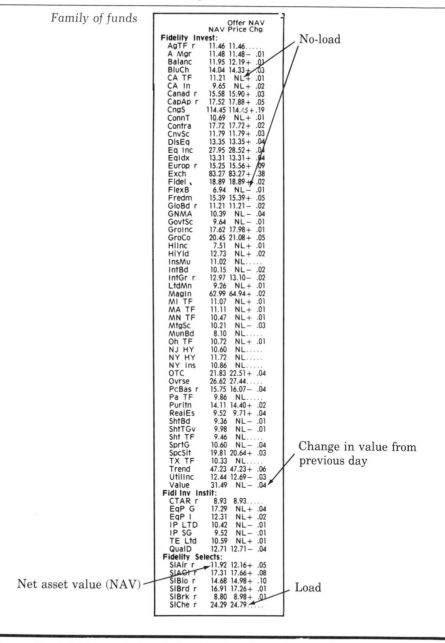

No-load

Change in value from previous day

Net asset value (NAV)

Load

Note: r: Redemption charge may apply the liquidation.

　　　p: Distribution costs may apply in the case of 12b-1 funds.

MUTUAL FUND CHARGES

Front-end load. An initial sales expense (three percent to 8.5 percent) that is charged before the shares are purchased. Some of this money goes to managing the fund but most of it goes to pay sales commissions.

Back-end load. A deduction taken from the proceeds of the sale of shares. The percentage charged usually decreases as the length of time over which shares are held increases.

Re-load. A charge to reinvest the gains and/or cash dividends.

Exit fee. A charge to cash in any shares of the fund. It's usually a flat rate or one to two percent of the proceeds.

Managing fee. Used to cover costs like salaries, expenses, and so on.

12b-1 fee. Fee used to cover advertising, commissions, and other costs.

Transfer fee. A charge to switch from one fund in the company to another. It is usually .5 to one percent.

No-Load (NL)

If the purchase price of a fund equals its net asset value, it is a no-load fund and is designated by the letters NL. The Value Fund is one of the no-load funds in this family.

Offer Price/Load

Sometimes called buy price, this is the sum of the fund's net asset value and its maximum front-end load, if the fund charges one. For instance, on November 20, 1989, the offer price for Fidelity Magellan was $64.94, whereas its NAV was $62.99. The difference of $1.95 was its front load; it calculated to around three percent.

AT LAST, A WAY TO COMPARE LOADS AND FEES

In the days when loads were loads and no-loads were no-loads, a mutual fund investor knew where he stood. If you wanted a broker's advice in selecting a fund, you paid for it up front in the form of an 8.5% sales load. If you didn't, you bought no-load fund shares by mail. Nothing is so simple anymore. Nowadays, you must contend with a thicket of new charges that make it difficult to figure out the real cost of investing in a fund. The worksheet and tables below, devised for *Money* by John Markese, research director for the American Association of Individual Investors, will enable you to compare all fees, including front-end loads, back-end loads or exit fees, if any, and annual expenses. (Annual expenses, usually lumped together and expressed as a percentage of the fund's total assets under "per share data" in the fund's prospectus, include management fees and so-called 12b-1 charges.)

The key to making the conversions work is to estimate how long you will own shares in any fund you are considering. The table at left (below) then converts front-end loads into the equivalent of fixed annual expenses. The table at right performs the same translation for back-end loads, assuming the fund grows at a 10% annually compounded rate. The worksheet makes it easy to come up with a total figure for annual expenses, expressed as a percentage of your investment.

Here's how the calculations work. Suppose you expect to hold a fund's shares for three years and want to compare the costs over that period for two funds—for example, Fidelity OTC, with a 3% front-end load and total annual expenses of 1.5%, and broker-sold Hutton Special Equities, which carries no front-end load but has total annual expenses of 2.2% and a back-end load. The charge is 5% on shares you redeem in the first year you own the fund; it declines by a percentage point each year thereafter.

By consulting the appropriate table,

you discover that OTC's 3% front-end load is equivalent to a 1% annual charge over three years (read across the row for years held—in this case three—until you reach its intersection with the column for a 3% front-end load). Using the worksheet, add the front-end load equivalent (line A) to the fund's 1.5% annual expense charge (line C); line B can be left blank. Total equivalent annual expense: 2.5%.

By reviewing the table at right in the manner described above, you find that Special Equities' back-end load (3% after three years) is equivalent to an annual charge of .75% over three years. Add that figure (line B) to the fund's annual expenses of 2.2% (line C) and you get an equivalent annual expense of 2.95%. The conclusion: the Hutton fund is the higher cost fund over three years. Thus, unless you believe the assistance of a Hutton broker is worth the extra cost, or unless you expect the Hutton fund to outperform the Fidelity fund by at least 0.45% per year over the next three years, OTC is the better bet.

FIGURING YOUR FUND'S TRUE COSTS

A. Annual equivalent expense for your fund's front-end load, if any (from table 1)   _____

B. Annual equivalent expense for your fund's back-end load, if any (from table 2)   _____

C. Your fund's annual expenses (from fund prospectus)   _____

D. Total equivalent annual expenses (add lines A, B and C)   _____ %

TABLE 1 Front-End Load						TABLE 2 Back-End Load					
Years held	3%	4%	5%	6%	8.5%	Years held	1%	2%	3%	4%	5%
1	3%	4%	5%	6%	8.5%	1	0.91%	1.8%	2.7%	3.6%	4.6%
3	1	1.3	1.7	2.0	2.8	3	0.25	0.50	0.75	1.0	1.3
5	0.6	0.8	1.0	1.2	1.7	5	0.12	0.25	0.37	0.50	0.62
10	0.3	0.4	0.5	0.6	0.85	10	0.04	0.08	0.12	0.15	0.19

Source: Money, May 1987, p. 37.

NAV Change (CHG)

This item shows how much the fund's net asset value changed over the previous close. The change is reported in cents per share. Thus, the net asset value of the Value Fund increased from $33.34 to $33.44, an increase of +10 or ten cents.

READING A MUTUAL FUND STATEMENT

Mutual fund investors receive a wealth of information from their monthly statements. Some of the information is mechanical. These include the name and address, account number, date of the statement, and shares on deposit. Other pieces of information are not so mechanical and easy to understand.

A detailed explanation of each of the important pieces of information contained in a mutual fund statement is presented in Figure 9-6. Note, however, that it is important to keep track of purchases and reinvestments for purposes of calculating gain or loss for tax computations. Also, for realizing maximum tax benefits, at the time of sale of mutual fund shares, it is necessary to identify which shares are to be liquidated. Without proper identification the IRS automatically assumes that shares with the longest holding are sold first, an assumption which may lead to undesirable tax consequences.

READING A MUTUAL FUND PROSPECTUS

Before making an investment decision, every investor should examine the fund's goals and objectives and the ability of its management to carry them out. Additionally, one must evaluate the services provided by the fund and the costs of such services.

A wealth of information is contained in the fund's prospectus which, by law, must be furnished to all potential investors before a purchase application can be accepted by the fund. In the following paragraphs, we will discuss statements of investment objectives and policies, risk factors, investment restrictions, costs and fees, and other miscellaneous information contained in a mutual fund prospectus.

Investment Objectives and Policies

Mutual funds can be classified into various categories according to their objectives.

1. *Capital gains or growth funds* cater to the needs of investors who prefer future long-term capital gains over immediate dividend income. Their

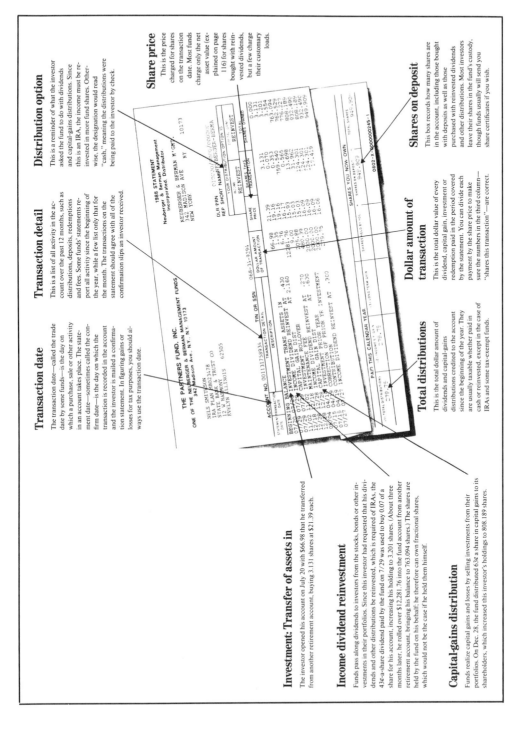

Transaction date

The transaction date—called the trade date by some funds—is the day on which a purchase, sale or other activity in an account takes place. The statement date—sometimes called the confirm date—is the day on which the transaction is recorded in the account and the investor is mailed a confirmation statement. In figuring gains or losses for tax purposes, you should always use the transaction date.

Transaction detail

This is a list of all activity in the account over the past 12 months, such as distributions, deposits, redemptions and fees. Some funds' statements report all activity since the beginning of the year, while a few list only that for the month. The transactions on the statement should agree with all of the confirmation slips an investor received.

Distribution option

This is a reminder of what the investor asked the fund to do with dividends and capital-gains distributions. Since this is an IRA, the income must be reinvested in more fund shares. Otherwise, the designation would read "cash," meaning the distributions were being paid to the investor by check.

Share price

This is the price charged for shares on the transaction date. Most funds charge only the net asset value (explained on page 116) for shares bought with reinvested dividends, but a few charge their customary loads.

Shares on deposit

This box records how many shares are in the account, including those bought with deposits as well as those purchased with reinvested dividends and other distributions. Most investors leave their shares in the fund's custody, though funds usually will send you share certificates if you wish.

Investment: Transfer of assets in

The investor opened his account on July 20 with $66.98 that he transferred from another retirement account, buying 3.131 shares at $21.39 each.

Income dividend reinvestment

Funds pass along dividends to investors from the stocks, bonds or other investments in their portfolios. Since this investor had requested that his dividends and other distributions be reinvested, which is required of IRAs, the 43¢-a-share dividend paid by the fund on 7/29 was used to buy 0.07 of a share for his account, increasing his holding to 3.201 shares. (About three months later, he rolled over $12,281.76 into the fund account from another retirement account, bringing his balance to 763.094 shares.) The shares are held by the fund on his behalf; he therefore can own fractional shares, which would not be the case if he held them himself.

Capital-gains distribution

Funds realize capital gains and losses by selling investments from their portfolios. On Dec. 28, the fund distributed 63¢ a share in capital gains to its shareholders, which increased this investor's holdings to 808.189 shares.

Dollar amount of transaction

This is the total dollar value of every dividend, capital gain, investment or redemption paid in the period covered by the statement. You can divide each payment by the share price to make sure the numbers in the third column—"shares this transaction"—are correct.

Total distributions

This is the total dollar amount of dividends and capital-gains distributions credited to the account since the beginning of the year. They are usually taxable whether paid in cash or reinvested, except in the case of IRAs and some tax-exempt funds.

FIGURE 9-6 Reading a mutual fund statement. Courtesy of Bruce Hager, "Those $☆&*!#% Statements," in *Money*, October 1988, p. 115. Reprinted with permission.

investments are largely made in established companies that have demonstrated their ability to expand faster than the nation's economy as a whole.

2. *Income funds* basically favor securities with above-average, current income potential, although growth possibilities are not ruled out. Because their objective is to select stocks with high and stable dividend payments, income funds offer greater price stability than capital gains and growth funds.

3. *Growth and income funds* invest for a combination of capital gains and current income. Of course, some funds seek income as the primary objective and growth as a secondary aim; still others seek an even balance between the two. Funds seeking both growth *and* income generally invest in a more broadly diversified group of securities than funds whose principal objective is current income.

4. *Index funds* are designed to match the performance of the aggregate stock market. These funds operate under the notion that matching the market averages will produce better long-run performance than the efforts of money managers who try to beat the market. An example of an index fund relates to the situation where the portfolio manager attempts to invest in the S&P 500 stocks.

5. *Balanced funds* hold bonds and preferred stocks in addition to common stocks in order to minimize market risk.

The important characteristics of objectives for various types of mutual funds are presented in the accompanying boxed insert.

Risk Factors

An important section contained in every prospectus deals with the risks fund managers are likely to assume. For instance, the fund may state that in seeking capital appreciation, it will purchase stocks of small companies which may trade on the OTC market and may have a history of price volatility greater than the stocks of more mature companies. Another prospectus may explain, "We expect to be fully invested in stocks under most market conditions." Also the fund's prospectus may identify if the fund deals in call and put options. These statements should be taken into account in determining the riskiness of the fund.

Investment Restrictions

It is desirable to study the investment restrictions as well. Every prospectus contains the usual investment restrictions imposed by the Investment Company Act of 1940. In addition, it may also impose other restrictions on the

CHARACTERISTICS OF SELECTED MUTUAL FUNDS

Type	Characteristics	
Aggressive Growth	Key Strength:	Growth potential in rising markets
	Main Weakness:	High vulnerability to slumps
	Investor Profile:	Risk takers who won't need cash for at least 3 years
Growth	Key Strength:	Long-term growth
	Main Weakness:	Scant protection from market drops
	Investor Profile:	Long-term investors who want capital growth with roughly market level risk
Total Return	Key Strength:	Comparatively steady gains in variety of market conditions
	Main Weakness:	Tepid results in high times
	Investor Profile:	Risk averse investors looking for capital growth and moderate income
International	Key Strength:	Can outpace U.S. stocks
	Main Weakness:	Vulnerable to currency fluctuations
	Investor Profile:	Growth investors who want diversity
Gold	Key Strength:	Gains not dependent on U.S. stock market
	Main Weakness:	More ups and downs
	Investor Profile:	Investors who want to hedge against inflation
Bond Fixed Income	Key Strength:	Dependable monthly income
	Main Weakness:	Rising interest rates can zap principal
	Investor Profile:	Income seekers and equity investors looking to diversify

Source: Walter L. Updegrave, *Money,* January 1988, p. 112.

portfolio managers. A list of typical restrictions is presented here:

1. The fund will not indulge in short selling.
2. The fund will not purchase securities on margin.
3. The fund's assets will be diversified so no more than 7.5 percent of the total is invested in a single industry group.
4. The fund will not borrow more than three percent of the total assets for meeting emergencies.

Naturally these investment restrictions should be carefully studied before investing in a fund.

Past Performance

Mutual funds generally present a five-year track record and compare their record with that of the Standard & Poor's 500 or the Dow Jones Industrial Average. In addition, the prospectus would reveal such important data as the ratio of expenses to average net assets and the portfolio turnover rate. While past performance does not guarantee future success, a good track record is certainly an attractive feature of any fund. Also, a ratio of expenses to average net assets of up to one percent and a high portfolio turnover rate (say, 30 to 40 percent) might demonstrate that the fund is being efficiently run.

Costs and Fees

The SEC requires every fund to include a table of all fees near the front of the prospectus, followed by a hypothetical total of all fees over several years. A pure no-load fund usually indicates this fact on the cover. Front-load, low-load, and back-load funds disclose their costs inside the prospectus. The investor may also have to be creative in interpreting additional costs. For instance, instead of saying that all dividends are subject to the usual full front-end load, one prospectus puts it this way: "Dividends will be reinvested in additional full and fractional shares at the public offering price (net asset value plus a sales charge)."

Miscellaneous Information

The back pages of the prospectus contain valuable information on additional services available through the fund. These include, among other items, share purchase, sale and exchange privileges, transfer between funds within the family, participation in a systematic withdrawal plan, dividend distribution, reinvestment, and automatic deposit and withdrawal plans. Information is also provided on telephone switch, check writing privileges, and other related services provided by the fund.

SALE OF MUTUAL FUNDS

The Basic Issue

Buying mutual fund shares completes only half the transaction. The other half consists of the decision to sell it at the most appropriate time—unquestionably the toughest decision one faces as a mutual fund investor. Unfortunately, matching the present value of a fund's share to its market price is not a viable approach. The reason is that the mutual fund is a portfolio of stocks, bonds, and other related securities, and the value of the portfolio is different from the value of individual securities included in it. Consequently, different strategies must be developed for assisting an investor to decide when to sell mutual fund shares. In the following paragraphs, we will present several of these strategies.

Change of Investment Objective

Buying into a fund, of course, is just the beginning of the investment process. A change in the stock or bond market or in the investor's risk preference might necessitate switching, or liquidating investment in mutual fund shares because of a change of the fund manager. Each fund is committed to a particular investment philosophy which dictates the type of securities it will hold. Although its managers may alter the holdings fairly frequently, they cannot completely change direction to capitalize on basic changes in investment conditions. In fact, by the terms of their prospectuses, many funds are required to invest only in certain types or grades of securities. For example, an income fund may replace certain stocks with others, but even the new stocks will primarily be income stocks. Consequently, an income fund investor who is unwilling to hold income stocks has little choice but to move the money to another type of fund with a different goal or method of operation.

Consistent Poor Performance

Mutual fund investment is for the long term, and one or two bad quarters should not be the compelling reason for liquidating the shares. However, if the fund's performance continuously ranks in the bottom fifth of funds of its type for several quarters, serious consideration should be given to liquidating the fund. Of course, in making this decision the back-end load charges if applicable must always be taken into account.

Size of the Fund

The general maxim for mutual fund investment in stocks is, "smaller is better." The critical size for a mutual fund appears to be assets of $200 million or less, as portfolio managers face increasingly difficult investment choices as the assets exceed $250 million. More specifically, investing large amounts of money makes it more difficult to accumulate meaningful positions in individual stock issues, especially if these issues are relatively small. There are exceptions, of course, as is evidenced by the extraordinary success of Fidelity Magellan which manages over $1 billion in assets. But these exceptions are rare, and investors would be well advised to get out when their fund gets too big for their taste. Interestingly, this small size criterion does not apply to bond mutual funds, since the more bonds a fund holds, the slimmer are the chances of its being badly hurt should some of its bond issuers default.

Miscellaneous Changes

If the portfolio manager of a fund, who was primarily responsible for the fund's admirable record, quits the fund, and the new manager does not have a comparable track record, it would be wise to liquidate the fund, or at least carefully watch its future performance under the new manager. Investors should also be leery of spectacular performance for several consecutive months. Such performance is usually the result of the manager's taking unusually high risks with investors' money. Finally, a change in economic conditions might warrant a shift from a stock or bond fund into a money market fund.

MUTUAL FUNDS AND TAXES

At tax time, every mutual fund shareholder is faced with a dual task: reporting fund distributions (dividend income and capital gains distribution), and calculating capital gains and losses as a result of the sale (redemption) or exchange of fund shares.

Fund Distributions

At the beginning of each year, each mutual fund sends its investors Form 1099-DIV for each of the regular, nonqualified accounts. This form lists the taxable dividend and capital gains distributions that the fund declared during the previous year and paid by January 31 of the current year. All dividend and capital gains distributions listed on this form are considered taxable regardless of whether they were received in cash or automatically reinvested in the fund, unless it is a municipal bond, fund in which case dividends are treated as tax-free distributions. It should be noted here that currently long-term capital gains distributions are taxed at the same rate as dividend distributions and other ordinary income.

The procedure for reporting distributions on tax returns is straightforward. First, itemized information needs to be provided on Schedule B if the total dividend and distribution income exceeds $400. This income is the sum of all dividend and capital gains distributions, plus all other dividend income received on individual stock holdings. If the total is $400 or less, the distributions can be directly reported on Form 1040. Second, the investors should submit Schedule D if other capital gains and losses have been realized. In that case, the mutual fund capital gains distributions will also be reported on Schedule D, along with other capital gain and loss transactions.

Selling and Exchanging Shares

If an investor sells or exchanges shares of a mutual fund with a fluctuating share price, the IRS considers the transaction a taxable event. A capital gain or loss must be calculated for each sale or exchange. At the beginning of each year, the mutual fund sends each shareholder Form 1099-B which lists the gross proceeds, share price, and number of shares for each sale/exchange of shares. For each transaction the investor is required to determine the cost basis (original cost), calculate the gain or loss, and report the results on Schedule D of the tax return. Incidentally, each capital gain or loss must be classified as short-term or long-term, even though both terms receive identical treatment under current tax law. Additional information of interest to financial planners is presented in the accompanying boxed material.

THE FUNDING IS MUTUAL

Mutual funds are popular investment vehicles based on a simple concept: Establish a clearly defined investment objective; combine the funds of a large number of investors; employ a manager to develop a diversified portfolio which will achieve the fund's objectives; and then let the investors share all income and expenses, as well as any capital gains and losses. But while the mutual fund concept is simple, selecting the proper fund is a complex decision, independent of the decision of whether to invest in one in the first place. Unfortunately, many investors make their decisions based on a number of misconceptions or myths.

Myth 1: The various mutual funds available today differ only in minor respects. This is not the case. Today there are more than 1,500 mutual funds which vary significantly in a number of important ways. (An annual publication, *Investment Companies,* by Wiesenberger Services, is an excellent source of information on the mutual funds available.) First and most obvious, funds differ by the type of securities in which they invest, such as common stocks, money market securities, corporate bonds, municipal bonds, etc. Mutual funds can also specialize within each of these categories. For example, within the common stock category there are funds which specialize in growth stocks, utility stocks, and stocks of small companies, to name a few. Second, funds also differ according to investment objectives. For example, one common stock mutual fund might stress earning long-term capital gains, while another stresses current income through dividends. Third, and less obvious, the investment style and abilities of the various fund managers also differ significantly. That is, each fund manager employs unique strategies and techniques to select securities to achieve a fund's objectives. Each also executes these strategies with varying degrees of success. Finally, there are many other important differences among funds, which include the expenses they incur for marketing and administration, management fees, and brokerage commissions. All of the above differences, both obvious and subtle, can significantly influence an investor's return over time.

Myth 2: Selecting the proper mutual fund is the only investment decision an individual has to make. The mutual fund handles everything else.   Unfortunately, while a mutual fund handles all decisions regarding which securities to buy and sell, it cannot make the following decisions for its investors: (a) when they should buy into the fund; (b) how much they should invest; and (c) when they should sell out of the fund. These decisions often can be more important in determining an investor's total investment return than the buy-and-sell decisions of the fund manager.

Myth 3: When deciding to invest in a mutual fund, always rely on the advice of a financial planning professional or investment advisor.   While many financial planning professionals offer sound advice on mutual funds, many others make biased recommendations to invest in certain funds because they receive a substantial commission for doing so. It is important to recognize that some mutual funds charge investors a sales fee to invest, while others do not. The former (known as load funds) are often marketed through persons connected with the financial planning business who receive part of the sales fee for "selling" the fund to the investor. Therefore, before investing in a mutual fund based on an advisor's recommendation, be very careful to select a knowledgeable, unbiased professional who will recommend the most appropriate fund, whether or not there is a sales fee attached. Unfortunately, selecting an investment advisor today can be more difficult than selecting one's own investments.

Myth 4: The best-managed mutual funds over a given time period are those that have earned the highest returns.   It seems logical to conclude that the best-managed funds are those that earn the highest returns; however, this may not always be the case. Suppose mutual fund A returned ten percent over a certain period, while mutual fund B returned eleven percent. But also assume that fund A invested in lower risk utility stocks, while fund B took much

greater risk by investing in shares of small, high technology companies. Even though fund B earned one percent more than fund A, the extra return might not have been enough to compensate adequately for the extra risk assumed. In this example, investors might have reasonably expected a portfolio of high-risk stocks to return much more than one percent above a low-risk portfolio, indicating that fund B was not better managed than fund A. In any case, investors should expect mutual funds with higher risk to earn higher returns, and not automatically attribute those higher returns to better management. Exactly what return should an investor expect from each of the various mutual funds with different risks? This is determined largely by individual preference, although there are statistical tools used by professionals to make reasonable estimations.

Myth 5: Mutual funds that charge a sales fee to invest (i.e., load funds) generally offer prospects for better investment performance than those that do not (no-load funds).   There is no evidence to conclude that, on average, load funds are better managed than no-load funds and offer prospects for superior investment results. Of course, there are certain load funds that have outstanding records and have clearly justified their up-front sales charge. However, there are certain no-load funds that have excellent performance records as well. The point is this: merely because a fund is more expensive to invest in does not mean it should be expected to perform better. Each fund must be analyzed individually to determine if it justifies a sales charge, which often can be as high as 8.5 percent of the amount invested.

Why do some funds charge a sales fee to invest while others do not? The answer is that load funds usually incur higher marketing expenses for items such as advertising or commissions to stockbrokers and financial planners who recommend their funds. In addition, sales fees are sometimes charged to earn extra profit for the fund distributor. It should be noted, however, that some no-load funds also charge the equivalent of a sales fee in hidden ways, as discussed next.

Myth 6: No-load funds, because they do not charge a sales fee to invest, are less costly to invest in than load funds. In many cases this is true; however, a number of no-load funds charge the equivalent of an up-front sales fee in different forms. First, some no-loads charge a sales fee on redemptions rather than initial investments. This is known as a back-end load. Also, some no-load funds have adopted controversial 12b-1 plans that allow them to reimburse themselves for certain selling expenses by taking money directly from the fund's portfolio each year.

In addition to sales fees, however, other costs should be examined when comparing mutual funds. These include fees paid by the fund to its investment manager, brokerage commissions to trade securities, and other administrative expenses. These costs (shared by all fund investors on a pro rata basis) can vary substantially among mutual funds, often by more than one percent of the fund's net assets each year. All factors considered, a no-load fund could actually be more costly to invest in than a load fund. Clearly, investors should examine the area of expenses very carefully.

Myth 7: In order for a mutual fund to be registered with the Securities and Exchange Commission, it must be managed by an experienced professional with a good record of investment performance. There is no such rule. Essentially, to manage a mutual fund one need only have a record which is free of fraud, securities violations, and certain other offenses. It is clearly the investor's responsibility to evaluate the ability and experience of the fund manager, which is a very important but difficult task.

Chris Gassen, "The Funding is Mutual," *Heritage*, October 1986, pp. 65–67.

Myth 8: There is no risk when investing in mutual funds which hold only fixed income securities issued or backed by the U.S. government. Although there is no risk regarding the payment of interest and principal on securities issued or backed by the U.S. government, there is a risk that the price of these securities will drop should interest rates rise. For a given increase in interest rates, price declines will be greater for fixed income securities with longer maturities. Consequently, mutual funds that hold longer-term government securities, such as bonds that mature in twenty to thirty years, carry considerable risk. In contrast, a fund that holds only U.S. Treasury bills (which mature in one year or less) is virtually risk-free.

Myth 9: The tax planning aspects of mutual fund investing can be easily controlled. Investors can actually lose considerable control of their tax planning with certain types of mutual funds, namely those which generate significant capital gains. This results because the fund manager decides when to sell securities in the fund portfolio and realize capital gains. These gains are then distributed to the investors, who must pay taxes on them for the tax year in which they are received, even if the timing of the distribution is inopportune.

Mutual funds can provide tremendous advantages to individuals by providing access to a diversified, professionally managed portfolio. However, investing in them can also be very complex, as demonstrated by the preceding myths. Clearly, a commitment to these investment vehicles should not be made without a thorough understanding of: (a) the mutual fund's objectives and strategies; (b) the risk characteristics of the securities it holds; (c) the abilities and record of the management; and (d) other factors, such as expenses and tax considerations. Such an understanding can come only through thorough and careful research, either by the investor or a qualified advisor. It is certainly no myth that mutual fund investors should be well informed.

OTHER INVESTMENT ALTERNATIVES

JUNK BONDS

In Wall Street terminology, corporate bonds rated below Baa by Moody's or below BBB by S&Ps are characterized as *junk bonds*, whereas bonds with higher ratings are identified as investment quality bonds. The connotation "junk" comes from the investment community's belief that, under unfavorable economic conditions, market prices of such bonds will significantly drop, producing at least a paper loss. Junk bonds should not be confused with deep discount bonds. Deep discount bonds sell at discount prices because they carry a low coupon rate; junk bonds sell well below par because they carry substantial default risk. Clearly junk bonds offer a higher yield, reflecting the substantial default risk they carry. This is borne out by the current woes of junk bonds. A recent study by Paul Asquith found that investors who bought a portfolio of all junk bonds issued in 1977 and 1978 and held them through late 1988 would encounter a default rate exceeding 34 percent. Another study by Barrie Wigmore pointed out that the default rates for bonds issued in 1986 to 1988 were expected to be much higher.

CONVERTIBLE BONDS

As previously mentioned, *convertible bonds* give the bondholder the right to convert bonds into common stock. Usually, the number of shares for which a convertible bond can be exchanged is fixed, and the conversion privilege lasts for the life of the bond.

Convertible bonds are considered a hybrid-type security because they combine the basic attributes of common stock (equity interest) *and* corporate bonds (debt) into a single security. Because these bonds can be exchanged for common stock at the initiative of the investors, they can participate in the appreciation potential of the associated equities. In addition, convertible bonds can provide the investor with downside protection in the event of a significant decline in equity prices. Equally important, convertible bonds represent an obligation on the part of the corporation to make regular interest payments.

ZERO COUPON BONDS

Zero coupon bonds are instruments that offer no periodic interest payments. Instead they are sold at a discount from their face value, and gradually increase in value representing interest income as they approach maturity. Yield to maturity is based solely on the difference between the initial investment and the amount received upon sale or maturity. Overall investment return is computed using a standardized formula which calculates price, interest rate, and interest reinvestment.

WARRANTS AND RIGHTS

Broadly speaking, warrants and rights are related to stocks and bonds. They neither represent ownership in the issuing company nor are they a form of debt; they only represent the privilege of purchasing a specified corporate security at a particular price within a specified limit of time. Ownership of these instruments, however, is somewhat episodic rather than of continuous interest.

Warrants

Warrants allow the holder to purchase a corporate security—usually common stock—at a given price within a specified period of time. This time period may be finite or indefinite. A company may issue warrants to shareholders or creditors when a new stock or bond issue is released as an inducement to purchase these securities. Warrants may be traded on stock exchanges after the security has been issued.

Rights

Rights differ from warrants in one important respect: Unlike warrants, rights have short expiration dates, generally extending between two to ten weeks. Rights to purchase a common stock are often given to shareholders when additional stock is issued. Shareholders are then entitled to purchase more stock in proportion to their current holdings in order to maintain their existing percentage equity in the firm. Depending on the particular issue, rights may or may not be traded by the original owner in a secondary market.

STOCK OPTIONS

Stock options are contracts that can be used to buy or sell stock. There are two types of options: calls and puts. A *call option* allows the holder to purchase a minimum of 100 shares of a stock at a given price within a specified period of time, usually three to nine months. Unlike warrants or rights, call options are not issued by the company, but are written—or sold—by other investors who contract to deliver the shares to the option holders if the options are exercised.

A *put option* allows the holder to sell a minimum of 100 shares of a stock at a given price within a specified period of time. Whereas a call option is purchased by an investor who expects the stock price to rise before the option

TABLE 9-3 Listed Options Quotations

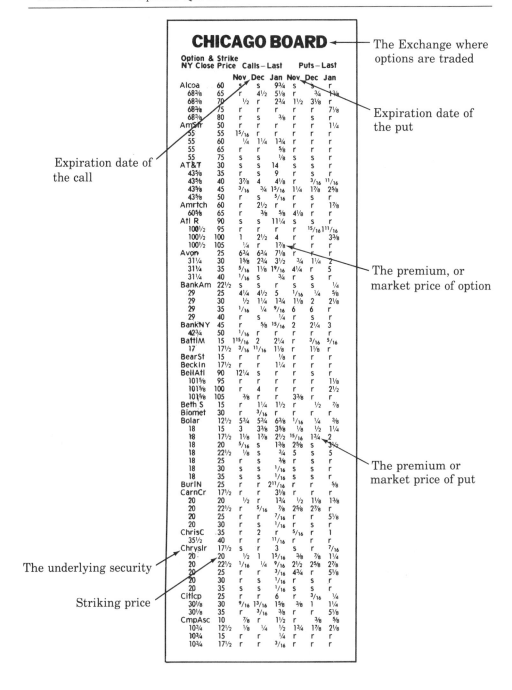

The Exchange where options are traded

Expiration date of the put

Expiration date of the call

The premium, or market price of option

The premium or market price of put

The underlying security

Striking price

r: Not traded   s: No option

expires, a put option is purchased by an investor who foresees a decline in the stock's price.

A typical option table is presented in Table 9-3. For instance, in November 1989 John Jones might purchase one Chrysler Jan 20 call, giving him the right to purchase 100 shares of Chrysler stock at $20 a share before the expiration of the option in January 1990. The Chrysler stock is known as the *underlying security*, and the $20 figure is referred to as the *striking price*. The writer of the option, Cindy Smith, receives the price (called the *premium*) and is required to deliver 100 shares of Chrysler stock at $20 per share if the holder of the option decides to exercise it before the option expires.

It can now be discussed how John and Cindy can benefit from this transaction. If before the expiration date Chrysler stock rises to, say, $25, John would be able to purchase the stock from Cindy at $20 a share and sell it at $25, thereby realizing a capital gain (ignoring commissions) of $5 per share. Cindy would lose the stock but keep the premium received for selling the option. Of course, if Chrysler stock does not appreciate and the option is not exercised, Cindy will wind up keeping the premium *and* the stock and John would lose the premium.

The put option works precisely in the reverse manner. If John Jones purchased a Chrysler January 20 put in November 1989, he would have the choice of selling 100 shares of Chrysler stock at the $20 striking price before the January 1990 *expiration date*. The writer of the put, Cindy Smith, of course would receive a premium and would be obliged to purchase the stock at $20 if the put option were exercised.

In purchasing a put option John expects to profit from a drop in Chrysler stock. If John is right, and Chrysler price drops to, say, $15 a share, John would purchase the stock at $15 and "put it" to Cindy at the striking price of $20. In this case, John would realize a capital gain (excluding commission) of $5 per share.

SHORT SELLING

Short selling is the reverse of the usual market transaction. Instead of buying a stock in the hope that it can be sold later at a higher price, a short trader *first sells stock* and later *buys it back* at what the seller hopes will be a lower price; that is, the short seller attempts to first sell high and then buy low. Short traders borrow stock to sell short from their brokers, who acquire their stock to lend from their margin account customers. At a subsequent time period, the short seller purchases the stock to cover the sale. At that point, the short seller realizes either a profit or a loss, depending on the purchase and sale price of the stock.

SINGLE PREMIUM WHOLE LIFE (SPWL)

One of the latest developments in the world of investment is the popularity of SPWL. As the name suggests, SPWL is purchased with a single payment, much as an investor would invest in a certificate of deposit (CD). The difference is that SPWL is an insurance policy with just enough insurance to qualify for tax-deferred status under the tax code. In fact, most policies subtract the cost of insurance before quoting the interest rate. Consequently, interest earned on a SPWL policy is generally less than what could be earned elsewhere; in addition, this loss is more pronounced if the insurance coverage is not desired.

A SPWL policy permits the tax-deferred build-up of cash value. Even more important, the law allows the investor to withdraw the accumulated interest as a loan (taxable for policies after June 20, 1989) and at zero or nominal cost. In addition, a large portion of the principal can also be borrowed out at a nominal interest. Finally, an investor is allowed to bail out of the policy, although the company imposes a surrender charge for this privilege.

SINGLE PREMIUM VARIABLE LIFE (SPVL)

SPVL differs from SPWL in one important respect: A large part of the single premium becomes the nest egg to be invested by the company in a variety of stock, bond, and other mutual funds. The investor can switch from one fund to another without paying tax. And all earnings compound tax-deferred. However, any withdrawal of gains, interest or dividend from SPVL is taxed at ordinary tax rates.

TANGIBLE ASSETS

REAL ESTATE

The Objective

Real estate often offers an average yield of two times that of most common stocks. However, the investor must be willing to take the risk of a long-term investment and experience greater liquidity risk.

Types of Real Estate Investment

Raw land and residential lots. Investment in raw land and residential lots is very speculative in nature. There are no special tax advantages and positive cash flow for this kind of investment. Raw land is usually located far from established communities, with no utilities or improvements. Residential lots are subdivided parcels of land with utilities, usually located near established communities. Investment in this type of real estate should be based on the premise that the investor will eventually build on the property, the land will appreciate significantly over the holding period, or comparable land will not be available in the future when needed by potential buyers.

Residential property. The natural real estate investment for most people is the single-family home or condominium. Owning a home has several tax advantages. First, interest payments on the mortgage and property taxes are fully deductible. Second, a homeowner can defer realizing a capital gain by buying another, more expensive, home. Third, if a homeowner is over 55 when the home is sold, up to $125,000 of the gains are tax-exempt.

There are risks in investing in residential property as well. In an inflation-stricken economy, adoption of a tight money policy by the Federal Reserve dries up the supply of funds to housing. High and increasingly volatile long-term rates cause a massive shift of funds from the long-term, fixed-rate market to other markets. A continuous increase in the prices of homes makes it progressively more difficult for most people to own homes, thereby adversely affecting their potential for capital appreciation. Another risk is the potential for a significant drop in real estate prices after a sharp rise. Other specific risks include lack of liquidity and diversity in residential investment, ever-increasing taxes on residential property, and a possible change in the size and type of homes in which people might invest in the future. Despite these risks, reasonably priced residential property in a good location continues to provide an attractive form of investment for the long term.

Income-producing properties. Residential units are properties such as houses, duplexes, apartments, and condominiums, designed for residential living, that have a potential to generate a profit. Making a profit in these properties often requires the investor to take an active interest in their management. Investors should seek properties offered at favorable prices with good underlying value that can be refurbished and sold at a profit or rented out.

Commercial properties are designed for business uses (e.g., office buildings, medical centers, motels, and so on) that have a potential to generate profit. These properties usually carry a higher risk of vacancy than residential units. Also, the numerous services required by the tenants are usually more expensive as well as extensive. Of course, higher rents can be charged on commercial property to compensate for higher risk.

When residential and commercial property is used to generate rental income, all expenses allocable to the rental use of the property become tax-deductible. Furthermore, if this results in a net loss, this loss can be used to shelter other income from taxes. All real estate income and losses are classified, respectively, as "passive income" and "passive losses." Passive losses can generally only be used to offset other passive income. However, if an investor has an adjusted gross income of under $100,000, up to $25,000 in passive losses may be used to shelter income from any source. This limit is gradually phased out, however, as the adjusted gross income moves from $100,000 to $150,000.

Syndicates and limited partnerships.   Syndicates facilitate the raising of capital and the sharing of investment risks. A syndicate is usually formed by a real estate manager who raises capital from individual investors. A syndicate offers the inexperienced real estate investor an opportunity to participate in a large real estate venture.

Syndicates are frequently organized as limited partnerships in which the risks of limited partners are limited to their investment in these partnerships. Limited partnerships often use leverage in an effort to enhance profits. Twenty investors may put up $10,000 each, totaling $200,000, for a down payment on a building costing $1 million. Tax laws permit partnership incomes, losses, depreciation, and appreciation to be passed directly through to investors, subject to the "at risk" rules (that is, as long as the losses do not exceed the investors' risk exposure), thereby avoiding double taxation. Consequently, investors generally receive substantial tax losses—known as passive losses—to offset passive income and can anticipate long-term capital gains on the value of the properties purchased by the partnership.

REITs.   The passage of an act of Congress in 1960 revived interest in the type of group real estate investments known as *real estate investment trusts*, or REITs. These institutions are exempt from taxation if they (1) have 75 percent of their assets in real estate, mortgages, cash, or government securities at the end of each quarter; (2) derive 70 percent of their gross income from real estate, and receive no more than 30 percent of their income from capital appreciation (to discourage investing in highly speculative projects); (3) distribute 90 percent of their income to shareholders (officially known as beneficiaries); and (4) have at least 100 shareholders, no five of whom can control more than half of the shares. In exempting the REITs from taxation, the lawmakers intended that these institutions be publicly held and that they be instrumental in diverting public funds primarily into the real estate industry.

There are two major types of REITs on the market: mortgage trusts and equity trusts. Mortgage trusts provide short-term financing for construction loans or for permanent mortgage loans for large projects. Equity trusts buy or build their own real estate property and hire management firms to run them.

REITs offer the investor the opportunity to invest in real estate without committing a large amount of money. Shares of REITs are generally readily marketable, especially those listed on exchanges or traded over the counter. Because a REIT is, in effect, a closed-end investment company, its price is determined on the open market. The price of REIT shares may be above or below the actual book value of the real estate holdings.

GOLD AND DIAMONDS

Gold

There are several methods of investing in gold; namely, gold bars, bullion coins, collectible coins, gold certificates, mutual funds, and mining shares. Each offers a different set of risks and rewards. A summary of these investments which can be used to determine their suitability for a given investor is presented in the accompanying boxed insert. It should be explicitly recognized that gold and diamonds are illiquid investments and they may have carrying costs associated with them. In addition, these investments do not generate any income other than a potential appreciation in value.

Diamonds

Precious stones, including diamonds, rubies, emeralds, and sapphires, have great appeal to investors because of their small size and easy concealment, their durability, and their potential as a hedge against inflation. Of these stones, diamonds are traded in more numerous wholesale markets and are worth more per carat than any other precious stone.

THE MIDAS MARKET

Which type of gold investment is best for you? To help you answer that question according to your motives for owning the metal, this rundown of the options sorts out the differences in terms of suitability, cost, and risk.

GOLD BARS

For whom: conservative investors prepared to hold large amounts of the metal for years; people who want insurance against political upheavals

Where to buy: large banks, coin dealers, stockbrokers

Smallest investment: tiny bars weighing one gram (0.032 of an ounce); more typically, one ounce, ten ounces, and one kilogram (32.15 ounces)

Price behavior: the same as the spot, or cash, price of gold on commodity markets

Advantages: low markup on large bars (2% to 3%); portability

Disadvantages: cost of storage (usually in a bank vault) and insurance (about $50 a year); cost of selling—dealers may require an assay at $25 or more a bar

BULLION COINS

For whom: conservative investors who wish to own small amounts of gold

Where to buy: most banks, stockbrokers, coin dealers

Smallest investment: 0.1-ounce coin; more typically one ounce

Price behavior: the same as the spot price of gold on commodity markets

Advantages: ease of buying and selling; portability

Disadvantages: higher markup than on bars; cost of storage and insurance (about $7 a year for each coin)

COLLECTIBLE COINS

For whom: collectors

Where to buy: bullion and coin dealers, auctions, numismatic shows

Smallest investment: quarter-ounce $10 (face value) American gold piece minted between 1867 and 1933; cost: about $165

Price behavior: usually rises and falls less than the spot price of gold

Advantage: value may hold up better than for bars and bullion coins

Disadvantages: poorly defined market value and difficulty of finding buyers willing to pay top price; cost of storage and insurance

GOLD CERTIFICATES

For whom: conservative investors, particularly those interested in buying small amounts at regular intervals

Source: "The Right and Wrong Ways to Buy Gold," *Money,* 1988, p. 71.

Where to buy: brokers, large banks, and one dealer, Deak International

Smallest investment: $250 in systematic buying programs that let you subsequently invest as little as $100 a month

Price behavior: the same as the spot price of gold on commodity markets

Advantage: low dealer markup (3% to 3.5%)

Disadvantage: annual storage fee (usually 1%)

MUTUAL FUNDS AND MINING SHARES

For whom: aggressive investors

Where to buy: stockbrokers, financial planners, by mail from no-load and low-load funds

Smallest investment: the price of one share of an individual company; usually $250 in a mutual fund

Price behavior: more volatile than the spot price of gold

Advantages: maximum gains when the gold price rises; dividend income; no storage costs; diversification and professional management in funds; ease of buying and selling

Disadvantages: maximum losses when gold prices fall; high political risk of South African mines; risk of loss if a mine becomes unprofitable

COMMODITIES

There are five principal commodity exchanges in the U.S.: The Chicago Board of Trade, Chicago Mercantile Exchange, New York Mercantile Exchange, Kansas City Board of Trade, and Mid-America Commodity Exchange in Chicago. Of these, the most active exchanges are the Chicago Board of Trade and the Chicago Mercantile Exchange.

A commodity futures contract is one that provides for the delivery of a specific commodity at a specific price at a designated time in the future. The person selling the contract does not necessarily have possession of the commodity. Almost all contracts are closed out before the actual physical transaction is to take place. While there is a large volume of trading in commodity futures markets, there is very little actual movement of goods. Investment in commodity futures is both complex and speculative. Hence, it is suitable for only the most sophisticated investors.

ART AND ANTIQUES

Art, antiques, etchings, and other exotic objects constitute a specialized form of investment. However, knowledgeable investors may benefit from observing the following guidelines.

First, the investor should learn to recognize the factors that can make the price of an investment object go up or down so that he or she can take advantage of such fluctuations. In the case of art objects, for example, value is determined by a combination of several factors: artistic quality, rarity, condition, authenticity, historic appeal, provenance, and fashion. Etchings, drawings, and pastels increase in price when they are authentic, have been produced by internationally famed artists, and are in demand as collectors' items.

Second, it helps to get reliable information from some reputable dealer or expert, and also from authentic publications such as the *International Art Market*, which deals with art, antiques, etchings, and other objects.

Finally—and this is important—if a person wishes to invest in an object, he or she should attempt to acquire it at an auction rather than from a dealer. As the *International Art Market* newsletter points out, "You are better off competing with a dealer when he's trying to buy at wholesale, than later on, paying *his* retail price."

In this chapter we have presented an overview of a wide variety of investments available in the marketplace. Also, the securities markets and stock market indices are discussed in the appendix. In the next chapter we will undertake a detailed discussion of investment theories, models, and concepts.

APPENDIX TO CHAPTER 9: SECURITIES MARKETS AND STOCK MARKET INDICES

In order to understand the process by which an investor's preference for a bond or stock is related to secondary markets and to the eventual execution of an order to buy or sell a security, it is desirable to understand the nature, functions, and operations of the securities markets in the United States.

THE PRIMARY MARKETS

The *primary markets* provide users of capital with a direct means of obtaining funds. Users of capital obtain cash from investors in two ways. Funds needed only for the short term are acquired in the *money market*, whereas long-term funds are obtained in the *capital market*.

The Money Market

The *money market* trades in short-term, highly liquid, negotiable debt instruments of one year or less in maturity. Borrowers in the market include corporations, financial institutions, and governments.

Suppliers of funds in the money market include almost every type of financial institution. The major participants are commercial banks, state and local governments, large nonfinancial businesses, and nonbank financial intermediaries, such as insurance companies and pension funds. Foreign banks and nonbank businesses, however, have become increasingly important suppliers of funds.

The Capital Market

In contrast to the money market, which brings together borrowers and lenders of short-term funds, the *capital market* facilitates long-term financial arrangements. In this market, there are two broad categories of issuers of new securities—corporations and governments. This market also includes the sale of real estate mortgages.

Corporations, state and local governments, and federal government agencies distribute to investors large amounts of new securities through intermediaries like securities brokerage houses, which serve as *investment banks*. These institutions may sell the securities of a company to the public, or assist in placing an issue directly with a large institutional investor (private placement). The federal government usually distributes its securities directly to investors through either the Federal Reserve System or the commercial banks.

Exactly where are these capital markets located? The center for the national capital market is in New York, although other major cities also act as important marketplaces. In fact, the capital markets are multifaceted. They can be national or regional in scope. A large fraction of all financial debt in the United States enjoys a broad market: Securities issued by the best-known corporations, the federal government, certain state governments, and other large investment companies can be sold to investors across the country.

THE SECONDARY MARKETS

After securities are issued and purchased in the primary markets, the *secondary markets* provide a mechanism for their systematic transfer of ownership. The principal function of secondary markets is to facilitate the trading of securities *among investors*. Because investors would undoubtedly be reluctant to purchase new securities if they could not sell them on short notice, the existence of secondary markets is essential for the successful operation of the primary markets.

There are two broad categories of secondary markets. Large, active, *organized exchanges*, such as the New York Stock Exchange and the American Stock Exchange, provide physical marketplaces for trading in existing securities. *Over-the-counter markets* provide a medium for the resale of the financial transactions between investors, but there is no physical marketplace for these markets.

Secondary Markets: Stocks

Functions of the stock markets. In the United States, the secondary markets for corporate equities perform two important functions. First, because the stock markets in this country are large and well organized, they can absorb and quickly execute a large volume of buying and selling with reasonable price changes. Second, the existence of secondary markets encourages potential savers to invest in new and outstanding corporate stock, thereby facilitating the process of real capital investment.

However, the primary economic function of the stock market lies elsewhere. As this secondary market evaluates the issued shares of different firms, in the primary market it facilitates the flow of capital to those companies with superior performance and simultaneously disciplines poorly managed firms. The primary function of the stock market is not the creation but the *allocation* of capital.

Stock market trading. The operations in the stock markets are similar to those that take place in any open market. On the various stock markets are traded thousands of issues, each of them unique because no two companies are alike. Yet, on our nation's stock exchanges and in the over-the-counter market—a sophisticated trading network equipped to handle trading in thousands of stocks—*crude bargaining* is still permitted as a means of determining the trading prices.

Trading activity in the stock markets is handled in one of two ways. A *two-way auction market* system governs activity on the New York, American, and several regional stock exchanges; *negotiated trading* controls trading in the over-the-counter market. It is important to mention here that listing on an organized exchange is not an indication of a company's quality. Many over-the-counter companies are considered of good quality.

The New York Stock Exchange. The *New York Stock Exchange* (NYSE) was established in 1792 as the nation's major stock exchange. It is a rather unusual form of enterprise; its purpose is neither to make a profit nor to act as a charitable organization. Rather, it is an incorporated association of brokers formed to provide facilities and services for the execution of customers' orders. Brokers are provided with a building in which to house trading activities, a trading floor, communications from the floor to offices of member broker-dealers, a ticker and communications equipment for reporting trades and prices, and regulations for the trading practices of the Exchange members.

Because only stocks listed on the NYSE may be traded on the Exchange floor, less than 2,000 corporations are listed (less than one percent of the thousands of corporations doing business in the United States and abroad). However, the aggregate value of these listed stocks is greater than half the value of all outstanding corporate stock.

A company qualifies for listing on the NYSE if it has at least 2,000 stockholders who are each holders of at least 100 or more shares; there must be a minimum of 1 million shares outstanding; the aggregate value of publicly held shares must exceed $16 million; and the company must have pretax income of $2,500,000 for the latest fiscal year.

The sales and prices of a NYSE listed stock are reported promptly over a nationwide network of tickers and displays and are published in newspapers. A NYSE listing is valuable because it provides greater familiarity with and marketability for a company's securities, thus making it easier and less costly for the company to sell new securities when additional financing is needed. However, comprehensive reporting requirements add administrative costs to the company in order to satisfy the NYSE.

The American Stock Exchange. The functioning of the *American Stock Exchange* (AMEX) resembles that of the NYSE in that trades are made in a similar way on both exchanges. However, there is one important difference: The listing requirements for companies on the AMEX are less stringent than those on the NYSE. Because the companies listed on the AMEX are generally less well established, it serves as a proving ground for new, small, or medium-size companies which meet certain basic standards and expect to grow rapidly. Although the AMEX is a small exchange in comparison to the NYSE, trading activity on the AMEX does accelerate when investor interest, particularly among the larger institutions, is incited by many of these smaller companies.

More than 800 corporations' common and preferred stocks are listed on the AMEX. About 300 corporate bond issues, approximately 270 bonds issued by the Treasury and various federal government agencies, and put and call options on over 100 corporate securities and various market indexes are also listed on the AMEX.

Regional stock exchanges. Regional stock exchanges were originally established for the purpose of affecting transactions in local interest stocks, but this is no longer the case. At present, a large majority of the securities traded on regional stock exchanges are also traded on the NYSE. The following is a brief description of several regional exchanges.

The Midwest Stock Exchange (MSE). This exchange, located in Chicago, is the center for futures trading in the U.S. The volume of trading in this market has exceeded the volume on the AMEX, making MSE the second largest exchange in the country.

The Pacific Stock Exchange (PSE). Trading floors for this exchange are located in both Los Angeles and San Francisco. One hundred West Coast corporations, over 800 NYSE-listed stocks and more than 150 AMEX-listed stocks are listed on the PSE.

The Philadelphia Stock Exchange (PHLX). This exchange is the only organized exchange in the U.S. that allows institutional traders such as pension funds, mutual funds, and banks to become members and exercise trading privileges commission-free.

Other Stock Exchanges. The Cincinnati Stock Exchange, The Boston Stock Exchange (BSE), the Spokane Stock Exchange, the Honolulu Stock Exchange, and the Intermountain Stock Exchange in Salt Lake City, Utah, are other active regional exchanges in the U.S.

Over-the-counter market. Negotiated trading takes place in the *over-the-counter (OTC) market*; the term "over-the-counter," however, is misleading because there is no counter and no market in the sense of a given place where buyers and sellers meet to trade securities. OTC is a complex national network of trade rooms; these locations are connected by telephones and sophisticated communication facilities. The OTC market, therefore, is actually a *way* of trading in stocks rather than a central marketplace. It is probably the least-known segment of the securities industry.

OTC stocks include not only most bank and insurance company stocks, but also some blue chip stocks that could qualify for trading on major exchanges. Because there are no minimum requirements for a stock to be traded, however, many OTC stocks represent small, often unknown companies. This market expands as more and more companies seek public funds for developing new products and markets. In addition to domestic stocks, most federal, municipal, and corporate bonds, and several foreign stocks are traded on the OTC market.

Third and fourth markets.   Since the 1950s, trading activities on the nation's stock exchanges, particularly the NYSE, have become increasingly dominated by such institutional investors as the pension funds, bank trust departments, insurance companies, and mutual funds.

One side effect of increased institutional trading has been the fragmentation of the equities market in the United States. As institutional trading increased during the 1960s, institutions began to execute trades for NYSE-listed securities on regional exchanges and in the *third* and *fourth markets.*

The *third market* is essentially an OTC market for NYSE- and AMEX-listed securities. During the 1950s a number of broker-dealer firms which were not members of the NYSE began to make markets, or trade, in these stocks. (By NYSE Rule 394, later Rule 390, NYSE member firms are not allowed to make a market, or act as dealers in NYSE securities.) Third-market firms act as both dealers and agents. As a dealer, a firm acts as principal to buy stock for its own account when it is offered by an institution, and sells shares when an institution wishes to buy. The dealer's profit comes from the markup or markdown on the trade. Acting as an agent, a third-market firm attempts to match buy and sell orders between institutions in much the same way as do specialists.

The *fourth market* is similar to the third market, except that there is no dealer or market maker. An institution wishing to sell stock, for example, attempts to deal directly with another institution that wishes to buy the stock. Block traders find each other through computerized communications networks operated by fourth-market organizations.

Types of orders.   There are several ways in which an investor can order the purchase or sale of stock in the two-way auction market.

Market Orders. An investor interested in buying or selling a stock immediately orders his broker to buy or sell *at the market.* This is known as a *market order.* The brokerage firm's representative goes to the position on the trading floor where the stock is traded and executes the order at the best obtainable price—either trading with another broker or with a specialist. The investor is certain of execution, but cannot be sure of the price.

Limit Orders. A *limit order* is often placed by investors who wish to buy or sell a stock only if the transaction can be made at a certain price or better. If a *buy-limit order* is entered to buy a stock at $50, it cannot be executed at a price higher than $50. Likewise, a *sell-limit order* cannot be executed below a certain price. In all cases, however, the broker will try to get the best price available on the floor.

Stop Orders. There are actually *two types of stop orders*—a stop order to buy and a stop order to sell. Imagine that an investor named Jane Smith bought 100 shares of Ford Motor Company at $48 per share. Jane could then place an order to sell the stock at any price *above or below this level.* For example, if Jane's stop order to sell were at "$45 stop," and Ford Motor declined to $45 or below, the order would automatically become a market order and would be executed at the best price available on the floor.

Conversely, suppose the Ford Motor stock is selling at $45 a share and Jane wishes to buy the stock at $48 to make sure that the stock has a clear upward potential. Jane can then put in a stop order to buy Ford at $48. Should the stock price hit the level of her stop order to buy, her broker would be instructed to make a purchase at the best prevailing market price. In any case, placing a stop order to buy or sell at a given price does not ensure that the order will be executed at this price. Once the stop order becomes a market order, the price of execution may then be made at, above, or below this level.

Other Orders. When using a limit or stop order, a customer can specify that it be good for one day, one week, one month, or *good till canceled* (*GTC*). A broker might be instructed to cancel a limit order if it cannot be executed immediately. This is known as a *"fill-or-kill"* order. Sometimes a *day limit order* may be placed to buy or sell at a specified price, even though the customer still desires to have the order executed that same day whether or not the stock reaches the limit price level. The customer can then have the order marked for execution at the close, regardless of the market level.

Other types of trading.

Margin Trading. When brokerage house customers purchase securities on margin, they are really buying on credit. Only a percentage of the purchase price of the stock is paid by the customer; the balance is loaned by the brokerage house at a specified rate of interest. For instance, if the margin requirement is 50 percent (which is the current margin requirement), the investor must pay cash equal to at least 50 percent of the value of securities purchased. Thus, the investor may borrow funds to pay for no more than the remaining 50 percent of the cost of the securities.

The Federal Reserve System specifies the *initial margin.* This margin may be periodically changed by the System to control economic expansions and recessions. In addition, brokerage firms usually specify a *maintenance margin* below which either more cash must be placed in the account or securities must be sold to wipe out the deficiency in the account.

The advantage provided by a margin account is clearly the increased leverage. For a given dollar of equity capital, a larger quantity of securities can be purchased. Naturally, this increased leverage raises both the expected returns on an equity investment and the risk associated with that investment. Of course, the disadvantage is that the cost of carrying a margin account can be high or even prohibitive if the stock price significantly declines.

Short Selling. As already mentioned, *short selling* is the reverse of the usual market transaction. Instead of buying a stock in the hope that it can be sold later at a higher price, a short trader *first sells stock* and later *buys it back* at what he hopes will be a lower price; that is, the short seller attempts to sell high and buy low. However, most short selling is now done not by the public, but by stock exchange members.

Secondary Markets: Bonds

Functions of bond markets. The secondary markets for bonds serve several important functions. Their most obvious function is to provide a ready means for bondholders to liquidate their debt claims before maturity. If bonds could not be sold in a secondary market, or could be liquidated only at a substantial expense, investors would not purchase them unless the issuers offered higher yields on their debt instruments.

The amount of outstanding debt claims and transactions in the secondary market is much larger than in the primary market. Consequently, the terms under which new issues can be sold at par (that is, $1,000) are greatly influenced by the bond prices prevalent in the secondary market. A new bond cannot be sold at a yield significantly below that of the most comparable outstanding issue in the secondary market, because investors buy new or outstanding issues interchangeably for an income stream rather than for capital gains.

Although bonds are traded in both auction (such as the bond trading room of the NYSE) and over-the-counter (through a large network of dealers) markets, the market for debt claims exists predominantly in the latter market. There is, of course, a significant volume of trading on the exchanges, particularly on the NYSE. However, the volume of bond trading on the OTC market far exceeds the combined trading volume of all other exchanges.

Securities of the federal government. Securities of the federal government—especially treasury bills, notes, bonds, and various federal agency issues—are purchased by almost every type of investor in the economy. The volume of these transactions in the secondary market is far greater than in any other securities market in the world. These transactions total billions of dollars every month, as commercial banks and other financial institutions buy and sell large volumes of treasury securities to adjust their liquidity positions. The Federal Reserve System uses this market to trade in government securities. The purchase and sale of government securities by the Federal Reserve are known as open market operations. These securities provide the highest level of safety.

Municipal bonds. Because of their tax advantages, municipal bonds are traded in the secondary market both by individuals in maximum income tax brackets and by institutions subject to federal income tax. Commercial banks are large holders of municipal bonds and, with broker-dealers, play major roles as dealers in the secondary market for these securities.

Corporate bonds. The market for corporate bonds centers heavily on dealers who stand ready to buy or sell bonds, frequently in large amounts. Dealers in corporate bonds function much like market makers for stocks. They often deal directly with institutional investors; smaller investors gain access through the large network of brokers available.

A large fraction of the outstanding corporate bonds is held by financial intermediaries, such as life insurance companies, investment companies, and pension funds. The corporate bond market is, therefore, mainly dominated by institutions that trade in large amounts.

REGULATIONS OF SECURITIES MARKETS

Any economic entity as sophisticated and complicated as the securities markets must be regulated if its efficient operation is to be assured. Through the Securities and Exchange Commission (SEC) as well as the National Association of Securities Dealers (NASD) the federal government has taken various legal and procedural measures to ensure that these markets offer a fair environment for the conduct of investment business. The key regulations are summarized next. It is worth noting that registration with the SEC is not an indication of investment quality but rather of compliance with disclosure requirements.

Insider Trading

Corporate directors, officers, and other executives who have a first-hand knowledge of the operations of the corporation are called *insiders*. These officials are prohibited by the SEC from earning speculative profits by trading in the securities of their respective firms. This law is enforced by requiring every holder of more than ten percent of a firm's stock to file an *insider report*, which lists the names of insiders whose holdings changed during the month.

Wash Sale

A wash sale is recorded when an investor buys and sells a given security quickly (usually the same day) to create a record of sale. This would be the case where an investor sells a stock to realize a tax loss and immediately buys it back to leave the original portfolio undisturbed. A wash sale can also be undertaken by a speculator who wishes to mislead the general public into believing that the stock's price has changed. Wash sales are considered illegal.

Churning

It is a common practice among many investors to open discretionary accounts which authorize their brokers to trade their accounts without seeking prior approval. This creates a potential conflict of interest situation since the brokers earn a commission on every buying and selling transaction. The law prohibits the *churning* of an account. This term is defined as abuse of the investors' confidence for the broker's personal gain by generating a disproportionately large number of stock transactions.

Cornering the Market

Cornering of the market occurs when a large speculator buys all (or almost all) of the supply of a security or a commodity. Once ownership is established, the speculator can raise the price to realize a capital gain or force a short seller into covering a short position at a higher price. Cornering is illegal under the present law.

STOCK MARKET INDICATORS

Stock market *averages* and *indexes* are used as more than simply a measure of the price performance of different segments of the market. Movements in stock market indicators are considered benchmarks for measuring the investment results of individual securities and portfolios. Moreover, an effective measurement of fluctuations in individual stock prices relative to fluctuations in the stock market is considered a prerequisite to a successful application of the modern portfolio theory.

One widely held belief among investors is that there exists a unique index or average which faithfully represents the state of the market. Actually, no single indicator occupies this venerable position. The basic factors which differentiate the many market indicators are the types and numbers of stocks used in the index or average—the sample—and the importance given to the price and number of securities outstanding—the weighting.

The Dow Averages

The Dow Jones averages are the best known and most widely quoted indicators. Although there are only four distinct Dow averages, it is necessary to understand how to interpret and use each of them.

The Dow Jones Industrial Average (DJIA). This average covers only 30 NYSE stocks. However, the DJIA stocks (blue chips) represent 30 large, well-established companies that are generally the leaders in their industry.

The DJIA is *price weighted*; that is, it measures changes in the price of 30 large, well-known industrial stocks. The average is derived by totaling the current prices of the 30 stocks and dividing the sum by the divisor that has been adjusted to take into account stock splits. Incidentally, the DJIA has been criticized for its rather narrow scope.

Other Dow Averages. Besides the popular DJIA, there are three other averages, all of which are computed in a similar manner. *The Dow Jones Transportation Average*—once comprised of 20 railroad common stocks—still consists of 20 issues, but now represents a broader sample of transportation companies because it includes air transportation and trucking firms. *The Dow Jones Public Utility Average* represents data for 15 electrical and natural gas utilities. Finally, the *Dow Jones Composite Average* is comprised of the 65 stocks included in the Industrial, Transportation, and Utility Averages.

Standard & Poor's 500 Index

The *Standard & Poor's 500 Index* covers 88 industry groups and is comprised of 400 industrial companies, 40 public utilities, 20 transportation companies, and 40 financial corporations. The Index is *value weighted*; that is, it gives weight to both the *size* (outstanding shares) and *price* of each stock. Consequently, the highest-priced stocks with the largest number of shares outstanding carry the greatest influence in the movement of this indicator. Besides the S&P 500, there are separate indexes for the industrial, transportation, utility, and financial companies which are included in this Index.

NYSE Composite Index

On July 14, 1966, the NYSE, also known as the big board, began to publish new price indexes of common stocks listed on the Exchange. The NYSE Composite Index covers all the common stocks listed on the Big Board. In addition, there are four separate indexes for the industrial, transportation, utility, and financial company stocks included in the composite.

Like the S&P 500, the *NYSE Composite Index* is value weighted; therefore, its major movements are dominated by the issues of larger companies. For example, although the S&P 500 Index represents only about 30 percent of the NYSE listings, that 30 percent represents approximately 75 percent of the market value of all NYSE stocks.

AMEX Market Value Index

The *AMEX Market Value Index* covers approximately 1,000 stocks listed on the American Stock Exchange; these account for less than five percent of the market value of all U.S. stocks. Unlike those in the NYSE Composite, the S&P 500, and the Dow Jones Industrial Average, movements in the AMEX Index are heavily influenced by the stocks of smaller companies.

TABLE A9-1 Stock Market Indexes

Stock Market Index	Sample	Representation	Weighting and Computation
Dow Jones Industrial Average	30 major NYSE industrial companies.	Less than 2% of all NYSE stocks and less than 1% of all actively traded stocks. Accounts for about 25% of market value of NYSE stocks and about 20% of all stock values.	Price weighted arithmetic average with divisor adjusted for stock splits.
S&P 500	400 industrials, 40 utilities, 20 transportation, 40 financial companies (mostly NYSE issues). Separate indexes for each of these groups.	About 75% of NYSE market value and 30% of NYSE issues. Large capitalization companies have heavy influence on index movement.	Value weighted index, as a percentage of the average during 1941–43.
NYSE Composite Index	Approximately 1,632 NYSE listed stocks. Separate indexes for industrial, utility, transportation, and financial stock groups.	Complete coverage of NYSE stocks. Major movements still dominated by stocks of large companies.	Value weighted index, with base of 50, average price of NYSE stocks on July 14, 1966.
AMEX Market Value Index	About 1,000 American Stock Exchange stocks.	Complete coverage of smaller companies listed on the American Stock Exchange. Accounts for less than 5% of market value of all stocks.	Value weighted index, with base of 100, base date August 31, 1973.
NASDAQ OTC Composite Index	Over 2,000 stocks traded over the counter. Separate indexes for industrial, insurance, and bank stocks.	Covers many small company stocks, but is heavily influenced by about 100 of largest NASDAQ stocks.	Value weighted index, with base of 100, started on February 5, 1971.
Value Line Composite Average	1,681 stocks, which include 1,484 industrials, 19 rails, and 178 utilities. Separate averages for each of these groups.	Broad representation of stocks, mostly from the NYSE. All stocks have equal influence on indicator's movement.	Equal weighting, with average expressed as a percentage of a 100 base value, prevailing on June 30, 1961.

The AMEX Index is value weighted. Its method of construction is similar to that of the NYSE Composite Index, except that it uses August 31, 1973, as the base date and 100 as the base value. If on a given day the Index stands at 115, this implies that the value of all American Stock Exchange stocks is 15 percent above its 1973 level.

NASDAQ OTC Composite Index

The *NASDAQ OTC Composite Index* is a value weighted index derived from over-the-counter trading in over 2,000 securities. The Index was started on February 5, 1971, with a base value of 100. Like the AMEX Market Value Index, this indicator is also more representative of smaller companies than the NYSE Composite, the S&P 500, or the Dow Jones Industrial Average. However, it is heavily influenced by about 100 of the largest stocks on the NASDAQ system, many of which are larger than the largest firms on the American Stock Exchange.

Value Line Composite Average

The Arnold Bernhard and Company Investment Service, publisher of the *Value Line Investment Survery*, also publishes the *Value Line Composite Average*. This average measures the value of 1,681 common stocks comprising 1,484 industrials, 19 rails, and 178 utilities. Most issues involved in this average are from the NYSE, although a few stocks are also traded on the AMEX and the OTC markets.

The Value Line Composite Average is unique in that it computes a daily new percentage change for the stocks, thereby giving each stock equal weight in the average regardless of its price or size. Incidentally, although this indicator is labeled as an average, it is expressed as a percentage of a base value of 100 prevailing on June 30, 1961, and can, therefore, be technically treated as an index.

Summing Up

The major stock market indicators discussed in this section are summarized in Table A9-1. This table includes the stock sample, representation, weighting, and computation of the indexes and averages. Because the many indicators presented here have different characteristics, they lend themselves to varying uses. For instance, it is often asserted that the broad coverages of the NYSE Composite Index and the Value Line Composite Average make them the best overall measure of stock prices. However, although the NYSE Composite is more comprehensive than the DJIA and the S&P 500, it is not influenced by small companies to the same extent as the NASDAQ or AMEX indices.

CHAPTER 10

Investment: Theories, Models, and Concepts

INTRODUCTION

In this chapter we will present the key elements of investment theories, models, and concepts. Clearly, for those financial planners who are not interested in valuing individual stocks, building portfolios for individual clients, or timing client portfolios, many of the topics discussed here will not be relevant. Nevertheless, we firmly believe that most serious financial planners should have some familiarity with modern investment theories and concepts, and are therefore presenting them in this chapter.

In the first section we will discuss the concept of risks associated with individual stocks, bonds, and portfolios. Next we will present an overview of fundamental and technical analysis. Then we will undertake a discussion of the asset allocation model and the use of this model in structuring various investment portfolios. Finally, we will discuss the concept of timing a portfolio.

THE CONCEPT OF RISK

AN OVERVIEW

Investment can be simply defined as the commitment of a given sum of money at the present time with the expectation of receiving a larger sum in the future. This definition underscores two important points. First, the process of investment involves the trade-off of *present* income for *future* income. Second, the objective of investment is to receive a *future* flow of funds larger than that originally involved.

In this context, it is important to differentiate between investment and speculation. Essentially, speculators concentrate on returns expected to be received over relatively short periods of time; in contrast, an investor's objective is to derive benefits from investment over a long horizon. Furthermore, speculators act quickly on the available information which has not yet been analyzed or acted upon by the general public, whereas investors generally base their judgment on investment analysis.

Chapter 9 was devoted to a description of various types of securities and investments. But securities are more than mere legal documents. They are analyzed in terms of risk and rates of return, or, more appropriately, income and capital appreciation, which an investor can expect to attain from them. It is of course true that many investors do not like to take risks. It is also true that virtually no investment is completely free from all risk. Consequently, every investor must learn how to deal with risk.

TYPES OF RISK

In order to effectively deal with risk it is important to understand the types of risk associated with equities and fixed income securities. For only then can we develop appropriate strategies to minimize the risk of a single security or that of a portfolio. Furthermore, since the risks associated with bonds are significantly different from those affecting a common stock, these risks should be separately discussed.

Fixed-Income Security Risk

Interest rate risk. In the event of an increase in the market interest rate, the price of an old bond with a coupon (interest) rate below that of the market rate must fall sufficiently to offer investors yields that compete with new issues with higher coupon rates. In contrast, when the market interest rate declines, prices of outstanding bonds rise because old bonds with a higher coupon rate will command a premium to make them as attractive as new bonds with a lower coupon rate. A change in the price of a bond due to a change in the market interest rate is known as the *interest rate risk*.

Inflation risk. When it issues a bond, the entity promises to pay future interest and principal with current dollars. If a contract is made under which a lender receives a return on a $1,000 bond of $100 at the end of one year, the *nominal* return is ten percent ($100/$1,000). However, if during the year the price level is found to have risen by five percent, then the *real* return would be only 4.762 percent {[($1,100/1.05) − ($1,000)]/($1,000)}. The possibility of inflation being higher than anticipated so the nominal yield would be insufficient to compensate for the change in price is known as *inflation risk.*

Maturity risk. Maturity risk refers to the contrasting perceptions of risk by lenders and borrowers. As a general rule, because borrowers fear increases in future interest rates, they prefer to borrow long-term by offering inducements to the lenders. However, the longer the period for which lenders part with their liquid funds, the more they are *uncertain* about the prospect of realizing a capital loss, and the higher the *maturity risk.*

Default risk. Uncertainty about the receipt of interest and principal payments is the basis for *default risk.* Although payment on time of both interest and principal is promised by the issuing entity, due to adverse financial conditions or bankruptcy, entities occasionally fail to fulfill their promises. Because this possibility always exists for corporate and municipal bonds, when these types of bonds are purchased investors are subject to default risk.

Callability risk. Under certain circumstances, the issuer of a bond may force bondholders to redeem their bonds before they reach maturity. If a bond is called during a period of falling market interest rates, the bondholders will probably be forced to reinvest the proceeds at a lower rate. This is known as the *callability risk.*

Liquidity risk. A bond may also be subject to *liquidity risk.* This risk refers to the price concession one must grant in order to quickly convert the bond into cash and receive the amount approximately put into it. In general, the less liquid a security, the higher its *liquidity risk.*

Common Stock Risk

When investing in a stock, an investor assumes the risk of realizing less than the expected return. Closer scrutiny reveals that this risk has two important components: namely, the risk that the variability in return would be caused by factors that affect the prices of all stocks—*market or undiversifiable risk*—and factors that are unique to a firm or industry—*nonmarket or diversifiable risk.*

More specifically, market or undiversifiable risk refers to both the economic and the market risk. The former refers to the risk that slower economic

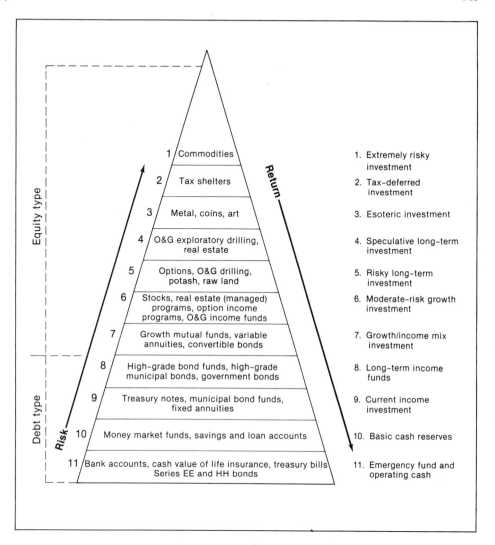

FIGURE 10-1 Risk-return pyramid

growth will cause investments in stocks to decline. Recessions can adversely affect shares of growth companies, cyclical companies, and other types of companies. In addition, market risk refers to risks associated with political developments, tax law changes, investor psychology, foreign domination of the U.S. investment market, leveraged buy-outs, and insider trading fiascos. In contrast to the undiversifiable risk, the diversifiable risk refers to that portion of the variability of a stock's return which is the result of unexpected events or developments within the company or the related industry.

Interestingly, different strategies are formulated in order to deal with the two types of risk just discussed. Investors deal with undiversifiable risks by requiring higher rates of return from investments with higher risks. The strategy, commonly known as the risk-return trade-off, refers to the higher returns demanded by investors to make it worthwhile to assume higher levels of risk. In contrast, investors attempt to reduce or eliminate diversifiable risks by constructing efficiently diversified portfolios. A risk-return pyramid, which demonstrates the risk-return trade-off between various types of investments, is presented in Figure 10-1.

MEASUREMENT OF RISK

Now that we have presented the nature of risk, it is appropriate to discuss the technique of risk measurement. Since the risks associated with bonds are different from those involving equities, it is appropriate to discuss the measurement of bond and stock risks separately.

Bonds

Bonds carry six types of risks which can be broadly measured in terms of the risk premium associated with each type of risk. The general nature of bond risk premiums is described below:

Risk	Description	Nature of risk premium
Interest rate	Variations in bond prices as a result of fluctuations in market interest rates.	The greater the uncertainty surrounding interest rate predictions, the higher the interest rate premium.
Inflation	Possibility that the value of coupon payments and the principal would be eroded.	Inflation risk premium should approximate the expected inflation.
Maturity	Lenders assume greater risk with longer-term bonds.	Maturity risk premium rises to about one percent as the maturity approaches one year. Thereafter, the premium rises very slowly, increasing by about 0.25 percent as the maturity approaches ten years.
Default	Possibility that the bond-holder would experience delay or failure in receiving coupon payments and the principal.	Default risk premium rises as bond ratings decline. These ratings are presented in Table 10-1.
Callability	Bonds may be called away before maturity.	Callability risk premium is the difference in yields between a callable and a noncallable bond.
Liquidity	Difficulty in converting the bond into cash without a significant loss.	Liquidity risk premium is the spread between dealers' bid and asked price.

Stocks

The measure of stock risk, which is popularly referred to as a *beta*, or beta coefficient, is an index of the risk that measures the volatility of the

TABLE 10-1   Investors' Services Rating Classification

Moody's	*General description*	*Standard & Poor's*
Aaa	Highest Quality	AAA
Aa	High Quality	AA
A	Upper Medium Grade	A
Baa	Medium Grade	BBB
Ba	Lower Medium Grade	BB
B	Speculative	B
Caa	Poor Standing (Perhaps in Default)	CCC-CC
Ca	(Generally) in Default	C for Income Bonds
C	Lowest Grade (in Default)	DDD-D

security's return relative to *the market*. The reference point is an aggregate measure of the market, such as the Standard & Poor's 500 Index. A beta of 1 means that the stock's return is moving exactly with the market index. A beta of less than 1 indicates that the stock's return fluctuates less than the market, and a beta of more than 1 suggests that the stock's return fluctuates more than the market. Put differently, if a stock has a beta of .65 it is 35 percent less volatile than the Standard & Poor's 500 Index; in contrast, if the beta is 1.40, it is 40 percent more volatile than the Standard & Poor's 500 Index.

Like an individual security, a portfolio of stocks and bonds can be assigned a beta value. The portfolio beta is a weighted average of betas for individual securities. The beta for each security in the portfolio is multiplied by that security's weight in the portfolio. The resulting betas are then added together to find the overall beta for the portfolio.

Since a beta coefficient indicates the risk associated with a particular stock, it can be used in security selection and portfolio construction. To induce investors to purchase high beta (larger than 1) securities, the expected return must be sufficient to compensate the investor for the additional risk. Beta values of individual securities are readily available in financial publications such as *Value Line Investment Survey*.

Beta values play an important role in the construction of an investor's portfolio. By constructing a diversified portfolio of assets (stocks, bonds, money market funds, and so on) issued by firms from different industries (manufacturing, utility, transportation, and so on) and by various levels of government (federal, state, local agencies), an investor attempts to eliminate, or significantly reduce, the diversifiable risk and arrive at an acceptable portfolio beta. The technique of risk reduction through the construction of an efficient portfolio is presented in Figure 10-2.

The basic nature of the reduction, and eventual elimination, of diversifiable risk through diversification can be easily explained. As noted, individual securities have risk-return characteristics of their own. The objective of con-

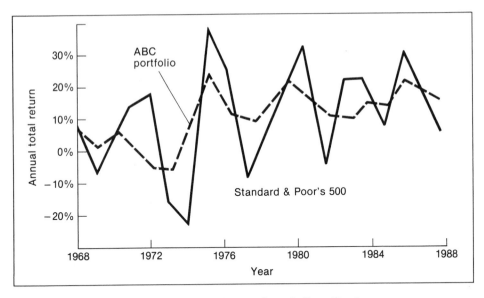

FIGURE 10-2   Risk reduction through diversification

structing an efficient portfolio is to reduce the portfolio risk below the aggregate risks of all securities included in it. This is achieved by selecting securities that do not fluctuate in tandem. In a diversified portfolio, the fluctuations of some stocks partly compensate for those of the others, so that the variability of the portfolio's return becomes significantly less than the average variability of the individual components of the portfolio.

FUNDAMENTAL AND TECHNICAL ANALYSIS

FUNDAMENTAL ANALYSIS

An Overview

A time-tested analytical method used by many financial planners is to identify, and eventually recommend, the purchase of undervalued securities. This strategy is based on the assumption that the price of an individual security always gravitates toward its value, or in technical jargon, its present value. This method, called fundamental analysis, examines general economic conditions, such as economic growth, and financial conditions, such as interest rates. This approach also requires the analysis of industry conditions and projected industry growth. Finally, fundamental analysis involves the examination of a firm's economic performance and its potential earnings growth. Ratios, financial data, and analytical savvy are the cornerstones of fundamental analysis. As mentioned, the ultimate objective of fundamental analysis is to calculate the present value of a security so it could be compared with its current market price to determine whether or not it is an undervalued security and therefore offers an attractive investment opportunity.

Forecasting Earnings

Essentially a dependable earnings forecast is the key to the calculation of the present value of a security. Consequently, forecasting earnings growth is at the heart of fundamental analysis. Accurate prediction of earnings growth, in turn, depends on a careful examination of the general economic conditions prevailing in the country, the industry conditions, and the overall growth of the company whose earnings are under analysis.

The economy.   In a nutshell, earnings of a company largely depend on prevailing economic conditions. Similarly, forecasting of earnings depends upon the forecasting of economic conditions. A study of two groups of variables is helpful in predicting the future of the economy.

Group I: Interest Rate, Inflation, and Leading Indicators. Rising interest rates generally signal trouble for a growing economy. They make bonds and other fixed securities more attractive and stocks less desirable. They also discourage economic activity, raising fears of a recession.

The rate of inflation is another key variable. The higher the rate, the greater the likelihood that the Federal Reserve will pursue a tighter monetary policy. Credit tightening is the bane of a growing economy.

The index of leading indicators is clearly one of the most important variables to watch. As its name (leading indicators) implies, the key to the end of a healthy economic growth, which signals the reversal of a bull market, is a downturn in the index. Traditionally, this index declines *prior* to the onset of a recession. The index of leading economic indicators is presented in Figure 10-3.

Group II: Price/Book Value, Dividend Yield, and Liquidity Ratio. A useful measure of a stock's market value is the ratio of share price to book value, which is the net worth of a company's assets. For all common stocks taken as a group, a book value ratio of more than 2 generally signals the onset of a recession and a bear market. On Black Monday (October 1987), the book value ratio of Standard & Poor's 500 Index stood at 2.9. It is generally claimed that the ratio of share price to book value (and not the P/E ratio) is a good measure of a stock's present value, if it is examined in relation to the company's earnings growth and return on equity.

Another measure of value is the dividend yield. Almost without exception, a dividend yield of below three percent of all stocks taken as a group signals the end of a growing economy and a bull market. On the

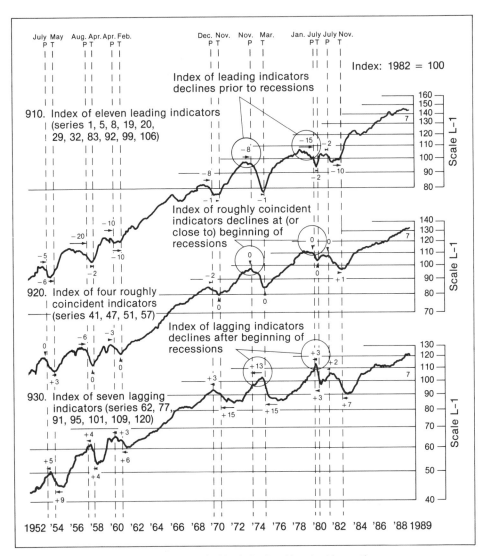

*Numbers entered on the chart indicate length of leads (−) and lags (+) in months
from reference turning dates. Current data for these series are shown on page 60.

FIGURE 10-3 Cyclical indicators: composite indexes and their components.*
Courtesy of Bureau of the Census, Department of Commerce, *Business Conditions Digest*, August 1989, p. 10.

eve of the 1973–74 recession, the dividend yield of the Standard & Poor's
500 Index was 2.67 percent. In October of 1987 the yield dropped to 2.9
percent.

A third measure of prevailing economic conditions is the existing liquidity situation. Stock prices increase dramatically to artificially high levels when an ever-expanding supply of money starts chasing a dwindling supply of stocks. Mergers, leveraged buyouts, and corporate stock buy-backs during 1984 to 1986 resulted in a net decrease of $214 billion in publicly traded stocks, while the money supply initially rose by an equivalent amount. During the same period, $25 to $30 billion came from overseas investors, thereby aggravating the liquidity situation even further.

Analysis of the nation's general economic conditions is important because there is a direct relationship between the economy and the performance of an individual firm, of which earning power is a key measure. In general, the growth in the real GNP, reflecting the nation's economic

TABLE 10-2 Key Industry Fundamentals

Indicator	Description
Historical Performance Industry Life Cycle	Three distinct phases
	Pioneering Stage—Rapid sales and earnings growth
	Investment Maturity Stage—Consolidate market positions and begin to encroach on competitors' market share by broadening capital base and establishing earnings and dividend policy.
	Stabilization—Unit costs become stable and market becomes saturated.
Performance During a Business Cycle	Cyclical or countercyclical performance of a company during an economic cycle.
Economic Structure	Degree of competition which prevails within the industry.
Capital Investment	Highly capital intensive industries usually make effective long-term plans for capital investment, are generally technologically more advanced than less capital intensive industries, and have a much larger growth potential than labor intensive industries.
Government Regulations	Some industries are subject to continual government intervention.
	Others may be subject to antitrust suits or attacks from environmental groups.
Labor Conditions	History of labor negotiations and impact of previous labor strikes can help determine the risks associated with certain industries.
Miscellaneous Factors	Price and income elasticities of demand for products, changes in consumer tastes, foreign competition, and the availability and cost of raw materials.

health, and changes in earning power, representing the performance of individual firms, are positively related.

The industry. Variations in earnings of individual companies are closely related to variations in earnings of related industries. This can be inferred from the fact that a significant portion of the price variations of an individual stock is the result of average price variations of all companies within related industries.

The key industry fundamentals are presented in Table 10-2. Analysis of these fundamentals can help an investor identify those industries that are likely to record superior performance.

The company. Thus far we have seen that a company's earning power is influenced by national economic and industry conditions. However, to a large degree, earning power is also determined by the company itself. There are several ways of analyzing the earnings potential, and therefore the future expected stock price, of a company.

Annual Reports.[1] A detailed study of the annual report of a company is essential to forecasting its future earnings. The balance sheet of ABC Corporation for 1988 and 1989, with the key items numbered for easy reference, is presented in Table 10-3. The following is a brief discussion of ABC's balance sheet:

1. Total Assets: Assets owned by ABC.
2. Total Liabilities: What ABC owes.
   #1 must exceed #2 for ABC to have a positive net worth.
3. Total Current Assets: These assets can be converted into cash quickly.
4. Total Current Liabilities: Liabilities to be paid off within one year.
5. Long-term debt: Debt to be paid off after one year.
6. Total inventory: Finished products ready to be sold.
7. Equipment sales: Ratio of #7 to #6 shows how fast the company is selling its warehoused products.
8. Stockholders' equity: This is the net worth of the company.
9. Interest expense.
10. Operating income.
11. Interest income.

---

[1] This section is based on Gretchen Morgenson, "Annual Reports," *Money Guide: The Stock Market*, 1986, pp. 79–85.

TABLE 10-3   Balance Sheet of ABC Corporation

Assets	Dec. 31, 1989	Dec. 31, 1988
Current Assets		
Cash and temporary cash investment	$1,080,180	$ 476,150
Accounts receivable, net of allowance of $40,930		
and $38,512	1,538,955	1,527,257
Inventories		
Raw materials	512,670	456,490
Work-in-process	545,765	614,766
Finished goods	697,732	780,912
(6) Total Inventories	1,756,167	1,852,168
Prepaid expenses	64,569	57,030
Net deferred Federal and foreign income tax		
charges	197,957	169,308
(3) Total Current Assets	4,637,828	4,081,913
Property, Plant and Equipment, at cost		
Land	97,492	97,517
Buildings	745,825	678,895
Leasehold improvements	190,692	150,985
Machinery and equipment	1,793,623	1,424,389
Gross Property, Plant and Equipment	2,827,632	2,351,786
Less accumulated depreciation	1,096,603	840,446
Net Property, Plant and Equipment	1,731,029	1,511,340
(1) Total Assets	$6,368,857	$5,593,253
Liabilities and Stockholders' Equity Current Liabilities		
Loans payable to banks	$ 12,251	$ 13,181
Accounts payable	185,202	278,111
Federal, foreign and state income taxes	267,900	312,871
Salaries, wages and related items	165,933	224,036
Deferred revenues and customer advances	160,105	126,454
Current portion of long-term debt	1,411	1,374
Other current liabilities	150,807	124,517
(4) Total Current Liabilities	943,609	1,080,544
Net deferred Federal and foreign income tax		
credits	33,704	92,180
(5) Long-term debt	836,945	441,313
(2) Total Liabilities	1,814,258	1,614,037

TABLE 10-3 (*continued*)

Assets	Dec. 31, 1989	Dec. 31, 1988
Stockholders' Equity		
Common stock, $1.00 par value; authorized 225,000,000 shares; issued and outstanding 59,252,782 and 57,811,416 shares	**59,253**	57,811
Additional paid-in capital	**1,737,834**	1,610,575
Retained earnings	**2,757,512**	2,310,830
(8) Total Stockholders' Equity	**4,554,599**	3,979,216
Total Liabilities and Stockholders' Equity	**$6,368,857**	$5,593,253

		Year Ended	
Revenues	*Dec. 31, 1989*	*Dec. 31, 1988*	*Dec. 31, 1987*
(7) Equipment sales	**$4,534,165**	$3,831,073	$2,867,428
Service and other revenues	**2,152,151**	1,753,353	1,404,426
Total operating revenues	**6,686,316**	5,584,426	4,271,854
Costs and Expenses			
Cost of equipment sales, service and other revenues	**4,087,475**	3,379,632	2,605,970
Research and engineering expenses	**717,273**	630,696	472,392
Selling, general and administrative expenses	**1,431,769**	1,179,529	830,564
(10) Operating income	**449,799**	394,569	362,928
(9) Interest expense	**82,003**	35,096	13,078
(11) Interest income	**(63,026)**	(41,477)	(61,195)
Income before income taxes	**430,822**	400,950	411,045
Income Taxes			
Provision for income taxes	**47,390**	72,171	127,423
Reversal of DISC taxes[1]	**(63,250)**	—	—
Total income taxes	**(15,860)**	72,171	127,423
Net income	**$ 446,682**	$ 328,779	$ 283,622
(12) Net income per share	**$ 7.42**	$ 5.73	$ 5.00
Weighted average shares outstanding	**62,056**	57,364	56,676

[1] Reversal of DISC taxes accrued prior to 1984 due to a change in U.S. tax law.

The accompanying notes are an integral part of these financial statements.

In thousands except per share data.

Source: Adapted from Gretchen Morgenson, *Money Guide: The Stock Market,* 1986, pp. 80–81.

Note that the two income items (#10 and #11) for 1989 total $513 million—over six times the interest expense (#9) for that year. However, even when interest expense jumped from $35 million to $82 million in 1989, the company maintained a wide margin of safety, since the ratio of operating and interest income to interest expense of 3 is considered quite adequate.

12. Net income per share: This is the bottom line figure of how much the company makes after expenses. The balance sheet shows that it grew by almost 30 percent—indeed an impressive performance record.

Published Reports. An investor need not depend totally on the annual report published by the company. Both Value Line and Standard & Poor's publish extensive data on approximately 1,700 stocks that are most actively traded. A typical Value Line full-page report is presented in Figure 10-4. This report not only publishes the net profit for the year but also rates each stock from 1 to 5 for timeliness and safety. Similarly, Standard & Poor's stock reports (Figure 10-5) offer comprehensive financial data on numerous stocks and assign companies one of eight grades.

EPS Model. The annual report and the published reports just discussed provide a basis for predicting a company's future earnings. The techniques for estimating future earnings are based on a detailed examination, and eventual prediction, of several financial ratios.

The construction of the earnings per share model for XYZ company is presented in Figure 10-6. It shows that, for the EPS to increase, one or more of the key variables (production efficiency, coverage ratio, leverage ratio, and so on) must also increase. For instance, the company can increase its EPS from its current level of $13.35 by improving its production efficiency ratio of 14.4 percent, turnover ratio of 1.94, leverage ratio of 2.28, and so on.

P/E Ratio. The main purpose of undertaking fundamental analysis is to calculate the present value of a stock. It can then be compared with the current price to determine whether or not it is undervalued. A time-tested yet simple method is to estimate the present value by multiplying the projected future earnings by its P/E ratio.

Essentially, the P/E ratio is the amount of money investors are willing to pay for each dollar of a company's earnings. Literally, it is the price of a company's stock divided by its annual earnings. If a stock sells for $50 a share and the company's next year's expected earnings are $5, it carries a P/E ratio of 10. It should be pointed out that the P/E ratio of a company with negative or negligible earnings is meaningless. However, the vast majority of stocks have meaningful P/E ratios as do most popular stock indexes.

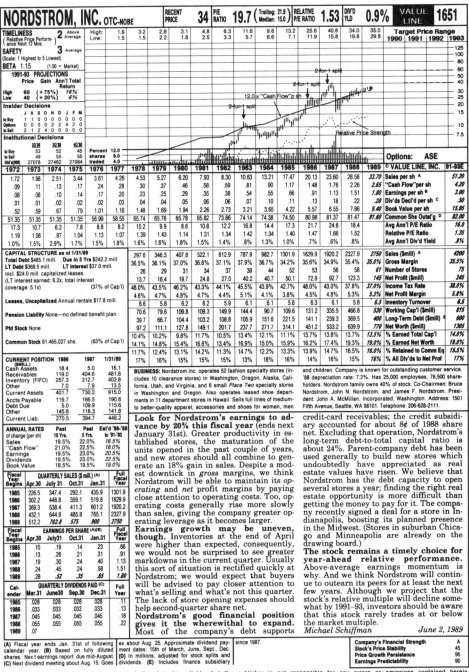

FIGURE 10-4 Value Line Report: Nordstrom, Inc. Copyright © 1989 by Value Line, Inc.; used by permission.

Nordstrom, Inc. 4793

NASDAQ Symbol NOBE (Incl. in Nat'l Market) Options on ASE (Jan-Apr-Jul-Oct) In S&P 500

Price	Range	P–E Ratio	Dividend	Yield	S&P Ranking	Beta
Apr. 13'89	1989					
33⁵/₈	34¹/₄–29³/₄	22	0.28	0.8%	A+	1.38

Summary

This specialty retailer of apparel and accessories, widely known for its emphasis on service, is expanding its business to the East Coast, having recently opened a store outside Washington, D.C. The company's $500 million capital expenditure program over the next three years, which includes several new stores, augurs well for future sales and earnings growth.

Current Outlook

Share earnings for the fiscal year ending January 31, 1990, are projected at $1.80, up from the $1.51 of 1988-9.

The quarterly cash dividend has been increased frequently.

Sales gains for 1989-90 should reflect higher productivity in recently constructed stores. Gross margins should remain about level, reflecting a more-competitive pricing environment. Expense ratios may weaken as a result of store additions. Expansion into the East Coast provides a good base for long-term growth.

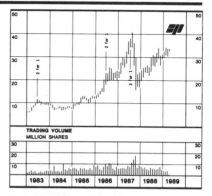

Net Sales (Million $)

Quarter:	1988-9	1987-8	1986-7	1985-6
Apr.	432	369	302	227
Jul.	645	538	449	347
Oct.	486	411	359	292
Jan.	765	601	520	436
	2,328	1,920	1,630	1,302

Sales for the fiscal year ended January 31, 1989, rose 21% from those of 1987-8. Margins widened slightly, and pretax income increased 22%. After taxes at 37.8%, versus 43.0%, net income rose 33% to $1.51 a share, from $1.13.

Common Share Earnings ($)

Quarter:	1988-9	1987-8	1986-7	1985-6
Apr.	0.24	0.19	0.13	0.10
Jul.	0.45	0.30	0.26	0.18
Oct.	0.24	0.24	0.21	0.14
Jan.	0.58	0.40	0.32	0.24
	1.51	1.13	0.91	0.65

Important Developments

Apr. '89— Nordstrom planned to open two large specialty stores in 1989-90—one in Pentagon City, Virginia (its second store on the East Coast), and one in Sacramento, California. In February, NOBE opened a 195,000-sq.-ft. store in Brea, California, that replaced a smaller one. In addition, the company planned four new stores in 1990 (three in California and one in New Jersey) and three new stores in 1991 (one in Chicago and two in Maryland). Beyond 1991, the company is looking at sites in the Denver, Minneapolis and Boston areas. Over the next three years, capital expenditures are projected at about $500 million, of which $300 million will be borrowed.

Next earnings report expected in mid-May.

Per Share Data ($)

Yr. End Jan. 31	1989	¹1988	1987	1986	1985	1984	1983	1982	1981	1980
Book Value	7.86	6.55	5.57	4.22	3.65	3.21	2.73	2.26	1.94	1.69
Earnings	1.51	1.13	0.91	0.65	0.54	0.54	²0.40	²0.38	²0.30	0.25
Dividends	0.22	0.18	0.13	0.11	0.10	0.07	0.06³/₈	0.05¹/₂	0.04¹/₂	0.04
Payout Ratio	15%	16%	14%	16%	18%	13%	16%	15%	15%	16%
Calendar Years	1988	1987	1986	1985	1984	1983	1982	1981	1980	1979
Prices—High	34	40³/₄	25⁵/₈	13¹/₄	9³/₄	11⁵/₈	6¹/₂	4³/₄	3¹/₈	2⁷/₈
Low	19³/₄	15³/₄	11⁷/₈	7¹/₈	6³/₄	5⁷/₈	6¹/₂	2¹/₂	1⁷/₈	2¹/₄
P/E Ratio—	23–13	36–14	28–13	20–11	18–12	22–11	16–8	13–7	10–6	11–9

Data as orig. reptd. Adj. for stk. divs. of 100% Jul. 1987, 100% Jun. 1986, 100% Jun. 1983. 1. Refl. acctg. change. 2. Ful. dil.: 0.38 in 1983, 0.35 in 1982, 0.29 in 1981.

FIGURE 10-5 Standard & Poor's Report: Nordstrom, Inc. Courtesy of Standard and Poor's Corp., Standard OTC Stock Reports, vol. 55, no. 45, sec. 24, April 21, 1989.

4793   Nordstrom, Inc.

Income Data (Million $)

Year Ended Jan. 31	Oper. ¹Revs.	Oper. Inc.	% Oper. Inc. of Revs.	Cap. Exp.	Depr.	Int. Exp.	Net Bef. Taxes	Eff. Tax Rate	Net Inc.	% Net Inc. of Revs.
1989	2,238	241	10.4	153	60.4	45.1	198	37.8%	123	5.3
²1988	1,920	192	10.0	129	49.9	37.1	163	43.0%	93	4.8
1987	1,630	172	10.6	79	46.6	7.1	³140	48.0%	73	4.5
1986	1,302	119	9.1	124	37.4	23.2	³87	42.7%	50	3.8
1985	981	116	11.8	135	26.3	22.1	³73	43.9%	41	4.1
1984	788	106	13.4	61	19.7	13.6	74	45.5%	40	5.1
1983	613	77	12.5	36	16.8	14.2	48	44.1%	27	4.4
1982	522	65	12.5	48	13.3	11.4	44	43.3%	25	4.7
1981	408	53	12.9	34	10.6	8.0	37	46.2%	20	4.8
1980	346	41	11.8	41	7.7	²5.0	29	43.5%	16	4.7

Balance Sheet Data (Million $)

Jan. 31	Cash	Curr. Assets	Curr. Liab.	Ratio	Total Assets	% Ret. on Assets	Long Term Debt	Common Equity	Total Cap.	% LT Debt of Cap.	% Ret. on Equity
1989	16.1	915	448	2.0	1,512	9.0	370	640	1,064	34.7	21.0
1988	4.9	730	395	1.9	1,234	8.7	239	533	840	28.5	18.8
1987	18.4	402	271	1.5	892	8.5	141	451	621	22.7	18.4
1986	7.3	317	207	1.5	763	7.3	221	314	556	39.8	17.1
1985	5.9	256	166	1.5	601	7.3	152	272	436	34.8	16.0
1984	2.6	309	165	1.9	515	8.7	106	238	350	30.3	18.3
1983	11.2	241	91	2.6	405	6.8	109	202	314	34.7	14.6
1982	5.1	202	93	2.2	347	7.7	103	149	254	40.6	17.9
1981	31.4	174	65	2.7	297	7.5	104	128	232	45.0	16.5
1980	3.4	132	52	2.5	230	8.0	67	111	178	37.5	15.8

Data as orig. reptd. 1. Incl. sales of leased depts. 2. Refl. acctg. change. 3. Incl. equity in earns. of nonconsol. subs.

Business Summary

Nordstrom is a specialty retailer selling primarily full lines of medium-to-upscale apparel, shoes and accessories for women, men and children. At January 31, 1989, it was operating 58 stores (occupying an aggregate of 6,374,000 sq. ft. of space), versus 56 stores (5,527,000 sq. ft.) at 1987-8 year-end. Nordstrom stores are located in Washington, Oregon, Alaska, California, Utah, Montana and Virginia. The company also operated leased shoe departments in 11 department stores in Hawaii.

Sales in recent years were derived as follows:

	1988-9	1987-8
Women's apparel and accessories	59%	59%
Shoes	18%	18%
Men's apparel and accessories	17%	17%
Children's apparel and accessories	4%	4%
Other	2%	2%

Nordstrom stores feature a wide selection of style, size and color in each merchandise category. Emphasis is placed on fashion and customer service.

The company also places importance on store design and fixturing to enhance its merchandise presentations. As of January 31, 1989, Nordstrom operated 42 large specialty stores and six smaller "Place Two" units, as well as 10 clearance stores. Sales per square foot of selling space were $380 in 1988-9, $349 the year before and $322 in 1986-7.

Dividend Data

Cash has been paid in each year since 1971.

Amt. of Divd. $	Date Decl.	Ex-divd. Date	Stock of Record	Payment Date
0.05½	May 17	May 24	May 31	Jun. 15'88
0.05½	Aug. 16	Aug. 25	Aug. 31	Sep. 15'88
0.05½	Nov. 15	Nov. 23	Nov. 30	Dec. 15'88
0.07	Feb. 21	Feb. 28	Mar. 6	Mar. 15'89

Capitalization

Long Term Debt: $369,520,000 (1/89), incl. lease obligs.

Common Stock: 81,524,130 shs. (no par).
About 40% is owned by the Nordstrom family.
Institutions hold some 35%.
Shareholders: About 76,500 of record.

Office—1501 Fifth Avenue, Seattle, Washington 98101. **Tel**—(206) 628-2111. **Co-Chrmn**—B. A. Nordstrom, J. F. Nordstrom & J. N. Nordstrom. **Pres**—J. A. McMillan. **Secy**—Karen E. Purpur. **Sr VP, Treas & Investor Contact**—John A. Goesling. **Dirs**—R. E. Bender, B. H. Franklin, D. W. Gittinger, J. F. Harrigan, C. A. Lynch, J. A. McMillan, B. A. Nordstrom, J. F. Nordstrom, J. N. Nordstrom, A. E. Osborne Jr., W. D. Ruckelshaus, M. T. Stamper, E. C. Vaughan. **Transfer Agent & Registrar**—First Interstate Bank of California. **Incorporated** in Washington in 1946. **Empl**—25,000.

Information has been obtained from sources believed to be reliable, but its accuracy and completeness are not guaranteed. Karen J. Sack

FIGURE 10-5   (continued)

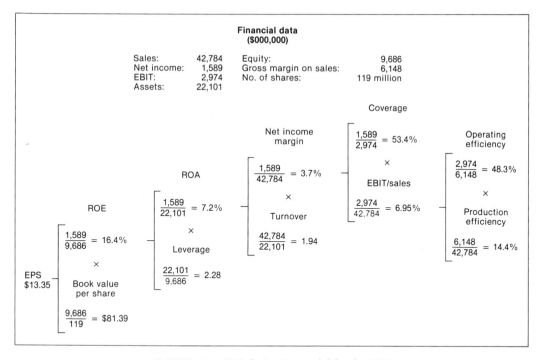

FIGURE 10-6 EPS derivation model for the XYZ company

The P/E ratio can be used to estimate the attractiveness of a stock. Consider first the big picture. The Standard & Poor's normal P/E range is 13 to 15 during a bull market and 8 to 10 in a declining, or bear, market. So, when the Standard & Poor's P/E ratio shoots up to 21.1, as was the case prior to the infamous Black Monday of October 19, 1987, there is definite cause for alarm. In the fall of 1988, the Standard & Poor's P/E ratio declined to around 10.

Two observations are apropos at this point. First, the case for stocks with low P/Es is compelling. A recent study shows that stocks with P/Es below the market average of 12.7 percent significantly outperformed other stocks. This study showed that low P/E stocks return 16.8 percent annually, compared with 9.9 percent for the stocks included in the Standard & Poor's 500. Second, the P/E ratio is not a fixed number. Every company actually has several P/Es, which can significantly vary over time. Hence, care should be exercised when using this ratio to estimate the future value of a stock.

TECHNICAL ANALYSIS

An Overview

To this point, the discussion has centered around the selection of stocks by engaging in fundamental analysis. The techniques of technical analysis are at odds with fundamental analysis. Proponents of technical analysis argue that, because the market price of a stock reflects *all* factors affecting it, a study involving only stock price movements is necessary. Technical analysts believe that the future expected price of a stock—the only variable that matters—can be predicted by carefully analyzing its past price behavior, because movements in past prices create discernible patterns that tend to repeat themselves in a predictable manner. Consequently, technicians concern themselves with predictions of short-term price movements in an effort to determine the best *timing* for purchases and sales of common stocks. For these reasons, it is sometimes claimed that the fundamental technique is generally best for selecting *what* to buy or sell, whereas technical analysis primarily helps one decide *when* to trade in stocks. The factors used by technical analysts in making their buy and sell decisions are presented in Table 10-4.

Charting

Technical analysis of individual stocks involves the interpretation of important chart patterns known by such esoteric names as head and shoulders, necklines, triangles, wedges, flags, and saucers. Each pattern signals to technical analysts a major or minor upward or downward movement in the stock. Several popular chart patterns are discussed next.

Support and resistance levels.   One of the most important aspects of chart analysis is the identification of support and resistance levels, as shown

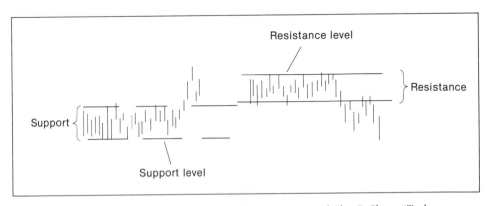

FIGURE 10-7   Support and resistance levels. Courtesy of Alan R. Shaw, "Technical Analysis," in *Financial Analyst's Handbook,* ed. Sumner N. Levine (Homewood, Ill.: Dow Jones-Irwin, 1975), p. 958.

TABLE 10-4 Factors Used in Technical Analysis

	Description	Claim by technical analysts
Activity factors		
High-Low Index	Average number of NYSE stocks making new highs (surpassing their previous highest price levels for preceding 52 weeks) minus the number making new lows.	During a rising market an increasing number of stocks reach new highs and a decreasing number reach new lows (market technically strong). The reverse is true in a declining market (market is technically weak).
Advances-Declines Index	Ratio of the number of issues that advanced to the number that declined, relative to the total of stocks that changed in price.	Changes in the ratio predict short-term market trends.
Most Active Stocks	Wall Street Journal listing of most actively traded stocks, their high, low, and closing prices on the New York and American stock exchanges.	Because of degree of risk involved in holding low quality stocks, market is generally more vulnerable when low quality stocks become popular.
Lo/Price Activity Ratio	Compares activity in speculative stocks to that in quality issues. Represents the weekly ratio of volumes in Barron's Lo/Price Stock Index to volume in DJIA.	High speculative activity usually occurs at the top of the market, whereas low speculative activity occurs at the bottom.
Dow Jones Momentum Ratio	Measures spread between the DJIA and its 30-day moving average.	Assumed to pinpoint turning points in the market. In a bull market, difference of 30 to 40 points indicates the market has reached the top; -30 to -50 suggests the market has reached the bottom. In a bear market, a spread of 20 to 30 signals a market top, whereas -50 to -70 signals a market bottom.

TABLE 10-4 (continued)

	Description	Claim by technical analysts
Market strength factors		
Breadth Index	Computed by subtracting the number of advances from the number of declines every week and dividing the result by the number of stocks that remain unchanged during that week. Index for the week is added to the previous week's figure.	When plotted on a graph, the trend in the market is determined from the direction of movement in the breadth index.
Relative Strength Index	Ratio of the price of a stock to the DJIA.	As long as the ratio continues to rise, that stock price is rising at a faster rate than the market and vice versa.
Volume of Trading	The number of issues changing hands daily.	Rise or decline in stock prices on high volume signals a continuation of the existing price trend; whereas a low volume points to an impending reversal of price trend.
Large Block Transactions	Financial journals regularly publish data concerning large transactions (25,000 shares or more) in specified stocks and prices at which these transactions were made.	Large blocks of shares traded on a downtick indicate a weak market. Conversely, large transactions on upticks suggest a strong bull market.
Directional factors		
Daily Trading Barometer	A weighted composite of three oscillating factors: (1) Last 7 days of advances and declines on the NYSE; (2) Algebraic sum of the last 20 days of plus and minus volumes on the NYSE; and (3) Ratio of the closing value of the DJIA to the average closing price for the last 28 days.	Proponents argue that it is a reliable indicator of overbought and undersold market conditions.

Directional Moves	Directional moves of the various Dow Jones Indicators. While divergence is not unusual, it is assumed that this divergence is not likely to persist for long.	Movements in weaker segment of the market (transportation) precede movements in the stronger counterparts (industrials and utilities).

Contrary opinion factors

Short Interest	Measure of short sales. An investor is selling short when, without first owning a stock, he/she sells it at a certain price in the hope of later being able to buy it at a lower price and realizing a profit.	Two interpretations: (1) Large short interest indicates widespread expectation of a price decline and is bearish. (2) Indicates a strong potential demand for stock and is, therefore, bullish.
Odd-Lot Index and Odd-Lot Sales Index	Ratio of odd-lot sales to odd-lot purchases (less than 100 share units).	Small investors are ill-informed and can be counted on to make the wrong moves at critical moments. If odd-lotters are net-buyers, "smart money" will get out of the market.
NYSE Specialists Short Sales Ratios	Ratio of specialists short sales to total NYSE short sales.	Measures extremes of sentiment of NYSE specialists who sell short most heavily at market tops when nonmember enthusiasm for buying is greatest and less heavily at bottoms when public selling is accelerated.
Advisory Service Sentiment	Weekly index of the percentage of leading bearish advisory services.	When the advisory service becomes overly one-sided, technical analysts view it as a contrary indicator because services follow trends rather than anticipate changes.

Confidence factor

Barron's Confidence Index (CI)	Ratio of high grade to low grade bond yields. High quality bond yields are always lower than low quality bond yields because investors have more confidence in them.	In a rising market, the CI rises. When the CI slides downward, the market is believed to be getting ready for a downturn because investors are reluctant to place confidence in lower quality bonds.

367

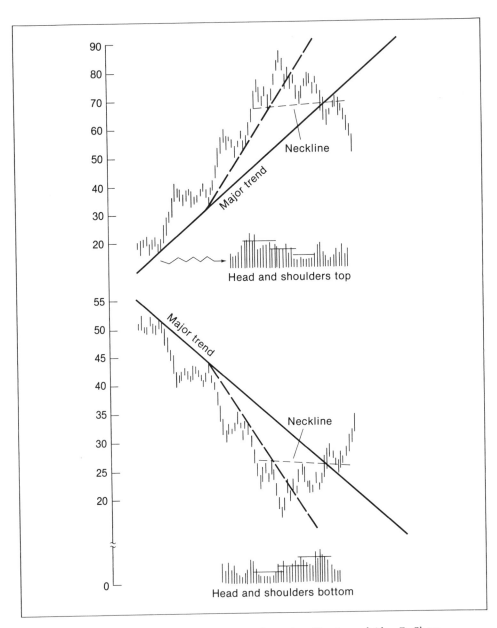

FIGURE 10-8 Head and shoulders configuration. Courtesy of Alan R. Shaw, "Technical Analysis," in *Financial Analyst's Handbook*, ed. Sumner N. Levine (Homewood, Ill.: Dow Jones-Irwin, 1975), p. 963.

in Figure 10-7. A support level is a barrier to a price decline; a resistance level is a barrier to a price advancement. Although the barrier is an obstruction, it is by no means impassable: Stock prices do break support and resistance barriers.

Head and shoulders configurations. Basic reversal patterns help analysts identify the turning points so that they can decide when to buy or sell stock. The key reversal pattern is popularly known as the head and shoulders configuration. This configuration, shown in Figure 10-8, is merely another name for an uptrend or a downtrend in a stock; "neckline" is the familiar resistance or support level.

A head and shoulders formation should be analyzed against the background of volume trend. As the head and shoulders top is formed, resistance

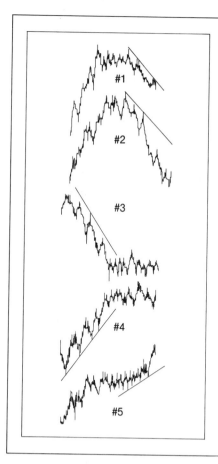

Chart Pattern #1
Stocks with vulnerable trends and/or possible downside potential.

Chart Pattern #2
Stocks with less vulnerability that appear to have reached possible lows, but need consolidation.

Chart Pattern #3
Stocks that have declined and experienced consolidation, and could do well in a favorable market.

Chart Pattern #4
Stocks that have performed relatively well but are currently in "neutral" trends.

Chart Pattern #5
Stocks in established uptrends and/or with possible upside potential.

FIGURE 10-9 Various chart patterns. Yale Hirsch, *The 1971 Stock Trader's Almanac* (Old Tappan, NJ: The Hirsch Organization, 1970), p. 37.

to further price increases dampens investor enthusiasm; therefore, the volume decreases on each of the rally phases within the top formation. The reverse is true when the head and shoulders bottom is under formation. It should be emphasized that the completion of a head and shoulders top or bottom is not considered final until the penetration of the neckline is apparent.

Five broad patterns. It is worth noting that of all the many chart patterns and techniques just discussed, five broadly classified patterns are claimed to best describe the price behavior of most stocks. These patterns, shown in Figure 10-9, should be self-explanatory.

ASSET ALLOCATION MODEL

THE BASIC CONCEPT

At the heart of investment planning is the Asset Allocation Model (AAM) which refers to the technique of allocating capital to diverse asset classes to maximize returns within specific risk tolerances. Another way of stating this concept is to say that AAM is a rational system for managing portfolio risk through diversification without compromising portfolio return. Regardless of whether the AAM is used to maximize the portfolio return for a given level of risk, or minimize the portfolio risk for a given level of return, it provides the financial planner with a dynamic tool for efficiently handling both the changing economic environment and the ever-changing needs and goals of the investor.

THE KEY BENEFITS

The AAM offers a variety of important benefits. More specifically, the AAM:

1. Provides a long-term perspective to portfolio management, although the need for short-term adjustments is not ruled out.
2. Helps the financial planner incorporate the investor's life-cycle needs, objectives, and risk tolerance level into the development of the investment portfolio.
3. Bridges the gap between tax-base planning and the investment-based planning.
4. Helps reduce the investment risk through diversification. A study, conducted by C. D. Brinson, J. J. Diermeir, and G. G. Schlarbaum published in the March/April 1986 issue of the *Financial Analyst Journal* concluded that over 90 percent of the average portfolio's risk can be controlled by

adjusting the asset class mix, rather than by using individual securities selection or mechanical market timing formulas.

5. Rationalizes the recommended portfolio strategy by comparing it with a "standard portfolio allocation." This benefit is derived from the basic premise that after the completion of asset reallocation, the percentage allocated to each individual class should approximate the "standard portfolio."

SEVEN KEY STEPS

The development of the AAM involves seven key steps.[2]

Step 1. Long-term direction of inflation.   There are two broad categories of investment: tangible or hard assets, known as direct investments, and financial assets, called indirect investments. Each category behaves differently during inflationary and deflationary periods. Assets in the direct investment category perform best during inflationary times, while those in the indirect investment category are more attractive during periods of disinflation.

Step 2. Asset split.   Assets can be divided between direct and indirect investments. The split between direct and indirect investment is somewhat subjective based upon the planner's degree of confidence in predicting the inflationary environment. Strong, confirmed inflationary periods might make it desirable to have a 90/10 split between direct and indirect investments. If no clearly discernible inflationary pattern exists, a 50/50 split might be more appropriate. Finally, if disinflationary pressures are strong, then a 20/80 or even a 10/90 split would appear desirable.

Step 3. Selection of investment areas.   Favored investments arise from three scenarios: (1) those which are opposite to the risk side of an economic crisis; (2) those which have not been completely exploited by the marketplace; and (3) those which can be extensively diversified.

Step 4. Percentage assignment to favorite investments.   Definite percentages can be assigned to favorite investments. In making this assignment, investor's risk tolerance, concerns for liquidity, taxes, time horizon, and temperament should be taken into account.

Step 5. Identification of specific investments.   Specific investments should be identified which are not only undervalued but which also meet the investor's preferences and objectives articulated in Step 4.

---

[2] Harold Georgues has developed these seven key steps for successful asset allocation.

Step 6. Estimation of risk level.   Client's assets should be segmented into categories of working capital, and an estimated total return should be assigned to each category. This will lay the foundation for the calculation of weighted average total return, which, in turn, will help approximate the investor's risk level. AAM addresses the process whereby assets are realized in terms of amount, type, and risk level desired by the investor.

Step 7. Matching of investment names and choices.   The time period within which an investor wishes to achieve certain financial objectives should be determined. This will lay the foundation for calculating how fast the selected investments should reach their stated destination. It is this singular premise which solidifies the process of asset allocation.

BUILDING AN ASSET ALLOCATION MODEL

The AAM uniquely combines three major building blocks: namely, inflation expectations, market trends for each asset class, and the investor's financial profile. Each block is discussed next.

Inflation Expectations

The most fundamental building block of the AAM is the articulation of future inflation expectations. The reason is that, as mentioned, direct assets are favored during periods of rising inflation, whereas indirect or financial assets are better investments during periods of low inflation, or disinflation. This fact is clearly revealed in Table 10-5. Systematic asset class diversification assures that a portfolio is protected from the negative impacts of different inflationary cycles.

Market Trends for Each Asset Class

Notwithstanding inflationary cycles, changing market conditions affect different asset categories in varying degrees. For instance, at certain times, such as during the period of rising inflation, the market would favor hard and tangible assets over financial assets. At other times, unrelated to inflationary expectations, the market would favor financial securities. AAM must take appropriate steps to take advantage of favorable market conditions and protect the portfolio against erosion due to hostile trends prevailing in the market.

Investor's Financial Profile

Another crucial building block is the construction of the investor's financial profile. While each investor goes through many stages of the financial life cycle, for simplicity these cycles can be classified into two broad categories: namely, accumulation cycle for preretirement investors and preservation cycle

TABLE 10-5 Inflation and Asset Category Behavior

Asset category	Inflation scenario				
	−5%–0%	0%–3%	3%–6%	6%–12%	12%–20%
Fixed Income:					
Bonds (Intermediate and Long-term)	Excellent	Good	Good	Poor	Poor
Cash Equivalents	Fair	Fair	Fair	Fair	Fair
Equities	Excellent	Good	Good	Poor	Poor
Natural Resources	Poor	Fair	Fair	Good	Excellent
Real Estate	Poor	Fair	Good	Excellent	Poor*
Tangibles	Poor	Poor	Fair	Good	Excellent

Asset behavior definitions

Excellent: Substantial real return
Good: Reasonable real return
Fair: Tend to track inflation
Poor: Loss of purchasing power

* This assumes project financed with expensive debt. Results likely to be excellent under other financing scenarios.

Source: J. L. Joslin, S. G. Lorant, and R. E. C. Wegner, "The Multi-Asset Association Model: A Financial Planning Framework for Long-Term Investment Management," *Tax Management Financial Planning Journal*, October 21, 1986, p. 528.

for postretirement investors. Frequently, the asset allocation strategies are different for each cycle (for simplicity, this feature is not shown in Figure 10-10). In general, the accumulation investor is more of a risk taker and can afford greater diversification than the preservation investor, who is generally risk averse.

A Simple Application

We are now in a position to construct an integrated AAM for both accumulation and preservation investors under conditions of both high and low inflation periods. The manner in which client profiles affect allocation strategies in a high inflationary environment is demonstrated in Figure 10-10. Other things being equal, the accumulation investor is able to assume medium risk levels during a period of high inflation (six to 12 percent). The preservation investor, by contrast, is a risk-averse person; consequently, lower percentages are allocated to equities, real estate, and natural resources, whereas the cash equivalents percentage is higher than in the former case.

In Figure 10-11 the model is reproduced under low inflationary conditions (zero to three percent). Here again, the relative risk aversion of the preser-

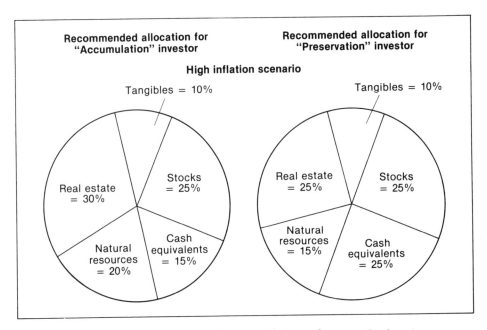

FIGURE 10-10 Asset allocations for accumulation and preservation investors. J. L. Joslin, S. G. Lorant, and R. E. C. Wegner, "The Multi-Asset Association Model: A Financial Planning Framework for Long-Term Investment Management," *Tax Management Financial Planning Journal*, October 21, 1986.

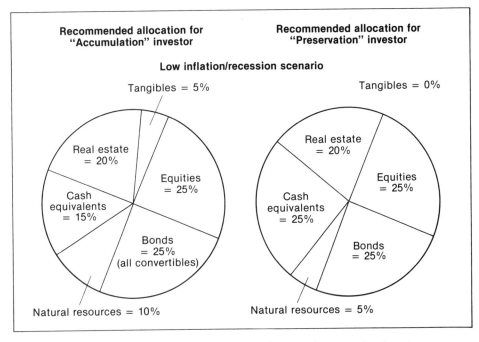

FIGURE 10-11 Asset allocation for accumulation and preservation investors. J. L. Joslin, S. G. Lorant, and R. E. C. Wegner, "The Multi-Asset Association Model: A Financial Planning Framework for Long-Term Investment Management," *Tax Management Financial Planning Journal*, October 21, 1986.

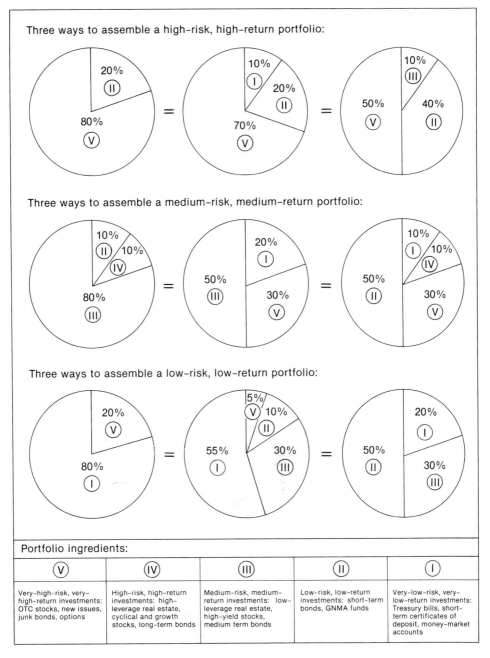

FIGURE 10-12 High, medium, and low risk portfolios. Adapted from Clint Wills, "Managing Your Portfolio Like A Pro," *Money*, May 1986, Reprint, p. 4.

vation investor is evidenced by the fact that this portfolio eliminates tangibles, lowers percentages allocated for natural resources, and increases the cash equivalents ratio.

Thus far the discussion has centered around the fact that asset allocation means maximizing returns for a given amount of risk, by maintaining an efficient combination of stocks, bonds, cash, hard assets, and a variety of other kinds of investments. It has also been emphasized that it is a dynamic process, since what works out at one stage of the business cycle or the investor's life cycle may be inappropriate for another.

The previous discussion on AAM might lead one to conclude that the science of model construction is so precise that it enables a financial planner to put together a combination of assets that is *right* for both the prevailing economic conditions and the investor for whom the portfolio is developed. That is simply not true. There are no magic formulas which can guide a planner to construct an ideal or a target portfolio for a given investor. Furthermore, the Target Investment Portfolio (TIP) developed with the help of the AAM is likely to require an updating as economic conditions change. It is therefore safe to conclude that portfolio construction is a flexible art and an astute planner should permit the investor to choose from several portfolios with comparable risks the one that is most preferable. Nevertheless, it can be claimed that the AAM concept attempts to utilize the "buy-low-and-sell-high" approach.

Three sets of portfolios in each of the risk categories (high, medium, and low) are presented in Figure 10-12. For instance, having settled on an appropriate level of risk for a portfolio, an investor can decide on the comfort level and allocate the funds designated by one of the choices available in that category. With this flexible strategy, an AAM can succeed in balancing the fears and hopes, or more appropriately, the risks and rewards, of an investor. Even more important, the risks of an AAM-directed portfolio can be further controlled with the help of a technique known as portfolio timing.

CONCEPT OF PORTFOLIO TIMING

INTRODUCTION

We have observed that the asset allocation model (AAM) is used for developing an appropriate investment portfolio with the proper mix of equities, bonds, and money market instruments, given the investor's age, investment objectives, and willingness to assume risk. This point is elaborated with the help of Figure 10-13. For example, a 25-year-old investor willing to assume moderate risk and planning a home purchase or other large outlay in the near future might be advised to put the largest percentage of the portfolio in treasury bills, short-term certificates of deposit, or other cash equivalents (Portfolio A). However, for an aggressive investor at age 45, such liquidity might not be

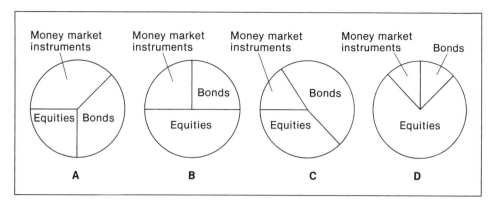

FIGURE 10-13 Portfolio reorganization strategy

needed, and it might be prudent to put far more emphasis on moderate-growth investments, such as common stocks and variable annuities (Portfolio D).

The preceding discussion fails to recognize an important fact: A target investment portfolio (TIP) developed with the help of the AAM is likely to require updating as economic conditions change and the economy moves from

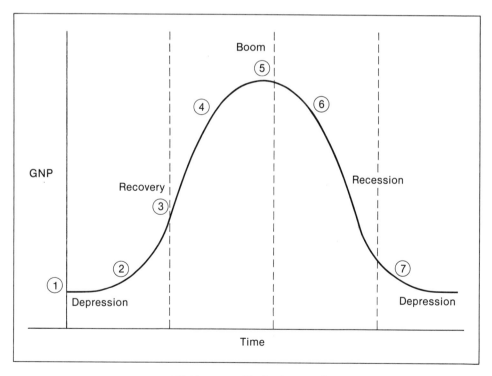

FIGURE 10-14 The business cycle

one stage of the business cycle into another. It is of course clearly understood that financial planners are not economists or forecasters and it is not their responsibility to call business cycle turns or analyze complicated forecasting data. Nevertheless, serious financial planners should assume responsibility for identifying the stage of the business cycle, define the short-term and long-term direction of inflation and interest rates, and reorganize their clients' portfolios to make them consistent with the prevailing economic environment.

TIMING OVER BUSINESS CYCLE

The four stages of a business cycle are presented in Figure 10-14. The National Bureau of Economic Research regularly publishes data on booms (peaks) and recessions (troughs). Financial planners can also make an attempt to predict the business cycle turns by analyzing the index of leading economic indicators. Although there are exceptions, in general, growth or equity investment is preferable during the recovery periods until the cycle approaches a peak. Near the peak of the boom period, it is desirable to liquidate growth securities and hold liquid funds. As the economy begins a downturn, interest rates begin to

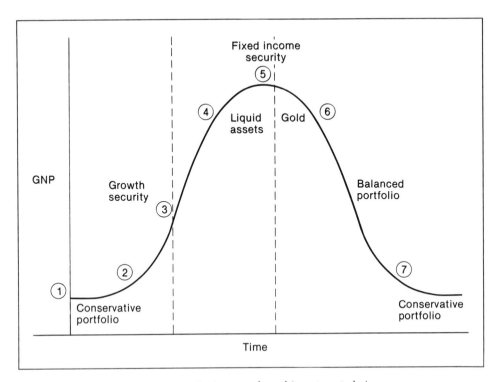

FIGURE 10-15 Business cycle and investment choices

decline from their peaks. This is the time to invest liquid funds in fixed income securities, since falling interest rates lead to an increase in the prices of these securities. It is also desirable to invest in gold during an inflationary period which is associated with a period of recovery leading to the business cycle peak. The preferred investments during different stages of the business cycle are presented in Figure 10-15.

INTEREST RATES

The pulse of the economy can be felt by watching interest rates. Interest rates tend to move directly with the business cycle (dashed vertical lines), as revealed in Figure 10-16. While there are exceptions, as a general rule interest rates

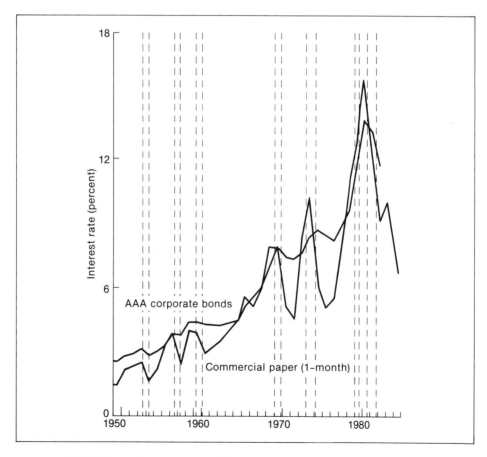

FIGURE 10-16 Interest rates and business cycles. Courtesy of The Board of Governors of The Federal Reserve System.

are relatively high when the economy is close to full employment and relatively low when the economy experiences recessions and high levels of unemployment. As mentioned, fixed income securities become attractive at or near the peak of the business cycle when the interest rates are high, while investment in growth securities or equities is preferable when interest rates are low.

MONEY SUPPLY

One of the financial indicators closely watched by financial planners is fluctuations in the money supply. When the money supply grows rapidly, interest rates generally decline and the economy speeds up, boosting corporate profits. As a result, stock prices usually rise. And when the rate of growth of the money supply declines, interest rates rise, thereby slowing down the economy and

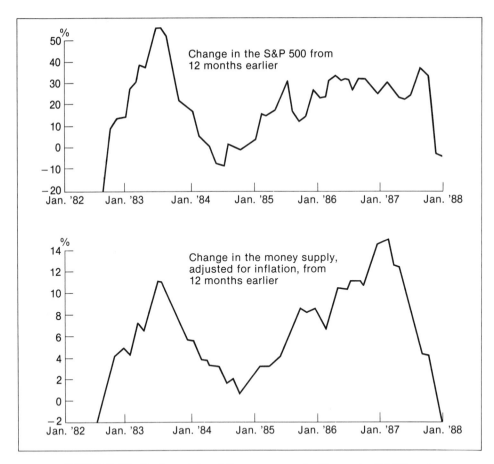

FIGURE 10-17   Stock market and the money supply. *Money,* April 1988, p. 8.

pushing down the stocks, as revealed by Figure 10-17. Thus, as a general rule stocks become attractive during periods of a rising money supply and vice versa.

U.S. DOLLAR AND PRICE INDICES

The exchange rate on the U.S. dollar, particularly on foreign markets, has become important to financial markets. In general, the stronger the dollar relative to other foreign currencies, the more it attracts foreign investors and harms U.S. exports because it makes U.S. exports more expensive for foreigners.

The Producer Price Index (PPI) makes information available on crude materials and semifinished goods. This is a leading indicator of the Consumer Price Index (CPI), which reflects prices on fixed markets of consumer goods and services. While the CPI should fall during recessions and rise during periods of rapid and sustained growth (solid vertical lines), that has not been the case during most of the 1970–1987 period, as revealed by Figure 10-18.

Notwithstanding the erratic behavior of the CPI, it is still widely believed that if the CPI rises $\frac{3}{4}$ percent per month for six consecutive months, planners should be aware of higher interest rates, which should follow along with the new round of inflation.

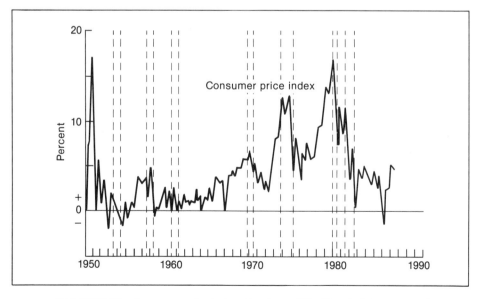

FIGURE 10-18 Consumer price index. Courtesy of The Board of Governors of the Federal Reserve System.

RIDING THE YIELD CURVE

The yield curve, which shows a relationship between bond yields and short-, intermediate-, and long-term maturities, is an excellent predictor of a recession. Generally, short-term interest rates are lower than their long-term counterparts because the more distant the future, the greater the risk associated with the investment. Put differently, in theory the higher yields compensate investors for the extra risk they take by tying up their money for a longer period of time. However, when the yield curve is inverted, that is, the short-term interest rates are more than a percentage point above long-term rates, then a recession will very likely follow. This was the case in January 1981, as can be seen from Figure 10-19. As we learned, the end of a recession calls for an equity-dominated portfolio (Portfolio B in Figure 10-14) or a balanced portfolio (Portfolio C).

The yield curve is also helpful in identifying the end of a bond market rally. For instance, the Treasury's inverted yield curve on June 9, 1989, presented in Figure 10-20, reversed itself on July 6, 1989. More specifically, bond equivalent yields were 8.0 percent on three-month treasury bills, compared with a yield of 8.1 percent on the benchmark 30-year treasury bond. The July 6, 1989, curve was a warning signal that the yields on long-term bonds were likely to drop and the end of the prevailing bond market rally was approaching.

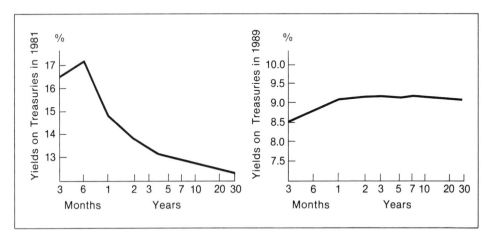

FIGURE 10-19 The yield curve. Adapted from Jerry Edgerton and Jordan E. Goodman, "How to Steer Your Investments Around a Twisting Yield Curve," *Money*, February 1989, p. 7.

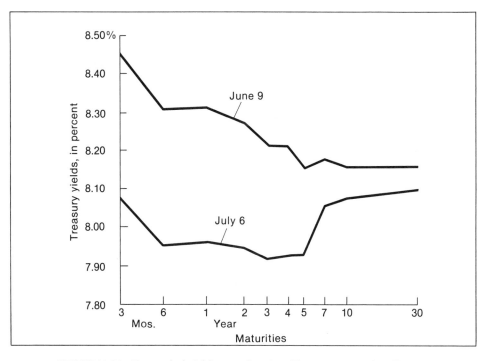

FIGURE 10-20   Reversal of yield curve. Reprinted by permission of *Wall Street Journal*, © Dow Jones & Company, Inc., July 7, 1989. All Rights Reserved Worldwide.

MARKET TIMING

Not all financial planners and investment timers reorganize investment portfolios over the stages of business cycles. A group of people, popularly known as market timers, are believers in technical analysis and they time individual stocks, bonds, and mutual funds on a day-to-day basis.

Explained simply, rather than poring over financial reports of corporations, a market timer looks at price trends in the stock and bond markets to put investors in a better position to catch major advances or avoid large losses when stocks or bonds decline. Clearly, if investment in a stock or bond fund can be consistently moved into a money fund before a market decline, and moved back into a stock or bond fund just before a market rise, market timing can, optimally, produce significant returns even in lackluster years. The critical question, of course, is this: Can a market timer consistently predict market turns and successfully forecast them? While the answer to this question is a definite no, that does not negate the value of market timing, as should be clear from the following discussion.

The technique of market timing is presented in Figure 10-21. In this hypothetical example, the market timer quadruples the initial investment of $1,000 even after missing the top ($27) and the bottom ($3) of the market. Even more important, the stock was sold at the same price at which it was purchased ($10).

Let there be no misunderstanding, however. The preceding illustration does not address the difficulties associated with determining market timing. Although market timing services differ in their interpretations and use of indicators, there are some basic measures common to many timing systems. These include the moving average of the market index, advancing versus declining stocks, interest rates, money supply, market sentiment, book value of the stock index, and the market's price-to-earnings ratio. As can be expected, some market timers achieve more success than others. Their success in part depends on which mutual funds and stocks are timed by them, for some funds and stocks lend themselves to market timing much more than others.

A sampling of timing newsletters and their performance in 1987 is presented in Table 10-6. Also, a buy-and-hold strategy is contrasted with market timing in Figure 10-22. Both illustrations attest to the value of market timing. However, almost all studies consistently show that market timing succeeds in reducing the market risk only when it is applied as a long-term strategy. Also,

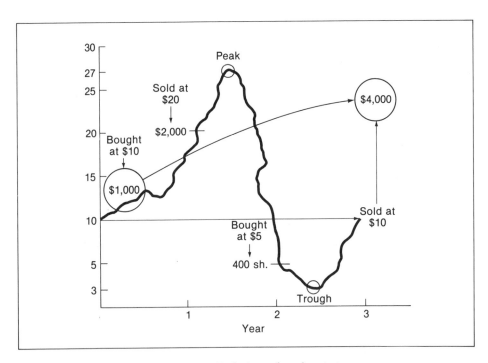

FIGURE 10-21   Technique of market timing

TABLE 10-6 Sampling the Top Timers

The 10 timing newsletters below performed well in 1987. The first five specify mutual funds to switch in and out of the stock market. The second five give you the choice of funds. The performance of the second group was measured by their return on the New York Stock Exchange composite index.

Group 1	Gain
Fund Exchange Report—Aggressive Growth Margined	**45.4%**
(206) 285-8877	Annual fee: $125
Investors Intelligence	**41.1%**
(914) 632-0422	Annual fee: $108
Dowes Market Letter	**33.8%**
(Equity Portfolio)	
(415) 981-0516	Annual fee: $200
Lynn Elgert Report	**32.8%**
(Mutual Fund Portfolio)	
(308) 381-2121	Annual fee: $190
Investech Mutual Fund Advisor	**28.8%**
(406) 862-7777	Annual fee: $150

Group 2	Gain
Lynn Elgert Report—Advice for Switch Fund Traders	**38.3%**
	Annual fee: $190
Dow Theory Letters—Grading of Primary Trend	**31.9%**
(619) 454-0481	Annual fee: $225
Investors Intelligence—Switch Fund Portfolio	**38.3%**
	Annual fee: $108
Elliot Wave Theorist	**38.8%**
(404) 536-0309	Annual fee: $233
Dowes Market Letter	**28.0%**
(Equity Timing Model)	
	Annual fee: $200

Note: All data are through November 1987

USN&WR—Basic data: *Hubert Financial Digest*

Source: Copyright February 1, 1988, *U.S. News & World Reports.*

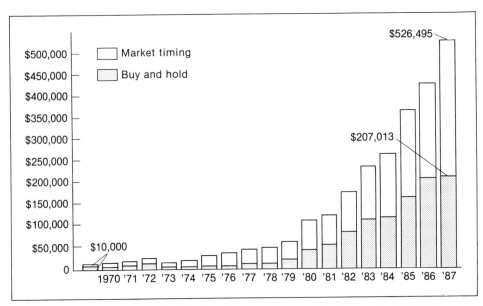

Note: All figures are at year's end. Paul Merriman & Assoc. began managing funds with the Merriman Equity Switch Model on July 31, 1983. This model is applied to the Fidelity Magellan mutual fund from Jan. 1970, through July 31, 1983. Average rates for 90–day U.S. Treasury bill are assumed while in money–market funds. Results do not include taxes or management fees and assume dividends and capital gains are reinvested.

FIGURE 10-22   Two strategies: timing the market vs. buy and hold. Copyright, February 1, 1988, *U.S. News & World Reports.*

in many instances, the annual returns *net* of all timing fees and charges do not appear to be as attractive as before-fees returns, especially in the short- and intermediate-term.

In this chapter we have discussed those investment theories, models, and concepts that are most important and appropriate for financial planning. The application of these theories and concepts in the context of investment planning will be presented in the next chapter.

CHAPTER 11

Investment Planning: Concepts and Strategies

INTRODUCTION

Investment planning can be a complex and often overwhelming task. However, the basic definition of investment planning is simple: the development and implementation of an investment portfolio designed to achieve the short- and long-run investment objectives articulated by an investor. This definition suggests that, for the investment planning process to be successful, a financial planner must not only understand the investor but also play a crucial role in achieving a delicate *balance* between risk and return, concentration and diversification, current income and growth, taxable and tax-advantaged investment, and liquid and nonliquid investments. An overview of the concept of investment planning is presented in Figure 11-1.

This chapter is divided into three parts. First we will analyze in detail the investment planning process. The key investment planning strategies will be discussed next. Finally, we will present a real world investment plan developed by using the investment planning process presented in the first part of this chapter.

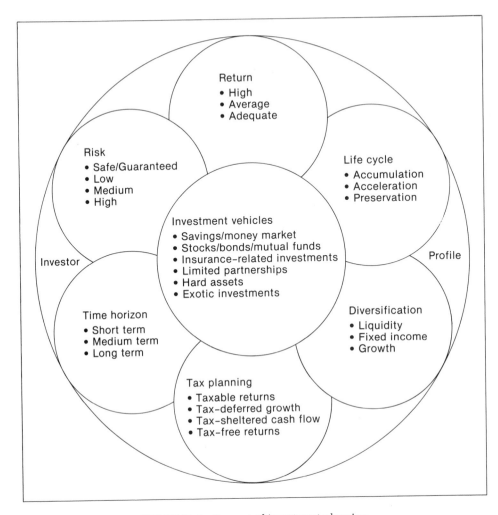

FIGURE 11-1   Concept of investment planning

INVESTMENT PLANNING PROCESS

INTRODUCTION

The investment planning process generally consists of five major steps: (1) identification of client goals; (2) determination of the client's risk tolerance level; (3) articulation of the client's investment preferences; (4) analysis of current investment portfolio; and (5) reorganization of current investment portfolio. In discussing these steps in this section, we will draw upon the investment models, theories, and concepts developed in the previous chapter. In our discussion we will also make extensive use of the basic investment alternatives presented in Chapter 9. A generous use of forms and questionnaires will also be made to determine client's goals, risk tolerance level, and investment preferences.

GOAL SETTING

An Overview

The investment planning process is initiated with the identification of a client's goals. This is easier said than done for several reasons: (1) Investment goals are likely to change as the client passes through different stages of life cycle; (2) Investment planning objectives are harder to verbalize than other (education, risk management, and so on) planning goals. For instance, it is difficult for many clients to state with any degree of certainty their needs for liquidity, current income, and desired rate of growth of investible funds; (3) As a general rule, few clients truly appreciate the power of diversification and the value of using the asset allocation model in the construction of an investment portfolio; (4) Since the Tax Reform Act of 1986 removed some of the effects of tax considerations in investment planning, many clients naively assume that tax saving strategies no longer play an important role in investment goal setting; (5) Few clients realize that sometimes the time horizon associated with a specific goal can become the dominant factor in determining the appropriateness of a specific investment to achieve that goal. For instance, the type of investment selected to fund a child's education may depend upon the number of years remaining before the funding begins; and (6) In setting investment goals, an unrealistic expectation of investment returns can frustrate the achievement of these goals. An appreciation of *reasonable* returns from different types of investment is therefore necessary before realistic investment goals can be established. Development of strategies for dealing with these issues will provide the framework for a meaningful discussion of the process of setting investment goals.

Life Cycle

The starting point of the goal-setting process is the recognition of the stages of financial life cycle. Although an investor passes through many stages of life cycles, for reasons of practicality, these stages can be classified into three broad categories: namely, accumulation, acceleration, and preservation.

The *accumulation* stage begins at the start of the investor's financial life. During this stage the investor's preoccupation is with: (1) protecting the growing family from a potential financial disaster due to death or disability; (2) providing for children's education; (3) accumulating basic assets like home and furnishings; and (4) building cash reserves and emergency funds to meet un-expected contingencies. An investment portfolio suited for this stage invari-ably consists of a large percentage of cash reserves and a variety of safe and low risk investments designed to help the investor's savings grow at a slow but steady rate.

The *acceleration* stage is ushered in when the investor enters the peak earning years and feels secure about having taken care of the family's basic needs and emergency situations. During this stage the investor may change from being extremely risk averse to being more willing to take risks, since the investor feels he or she has the time and resources to recover from potential losses generated by assuming investment risks. Naturally, during the accel-eration stage, for a risk taker the portfolio is transformed from a relatively riskless variety into a relatively risky type. This is done by including higher-risk investments so as to obtain higher investment returns and maximize the growth of net worth.

The third stage, known as the *preservation* stage, begins when the inves-tor starts preparing for retirement. Gone are the peak earning years. Also gone is the capacity to bounce back from investment losses resulting from taking high risks. During this stage the major preoccupation is the preser-vation of capital accumulated during the previous stages so the maximum amount of capital is still available to generate current income when regular sources of earned income are exhausted. Once again, the portfolio is trans-formed into a relatively risk-free type developed during the accumulation stage, although the major emphasis shifts from low-risk, slow-growing in-vestments to those products that are capable of generating maximum current income.

The concept of shifting investment goals as the investor passes through the three stages of life is presented in Figure 11-2.

Basic Investment Objectives

The second consideration in goal setting is an accurate verbalization by the investor of the basic investment objectives which, in turn, provides the foundation for the articulation of other, broad-based objectives like a proper balance between risk and investment return. The three basic investment ob-jectives relate to an investor's need for liquidity, current income, and invest-ment growth.

Liquidity. An essential component of a well-designed investment port-folio is the percentage allocated for cash reserves. The investor's liquidity needs can be classified into three categories: operating funds, emergency funds, and funds earmarked for capitalizing on future investment opportunities. The cash reserves portion of an investment portfolio satisfies all three liquidity needs of an investor.

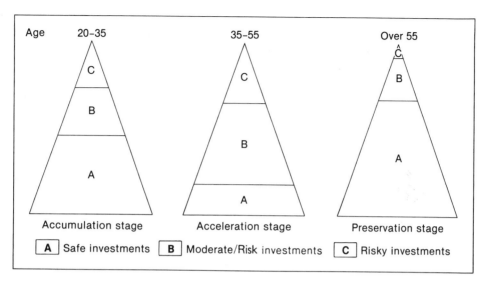

FIGURE 11-2   Life cycle stages and distribution of investment

Current income.   The types and amounts of fixed income securities and annuities included in an investment portfolio are influenced by the investor's current income needs. There are two major considerations in determining these income needs. First, the total of all the income sources—salary, pension, current investment income, bonus, and so on—should be compared with the current income needs which, in turn, are determined by the desired standard of living of the investor. The excess of income needs over total income sources, if any, is the amount of additional income which must be generated by new investments. Second, the investor must recognize the trade-off involved in this process: The higher the amount invested in securities generating current income, the lower the amount available for investing in growth securities, and the smaller the potential for future growth of the principal.

Investment growth.   One of the major objectives of investment planning is to maximize the growth of the total investment portfolio. Several major considerations determine the amount of investable funds to be allocated to growth investments and the types of investment products selected to achieve this objective. These considerations include the returns desired, the investor's risk tolerance level, and the investor's future income needs and time horizon.

Diversification and Asset Allocation

The third element in the goal setting process is the realization of the benefits offered by the use of the asset allocation model. One of the most celebrated bits of investment advice was given by Andrew Carnegie: "Put all your eggs in the same basket and watch it carefully." Unfortunately, this advice is improper for most investors, for rarely do they have the time or the expertise to select the *right investments* and liquidate them at the *right time* when they are no longer attractive. Consequently, with rare exceptions, the use of the asset allocation model becomes essential in investment planning.

It was explained in Chapter 10 that the asset allocation model provides a system for diversifying a portfolio among several asset classes to maximize the portfolio return for a given level of risk. This diversification is the process of reducing risk within a particular asset class by spreading individual issues of stocks, bonds, or other investments within a broad range. While the value of diversification is generally comprehended and hence the diversification objective is accomplished with relative ease, the extent to which the asset allocation model can be successfully used in any given situation depends upon the investor's goals and level of sophistication. For instance, a sophisticated investor may wish to use the asset allocation model for maximizing the portfolio return and simultaneously achieving a delicate balance between the degree of risk; the percentage return, short-, intermediate-; and long-term goals; and the perfect mix between liquid, fixed, growth, and nonliquid funds. In contrast, a not-so-savvy investor may be content with a much more modest asset allocation objective of a safe portfolio with a reasonable return.

Tax Considerations

In addition to the considerations already mentioned, at the heart of comprehensive investment planning are the tax ramifications of constructing and managing an investment portfolio. The reason is that in the final analysis the return which is meaningful to an investor is the net after-tax return. The tax issues relating to various investments were discussed at length in Chapter 8 and need not be repeated here. It is important to point out, however, that returns on various investment products can be classified as taxable, tax-deferred, tax-sheltered, and tax-free. Municipal bonds are tax-free. Many limited partnerships generate tax-sheltered cash flows. Insurance-related investments, such as annuities, single premium whole life, and universal life, as well as all qualified plan investments, generate tax-deferred returns. Finally, returns on all other investments are fully taxable. Other things being equal, an investor prefers investments that maximize after-tax returns.

Time Horizon

Timing is of the essence in selecting the right investment. Product choices are frequently shaped by the amount of time the investor has to reach financial goals. Classification of various investments into short-term, medium-term, and long-term, and the trade-offs associated with investments in different term categories, are presented in Table 11-1. Clearly, for an investor who wishes

TABLE 11-1   Terms of Investment

Investment examples	What they offer	Trade-offs
Short *(less than 2 years)*		
Money-market funds Short-term CD's Short-term bonds	Low volatility—price changes slightly or not at all Moderate yields Regular income Ready access to funds	Lower overall returns Frequent reinvestment decisions
Medium *(3 to 5 years)*		
Intermediate-term bonds Flexible-rate CD's High-income conservative stocks GNMA's	Moderately high yields Price moves in narrow range Regular income	Less safe than short- term investments Can be vulnerable to inflation Income can vary
Long *(more than 5 years)*		
Long-term bonds Long-term CDs Real estate Growth stocks (if held) Gold and silver	Highest yields or capital- growth potential Returns usually outpace inflation	Most volatility Less liquid Principal can be vulnerable to inflation

Source: Copyright June 6, 1988, *U. S. News & World Report.*

to have a lump sum in two years to make a down payment on a home, medium- and long-term investments would not be appropriate.

Investment Return

We have learned in Chapter 10 that risk and return are positively related. That is, the higher the return of an investment, the higher the risk it carries. This is the cornerstone of investment planning. In constructing a *target investment portfolio* (discussed in Chapter 10), given the investor's risk tolerance, a financial planner selects those products that maximize the portfolio's returns.

An important dimension of the problem of maximizing investment return is revealed by asking the question: What is a reasonable return that an investor can expect from a given security or portfolio? This question is not easily answered, for a great deal of myth surrounds the topic of what constitutes a reasonable return from an investment.

Long-term returns on common stocks and bonds are presented in Figure 11-3. This chart reveals several important facts. First, on a year-to-year basis common stocks have yielded an annual return of as much as 54 percent, but they have also lost up to 43 percent during any given year (Bar 1). Put differently, an investor expecting to double the value of the common stock in-

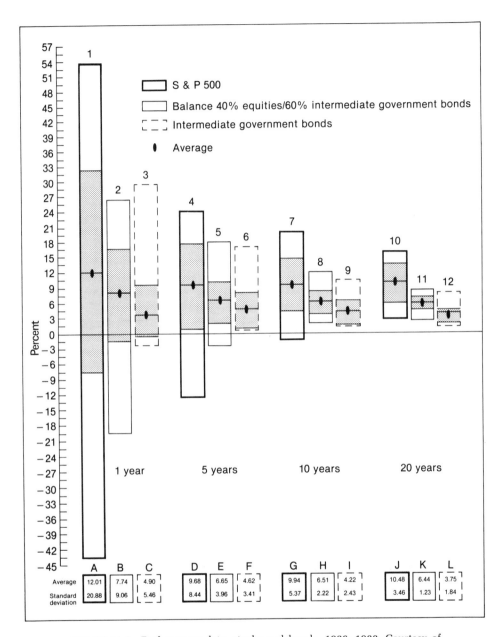

FIGURE 11-3 Performance data: stocks and bonds, 1926–1988. Courtesy of Ibbotson, Roger G., and Rex A. Sinquefield, *Stocks, Bonds, Bills, and Inflation* (SBBI), 1982, updated in *Stocks, Bonds, Bills, and Inflation 1989 Yearbook™*, 1989, Ibbotson Associates, Inc., Chicago. All rights reserved.

vestment portfolio every two years could also suffer a massive loss of principal. Second, the longer an investor's time horizon, the smaller the risk of losing the principal; however, it also reduces the potential for higher return. For instance, a five-year (Bar 4) time horizon reduces the potential for an annual loss to 13 percent but it also reduces the potential for gain to 24 percent. Third, the average long-term annual return on common stock on a one-year basis is around 12 percent (Box A). This means that, following the Rule of 72, an investment earning a 12 percent annual return can be expected to double every six years ($72/12 = 6$).

Prioritizing of Goals

It is important for financial planners to learn about the priorities their clients place on various investment goals. A convenient worksheet is presented in Table 11-2 which can be used to gather this information. It should be pointed out that this worksheet not only reveals how strongly investors feel about various investment goals but also helps them identify some of the goals which may otherwise be missed when articulating their investment objectives. Also, a rating of 1 or 2 selected for a specific goal would clearly suggest that the investor does not consider that goal to be of any significance.

Summing Up

The success of an investment planning process largely depends upon the ability of financial planners to help their clients clearly define their investment planning goals. Some investors can state their investment goals in broad terms, such as diversification of investments, achievement of a reasonable mix of liquid and nonliquid investments, and striking a reasonable balance between investment risk and return. In contrast, other investors may wish to achieve a specific investment goal like a net, after-tax real rate of return of four percent.

TABLE 11-2   Prioritizing Investment Goals

	Weak				*Strong*
Diversification	1	2	3	4	5
Liquidity	1	2	3	4	5
Safety of principal	1	2	3	4	5
Capital appreciation	1	2	3	4	5
Current income	1	2	3	4	5
Inflation protection	1	2	3	4	5
Future income	1	2	3	4	5
Tax reduction/deferral	1	2	3	4	5
Ease of management	1	2	3	4	5

While both are acceptable forms of stated goals, a written set of clearly specified goals helps the planner appreciate more fully the client's risk and investing preferences, fears, and level of sophistication.

RISK TOLERANCE LEVEL

Risk Versus Return

In Chapter 10 it was explained that the risk associated with an investment refers to the probability of loss of invested capital, future returns, and purchasing power of this investment. It was also pointed out that, as a general rule, risk and return are positively related. That is, investments offering higher returns generally carry higher risks.

Translating the concept of the positive risk-return relationship into the selection of various investment products, we can observe two important facts. First, debt securities generally carry lower risks and offer lower returns, whereas equity type securities offer higher returns but also carry higher risks. Second, as the investor climbs the risk-return pyramid (see Figure 10-1), both risk and return increase; the reverse is true when a move is made in the opposite direction.

It is necessary to reiterate that fixed income securities suffer a loss during inflationary periods when interest rates rise; however, they also offer a greater assurance of return of the principal upon maturity. In contrast, equity type investments offer a much greater potential for growth but have an increasing risk of losing the principal. Finally, the highly risky investments, such as tax shelters, commodities, and hard assets, have the best potential for highest returns over time. However, they are illiquid and carry the maximum risk of losing the principal; in addition, some investments may also carry additional risks of the eventual loss of some of the tax benefits originally enjoyed by the investor if phantom income is received or the IRS denies some of the previously realized tax benefits.

Risk Tolerance Level

The determination of an investor's risk tolerance level is not a precise technique. Although in certain instances measuring risk tolerance *can* be objective, generally it is a *subjective* measure of the emotional and financial ability of an investor to withstand investment losses. Even more important, over time the risk tolerance level may rise with an increase in net worth, income, investment knowledge, and sophistication, and may decline as the client approaches retirement. Nevertheless, it is essential for financial planners to make a concerted effort to determine this level for every client.

We mentioned earlier that the risk tolerance level is not a precise measure and hence is difficult to express as a specific number. Consequently, as a practical matter, investors can be classified as high, medium, low, and zero risk takers. The most effective way of making this determination is to give the investor a series of well-designed tests. A *sample* test presented in the box entitled "Do You Take Risks?" is designed to determine the investor's risk tolerance level. Another questionnaire, presented in the boxed material on page 399, helps record an investor's general attitude toward risk.

DO YOU TAKE RISKS? A QUIZ

1. An investment loses 15% of its value in a market correction a month after you buy it. Assuming none of the fundamentals have changed, do you:
   (a) Sit tight and wait for it to journey back up?
   (b) Sell it and rid yourself of further sleepless nights if it continues to decline?
   (c) Buy more—if it looked good at the original price, it looks even better now?

2. A month after you purchase it, the value of your investment suddenly skyrockets by 40%. Assuming you can't find any further information, what do you do?
   (a) Sell it.
   (b) Hold it on the expectation of further gain.
   (c) Buy more—it will probably go higher.

3. Which would you have rather done:
   (a) Invested in an aggressive-growth fund that appreciated very little in six months.
   (b) Invested in a money-market fund only to see the aggressive-growth fund you were thinking about double in value in six months.

4. Would you feel better if:
   (a) You doubled your money in an equity investment.
   (b) Your money-market fund investment saved you from losing half your money in a market slide.

5. Which would make you happiest?
   (a) You win $100,000 in a publisher's contest.
   (b) You inherit $100,000 from a rich relative.

   (c) You earn $100,000 by risking $2,000 in the options market.
   (d) Any of the above—you're happy with the $100,000, no matter how it ended up in your wallet.

6. The apartment building where you live is being converted to condominiums. You can either buy your unit for $80,000 or sell the option for $20,000. The market value of the condo is $120,000. You know that if you buy the condo it might take six months to sell, the monthly carrying cost is $1,200, and you'd have to borrow the down payment for a mortgage. You don't want to live in the building. What do you do?
   (a) Take the $20,000.
   (b) Buy the unit and then sell it.

7. You inherit your uncle's $100,000 house, free of any mortgage. Although the house is in a fashionable neighborhood and can be expected to appreciate at a rate faster than inflation, it has deteriorated badly. It would net $1,000 monthly if rented as is, or $1,500 per month if renovated. The renovations could be financed by a mortgage on the property. You would:
   (a) Sell the house.
   (b) Rent it as is.
   (c) Make the necessary renovations, and then rent it.

8. You work for a small but thriving privately held electronics company. The company is raising money by selling stock to its employees. Management plans to take the company public, but not for four or more years. If you buy stock, you will not be allowed to sell until shares are traded publicly. In the meantime, the stock will pay no divi-

dends. But when the company goes public, the shares could trade for ten to 20 times what you paid. How much of an investment would you make?
(a) None at all.
(b) One month's salary.
(c) Three months' salary.
(d) Six months' salary.

9. Your long-time neighbor, an experienced petroleum geologist, is assembling a group of investors (of which he is one) to fund an exploratory oil well, which could pay back 50 to 100 times its investment. If the well is dry, the entire investment is worthless. Your friend estimates the chances of success at only 20%. What would you invest?
(a) Nothing at all.
(b) One month's salary.
(c) Three months' salary.
(d) Six months' salary.

10. You learn that several commercial-building developers are seriously looking at undeveloped land in a certain location. You are offered an option to buy a choice parcel of that land. The cost is about two months' salary and you calculate the gain to be ten months' salary. Do you:
(a) Purchase the option.
(b) Let it slide—it's not for you.

11. You are on a TV game show and can choose one of the following. Which would you take?
(a) $1,000 in cash.
(b) A 50% chance at $4,000.
(c) A 20% chance at $10,000.
(d) A 5% chance at $100,000.

12. It's 1989, and inflation is returning. Hard assets such as precious metals, collectibles and real estate are expected to keep pace with inflation. Your assets are now all in long-term bonds. What would you do?
(a) Hold the bonds.
(b) Sell the bonds, put half the proceeds into money funds and the other half into hard assets.
(c) Sell the bonds and put the total proceeds into hard assets.

Source: Donoghue's *Moneyletter*—P.O. Box 6640 Holliston, MA, 01746. For a free sample call 1-800-343-5413.

(d) Sell the bonds, put all the money into hard assets and borrow additional money to buy more.

13. You've lost $500 at the blackjack table in Atlantic City. How much more are you prepared to lose to win the $500 back?
(a) Nothing. You quit now.
(b) $100.
(c) $250.
(d) $500.
(e) More than $500.

SCORING

Total your score, using the point system listed below for each answer you gave.

1. (a) 3 (b) 1 (c) 4
2. (a) 1 (b) 3 (c) 4
3. (a) 1 (b) 3
4. (a) 2 (b) 1
5. (a) 2 (b) 1 (c) 4 (d) 1
6. (a) 1 (b) 2
7. (a) 1 (b) 2 (c) 3
8. (a) 1 (b) 2 (c) 4 (d) 6
9. (a) 1 (b) 3 (c) 6 (d) 9
10. (a) 3 (b) 1
11. (a) 1 (b) 3 (c) 5 (d) 9
12. (a) 1 (b) 2 (c) 3 (d) 4
13. (a) 1 (b) 2 (c) 4 (d) 6 (e) 8

Below 21: You are a conservative investor who's allergic to risk. Stick with the sober, conservative investments until you develop the confidence or desire to take on more risk.

21–35: You are an active investor who's willing to take calculated, prudent risks to achieve greater financial gain. Your investment universe is more diverse.

36 and over: You're a venturesome, assertive investor. The choices that are available to you promise dynamic opportunities. Remember, though, the search for more return carries an extra measure of risk.

Summing Up

We have barely scratched the surface regarding the task of developing an investor's risk profile. Clearly, additional issues, such as the state of the investor's financial life, degree of affluence, and a host of other factors need to be analyzed before an accurate risk profile can be compiled. Because of space constraints, however, we present in the box entitled "Strategic Investment Planning" a simple worksheet which can assist a financial planner in developing a functional risk profile for the investor.

MEASURING ATTITUDE TOWARD RISK

For each statement, choose the answer that most resembles your attitudes toward investing over the next five years. Remember: There are no right or wrong answers.

	True	False	Not Applicable
1. I cannot afford any loss of principal regardless of potential return.	____	____	____
2. I cannot afford any significant loss of principal but I want the best return I can get.	____	____	____
3. Since I can get high yields from bonds, I don't wish to suffer through market ups and downs.	____	____	____
4. I want both the investment income for current needs and the potential for growth.	____	____	____
5. I want both the compounding of investment income and the potential for gain from stocks.	____	____	____
6. Although over the long haul stocks earn better return than other types of securities, I will forgo some future gains in order to earn a steady stream of income.	____	____	____
7. Higher-risk investments earn higher returns and I must earn higher returns at any cost.	____	____	____
8. I like my portfolio to show superior results and I believe I need a professional to help me achieve my goal.	____	____	____
9. I like to *play* the stock market and long-term investment is not for me.	____	____	____
10. There is no way to successfully compete with big investors, so I should concentrate on safe, guaranteed investment products.	____	____	____

INVESTOR PREFERENCE

Investor preference refers to an investor's predisposition toward or away from specific investment products. As a result of past experiences, as well as previous training, most investors form opinions about various investments. It is therefore critical for the financial planner to learn not only about such opinions but also about the depth of these feelings. A simple questionnaire, presented in the box entitled "Attitudes Toward Investment Products," (p. 404) is designed to help the planner determine an investor's predisposition toward specific investments.

THE INVESTMENT PORTFOLIO

The objective of constructing a *target investment portfolio* (TIP) is to bring about a synthesis between the various competing investment objectives just discussed. This goal is achieved by including the right combination of investments in the portfolio. In Chapter 10 we presented the basic investment alternatives. We will now discuss the place of these investments in the TIP.

Cash Reserves and Emergency Funds

The starting point of constructing every investment portfolio is to determine the percentage allocation for cash reserves and emergency funds. Every investor should recognize that in a family's financial life there will occur unforeseen contingencies which must be successfully met if catastrophic consequences are to be avoided. In addition, cash reserves provide liquidity to the portfolio which allows the investor to respond to occasional changes in lifestyle and capitalize on emerging investment opportunities. The primary considerations in selecting these assets are safety and liquidity with a clear understanding that the trade-off is a low return. Investments listed in Table 11-3 under "Cash Reserves and Emergency Funds" fall in this category.

Income Flow

An important consideration of an investment portfolio especially appropriate for—but not limited to—the preservation stage is the amount of income which it can generate to help maintain the desired lifestyle. Income-oriented investments generally emphasize current income but may sacrifice growth of the principal. Most, though not all, fixed income investments have a fixed maturity date when the principal can be expected to be returned to the investor. These investments appreciate in value during periods of falling interest rates and tend to lose their value during periods of rising interest rates.

Let us add an important caveat here. Bonds are usually thought of as the primary vehicle for generating current income. That view is too parochial. There are a number of other reliable investments that are attractive as income generators. These include utility stocks, high-yield stocks, mortgage-backed securities, fixed annuities, master limited partnerships, and real estate in-

---

STRATEGIC INVESTMENT PLANNING WORKSHEET

A. TIME HORIZON

In order for historic rates of return and risk measurements to be a meaningful basis for investment planning, the investment time horizon ought to be at least five years. For most individuals and qualified plans this will be the case. While the plan will be reviewed and possibly revised on a regular basis, allocations should be based on long-term expectations.

1. Is your time horizon in fact five years or more? Yes_____ No_____

2. Do you foresee any specific need to withdraw principal during that time? Yes_____ No_____
   If so, what amount? $_____

3. What is a comfortable emergency reserve to meet unanticipated needs? $_____

B. RATE OF RETURN OBJECTIVES

Prior to considering rate of return, it is necessary to define the total amount of funds to be invested. Liquid investable assets refers to those assets which are earmarked for long-term investment in financial instruments (stocks, bonds, Treasury bills, and so on). For individuals, this means liquid net worth, less emergency cash reserve. Do not include illiquid funds targeted for real estate, metals, and other tangible assets. For qualified plans, liquid investable assets refers to total plan assets less any required reserve.

$_____ − $_____

Liquid net worth   Cash reserve

= $_____
Total liquid investable assets

Following are three different ways to quantify return objectives (I–III). If only one is meaningful, fill out only the applicable section. If more than one, please prioritize. While hopefully a plan can be presented to meet all parameters, it may be necessary to make tradeoffs, and thus to know which set of objectives is most important to you.

I. Absolute Returns:

1. To what dollar amount would you like to see your assets grow in 5 years? $_____ in 10 years? $_____

2. Alternatively, what compound annual rate of return would you like to achieve on your entire investment portfolio? _____%

3. Do you look for these assets to provide you an income at some point in the future?
   Yes_____ No_____
   If so, what amount (in today's dollars)?
   $_____ When_____?
   Some facts to help you answer the above:

Rates of return on the various asset classes have been as follows:

Equities	Historic (1920–1987)	11.8%	Current	?
Bonds		5.2%		8–9%
Cash Equivalents		3.6%		6–7%

$10,000 will grow to the following amounts at various rates of return:

	5 yrs.	10 yrs.
6% (approximate bond history)	$13,382	$17,908
8% (approximate current bond rate)	$14,693	$21,589
12% (approximate equity history)	$17,623	$31,058

II. Inflation Adjusted (Real Returns):

Would you prefer to confine the analysis to dollar returns or are goals more meaningful to you when restated to reflect purchasing power?

Dollar returns _____ Purchasing power _____ (If dollar returns, proceed to section III).

(a) In today's dollars, to what amount would you like to see your assets grow in 5 years?
$_____ in 10 years ? $_____

(b) What real rate of return (after inflation) would you like to realize over the long term?
_____%

III. Relative Return:

Most people like to set standards by which to measure the long-term performance of their equity managers. Which standard is most relevant to you?

_____ Outperform S&P 500.
_____ Outperform S&P 500
by _____%.

Source: Adapted from questionnaire developed by Investment Advisory Services (IAS), a division of Raymond James & Associates, Inc., St. Petersburg, Florida.

C. RISK

Most individuals and fiduciaries have a strong concern for "safety" or "preservation of capital." Yet most investments carry some risk of fluctuation in principal value. In fact it is *because* one assumes this risk that higher returns are expected. Risk can be quantified by the response to the following two questions concerning the overall portfolio.

1. Is a risk of loss once every three years tolerable to you? One in 10? 20? Never? Indicate one of the following:

_____ one out of _____ years
_____ never

2. Is a risk of extreme loss (greater than 15%) tolerable to you once every 10 years? 20? Never? Indicate one of the following:

_____ one out of _____ years
_____ never

To aid you in answering the above questions, the long-term rate of equity return mentioned earlier (11.8%) was achieved with approximately three loss years every ten. Moreover, extreme losses were suffered about one out of every 11 years while producing this return.

IAS utilizes the answers to this questionnaire to help clients allocate their assets in concert with their individual time horizon and risk tolerance.

TABLE 11-3 Investment Vehicles and Their Objectives

Objective	Type	Investment vehicles
Cash Reserves and Emergency Funds	Cash Reserve	Cash Money Market Funds Savings and Loan Accounts Checking Accounts Short-term CDs Cash Value of Life Insurance Treasury Bills
Income Flow	Fixed Income	Corporate Bonds Government (Treasury) Bonds Municipal Bonds GNMA Bond Mutual Funds Fixed Annuities Convertible Bonds Real Estate Investment Trusts Utility Stocks Master Limited Partnerships
Growth	Equity	Common Stocks Variable Annuities Stock Mutual Funds Real Estate (Managed) Programs Option Income Programs Oil & Gas Income Funds
Long-term Growth and Tax Advantages	Real Estate Tax Shelters Hard Assets Miscellaneous	Real Estate Oil & Gas Drilling Programs Equipment Leasing Programs Hard Assets (Gold, Coins, Art) Commodities Series EE and HH Bonds

vestment trusts. Each has distinct investment characteristics and provides a valuable tool for income planning. A list of investments satisfying the income flow objective is listed in Table 11-3.

Growth

Most equity investments offer a potential for appreciation in value but generate relatively limited amounts of cash flow. These investments are subject to market as well as industry- and company-related risks, and can result in losses if the investor is compelled to sell them under adverse market conditions. Investments listed in Table 11-3 under the category "Growth" are examples of products which can satisfy the growth objective of an investor.

ATTITUDES TOWARD INVESTMENT PRODUCTS

Please indicate the level of comfort with   following criteria:
each of the following investments using the

1	2	3	4	5	6	7
Can't sleep at night	Jittery	No feeling either way	Comfortable	Extremely comfortable	Don't know	Don't care

_____ Savings account   _____ Treasury bills
_____ Commodities futures   _____ Real estate ltd. partnership
_____ Antique paintings   _____ AAA corporate bonds
_____ Cattle ltd. partnership   _____ Blue chip common stocks
_____ Equipment leasing   _____ Utility stocks
_____ Private placement: real estate   _____ Money market acct (uninsured)
_____ Silver coins   _____ Municipal bond funds
_____ Zero coupon bonds   _____ High yield mutual funds
_____ Growth mutual funds   _____ U.S. stamps
_____ Gold coins   _____ Chinese ceramics
_____ Diamonds   _____ High grade bond funds
_____ Universal life ins.   _____ Speculative stocks
_____ Prime farmland   _____ International mutual funds
_____ High yield bond funds   _____ Aggressive stock funds
_____ Government bond funds   _____ Oil & gas ltd. partnerships
_____ High quality stock funds   _____ Single prem. deferred annuity
_____ Single prem. whole life   _____ Brokered CDs
_____ GNMA   _____ Single prem. immediate annuity

Long-Term Growth and Tax Advantages

The objectives of long-term growth and tax savings are achieved through investments in a variety of vehicles listed in Table 11-3. The main categories of these investments are discussed next.

Real estate investments. An important component of an investment portfolio is investments in real estate. There are various ways in which an investor can participate in real estate. These include real estate partnerships, real estate investment trusts, investment in apartment complexes and shopping centers, and investment in undeveloped lands. Each has a different degree of risk associated with it and great care should be exercised in making sure that the risk of a real estate investment is consistent with the risk tolerance level of the investor.

In general, real estate investments perform well during periods of economic growth and moderate inflation. However, history suggests that high interest rates are generally disastrous for real estate investments and real estate markets could be depressed for long periods. It is also important to recognize that real estate investments are illiquid and can rarely be converted into liquid funds in an emergency.

Tax-sheltered investments. As a general rule, tax-sheltered investments generate cash flows which are sheltered from income taxes. This is accomplished by deducting depreciation, loan interest, and other deductible expenses against cash flow.

Although a number of tax shelters are still available on the marketplace, their number has greatly reduced following the passage of the Tax Reform Act of 1986. The reason is that this Act eliminated the benefits of many tax shelters and severely reduced the tax benefits of others by requiring that the tax losses (called passive losses) be used to reduce only income from these limited partnerships (called passive income). Consequently, only those tax shelters which are economically sound and offer attractive economic returns are worthy of consideration.

Hard assets. Generally, investments in gold, silver, rare coins, stamps, and precious metals, which are popularly known as hard assets, become attractive during periods of actual or anticipated high inflation and are therefore called inflation hedges. Ostensibly, investments in hard assets are good only for those risk takers who can afford large losses and are not affected by their total illiquidity.

TABLE 11-4 Ron and Sarah Brown, Investment Portfolio, May 1, 1990

Type (1)	Current amount (2)	Distribution (3)	Target distribution (4)	Recommended action (5)
Cash reserve	$ 2,500	1%	10%	+ $15,750
Fixed income	10,000	6	33	+ 50,225
Equity	110,000	60	33	− 49,775
Real estate	25,000	14	16	+ 4,200
Tax shelters	30,000	16	5	− 20,875
Hard assets	5,000	3	3	+ 475
Miscellaneous	0	0	0	0
Total	$182,500	100%	100%	$ 0

Miscellaneous investments. There are other investment products, such as commodities, exploratory oil and gas programs, and race horses, which have not yet been discussed. The list of these investments is long. It is, however, sufficient to say that these exotic investments are inappropriate for all but a chosen few who are highly sophisticated, affluent, and resourceful.

Target Investment Portfolio

Now that we have reviewed the investment alternatives available for portfolio construction, it might be interesting to review the target investment portfolio of a hypothetical family.

Let us analyze the current investment portfolio of the Brown family. The family consists of Ron, age 38, Sarah, 35, John, 10, and Susan, 7. The family's gross annual income is $85,000. The Brown family's investment portfolio is presented in Table 11-4 (Columns 1 and 2). The portfolio reveals that the Browns: (1) favor equity investments over fixed income investments (60 percent versus six percent); (2) have a low level of cash reserves (one percent); and (3) have invested disproportionately high percentages in real estate (14 percent) and tax shelters (16 percent). However, construction of a target investment portfolio by using the portfolio repositioning technique requires a great deal more *analysis* than just a superficial review of the current portfolio, as we shall now observe.

PORTFOLIO REORGANIZATION

The Basic Steps

An in-depth analysis of the technique of portfolio reorganization and the development of appropriate recommendations for a hypothetical client will be undertaken in the final part of this chapter. At this stage it would suffice to make some basic remarks about this technique.

Conceptually, an existing portfolio is reorganized and a TIP developed on the basis of the completion of the following four steps:

Step 1. Application of the seven-step asset allocation model presented in Chapter 10 and development of a percentage distribution of various investment types.

Step 2. Determination of the client's investment goals by taking into account the client's life cycle, investment needs, time frame, and tax considerations.

Step 3. Calculation of the client's risk tolerance level.

Step 4. Articulation of the client's special needs, if any, which must be taken into consideration in developing the TIP.

The Strategy

After we complete the four steps just listed we can start applying the portfolio reorganization strategy to Ron and Sarah Brown's portfolio. To make the discussion meaningful, let us assume we have determined that the Browns: (1) are basically risk averse; (2) must generate additional current income in order to maintain the standard of living with which they are most comfortable; and (3) realize that they should build up their cash reserve. On the basis of these considerations, and taking into account the desired percentage distribution of assets generated by the asset allocation model, a *target distribution* of investments is generated and presented in Table 11-4 (Column 4). We notice that recommended actions (Column 5) include: (1) building up the cash reserve by adding $15,750 to this category; (2) investing an additional $50,225 in fixed income securities to generate additional current income to meet their income needs; and (3) purchasing additional real estate ($4,200) and hard assets ($475). Funds for these investments are to be generated by liquidating $49,775 worth of equities and $20,875 currently invested in tax shelters.

At this point it is appropriate to add an important caveat. The target distribution developed in the previous section represents the *conceptual* TIP for the Browns based on the asset allocation model, their risk tolerance level, current income needs, and desire for growth. However, this TIP may not be achievable for a number of compelling reasons. For instance, because of their illiquidity, it may be impossible for the Browns to reduce their investment in tax shelters. Similarly, because of weak conditions which might be prevailing in the stock market, at this time it might be undesirable to reduce the equity investment as recommended. Other reasons for deviating from the TIP include: (1) investment recommendations conflicting with other financial goals; (2) unavailability of recommended investments; and (3) unfavorable tax consequences of investment recommendations.

Notwithstanding the difficulties associated with implementing all the TIP recommendations, at least in the short run, the financial planner has the responsibility for selecting specific investment products so the client may invest in them by way of reorganizing the portfolio. A financial planner, who is also a Registered Investment Advisor and feels qualified to do so, may perform this function. Alternatively, the responsibility for selecting specific products may be shifted to other investment professionals or advisors. Regardless of the strategy used, the financial planner must bear the responsibility for making sure that: (1) appropriate due diligence on each product is performed; (2) the recommended products fit the investor's portfolio; and (3) the client fully understands and accepts the advantages and drawbacks of each recommended product before investing in it.

INVESTMENT PLANNING STRATEGIES

INTRODUCTION

In the previous section we undertook a detailed discussion of the investment planning process. We learned that this process consists of a five-step operation, beginning with the identification of client goals and ending with the construction of a target investment portfolio by reorganizing the current investment portfolio. In this discussion no mention was made of various investment strategies which a financial planner can use when constructing or reorganizing an investment portfolio. In this section we will analyze some of the key time-tested strategies available to the financial planner.

BUY-HOLD-SELL STRATEGIES

Buying a Stock

The key to successful stock market investment is the ability to size up a stock in order to determine whether or not it should be purchased. The time-tested strategy is to invest in an undervalued stock because, over time, the market price of a stock tends to gravitate toward its present value. Another way of stating this fact is to say that an investor should invest in a stock which is fundamentally strong and offers good value.

It may be of some value to summarize here the techniques of fundamental analysis which were discussed in detail in Chapter 10. The single most important variable in fundamental analysis is the projection of future earnings. With that in mind, the first order of business is to construct a comprehensive company profile. This profile would provide the basis for an analysis of the price/earnings ratio, the dividend rate, the yield, the expected price appreciation, the growth in future earnings, and, finally, the analysis of expected price appreciation. The company's position in the industry, the prevailing economic conditions, and the investor's risk tolerance level would help the investor determine the discount rate with which the future earnings should be discounted to determine the present value of the stock. The final step in this analytical process is to select the stock whose present value exceeds its current market price.

While the identification of a fundamentally strong stock is the basis for stock market investment, the timing issue is equally important. The market does not always spot an attractive stock and frequently undervalued stocks perform poorly in a given market. Investing in such a stock at that time might mean a longer than anticipated holding period and even a temporary loss in the market value of the holding. Consequently, an attempt should be made to invest in only those stocks which are not only undervalued but also exhibit technical strength. These securities are commonly referred to as stocks which are both *fundamentally* and *technically* strong.

Buying a Bond

As a general rule (with the exception of government bonds which are always presumed to be appropriately priced) it is advisable to purchase an undervalued bond. However, since bonds are long-term obligations to pay a fixed number of dollars at maturity, several special factors should be taken into account when purchasing a bond.

Bond yield. The critical variable in bond investment is its yield: Given a fixed coupon rate, the lower the price of a bond, the higher its yield. Although there are exceptions, generally when the stock market is up, the bond market weakens and vice versa. Consequently, the stock market bears careful watching when selecting a bond.

Two important caveats of bond yields deserve special mention. First, during periods of restrictive monetary policy, interest rates generally rise, thereby depressing bond prices and pushing up bond yields. Second, when short-term interest rates decline, investors start investing in long-term securities, which ultimately leads to a decline in the long-term rates as well. These factors should help a financial planner determine the right time for investing in bonds.

Bond ratings. The task of selecting an attractive bond is facilitated by the availability of bond ratings which are regularly published by Standard & Poor's and Moody's. The ratings range from AAA for the safest bonds to D for highly speculative bonds which may even be in default. The ratings of A or better are given to investment grade bonds, while speculative bonds are rated lower than BBB.

Current yield and yield to maturity. The *current yield* on a bond is the ratio of the current coupon payments to the current market price of that bond. For instance, if a $1,000 bond with a 20-year maturity and a coupon of eight percent is currently selling for $950, the current yield is 8.42 percent [($80/$950) × 100]. However, if the same bond is held until maturity, a different measure, known as *yield to maturity* (YTM) must be calculated. The YTM takes into account the capital gain or loss the investor would realize by holding the bond until maturity when the issuer returns to the bondholder the face value (and not the current price) of the bond. Naturally, if the maturity price of the bond exceeds the current market price, the YTM will exceed the current yield; the reverse will be true if the current price exceeds the maturity price. For instance, in the case of the preceding bond currently selling for $950, if held until maturity, the bondholder will receive the maturity price of $1,000 and the YTM will equal 8.53 percent.

Selling a Stock

The basic strategy.   The first law of successful stock investing is: Buy a stock which is both fundamentally and technically strong. The buying part may be relatively easy. Without a strict investment discipline, however, determining the right time to sell a stock might be extremely difficult. For one thing, when prices fall, it appears reasonable to postpone selling in hopes of a recovery. And when prices rise, greed can get in the way of taking profits. Notwithstanding the difficulties associated with the sale of a security, for good investment results, the task must be successfully performed. The reason is that, in the final analysis, in investing the potential gain is of little value unless it is actually realized. There are several key selling strategies which provide a financial planner with broad guidelines for selling a stock.

Theory of undervalued security.   A good test of the attractiveness of a security at a given time is whether or not it is still an undervalued security. That is, if a stock which was undervalued when it was first selected is still undervalued, then it makes sense to hold it until it becomes appropriately valued. If not, then it is a prime candidate for sale, regardless of how well it is performing at this time. This rule keeps emotions of greed out of the decision process.

Realization of goals.   After a stock has met the investor's goals, unless there are overriding considerations, it should be disposed of. For instance, suppose an investor purchases a stock at $25 because its book value is $40 and it generally sells at 85 percent of its book value. There is no law that says stocks have to sell at book value. But if the company is fundamentally sound, there is good reason to believe the stock will return to near its historic price/book value ratio of 85 percent. So, if the price approaches $34 (85 percent of the book value of $40), other things being equal, it would be appropriate to seriously consider selling the stock.

Change of conditions.   It is also appropriate to sell a stock if the reason for which the stock was purchased is no longer valid. Suppose an investor purchases the stock of a drug company which introduced a miracle drug on the market. If the product fizzles, it is best to face the new facts and sell the stock.

Spectacular success syndrome.   Quite often a spectacular price increase signals trouble for a stock. In 1985, Alfin quadrupled in a few months when a skin-care product was promoted as an anti-aging cream. Home Shopping Network stock experienced a similar success. Both stocks currently trade at mere fractions of their all-time highs.

Myth of break even strategy. One of the myths that never seems to die is that a depressed stock should be held until the current losses are recouped. In order to appreciate the fallacy of this line of thinking, one needs to only consider the following table:

Current loss	% Gain required to recoup the loss
10%	11%
15	18
20	25
30	43
40	67
50	100
75	300

Note that if a stock loses 75 percent of its value, which was the case in October 1987 for many stocks, then the stock must appreciate 300 percent merely to recoup the past losses. A far more sensible and practical strategy would be to decide at the time of purchase the loss point which is the maximum the investor is willing to bear. The stock should be sold when it hits the loss point.

In this context, a mention should be made of the use of *stop loss orders* which are designed to minimize an investor's exposure to loss. When a stock is purchased, or any time thereafter, the investor can instruct the broker to sell the stock if the price falls to a certain level, such as five or ten percent below the purchase price. This would generally protect the investor against an extended drop, although the broker cannot guarantee a sale at the specified price. In the event of panic selling, such as that which occurred on the infamous Black Monday in 1987, there might not be any buyers. To avoid such a contingency, the investor could also place a *stop limit order*, authorizing the broker to sell at a specified price.

Tax considerations. While as a general rule tax considerations should not be allowed to influence a decision to sell a stock, sometimes it is desirable to resort to tax selling at an opportune time. Basically, selling at a gain or a loss is a taxable event. Consequently, if a decision has been made to sell a security on fundamental grounds, selling it at a given time (for instance, before year-end) could produce favorable tax outcomes.

Selling a Bond

Like stock, a bond should be sold when it becomes appropriately valued or overvalued. However, since bonds are interest-sensitive securities, fluctuations in interest rates as well as predictions of future interest rates play a major role in determining the time of sale of fixed-income securities.

TABLE 11-5 Bond Swapping Techniques

	Buy/sell	Company	Maturity (years)	S&P rating	Coupon (%)	Price ($)	Yield to maturity (%)	Type of swap	Purpose of Swap
Example 1	Sell	ABC	10	A	9.0	1,000.00	9.00	Equivalent securities with different prices	Take advantage of short-term market imperfection
	Buy	XYZ	10	A	9.0	990.00	9.16		
Example 2	Sell	ABC	10	A	8.0	935.82	9.00	Different coupons	Earn additional interest income
	Buy	XYZ	10	A	12.0	1,192.53	9.00		
Example 3	Sell	ABC	10	AA	9.0	1,000.00	9.00	Different quality ratings	Increase return by assuming higher risk
	Buy	XYZ	10	BB	9.0	882.22	11.00		
Example 4	Sell	ABC	10	A	9.0	1,000.00	9.00	Different categories with contrasting tax features	Take advantage of a favorable tax situation
	Buy	XYZ	10	A	7.0 (tax-free)	1,000.00	7.00		

Note: In these examples transaction costs are ignored.
Source: Adapted from Sid Mittra and Chris Gassen, *Investment Analysis and Portfolio Management*, Harcourt Brace Jovanovich, Inc., 1981, p. 277.

In this context, it is appropriate to briefly discuss bond *swapping* techniques. Our discussion will demonstrate the nature of several swapping operations by means of simplified examples, given in Table 11-5. All transaction costs are ignored in these examples, and, for simplicity, the inherent risks associated with these cases are not thoroughly explored. In each of the four examples shown in this table, the investor switches from ABC to XYZ bond but the reason for the swap differs in each case. In Example 1, the ABC bondholder feels that ABC and XYZ are identical bonds, but notices that the market favors the XYZ over the ABC bond. This is evidenced by the fact that the XYZ bond offers a higher yield to maturity than that offered by ABC. The investor therefore swaps ABC for XYZ to capitalize on what she feels is the prevailing yield differential. In Example 2, the purpose of the switch is to earn additional current interest income (12 percent instead of 8 percent), although a higher price must be paid to purchase the XYZ bond. Presumably, in this case the investor predicts that the higher coupon payments can be invested at more attractive rates to make this swap worthwhile.

In Example 3, the investor is aggressive and switches to XYZ to improve his yield. He realizes, of course, that the rating of XYZ is much lower than that of ABC, but is willing to assume the extra risk for an additional yield of two percent (11 percent versus nine percent). Finally, in Example 4, the investor switches from ABC corporate bond yielding nine percent to the XYZ tax-exempt municipal bond which has a tax-free yield of seven percent. Apparently, this investor is in a sufficiently high income tax bracket—say 33 percent—so she finds the swap attractive.

LIMITING THE RISK

Weathering the market's ups and downs is a key concern for most investors, regardless of their risk tolerance level, age, tax bracket, or net worth. While the risk associated with stocks, bonds, and other investment vehicles cannot be completely eliminated, there are ways in which investors can reduce risk to manageable levels. Some of the better known techniques of weathering the market's fluctuations are discussed next.

Dollar Cost Averaging

Dollar cost averaging (DCA) is a systematic program of investing equal sums of money at regular intervals, regardless of the price of shares. Clearly, DCA cannot guarantee a profit or prevent a loss. However, it does reduce the effects of market fluctuations over the long term. The reason is that instead of timing the market, the individual invests the same amount of money whether the share price is high, low, or in between. Hence, the investor buys more shares when the price is low and fewer when it is high, thereby avoiding the common mistake of buying high and selling low.

The key advantage of DCA is that, in the long run, it has the effect of making the average share cost less than the average share price. Two illustrations, covering a weak market and a strong market, demonstrate this strategy. In each illustration, it is assumed that the investor has decided to invest $100 each month.

A DCA program during a period of declining market is presented in Table 11-6. After four months and a total investment of $400, the average price of this investment is $7.00 while the average cost is $6.23. This situation is the result of purchasing progressively larger number of shares for $100 as the market price consistently declines, assuming that the stock continues to be undervalued and fundamentally strong. In the second illustration presented in Table 11-7, the average cost of the investment is $12.61, but the average price is slightly higher ($13.00) than the average cost. This is the result of an appreciation in the stock price in a rising market.

A word of caution should be added here. While both illustrations demonstrate its power as an investment tool, DCA is not appropriate for short-term investments and, as mentioned, cannot guarantee a profit or prevent a loss. However, this technique does provide investors with the benefit of a disciplined investment program that eliminates the need for market timing and helps alleviate the effects of a fluctuating market.

Constant Ratio Plan

The *constant ratio plan* (CRP) is a variation of DCA in which the monthly contribution is equally divided between a stock fund and a money market fund. Subsequently, if an increase in the share price makes the equity portion worth considerably more than the value of the money fund, then part of the equity fund would be liquidated and the proceeds transferred into the money fund. The reverse action would be taken if equity prices drop, thereby making the money fund worth more than the equity fund.

A 55/45 ratio is generally applied to the CRP, although other ratios would work equally well. This means that whenever the value of either fund exceeds 55 percent of the total value of the portfolio, an automatic readjustment plan

TABLE 11-6 Dollar Cost Averaging in a Declining Market

Investment	Total invested	Market price	Shares bought	Total shares	Average price/ share	Average cost/ share
$100	$100	$10	10.0	10.0	$10.00	$10.00
100	200	8	12.5	22.5	9.00	8.89
100	300	6	16.7	39.2	8.00	7.65
100	400	4	25.0	64.2	7.00	6.23

TABLE 11-7   Dollar Cost Averaging in an Advancing Market

Investment	Total invested	Market price	Shares bought	Total shares	Average price/ share	Average cost/ share
$100	$100	$10	10.0	10.0	$10.00	$10.00
100	200	12	8.33	18.33	11.00	10.91
100	300	14	7.14	25.47	12.00	11.78
100	400	16	6.25	31.72	13.00	12.61

is put into motion to make the ratio equal (50 percent). For instance, if the value of the stock fund rises to 55 percent, the investor shifts cash from the partially liquidated equity fund into the money fund to make them of equal value. Likewise, if the equity fund drops to 45 percent of the portfolio, the investor quickly shifts funds from the money fund into the equity fund to make them of equal value.

Variable Installment Plan

A refined approach to investing in stocks is known as the *variable installment plan* (VIP), which begins with an equal investment in both stock and money funds, but shifts the emphasis on stock investment when the fund's share price declines. A simple rule is for the investor to direct the entire monthly contribution to the stock fund whenever its share price falls by a predetermined (for example, ten percent) percentage. Similarly, the investor would skip the monthly stock fund investment if its share price rises by ten percent and invest the entire monthly contribution into the money fund.

A more sophisticated VIP strategy requires the investor to keep track of the average cost of the stock fund shares, including those purchased with reinvestment dividend and capital gains distributions. When the fund's current share price is higher than the average cost, the investor invests less in the stock fund. Conversely, when the share price is lower, more is invested in the stock fund.

A simple rule, which can be devised to determine how much of a contribution should be made to the stock fund, is described here:

$$\text{Amount of Contribution} = \frac{\text{Average Cost of Shares}}{\text{Current Price}} \times \begin{array}{l}\text{Original}\\\text{Contribution}\end{array}$$

For example, suppose an investor started investing $1,000 a month in a stock fund when the share price was $10.00. If, after a month, the price jumps to $12.00, the contribution for the second month would be $833.00 [($10/$12) × $1,000]. The difference ($167) would be invested in the money market fund.

In passing, it should be mentioned that investors can use other, more sophisticated, variations of the VIP just described. One such variation is known as the *leveraged variable investment plan* (LVIP), which requires the calculation of a leverage factor to minimize the average cost of a stock fund. In fact, an imaginative and sophisticated investor can design a variety of complex plans to suit his or her investment objectives.

Strategy of Covered Calls

The market risk can also be reduced by the sale of covered call options. A call option gives the buyer the right to purchase a stock at the "strike" or set price within the call option period. The option is covered by the stock the investor owns at the time of the option sale. A covered call option reduces the investor's risk exposure, although it simultaneously reduces the potential for profit. An illustration should make this strategy clear.

Let us assume Susan Bohn owns 100 shares of Marvin stock, trading at $30 a share. Susan sells a contract giving the buyer the option to buy these shares for $30 within the next six months; in return she receives a premium of $3 per share, or a total of $300. If Marvin's price drops to, say, $28 a share in the next six months and the option is not exercised, Susan's investment drops to $2,800 (100 shares × $28). However, the loss is more than compensated by the $300 option price, so she winds up with a profit.

But what if the stock price rises to $35 and the option is exercised? In that case, Susan must surrender the stock at $30 a share. The result will be that she will end up with $3,300 ($3,000 from the stock sale plus $300 option price) instead of $3,500 which she would have received from the sale of the stock had she not sold the option. It is now easy to see why a covered call option reduces the risk exposure but also simultaneously reduces the potential for profit.

Call Option With Stock Sale

A reverse strategy is to lock in profits by selling an appreciated stock and simultaneously buying call options on the same stock. As mentioned, a call option gives the buyer the right to buy 100 shares of the stock at a certain price for a fixed time period.

This strategy works in the following manner. Suppose Bob Kirk owns 100 shares of Chrysler in which currently he has a $1,200 profit. Bob thinks the stock is overpriced and will eventually plunge. However, he notices that Chrysler is hot and thinks it might still make one or two upward moves before taking a nose dive. Consequently, Bob sells Chrysler at $40 thereby locking in the $1,200 profit and buys a six-month call option on the stock for $300. If the stock does rise, Bob will exercise the option and realize additional profit. If not, all Bob would lose would be the $300 option price but he would have locked in the $1,200 capital gain on that stock.

A REAL WORLD INVESTMENT PLAN

INTRODUCTION

In the previous sections we have presented the investment planning process and several key investment planning strategies. We are now in a position to apply these concepts to the analysis and reorganization of a real world investment portfolio.

By way of a case study, we will now present a comprehensive approach to the construction of a target investment portfolio. The client is Dr. John Klein, age 61, who has just engaged a financial planner named Ted Bower to analyze his current portfolio, recommend a portfolio reorganization plan, and help him construct the target investment portfolio. The plan presented next is directly addressed to him.

We would like to mention here that the recommendations contained in this plan are based on the financial planner Ted Bower's understanding of Dr. Klein's short- and long-term goals and aspirations. Consequently, it is entirely possible—in fact likely—that another financial planner, who views Dr. Klein's goals and priorities differently, would develop an investment plan with a different orientation. This fact should be borne in mind in reviewing this plan.

COMPREHENSIVE INVESTMENT PLAN FOR DR. AND MRS. JOHN KLEIN

Dr. and Mrs. Klein, several weeks ago you invited us to develop for you a comprehensive investment plan. Dr. Klein, during the initial interview we learned that you are a 61-year-old physician and still maintain an active practice. Your wife, Debby, is 59 and is a homemaker. Both of your children are well settled in life and you have no financial responsibilities toward them. You believe that in the past you have done a good job of managing your portfolio. However, now that you have decided to retire in two years, you are not sure how to reorganize your portfolio to make it consistent with your retirement goal.

GOAL SETTING

During our goals and objectives interview we discovered that after retirement your major objective will be to have sufficient income from your investments so you may maintain your current lifestyle. Once that is accomplished, you want to maintain a proper balance between safety, liquidity, and growth. Furthermore, you made the important point that you must thoroughly understand the pros and cons of investing in a specific product before actually investing

TABLE A   Monthly Retirement Budget

Dr. and Mrs. John Klein

Total income	
Money market fund	$105
Dividends and interest	200
Notes receivable	1,528
Monthly benefits from employer	1,600
Social Security benefits	650
	$4,083
Total expenses	
In current dollars	3,500
Monthly savings	$583

any money in it. We will keep these facts in mind when making our investment recommendations.

As a starter, let us determine your retirement income needs by reviewing your tentative retirement budget presented in Table A. Clearly, during retirement, you do not need additional investment income to supplement your other sources of income. We have taken this fact into account in developing your target investment portfolio.

RISK TOLERANCE LEVEL

A careful analysis of your risk tolerance questionnaires has clearly demonstrated that basically you are a risk averse person. However, we have also discovered that you did not recognize that risk has many faces and that in the past the loss of principal is only one of many risks you have assumed. For instance, you had honestly believed that there was no market risk associated with investing in a "safe" government bond mutual fund when in reality only the reverse was true. However, after an extensive discussion we had with you on the key stock and bond risks, and after studying a variety of published information we provided, we believe you have acquired a good working knowledge of what constitutes investment risk.

It is important to recognize here that even though you are basically a risk averse person, you do wish to assume *some* risk by investing a small portion of your funds in one or more relatively high-risk products. We will certainly take this fact into account in developing our recommendations.

CURRENT INVESTMENT PORTFOLIO

Your current investment portfolio is presented in Table B. The following points should be noted:

1. Funds placed in cash reserve (30 percent) and tax shelters (13 percent) appear to be disproportionately high.

TABLE B Investment Portfolio for Dr. and Mrs. John Klein, February 14, 1990

	Date	Cost	Interest	Qualified plan?	Market value	Group total	% to total
Cash reserve							
Bank account					$ 1,500		
Money market (1)			6.7%		160,584		
Money market (2)			7.3%	yes	40,328		
Money market (3)			7.1%		100,180	$302,592	30%
Fixed income							
CD (1)	11-28-86	$93,000	12.0%	yes	100,000		
CD (2)	4-8-85	2,000	13.0%	IRA	3,116		
CD (3)	4-8-85	2,000	13.0%	IRA	3,116		
XYZ bond (1)	2-13-87	1,800	11.0%	yes	2,011		
XYZ bond (2)	2-12-87	1,800	11.0%	yes	2,011		
Fixed note	6-26-86	25,000	10.0%	yes	25,000		
Hospital bond	1-9-88	10,000	8.0%		10,000		
Municipal trust	9-28-87	10,000	7.0%		10,000	$155,254	15%
Equity							
Mutual fund (1)	2-1-86	4,000		IRA	6,178		
Mutual fund (2)	4-15-87	12,000		IRA	17,401		
ABC bank stock	4-20-82	150,000			200,500		
Mutual fund (3)	7-10-85	5,000			6,404		
Mutual fund (4)	9-17-86	10,144			10,144		
Mutual fund (5)	10-10-86	3,000			4,584		
Mutual fund (6)	10-10-86	10,539			10,645		
Mutual fund (7)	2-9-87	7,000			7,286	$263,142	26%
Real estate							
Office building	1-1-80	40,000		yes	75,000		
Apartment	4-19-75	90,000			69,500	$144,500	15%
Tax shelters							
Cable TV*	3-17-74	25,000			25,000		
Equipment leasing*	9-18-76	35,000			35,000		
Cattle*	12-30-85	50,000			50,000		
Oil & gas drilling*	12-1-87	18,000			18,000	$128,000	13%
Hard assets							
Gold coins		10,000			5,000	$ 5,000	1%
Miscellaneous					0	0	0%
			Total			$998,488	100%

* Current market value cannot be determined; it is assumed that the market value equals the cost of this investment.

2. Given the fact that you are about to retire, the percentage of the portfolio allocated to fixed-income securities appears to be low.

3. The amount of $200,500 invested in ABC Bank stock, which constitutes 20 percent of your total portfolio, is disproportionately high, even if this bank stock offers an attractive investment.

TARGET INVESTMENT PORTFOLIO

We have made an extensive analysis of the asset allocation model, your risk tolerance level, and your need for current income and growth. On the basis of this analysis we have developed for you a target investment portfolio (TIP). However, before making a formal presentation of your TIP, let us specify the intermediate steps we completed as the basis for the construction of the TIP: (1) Initially we developed a *preliminary* TIP by applying our current asset allocation model. In developing this model we analyzed the current business cycle, prevailing financial market conditions, inflationary expectations, interest rate predictions, and other ancillary factors; (2) On the basis of the goals and objectives interview we conducted several weeks ago, we developed a realistic risk profile for you; (3) We analyzed your current financial situation and calculated the tax consequences of your capital gains or losses during the current year resulting from the sale of appropriate investment products; and (4) We carefully considered the financial ramifications of your expressed desire to retire in two years. On the basis of the conclusions we reached by analyzing these factors, we finalized your TIP, which is summarized in Table C. We would like to explain here the reasons for making these recommendations:

1. We believe that the liquid assets included in the "Cash Reserve" category should be reduced to $99,848 or ten percent of the portfolio. Of this amount, $60,000 should be reserved for the down payment you wish to make on the home you intend to build in West Palm Beach, Florida. The balance of approximately $40,000 (four percent) should be maintained to satisfy your current liquidity needs.

2. Our analysis has clearly indicated that you would prefer not to be exposed to day-to-day market fluctuations. You have also expressed a strong desire to move a large portion of your funds into relatively safe, tax-deferred, single premium deferred annuities (SPDA), which provide long-term (five year) interest rate guarantees. What you really like about this investment is that: (1) the income generated by it can be automatically reinvested until you need additional monthly income to supplement income from other sources; and (2) you will be offered a variety of attractive choices when you are ready to annuitize. We therefore recommend that an additional $343,990 be invested in the fixed income category, a significant portion of which will be represented by the SPDA investment.

TABLE C Target Investment Portfolio: A Summary, Dr. and Mrs. John Klein, May 1, 1990

Type (1)	Current amount (2)	Distribution (3)	Target distribution (4)	Target amount (5)	Recommended action (6)
Cash reserve	$302,592	30%	10%	$ 99,848	− $202,743
Fixed income	155,254	16	50*	499,244	+ 343,990
Equity	263,142	26	20	199,698	− 63,444
Real estate	144,500	14	15	149,773	+ 5,273
Tax shelters	128,000	13	2	19,970	− 108,030
Hard assets	5,000	1	3	29,955	+ 24,954
Miscellaneous	0	0	0	0	0
TOTAL	$998,488	100%	100%	$998,488	$0

* We have recommended that 50 percent of your portfolio be invested in fixed income securities to satisfy your explicitly stated needs for current income. However, you should realize that, over time, inflation will undoubtedly take its toll on this income.

3. Since you do wish to reduce market risk, and since it is inadvisable to invest $200,000 in one bank stock, we recommend that investment in this bank stock be reduced by $63,444 to $199,698, thereby lowering your equity investment to 20 percent. This recommendation is partly based on the fact that the ABC Bank stock is still grossly undervalued.

4. A risk averse investor like you should not invest $128,000 in various nonliquid, highly risky tax shelters. Therefore, assuming their salability and no adverse tax impact, we recommend that investment in these shelters be reduced by $108,030 to $19,970, which will represent two percent of your total portfolio.

5. You have convinced us that, because of your personal connections with a dealer both in terms of purchase and eventual disposal, you have the opportunity of making a sound investment in a gold coin collection. We therefore recommend that you increase your investment in hard assets from $5,000 to $24,954 by purchasing these coins, which will then constitute three percent of your total portfolio.

Before leaving this topic we would like to make an important point. The TIP we have presented here represents an *ideal* investment portfolio which could be constructed only if undesirable products could be instantly liquidated and desirable investment products could be purchased now at attractive prices. Unfortunately, that does not represent the real world in which we must operate. For instance, because of their illiquidity, it might be impossible for you to quickly liquidate your tax shelters even though we have recommended such an action. Similarly, you may wish to postpone making investments in SPDAs simply because the guaranteed interest rates currently offered on this product are predicted to rise in the near future. We believe we should emphasize these facts so you will not consider the delay in implementing our recommendations and reaching the TIP goal as noncompliance on your part.

THE TRIP TICK

Now that we have explained to you in detail the reasons behind our *generic* investment recommendations, we are ready to make *specific* investment recommendations. We will do so in the form of a trip tick, presented in Table D, so you will have an organized action plan to guide you through the investment product maze. In this connection we would like to reiterate that you should not invest in the new products we have recommended without first gaining a complete knowledge of the risks, costs, limitations, and return expectations associated with each of them. You should also note that if you literally follow the trip tick, you will only wind up with the realistic investment portfolio presented in Table E, which is different from the TIP we have recommended (Table C). The TIP presents our recommendations which could be carried out only under *ideal* conditions, whereas the realistic investment portfolio is based on the *realistic* environment within which you must operate. More specifically, you cannot implement all of our recommendations at this time because: (1) you cannot unload your tax shelters; (2) it is impractical to buy only $5,000

TABLE D Trip Tick for Dr. and Mrs. John Klein, May 1, 1990

Recommended action date	Action	Reason	Balance available in cash reserve category
2-14-90			$302,592
2-19-90	Sell $63,500 worth of ABC Bank stock.	Reduce concentration.	366,092
4-16-90	Purchase SPDA worth $200,000. Consider four companies for diversification.	Convert risky investment into relatively safe, 3–5 year interest rate guaranteed investment.	166,092
4-20-90	Purchase $66,000 worth of high grade corporate bonds with intermediate maturity.	Invest in income producing investment.	100,092

TABLE E   Realistic Investment Portfolio for Dr. and Mrs. John Klein, May 1, 1990

	Date	Cost	Interest	Qualified plan?	Market value	Group total	% to total
Cash reserve							
Bank account					$ 1,500		
Money market (2)			7.3%	yes	40,328		
Money market (3)			7.1%		58,264	$100,092	10%
Fixed income							
CD (1)	11-28-86	$93,000	12.0%	yes	100,000		
CD (2)	4-8-85	2,000	13.0%	IRA	3,116		
CD (3)	4-8-85	2,000	13.0%	IRA	3,116		
XYZ bond (1)	2-13-87	1,800	11.0%	yes	2,011		
XYZ bond (2)	2-12-87	1,800	11.0%	yes	2,011		
Fixed note	6-26-86	25,000	10.0%	yes	25,000		
Hospital bond	1-9-88	10,000	8.0%		10,000		
Municipal trust	9-28-87	10,000	7.0%		10,000		
SPDA (1) *Single-Premium*	4-16-90	50,000	9.3%		50,000		
SPDA (2) *deferred Annuity*	4-16-90	50,000	9.3%		50,000		
SPDA (3)	4-16-90	50,000	9.3%		50,000		
SPDA (4)	4-16-90	50,000	9.3%		50,000		
Corporate bonds	4-20-90	66,000	9.1%		66,000	$421,254	42%
Equity							
Mutual fund (1)	2-1-86	4,000		IRA	6,178		
Mutual fund (2)	4-15-87	12,000		IRA	17,401		
ABC bank stock	4-20-82	150,000			137,000		
Mutual fund (3)	7-10-85	5,000			6,404		
Mutual fund (4)	9-17-86	10,144			10,144		
Mutual fund (5)	10-10-86	3,000			4,584		
Mutual fund (6)	10-10-86	10,539			10,645		
Mutual fund (7)	2-9-87	7,000			7,286	$199,642	20%
Real estate							
Office building	1-1-80	40,000		yes	75,000		
Apartment	4-19-75	90,000			69,500	$144,500	15%
Tax shelters							
Cable TV	3-17-74	25,000			25,000		
Equipment leasing	9-18-76	35,000			35,000		
Cattle	12-30-85	50,000			50,000		
Oil & gas drilling	12-1-87	18,000			18,000	$128,000	13%
Hard assets							
Gold coins		10,000			5,000	$ 5,000	1%
Miscellaneous					0	0	0%
				Total		$998,488	100%

worth of real estate; and (3) you have a shortage of funds so you must postpone investment in hard assets. Despite these limitations, however, by following the trip tick (Table D) you will have the realistic investment portfolio which in our judgment will effectively meet most of the intermediate- and long-term investment goals articulated by you.

FINAL THOUGHTS

Dr. and Mrs. Klein, the TIP we have presented to you is quite comprehensive. This is borne out by the fact that in developing it we have taken the following investment planning principles into account, some of which may not be evident to you:

A. *A*fter-tax return: Maximize, subject to income needs and risk tolerance level.

B. *B*alanced approach: Maintain a balance between liquidity, current income, and growth.

C. *C*lient's risk: Match investment diversification with investor's risk tolerance level.

D. *D*iversify: Diversify: (i) in terms of investment vehicles, (ii) within a class or type of investment; and (iii) through different maturities and time horizons.

E. *E*liminate the tax of wealth: Use investment techniques to reduce or eliminate federal estate tax.

F. *G*rowth over time: Use the time-honored time value of money concept to maximize growth of investable funds.

In addition, we have taken great pains in ensuring that the TIP is attuned to your attitudes toward risk, stability, investment return, liquidity, and ease of management.

Dr. and Mrs. Klein, it is worth reemphasizing that since we do not live in a utopia, for reasons of practicality we had no choice but to deviate from the target plan. The trip tick we have developed for you is indeed a practical plan which can be implemented to maximize the benefits that can be derived from the realistic investment portfolio. We are ready to assist you in expeditiously completing the implementation process. In addition, we will constantly monitor your progress and hereby make a commitment to be of service to you for a long time.

CHAPTER 12

Basic Structure of Retirement Income

INTRODUCTION

Of all the many strategies which might be developed to meet different financial objectives, none are more difficult than those relating to financial independence and retirement planning. This is because, for most people, financial independence or retirement seems far away, and in these uncertain times planning for the distant future is virtually impossible. However, no matter how far away retirement age seems at the moment, we should prepare for the day *now*. There is nothing worse than discovering on the 65th birthday that, given the existing financial position, it is impossible to maintain a desired standard of living.

The argument for planning early for retirement is indeed compelling. By one count, out of 100 persons reaching retirement age today, only two are financially independent. In addition, over 20 percent of persons over 65 find it necessary to continue to work out of financial necessity. By another count, by the year 2010, a record 75 million Americans will be over 65, as compared to about 30 million today. Since the average life expectancy is now nearly 80

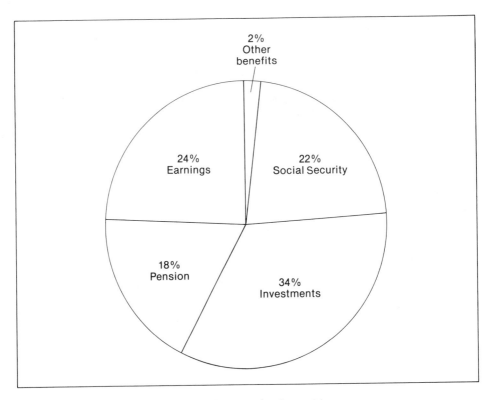

FIGURE 12-1   Sources of retirement income

and still on the rise, a person could need retirement income for 20 to 30 years. To further complicate matters, many young Americans want to become financially independent and retire before age 55 or 60.

While it may be difficult for a 30- or 40-year-old to visualize life in 25 or 30 years, financing the lifestyle this person hopes to lead will have a dramatic impact on the rate of accumulation of savings needed for retirement. For instance, if a 30-year-old earning $40,000 a year hopes to retire at age 65 with an annual income of $50,000 in today's dollars, assuming a four percent inflation-adjusted interest rate and a life expectancy of 85, at age 65 (year 2023) this youngster would need to amass savings of $2.68 million as shown next:

Step 1

$$PV = \$50,000$$

$$n = 35$$

$$i = 4$$

$$FV = \$197,304$$

Step 2

$$PMT = 197{,}304$$

$$n = 20$$

$$i = 4$$

$$PV = 2{,}681{,}425$$

$$= \$2.68 \text{ million}$$

The picture dims even further when we add to this scenario the fact that pensions and Social Security might not provide enough of a cushion for retirement. As revealed by Figure 12-1, Americans hoping to retire with an annual income of $20,000 or more should expect to receive on average no more than 40 percent of this retirement income from pension and Social Security. On the expenses side, a key concern is the health care cost during retirement which increased 81 percent from 1981 to 1986, nearly four times the general

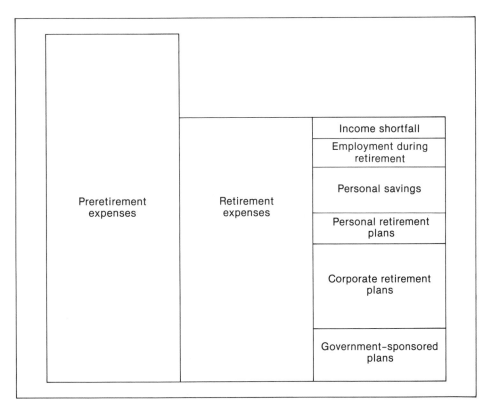

FIGURE 12-2   Planning for retirement

inflation rate over the same period. Today Medicare pays only part of the retiree's medical bills (see Chapter 4). Many of the costs of long-term care, such as that required for Alzheimer's disease and for nursing care, are not covered at all. When we put it alltogether, we begin to realize how important it is to develop and implement an effective retirement plan at the earliest possible opportunity.

Planning for retirement involves taking four major steps: (1) The pre-retirement expenses should be estimated; (2) On the basis of Step 1 monthly or annual retirement expenses needed to maintain the desired standard of living should be determined; (3) The total expected income from all sources, including government-sponsored plans (such as Social Security), corporate retirement plans, personal retirement plans (such as IRAs and Keoghs), personal

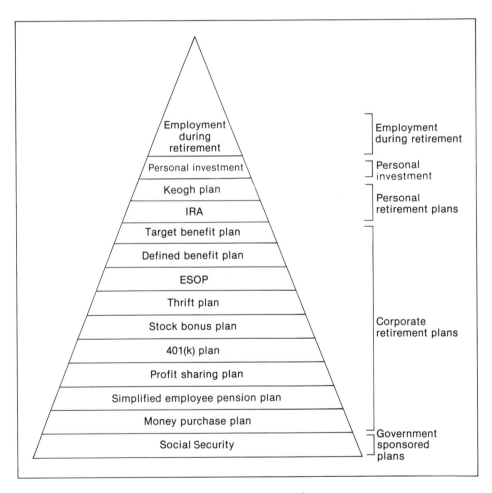

FIGURE 12-3 Retirement earnings tree

savings, and employment during retirement should be estimated; and (4) If the expected income falls short of the expected expenditure needs, appropriate steps should be taken *now* to alleviate the anticipated retirement income deficit problem. This concept of planning for retirement is clearly presented in Figure 12-2.

This chapter will be devoted to a discussion of the major sources of retirement income. The techniques of estimating capital needs during retirement, taxation of a distribution from qualified plans, and the key retirement planning techniques will be discussed in the next chapter.

The key sources of income available upon retirement can be conveniently classified into the following categories: (1) government sponsored plans; (2) corporate retirement plans; (3) personal retirement plans; (4) personal investment; and (5) employment during retirement. These sources are listed in Figure 12-3. Of these, personal investment strategies were fully discussed in Chapters 9–11 while employment during retirement needs no further consideration. Consequently, in the first, second, and third parts of this chapter we will analyze the first three sources of income just listed.

GOVERNMENT SPONSORED PLANS

SOCIAL SECURITY

General Remarks

Franklin Roosevelt's Social Security Act of 1935 was a historical landmark with a modest beginning. In 1940, the first year of the benefits, barely one person in six hundred received assistance, compared with one in six now. The maximum monthly payment in 1940 was $41. In 1989, it was around $899.

"The essence of Social Security insurance" said Winston Churchill, "is bringing the magic of averages to the rescue of millions." This statement brings to mind the long soup lines in which old people were forced to stand for hours to receive their handouts. Actually, Social Security is anything but a scheme to rescue millions of impoverished people. It includes old age retirement, survivors' benefits, disability insurance, and Medicare—all of which are administered by the federal government. In addition, Social Security includes state and local government administered programs, such as unemployment insurance and public welfare.

Even a casual review would show that the growth of Social Security over half a century has been phenomenal. However, such an overview conceals a basic fact. Data show that through 1949, no worker paid into the system more than $30 a year. The maximum Social Security tax in 1989 was $3,604—over 120 times the original tax. Furthermore, in 1989, a couple could get the maximum monthly benefit of only $1,348, not an attractive return on the thousands of dollars contributed over the working life of these people.

TABLE 12-1   Retirement Plans: Social Security

Title	Major responsibility for funding rests on	General characteristics	Where appropriate	Vesting rules
Social Security	Federal Government	Starting at the earliest age of 62, upon application, payments begin. Monthly income is based on several factors. No age restrictions apply for payments due to disability or death.	Every working person is entitled to Social Security benefits.	8¼ to 10 years of work.

An overview of Social Security is presented in Table 12-1. We will now present the key features of Social Security plans.

The Eligibility Issue

Commonly called OASDHI (Old Age, Survivors', Disability, and Health Insurance), the Social Security program is financed by payroll taxes. Social Security taxes are paid by both the employer and employee in equal amounts. In 1989 the tax rate was 7.51 percent each for the employee and the employer, and the maximum wage base on which the tax was imposed was $48,000.

Before a person or family becomes eligible to receive monthly cash benefits under Social Security, a minimum amount of work credit must be earned. Social Security credit is measured in "quarters of coverage." In 1989, employees and self-employed persons received one quarter of coverage for each $500 of annual earnings subject to Social Security taxes. The amount of earnings needed to receive a quarter of coverage will increase automatically in the future in order to keep pace with average wages.

No more than four quarters of coverage can be credited for one year. In 1989, 38 quarters of work credit were necessary to become eligible for Social Security. The minimum work credit quarters increase to 39 in 1990 and to 40 in 1991 or later. Incidentally, the work credit requirements for receiving disability benefits are considerably lower than those for normal Social Security benefits. For instance, if a person becomes disabled before age 24, only 1½ years of work out of the three-year period ending when the disability begins are required for receiving disability benefits. Persons meeting the minimum work credit requirements are called *fully insured* while those meeting the disability requirements are called *currently insured*. These work credit requirements and other related data are presented in Table 12-2.

TABLE 12-2 Length of Work Requirements for Social Security Benefits

Type of benefits	Payable to	Minimum years of work under Social Security
Retirement	You, your spouse, child, dependent spouse 62 or over	10 years (fully insured status) (If age 62 prior to 1991, you may need only $7\frac{3}{4}$ to $9\frac{3}{4}$ years.)
Survivors[a]		
Full	Widow(er) 60 or over Disabled widow(er) 50–59 Widow(er) if caring for child 18 years or younger Dependent children Dependent widow(er) 62 or over Disabled dependent widow(er) 50–61 Dependent parent at 62	10 years (fully insured status)
Current	Widow(er) caring for child 18 years or younger Dependent children	$1\frac{1}{2}$ years of last 3 years before death (currently insured status)
Disability	You and your dependents	If under age 24, you need $1\frac{1}{2}$ years of work in the 3 years prior to disablement. If between ages 24 and 31, you need to work half the time between when you turned 21 and your date of disablement. If age 31 or older, you must have 5 years of credit during the 10 years prior to disablement.
Medicare		
Hospitalization (Part A: automatic benefits)	Anyone 65 or over plus some others, such as the disabled	Anyone qualified for the Social Security retirement program is qualified for Medicare Part A at age 65. Others may qualify by paying a monthly premium for Part A.
Medical expense (Part B: voluntary benefits)	Anyone eligible for Part A and anyone else 65 or over. (Payment of monthly premiums required.)	No prior work under Social Security is required.

[a] A lump-sum death benefit no greater than $255 is also granted to dependents of those either fully or currently insured.

Source: U.S. Department of Health and Human Services, 1987.

Types of Benefits

Basically there are three types of benefits offered by Social Security: (1) The Old Age and Survivors Insurance Trust Fund provides monthly checks to retirees, their families, and to families of deceased workers; (2) The Disability Insurance Trust Fund pays benefits to disabled workers and their families; and (3) The Hospital Insurance Trust Fund pays Medicare claims.

Retirement benefits. Social Security offers pension benefits to workers who are fully or currently insured. If born prior to 1939, an insured worker can retire any time on or after the 65th birthday with full benefits. The monthly Social Security benefits in 1989 were $899 for an insured worker retiring at age 65. The normal retirement age is gradually being raised to 67 over a 27-year period.

The minimum—or early—retirement age is 62, regardless of the normal retirement age. The monthly benefits for an early retiree are anywhere between 70 to 80 percent of the maximum benefits. For instance, if the normal retirement age is 66, the worker will receive 75 percent of the full benefits if an early retirement is taken at age 62.

The law does not make it mandatory for anyone to retire at age 65. If a person continues to work past the normal retirement age, the Social Security Administration will raise the monthly benefits. The increase is three percent a year for each month of working past the normal retirement age. The increase is not available for work past age 70. Over the next ten years, the present three percent per year increment for each additional year of work past the normal retirement age will be increased to eight percent.

An increase in the monthly benefits for persons working beyond the normal age only tells one side of the story. On the other side, the law taxes the earned incomes retirees receive to supplement their benefits. This topic will be discussed in a subsequent section.

Benefits for spouse and children. Social Security benefits of a fully insured retiree are extended to spouse and children as well. If the insured worker applies for Social Security at age 65, the spouse receives 50 percent of the retiree's primary insurance amount (PIA). The PIA is reduced by $\frac{25}{36}$th of one percent for each month before age 65, or if a spouse applies for Social Security benefits before age 65. In addition, a child under age 18 (or under 19 if in high school), or a child of any age if disabled mentally or physically before age 22, is entitled to 50 percent of the insured's PIA.

In the case of death or divorce, a widow, widower, or surviving divorced spouse will receive 100 percent of PIA of the deceased or divorced spouse, if the benefits began at age 65. If the distribution of the benefits begins before age 65, a different formula is applied by Social Security Administration to determine the benefit amount.

Disability benefits. A *covered* individual who suffers from long-term disability can collect for life disability benefits of 100 percent of the PIA, regardless of age. An individual qualifies for disability benefits in any month if the individual: (1) would have been fully insured had he or she attained age 62 and filed an application for retirement benefits on the first day of the month; (2) has at least 20 quarters of coverage in the 40-quarter period ending with the quarter in which disability began (less stringent requirements if disability occurs between ages 24 and 31); (3) has a medically determinable physical or mental impairment that is expected to result in death or last for at least 12 months; and (4) has been disabled for at least six months.

Disability benefits offered by private insurance companies were discussed in Chapter 4 in detail. Disability benefits under Social Security are similar to private disability policies in some respects but are different in other respects. For instance, under Social Security rules, after becoming eligible for disability benefits, an individual or family can receive benefits for the duration of the disability, even if it lasts for life. In contrast, a private insurance policy issued to age 65 would automatically lapse upon the insured's attaining that age. Also, under Social Security the amount of the monthly family benefit paid on behalf of the disabled worker, say, under age 35, would range between 40 and 80 percent of the pre-disability monthly earnings. The private disability policy would pay only the monthly amount specified in the contract. Finally, all disability payments under Social Security are automatically adjusted periodically to reflect increases in the cost of living. In contrast, only those privately insured policies which have a COLA (cost of living adjustment) feature will offer to make a predetermined inflation adjustment in disability payments.

Medicare

Medicare is a two-part, government sponsored, health insurance program for persons over age 65 and certain disabled persons. The basic plan provides automatic coverage of hospital and nursing care expenses when a person becomes eligible. The other part of the program, the supplementary plan, is voluntary and covers only those individuals who make the required premium payments. Incidentally, the Medicare service is handled by the Health Care Financing Administration, not by the Social Security Administration.

The hospital insurance part of Medicare pays for the cost of inpatient hospital care and certain kinds of follow-up care. The medical insurance part of Medicare helps pay the costs of physicians' services, outpatient hospital services, and for certain other medical items and services not covered by hospital insurance. Premiums are paid by eligible individuals for appropriate coverage, whether or not they are currently receiving Social Security benefits.

Taxation of Social Security Benefits

Social Security benefits consisting of retirement, disability, and survivor payments are currently subject to federal taxes if the annual income from other sources exceeds $32,000 for married taxpayers filing jointly or $25,000 for a single taxpayer (zero for married taxpayers filing separately). For the purposes of Social Security taxes, the annual income comprises adjusted gross income, all municipal bond and other nontaxable interest income, and one-half of the Social Security benefits received. An example should make this clear.

Let us assume Mr. and Mrs. John and Betty Brown are both over 65 and have pension income from their respective employers. In 1989, the Browns had $26,000 in fully taxable pension income, $5,000 in taxable dividends and interest, and $2,000 in tax-free municipal bond interest. They also received $10,000 in Social Security benefits. The mechanics of Social Security tax on the Browns are presented in Table 12-3. The table reveals that the Browns' Social Security benefit subject to tax is $3,000, since that figure is less than $5,000 (one half of Social Security benefits). Also, since the total taxable income for the Browns puts them in the 28 percent tax bracket, their Social Security tax liability works out to $840 (.28 × $3,000).

It should be mentioned here that beginning in 1990, those under age 70 will lose $1 in Social Security benefits for every $3 in earnings above the annual limit. However, there are no earnings limits for retirees age 70 and over.

Social Security Income Estimate

The success of retirement planning depends partly upon an accurate estimate of Social Security income to be received upon retirement. In addition, knowing where one stands with Social Security is essential for analyzing life insurance and disability insurance coverage.

Fortunately, the Social Security Administration promptly mails a personalized accounting of Social Security payments and expected income. All the

TABLE 12-3 Social Security Tax for the Brown Family

The test		The tax	
Pension	$26,000	Add to taxable income the lesser of:	
Taxable dividend and interest	5,000	½ S.S. Benefit	$5,000
Tax-free interest	2,000	"Test" Result	$3,000
½ S.S. benefit	5,000		
Total	$38,000		
Base amount	−32,000	$3,000 × 28% = $840	
	$ 6,000	(Marginal Tax Bracket)	
Divide by 2: Test result	$ 3,000		

person has to do is mail a completed Form SSA 7004 entitled, Request for Earnings and Benefit Estimate Statement. This form can be obtained by calling 1-800-937-2000. If the Administration has made an error in correctly recording past payments, this error should be promptly rectified to avoid future problems.

CORPORATE RETIREMENT PLANS

GENERAL DISCUSSION

Corporate retirement plans, commonly known as qualified plans, provide an excellent means of accumulating wealth on a tax-deferred basis. Furthermore, the distribution of this wealth can be timed so the owner receives during retirement the maximum after-tax income. Finally, distributions under the plan may be accorded favorable tax treatment.

More specifically, corporate retirement plans offer tax advantages both to the employer and to the employee. The company gets a current tax deduction for amounts contributed to the plan, while the employees are not taxed on their contributions to the plan when the contributions are made. Also, the plan is not taxed on its earnings, so there is a tax-deferred buildup of retirement benefits. At the time of distribution of retirement benefits, depending on the method of distribution, lump sum distribution rules or annuity rules apply, unless the benefits are rolled over into an IRA. In Chapter 13 these tax distribution rules will be discussed in detail.

SPECIFIC REQUIREMENTS

All retirement plans must comply with certain minimum participation standards set out in Employee Retirement Income Security Act (ERISA) and the Tax Reform Act (TRA) of 1986. To be sure, the law does not require a company to provide retirement benefits, and in fact certain provisions appear to discourage retirement plans. However, if an employer elects to provide retirement benefits, the minimum requirements set by ERISA or TRA must be met if the plan is to be considered qualified.

The basic requirements under ERISA, which have been significantly changed by subsequent tax laws, are presented in Table 12-4. The table reveals that many of the requirements are both stringent and complicated. Clearly, ERISA sets rigid standards of fiduciary responsibility, imposes restrictions on certain types of investments, prohibits discrimination against non-highly paid employees, and penalizes especially prohibited transactions.

TABLE 12-4   Basic Requirements Under ERISA

Category	Key factors	Special rules
Participation Requirements	1. Employees 21 or older and with one year's service must be covered. 2. A plan providing for immediate vesting may require two years of service for coverage.	
Coverage Requirements	1. *Percentage Test.* Either (1) 70% or more of all employees participate; or (2) 70% or more of all employees are eligible to participate and at least 80% of them actually participate. 2. *Ratio and Average Benefits Test.* A plan meets the test if (1) the plan does not discriminate in favor of highly compensated employees; and (2) the average benefit percentage of non-highly compensated employees is at least 70% of the average benefit percentage for highly compensated employees. 3. *Minimum Participation Requirement.* The plan must benefit the lesser of (1) 50 employees or (2) 40% of all employees.	1. Special definition for highly compensated employees. 2. Special rule for SEP
Vesting Requirements	1. *Five-year vesting.* An employee must be fully vested after five years of covered service. 2. *Graded vesting.* Employees are vested depending on their years of service. Full vesting after seven years.	Special values apply to certain types of plans.
Funding	1. The *minimum funding requirement* is the sum of normal costs of plan, experienced gains and losses and amounts necessary to amortize past service costs. 2. Not every retirement benefit is subject to minimum funding standards. Plans exempt from this requirement include profit sharing plans, government plans, unfunded plans, and IRA plans.	

TABLE 12-4 *(continued)*

Category	Key factors	Special rules
Maximum Contributions and Benefits	1. Defined Contribution Plans: the lesser of $30,000 or 25% of compensation.	1. For employees of less than ten years of work the limit is proportionately reduced.
	2. Defined Benefit Plans: the lesser of $90,000 (adjusted for inflation) or 100% of average compensation for highest three consecutive years of service (taking into account only the first $200,000 of compensation), actuarily reduced for retirement before age 65.	2. A combined limit is applied where an employee participates in both types of plans.
Nondiscriminating Rules for 401(k)	The plan must meet *one* of the two criteria to be nondiscriminatory: 1. The contribution percentage is no greater than 125% of the contribution percentage for all other eligible employees. 2. The contribution percentage for highly compensated employees is no greater than the lesser of 200% of the contribution percentage for all other eligible employees (or this percentage plus 2%).	Different rules apply to 401(k) plans.

PARTICIPATION REQUIREMENTS

All qualified plans must cover employees who have reached the age of 21 and have one year of service. However, the law allows one exception to this general rule. If a plan provides for immediate vesting, two years of service may be required for coverage. If eligibility requires two years of service, the participant becomes 100 percent vested upon entry.

COVERAGE REQUIREMENTS

A plan must satisfy one of the following tests in order for it to be considered qualified.

The Percentage Test

A plan may qualify for favorable tax treatment if either: (1) 70 percent or more of all employees participate in the plan; or (2) 70 percent or more of all employees are eligible to participate *and* at least 80 percent of them actually participate. Employees who do not meet the plan's minimum age or service requirements are not counted. Union members do not count if retirement benefits have been the subject of good faith bargaining between the company and the union.

The Ratio Test

A plan may also qualify for favorable tax treatment if the plan benefits a portion of non-highly compensated employees. That is, the average benefit of non-highly compensated employees must be at least 70 percent of the average benefit percentage for highly compensated employees for the plan to qualify.

The Average Benefits Test

A plan meets the test if it does not discriminate in favor of highly compensated employees. For plans that began in 1989 or after, the following requirement has been added as a qualification. The plan must benefit the lesser of: (1) 50 employees; or (2) 40 percent of all employees. This percentage may not be satisfied by aggregating comparable plans.

VESTING REQUIREMENTS

For plan years that began in 1989 or after, there are two permissible vesting schedules: (1) full vesting upon the completion of five years of service; or (2) graded vesting beginning at 20 percent per year after three years of service and increasing by 20 percent for each subsequent year of service until full vesting is attained after seven years of service.

Incidentally, a few types of plans provide for immediate 100 percent vesting. These are plans requiring more than one year of service before participation, plans maintained by certain educational organizations, simplified employee pension plans, and some employee stock ownership plans. Other plans, called top heavy plans, must either provide for 100 percent vesting after three years of service or for 20 percent vesting after two years of service and 20 percent additional vesting each year (called the six-year vesting rule).

FUNDING REQUIREMENTS

There are several plans which are not subject to minimum funding requirements. These include profit sharing plans, government plans, unfunded plans, and IRA plans. The minimum amount that an employer is required to contribute annually to a plan subject to a minimum funding requirement is the sum of two elements: (1) normal costs of the plan which consists of current contributions; and (2) amounts necessary to amortize past service costs representing payments for costs of the employees' services prior to the adoption of the pension plan.

In general, all plans are concerned with the general funding rules. Additionally, employers have to fund their defined benefit, money purchase, and target benefit plans by contributing annually an amount at least sufficient to fund the normal costs of the plan.

The IRS charges employers with interest for underfunding their plans. Conversely, an employer who has funded more than the maximum permitted contribution is charged a ten percent excise tax for overfunding. These penalties will be discussed more fully in a subsequent section.

PLAN INVESTMENT RULES

In developing plan investment strategies, federal regulations require that the plan trustee exercise care, skill, prudence, and diligence. In addition, federal guidelines indicate that investments should be: (1) sufficiently liquid to allow for timely distribution of benefits; (2) sufficiently diversified to minimize risk potential; and (3) sufficiently conservative to provide dependable growth without undue risk. Within these guidelines, plan contributions can be invested in a bank account, stocks, bonds, mutual funds, government securities, life insurance, money market funds, and fixed and variable annuities.

TYPES OF PLANS

There are two major categories of qualified plans: defined contribution plans and defined benefit plans. A third category, target benefit plans, is a hybrid of a money purchase (a form of defined contribution) and defined benefit plans. These categories are presented in Figure 12-4. Simply stated, a defined contribution plan is a plan providing for an individual account for each participant and for benefits based solely upon the amount contributed to the participant's account, plus any income, expenses, gains and losses, and forfeitures which may be allocated to the account. In contrast, defined benefit plans *define* the *benefits* to be paid to plan participants at retirement. These plans pay the plan

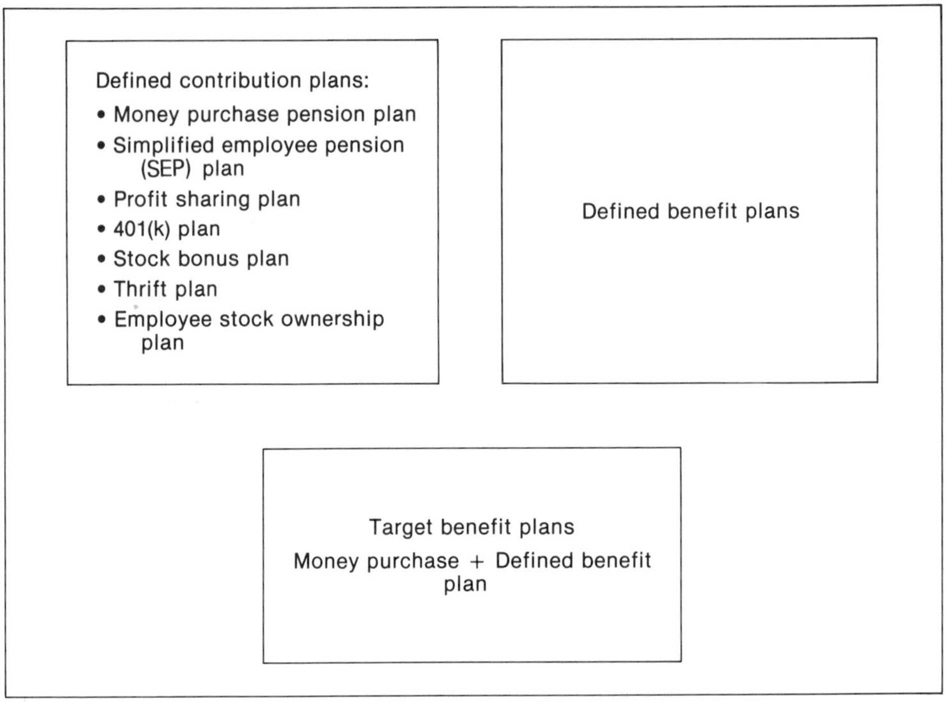

FIGURE 12-4   Major categories of corporate retirement plans

participants the specific benefit which is promised (defined) in the plan document.

Defined Contribution Plans

The annual contribution to a defined contribution plan is usually defined as a percentage of the compensation of plan participants. For a money purchase plan, the legal document establishing the plan describes the percentage of compensation which the employer (business) is required to contribute. Allocations to all other (except target benefit) plans are determined by a formula. The mechanism for determining the plan contribution by the employer is presented next, assuming a ten percent contribution for participants earning $118,000:

Percentage specified in plan document		Compensation of plan participants		Annual contribution to plan
10%	×	$118,000	=	$11,800

Federal regulations limit the maximum tax-deductible contribution which a business can make to a defined contribution plan. As mentioned, the annual addition to each participant's account is comprised of the employer's contribution, any employee contribution, and any forfeiture allocation. The maximum limits under different types of plans (except SEP plans) are as follows:

Type of plan	Maximum annual addition
Money Purchase	Lesser of 25% of compensation or $30,000
Profit Sharing	same
Target Benefit	same
Money Purchase and Profit Sharing	same

It should be mentioned here that while during any given year the maximum annual addition for certain employees in a profit sharing plan could be as much as 25 percent of their compensation or $30,000, whichever is less, the overall annual addition is limited to 15 percent of the total compensation of all employees of the corporation. In the case of a SEP plan the maximum allowable contribution is the lesser of $30,000 or 13.04 percent of the owner's net profits or 15 percent of an employee's taxable wages.

Except for a profit sharing plan, the plan document defines the amount of the employer's contribution to be allocated to each participant's account. It is defined as a percentage of compensation, as shown here:

$$\text{John's compensation} \times 10\% = \text{John's allocation}$$

15 KEY QUESTIONS

How much do you know about your own pension plan or that of a prospective employer? Here's what to ask your plan's administrator:

1. What type (or types) of plan do I have? (Remember, if it's a defined benefit plan, benefits are guaranteed and insured by the government.)
2. When will I become a member?
3. When will I be vested?
4. What happens if my employment is interrupted?

5. What provisions are there for early retirement?
6. How much would I receive if I decided to retire early?
7. Can I receive benefits if I keep working after age 65?
8. Is there any inflation protection?
9. Are disability benefits provided?
10. What about death benefits?
11. How is the plan funded?
12. How fast are benefits accrued?
13. What is the current financial condition of the plan?
14. Do you anticipate any difficulty in paying benefits?
15. Do I have any say in how my share of the money is invested?

Source: Changing Times, January 1988, p. 82. Reprinted with permission.

The employer's contribution may also be defined as a proportional amount of the contribution:

$$\frac{\text{John's compensation}}{\text{Total compensation}} \times \frac{\text{Total plan}}{\text{contribution}} = \text{John's allocation}$$

Similarly, amounts forfeited by terminating participants who are not yet eligible for full benefits under the plan may also be allocated proportionately to each participant based on compensation:

$$\frac{\text{John's compensation}}{\begin{array}{c}\text{Total compensation}\\\text{of all participants}\end{array}} \times \begin{array}{c}\text{Forfeitures}\\\text{to be}\\\text{reallocated}\end{array} = \begin{array}{c}\text{John's share of}\\\text{forfeitures}\end{array}$$

Incidentally, in the case of a money purchase pension plan, forfeitures may also be used to reduce the employer's required contribution.

Each participant in a defined contribution plan is considered to have an individual account. Every year all the investment data for the plan for its 12-month period is reviewed. The gain or loss of the plan's assets is calculated and allocated among the individual participant accounts. More specifically, the allocation is determined by using the following formula:

$$\frac{\begin{array}{c}\text{Individual participant}\\\text{account value}\end{array}}{\text{Total plan assets}} \times \begin{array}{c}\text{Investment}\\\text{gain/loss}\end{array} = \begin{array}{c}\text{Participant's}\\\text{gain/loss}\end{array}$$

For instance, suppose the following information is provided:

$$\text{Account value of Employee \#1} = \$10,000$$

$$\text{Account value of Employee \#2} = 8,000$$

$$\text{Account value of Employee \#3} = 2,000$$

$$\text{Total assets of the plan} = \$20,000$$

$$\text{Investment gain for the year} = \$2,200$$

Based on the preceding data the following allocations are made:

$$\text{Employee \#1: } \frac{\$10,000}{\$20,000} \times 2,200 = \$1,100$$

$$\text{Employee \#2: } \frac{\$8,000}{\$20,000} \times 2,200 = \$880$$

$$\text{Employee \#3: } \frac{\$2,000}{\$20,000} \times 2,200 = \$220$$

The benefit which a participant receives at retirement or termination is the current value of the account in which the participant has a vested interest. The value of the account is the sum of the annual contributions made to the account, its share of the forfeitures, and its share of the investment return of the plan assets. The calculation is done in two steps:

Step 1

$$\begin{array}{c}\text{Sum of} \\ \text{contributions} \\ \text{to account}\end{array} + \text{Forfeitures} + \begin{array}{c}\text{Investment} \\ \text{gains/losses}\end{array} = \begin{array}{c}\text{Participant's} \\ \text{account balance}\end{array}$$

Step 2

$$\begin{array}{c}\text{Participant's} \\ \text{account} \\ \text{balance}\end{array} \times \begin{array}{c}\text{Vested} \\ \text{percentage}\end{array} = \begin{array}{c}\text{Participant's} \\ \text{benefit}\end{array}$$

To conclude, defined contribution plans have certain basic characteristics which are common to all plans included in this category. For instance, the contribution to be made, as defined in the plan document, is usually defined as a percentage of compensation. In addition, the value of a participant's individual account is the benefit to be paid out at the time of retirement or termination. However, each type of defined contribution plan has its own unique characteristics, as is revealed in Table 12-5. We will now undertake a detailed discussion of each type of defined contribution plan.

Money purchase pension plan. The money purchase pension plan permits the employer to make a tax-deductible contribution according to a predetermined formula. An employee's benefit depends upon: (1) the length of time the employee worked while covered under the plan; (2) the amount of money contributed each year by the employer; (3) forfeitures; (4) contributions; and (5) investment results.

The contribution formula can take one of two forms. Under the *flat amount formula,* a set amount of money is contributed to the plan each year on behalf of each participating employee. This formula does not recognize either the length of service or the income of an employee and is therefore considered not as attractive as the *flat percentage of earnings formula* form. The latter type fixes the percentage of income contributed annually to the plan by the employer on behalf of the employee. Maximum contribution under either formula is the lesser of 25 percent of the participant's compensation or $30,000 per year.

Let us summarize here the four major characteristics of money purchase pension plans:

1. They may permit a contribution formula of up to 25 percent of compensation, or $30,000, whichever is less.

TABLE 12-5 Defined Contribution Plans

Title	Major responsibility for funding rests on	Types of investment permitted	General characteristics	Where appropriate	Vesting rules
Money Purchase Pension Plan	Employer.	Determined by trustees.	This plan fixes the employer's contribution by a predetermined (flat amount or flat earnings) formula. The benefit depends upon the length of service, annual contributions of each employee, and corporate earnings.	All employees can benefit from it.	Minimum vesting rules apply.
Simplified Employee Pension Plan (SEP)	Employer.	Only highly risky investments are not permitted.	A SEP is an IRA funded by employer. An IRA account is set up by an employee. Then employer makes an annual contribution of 15% of salary or $30,000, whichever is less.	All employers unable or unwilling to pay lawyer's fees and annual administrative fee can set up SEPs.	Immediate.
Profit Sharing Plan	Employer.	Determined by trustees.	Through this plan, employers allow their employees to participate in the profits. Employer contributions to the plan are allocated among the employees under a defined formula. The benefit is equal to the value of contributions, plus earnings, that have accumulated in each account. The company must make recurring and substantial contributions to keep the plan in force.	This plan is appropriate where employers want their employees to share in the success of the company. A company need not have made a profit to take advantage of making a deductible contribution.	Minimum vesting rules apply.
401(K) Plan	Employee.* Employer may match a portion of	Employee's choice of stock or bond mutual funds, fixed	401(K) plan may be a part of a profit sharing or a stock bonus plan. Majority of	Employees in need of sheltering part of their taxable income while	Immediate.

	employee's contribution.	income account, or company stock.	contributions come from employees, so the employer's cost is low. This plan allows employees to defer taxation on part of their compensation, while still providing access to the money for certain emergencies.	retaining the right to borrow from the plan for specified reasons may select this plan.	Minimum vesting rules apply.
Stock Bonus Plan	Employer.	Corporation's stock or cash.	Stock bonus plan provides benefits similar to a profit sharing plan, except that employer's contributions are not necessarily dependent upon profits and benefits are distributable in company stocks.	This plan is appropriate where employers want their employees to share in the success of the company but wish to retain cash in the company.	Minimum vesting rules apply. Immediate vesting for employee contributions.
Thrift Plan	Employer. Employees may make contributions with after-tax dollars.	Determined by trustees.	This plan is hybrid of pension, profit sharing, and stock bonus plans.	This plan is appropriate where the important features of several types of plans are described.	Minimum vesting rules apply.
Employee Stock Ownership Plan (ESOP)	Employer.	Company stock.	Employer contributions of company stock are discretionary and don't have to be made from profits. Starting at age 55, employees must be given a choice of investments other than company stock for a portion of their account balance.	Employers interested in retaining employees on a long-term basis may opt for this plan.	Immediate.

* Employee contributions are tax-deductible.

2. They require a *fixed* annual contribution commitment by the employer, regardless of the performance of the business.

3. The plans' investment gains or losses are proportionately allocated among the participants.

4. Forfeitures may either be reallocated to the accounts of the remaining participants or used to reduce the employer's required contribution.

Simplified employee pension plan. A simplified employee pension (SEP) plan combines the simplicity of an IRA with the generous contribution limits of a formal pension plan. Essentially, SEPs allow employers to use IRAs to build tax-sheltered retirement funds for themselves and their employees with minimal paperwork and cost. A SEP plan is adopted by the employer with each eligible employee establishing an IRA to receive his or her share of the employer's contribution. Having individual IRAs as the funding vehicle obviously minimizes the record-keeping function, as the employee's "account balance" at any time is the value of the IRA at that time. No earnings allocation is required by the company. The level of effort involved in the implementation and administration of SEP plans directly depends on whether the employer uses as the plan document the IRS model SEP Form 5305-SEP or the presumably simpler SEP prototype.

The law requires that SEP plans cover all employees at least 20 years old who have worked for three of the past five years. By this definition, even part-timers and seasonal employees must be included in the plan.

Employer contributions to the SEP must be made according to a written allocation formula. The maximum allowable contribution is the lesser of $30,000 or 13.04 percent of the owner's net profits or 15 percent of an employee's taxable wages.

A SEP plan can be set up so the employees can make their own deductible contributions to the plan. As with the IRA, each employee can contribute up to $2,000 of earnings to the account.

Distributions from a SEP plan are covered by the same rules as those governing IRAs. Each SEP participant has the right to extend payments over the beneficiary's life. It should be noted here that the employer's SEP contribution for an employee is included on the employee's W-2 form; this amount is deducted from taxable income on the employee's tax return if the contribution is deductible.

Profit sharing plan. A major type of defined contribution plan is a profit sharing plan. In this type of plan, each year the employer may make contributions to the retirement plan trust whether or not the company realizes a profit for that year. Employees are not taxed on employer's contributions. In addition, the contributions grow tax-deferred until they are distributed.

The company has a choice of selecting a definite contribution formula. For example, a profit sharing plan may provide for a flat percentage of pre-

or post-tax profits to be contributed to the plan. Alternatively, it may have a sliding scale formula which increases as profits rise, or it may provide that profits are to be shared only if they exceed a predetermined level. Generally, the employer's overall annual contribution to a profit sharing plan is limited to 15 percent of the total compensation of all employees of the corporation.

Under the profit sharing plan rules, a company is not required, but may choose, to make contributions when no profits exist or even when the company makes profits. However, the law does state that the continuation of such a plan is contingent upon the company's making recurring and substantial contributions, and many employers make a contribution even when the associated companies had an operating loss.

In the case of five-year vesting in a non-top heavy plan, the vesting rules covering a profit sharing plan require a complete vesting of each year's contributions to an employee's account by the end of the fifth plan year after the employer's contribution is made. The plan may also choose a seven-year graded vesting, in which case seven-year vesting rules will apply. If an employee leaves the firm before his or her contributions are fully vested, the funds are "forfeited"; these funds are typically used to increase other participants' accounts.

It is interesting to note that three other plans—401(k), stock bonus, and employee stock ownership plans—operate as profit sharing plans, but each has its own additional unique characteristics, as we shall now observe.

401(k) plan. A 401(k) plan may be part of a profit sharing or a stock bonus plan. Under this arrangement, the tax law allows the employee to contribute up to $7,627 (1989), which is annually adjusted for inflation. The employee agrees to take a salary reduction equal to the contribution and is not taxed on the contribution except for FICA (Social Security) taxes. In addition, the company may match part of the employee's contribution. However, the sum of the employee contribution plus the company's contribution is limited by the maximum of 15 percent of the eligible compensation. The law also allows a plan to accept after-tax employee contributions, on a nondiscriminatory basis, which grow tax-deferred.

Income earned on the 401(k) plan accumulates tax-deferred until it is withdrawn. Funds may be withdrawn after an employee reaches the age of $59\frac{1}{2}$, is separated from service, becomes disabled, or shows financial hardship. Withdrawals are also allowed if the plan is terminated.

An attractive feature of a 401(k) plan—or for that matter of all plans (except SEPs and Keoghs) with an appropriate document permitting loans—is its loan provision. An employee may be permitted to borrow from the plan up to a maximum amount. The loan amount is limited to the lesser of: (1) $50,000, reduced by the employee's highest loan balance during the past 12 months; or (2) 50 percent of the present value of the employee's vested interest in the plan, or $10,000, whichever is greater. Interest, which is usually charged at a rate slightly higher than the prime rate, is deductible (as consumer loan interest) from federal taxes up to the permissible limits and is added back to the borrower's account. With the exception of money borrowed to purchase a home, the loan must be repaid within five years, and the interest and principal must be amortized at least on a quarterly basis.

Stock bonus plan. A stock bonus plan is similar to a profit sharing plan except that the employer's contribution may be made in either stock or cash. A "cashless" contribution in the form of stock keeps needed cash in the company, but still provides the company with the same tax deduction. The amount of the employer's contribution is the fair market value of the stock.

An interesting feature of the stock bonus plan is that the contribution is generally fully invested in the employer's stock. This is in contrast to a profit sharing plan which cannot invest more than ten percent in employer stock. Another feature of this plan is that if a distribution is made in a lump sum, the appreciation realized while the stock was held in the trust is usually not taxed until the stock is sold.

Thrift plan. A thrift plan is a hybrid of pension, profit sharing, and stock bonus plans. It may resemble a profit sharing plan by making employer contributions contingent on current profits or accumulated earnings; it resembles a stock bonus plan by allowing employer securities as an investment; and it resembles a pension plan by making employer contributions mandatory.

In thrift plans, which are also called savings plans, contributions by employees must be made with after-tax dollars. Also, employees may withdraw their own contributions at will, although they may forfeit employer contributions by doing so.

Employee stock ownership plan. An employee stock ownership plan (ESOP) is an employee benefit plan designed to invest primarily in the common stock of the corporation sponsoring the plan. An ESOP must meet all the IRS rules requiring nondiscrimination, vesting, and participation, as well as other rules applicable to ESOPs.

Generally, the basic element of an ESOP is a stock bonus plan. It may also be a combination of a stock bonus plan and a money purchase pension plan. As mentioned, a stock bonus plan is established and maintained to provide benefits similar to those of a profit sharing plan. The exception is that employer contributions are not necessarily dependent on profits, and benefits can be distributed in employer stock.

Essentially, an ESOP is a defined contribution plan. Consequently, the maximum contribution is limited to $30,000 or 25 percent of the total of all employees' compensations, whichever is less.

Defined Benefit Plans

Defined benefit plans differ significantly from defined contribution plans. For example, the benefit an employee wishes to receive upon retirement is first established and then the contributions are set at the level necessary to achieve the targeted benefits. The benefit formula consists of either a flat dollar amount or a flat percentage of earnings. The maximum annual deductible contribution for retirement at age 65 (provided the person was born prior to 1939) is limited to the amount it takes to generate the lesser of: (1) an annual income of $98,064 (adjusted for inflation); and (2) 100 percent of average compensation for the employee's compensation for three highest consecutive years.

Defined benefit plans include: (1) fixed benefit plans in which all employees receive the same benefits; (2) flat benefit plans in which the benefit is a percentage of salary; and (3) unit benefit plans in which the benefit depends on the income *and* time of service.

The basis of the contributions made by the employer to a defined benefit plan is the total amount of benefits which must be paid to all participants when they retire. The employer must contribute the amount necessary to fulfill the benefit promises specified by the plan. The amount of the employer contribution is determined by an actuary each year. Salient features of a defined benefit plan are presented in Table 12-6.

Since the funding method of a defined benefit plan is so different from that of a defined contribution plan, it is appropriate to briefly comment on the actuarial method of calculating a plan contribution. An actuary reviews the plan each year to calculate the portion of the ultimate assets needed by the plan which should be contributed in a specific year. The actuary bases the amount of the plan contribution on factors which include: (1) the benefits promised by the plan; (2) the ages, sex, salaries, and retirement ages of the participants; and (3) the assumptions, or mathematical projections, of the interest to be earned by the plan's assets, future salary increases of the participants, and the projected mortality of the plan's participants. This calculation method can be summarized in the following manner:

$$
\begin{array}{c}
\text{Benefit} \\
\text{formula} \\
\text{provisions}
\end{array}
+
\begin{array}{c}
\text{Characteristics} \\
\text{of plan} \\
\text{participants}
\end{array}
+
\begin{array}{c}
\text{Assumptions} \\
\text{of future} \\
\text{plan} \\
\text{performance}
\end{array}
=
\begin{array}{c}
\text{Contribution} \\
\text{required to} \\
\text{fund future} \\
\text{benefits}
\end{array}
$$

In a defined benefit plan, the participant receives the promised income upon retirement. However, if the service is terminated prior to the anticipated retirement, the participant receives only the present value of the vested "accrued benefits." The value of accrued benefits is determined by a mathematical formula known as the fractional rule.

TABLE 12-6 Defined Benefit Plans, TBP, and TSA

Title	Major responsibility for funding rests on	Types of investments permitted	General characteristics	Where appropriate	Vesting rules
Defined Benefit Plan	Employer.	Determined by trustees.	This plan defines the benefit to be received at retirement. Then the actuary determines what contributions must be made each year to meet the benefit target. However, the benefit paid is not necessarily the benefit chosen; it depends on the accumulated amount at the time of distribution.	This plan is especially beneficial for highly paid employees who are 50 and over. They can shelter a significant portion of their taxable earnings by participating in this type of plan.	Minimum vesting rules apply.
Target Benefit Plan (TBP)	Employer.	Determined by trustees.	This plan is a hybrid of defined benefit and money purchase plan. Benefits targets are established and contributions are set at levels necessary to meet the target. However, the benefits actually paid are not necessarily equal to the target chosen but depend on the account upon distribution.	This plan is best for older clients with a budget. Target plans are also suitable where maintenance of individual participants' accounts is desired.	Minimum vesting rules apply.
Tax-Sheltered Annuity (TSA or 403(b) Plan)	Employee. Employer may elect to contribute as well.	Employees's choice of almost any type of investment	Employees of Section 501(c)(3) organizations and public school teachers can buy special, nonforfeitable, tax-deferred annuities or face amount certificates of mutual funds to provide funds for their retirement.	All eligible employees may take advantage of TSA to plan for retirement.	Immediate.

Target Benefit Plans

Target benefit plans are a combination of defined benefit and money purchase plans. In this type of plan, the benefit is established and then contributions are set at the level necessary to achieve the targeted benefit. But the benefit actually paid out is not necessarily the benefit chosen. The amount finally distributed depends on the amount that has accumulated in the account.

In a target benefit plan, the contribution is fixed and will not change regardless of the plan's actual investment return. It must be made each year regardless of the business situation. Target Benefit plans permit a maximum contribution up to the lesser of 25 percent of compensation or $30,000 for each participant.

An important feature of target plans is that individual account balances are kept for all participants. The contribution is allocated into separate accounts for each participant. All accounts share in the investment gains, losses, expenses of the plan assets, and forfeitures if they are reallocated. The benefit provided to the participant is the balance in the account at retirement which, as mentioned, could be different from the targeted amount.

Tax-Sheltered Annuity

A tax-sheltered annuity (TSA) represents a special retirement plan open only to the employees of certain nonprofit, religious, charitable, and educational institutions specified in Section 501(c)(3) of the IRS code as well as teachers of public school systems.

An employee may contribute up to $16\frac{2}{3}$ percent of annual compensation to a TSA under a salary reduction agreement. Participation by the employer may be in the form of additional, matching, or total contributions. Premiums paid by employers to buy TSAs are excluded from the employee's gross income to the extent of the employee's "exclusion allowance" for that year. The exclusion allowance equals 20 percent of the employee's annual compensation times the years of service, less the amount contributed by the employer and excluded from income by the employee in earlier years. The total contributions by the employer are determined by a sophisticated formula.

The laws governing distribution from TSAs are similar to those relating to withdrawals from an IRA. For instance, in both cases early withdrawals prior to age $59\frac{1}{2}$ are subject to a ten percent penalty, and minimum compulsory distributions must begin at age $70\frac{1}{2}$.

A TSA account can be rolled over into another TSA account or into an IRA. However, a TSA cannot be rolled over into another pension or profit sharing plan. A rollover from a TSA account must be completed within 60 days of receipt of the funds from that account.

TSA funds can be invested in life insurance annuity contracts or in mutual funds. Other forms of basic investments, such as investments in stocks, bonds, GNMAs, and real estate investment trusts, are also approved for this plan.

PERSONAL RETIREMENT PLANS

INDIVIDUAL RETIREMENT ACCOUNT (IRA)

An Overview

Anyone who has earned income is eligible to open an individual retirement account (IRA), whether self-employed or an employee, full-time or part-time. The key restriction on an IRA is that a tax-deductible IRA contribution cannot be made in any year in which the person is eligible to participate in a tax-qualified plan and earns more than a specified amount, as described next.

The provisions regarding the deductibility of an IRA are summarized in Table 12-7. The following facts are revealed by the table. First, if neither spouse is covered by a qualified plan, the law allows a tax deduction of $2,000 per worker or $2,250 per one-income couple, regardless of income. Second, married couples covered by a corporate plan, and having an adjusted gross income of less than $40,000, keep the full deduction. The deduction tapers off after that if either spouse is in a corporate retirement plan. It vanishes altogether when adjusted gross income exceeds $50,000, but is prorated between $40,000 and $50,000. The comparable limits for a single person are $25,000 and $35,000, respectively.

Deduction limits for an active participant in a qualified plan who is married and files separately are not as straightforward as those for the categories just discussed. In general, for such a person no deduction is allowed if the adjusted gross income is over $10,000. If the adjusted gross income is less than $10,000, a partial deduction is allowed, and the amount of the deduction is calculated by using a special formula. For instance, suppose John Johnson is

TABLE 12-7 Deductibility of IRA

	Adjusted gross income	Participating in pension plan?	
		Yes	No
Joint	$40,000 or less	$2,000	$2,000
	$40,000–50,000	$200–2,000	$2,000
	Above $50,000	None	$2,000
Single	$25,000 or less	$2,000	$2,000
	$25,000–35,000	$200–2,000	$2,000
	Above $35,000	None	$2,000
Married filing separately	$10,000 or less	Partial	$2,000
	Over $10,000	deduction*	$2,000

* Special deductibility rules apply.

TABLE 12-8 Long-Term Accumulation of IRA Contribution

Investment return	Years					
	5	10	15	20	25	30
7%	$12,307	$29,567	$53,776	$ 87,730	$135,353	$202,146
8	12,672	31,291	58,649	98,846	157,909	244,692
9	13,047	33,121	64,007	111,529	184,648	297,150
10	13,431	35,062	69,899	126,005	216,364	361,887
11	13,826	37,123	76,380	142,530	253,998	441,826
12	14,230	39,309	83,507	161,397	298,668	540,585

Note: Annual contribution of $2,000 is made at the beginning of each year.

married, files a separate return, and is an active participant in an employer plan. John's adjusted gross income is $7,500. The maximum deductible IRA contribution is $500:

Step 1: $7,500 ($7,500 − $0)
Step 2: $2,500 ($10,000 − $7,500)
Step 3: $500 ($2,500 × .20)

Long-Term Accumulation

The magic of compounding and the concept of the time value of money are demonstrated nowhere more clearly than in the long-term accumulation in an IRA account. For instance, Table 12-8 reveals that $2,000 invested at the beginning of every year at ten percent for 30 years would total $361,887. If the investment earns a 12 percent return, in 30 years the IRA fund would grow to approximately half a million dollars.

Deductible versus Nondeductible Contributions

As mentioned, qualified plan participants whose adjusted gross income exceeds designated amounts can no longer make tax-deductible contributions into an IRA. However, their contributions are still allowed to grow tax-deferred until distribution. For these people to contribute to an IRA or not becomes the key question.

The difference between the tax-deferred and taxable IRA contributions is presented in Table 12-9. In this illustration it is assumed that the investor is in the 28 percent tax bracket and the investment grows at ten percent. According to this table, in ten years the excess of savings will be $9,817; in 30 years these savings will amount to $101,328. Of course, taxes on before-tax IRA contributions would have to be deducted in order to arrive at more

TABLE 12-9   IRA: Before versus After-Tax Contribution

Years (1)	IRA: Before-tax (2)	IRA: After-tax (3)	Difference (4)
10	$ 35,062	$ 24,245	$ 9,817
20	126,005	90,724	35,281
30	361,887	260,559	101,328

Note: 1. Investor's marginal tax bracket remains constant at 28 percent.
2. Annual contribution of $2,000 before-tax, or $1,440 after-tax, is made at the beginning of each year.
3. IRA funds grow at a constant return of ten percent.

accurate excess savings figures. Also, on the negative side, the investor will be required to keep very detailed records: income tax forms and a copy of Form 8606 for any year with a nondeductible contribution; Forms 1099-R and W-2P, showing distributions from the IRA, and Form 5498, showing the value of the IRA at the end of each year. On balance, nondeductible IRA contributions do offer economic benefits, but the burden may prove to be onerous. In this connection it should be mentioned that a tax-deferred annuity may be a better alternative than a nondeductible IRA since unrestricted amounts may be invested in an annuity which grows tax-deferred.

Types of IRAs

IRA assets must be invested in one of two plans: an individual retirement account that has a bank or other qualified organization as trustee or custodian; or an individual retirement annuity.

Individual retirement plan.   An IRA account must be a trust or custodial account, although it may be in a self-directed IRA. The individual's interest in the account must be nonforfeitable. Unless the contributor becomes disabled or dies, the account must be held exclusively for the purpose of providing retirement benefits. The IRA benefits can be distributed starting with the earliest of 59½ years or time of death or disability. In addition, the distribution must begin by no later than age 70½.

An IRA trust may accept only cash contributions. The IRA funds may be invested in savings accounts, stocks, bonds, mutual funds, real estate, limited partnerships, approved government coins, gold, and endowments. However, the rules prohibit the investment of IRA funds in highly speculative products including collectibles, art, and gems.

Individual retirement annuity plan.   This is an annuity issued by an insurance company. It may be either an individual annuity contract or a joint and survivor annuity for the benefit of the annuitant and spouse. The investment must be nontransferable and its distribution must begin when the annuitant is no older than $70\frac{1}{2}$.

Rollover versus Transfer

The terms *rollover* and *transfer* are applied to any movement of funds from a qualified plan or an IRA to another IRA investment. There are, however, important distinctions between a rollover and a transfer.

An investor rolls over an IRA when a plan is liquidated and a check or wire transfer is sent by the trustee to the IRA investor. This would be the case when a lump sum distribution is received from a qualified plan or the money is withdrawn from an IRA investment. In this case, from the time the money is received, the investor has 60 days to reinvest in another IRA account without paying current taxes on the rollover amount. Only one rollover is allowed per year per IRA account. Thus, if a person has five separate accounts, the person could roll over each account once a year.

In contrast, an IRA is "transferred" when the money is sent directly by one trustee to another trustee, completely bypassing the investor. There are no legal restrictions on the number of times a transfer can take place in a year. However, some custodians impose restrictions on how many transfers will be permitted during any given year and may also impose fees on such transfers. It is therefore advisable to investigate these restrictions and costs before transferring IRA funds.

An important caveat should be added here. An employee receiving a lump sum distribution from a qualified plan has the opportunity to roll over part or all of the distribution into an IRA, thereby deferring taxation on the amount rolled over into an IRA. Any amount not rolled over is currently taxed as ordinary income. However, by rolling over the lump sum distribution into an IRA, the employee forfeits the right to subject this amount to a favorable tax treatment known as five-year or ten-year forward averaging, which is explained in the next chapter.

KEOGH PLAN

Introduction

If IRAs are the best tax shelter for employees, Keogh or H.R. 10 plans are the best for the self-employed. A Keogh plan, or more accurately, the qualified plan of an unincorporated entity, is simply a retirement plan for self-employed business people or professionals. The self-employed person gets a deduction for the contributions and the earnings in the fund accumulate on a tax-deferred basis.

TABLE 12-10 Keogh Plan: An Overview

Type	Who is interested?	Its nature	Maximum annual contributions	Maximum vesting	Legal reporting
Keogh: Money Purchase	Persons who can commit to a fixed annual obligation.	Contributions are a fixed percentage of compensation and must be made annually.	Lesser of $30,000 or 20% of net profit for owner and 25% of total taxable wages for employees.	Full vesting after three years, or six-year graded vesting. Part-time and seasonal employees may be excluded.	Form 5500-C must be filed annually.
Keogh: Profit Sharing	Persons who wish to tie contributions to profits or are unable to commit to a fixed obligation.	Discretionary contributions are based on profits. No contributions during a given year are permitted.	Lesser of $30,000 or 13.04% of net profit for owner and 15% of total taxable wages for employees.	Same as above.	Same as above. If both money purchase and profit sharing plans are adopted and the accounts are at different institutions, Form 5307 must be filed.
Keogh: Defined Benefit	Persons 50 and over who are anxious and able to make the highest contributions possible.	Contributions must be made annually to fund a predetermined retirement benefit.	Amount necessary to fund a maximum benefit of $90,000 (indexed for inflation) per year at retirement, up to 100% of income.	Same as above.	Form 5500-B. Also, annual review by an actuary to determine annual contributions.

The ceilings on Keogh contributions have been made competitive with those of tax-protected corporate pension plans. This means that a self-employed person can make an annual contribution of up to $30,000 or 25 percent of net income.

Types of Keogh Plans

An overview of Keogh plans is presented in Table 12-10. The simplest Keogh to establish is a *defined contribution* plan. There are three kinds of defined contribution Keoghs: money purchase, profit sharing, and defined benefit. The maximum contribution allowed in money purchase Keoghs is either $30,000 or 20 percent of the owner's net profit (or 25 percent of total employees' taxable wages), whichever is less. The law is very strict, however, with respect to the minimum contribution requirements. The participant must contribute the same minimum percentage each year or risk a fine equal to five percent of the amount of any underfunding.

Those who wish to avoid the risk of a penalty or who like to tie their contributions to the profitability of their enterprise prefer the profit sharing Keogh. In this plan the limits are the lower of $30,000 or 13.04 percent of the owner's net profits (or 15 percent of total employees' taxable wages).

It is important to note that the two plans just described are not mutually exclusive. The law allows a person to set up both types of plans as long as the total contribution does not exceed the lesser of $30,000 or 20 percent of the owner's self-employment income (25 percent of total employees' taxable income).

Frequently, employees of corporations who are also self-employed business persons wish to shelter most or all of their self-employed earnings. This is especially true for older self-employed persons who also have secured positions with corporations. For them, the *defined benefit* Keogh provides a rare opportunity. With this type, the individual decides not how much to put in the plan each year, but how much the plan should pay out on maturity—up to the maximum allowable contribution limit of $98,064 a year (1989), adjusted for inflation. Annual contributions to this plan will vary according to the age of the participant and other factors, such as the return on the plan investment. For this reason, defined benefit Keoghs require detailed actuarial computations every year in order to determine how much contribution would be legally allowed for that year.

Finally, regardless of which Keogh is selected, the law allows an additional nondeductible contribution of six percent of the self-employed income net of deductible contribution, but 401(k)-type nondiscrimination rules apply.

In this chapter we have analyzed in detail the basic structure of retirement income. In the next chapter we will undertake a detailed review of the key concepts and strategies relating to retirement planning.

CHAPTER 13

Retirement Planning: Concepts and Strategies

INTRODUCTION

For the past couple of generations, Americans have relied on the venerable three-legged stool to provide for their retirement: Social Security benefits, private pensions, and personal savings. Many factors currently threaten the stability of this stool. For instance, retirees of the next century will grow far older. When Social Security was enacted in 1935 and retirement was set at 65, the average male that age could expect to live an additional 12 years. In 1989, he could expect to live for 15 more years, and by 2025, it could be 20 more years. At the same time, the age at which full Social Security benefits can be collected will rise to 67, and the portion of benefits individuals sacrifice when they retire will be greater.

Longer lives will require more financial support. Yet the ability of Social Security to provide this expanded support appears questionable. The reason for this concern is clear. More than three people now work and pay Social Security taxes for each retiree collecting; by 2030, that ratio will drop to below 2 to 1. In addition, the viability of many corporate plans is also in doubt.

Clearly, those who save for retirement starting an early age will become the envy of the retirement generation.

Retirement planning, or planning for financial independence, is one of the key areas of personal financial planning. We work all our lives, expecting to earn the privilege of maintaining a desired lifestyle upon retirement. It is conceivable, however, that without proper planning, this retirement dream could turn into a nightmare. The reasons for this potential problem are not hard to find. As mentioned, without proper planning and systematic directive actions, a retiree might not have an adequate income upon retirement. An accumulated capital fund might not last as long as both spouses live. Retirees might not make the right decisions with regard to: (1) tax-wise distribution of retirement funds; (2) picking the right retirement age; and (3) selecting the appropriate strategies for investing retirement funds.

In retirement planning, individuals first define their goals for quality of life after retirement. Next, they measure their ability to meet their goals and develop strategies for improving their progress. In the final analysis, success in retirement planning is assured if the individual is able to retire at the desired retirement age with the desired level of income.

This chapter is divided into four parts. First an in-depth analysis of retirement income needs is undertaken. Then distribution requirements and tax implications of retirement fund distribution are explored. Next several methods of receiving retirement income are presented. Finally, several retirement planning strategies are discussed.

At this point it is necessary to make an important observation about the discussions which follow. Any sophisticated discussion on retirement planning should take into consideration the different types of individuals, such as: (1) the financially sophisticated person; (2) the dual-career couple; (3) the highly compensated executive; (4) the owner of a professional practice; (5) the owner of a closely held business; and (6) the salaried employee. However, since such sophistication is beyond the scope of this book, in our discussions on retirement planning we will treat all individuals as part of a homogeneous group. While that will inevitably create distortions, by so doing we will be able to focus our attention on the *major issues* relating to retirement planning.

RETIREMENT INCOME NEEDS ANALYSIS

RETIREMENT BUDGET

The retirement income needs analysis begins with the construction of a realistic retirement budget, which involves the estimation of income and expenses during retirement years. We will now turn to the construction of such a retirement budget for a hypothetical family. John and Betty Jones are an affluent couple. John is a corporate executive and Betty is a dental hygienist. Both participate in corporate retirement plans. John is 40 and wishes to retire in 20 years. Betty is 38 and intends to retire with John.

Retirement Expenditure Analysis

We will begin with the Jones's current expenditures, which are presented in Table 13-1. It is important to note here that these expenditures are strictly for the Jones family and do not necessarily represent either a national average or an ideal expenditure pattern. In fact, in analyzing retirement budgets it may be counterproductive for financial planners to make value judgments about their clients' expenditure patterns.

Once the current expenditures are recorded, our next task is to estimate those expected during retirement. There are, of course, no hard and fast rules for precisely estimating retirement expenses. The accepted rule of thumb is that a retiree will spend 70 or 80 percent of the preretirement expenditure level. This rule, however, appears too rigid and often misleading, because it does not specifically recognize the differences between (1) various categories of expenditures and (2) people who aspire to maintain different lifestyles after retirement.

A better approach to estimating expenditures during retirement is to divide fixed and flexible expenditures into several key categories and encourage the client to estimate the retirement expenditure in each category. This approach provides individuals with an opportunity to fine tune their retirement income estimates. For instance, Table 13-1 reveals that the Joneses plan to keep on making mortgage payments after retirement; consequently, after retirement their housing expenditures remain virtually unchanged. For another family expecting to own a home free and clear before retirement, these expenses would be drastically reduced after retirement. Another area of interest is entertainment expenditure. Some families may wish to drastically reduce their entertainment expenses after retirement, while others may plan to spend a great deal more by undertaking world travels or developing other expensive hobbies.

Returning to the Jones family, we find that after retirement the Joneses expect to spend $73,804 per year, which is 46 percent of their current expenditure.

Retirement Income

We now turn to an estimate of the retirement income for the Joneses. The family expects to receive an annual income of $55,800 from corporate and

TABLE 13-1 Retirement Budget Estimate

Income/expenditures	Current year	At retirement
Current Income	$196,396	$55,800*
Expenditures		
Housing		
Rent, mortgage, property taxes, utilities (gas, oil, electricity and water), telephone, home furnishings, household services, maintenance, improvements	39,012	36,904
Clothing		
Purchases and cleaning	1,846	1,100
Food	7,800	8,000
Transportation		
Car repair and maintenance, installment payments, gas, commuting costs, etc.	3,854	1,200
Gifts	2,700	1,500
Contributions	4,188	1,500
Education, books, subscriptions	6,456	1,500
Insurance		
Life, medical, auto, property, liability	4,236	950
Medical and dental care		
Premiums, deductible and out-of-pocket costs	132	350
Loan-repayment costs	2,880	0
Personal care		
Grooming, health club, other	0	0
Entertainment		
Vacations, dining out, movies, plays, concerts, sports events, cable TV, videocassettes, entertaining, sports, hobbies, other	11,244	10,000
Domestic help	0	200
Savings and Retirement		
Contribution to company plans IRAs, Keoghs, SEPs, other savings	17,000	0
Taxes		
Federal, FICA, state, local	53,500	8,600
Miscellaneous	4,500	2,000
Total expenditure	159,348	73,804
Surplus(+)/deficit(−)	+37,048	−18,004

* Expected income from corporate and noncorporate qualified plans, and Social Security and IRA plans.

noncorporate qualified plans as well as from Social Security, as shown next:

Social Security	$10,200
Pension/Profit Sharing Plans	32,400
401(k) Plan	9,000
IRA Plan	4,200
	$55,800

The Social Security benefits can be calculated with the help of a Social Security pamphlet called *Estimating Your Social Security Retirement Check*. The company benefits department can estimate the income from pension, profit sharing, and 401(k) plans. Annual income from IRA and Keogh plans can be calculated by estimating the value of each plan upon retirement and acquiring from a life insurance company the lifetime annuity value for the accumulated amount.

To sum up, at retirement, the Joneses expect to have annual expenses of $73,804, whereas their income from corporate and noncorporate qualified plans and Social Security are expected to be $55,800. The balance of $18,004 must come from personal investment if the family expects to meet its retirement goals.

The Potential Shortfall

Now that we have learned that the Joneses must receive $18,004 every year from personal investments in order to meet their retirement goal, we can determine if they can reasonably expect to meet this goal.

The analytical framework for calculating the savings required for retirement is presented in Table 13-2. In constructing this table we have made the following assumptions: (1) the Jones's current personal, nonqualified savings amount to $85,954; (2) number of years to retirement is 20; and (3) both qualified and personal savings will grow at an inflation-adjusted real rate of three percent. As we can see, in this table line 3 confirms that after retirement the Joneses must receive an annual income of $18,004 from nonqualified investment sources.

We recall that John Jones is 40 and wishes to retire in 20 years. Assuming his life expectancy to be 80, the first step is to determine how much savings is required to generate $18,004 a year at the end of each year for 20 years. We calculate that amount to be $267,854:

$$PMT = 18,004$$

$$i = 3$$

$$n = 20$$

$$PV = 267,854$$

TABLE 13-2 Determination of Savings Required for Retirement

Line 1	Annual budget after retirement		$ 73,804
Line 2	Annual distribution from:		
	a. Social Security	$10,200	
	b. Pension/profit sharing plans	32,400	
	c. 401(k) plan	9,000	
	d. Keogh plan	—	
	e. IRA plan	4,200	
	f. Total:		55,800
Line 3	Annual income needed from nonqualified Investments (#1 minus #2f)		18,004
Line 4	Savings required by retirement date, in current dollars $PMT = 18,004, i = 3, n = 20,$ $PV = 267,854$		267,854
Line 5	Current personal savings		85,954
Line 6	Value of personal savings at retirement $PV = 85,954, i = 3, n = 20,$ $FV = 155,242$		155,242
Line 7	Amount of savings required to cover the deficit (#4 minus #6)		112,612
Line 8	Savings required each year $FV = 112,612, i = 3, n = 20,$ $PMT = 4,191$		4,191

Assumptions: 1. Current personal savings = $85,954
2. Years to retirement = 20
3. Inflation-adjusted real rate of return = 3%

Next, we estimate the value of personal savings on the day of retirement. Currently, personal savings of the Joneses are $85,954 (line 5). If these savings grow at an after-tax, inflation-adjusted rate of return of three percent, the value of the savings in 20 years will be $155,242:

$$PV = 85,954$$

$$i = 3$$

$$n = 20$$

$$FV = 155,242$$

We have determined that, at retirement, the Joneses need a total personal savings of $267,854 (line 4), whereas their expected savings would be only $155,242 (line 6). That is, the expected shortfall of savings is $112,612 (line

7). This shortfall can be met if the Joneses save at an annual rate of $4,191 for 20 years and realize an after-tax, inflation-adjusted rate of return of three percent:

$$FV = 112,612$$

$$i = 3$$

$$n = 20$$

$$PMT = 4,191$$

An oversimplified framework for the retirement income shortfall is presented in Figure 13-1. This figure reveals that without additional savings the Joneses would experience an annual shortfall of $7,569 when they retire in 20 years. While the Joneses realize that the additional annual savings of $4,191 required to meet their retirement goal can quickly change with a change in the key variables (e.g., inflation rate), this analysis does provide them with a basis for effective retirement planning.

Given the basic assumptions made in this example, the Joneses have four distinct options:

Option 1: They can retire on time if they manage to save an additional $4,191 per year and make it grow at a three percent after-tax real rate of return.

Option 2: Even if the Joneses cannot save additional funds, they still can conceivably meet their retirement goal if they succeed in having their savings grow at a rate faster than the three percent after-tax real rate assumed in the previous discussion.

Option 3: The Joneses can lower their retirement income goal.

Option 4: John Jones can extend his desired retirement age beyond age 60.

To recap, a potential shortfall in the retirement budget requires the development of specific strategies to solve the problem. These strategies can be conveniently divided into the following categories.

1. *Tax-Advantaged Investment Planning.* This strategy requires that the family consider the possibility of making the maximum contribution to the qualified plans and the IRAs, if that is not currently being done.

2. *Savings Planning.* Increasing the amount of annual savings may entail a thorough examination, and eventual reduction, of current monthly expenses. A more austere budget may force the family to choose between nonessential current expenditures and a better standard of living at retirement.

3. *Asset Repositioning Planning.* A review of the existing investments may induce the family to shift the current portfolio into more aggressive in-

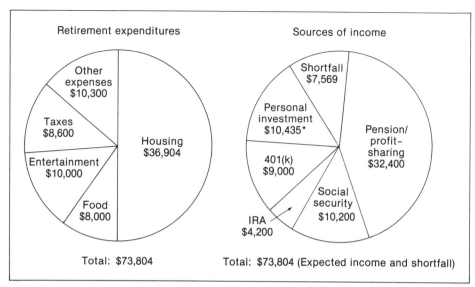

Total: $73,804

Total: $73,804 (Expected income and shortfall)

*Total savings of $155,242 at retirement will generate
an annual income of $10,435 for 20 years.

FIGURE 13-1 Retirement income needs analysis

vestments if there are strong feelings about the desired level of retirement income. Of course, if these planning strategies do not produce the desired results, the family would be forced to lower the desired retirement income or advance the retirement age, neither of which might offer an attractive alternative.

The Potential Surplus

It should be clearly recognized that not every retirement plan has a potential shortfall. For instance, assume the Joneses wish to have annual retirement expenses of $73,804 (Table 13-2), but at retirement expect to receive an income of $75,800 instead of $55,800. In that case they will have a potential surplus in their retirement budget, and no further action will be necessary on their part.

DISTRIBUTION FROM QUALIFIED PLANS

INTRODUCTION

Qualified plans are subject to strict rules about when and how they can make distributions to participants. As a general rule, some deferral is required before employees can receive distributions. Also, employee contributions are generally subject to fewer restrictions than employer contributions. In addition to these general rules, however, there are specific rules which apply to different types of qualified plans. A description of various types of plans and the key distribution rules governing them is presented next.

PENSION PLANS

Pension plans are subjected to the most stringent distribution rules. Furthermore, within the pension plans, rules applying to defined benefit plans are stricter than those applicable to the defined contribution plans. As a general rule, the law allows distribution from a pension plan: (1) at retirement; (2) upon the attainment of normal retirement age; (3) upon the separation of service; (4) upon death; (5) in the event of permanent disability; or (6) upon the plan's termination.

PROFIT SHARING PLANS

The rules governing profit sharing plans are less restrictive than those governing pension plans. In general, distribution from a profit sharing plan is allowed: (1) upon the attainment of age $59\frac{1}{2}$; (2) when certain specified events like layoff, illness, disability, or termination of employment occur; or (3) after the passage of a prespecified time period.

OTHER QUALIFIED PLANS

Other types of qualified plans are subject to varying distribution rules. For instance, 401(k) plans cannot make the distributions because of the passage of time, but these plans can make distributions at retirement, death, disability, separation from service, or attainment of age $59\frac{1}{2}$. These plans are also allowed to distribute elective contributions, but not earnings on them, because of hardship. Obviously, these rules apply only to 401(k) plans. Other plans, such as thrift plans, ESOPs, SEPs, and so on are governed by a slightly different set of rules.

It should be mentioned that employee contributions to various types of plans are not subject to the same restrictions as those imposed on other contributions. However, a waiting period is generally imposed before employee contributions can be distributed.

REQUIRED DISTRIBUTIONS

All qualified plans are required to make compulsory distributions to the participating employees when certain conditions are met. Chief among these conditions is the participants' attaining age 70½. The law requires that when a person reaches age 70½, a minimum distribution (which is determined by using a predetermined formula) from a qualified plan must be started. The penalty for failure to start the minimum distribution process at that age is a 50 percent excise tax on the difference between what should be distributed and what is actually distributed.

The distribution from a qualified plan must also begin after an employee's death. If the distribution has already started in the form of an annuity, after death the remaining portion of annuity interest must be distributed at least at the same rate at which the distribution would have been made had the employee survived. On the other hand, if no distribution had started, the distribution process must start within five years after the employee's death. One exception to this general rule relates to the situation in which the benefit is payable to a designated beneficiary. Amounts in these plans may be distributed over the life of the beneficiary as long as the distribution begins no later than one year after the employee's death.

TAXATION OF PLAN BENEFITS

The tax consequence of a distribution from a pension plan depends upon the mix of before-tax and after-tax dollars used to make the contributions. If the employer uses before-tax dollars to fund the entire cost of the retirement plan, upon distribution, qualified plan benefits to the recipients become fully taxable. However, if the employee made contributions to the plan with after-tax dollars, or was previously taxed on benefits, such as life insurance premiums, and the benefits represent both types of contributions, only that part of each distribution representing the employer's contribution become taxable. Of course, earnings accumulated in a qualified plan on a tax-deferred basis are fully taxable as ordinary income.

Once the amount of distribution which is subject to taxation has been identified, the tax treatment of this amount would depend upon whether the distribution is taxed under the lump sum distribution rules or the annuity rules. The tax treatment under each method is discussed below.

Lump Sum Distribution

Although the law does not require them to do so, as an alternative to the annuity option, many qualified plans offer persons who have been participants for at least five tax years—the minimum required for lump sum distribution—

a choice of receiving the money in the form of a lump sum distribution. Under IRS rules, employees favoring this option may choose between two methods of computing the tax: as part capital gain, or as all ordinary income subject to the five-year (or in certain cases ten-year) forward averaging rule.

Capital gains treatment. The portion of a lump sum distribution attributable to employer contributions for service before 1974 is eligible for capital gains treatment. This treatment is being phased out over a six-year period which began in 1987. But employees who attained age 50 before January 1, 1986, can choose to remain eligible for capital gains treatment.

Participants who choose the capital gains tax option are permitted to use 20 percent as the favorable tax rate to compute the tax separately on accumulations eligible for capital gains in their plan accounts.

Forward averaging. Participants of qualified plans can choose the alternative method of taxation known as forward averaging. For distributions after 1986, the period over which income may be averaged is five years, although employees who attained age 50 before January 1, 1986, can elect to use the ten-year averaging method. However, in that case, they must use the tax rates in effect on December 31, 1986. The forward averaging technique is discussed more fully in a subsequent section.

Annuity Distribution

The second option available to plan participants is to receive the distribution as an annuity. Distributions received as an annuity, less the return of the participant's cost basis, are taxed as ordinary income. This cost basis represents the contributions made by the employees with after-tax dollars and the previously taxed employer's contributions.

Incidentally, under the annuity rules the amount of monthly distribution that escapes taxation is identified by an *exclusion ratio.* This ratio is calculated by dividing the employee's total investment in the plan (cost basis) by the total expected return under the contract. For instance, assume Judy Clark contributed $50,000 of after-tax funds to a pension plan and is expected to receive $1,000 per month for life. Given her life expectancy the actuary has determined that during her lifetime Judy will receive a total of $91,000. The exclusion ratio in this case is 55 percent ($50,000/$91,000). This means that 55 percent of each month's annuity income of $1,000, or $550, will escape taxation.

Rollovers

It is of course possible to postpone the taxation of qualified plan benefits at the time of lump sum distribution. This is accomplished by rolling over within 60 days the total distribution into an IRA or into another qualified pension or profit sharing plan. The earnings will then accumulate tax-deferred until withdrawals are made.

It is not necessary for a plan participant to roll over the entire retirement fund. However, partial distributions have several restrictions associated with them:

1. They can be rolled over only into an IRA and not into another qualified plan.
2. The partial rollover is allowed only if the distribution is due to the participant's death, disability, or separation from service.
3. Partial distributions must equal at least 50 percent of the balance to the credit of the employee, determined immediately before distribution.
4. After a partial rollover, no part of the amount that remains in the qualified plan is eligible for five- or ten-year averaging or for capital gains treatment.

TAXATION OF IRAs

Earnings in the IRA accounts are tax-deferred until these earnings are withdrawn; upon distribution, all earnings are taxed as ordinary income.

The rules governing the taxability of IRA contributions are a little more involved. If contributions were made with tax-deductible dollars, upon distribution these will be fully taxed. Distributions attributable to nondeductible contributions are treated as a return of capital basis and are not taxable. Finally, if nondeductible and deductible contributions are made by the same individual, all distributions are apportioned between them.

TAXATION OF KEOGH PLANS

Since Keogh plans are for the self-employed, there is no lump sum distribution for such a plan after retirement. Consequently, the treatment is limited to distributions by reason of death, attaining age 59½, or disability.

Keogh plan withdrawals must begin by April 1 of the year after a person reaches 70½. If the participant is married, a minimum withdrawal is based upon the life expectancy of the individual and his or her spouse. All deductible Keogh contributions and earnings are taxed as ordinary income. However, nondeductible contributions are distributed tax-free.

As in the case with corporate plans, the five-year, or ten-year, forward averaging rule applies to Keogh plans. However, a person can take advantage of a special tax break only once, whether it applies to a lump sum distribution from a Keogh plan or a corporate plan. Because of this limitation, depending on individual circumstances, it may be advisable to roll over the corporate lump sum payment into a Keogh plan if one is available. That way the five-year—or ten-year—forward averaging rule can be applied to the lump sum distributions from *both* plans.

OTHER TAX CONSIDERATIONS

Premature Distributions

If an individual makes a withdrawal from an IRA account prior to reaching age 59½, an additional tax of ten percent is imposed on the taxable portion of the withdrawal. Of course, this additional tax is waived if the distribution is: (1) triggered by either death or disability; (2) used to purchase a single or joint lifetime annuity; or (3) rolled over within 60 days into another IRA.

The ten percent penalty tax on early distribution is also imposed on qualified defined benefit and defined contributions plans, tax-sheltered annuities, SEPs, and custodial accounts. However, the exceptions to this additional tax are: (1) death; (2) disability; (3) single or joint lifetime annuity distributions; (4) distributions to employees who have attained age 55, separated from service, and who received the distributions as part of an early retirement arrangement; (5) distributions made to pay deductible medical expenses; (6) distributions of dividends from profit sharing or stock bonus plans; and (7) distributions from ESOPs (employee stock option plans) that have been invested in employer securities for five years.

Excess Contributions

If contributions made to a qualified plan exceed the maximum allowed by law, the excess contribution is subject to a six percent excise tax. In the case of an IRA, an individual can avoid paying this tax by withdrawing the excess from the IRA account before the deadline for the IRA contributions, which is April 15 of the year following the year for which the contribution is made.

The IRS provides a formula which can be used to determine how the *earnings* relating to the excess contributions to qualified plans must also be withdrawn. Also, if the client is under 59½ years of age, then the withdrawal of earnings is treated as a premature distribution and a ten percent penalty tax is imposed on them. Form 5329 is required to be filed distinguishing between the: (1) IRA earnings; (2) IRA distribution; and (3) the penalty tax. These steps are all necessary to cover timely removal of the excess contributions.

Excess Distributions

There is a penalty tax of 15 percent on annual distributions exceeding the greater of (1) $122,580 (1989) as indexed for inflation, or (2) $150,000. This penalty applies to the total of all distributions to the individual in one year from all qualified plans, 403(b) tax-deferred annuities, IRAs, and SEPs. If the recipient elects lump sum treatment on the distribution, the limits are increased to five times the preceding limit—that is, $612,900 in 1989 or $750,000. If both annual and lump sum distributions are received in the same year, the excess distributions are determined separately.

There are potentially favorable "grandfather" provisions for participants whose accrued plan benefit on August 1, 1986, exceeded $562,500. To take advantage of these provisions, an election must have been made on the participant's 1987 or 1988 tax return, before the due date of the return. If grandfathering was elected, the taxpayer forfeits the use of the $150,000 applicable annual exclusion but still has the use of the $122,580 (1989) exemption which is indexed for inflation.

Exclusions from the 15 percent excess distribution tax are distributions: (1) from plans terminated prior to December 1986; (2) of the participant's after-tax investment in the plan; or (3) rolled over into an IRA or another qualified plan.

Insufficient Distributions

When an individual reaches age 70½, the law requires that compulsory minimum distributions from qualified plans, tax-deferred annuity plans, IRAs, SEPs, and governmental deferred compensation plans begin in one of the following forms: (1) full distribution; (2) minimum distribution; or (3) individual or joint and survivor annuity. If the actual distribution falls short of the minimum required distribution, there is a penalty tax of 50 percent on the shortfall. As mentioned, this shortfall represents the difference between the amount that has been calculated as the minimum distribution and the amount actually distributed from the plan.

RETIREMENT INCOME: THE ULTIMATE DECISION

INTRODUCTION

As retirement age draws near, every individual is faced with the dilemma: How can one make a rational decision on the most efficient means of distribution of qualified money? As revealed by Figure 13-2, the major sources of retirement income consist of income from personal investment, corporate sponsored qualified plans, Keogh plans for self-employed income earners, IRAs, and Social Security. Of these, personal investment income was discussed in great detail in Chapters 9 through 11 and need not be repeated here. The rest of the choices will be discussed in this section. Incidentally, since there is little difference between corporate sponsored qualified plans and Keogh plans insofar as distribution of retirement income is concerned, no distinction will be made between them.

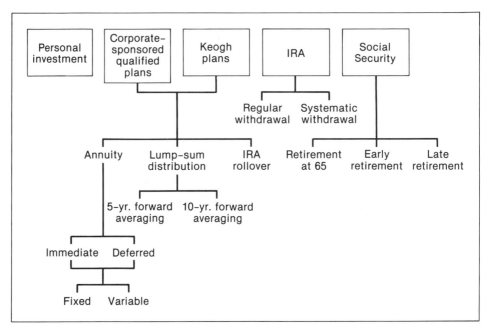

FIGURE 13-2 Major sources of retirement income

Company Sponsored Qualified Plan and Keogh Plan

There are three principal ways in which an individual can withdraw retirement money: an annuity, lump sum distribution, or IRA rollover. At stake is the bulk of the retirement wealth. Furthermore, since the choices open to the retiree are almost always irrevocable, and the outcomes of the distribution decisions are vastly different, great care should be exercised in making this important decision. We will now discuss in detail each of the three key distribution choices available to a retiree.

Annuity

The annuity principle. Life insurance enables an individual to purchase a contract providing a definite sum of money at the time of death. Such contracts are possible because the mortality of a large group of individuals can be predicted with reasonable accuracy.

A different problem, however, faces the individual who has accumulated a sum of money and wants to determine how much can be safely spent each year during her or his lifetime. If the money is spent too rapidly, the day will come when the funds will be exhausted—possibly with several years of life remaining. In contrast, if the funds are disbursed too slowly, at the time of death a portion of the funds will be left, money that could have been used to maintain a higher standard of living.

Confronted with this problem, no one person can be certain as to what sum can be *safely* spent each month. However, this uncertainty does not apply to a large group. Through the use of mortality tables, in return for the payment of a lump sum or a series of payments, insurance companies can make guaranteed life-income payments to various individuals, because the mortality rates of each group can be predicted with reasonable accuracy. Put differently, the greater total sum paid to those who live to unusually advanced ages can be balanced by the smaller payments made to those who die relatively early. Such payments are called annuities.

The word "annuity" implies payments made by an insurance company at fixed intervals, such as monthly, quarterly, or yearly. When an insurance policy is purchased, payments are made to the insurance company during the policyholder's lifetime and the company pays a stipulated amount when the policyholder dies. With an annuity, an individual pays a given sum to the insurance company and in return receives an income according to various options (discussed below). An annuity contract, therefore, is essentially the reverse of a life insurance policy, although it is *not* an insurance policy.

Under the classic, or original, type of annuity, the income ceases with the death of the annuitant, and the company is under no further obligation. Fortunately, however, many important variations of the original type are available in the marketplace today, as revealed in Figure 13-3. This figure

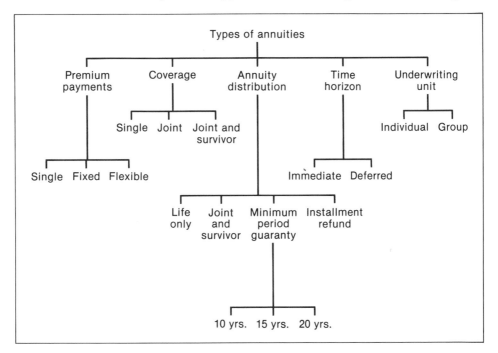

FIGURE 13-3   Forms of Annuities

reveals that annuity contracts vary according to how the payment for the annuity is made, how the proceeds are distributed, how earnings accrue, and when the benefits are received by the annuitant or beneficiary. Of these features, disposition of proceeds is of special interest for the individual planning to retire.

Before discussing various annuity distribution options it might be interesting to think of an annuity as a *liquidating* retirement payment plan. This principle is illustrated in Figure 13-4. For instance, suppose Betty Jones retires at age 65 with an after-tax lump sum distribution of $100,000. She purchases an annuity which guarantees an income for 20 years. During this 20-year period, in addition to receiving her principal of $100,000, Betty will receive an additional $10,185 representing the return on the principal in the form of dividends and interest. Put differently, the monthly income received by Betty will consist of interest, dividends, and a portion of the original investment. Consequently, at the end of the 20-year period, the entire investment will have been liquidated and the company will owe nothing to Betty Jones.

Disposition of proceeds. Various options available under an annuity plan, which were briefly discussed in Chapter 3, are presented in Figure 13-5. The figure reveals that the annuity can be fixed or variable. The former refers to an annuity contract which promises a fixed return during the life of

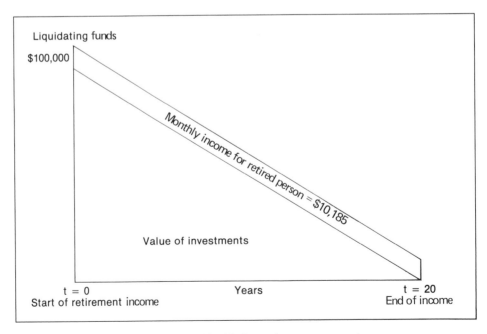

FIGURE 13-4 Liquidating retirement payout plan

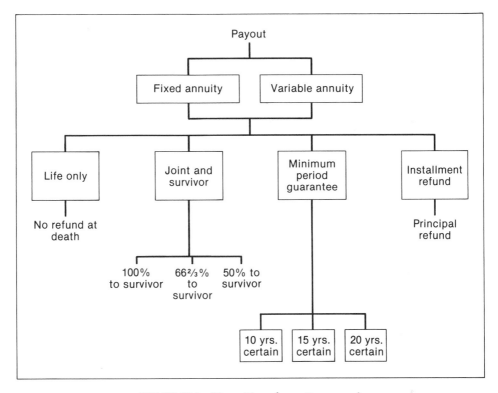

FIGURE 13-5 Disposition of annuity proceeds

the contract and is therefore not dependent upon the results of the vehicle in which the money is invested. However, typically the return is fixed on an annual basis (with a minimum guaranty of four percent) so the fixed return can—and often does—vary from year to year. In contrast, a variable annuity is a form of contract that is invested in one or several mutual fund portfolios. In this case, payments can vary in size, depending upon the rate of return on the portfolios selected. In both cases, the options available to the annuitant are identical, although generally the amount of the annuity payments will vary—sometimes greatly—between the two methods of payment. We will now discuss the key choices available to an annuitant.

- *Life only* pays for the annuitant's lifetime and pays nothing to the surviving spouse or other heirs.
- *Joint and survivor* pays a reduced amount to the annuitant during his or her lifetime and then continues 100 percent, 66⅔ percent, or 50 percent of the original sum over the remaining lifetime of the surviving joint annuitant. Payments stop after the death of the annuitant *and* the joint annuitant, and the company owes nothing to the beneficiaries.

- *Minimum period guaranty* promises that payments will continue for at least the minimum (for instance, ten, 15, or 20 years) guaranteed period even if the annuitant (or both annuitants) dies during this period. If the annuitant survives longer than the specified period, the annuity continues to pay the same amount until death.
- *Installment refund* pays the annuitant or the survivor until the payment equals the original investment in the annuity contract.

Tax treatment of annuity payments

Fixed Annuity. The basic rule of annuity payment taxation is that the investment portion of each payment is excludable from the calculation of gross income because it is a return of the purchaser's original investment in the contract. In the case of a fixed annuity, an exclusion ratio is calculated by dividing the investment in the contract by the expected return. For example, an annuitant purchases a $50,000 immediate five-year annuity. Based on current interest rates the monthly income would be $990.02. Therefore, the expected return is $59,401.12 ($990.02 × 60). The exclusion ratio is 84.2 percent ($50,000/$59,401.12). Under the 1986 Tax Reform Act, the exclusion ratio is applied until the entire initial investment is recovered. Thereafter, 100 percent of each payment is taxed as ordinary income.

Variable Annuity. Under the variable form of annuity payments, the monthly payments are paid from a variable account which fluctuates based on investment results. As such, the expected return cannot be determined in advance. Therefore, Treasury regulations make the assumption that the expected return is equal to the investment in the contract. The excludable portion of each payment is found by dividing the investment in the contract by the anticipated number of months of payout. In the preceding example, the $50,000 investment would be divided by the five years of payout [$50,000/($990.02 × 12 × 5) = 84.17%] and 84.2 percent of each monthly payment of $990.02, or $833.30, would be excluded from gross income. Essentially, the tax treatment is the same for both fixed and variable annuities.

The best choice.   Clearly the best choice of an annuity option depends upon the objective of the annuitant and the total amount of retirement income expected to be received from other sources. Individuals who wish to receive a guaranteed income for life to supplement Social Security and other investment income should definitely choose either the life only or joint and survivor option, possibly with a minimum period of guaranty of ten or 15 years. However, those who have other sources of income and wish to use up the lump sum in a relatively short period of time may choose a guaranteed income for, say, five or ten years. Finally, if the retiree can assume the market risk, serious consid-

eration should be given to a variable instead of a fixed annuity, be
is a greater potential for growth in the former type of annuity.

Lump Sum Distribution

An overview.   One of the valuable options available to most retirees is
to receive the nest egg in one lump sum instead of as an annuity. If a decision
to take the lump sum is made, then the retiree comes to the second crossroad:
whether to pay the tax on the lump sum right away or to postpone the reck-
oning by rolling over the money into an IRA. If the latter decision is made,
the money must be rolled over into an IRA within 60 days. If the first choice
is preferred, however, the employee must resort to a rather sophisticated tax
planning strategy, as described next.

Forward averaging option.   With the exception of IRAs, SEPs, and 403(b)
plans, distributions from qualified funds receive a special tax treatment provided they meet certain eligibility requirements. For instance, for a plan to
be eligible, a distribution must be of the *entire* account balance, made within
one taxable year, on account of retirement, or upon death or disability. In
addition, to be eligible, the participant is required to be in the plan for at least
five years. It should also be noted here that the participant must be $59\frac{1}{2}$ or
older; otherwise a ten percent penalty could be imposed on the distribution.

There are two special tax treatments available: five-year forward averaging and ten-year forward averaging. The former option is available to everyone; however, the latter option is available only to those who were over 50
years old on January 1, 1986. People over age 52 who participated in their
employer's pension plan before 1974 have yet another option. They can elect
to have the portion of the sum attributable to the pre-1974 contributions taxed
as capital gains at the top 1986 rate of 20 percent. Taxpayers in this category
can then use five-year or ten-year forward averaging for the remainder of their
payout.

The five-year forward averaging method requires taking the following
steps:

Step 1: Divide total distribution by 5.
Step 2: Compute tax on the amount calculated in Step 1 by using current
tax rates for a single taxpayer.
Step 3: Multiply the tax calculated in Step 2 by 5.

The ten-year forward averaging method requires a slightly different approach:

Step 1: Divide total distribution by 10.
Step 2: Add $2,480 to this amount.

Step 3: Compute tax on this total by using 1986 (not current) single tax-payer rates (even if the retiree files joint returns).

Step 4: Multiply the tax calculated in Step 3 by 10.

Clearly, the retiree should use whichever method minimizes the tax liability.

IRA Rollover

The third distribution option is to roll over the funds into an IRA within 60 days of receiving the lump sum distribution. With a rollover IRA the retiree avoids paying current taxes on the distribution. Instead, taxes are paid when money is withdrawn. The advantage in choosing this option is that no penalties are imposed for the rollover and the individual can choose how the money is invested through a self-directed IRA account. Most important, the entire distribution continues to grow tax-deferred, over the life of the IRA. A disadvantage of this option is that all IRA conditions are imposed on such rollovers.

LUMP SUM VERSUS IRA: A TAXING DECISION

The discussion undertaken in the previous section underscored an important point: To choose between a lump sum distribution and an IRA rollover is a taxing decision. There is no clear choice and the best alternative depends on a host of tax-related factors, as revealed in the following discussion.

Let us examine the case of John and Betty Jones, both of whom were 65 and were set to retire on December 30, 1988. John's employer offered to make a monthly payment of $2,000 to him for life or pay him a $250,000 lump sum. These choices with related data are presented in Table 13-3. Receiving the

---

TABLE 13-3   Retirement Distribution Choices

Option	Initial tax	Net sum invested	Income at age 65*	Income at age 75*	Balance at age 75**
Pension (Annuity)	$0	$0	$17,280	$10,608	$0
Lump sum with 10-year averaging	50,770	199,230	17,280	17,280	87,552
IRA rollover with immediate withdrawals	0	250,000	17,280	17,280	148,759

* In after-tax 1988 dollars, assuming inflation of 5% a year.

** Assuming the mutual fund performance matches its historical record.

Source: Adapted from *Money,* December 1988, p. 110.

annuity would shrink the annual income of $24,000 ($17,280 after taxes, assuming a 28 percent tax bracket) to $10,608 in 1988 dollars by the time John reaches 75 if inflation were to run at a modest 5 percent a year annual rate ($FV = \$17,280, i = 5, n = 10, PV = 10,608$).

If John Jones chose to receive the lump sum, he would have many investment options open to him for the retirement fund. Let us examine the two choices presented in Table 13-3.

The first choice relates to the payment of federal income tax by using the preferential treatment under the ten-year forward averaging rule. John's CPA has determined that the tax (1988) on the $250,000 lump sum distribution would be $50,770, so the *net* amount of distribution would be $199,230 ($250,000 − $50,770).

Next, John contacts his financial planner and asks him to recommend a municipal mutual bond fund which would permit him to withdraw tax-free $17,280 per year—the same income he would receive under the lifetime annuity plan. John further specifies that his annual withdrawals should increase by five percent, so his income would keep up with the expected annual inflation rate of five percent. That is, during the tenth year, at age 75, John would receive $28,147, which would have the purchasing power of $17,280 in today's dollars. Finally, John asks his financial planner to ascertain how much money would be left in the fund if he were to die at, say, age 75, assuming the mutual fund maintains its historical track record. The information supplied by the financial planner is summarized in Table 13-3.

A comparison of the results achieved by selecting the annuity option and the lump sum with ten-year forward averaging reveals the following interesting facts: (1) the income under the lump sum choice keeps up with inflation, whereas the annuity income is not protected against inflation; (2) if death occurs at age 75, John's heirs will receive a significant amount of money under the second choice ($87,552), whereas they would receive nothing if the annuity choice was selected; (3) although not shown in the table, it is quite conceivable that at some point (say, around age 80) the money under the second choice would run out, whereas under lifetime annuity John could never outlive his monthly income.

Table 13-3 reveals further that John could also roll over the total lump sum amount of $250,000 into an IRA, and immediately start withdrawing the desired after-tax annual income of $17,280. In this case John would not have to pay tax upon distribution. But if the money is invested in a fully taxable corporate bond fund, John would have to withdraw every year $24,000 to net an after-tax income of $17,280 ($24,000 − 28% × $24,000), assuming John continues to be in the 28 percent marginal federal income tax bracket. When compared with the first two choices, this last option offers the best alternative.

Before leaving this topic, an important caveat should be added. Besides the three choices presented here, John and Betty have other important choices which should be explored before making the final decision. More important, even the best choice under one set of circumstances could turn out to be the worst under a different set of circumstances. For instance, if John lives to age 100, the lifetime annuity, which appears to be the worst choice, would turn out to be the best option. Consequently, care should be exercised in making sure that the client clearly understands all the underlying assumptions before making the final decision.

To recap, the decision to annuitize, take a lump sum distribution and invest, or roll over into an IRA, must be made on an individual basis. In addition to examining the numbers, in those cases where the retirees cannot be expected to manage their own funds and need the assurance of an uninterrupted flow of current income until death, the annuity route provides the best alternative. However, people who can manage their own investments should either take a lump sum distribution or roll it over into an IRA, depending upon their current and future tax situation.

IRA DISTRIBUTION

The distribution rules from IRA funds are straightforward. At the lower end, except in the case of death or disability, any distribution prior to age $59\frac{1}{2}$ is subject to a ten percent penalty. At the upper end, the individual's funds in the account must be distributed starting no later than age $70\frac{1}{2}$. If not paid in a lump sum, the payments must be distributed over a period that does not exceed the life expectancy of the individual or of the individual and the spouse, if the individual is married. If the individual or the individual and the spouse die before receiving the entire amount, the balance must be distributed to the beneficiaries within five years or applied to the purchase of an immediate annuity contract that will be payable for life of the beneficiaries or for a certain term that does not extend beyond their life expectancy.

It should now be obvious that, subject to the restrictions just specified, an individual is free to choose any suitable distribution method for the IRA funds. However, purely for illustrative purposes, we will present here only two methods which are frequently used by IRA fund owners.

Systematic Withdrawal: Personal Investment

Let us take the case of John Klein. At age 45 he started investing $2,000 at the beginning of every year into an IRA investment which grew at an annual rate of ten percent. Now, 20 years later, the IRA investment has grown to $126,005 ($PMT = 2,000, i = 10, n = 20$). Now that John is retired he decides to start receiving, say, $500 per month from his IRA investment. Also, since the long-term inflation rate is expected to be around six percent, John wants his initial monthly income of $500 to increase by six percent every year so he would maintain the purchasing power of the monthly income at the current level. After some investigation John has identified the ABC stock mutual fund which has consistently generated a long-term annual return of ten percent. Satisfied with this record, John invests $126,005 into ABC stock mutual fund and simultaneously sets up a systematic withdrawal plan. Through this plan John will achieve his retirement objective of receiving an inflation-adjusted monthly income of $500 (that is, income increasing at six percent every year) and his IRA funds will hopefully last beyond John's 90th birthday.

Systematic Withdrawal: Insurance Plan

In the second illustration, we assume that John Klein, age 65, has decided to withdraw $126,005 from an IRA fund and invest it in a systematic withdrawal plan with ABC Insurance Company. In this case, the ABC Company guarantees that John will initially receive $524.99 per month, or $6,299.89 during the first year. However, monthly incomes will increase at progressively slower rates, starting with 8.1 percent per year. The annual income John receives will increase every year, although at a progressively slower rate, to a peak of $18,732.42 at age 85. Furthermore, even though John is receiving annual payments, the funds in the annuity will continue to exceed $126,005 through age 84.

To sum up, the systematic withdrawal plan selected by an IRA investor can be tailor-made to suit the family's needs. A wide variety of options is currently available, and possibly with external assistance, a withdrawal plan can be selected to achieve the family's stated objectives.

SOCIAL SECURITY BENEFITS

For purposes of receiving Social Security benefits, the current normal retirement age is 65. However, retirement age will increase in steps for workers born in 1938 and later years. For workers who reach 62 in year 2022, that is, those born in 1960 or later, the retirement age is 67. Social Security benefits expected to be received at the normal retirement age were discussed in detail in Chapter 12 and need not be repeated here.

The decision to start Social Security benefits at retirement, at age 62, or after the normal retirement age, should be coordinated with distribution from qualified plans and IRAs in order to derive the maximum retirement benefit. Also, the taxability of Social Security benefits should be taken into account in making this decision.

RETIREMENT PLANNING STRATEGIES

In this concluding section we will analyze several basic strategies which can be used to accomplish a variety of retirement planning objectives. Also, an advanced planning strategy will be presented in the appendix to this chapter.

LOANS FROM QUALIFIED PLANS

Loans within limits are permitted from qualified plans to all employees except owner-employees who are sole proprietors, more than ten percent partners, or more than 50 percent shareholders of S corporations.

As a general rule, loans must be repaid in equal payments at least quarterly over the term of the loan. Also, the $50,000 maximum loan limit on exempt loans must be reduced by the highest outstanding loan balance during the immediately preceding 12 months.

Following the passage of TRA of 1986, the rules for taking out loans from qualified plans significantly changed. Today, the advisability of borrowing from a plan depends on the individual's tax bracket, the time of contribution to the plan, and the type of the company savings plan from which the individual intends to borrow the money.

The pros and cons of *withdrawals* and *loans* from the three most popular types of retirement plans are presented in Table 13-4. In general, *withdrawing* money from a company plan makes sense only if it is an after-tax account and the employee is taking out money contributed before 1987. The reason for this argument is straightforward. Money invested after 1986 in an after-tax plan generally must include a prorated portion of the employee's account's earnings, and, if the money was matched, employer contributions. For instance, suppose an employee withdraws $1,000 from an after-tax plan in which he or she has a $10,000 balance—$7,000 from the employee's own 1987 and 1988 contributions, and $3,000 from earnings and the employer's contributions. Of the money the employee takes out, $700 would be considered a non-taxable withdrawal of after-tax contributions and $300 will be taxed at the employee's bracket. In addition, if the employee is under age $59\frac{1}{2}$, a ten percent penalty of $30 would be imposed on the withdrawal.

Withdrawing from a 401(k) plan may be a viable alternative, but the employee must prove that financial hardship is the basis for the withdrawal. Still, all withdrawals are taxable and a ten percent penalty is imposed if the person is under age $59\frac{1}{2}$ except when the money is used to pay for unreimbursed medical expenses exceeding 7.5 percent of the person's adjusted gross income.

Taking out a *loan* from a qualified plan may be a better alternative than withdrawal, since no tax or penalty is imposed on a loan. As Table 13-4 indicates, the maximum amount that can be borrowed at any time is the lesser of: (1) $50,000 minus the highest outstanding loan balance over the previous 12 months; or (2) half of the invested plan balance or $10,000, whichever is greater. Incidentally, Keogh plans do not enjoy parity with corporate plans in the area of borrowing. According to current rules, an owner-employee or 50 percent shareholder may qualify for a "prohibited transaction" exemption relating to loans from plans to plan participants if the Department of Labor approves a special exemption.

In deciding whether to borrow from a qualified plan an employee must

TABLE 13-4 Withdrawals and Loans From Qualified Plans

Type of plan	Withdrawals		Loans	
	Restrictions	Taxes	Maximum amount permissible	Deductibility of interest
After-tax savings	A company may limit the number of withdrawals or prohibit an employee from making future contributions for a certain period of time.	Withdrawals of an employee's contributions are tax-free. Earnings and company contributions are taxable and have a 10% penalty if the employee is under 59½. Withdrawals of contributions made after 1986 are partly subject to tax and a 10% penalty for those 59½ or younger.	Companies that permit loans allow the employee to borrow the lesser of (1) $50,000 minus highest outstanding loan balance over the past 12 months, or (2) half of the vested balance over $10,000, whichever is greater.	10% in 1990, none thereafter.
401(K)	If under age 59½, withdrawals are permitted only for financial hardship.	In addition to regular taxes, the employee must pay the 10% penalty on the amount withdrawn if under age 59½.	Most companies impose the same limits as the ones on loans from after-tax plans.	None.
Employee stock ownership	Few companies permit withdrawals.	Regular taxes are due upon liquidation.	Loans are seldom permitted.	10% in 1990, none thereafter.

take both loan costs and deductibility of interest into account. In general, most plan loans charge an interest rate equal to one or two percentage points higher than the prevailing prime rate in contrast to a home equity loan rate of around 11 percent. However, only ten percent of consumer interest paid on a loan from a qualified plan is deductible from individual federal taxes in 1990 and nothing after that, whereas 100 percent of the interest on a home equity loan of up to $100,000 is fully deductible.

PENSION ENHANCEMENT STRATEGY

We have learned that one of the distribution options of a retiree is to choose the joint and survivor annuity. This option continues to pay the spouse a stated percentage of the original monthly benefit (including 100 percent) after the death of the annuitant. However, this option generates a lower monthly payment than the life only option. An interesting alternative is to choose the life only option, and purchase an appropriate amount of cash value insurance policy with the higher monthly payout to duplicate the benefits of the joint and survival option.

An example should make this clear. Let us suppose John Quinn, age 55, intends to retire at age 62. His wife, Jane, is age 50. If upon John's retirement they select a joint and survival payout option that pays Jane 75 percent of their initial benefit at John's death, their annual retirement income while both are alive will be $26,671. If they select a life only option their annual income will be $31,452—an increase of $4,781 per year.

The pension enhancement proposal for John and Jane Quinn is provided in Table 13-5. First, we calculate the benefit of this strategy by multiplying the increase in pension income by John's life expectancy in retirement. We then estimate that $200,000 will replace Jane's survival pension benefit. This figure is arrived at taking 75 percent of the initial payout of $26,671, or $20,003, and capitalizing it at ten percent. As the table shows, the benefits range from $30,000 to $89,000 over the life of the plan.

The pension enhancement plan presents an interesting retirement strategy. However, it does not provide a panacea for all annuity problems, since the outcome can change dramatically in other family situations.

TABLE 13-5   Pension Enhancement Program

I. Increase in pension income to age 85
   $4,781 × 24 years   = $114,744

II. Amount of insurance needed

   $$\frac{\$26,671 \times 75\%}{.10}$$ = $200,000

III. Cost of insurance
   i. Lump sum payment   = $ 25,514
   ii. 10-year limited pay   = $ 39,160
       $3,916 × 10
   iii. Annual premiums   = $ 84,940
       $2,740 × 30

IV. Benefit of pension enhancement
   i.   Lump sum payment   = $ 89,230
        $114,744 − $25,514
   ii. 10-year limited pay   = $ 75,584
        $114,744 − $39,160
   iii. Annual premiums   = $ 29,804
        $114,744 − $84,940

Note: In this illustration, time value of money has been ignored.
Source: George M. Brockway and Susan A. Gillette, "Enhancement or Bust," *Financial Planning,* September 1988, p. 173.

SOCIAL SECURITY TAXES

As has been true since 1984, if a worker has a substantial income in addition to Social Security, a maximum of one-half the annual Social Security benefit may be included in taxable income. The amount included in gross income is the lesser of one-half the benefits received during the year or one-half the excess of the sum of the taxpayer's adjusted gross income and one-half of the benefits received over the base amount. The base amount is the following: (1) $32,000 for a married person filing a joint return; (2) zero for a married person filing separately if the taxpayer lived with his or her spouse at any time during the year; and (3) $25,000 for any other filing status.

The strategy for reducing Social Security taxes is similar to that used for reducing catastrophic taxes (now repealed). Let us recall that any income over $32,000 triggers a Social Security tax for a married couple filing a joint return. For instance, suppose Bob and Jane Smith earned $40,000 from various sources, as shown in Table 13-6. Since this taxable income is above the $32,000 threshold, half of the Social Security income will be included with taxable income and will be taxed. However, if the Smiths shift the municipal bond investment into a tax-deferred investment, like a single premium deferred annuity, the $8,000 interest income would not be included in the calculation,

TABLE 13-6 Social Security Tax Deferral

Plan A	
Pension	$24,000
Taxable interest on corporate bond	8,000
Municipal bond interest (nontaxable)	2,000
Half of Social Security benefits	6,000
Total	$40,000
Base amount	$32,000
Taxable amount	$ 8,000

Plan B	
Convert corporate bond investment into an annuity. The interest is tax-deferred.	
Pension	$24,000
Annuity interest included in calculation	None
Municipal bond interest (nontaxable)	2,000
Half of Social Security benefits	6,000
Total	$32,000
Base amount	$32,000
Taxable amount	None

with the result that their taxable income would drop to $32,000—the highest income exempt from Social Security taxes—and the Social Security income would completely escape taxation.

EARLY RETIREMENT

Preparing for early retirement takes extensive time and planning. Not everyone, however, has such luxury. If an employer makes an early retirement offer, the employee may only have a few weeks to make the decision to accept or reject it. This is not as farfetched as it may seem. Since 1986 more than 15 companies—including IBM and Metropolitan Life—have made such offers to over 100,000 employees.

The early retirement question has two distinct dimensions: psychological and financial. Before accepting such an offer, or voluntarily deciding to retire early, one should frankly ask the following question: Am I ready to retire? If the answer is negative, or if there are lingering doubts, then the idea of early retirement should be abandoned.

Assuming that the psychological issue has been satisfactorily resolved, the financial dimension should be handled by undertaking a preliminary review of the following four key areas.

Pensions

The terms of pension payments should be explored. As a general rule, an early retirement offer should pay a pension equal to or greater than the amount one would receive under normal retirement. In some cases, employers calculate the benefit by adding on three to five years to the employee's age or tenure. Both types of offers can increase the pension by as much as 30 percent over the expected normal pension income.

Health Insurance

The COBRA law, passed in 1986, requires every employer to continue group health insurance coverage (excluding dental insurance) at the employee's expense for up to 18 months after retirement. It is important to find out the cost and availability (regarding preexisting conditions or current health conditions) of buying individual health insurance after group coverage runs out.

Life Insurance

An early retirement may require switching from the company's group life policy to an individual policy. The cost of such a policy may run around $400 a year per $10,000 of coverage. The employer may also offer a decreasing term policy; the benefit would shrink each year and virtually disappear at age 70.

Income Limitation

Prior to tax reform, if an employee was due for the maximum $90,000 a year from the employer's defined benefit plan, the employee could start collecting retirement income at age 62. Today the employee has to wait until age 65. Also, if the employee was entitled to the maximum amount before tax reform, the plan could have paid the employee $75,000 a year if the individual retired as early as age 55. Under the current law the new payout can conceivably work out to only half as much.

POST-RETIREMENT EMPLOYMENT

Just as some people choose to retire early, there are others who resent the thought of retiring and wish to continue to work even after starting to draw pension and Social Security checks. While no one has the right to be critical of the *personal* decision involving post-retirement employment, it is appropriate to ask if such a decision is financially sound.

In Table 13-7 we illustrate (for the year 1987) how much two individuals—Ron Gray who is 66 and Cindy Karr who is 71—can add to their after-

TABLE 13-7 Tax Consequences of Post-Retirement Employment

At age 66: Ron Gray						
Post-retirement job income	$6,960	$10,000	$15,000	$20,000	$30,000	$40,000
Reduction in Social Security benefits	—	$1,520	$4,020	$6,520	$8,808	$8,808
FICA tax due	$466	$670	$1,005	$1,340	$2,010	$2,533
Federal, state, and local income taxes	$2,819	$4,520	$6,780	$10,000	$15,000	$22,840
Net gain (% of earnings retained)	$3,675 (53%)	$3,290 (33%)	$3,195 (21%)	$2,140 (11%)	$4,182 (14%)	$5,819 (15%)
At age 71: Cindy Karr						
Post-retirement job income	$6,960	$10,000	$15,000	$20,000	$30,000	$40,000
Reduction in Social Security benefits*	—	—	—	—	—	—
FICA tax due	$466	$670	$1,005	$1,340	$2,010	$2,533
Federal, state, and local income taxes	$3,146	$4,520	$7,500	$10,000	$17,130	$22,840
Net gain (% of earnings retained)	$3,348 (48%)	$4,810 (48%)	$6,495 (43%)	$8,660 (43%)	$10,860 (36%)	$14,627 (37%)

* After age 71 there is no reduction in Social Security benefits due to post-retirement job income.
Source: Money Guide, 1985, "Planning Now for Your Successful Retirement," p. 90.

tax income with a post-retirement job. We assume that both are single and collect the maximum Social Security benefits ($8,808 in 1987 for Ron Gray and $9,112 for Cindy Karr). Both people have pensions paying $17,000 a year and receive investment income of $15,500. Under current law, until he reaches age 70, Rob will lose $.60 in Social Security benefits for every dollar he earns above $6,960 a year. Both people will pay FICA taxes. Income tax figures assume state and local levies totaling 19 percent of the federal tax rate and reflect the Social Security tax. This illustration reveals that if Ron continued to work past age 66 and earned $40,000, after paying various taxes and suffering a loss of Social Security benefits, his net gain would be $5,819, which is less than 15 percent of the gross income earned. For Cindy Karr, the net income would be only $14,627, which is 37 percent of her gross earned income. So the moral of post-retirement employment is this: After retirement one may wish to keep on working for love of labor, but not necessarily for money.

SPECIAL SPOUSAL BENEFIT

A special retirement planning strategy can be used to help a small business owner who has no other employees. This strategy involves an increase in the maximum allowable contribution to a defined benefit plan when the client's spouse is unemployed and has never participated in a defined contribution plan of the employer. In such a situation it is possible to pay the spouse a minimum salary and fund the plan to provide a $10,000-a-year retirement benefit. The business owner must provide justification that the spouse is active in the business to use this strategy.

NONQUALIFIED DEFERRED COMPENSATON PLAN

Certain individuals can draw on payments from a nonqualified deferred compensation plan as an additional source of retirement income. This type of arrangement is nonqualified because the company chooses to benefit a selected group of employees without regard to the antidiscrimination rules of qualified plans. A deferred compensation plan is documented by an agreement between the company and the selected employee. The essence of the agreement is that the company promises to pay the employee for currently performed services at some date in the future. This type of arrangement has been attractive to highly compensated employees because considerable income tax savings could be achieved by deferring the receipt of income to retirement years, when it might be taxed at lower rates.

Incidentally, deferred compensation can be tied to an insurance policy. If the employee dies before retirement, proceeds from the policy can be used to pay the death benefit. If the employee reaches retirement age, the company may wish to keep the policy in effect and make payments to the employee out of the accumulated cash value.

Another strategy relates to Rabbi trusts which are irrevocable trusts used to fund nonqualified deferred compensation plans. If properly structured, they may provide a measure of security for the assets in executive deferred compensation plans because the employer does not have access to the assets. The trust, however, does not protect the plan assets from the employer's creditors. Because the trust's assets are subject to claims of the employer's creditors, the funding of the trust does not constitute a taxable event for the employee.

In this chapter we have discussed concepts and strategies relating to retirement planning. A review of the basic structure of estate planning will be undertaken in the next chapter. Also, the concept of distribution planning will be explained in the appendix to this chapter.

APPENDIX TO CHAPTER 13

DISTRIBUTION PLANNING[1]

In recent years the existence of several penalty taxes has become law. These include excise taxes on early and excess distributions, a 15 percent reversion penalty tax, a 50 percent tax on late distributions, and a ten percent tax on excess nondeductible contributions. Tax-free accumulation is still available, but an individual whose other assets place him or her in the 55 percent estate tax bracket may be surprised to discover how much of the pension plan will be lost upon death. For instance, consider the following:

Plan assets		$2,160,000
Excise penalty tax @ 15%	171,067	
Estate tax @ 55%	1,093,913	
Income tax to heirs @ 35%*	340,200	
Total tax		1,605,180
Net to family		$ 554,820

The result is an effective tax rate of 74.3 percent ($1,605,180/$2,160,000), which can be even higher under the generation skipping tax if some assets are passed on to grandchildren.

To protect the hard-earned wealth of individuals and families, a new strategy called *distribution planning* can be used. This strategy seeks ways to take assets out of a qualified plan with minimal taxation. Distribution planning is particularly suited for those who have substantial wealth outside the plan and who will allow the qualified assets to accumulate for the heirs' benefit. It may also help participants who intend to use some retirement income but wish to transfer as much of the principal as possible to their heirs.

In addition to estate and income taxes, problems relating to the excess distribution and accumulation taxes are also present in most cases. Thus, if the distribution is above an annual allowable amount, the individual faces an additional 15 percent excise tax on the remainder. The amount allowed will depend on whether the participant elected to grandfather the accrued benefits—an option open only to those whose plan assets exceeded $562,500 on August 1, 1986.

---

[1] For a detailed analysis of this strategy, see Alan D. Cohen and Steven W. Meistrich, "Distribution Planning," *Financial Planning*, June 1989, pp. 117–19, 122, 124.

* This rate is assumed for purposes of this illustration.

Those who did not make the grandfather election can take the greater of $150,000 a year or $122,580 a year (indexed for inflation) free of excise taxes. If the individual prefers to take a lump sum, the maximum amount is $150,000 times five, or $750,000. Those who did elect to grandfather can take a lump sum amount equal to five times the indexed amount ($612,900) or the amount that was grandfathered, whichever is greater. The amount of the annual distribution that can be taken before excise taxes will depend on the recovery method.

When the individual dies, the estate distribution becomes subject to the excess accumulation excise tax. If the accumulated assets are more than what would be needed to produce a theoretical life annuity of allowable distributions, the excess portion is subject to a 15 percent tax, which is deductible from the estate for estate tax purposes. As a result of the Technical and Miscellaneous Revenue Act of 1988 (TAMRA) the estate excise penalty tax may be deferred until the spouse's death; however, neither traditional offsets nor credits apply, and the amount of excise tax is not deductible when the heirs have to pay income taxes on their share of the estate.

TABLE A13-1 Choices for Grandfather Election and Qualified Plan Excise Taxes

	Nongrandfathered	Grandfathered	
Lump sum	5 × allowable annual distribution	5 × allowable annual distribution or grandfathered benefit (whichever is greater)	
Annual distributions	The greater of $150,000 or $112,500 indexed for inflation beginning 1987 (currently at 4.47%)	10% $112,500 indexed	100% Any amount up to 100% of grandfathered benefit is reduced by distribution
Exemption at death	Present value of 10% of (current annual) allowable distribution multiplied by life expectancy year prior to death	The greater of PV of annuity (as described) or remaining benefit (which has been reduced by 10% of each annual distribution)	The greater of PV of annuity (as described) or remaining benefit (which has been reduced by 100% of each annual distribution)
Penalty on excess amount at death	15%	15%	15%

Source: Alan D. Cohen and Steven W. Meistrich, "Distribution Planning," *Financial Planning,* June 1989, p. 117.

To continue the major theme, the person who grandfathered the assets has several choices. Any amount up to 100 percent of the grandfathered benefit can be taken out any year and the total grandfathered benefit can be reduced by the amount of the distribution. This individual can continue to do this until the grandfathered benefit is used up, at which point the annual limitations become applicable. Alternatively, each year ten percent of the distribution can be used to save as much of the total exemption as possible against the excess accumulation tax at death. The choices for grandfather election and qualified plan excise taxes are presented in Table A13-1. In conclusion, it is important to emphasize that distribution planning strategy deals with complex tax issues and should be used only by sophisticated planners.

CHAPTER 14

Basic Structure of Estate Planning

INTRODUCTION

As a general rule, the estate of a person consists of personal assets, real property, joint interests, qualified retirement plans, life insurance owned by the individual, life insurance policies gifted within three years of death, and any business interests. Upon death, the estate will pass by different means to other family members, friends, and designated entities. This estate can be likened to a funnel shown in Figure 14-1, through which all of the assets pass. What comes out at the bottom of the funnel is the amount of the estate remaining to be distributed. The amount of property actually transferred can be significantly affected by the form of ownership and the means chosen by the decedent to effectuate the transfer.

How people go about selecting the various forms of ownership and the means by which they expect to pass legal title is commonly referred to as "estate planning." The objectives of estate planning commonly include: (1) protecting the family; (2) ensuring that the estate property is adequate for family needs; (3) arranging for an orderly distribution of assets to the bene-

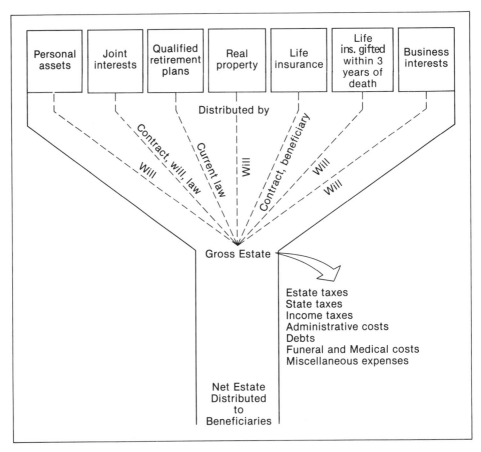

FIGURE 14-1 Estate distribution

ficiaries; and (4) taking steps to ensure that, upon death, the surviving family members would be able to obtain proper guidance and advice from professionals known to them.

AN OVERVIEW OF ESTATE PLANNING

ESTATE PLANNING: OBJECTIVES AND TOOLS

The Common Misconceptions

A popular myth in estate planning is that it is worth planning for only rich estates. That is simply not the case. Those at all levels need to plan for their estates. Besides, not every estate is as poor as it might appear, since appreciated values of solely owned homes, stocks and bonds, life insurance proceeds, and the prorated portion of jointly held properties are included in every estate.

Those who believe that estate planning can be dispensed with if husband and wife own everything jointly are also mistaken. In fact, when property is held in joint tenancy with right of survivorship, upon death, the property is included in the gross estate for estate tax purposes at either the proven portion of ownership or at 100 percent of the market value if it is not possible to prove the percentage of ownership. Later, when the surviving spouse dies, the estate could be taxed again, thereby shrinking it still further.

Some people believe that purchasing life insurance constitutes a complete estate plan. They are completely wrong. True, insurance proceeds paid to a named beneficiary do not have to pass through probate, since a life insurance policy is a contract. But it is still subject to federal estate taxes if the deceased had incidents of ownership at the time of death. Choosing the right option on a policy is also part of estate planning. Should it be paid to the surviving spouse in full or in installments? Should the beneficiary be solely responsible for managing the money, or should a trustee be given that task? These and other related questions must be answered as a part of estate planning.

Finally, a myth that never dies is that making a will is the ultimate tool of estate planning. A will does not govern the distribution of all assets. Retirement and profit sharing benefits or assets transferred to a living trust, for example, are not subject to the manner of distribution provided for in the will. The fact is that a will documents an individual's wishes relating to certain assets, but it is not by itself an estate plan. The will may not cover all the aspects of estate planning, since some of the assets may pass outside the will or may not be coordinated with the transfer of other assets to the beneficiaries.

Objectives of Estate Planning

A good estate plan has a single objective: to make sure that the maximum value reaches the intended beneficiaries in a manner directed by the deceased. To accomplish this goal, it is necessary to carefully consider the impact of federal estate and state transfer taxes in order to legally minimize the impact of current estate tax laws. The planning process can be both cumbersome and technical. It is therefore advisable to seek the help of a practicing estate attorney and a qualified financial planner.

Tools of Estate Planning

The word "estate" refers to everything solely or jointly owned by a living person. A good estate plan assumes an orderly transfer of an estate upon death in accordance with the wishes of the deceased.

Two major types of property are included in a person's estate: one passes through probate (probate estate), and the other passes outside the probate estate. The former type consists of the assets owned outright by a person. These assets can be disposed of by the person as desired. The latter type of assets includes, but is not limited to, life insurance policies, jointly owned property, retirement benefits payable to designated beneficiaries, and assets transferred to an inter vivos trust, commonly called a "living trust," which designates how the property is to be treated upon death. Incidentally, it should be recognized that even though certain properties may pass outside probate, they may still be subject to federal estate tax.

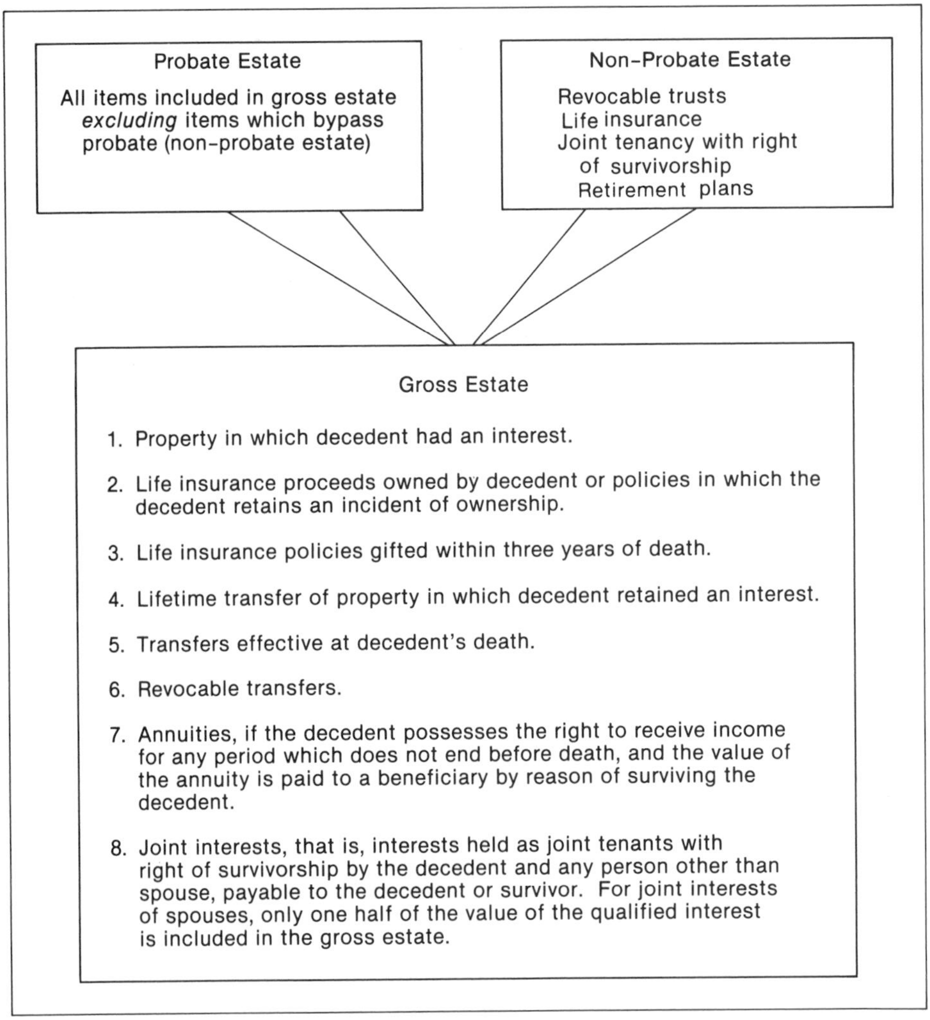

Probate Estate

All items included in gross estate *excluding* items which bypass probate (non-probate estate)

Non-Probate Estate

Revocable trusts
Life insurance
Joint tenancy with right
    of survivorship
Retirement plans

Gross Estate

1. Property in which decedent had an interest.

2. Life insurance proceeds owned by decedent or policies in which the decedent retains an incident of ownership.

3. Life insurance policies gifted within three years of death.

4. Lifetime transfer of property in which decedent retained an interest.

5. Transfers effective at decedent's death.

6. Revocable transfers.

7. Annuities, if the decedent possesses the right to receive income for any period which does not end before death, and the value of the annuity is paid to a beneficiary by reason of surviving the decedent.

8. Joint interests, that is, interests held as joint tenants with right of survivorship by the decedent and any person other than spouse, payable to the decedent or survivor. For joint interests of spouses, only one half of the value of the qualified interest is included in the gross estate.

FIGURE 14-2 Gross estate

There are four basic tools of estate planning. These are:

Wills
Joint Ownership
Trusts
Lifetime Gifts

In addition, when creating an estate plan, a skillful estate lawyer can create other documents designed to save thousands of tax dollars and make the estate plan more efficient. For instance, there are a number of ways to transfer assets from one spouse to the other which will qualify for the unlimited marital deduction. Assets which pass from one spouse to another in this manner will avoid the payment of federal estate taxes at that time.

At this point it is useful to make a distinction between assets which go through probate and those that completely bypass it. Both types of assets are included in the gross estate of the decedent as can be seen from Figure 14-2.

We will now turn to a discussion of the structure of each of the four basic tools of estate planning just listed. Use of these tools for developing estate planning strategies will be discussed in the next chapter.

THE WILL

Importance of a Will

Every person, single or married, old or young, healthy or ill, needs a will, which is a legal document activated upon death. This document can be used to designate: (1) to whom the property should go; (2) when it should go; (3) in what amount it should go; (4) how it should be safeguarded; (5) by whom it should be handled; and (6) who should be the guardian of minor children. By creating a valid will, a person exercises the legal right to bestow assets upon deserving or needy relatives, friends, or other beneficiaries, and designating the people responsible for taking care of minor children until they reach adulthood.

Absence of a Will

Whether or not a person has actually drafted a will, some form of will is used to distribute the estate. So even if a person dies without a will, state statutes known as the *laws of intestacy* take over and those statutes determine how the estate is to be distributed. Frequently, the state's notion of how the estate should be handled and the minor children managed is at odds with how the deceased would have proceeded. In particular, charitable organizations and individuals other than relatives will receive nothing. Consequently, dying intestate can be a real tragedy.

How an estate is distributed when a person dies intestate is shown in Figure 14-3. For instance, without a will, most states will make the spouse share the estate with children, siblings, or parents. Of course, it is important to recognize that the laws of descent and distribution vary from state to state.

There are other disadvantages to not leaving a will. Upon dying intestate, the estate will be handled by a personal representative appointed by the court. That representative may not be the one who would have been selected by the deceased. Another disadvantage is that legal procedures may force the personal representative to sell and distribute the estate or convert it into "legal investments" (government bonds, checking accounts, and so on) in accordance with the law. Most states limit the types of investments in which a personal representative can invest estate assets. Furthermore, the personal representative may be required to sell nonincome producing assets because there is no provision in the will permitting the personal representative authority to retain them. Thus, an investment which the decedent would like to have retained in the family, such as a closely held business, might have to be sold and the proceeds invested within prescribed statutory limitations. Finally, without the protection of a will, the estate could be reduced substantially by unnecessary administrative expenses and estate taxes, making the net estate value less than anticipated.

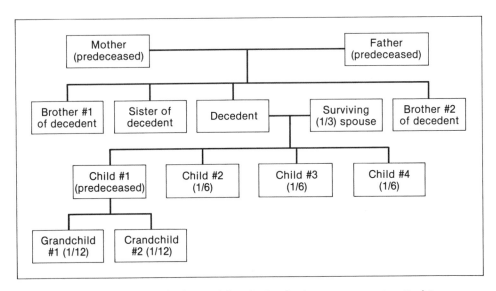

FIGURE 14-3 Typical scheme of distribution for intestate succession. Paul J. Lochray, *The Financial Planner's Guide to Estate Planning*, Prentice Hall, 1987, p. 67.

Drafting a Will

To draft a valid will, one must have a "testamentary capacity." That is, at the time the will was drawn, it must be demonstrated that the individual recognized the natural objects of his or her bounty, knew the assets comprising the estate, and also was certain of how the assets were to be distributed. Although there are literally hundreds of varieties of wills, they can be classified into a few categories as described next.

Simple will. The simple will is signed by the maker or testator, before the required witnesses (usually two in most states). The will states the disposition and the distribution of the estate involved. This is usually the shortest and easiest will to write and execute when the estate is relatively small.

Reciprocal will. If two persons—most often husband and wife—simultaneously execute their own wills, they will frequently leave their respective and totally distinct estates to each other. A reciprocal will can be drawn up as a unified document, although the most common practice is to draft two separate wills. For this type of will to be valid, the estates of the two parties need not be commonly owned. There could be separate property such as inheritances from previous wills, an estate that has nothing to do with the present marriage, or any other related holdings.

Mutual will. A mutual will is one instrument created by two parties to dispose of their respective properties. Mutual wills, or joint wills, are neither the simplest nor the most efficient form of will and should be avoided if possible.

Holographic will. This type of will is written entirely by hand by the individual, known as the testator or testatrix. Various states have differing opinions on their acceptability, and many legal battles have evolved over their validity. It is advisable to avoid making this type of will.

Basic Structure of a Will

A will can be a long, complicated document or it can consist of a single phrase, "I leave all my personal property and belongings to my spouse." Regardless of its complexity, the basic structure of a will should contain the following common clauses.

Exordium Clause. This clause identifies the name, address, and domicile of the testator. It also invalidates all prior wills and declares the current will as the testator's will.

Payment of Debt and Taxes Clause. This clause directs the payment of debt and taxes.

Disposition of Personal and Real Property Clause. This clause provides for the disposition of personal property, such as furniture, jewelry, automobiles, and clothing. It also directs the disposition of real estate property.

Trust Clause. This clause sets out the terms of any trusts created by the will.

Appointment of Fiduciary Clause. This clause designates the person or the fiduciary who will serve as the personal representative.

Powers Clause. This clause details the powers to be exercised by the personal representative. These include managing and selling property, handling the investable funds, and borrowing and lending of funds.

Appointment of Guardian Clause. This clause designates who will serve as guardian of minor children, if any.

Common Disaster Clause. This clause specifies which spouse would be presumed to have survived the other in the event of simultaneous death.

Testimonium and Attestation Clause. This clause establishes that the testator recognized the will and provides for compliance with other requirements, such as signatures of witnesses.

Codicil

Even the best-drawn wills may run into unexpected problems. Marriage or divorce might render a will obsolete. Other changes in the family, financial situation, or tax law might require revision of the existing will. An instrument, known as a *codicil*, can be used to make these alterations in the will, thereby avoiding the problem of making a new will. The codicil should be drawn up by a lawyer, properly witnessed, and attached to the will. Of course, there are certain situations in which it is more appropriate to draw up a new will rather than to *alter* the will by means of a codicil.

Letter of Last Instructions (Memorandum)

Settling an estate is no easy chore, and it can become complex and time-consuming. Since a person's interests are best served when family members promptly receive what is due them without losing an excessive amount in taxes and court costs, it is desirable for family members to assist the personal representative in every possible way. A person may also wish to assist a spouse in carrying out his or her responsibilities specified in the will. One way to help the personal representative and the surviving spouse is for the creator of the will to write a letter of last instructions. This letter, not normally legally binding, is usually addressed to a surviving spouse, and a copy is provided to the personal representative.

Ideally, a letter of last instructions should be both informational and directional. It should guide the surviving spouse in locating the will and other

MAKING A WILL: SOME POINTERS

Estate planning attorneys recommend that the following points be kept in mind when making a will.

1. The individual should work closely with the family, as the will is written by a professional. That way, family objectives can be met regardless of who dies first.

2. A beneficiary should not be chosen as a witness. If called upon to validate, the person may not be able to collect the inheritance.

3. The maker would be well advised to use in the will both percentages and absolute amounts rather than simply dollar amounts. For instance, if $25,000 is left to a charity and the remainder to the spouse, nothing would be left for the spouse if the estate shrinks to that level. Of course, these percentages and dollar amounts should be periodically reviewed to avoid such problems as the possibility of making a charitable contribution of a larger dollar amount than anticipated if the estate value rises in the future, or the shrinkage of the estate below a given level.

4. The will should be as flexible as possible. For instance, the heirs may suffer if the will insists on their holding certain stocks for the long term.

5. The will should be altered by a codicil and not by writing on the document itself.

6. The will should be kept up-to-date. Also, it should be reviewed whenever there are significant changes in the family and in the tax laws.

7. All will-related affairs should be kept in order. This includes making an inventory of all assets and purchasing additional life insurance to provide liquidity to compensate for an estate consisting largely of illiquid assets.

important papers (such as the birth certificate, Social Security card, marriage certificate, naturalization papers), finding the safety deposit box, arranging for organ donations, and making the funeral and burial arrangements. This letter should also contain details relating to the following: life insurance, bank accounts, savings and loan association accounts, securities, savings bonds, real estate, Social Security, homeowners', health and auto insurance, and financial obligations. Upon death, this information will be of great value and assistance to the family and to the personal representative.

THE PERSONAL REPRESENTATIVE

An important aspect of setting up a will is the appointment of a personal representative. The personal representative can either be one or more individuals or a corporate fiduciary such as a trust company. Designating a personal representative is not a precondition for setting up a will. Thus, a will would be valid even if the appointment of a personal representative is omitted. The court would then appoint the personal representative to administer the will.

TABLE 14-1 Estate Planning Data Requirements

Personal data:
  Names, addresses, phone numbers, family consultants
  Family birthdates, occupations, health problems, support needs
  Citizenship, marital status, marital agreements, wills, trusts, custodianships, trust beneficiary, gifts or inheritances, Social Security numbers, education, and military service.

Property (except life insurance or business):
  Classification, title, indebtedness, basis, date and manner of acquisition, value of marketable securities, and location

Life insurance

Health insurance:
  Disability income
  Medical expense insurance

Business interest:
  Name, address, ownership
  Valuation factors; desired survivorship control; name, address, and phone number of business attorney and accountant

Employee census data

Employee benefits

Family income:
  Income of client, spouse, dependent children, income tax information

Family finances:
  Budget information, investment preferences
  Ranking of economic objectives, capital needs, other objectives

Income and capital needs:
  Retirement: Age, required amount, potential sources
  Disability: Required amount, sources
  Death: Expected sources of income

Liabilities:
  Classification of liabilities, creditors, amounts, whether insured or secured

Factors affecting plan:
  Gift propensity, charitable inclinations, emotional maturity of children, basic desires for estate distribution

Authorization for information:
  Life insurance

Receipt for documents:
  Personal and business

Source: Copyright © 1988 by The American College. Reprinted with permission. The Financial and Estate Planning Fact Finder is part of the Advanced Estate Planning course.

The main responsibilities of a personal representative are as follows: (1) probate, or prove, the will's validity in probate court; (2) assemble all property belonging to the estate, including life insurance benefits, household effects, securities, mortgages, real estate interest, and cash; (3) collect money owed the estate; (4) appraise, manage, and protect business interests; (5) liquidate or invest funds in accordance with the will; (6) pay all debts, federal, state, and local taxes as well as all death-related expenses incurred; (7) defend against claims when necessary; and (8) distribute the residue and close the estate.

Because the personal representative plays such an important role in overseeing the orderly distribution of an estate, this person benefits from having access to an up-to-date data sheet. A condensed and simplified version of such a sheet is presented in Table 14-1.

GUARDIAN FOR MINOR CHILDREN

It is customary to assume that a parent is the best person to act as guardian for his or her minor children. While this is generally true, an important consideration might induce a person to appoint someone other than the spouse in this capacity. Both husband and wife might die simultaneously, in which case the court might appoint a guardian not acceptable to either of them. Naming an alternative instructs the court to consider appointing a guardian who the individual considers acceptable to assume such a significant responsibility. Furthermore, as a result of divorce, the surviving parent may not have been involved for some time in the care and rearing of the children of a previous marriage. In such a case, or in a case where the surviving parent is ill-prepared to deal with both the children and the property, an individual has the opportunity to designate separate persons to act as the guardians of the *person* as well as the trustee of the *property*. These individuals will be entitled to be compensated for their services. Separating the responsibility of managing the money from managing the children provides an added degree of protection to the family. Clearly, the well-being of the children and the children's property are of great importance, and it is imperative that careful consideration be given to the selection of a guardian. A will establishes the guardianship of minor children, subject to court approval.

PROBATE

An estate plan deals with two kinds of property—probate and nonprobate assets. The personal representative disposes of the probate assets in accordance with the instructions contained in the will. Nonprobate assets bypass probate, and contractual arrangements by the testator (that is, beneficiary designations for insurance) frequently control their transfer to specific individuals.

The literal meaning of probate is "to prove." Probate occurs under the supervision of a local court known as probate, surrogate, or orphan's court. It is a procedure established by law for the orderly distribution of estates. It is designed to assure that all of the deceased's property is collected and protected; that all debts and taxes are paid; and that the beneficiaries promptly receive the designated assets.

Upon death of an individual, the personal representative submits the will to the court and asks that it be probated. Before the court can probate a person's estate, however, it must be satisfied that the will submitted by the executor is indeed the final will. Therefore, the court will want to know if the will is valid, if it avoids all restricted actions, and if it recognizes the limitations on the types of property (Social Security, qualified plan benefits, and so on) that may pass through the will. The court will also provide the opportunity to all interested parties to contest the will. If all goes well, the will is probated and the personal representative is granted "Letters Testamentary"—the legal authority to act on behalf of the deceased.

In addition to approving the will, the probate court rules on the legitimacy of creditors' claims and oversees the personal representative until the estate is distributed. If minor children are involved, the court also supervises the guardian until the property is finally distributed to the children after they reach their age of property distribution specified in the will.

The probate process is usually long, complicated, and costly. Consequently, it pays to take the necessary steps to avoid delay in the probate process. These steps include assigning broad powers to the personal representative to settle disputes, keeping the will up-to-date, maintaining a complete inventory of all assets, and purchasing life insurance to provide additional liquidity for the estate.

The technique of bypassing probate as an estate planning tool will be discussed in the next chapter.

JOINT OWNERSHIP

Introduction

The gross estate consists of those assets to which a person has title or legal rights of ownership. These rights depend not only on the method by which the property was acquired but also on state statutes governing marital property. Some states consider marital property to be community property while others do not.

Community Property States

In the nine community property states (Arizona, California, Idaho, Louisiana, Nevada, New Mexico, Texas, Washington, and Wisconsin), both spouses own a separate, undivided, *equal* interest in the property. Furthermore, even if only one of the spouses initially acquires property or earns income that is used to benefit the couple, community property states emphasize the efforts of both spouses that lead to the acquisition of property. Also, not only do both spouses have equal rights of ownership in this property and its earnings, but they also share such equal ownership rights in the income derived from salaries, wages, or other compensation for services.

Noncommunity States

In the noncommunity states, the nature of distribution of assets held jointly depends on the form of joint ownership. Of the three types of joint ownership permitted in these states, one is designed specifically to process all assets through probate, whereas the other two completely bypass probate. Each of the three types of joint ownership has its own distinct characteristics.

Joint tenancy with right of survivorship. This type of ownership can be set up by any two or more persons. Each owner is known as a joint tenant and owns an equal share of the property. Co-owners may not sell or give away their interests without the partners' permission. When death occurs, the share of the deceased passes to the surviving joint owner. It is possible to have more than one joint owner. Upon death the property is divided equally among the surviving joint owners. This type of ownership completely bypasses the probate process, but is includible in the gross estate for estate tax purposes at either the proven portion of ownership or at 100 percent of the market value if it is not possible to prove the percentage of ownership. Generally, it is not a recommended form of ownership except under certain circumstances.

Tenancy by the entirety. This form of joint tenancy differs from the joint tenancy with the right of survivorship in two respects. First, in those states that permit it, tenancy by the entirety can be established only by married couples. Second, neither spouse can sell or give away any property without the consent of the other. When death occurs, the deceased's share passes to the survivor. This form, too, bypasses probate.

Tenancy in common. This type of ownership directs all property not to the co-owners but rather to the heirs named in the will or to the heirs at law if the person died intestate. Consequently, its major objective is to insure that all assets pass through probate court and that tenancy in common is not used to save on probate costs and delays by bypassing probate.

A comparison of the advantages and disadvantages of sole ownership, joint tenancy, and tenancy in common is presented in Table 14-2. It should be clear from the table that many factors should be considered before the most appropriate form of property ownership can be selected for the client.

TABLE 14-2 A Comparison of the Advantages and Disadvantages of Sole Ownership, Joint Tenancy, and Tenancy in Common Property

	Sole ownership	Joint tenancy WROS	Tenancy in common
Avoids probate?	No	Yes	No
Can be disposed of by will?	Yes	No	Yes
Does decedent have postmortem control?	Yes	No	Yes
Receive a partial step-up in basis at decedent's death?	Receives step up in basis on entire amount when it passes to beneficiary or heir	Yes	Same as sole ownership on the tenant's proportional interest
Consent of others needed prior to conveyance?	No	Yes—if there is a spousal joint tenant	No
Amount included in gross estate of decedent?	All	One-half if spouses; otherwise, the portion or percentage which is proved as actual contribution; if survivor cannot prove contribution, then all	Tenant's undivided fractional interest
Survivorship rights upon death of decedent owner?	No	Yes	No

If gifted, subject to payment of gift tax?	Yes	No—if gifted to spouse; otherwise, yes	Yes
Effective means of splitting income?	No	Yes	Yes
Reduced administrative expenses and costs?	No	Yes	No
Difficult to dispose of or convey?	Generally, no	Generally, no	Can be a problem if tenants in common cannot agree to buy or sell their interest to others—can result in a co-ownership discount
Can interest qualify for marital deduction?	Only if bequeathed to spouse in decedent's will or if transferred to spouse pursuant to intestacy statute	Yes—if surviving joint tenant is spouse	Yes—if tenant in common bequeaths it to spouse in will or if transferred to spouse pursuant to intestacy statute
Subject to creditors' claims?	Yes	No—possibly free in some states, but state law must be checked	Yes
Lifetime control?	Yes—total	Yes—partial	Yes—partial

Source: Paul J. Lochray, *The Financial Planner's Guide to Estate Planning*, Revised Edition, © 1989, pp. 121–22. Reprinted by permission of Prentice Hall, Inc., Englewood Cliffs, New Jersey.

TRUSTS

An Overview

A trust is a legal entity created to hold, manage, and eventually (upon death) distribute assets to the beneficiaries in accordance with the grantor who sets up the trust. Assets included in the trust—stocks, bonds, real estate, life insurance, business interests, artwork, and so on—are called trust property, principal, or corpus. The basic elements of a trust are presented in Figure 14-4.

Trust property is managed by a trustee. The trustee must carry out the grantor's instructions contained in the trust. These include the management of trust property and its distribution to the beneficiaries.

The beneficiary is the one who benefits from the distribution of trust property. The law does not place any restrictions on who, or how many, might benefit from a trust. Thus, a beneficiary might be the spouse, children, brothers and sisters, other relatives, charitable and educational institutions, or business associates. Finally, the trustee controls and manages the trust.

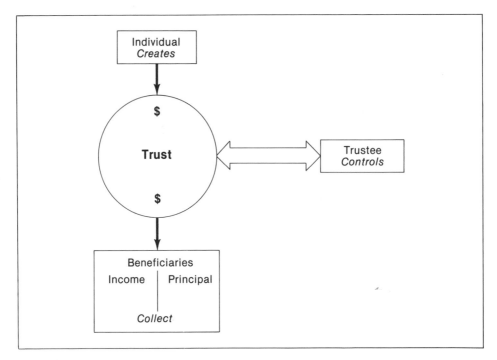

FIGURE 14-4 Diagram of a trust. Paul J. Lochray, *The Financial Planner's Guide to Estate Planning*, Revised Edition; © 1989, p. 68. Reprinted by permission of Prentice Hall, Inc., Englewood Cliffs, New Jersey.

There are two principal forms of trusts: *inter vivos* or living trust and *testamentary trust*. The former comes into effect immediately upon its creation, whereas the latter is written into the will and comes into existence upon death.

The living trust can be either revocable or irrevocable. The former begins to operate during the owner's lifetime. The owner or grantor—the person who creates the trust—frequently acts as his or her own trustee. The owner can also name another trustee to manage the assets in the event of disability or incompetence. The assets are held in the trust during the owner's lifetime and, upon death, the trust estate avoids probate, but is included in the gross estate. In contrast, an irrevocable living trust can be created to pass assets free of federal estate taxes to the beneficiaries. In creating this trust, a person gives up any right to trust income and principal as well as the right to change the beneficiary or other terms of the trust agreement.

The Purpose of Trusts

It is not necessary for everyone to create a trust for an orderly transfer of an estate to the beneficiaries. However, most people have specific objectives which are difficult—in fact, nearly impossible—to carry out without a trust. For instance, with the help of a trust, a person can provide a life income for the spouse and children. Subsequently, the assets could pass to the grandchildren. In another instance, if the spouse is too inexperienced, or incapable of managing investments, a trust can safeguard investable funds by letting a trustee manage them while providing adequate income for the spouse and children. A trust might also be necessary where a person has remarried. In this case, a trust can provide life income to the second spouse and upon death of this spouse distribute the assets to the children of the first marriage. Another situation in which a trust can be extremely useful relates to the care and support for a physically or mentally incapacitated person. Finally, a trust becomes the most important document where there is a possibility of a simultaneous death of both spouses. It is therefore safe to conclude that, with the exception of extremely simple cases, most people need some type of trust as an integral part of their estate plan.

Selection of a Trustee

The decision to create a trust—be it inter vivos or testamentary—carries with it the burden of selecting a trustee. The duties and responsibilities of a trustee may vary, depending upon the size and complexity of the trust. However, it is highly desirable that the trustee be sensitive to the needs of the beneficiaries and possess financial savvy. A trustee can also become an all-important person if the grantor of the trust is suddenly incapacitated and is unable to manage the trust properly.

As a general rule, it is always desirable to engage as a trustee a fiduciary company with perpetual life or a professional financial advisor. Such a trustee can not only manage a trust professionally but can also provide continuity, which is always desirable. However, annual fees for professional trustees can range from about ¾ percent to 1 percent of a trust's assets. Consequently, people with relatively small trusts may wish to sacrifice the use of a professional trustee and select a friend or a relative for little or no compensation. Regardless of how a trustee is selected, in case of a bank or a fiduciary it is prudent to leave the original trust agreement with the trustee, and keep one copy of the trust with the attorney, one copy with the grantor, and another in a safety deposit vault.

The use of a trust as a tool of estate planning is discussed more fully in the next chapter.

LIFETIME GIFTS

Another effective tool for reducing the size of the probatable assets is gift giving. During one's lifetime, gifts can be given in a variety of ways to individuals and institutions. However, there are pitfalls in giving gifts, and these must be carefully considered when designing a program of lifetime giving.

The law allows every person to gift each year up to $10,000, gift tax-free to any person (or $20,000 for husband and wife). The law does not limit the number of recipients. At the time of death, the IRS totals the *taxable* gifts made during a lifetime, and subtracts this total from the estate exemption limit of $600,000 in order to determine whether or not estate taxes are due. For instance, if John makes $80,000 of taxable gifts during his lifetime, upon death he would only have a $520,000 estate tax exclusion ($600,000 minus $80,000). If his taxable estate totals $600,000, he would be taxed on only $80,000 ($600,000 minus $520,000).

COMPUTATION OF ESTATE TAX

FEDERAL ESTATE TAXES

An Overview

The estate built during one's lifetime may not entirely belong to the beneficiaries. The federal government and at least one state government have the right to claim their shares before the estate can be distributed.

The federal estate tax is a tax on the right to transfer property at death. It is not a tax on the right of the beneficiary to receive the property. Generally the federal estate tax must be paid by the estate. In addition to federal estate taxes, an estate is also subject to a state inheritance tax, which will be discussed in a subsequent section.

For the purposes of calculating federal estate taxes, an estate includes not only real estate, bank deposits, personal property, and other obvious types of assets, but also insurance proceeds, interests in trusts, and jointly held property. In addition, certain interests a deceased may have in other estates are also included in the estate.

The 1976 Tax Act created a *unified* federal estate tax rate schedule applicable to both lifetime gifts and transfers at death. This provision was adopted to discourage the transfer of assets "in contemplation of death." The tax on gifts is imposed on the right to transfer property and is measured by the value of the property transferred. The donor is primarily liable for the tax. A graduated table of rates is used for both gift and estate tax purposes and is known as the unified rate schedule. These rates are applied to all taxable gifts after appropriate adjustments.

The federal estate tax is calculated by: (1) adjusting the value of the gross estate to determine the tentative tax base; (2) calculating the tentative tax; and (3) arriving at the net tax liability by subtracting the gross tax paid during lifetime as well as the applicable tax credits. The format for calculating the federal estate tax is presented in Table 14-3. We will now discuss the key items associated with the calculation of federal estate tax.

Gross Estate

Includible items. The key items includible in the gross estate are listed in Table 14-4. While most of the items are self-explanatory, it may nevertheless be of some interest to make a few basic comments about them.

As a general rule, items included in a gross estate are cash, real estate, securities, rights in property, collectibles, life insurance payable to anyone if the deceased had an ownership in it, and gifts of life insurance made within three years of death. Assets which are gifted away but in which the deceased

---

TABLE 14-3   Computation of Federal
Estate Tax

Gross estate
  Less deductions
Equals taxable estate
  Plus adjusted taxable gifts
Equals tentative tax base
  Times rate of tax
Equals tentative tax
  Less gift tax paid after 1976
Equals gross tax
  Less credits
Equals net tax liability

TABLE 14-4 Includable Items in Gross Estate

   I. Property in which decedent had an interest
      a. Personal assets
      b. Real property
      c. Intangible property
      d. Retirement assets
      e. Closely-held business
      f. Equity investments
      g. Hard assets
  II. Gifts of life insurance made within three years of death
 III. Incomplete lifetime transfers
 IV. Annuities payable to beneficiary
  V. Half of joint property (married couple)
 VI. Power of appointment (general) trust
VII. Proceeds of life insurance owned by deceased

---

retained some control are also included in the gross estate. The value of an annuity payable to any beneficiary upon death is included in the gross estate if during life the deceased had the right to receive income from the annuity. However, only the share of the annuity that was purchased by the individual is taxable. In the case of joint ownership of property, one-half of the value of the property is included in the gross estate if the parties are a married couple. If the joint tenants are not a married couple, the entire property is included in the gross estate of the deceased unless the survivor can claim to have paid for the property. Finally, if the deceased did not give an unconditional or *general* power to the donee to direct the disposition of certain assets, that is, if the deceased had imposed any restrictions on the disposition, these assets are also included in the gross estate of the deceased.

Valuing the estate. The process of calculating estate taxes begins with determining includibility. Once it is determined which assets are to be included, the values of the items comprising the gross estate can be calculated. In most instances, such as in the case of bank deposits, investments, pension, profit sharing, Keogh, 401(K) plans, and life insurance proceeds, determining the market value poses no problem. In the case of other assets, however, determination of fair market value at the time of death, or an alternative date six months after death, may be more difficult. Examples of these assets include family business, farm land, and stocks in closely held corporations.

The method of determining a couple's gross estate is presented in Table 14-5. Naturally, the method would be a lot more involved in the case of a more complicated estate. However, the process would be very similar to the one presented here.

Deductions

The IRS allows certain expenses and liabilities to be deductible from the gross estate. The key deductions are listed in Table 14-6. Most of the items

TABLE 14-5 Property Ownership and Gross Estate

Property	Ownership				
	Est. current value	Community	Joint	Property	
				Husband's	Spouse's
1. Net worth					
a. Liquid assets other than cash value of life insurance	$30,000		$30,000		
b. Investment assets, Other than retirement funds	225,000	150,000	50,000		25,000
c. Personal assets	500,000	500,000			
d. Total assets	755,000	650,000	80,000		25,000
e. Liabilities	(100,000)	(100,000)			
f. Total	655,000	550,000	80,000		25,000
2. Insurance owned					
a. On husband's life	250,000				250,000
b. On spouse's life	100,000			100,000	
c. Total	350,000			100,000	250,000
3. Other estate assets					
a. Retirement plans	200,000	200,000			
b. Other					
c. Total	200,000	200,000			
4. Total gross estate	1,205,000	750,000	80,000	100,000	275,000
5. Total gross estate for husband and spouse					
a. Husband's gross estate	515,000	375,000	40,000	100,000	
b. Spouse's gross estate	690,000	375,000	40,000		275,000
c. Total	1,205,000	750,000	80,000	100,000	275,000

TABLE 14-6   Allowable Deductions from Gross Estate

---

1. Funeral expenses
2. Expenses of last illness
3. Casualty losses
4. Administration expenses
5. Claims against the estate
6. Mortgage and other indebtedness
7. Charitable deductions
8. Marital deduction
9. Power of appointment (general) trust
10. Qualified terminable interest property (QTIP) trust
11. Sale of employer's stock to ESOPs (50 percent)

---

listed in this table are self-explanatory. A few, however, require a brief explanation.

Claims against the estate.   Claims are limited to a legitimate contractual obligation for which there was full consideration in money.

Charitable deductions.   The estate is allowed to make an unlimited deduction for property donated to a *qualified* charity. This is unlike the income tax charitable deduction, since there are no percentage limitations placed on the estate tax deduction for charitable gifts.

Marital deduction.   The estate may deduct *all* property bequeathed to a surviving spouse. This is known as the unlimited marital deduction.

Power of appointment trust.   The unlimited marital deduction will be available for a Power of Appointment Trust if: (1) the surviving spouse is entitled to all of the income from the trust; (2) the spouse actually receives the income at least annually; and (3) the surviving spouse's power of appointment is unconditional.

Qualified terminable interest property (QTIP) trust.   Property included in this trust will qualify for the estate tax marital deduction. This is because the entire interest and the property—both income and remainder—will be treated as passing to the spouse.

Sale of stock to ESOPs.   The estate may deduct 50 percent of the proceeds of a sale of employer's securities to an Employee Stock Option Plan (ESOP) as long as the sale occurs before the due date of the estate tax return. The deduction is not available for sales after December 31, 1991.

Estate Tax Calculation

A single unified rate schedule is applied to a decedent's estate and all the post-1976 lifetime gifts over the annual gift tax exclusion. Under the unified gift and estate tax rate, the overall tax on the taxable estate is the same regardless of whether or not a lifetime gift is made. Of course, lifetime gifts may reduce the estate tax by reducing the taxable estate.

For those estates where lifetime taxable gifts (that is, in excess of $20,000 per year for married couples) are nonexistent, the calculation of estate tax is straightforward. Taxable estate is simply the gross estate less certain allowable deductions. The unified credit is subtracted from the tax calculated on

TABLE 14-7   Estimated Federal Estate Tax: Husband's Estate

1. Gross estate		515,000
2. Deductions		
a. Funeral expenses	5,000	
b. Administrative expenses	15,000	
c. Total expenses	20,000	
3. Marital deduction for property passing to spouse:		
a. Jointly held property	40,000	
b. Transferred by contract (retirement plan)	100,000	
c. Transferred by will or living trust (personal assets)	250,000	
d. Total marital deductions	390,000	
4. Charitable deduction	———	
5. Total deductions		(410,000)
6. Tentative taxable estate		85,000
7. Post-1976 taxable gifts other than gifts includible in gross estate		———
8. Total taxable estate		85,000
9. Tentative federal estate tax		19,600
10. Less:		
a. Gift taxes paid on post-1976 gifts	———	
b. Unified credit	192,800	
c. Total		(192,800)
11. Federal estate tax*		0

* Since the tentative federal estate tax is $19,600, whereas the unified tax credit is $192,800, no federal estate tax is due.

the taxable estate. Other credits, including the state death tax credit, further reduce the estate tax.

The estate tax is cumulative on those estates where taxable lifetime gifts are present. In these cases, the unified tax rate is applied to the sum of the taxable estate at death and taxable lifetime gifts made after 1976. Of course, gifts that are already included in the gross estate would be excluded from this calculation. The tax calculated on the combined estate is reduced by gift taxes payable on gifts made after 1976. The unified credit and other credits are then subtracted from the remaining amount.

Federal estate taxes. The process of calculating the federal estate tax on the estate of the husband, presumed to die first, and on the estate of his spouse upon her death, is presented in Tables 14-7 and 14-8. The estate tax is calculated by using the unified gift and estate tax rates presented in Table 14-9. It should be noted here that, because of the existence of a comprehensive

---

TABLE 14-8   Estimated Federal Estate Tax: Wife's Estate

1. Gross estate		$1,080,000
2. Deductions		
a. Funeral expenses	$ 5,000	
b. Administrative expenses	$25,000	
c. Total expenses	$30,000	
3. Marital deduction for property passing to spouse:		
a. Jointly held property	————	
b. Transferred by contract	————	
c. Transferred by will or living trust	————	
d. Total marital deductions	————	
4. Charitable deduction	————	
5. Total deductions		$ (30,000)
6. Tentative taxable estate		1,050,000
7. Post-1976 taxable gifts other than gifts includible in gross estate		————
8. Total taxable estate		1,050,000
9. Tentative federal estate tax (0.41 × $1,050,000)		366,300
10. Less:		
a. Gift taxes paid on post-1976 gifts	————	
b. Unified credit	$192,800	
c. Total		$ (192,800)
11. Federal estate tax		$ 173,500

TABLE 14-9   Unified Estate and Gift Tax Rates

1988–1992

If the amount is: Over	But not over	Tax	Plus % on excess over
0	$ 10,000	0	18
$ 10,000	20,000	$ 1,800	20
20,000	40,000	3,800	22
40,000	60,000	8,200	24
60,000	80,000	13,000	26
80,000	100,000	18,200	28
100,000	150,000	23,800	30
150,000	250,000	38,800	32
250,000	500,000	70,800	34
500,000	750,000	155,800	37
750,000	1,000,000	248,300	39
1,000,000	1,250,000	345,800	41
1,250,000	1,500,000	448,300	43
1,500,000	2,000,000	555,800	45
2,000,000	2,500,000	780,800	49
2,500,000	3,000,000	1,025,800	53
3,000,000	* * * * * *	1,290,800	55

1993 and thereafter

If the amount is: Over	But not over	Tax	Plus % on excess over
0	$ 10,000	0	18
$ 10,000	20,000	$ 1,800	20
20,000	40,000	3,800	22
40,000	60,000	8,200	24
60,000	80,000	13,000	26
80,000	100,000	18,200	28
100,000	150,000	23,800	30
150,000	250,000	38,800	32
250,000	500,000	70,800	34
500,000	750,000	155,800	37
750,000	1,000,000	248,300	39
1,000,000	1,250,000	345,800	41
1,250,000	1,500,000	448,300	43
1,500,000	2,000,000	555,800	45
2,000,000	2,500,000	780,800	49
2,500,000	* * * * *	1,025,800	50

Note: A five percent surtax is imposed on taxable transfers between $10 million and $21,040,000, made after December 31, 1987, and before 1993. For decedents dying and gifts made after 1992, the ceiling drops to $18,340,000.

estate plan, there was no federal estate tax due on the $515,000 estate upon the first death. Furthermore, even though the surviving spouse's estate was $1,080,000, the federal estate tax was only $173,500.

State inheritance taxes.   There are two types of death taxes: federal estate taxes and state inheritance taxes. While the federal government imposes a federal estate tax, which is payable by the estate of the deceased, most states impose an inheritance tax, often based upon federal estate tax liability, which is payable by the recipient of the inheritance. The amount that the state extracts from the heir is determined by the amount the heir inherits and the heir's relationship to the deceased. State inheritance taxes are deductible in determining federal estate taxes.

In this chapter we have presented the basic structure of federal estate taxes. The next chapter will be devoted to a detailed discussion of estate planning techniques.

CHAPTER 15

Estate Planning: Concepts and Strategies

INTRODUCTION

The major objective of estate planning is the preservation of assets that were accumulated during a person's lifetime and the development of strategies for passing them on to the intended beneficiaries. The minimization of estate taxes is also an important estate planning goal, although it should not take precedence over the individual's personal and financial goals. A will is the primary document for passing the estate upon death to the beneficiaries. However, a will is an integral part of, and not a substitute for, estate planning.

A comprehensive estate plan is a complex document. Consequently, drafting an estate plan requires the working knowledge of several fields, including finance, law, economics, accounting, insurance, and taxes. In addition, depending upon individual circumstances, the estate plan may contain provisions for such esoteric topics as generation skipping tax, qualified terminable interest property trust, and buy-sell or business continuation agreements. Consequently, it is highly desirable, if not mandatory, for an individual to seek the help of a competent financial planner, an attorney, or accountant in developing an effective estate plan. Put differently, complex estate planning is frequently a team effort and an individual may need the help of all three professionals working together to design the best possible estate plan.

This chapter is divided into three parts. First we will present estate tax reduction strategies. Next we will analyze estate preservation and distribution rules. Finally, we will present miscellaneous estate planning techniques.

ESTATE TAX REDUCTION STRATEGIES

INTRODUCTION

One of the major objectives of estate planning is to eliminate or significantly reduce potential estate tax. Direct lifetime gifts can be made to remove future appreciation on property from an individual's estate. Ownership of life insurance can be changed to avoid estate tax. The will may provide for bequests that will qualify for the marital and charitable deductions.

To be sure, maximum reduction of the estate tax upon the first death is not always the best strategy. Sometimes it is desirable to pay the estate tax upon the first death if that will help minimize total estate taxes ultimately paid upon both deaths. At other times, paying estate taxes may well be the appropriate strategy for achieving other objectives. Nevertheless, it is desirable to discuss here the key estate tax reduction and elimination strategies, because for most people that is one of the primary objectives of estate planning.

MARITAL DEDUCTION

The 1981 Economic Recovery Tax Act (ERTA) made it possible to entirely avoid estate taxes on the death of the first spouse. Property passing to a spouse is generally free from estate or gift tax because of an unlimited marital deduction. To qualify for the marital deduction, the property must generally be given to the spouse outright or by other legal arrangements that are equivalent to ownership in law. There is an exception in the case of income interests in charitable remainder annuity or unit trusts and in qualified terminable interest property (QTIP), for which the executor makes an election. It should be mentioned in this connection that if the spouse is made the unconditional beneficiary of life insurance proceeds with unrestricted control over any unpaid proceeds, life insurance proceeds will also qualify as marital deduction property.

We have already learned that transfers between spouses are exempt from both estate and gift taxes. The unlimited marital deduction opens up exciting ways for large estates to save on taxes—especially when the deduction is combined with the unified credit. However, despite the unlimited marital deduction and the unified credit, for most families, estate planning is still necessary. The reason is that while there is no estate tax when the property passes to the surviving spouse, large estate taxes might be due when the property is transferred to the children upon the death of the second spouse. We will illustrate this point by using three examples.

Example I. Mr. John Becker's $1 million in assets are left outright to his wife, Betty Becker. Betty's will provides for everything to be left to the children. In this case, upon John's death because of the unlimited marital deduction the entire estate of $1 million passes to Betty free of estate taxes. However, upon Betty's death only $600,000 will pass estate tax-free to the children. The balance of $400,000 will be subject to estate taxes. Note that if John had used both a will and a trust, and the trust sheltered his $600,000 exemption, upon his death that amount would have been transferred to a bypass trust (discussed later) for Betty and only $400,000 would have been used for the marital deduction. In that case, upon Betty's death, the $400,000 amount would pass estate tax-free to the children (because of $600,000 unified credit), and the balance of $600,000 in John's bypass trust would also pass to the children estate tax-free, since this amount was not a part of Betty's estate. Clearly, by not using the bypass trust strategy, John Becker wasted his own $600,000 exemption.

Example II. In this example, John Becker leaves $600,000 to his wife and the balance of $400,000 to his children. In this case, no estate taxes would be payable upon either death. However, since $400,000 is left to John's children, Betty receives no economic benefit from this money. A better strategy would be to put the $400,000 in trust for the children (explained more fully in the Trust section), with Betty Becker receiving income from the trust during her lifetime. Such an arrangement would give Betty the right to the income from the trust, an option to receive five percent of the principal every year, and the right to receive principal for her health, education, support, and maintenance. To sum up, in this case, $600,000 passes tax-free from Mr. Becker to Mrs. Becker because of the unlimited marital deduction and then to the children under Betty's estate tax credit umbrella. And so does the $400,000 in John's estate. The reason is that John's $600,000 unified credit shelters the $400,000 he has transferred in trust to his children, and it bypasses Betty's estate. However, the trustees of the trust have the limited right to invade the principal of the trust for Betty's benefit.

Example III. The third example refers to a large estate of $2.5 million. The estate is almost entirely owned by John Becker whereas Betty Becker has a negligible estate. If John leaves his entire estate to Betty, upon John's death his estate pays no tax. But Betty Becker's estate pays tax on the full $2.5 million less a $600,000 exemption. However, if John were to leave $1.25 million to Betty and the rest to his children, and then she leaves her $1.25 million to her children, the Beckers shelter $600,000 in each estate and avoid the top estate tax rates.

In passing, it should be mentioned that when using the marital deduction, the consequences of leaving a large estate to a surviving spouse should be carefully weighed. This is especially true when the spouse is incapable of managing large assets. In that situation, upon the death of the first spouse it may be better to leave the assets in certain trust arrangements that are considered equivalent to complete or total ownership and thereby completely avoid paying estate taxes.

JOINT OWNERSHIP

In Chapter 14 we learned that upon death the nature of distribution of assets held jointly depends on the form of joint ownership. We will now discuss some of the advantages and disadvantages of joint ownership.

Key Advantages

The advantages of joint ownership are many. First, if property is held in joint tenancy with right of survivorship—which is often the case between family members—the surviving joint owner automatically owns all the jointly owned property without the necessity of probate. The reason is that, under the law, there is a presumption that the decedent intended the property to automatically pass to the surviving joint owner. Second, property held jointly cannot be taken away in settlement of a debt. For example, if a person owes a certain amount of money to a loan company and becomes delinquent on loan payments, the company cannot seize the car, or some other jointly owned property to cover the loan. However, jointly held property can be subject to a debt claim where the debt is incurred jointly by the same parties. This would be the case where the lender has both spouses sign the note. Third, if a person is the sole owner of a vacation home located out of state, the will must be probated in two states. Joint ownership would eliminate this requirement. Fourth, joint ownership can be used to shift income to a family member in a lower tax bracket. For instance, a father and his son age 15 holding stock jointly would each be taxed on only half the dividends, frequently resulting in significant income tax savings. Finally, joint property can be used to achieve special objectives. If a mother wants to allocate $10,000 to her daughter, but still wants to be able to use the money for her own benefit, she can place the money in a joint bank account both in her and her daughter's name. She can then draw money from this account, or if she wants to minimize her access to that money she can have it set up so that both signatures are required for withdrawal.

Key Disadvantages

There are also disadvantages to joint ownership of property. Since jointly owned assets automatically pass to the surviving joint tenant, the survivor could end up with an estate exceeding $600,000 if the couple had all of their assets in joint tenancy. This may result in higher estate taxes upon the death of the surviving spouse. Another disadvantage of joint ownership is that people often tend to use this as a substitute for a valid will. In situations where all properties are jointly owned and there is no will, if both spouses die in an accident, the entire property will be distributed according to rigid, unalterable rules commonly known as the laws of intestate succession (also known as the laws of intestacy).

An important problem associated with joint ownership of highly appreciated assets involves both federal income and federal estate taxes. For example, assume John and Betty Jones bought a house for $30,000 in 1966 and held it jointly until John died in 1989, when the house was worth $200,000. Half of the house's value ($100,000) was included in John's gross estate, leaving Betty with his $100,000 interest plus her own $100,000 interest in the house. The IRS assumes that Betty bought her interest with $15,000 (one-half of $30,000) in 1966. If she sells the house for $200,000, she incurs $85,000 ($100,000 − $15,000) in capital gains which will be taxed at her highest marginal income tax bracket. This tax liability could have been avoided had John owned the house alone and bequeathed it to Betty via a will. In that case Betty's cost basis for the house would have been $200,000 and the only amount taxable on the sale would be the appreciation from the date of John's death (not from initial purchase). Of course, Betty could also avoid paying taxes on this amount if she was over 55 and used the one-time $125,000 exclusion pertaining to the capital gains realized from the sale of her principal residence.

Finally, unmarried joint tenants can increase estate tax liability for their heirs by owning property jointly. The face value of a jointly owned interest is included in the estate of the decedent, except to the extent the decedent's estate can prove that the surviving tenant contributed consideration to the purchase of the property.

In passing, it should be mentioned that this section assumes married and family joint tenants. Consequently, the major disadvantages of joint tenancy are not discussed here.

Having completed a review of the key advantages and disadvantages of joint ownership, we turn to a discussion of the major estate planning strategies involving joint ownership with right of survivorship.

Planning Strategies

We have learned that only one half of the value of property held in joint tenancy by a husband and wife is includible in the gross estate of the first spouse to die. Generally, the decedent's surviving spouse has an income tax basis that consists of two elements: (1) one-half of the original cost of property (that is, the surviving spouse's half); plus (2) half the fair market value of the property at the decedent's death (that is, the half that is included in the estate). An example should make this clear.

Assume several years ago Mr. and Mrs. John and Betty Roe bought property as joint tenants. The cost of the property was $10,000 and at John's death the fair market value of that property is $100,000. One-half, or $50,000, of the value of this property is included in John's estate, but this amount will pass to Betty free of federal estate tax because of the unlimited marital deduction. Betty's income tax basis for the entire property is $55,000—$5,000 representing half of the original cost plus $50,000 representing one-half of the value of the property at John's death. If Betty sells the property for $100,000, she would have a taxable long-term capital gain of $45,000 ($100,000 minus $55,000).

The tax situation just described could be dramatically improved if John holds the property only in his name. In that case, upon his death the property valued at $100,000 would be included in his gross estate. However, it will still be sheltered by the unlimited marital deduction. In addition, for income tax purposes Betty's cost basis on this property will be $100,000. So, if she sells it for $100,000, she will not realize any capital gains and no income taxes will be due on the sale of this property.

Another strategy concerning joint ownership involves splitting the property down the middle during the individuals' lifetimes. Each spouse then leaves his or her estate in trust to the children with an income interest to the other spouse. The result is a total avoidance of estate taxes upon both deaths. Here is an illustration to demonstrate this point.

Let us assume John and Betty Becker are both 55 years old. John owns property worth $1 million and she owns none. Instead of owning this property jointly, John makes a gift of one-half ($500,000) of his assets to his wife. His will provides that the other $500,000 goes to his children in trust. Betty Becker has the right to the trust income, and the right to receive a limited amount of principal. Upon Betty's death, the $500,000 in trust goes to the children. Betty's will reads exactly the same way. If she dies first, her $500,000 in assets goes to the children in trust with John Becker's right to trust income during his lifetime.

There is no estate tax involved in this case no matter which spouse dies first. This strategy also assures the surviving spouse the full use of the estate for life. If Betty Becker dies first, her $500,000 goes directly to the trust for the children. This amount is sheltered by the unified credit and passes automatically to the children when John Becker dies. Thus, John owns $500,000 outright and is entitled to life income from the $500,000 Betty Becker left in the trust. When John Becker dies, the $500,000 left in trust bypasses his estate and goes directly to the children. The remaining $500,000 goes directly to the children under the terms of his will, since it is fully sheltered from estate taxes by the unified credit. The situation is reversed if John Becker dies first, but the end result is the same. The children ultimately receive everything and the estate completely escapes federal estate taxes.

LIFETIME GIFTS

An Overview

The tool of the lifetime gift, initially discussed in Chapter 14, is extremely valuable for reducing the overall estate taxes. Here is a summary of the rules governing lifetime gifts.

1. Annual gifts of $10,000 per donee—or $20,000 per married couple for split gifts—are exempt from gift taxes. Thus, an individual can give away multiples of $10,000 (or $20,000 for married couples) annually to an unlimited number of persons and pay no gift taxes.
2. In addition to the annual gifts of up to $10,000, an individual can also make lifetime gifts, although these gifts are added back to a decedent's estate for estate tax purposes.
3. If death occurs within three years of a lifetime gift of a life insurance policy, such a gift is treated as if it never occurred.
4. If a property of a certain value is gifted, upon death the *original* value of the property, and not its current market value, is added back to a decedent's estate for purposes of calculating estate taxes.

Gift Tax Calculation

The gift tax applies to all gifts of property which exceed the $10,000 annual exclusion and the allowed deductions. Each gift is valued as of the date of the transfer. The value of the gifted asset or property is its fair market value on the date of transfer. However, the basis is the donor's cost, unless the gift tax is paid by the donee. The gift tax is assessed from the unified rate schedule and is reduced by the allowable credits.

The federal gift tax is computed by using the following steps:

Step 1. Determine the amount of taxable gifts for a given period. Taxable gifts refer to the gross amount of the gift made less the allowable deductions and exclusions.

Step 2. Obtain the sum of the taxable gifts for each of the preceding calendar years.

Step 3. Add the amounts determined under Steps 1 and 2.

Step 4. Compute the tax on the Step 3 amount, using the unified rate schedule.

Step 5. Compute the tax on the Step 2 amount using the unified rate schedule.

Step 6. Subtract the Step 5 tax amount from the Step 4 tax amount. The difference is the gift tax for the period for which the return is being prepared.

The objective of developing estate planning strategies involving gifts is to reduce or eliminate gift taxes. We will now explore several planning ideas involving gifts.

Planning Ideas Involving Gifts

Annual exclusion. The annual exclusion of a $10,000 gift per donee provides an excellent opportunity for planning. Assume Mr. and Mrs. Litle have two children and an estate of $1.5 million. They make gifts of $20,000 to each child for eight years, or a total of $320,000, thereby reducing the estate to $1,180,000. Mr. Litle leaves $600,000 directly to his wife and the balance of $580,000 in a trust. The $1.18 million ($600,000 plus $580,000) goes to the children at the deaths of Mr. and Mrs. Litle. The result is that the entire $1.5 million is transferred to the children, and no tax is paid either when the lifetime gifts are made or when the $1.18 million passes to the children.

Special property. Another strategy relates to the gift of property with a potential for significant appreciation. Let us assume Lisa Brown owns an undeveloped piece of real estate property which she hopes will greatly appreciate in value. The current value of the property is $300,000 and she gifts it to her daughter. Several years later when Lisa dies, the fair market value of the property is estimated at $1 million. However, the gift is added back to Lisa's estate at the original value of $300,000 and not at the fair market value of $1 million estimated at the time of her death.

Gifting via a trust. Gifting to minors via trusts constitutes the third gift planning strategy. Trusts permit the grantor to postpone the donee's receipt of the trust property at a prespecified age. Under the terms of a trust a trustee can be given broad investment powers, and through the use of a trust the donor is able to designate the distributions of trust property to the minors at the ages considered most desirable by the donor.

Gifts to charity. Gifts to qualified charities offer another important estate planning strategy. As a general rule, gifts to qualified charities are deducted from the gross estate before estate taxes are calculated. Gifts to charities can be made either outright or through the use of a trust. Depending upon the type of charitable trust selected by the donor, the trust property can assure an income stream to the donor, the surviving spouse, or other beneficiaries. For instance, an *inter vivos* or living charitable remainder trust (ex-

plained later in the chapter) provides a cur
the present value of the remainder interest
donor's estate is reduced by the value of tl
income from the asset is taxed to the incom

Disadvantages of Gifts

While gift giving has great potenti
and future estate taxes, it has several d
eration for future needs, a person may
earning years and experience financial
band decides to give substantial gifts t
both will continue to live together, but later on is a
given the gift to someone who no longer shares his life. Similar minuc.
apply to charitable gifts; and (3) if a taxable gift or bequest is given to grandchildren, a generation skipping tax may be imposed on the gift. The tax is
imposed at a flat rate of 55 percent, but there is a $1 million exemption to be
allocated amongst all of the grandchildren. Consequently, it is safe to conclude
that lifetime gifts should not be allowed to compromise the trade-offs among
various objectives established for maximizing financial welfare.

TRUSTS

The topic of trusts was briefly discussed in Chapter 14. Because the use of the
right type of trust is one of the most valuable estate planning tools, it is appropriate to discuss here in detail how different types of trusts can be used to
reduce or eliminate federal estate taxes.

Estate Taxes and Trusts

The law provides a variety of trust-related tools which can be used to
minimize federal estate taxes. These tools, presented in Table 15-1, will be
discussed in detail in the following pages.

The key issues. The avoidance of the federal estate tax frequently involves two key features: the estate tax exemption limit of $600,000 and the
unlimited marital deduction. The law offers a credit that allows every person
to give away during his or her lifetime, or after death, up to $600,000 to be-
neficiaries free of federal estate taxes. The second feature is even more generous. It states that a person can leave an unlimited amount of assets to the
surviving spouse free of federal estate taxes. These two provisions of the law
allow married couples to pass to the beneficiaries an estate up to $1.2 million
without federal estate taxes. Frequently the use of a trust commonly known
as a *bypass* or *family* trust is used to accomplish this objective.

TABLE 15-1 Trusts and Taxes

Type of trust	Nature of trust	Advantages	Disadvantages	Included in gross estate	Qualifies for marital deduction	Recipient of income	Recipient of assets
Bypass (family) trust	Property allocated to this trust so as to not overqualify for marital deduction.	Bypasses the survivor's taxable estate.	Surviving spouse does not have ownership of trust property.	Yes, subject to $600,000 exclusion.	No	Personal choice†	Personal choice†
Marital trust	Surviving spouse receives all income and the right to designate the beneficiary.	All income goes to spouse. Also, this trust, plus the pour-over trust,* can eliminate estate tax.	Spouse does not receive property outright.	No	Yes	Surviving spouse	Surviving spouse's choice
QTIP trust	This trust controls the distribution of property upon death of second spouse. Surviving spouse receives all income.	Property owner can direct distribution of property after death of surviving spouse.	Surviving spouse has no control over property.	No	Yes	Spouse	Personal choice†
Estate trust	This trust terminates on the death of the surviving spouse at which time assets and accumulated income are paid to the probate estate.	Appropriate where current income is not desired. Trust is not required to distribute income.	Tax rates are steeper.	No	Yes	Spouse	Surviving spouse's choice
Life insurance trust	Irrevocable inter vivos trust funded by life insurance policy.	Proceeds bypass estates of both spouses, if trust is irrevocable.	Loss of control over policy.	No (except when death occurs in 3 years).	No	Personal choice†	Personal choice†

* Proceeds from other trusts (e.g., life insurance trust) can pour over into this trust upon the occurrence of certain events such as death.
† Choice of the person who creates the trust.

Bypass trust. A bypass or family trust is created as a testamentary trust which comes into existence upon death. Following death, the decedent's assets are reallocated in such a way that no estate taxes would be due either upon the first or the second death. An illustration should make this clear.

Suppose John Jones owns $1.2 million, and Betty Jones does not own any assets. If John's assets are transferred to Betty upon John's death, no estate taxes would be due because of the unlimited marital deduction. However, upon Betty's death, only $600,000 would pass estate tax-free, thereby subjecting the balance to estate taxes.

The Joneses can adopt an alternative strategy to minimize estate taxes. John modifies his estate plan to create a bypass trust. Upon John's death, $600,000 worth of assets will be transferred into the bypass trust, while the remaining $600,000 would be directly received by Betty. The situation would now be as follows: assets received directly by Betty would qualify for the marital deduction and would escape estate taxes upon John's death. Although assets transferred into the bypass trust would not qualify for the marital deduction, they would escape estate taxes because John is entitled to the $600,000 unified credit. In short, upon John's death, the entire $1.2 million would be available for Betty's benefit free of federal estate taxes.

The story would be repeated upon Betty's death. If she does not remarry, Betty would not have a marital deduction but would be entitled to the $600,000 estate tax credit. Assuming that Betty's estate was not more than $600,000, the entire asset would pass to her beneficiaries tax-free. The tax code excludes the assets in the bypass trust from Betty's estate because she does not have control of the property in the trust. In addition, the bypass trust would remain

TABLE 15-2   Use of Bypass Trust

	Property willed to Betty Jones		Use of bypass trust	
	John Jones	Betty Jones	John Jones	Betty Jones
Estate value	$1,200,000	$1,200,000	$1,200,000	$600,000
Marital deduction	$1,200,000	0	$ 600,000[1]	0
Taxable estate	0	$1,200,000	$ 600,000[2]	$600,000
Tax, before credits	0	$ 427,800	$ 192,800	$192,800
Unified credit	0	$ 192,800[3]	$ 192,800[3]	$192,800[3]
Estate tax	0	$ 235,000	0	0

[1] Property passing directly to Betty.

[2] Property in a bypass trust.

[3] The $192,800 unified credit refers to the estate tax on a $600,000 estate. This is another way of stating that up to $600,000 of an estate passes federal estate tax-free.

tax-exempt no matter how large the assets grow, as long as the initial size of the trust was limited to $600,000. These facts are clearly illustrated in Table 15-2.

Marital trust. In the previous illustration, Betty received $600,000 from John's estate with unlimited powers to dispose of these assets as she saw fit. If John did not want to leave property directly to Betty for medical or psychological reasons, he could have transferred these assets into a *marital trust*, also known as *power of appointment* trust. In this case, Betty would be given the right to designate by will who would receive the assets of the marital trust (hence the name "power of appointment" trust) and such appointment may be made to anyone she chooses. Betty would receive all of the income from the marital trust and may also be given the right to withdraw any part of the trust's assets during her lifetime.

The marital, or power of appointment, trust is an extremely valuable estate planning tool. However, the law specifies that in order for the marital trust to qualify, the following strict conditions must be fully met:

1. The surviving spouse must be entitled to all of the income produced by the assets and it must be distributed at least once every year.
2. The surviving spouse must be given a general power to appoint the property to: (1) herself or himself; (2) the estate; (3) the creditors; or (4) the creditors of his or her estate.
3. No one else can appoint any part of the trust assets to anyone except the surviving spouse.

Tax considerations of a marital trust differ significantly from those relating to a bypass trust. Initially, assets transferred to a marital trust qualify for the marital deduction, even though the surviving spouse does not directly control the assets. This is because, in the eyes of the law, the spouse receives sufficient benefits from this trust to warrant such classification. Upon the death of the surviving spouse, however, the assets of the marital trust would be added to his or her estate. Naturally, the entire estate would pass to the beneficiaries tax-free if the total value of the marital trust added to the value of other assets does not exceed $600,000.

QTIP trust. As mentioned, a marital trust gives the surviving spouse unlimited power to dispose of the assets in any manner he or she chooses, including to a new partner after remarriage. For instance, if John creates a marital trust, he will have no guarantee that after his death the assets will ever reach his children. To allay that fear, John can create a *qualified terminable interest property* trust, or QTIP trust, also known as the current interest trust. The QTIP trust agreement, and not the surviving spouse, controls the distribution of the assets upon the death of the spouse.

Assets transferred into a QTIP trust will qualify for the unlimited marital deduction, provided all of the income of the trust is paid, at least annually, to the surviving spouse. Also, no provision for invasion of the trust assets can be made for anyone other than the surviving spouse. Finally, if the assets of a QTIP trust qualify for the marital deduction, then these assets must be included in the estate of the surviving spouse.

A QTIP trust is generally used as an estate planning tool for one or both of the following reasons:

1. It allows the marital deduction to apply to the value of QTIP trust property, even though the client making the will controls who will be the trust's ultimate beneficiary.

2. It allows the personal representative of the estate to elect to have the property included either in the estate of the decedent or in the estate of the surviving spouse.

Since the QTIP trust is a valuable planning tool, it might be appropriate to use an example to illustrate its use. Assume John and Mary Dow have two children, Jeffrey and Lisa. Also, John has a daughter, Cindy, and Mary has a son, Robert, from previous marriages. John is concerned that, upon his death, Mary will favor her son Robert in her will. John's will can provide that certain property can go into a QTIP trust. This trust will pay Mary income for life, with the remainder of the trust going to Cindy, or if John prefers, to Cindy, Jeffrey, and Lisa, upon Mary's death. If the trust meets with all the legal conditions, the value of the property going into the QTIP trust will qualify for the marital deduction.

Estate trust. An estate trust is one that terminates on the death of the surviving spouse and at that time, assets and accumulated income are paid to the probate estate. The estate trust is particularly suitable in situations where there is a desire to invest in nonincome producing property and the survivor does not need the income from the trust. An added advantage is that since the trust is not required to distribute income, the trust can become a separate taxpaying entity.

Now that we have reviewed the four major types of trusts, it might be interesting to compare their important features. This comparison, presented in Table 15-3, assumes that the surviving spouse is the income beneficiary of the trust. A quick glance at this table reveals that no one trust is better than the others and that individual circumstances will dictate the selection of the best trust.

Life insurance trust. The trusts described thus far are primarily designed to shelter up to $1.2 million from federal estate taxes. One asset, which can

TABLE 15-3   Comparative Features of Key Trusts

Particulars	Bypass trust	Marital trust	QTIP trust	Estate trust
Value of trust property subject to marital deduction?	No	Yes	Yes	Yes
Value of trust property included in decedent's taxable estate?	Yes	No	No	No
Trust income must be distributed annually?	No	Yes	Yes	No
Remainder of trust distributed to persons named by decedent?	Yes	No	Yes	No
Remainder of trust distributed to persons named by surviving spouse?	No	Yes	No	Yes
Value of trust property included in surviving spouse's estate?	No	Yes	Yes	Yes

easily push the estate beyond that limit, is a sizable life insurance policy. One trust that is designed to solve that problem is known as *life insurance trust.*

To shelter life insurance proceeds from estate taxes, one must sacrifice ownership rights, such as the right to change beneficiaries, the right to surrender or cancel the policy, the right to assign it, and the right to borrow against it. This may be accomplished by irrevocably transferring the ownership of a policy to a life insurance trust. If the insured's death occurs more than three years from the time of the transfer, the life insurance proceeds will be poured over into the trust, completely bypassing the estate of the deceased. The surviving spouse may continue to receive income from this trust for life and the trustees of the trust may be given the discretion to invade the principal in accordance with the trust's provisions. After the surviving spouse dies, the assets will be distributed to the named beneficiaries.

An important limitation imposed by law on life insurance trusts relates to the timing of the assignment of the policy. The law states that the assignment must occur more than three years prior to the death of the insured in order to exclude the proceeds from the estate of the deceased. Consequently, it may be wise to arrange the plan in a way that would automatically transfer the life insurance proceeds into a marital trust should death occur within three years of the trust's creation. If the plan is arranged in this manner, even when death occurs within three years of transfer of a life insurance policy, the estate of the deceased would escape the estate tax via the marital deduction route.

Charitable trust.   A life insurance trust is but one way to reduce the estate tax burden on sizable estates. An estate can also be reduced by outright gifts to individuals and charities as well as by creating charitable trusts. Gifting to charities as an estate planning tool was discussed in a previous section. Charitable trusts are discussed in this section.

Charitable trusts involve an *income interest* and a *remainder interest*. The former is the right to receive the earned income, while the latter is the property which remains after the income interest is satisfied. Through the use of a charitable trust, a person may be able to currently receive an income tax benefit for contributing a remainder interest or income interest to charity while retaining the other interest for personal use.

There are four types of charitable trusts which can be used to qualify for the unlimited estate tax charitable deduction. These are described next.

Charitable remainder annuity trust. This trust permits the annual payments of a fixed income to one or more beneficiaries during their lifetime or for a term no greater than 21 years. The trust assets cannot be invaded, nor can the trust be amended or revoked. Upon the termination of the trust the assets are transferred to the designated charity. In this type of trust the donor retains a life income interest in the contributed property. Consequently, the entire value of the assets is included in the person's gross estate. However, the donor receives a charitable deduction for the present value of the property passing to the charity as a remainder interest in the year of the transfer to the trust for federal income taxes.

It is important to note here that in order for a charitable remainder annuity trust to qualify as an estate deduction it must meet the following tests:

1. A fixed amount or fixed percentage of the beginning value of the trust must be paid to the noncharitable beneficiary.
2. The annuity must be no less than five percent of the initial fair market value of the property transferred to the trust.
3. The specified amount must be paid at least annually.
4. The trust must be irrevocable.
5. The trust must be for the benefit of one or more individuals.

Charitable remainder unitrust. In this trust, the individual or other designated beneficiaries receive variable—rather than fixed—annuity income. The variable amount is determined by taking a specified (not less than five) percentage of the fair market value of the trust's assets. Thus, a unitrust must revalue its assets annually to determine its income payout amount. Other than these provisions, a unitrust is similar to the charitable remainder annuity trust.

Charitable lead trust. A charitable lead trust is basically the opposite of a charitable remainder trust. Instead of transferring the remainder interest to charity, the lead trust distributes an interest to charity while the remainder interest is retained by the donor or the beneficiaries. Since the charitable income interest must be in the form of an annuity or unitrust interest, there is the possibility that very little trust income will be distributed to the donor or other beneficiaries.

Pooled income fund. A pooled income fund is a remainder trust created and maintained by a public charity. These investment funds consist of funds pooled together from the contributions of many individuals. Since a donor's retained life estate is based upon the trust's income, a pooled income fund is of particular benefit to an individual with limited assets. The deduction of property transferred to a pooled income fund is equal to the difference between the fair market value of the property contributed and the present value of the retained income interest. The gift and estate tax consequences are the same as for transfers to a charitable remainder trust.

More specifically, the donor to a pooled income fund will be entitled to an income and gift tax deduction if the following requirements are met:

1. The donor must contribute an irrevocable remainder interest to the charitable organization.
2. The property transferred by the donor must be commingled with the property transferred by other donors.
3. The fund cannot invest in tax-exempt securities.
4. No donor or income beneficiary can be a trustee.
5. The donor must retain for himself or herself, or other named beneficiaries, a life income interest.
6. Each income beneficiary must be entitled to receive a pro rata share of the annual income based upon the rate of return earned by the fund.

Irrevocable Living Trust

Finally, an irrevocable living trust can be created to pass assets free of federal estate taxes to the beneficiaries. In creating this trust, a person gives up any right to trust income and principal as well as the right to change the beneficiaries or other terms of the trust agreement. Clearly, upon the transferor's death, the assets transferred into the trust for longer than three years will not be included in his or her estate.

Basically, to keep the property out of the estate, the grantor cannot: (1) retain a reversionary interest in the assets; (2) retain the power to amend, revoke, or change the trust; (3) maintain a right to the income or enjoyment of the property; (4) retain the power to control the disposition of the property; and (5) maintain any incidence of ownership in insurance included in the trust.

There are two major advantages to creating an irrevocable living trust over outright gifts. First, the individual can have the income distributed from the trust to one or more beneficiaries. Second, the person can specify who would inherit the principal upon death. Incidentally, the beneficiaries need not be the same persons who receive the income from the trust.

SOPHISTICATED ESTATE TAX REDUCTION STRATEGIES

IRS Section 2036(c)

As a prelude to the discussion of sophisticated estate tax reduction strategies, it is important to briefly review the IRS advance notice concerning Section 2036(c), which was published in September 1989. This section applies to a person who holds a substantial interest in an enterprise and transfers property having a proportionately large share of the potential appreciation of such interest while retaining an interest in the income of that enterprise. The effect of this section is to include in the transferor's gross estate the value of the portion of the enterprise that corresponds to the portion of the transferred appreciation which is *disproportionately large*. Whether or not the transfer is disproportionately large is determined by the amount of transferor's retained interest in the income generated by that property. Clearly, in amending Section 2036(c), Congress intended to limit the use of techniques used to circumvent the transfer tax system through the creation and transfer of interests with disproportionate shares of income, appreciation, and other attributes of ownership. Several of the sophisticated strategies discussed in this section are subject to Section 2036(c) rules.

The Split

The split, or split purchase, strategy involves the purchase of real estate or other types of investment property. Assume John Root and his son Mike pool their resources to buy an investment. John purchases a life estate and Mike buys the remainder which refers to the ownership after John's death. Each pays the actuarial value of his respective interest; that is, the longer John's actuarial life expectancy, the less Mike has to put up for the remainder interest.

In a split, since John has only a lifetime interest in the property, there is nothing to pass on at death. So the amount John paid for the life estate, plus all appreciation in the asset's value, would pass to Mike completely free of gift and estate taxes. The split is subject to Section 2036(c) rules.

The GRIT

The GRIT, or grantor retained income trust, permits the receipt of income from a trust for a specified period. After the trust's term lapses, ownership of the property goes to the beneficiary, removing it from the estate of the original owner. GRITs are most attractive to wealthy people who can contribute more than the $600,000 exclusion to the trust and still avoid estate and gift taxes. An example should make this clear.

Suppose Martha Cool puts real estate valued at $1.2 million into a GRIT for her daughter Linda, who gets the property when the trust terminates in ten years. Martha receives any income the trust produces during that period while Linda would get the real estate in a decade. But if the IRS assumes that assets placed in a GRIT earn, say, an eight percent annual return, the IRS view property that will be valued at $1.2 million in ten years to have a present (residual) value of $555,800 today, which is less than the $600,000 exclusion, thereby avoiding gift taxes. The $644,200 difference between the IRS's valuation and the real estate's current worth is Martha's projected income.

The SCIN

The SCIN, or self cancelling installment note, is most appropriate when the owner does not live until the natural end of the transaction. Typically, under the SCIN strategy, the individual sells a valuable asset to a child for installment payments with the provision that the installment obligation will cease in the event of the owner's death. This results in a tax-free transfer of the value of the property above the installments already paid. Of course, the child must pay market interest on the installments, and the sale price must also include an appropriate premium for the cancellation feature. The SCIN is subject to Section 2036(c) rules.

Generation Skipping Transfers

The generation skipping transfers are designed to pass property to a third- or fourth-generation beneficiary while bypassing the second generation. The current tax law establishes the following rules: (1) in the case of a direct transfer to a trust for a beneficiary, or an outright gift to a person who is two or more generations younger than the grantor, the generation transfer tax will be imposed on the transferor; and (2) if distributions are made of income or principal to a trust beneficiary who is two or more generations younger than the grantor, then the transferee is responsible for the tax liability.

While the new tax law has severely limited the usefulness of the generation skipping transfer as a valuable estate planning tool, several exemptions from this tax provide an opportunity for wealthy individuals to save on estate taxes. These exemptions include: (1) a $1 million exemption per transferor or $2 million exemption for both spouses; and (2) an exemption for all transfers to a grandchild, if the grandchild's parent, who is also the transferor's child, is deceased.

ESTATE PRESERVATION AND DISTRIBUTION STRATEGIES

In the previous section we discussed various strategies for reducing federal estate taxes. In this section we will analyze strategies for preservation and effective distribution of an estate.

THE WILL

Regardless of the size of an estate and the kind of property included in it, the best way to protect a family's interest is for each spouse to have a will. A valid will is the basis for answering four critical estate-related questions: (1) Who will get the property? (2) Who will raise the children? (3) Who will administer the estate? (4) How much tax will the estate pay? Clearly, the importance of a valid will cannot be overemphasized.

The topic of wills was presented in Chapter 14 in detail. We will now discuss the use of the will in the development of estate planning strategies.

There is no simple way to summarize the salient features of a will that is appropriate for the estate planning needs of all families. Single persons and young couples may get by with a fairly simple will. The estates of a couple can escape estate taxation as long as a person's bequest does not raise the surviving spouse's estate beyond the $600,000 exclusion.

The importance of making a more comprehensive will rises as soon as children enter into the picture. The family then has to make several difficult decisions: (1) Who will raise the children should both parents die? (2) Where do the children best fit in? (3) How do the parents like the job the candidates are doing raising their own children? Additionally, at this time a revocable trust should be drawn up that takes effect if both parents die, to support the children until they are mature.

As the estate approaches the $600,000 level, the will can be supplemented by a bypass trust. As mentioned, upon the death of the first spouse, up to $600,000 can be transferred into this trust, which escapes estate taxes because it falls within the estate tax exclusion. The property in the bypass trust will support the surviving spouse, upon whose death the money will pass to the beneficiaries.

Finally, for estates over $1.2 million, the will can be supplemented by other, more sophisticated, instruments like a marital deduction trust, QTIP trust, and life insurance trust. These trusts, like others just described, are part of a valid estate plan designed to preserve and distribute the estate in an orderly fashion.

PROBATE

In Chapter 14 we learned that an estate plan deals with two kinds of property: probate and nonprobate assets. The former are those assets that pass to the personal representative, who disposes them in accordance with the instructions contained in the will. Nonprobate assets are those that bypass probate, either by operation of law or by contract, such as life insurance to specific individuals.

There are several important reasons why people may want to bypass probate: (1) the probate process is both slow and expensive. It involves attorney's fees and court costs. There are still more costs involved if the court finds it necessary to appoint a personal representative for the estate or a guardian for the children; (2) some of the heirs may not have access to their full inheritances from a few months to the two or more years that probate can last; (3) if the property is owned in more than one state, the heirs will have to contend with two or more probate procedures; and (4) probate court records are open to anyone who cares to look at them, from curious neighbors to newspaper reporters.

While there are many reasons for establishing a plan to bypass probate, it may not always constitute the best strategy. For instance, where substantial assets are involved, it may be best not to leave everything to the spouse. Also, there may be large estate tax savings in arranging the disposition of some of the assets in other ways. Finally, in the case of a common disaster where both spouses die simultaneously, a joint ownership without a will instituted to bypass probate may spell disaster, because it may increase the estate tax liability upon the death of the last person. It should also be recognized that some of the disadvantages of bypassing probate can be minimized by administering the system known as *independent probate*. This system allows for privacy and expeditiousness, with minimal court intervention. It is therefore advisable to scrutinize every situation carefully before deciding whether bypassing the probate strategy makes the most sense.

REVOCABLE LIVING TRUST

Perhaps the most effective method for estate preservation and distribution is the creation of a revocable living trust. Two trusts which fall in this category are presented in Table 15-4.

As a general rule, a revocable living trust is created to inform the trustee: (1) to whom the income and principal are to be distributed; (2) when the distributions are to be made; (3) how the property held in trust should be managed; and (4) how long the trust should be continued. A revocable living trust provides no federal tax advantages to the creator of the trust, since the creator has the power to revoke the trust at any time. This is tantamount to complete control and for federal tax purposes the creator is assumed to be in control and

TABLE 15-4 Trusts and Estate Preservation

Type of trust	Nature of trust	Advantages	Disadvantages	Included in gross estate	Gift taxation	Income taxation	Estate taxation
Revocable Inter Vivos	May be revoked by grantor.	Avoids probate. Permits flexibility.	No tax benefits.	Yes	None	Grantor pays taxes.	Grantor
Minor's Trust 2503(c)	Income or principal may be paid out or accumulated before minor attains age 21; any property left is payable to minor.	Protects children's inheritances. Qualifies for annual exclusion.	If minor dies, property may pass to parents.	Yes	Value of principal taxable; annual exclusion available.	Beneficiary if distributed; trust if undistributed.	If minor dies property may be included in parent's estate.

to own all of the trust property. Trust income is taxable to the creator of the trust no matter to whom it is paid, and upon death the assets included in the trust are included in the creator's gross estate for federal estate tax purposes.

There are additional advantages to creating such a trust. First, property placed in a revocable trust bypasses probate. This can avoid delays and probate costs. Second, a living trust can be established as a depository of a variety of cash assets. Third, a person can act as trustee when in good health, but a successor trustee can take over if the owner becomes incapacitated.

Even though a revocable trust is designed to act as a substitute for a will, the creator of the trust still needs a will, since an individual may forget to put all of the possessions in the trust. The will should include a "pour-over" provision that will sweep any remaining property into the trust at the owner's death. The will can also be used to distribute personal belongings, name guardians for children, and provide for a personal representative to take care of any unfinished business.

Setting up a revocable trust requires some work. The lawyer must draft a trust document that names the owner, the trustee, and others as co-trustees. The document must include instructions on how to manage the property if the owner becomes disabled, and also after the owner's death. The owner will also have to change bank accounts, brokerage accounts, and retitle other assets to the name of the trust. So long as the owner of the trust retains the power to alter, amend, revoke, or terminate the trust, the owner (but not the trust) will continue to be required to file an annual tax return. Every time a new account is opened or a property is purchased, it must be purchased in the name of the trust.

STANDBY OR CONVERTIBLE TRUST

A major drawback of a revocable trust is the hassle of transferring all assets into such a trust at a time when a person is healthy and feels no compulsion to do so. This problem can be obviated by the use of a standby or convertible trust. Simply stated, an attorney simultaneously creates two documents: a standby trust and a durable power of attorney. The former stands unfunded, whereas the latter gives a designated person power of attorney over the property. No further action is necessary at this time. If the grantor of the revocable trust is incapacitated, the designated person transfers the assets into the standby trust. The outcome is the same as though all the assets had been systematically transferred to the revocable trust in the first place.

MINOR'S TRUST (POWER IN TRUST)

Sometimes a parent may be fearful that a court-appointed guardian, or one appointed by the parent, may misuse the assets left for the benefit of minor children. These fears can be allayed by the establishment of a minor's testamentary trust. As the name implies, this trust is activated upon the person's death. The trustee is required to follow to the letter all the instructions contained in the trust agreement. This will insure that the assets are managed and ultimately distributed according to the wishes of the deceased. Note, however, that since the trust assets are controlled by the owner, upon death they are included in the estate of the deceased and, consequently, this trust does not avoid estate taxes.

MISCELLANEOUS ESTATE PLANNING ISSUES

In this concluding section we will discuss several important issues which must be taken into consideration when developing a comprehensive estate plan. While some of these issues have been mentioned in previous discussions, they will now be brought into sharper focus to wrap up our discussion on estate planning.

ESTATE LIQUIDITY

At death, there will be an immediate need for ready cash to pay for certain expenses before the estate can be distributed to the beneficiaries. These typically include funeral costs, administrative expenses, liquidation of debts and liabilities, and cash bequests to heirs. In addition, ready cash must also be available to pay for personal income, state inheritance, and federal estate taxes.

Several major sources of liquidity are generally available to meet the liquidity needs of an estate. These include: (1) ready cash, such as bank accounts, money market accounts, and certificates of deposit; (2) a broad range of assets that can be turned into cash quickly without sacrificing value; (3) life insurance proceeds which provide instant liquidity upon death; (4) proceeds of buy-sell agreements which generate ready cash; and (5) all other convertible assets. Clearly, the first four sources listed here should provide sufficient liquidity to meet the estate liquidity needs. It is important to recognize that if insurance is heavily relied upon to provide liquidity, the amount of life insurance carried should be reviewed on a periodic basis and adjusted upward when necessary.

FEDERAL INCOME TAX CONSIDERATIONS

After death of a person, one of the most important decisions to be made by a personal representative relates to the filing of a single or joint federal income tax return. Since the surviving spouse's taxable income does not end upon death of an individual, it is possible to minimize the federal income tax liability by manipulating income and deductions to utilize the joint tax rates.

In filing an income tax return, it is desirable to take full advantage of all the allowable deductions. For instance, medical expenses paid within one year of death are deductible. So are the bad debts or investments that have become worthless in the year of death as well as all the administrative expenses relating to the settlement of the estate.

Acceleration or postponement of income is another strategy relating to the reduction of the federal income tax liability. The law states that any income *constructively* received prior to death must be treated as income, even if such income is *actually* received after death. Consequently, if reduction of income is desired, and if it can be demonstrated that such incomes were not constructively received by the decedent, then they can be excluded from the decedent's final tax return. In addition, if the decedent was receiving an annuity, but had not received all of the investment, the unrecovered portion can be deducted on the decedent's final return.

STEPPED UP BASIS RULES

For income tax purposes, the basis—or cost—of property acquired from a decedent is the fair market value of the property at the date of the decedent's death or, if elected by the personal representative, the alternative valuation date. This rule, known as the *stepped up basis rule* (not available for gifting), offers an extremely valuable estate planning tool. Here is a simplified example to illustrate this point.

Several years ago Steve Stahl purchased 1,000 shares of ABC stock for $10 a share which has now appreciated to $110 a share. Assuming his marginal income tax bracket to be 28 percent, if Steve were to sell the stock now he would realize an after-tax profit of $72 per share, plus the $10,000 ($10 × 1,000 shares) by way of cost recovery, or a total sum of $82,000. Assuming an estate tax rate of 50 percent, Steve's heirs will ultimately receive only $41,000 (50 percent of $82,000). If, however, Steve keeps the stock until death, the stepped up basis for that stock will be $110 per share. Estate taxes of 50 percent will consume half of the total value of $110, so the beneficiaries will receive a net amount of $55,000. Hence, the net savings on this transaction will be $14,000 ($55,000 minus $41,000).

SURVIVORSHIP LIFE INSURANCE

A relatively new concept in estate planning, called "survivorship" or "second to die" insurance, is a form of whole life insurance policy that pays off only after both spouses have died. Essentially, such a policy provides coverage for two lives, with death benefits paid after the second death. The premium, cash values, and dividends are based on the "joint equal age concept." That is, the insurance company has to set reserves aside for only one death benefit payment, rather than two separate ones. Consequently, the premium cost is only 50 or 60 percent of what two people would pay to purchase the same amount of individual whole life coverage.

Survivorship insurance can be used effectively in estate planning. For instance, if a couple buys a survivorship policy in the children's name, the proceeds are exempt from both estate and income taxes. So, a policy geared to the estimated size of the estate taxes can provide the heirs with cash to cover the taxes after both deaths. This policy can also be used by two partners in a business with their children as beneficiaries. When the second partner dies, the money can defray the cost of inheritance taxes without putting undue financial burden on the business.

ESTATE PLANNING FOR BUSINESS OWNERS

Finally, some of the estate planning strategies used for business owners might be discussed. Of necessity, these are sophisticated strategies and their implementation requires technical knowledge and a high level of competence. Our objective is to present here only a highly simplified—and therefore somewhat distorted—view of several key strategies.

Installment Sale

A common estate planning problem is the distribution of a closely held business to family members when only some of them are directly involved in running the business. The technique used in such a case is known as the installment sale.

The installment sale is a device whereby the purchase price will be paid by the buyer in a series of installment payments over a period of several years. Typically, this device is used to spread out the taxable gain and thereby defer the income tax on the sale of property. But it can also be used to sell the closely held business to those family members who are involved with the business and invest the money for the benefit of *all* the children, including those who are not associated with the business. Another attractive feature of this strategy is that it removes the future appreciation of the business from the seller's estate without triggering a gift tax. The installment sale is subject to Section 2036(c) rules.

Private Annuity

A private annuity is an arrangement between two parties, neither of whom is an insurance company. The transferor or annuitant transfers complete ownership of a property to a transferee who, in turn, promises to make periodic payments to the transferor for a period of time. Usually, this period is the transferor's lifetime or the lifetime of both spouses.

A private annuity is an excellent estate planning tool for removing a sizable asset from the estate of a wealthy individual. For instance, John Kerr is the sole shareholder of the closely held Real Estate Corporation. He has two sons presently working in the business. He could sell his company to his sons in return for their agreement to pay an annuity for life. This will result in a reduction in John's estate because the value of the business will be removed from his estate for federal estate tax purposes. At John's death, annuity payments cease and neither the closed corporation stock nor the promised payments will be included in his estate.

Business Purchase Agreement

A business purchase agreement, commonly known as a stock purchase or a buy-sell agreement, is an arrangement for the disposition of a business interest in the event of an owner's death, retirement, or upon withdrawal from the business. Such an arrangement is frequently structured in one of the two following forms:

1. *Stock Redemption Agreement.* This agreement is reached between the company itself and the individual owners.
2. *Cross-Purchase Agreement.* This arrangement is made between individual owners.

A business purchase agreement is used when it is desirable to "peg" the value of the business for federal estate and state inheritance tax purposes. It is also used when a guaranteed market can be created for the sale of a business interest in the event of death or retirement.

Let us use a simple example to illustrate the use of a business purchase agreement in estate planning. John and Bob are equal stockholders in a business valued at $500,000. The business purchases $250,000 of life insurance and a policy providing $2,850 a month of disability insurance on both men.

At John's death, his stock passes to his estate. The proceeds of life insurance on John's life are paid to the business. Then the business pays the cash proceeds to John's estate according to the agreement. In return for the cash, John's personal representative transfers the stock to the business. Consequently, Bob ends up with ownership of all of the outstanding voting stock.

Under the buy-sell agreement, should John become totally disabled prior to retirement, he would receive his full salary for one year. At the end of the year of total disability, John's interest would be sold to the business. The business would pay at least $25,000 (ten percent of $250,000) as a down payment to John. The business would also issue John a ten-year note for the remaining value of the stock, $225,000. The business would pay nine percent interest on the note. Thus, John would receive approximately $2,850 a month for ten years. In order to help pay off the note, the business would receive $2,850 a month of disability income insurance proceeds from a policy owned by, and made payable to, the business.

PREPARING THE FAMILY

The Basic Needs

Some people have the short-sighted attitude that what they earn they should enjoy by spending here and now. Many, however, know that present pleasure is really enjoyed at their own or another's expense. But not all know how to strike a balance between immediate enjoyment and the future comfort of their dependents after they are gone.

A husband, for example, owes his wife more than an insurance policy. He should present her the opportunity for full financial security. He should share with her the full range of information involved in financially managing a family. Consequently, much more is involved than simply preparing a will or designating her as the beneficiary of his insurance.

Young families stand to lose more than the retired couples when the breadwinner dies. As is often the case, a young widow finds that she must shoulder full family responsibilities. Younger children require more care; fewer years have passed for building an estate and accumulating resources; in fact, young families tend to be chronically in debt. And a young widow faces many more years of struggling alone with young children than does a widow in the middle or later years. Furthermore, should a young widow with children remarry, the new family may have additional members, making its future even more precarious. What is essential at such a time is an effective estate plan. An example of the key elements of an estate plan designed to help a family is presented in the accompanying boxed insert.

Preparing the Wife

A typical husband is about four years older than his wife. It is thus likely

PREPARING THE FAMILY
FOR BREADWINNER'S DEATH

Name	Purpose of relationship	Method of assistance	Timing of assistance	Payment	Type of property
Betty	Wife	Provide lifetime income.	During Betty's lifetime, starting with John's death.	Income from bypass trust.	Mutual funds, bonds, income producing real estate.
Robert	Son	Gift.	Upon death.	Transfer of property.	Car (collector's item), china, furniture.
Susan	Daughter	Increase her income.	Upon death.	Transfer of assets to trust with provisions to make annual distribution of income.	Bonds, income producing real estate.
Bhutto	Adopted son	Help his parents raise the boy.	Upon death.	Transfer life insurance proceeds in a trust.	Life insurance.
MMC School	Charity	Assistance to needy students.	Upon death.	Trust setting up a scholarship fund.	Life insurance.

that a wife will be a widow for a decade or so (five years plus the difference in spouses' ages). For a husband, then, an essential aspect of estate planning is to prepare his wife to be a widow so that she may be *financially* prepared when his death occurs.

At a time of deep shock a widow must necessarily perform three major tasks: pay the bills, distribute the assets according to her husband's wishes, and maintain continuity in the lives of survivors. These are onerous tasks under the best of circumstances, and the widow deserves all the help she can get from her husband.

Paying the Bills

Upon the husband's death, the wife must pay funeral expenses, probate costs, and estate taxes. These costs can easily run into thousands of dollars, not to mention the delays in meeting the family's normal expenses. To defray these expenses, as well as to meet other contingency expenditures, there should be some money in a checking or savings account, or some other liquid form, that is in the spouse's name only. That is because at least half of any joint account with the deceased's name on it as well as all of any account in his name alone could be frozen for a few days for tax purposes.

Locating Important Papers

Taken by itself, a widow's job of clearing her husband's estate through the probate court, paying all the legal taxes, and distributing the remaining assets according to her husband's wishes is a formidable one. If she does not have a personal financial planner who maintains up-to-date records, or if she cannot locate all the important papers and quickly gather all the relevant information, this job can turn into a nightmare. The two most important papers that a widow must be able to locate quickly are the will and the letter of last instruction. In addition to these papers, a widow must have details of the life insurance policies in existence, names and account numbers of bank accounts as well as accounts with savings and loan associations and credit unions, the name of her husband's stockbroker, a list of stocks and bonds and his investments in mutual funds, Social Security information, the number of his safety deposit box, information on investments in real estate property, bills her husband owes, and other miscellaneous information such as the names of the professional advisors and various obligations to others.

The Survivors

Once the estate plan has been executed and the initial expenditures have been met, the lives of the survivors must go on, especially if minor children are involved. The widow can bear this burden more gracefully if her husband and she have previously discussed in great detail how she might meet both the financial and emotional challenges of maintaining the family during widowhood. There are various ways in which these responsibilities can be met. For instance, a trust can be set up to handle the family finances. A guardian can be appointed to oversee the welfare of the minor children. Perhaps a combination of these, as well as access to good advice from close family friends, would be ideal. ·

PART III

Putting it all Together

In Part I we described the emerging role of the professional financial planner in a highly complex economic and financial environment. We also discussed how the financial planner begins the planning process by selecting and interacting with clients.

Part II was devoted to a detailed analysis of the six key financial planning areas; namely, risk management planning, budget, debt and credit planning, tax planning, investment planning, retirement planning and estate planning. In our presentation, the structure and concept of each area was first developed, followed by a detailed discussion of the planning strategies associated with that area.

In Part III we will demonstrate the process of developing a comprehensive financial plan for a hypothetical family and conduct an annual review of that family's comprehensive plan. We will also discuss briefly the essentials of business planning for a financial planning practice.

CHAPTER 16

Development, Implementation, and Monitoring of a Comprehensive Financial Plan

INTRODUCTION

We have just completed a detailed study of the following six key areas of financial planning:

R: Risk Management Planning
E: Essentials of Budgetary, Savings, and Credit Planning
T: Tax Planning
I: Investment Planning
R: Retirement Planning
E: Estate Planning

In this chapter, we will learn how to develop a comprehensive financial plan, monitor it, and conduct a periodic review of the plan.

On March 1, 1989, Louis and Alice Johnson of Pickesville, CT contacted professional financial planner Wyn Webb to explore the possibility of his developing a comprehensive financial plan for the Johnson family. After a preliminary interview which lasted two hours, Webb accepted the Johnsons as his clients. Two days later, the Johnsons submitted to Wyn Webb the completed financial planning questionnaire. Webb reviewed the questionnaire and immediately set up an appointment for the goals and objectives interview. The interview was conducted on March 20, 1989. A transcription of the interview was mailed to the Johnsons for their confirmation.

Following the goals and objectives interview, Wyn Webb undertook a detailed analysis of the data supplied by the Johnsons and developed a comprehensive financial plan for them. This was presented to Louis and Alice Johnson on May 8, 1989.

Finally, on April 10, 1990, financial planner Wyn Webb sent the Johnsons a new questionnaire as a first step towards completing the first annual review. The annual review was presented to the Johnsons on May 8, 1990.

A SPECIAL NOTE

The Comprehensive Financial Plan presented here is INTRODUCTORY IN NATURE. We have deliberately made it simple yet complete in order to convey the *basic* nature of a comprehensive financial plan. We would like to emphasize here that, as a general rule, professional financial planners develop far more sophisticated financial plans than that presented on the following pages.

COMPREHENSIVE FINANCIAL PLAN FOR LOUIS AND ALICE JOHNSON, MAY 8, 1989, PREPARED BY WYN WEBB FINANCIAL PLANNERS, INC.

WYN WEBB FINANCIAL PLANNERS, INC.

May 8, 1989

Mr. and Mrs. Louis Johnson
1565 Main Street
Pikesville, CT 07589

Dear Mr. and Mrs. Johnson,

The enclosed Financial Plan, which is the result of an extensive analysis of the current quantitative and qualitative data you have provided us, has been developed especially for you. In generating this Plan, we have been guided by the fact that the success you have achieved in life should be matched by thoughtful planning for the maximum accumulation, conservation, and final distribution of your estate.

The Financial Plan presented here is comprehensive. In developing this Plan, we have applied basic principles from the fields of finance, investment, taxation, estate planning, and insurance. Our recommendations are formulated to meet the needs and the goals expressed in your confidential questionnaire as well as during the goals and objectives interview.

Of course, no one can ensure that all of your financial objectives will be met; however, if you follow your Plan, you will be using the same prudent principles that have been successful for many others. This carefully generated and realistic Financial Plan, periodically reviewed and updated, not only helps us discharge our professional obligation to you, but is also your best assurance for a secure financial future.

This Plan is intended to offer an initial evaluation of your financial situation and suggestions for improvement. We recommend that you consult and rely upon the advice of your personal accountant and attorney for answers tax and legal questions regarding the recommendations contained in this Plan.

If you have any questions, or need further clarification on the issues discussed here, please feel free to contact us.

Cordially,

Wyn Webb
President

FINANCIAL PLANNING QUESTIONNAIRE

QUESTIONNAIRE

Page 1 of 5

1. **Your Name** <u>LOUIS</u> <u>JOHNSON</u>
2. (Check) Mr. <u>x</u> Mrs. __ Miss __ Ms. __ Dr. __   Male <u>x</u> Female __

3. **Home Address** <u>1565 MAIN STREET</u>
   <u>PIKESVILLE</u>   CT   <u>07589</u>

4. a. **Home Phone** <u>313-333-4444</u>   b. **Business Phone** <u>313-333-5555</u>
5. **Marital Status** (Check)   Married <u>x</u>   Unmarried __   Separated __
6. **Your Social Security Number** <u>000-00-0002</u>

7. **Spouse's Name** <u>ALICE</u> <u>JOHNSON</u>
8. (Check)   Mr. __   Mrs. <u>x</u>   Ms. __   Dr. __
9. **Spouse's Social Security Number** <u>000-00-0003</u>

10. **Your Date of Birth** <u>03/09/45</u>   **Spouse's Date of Birth** <u>05/11/45</u>

11. a. **Your Employer**   b. **Spouse's Employer**
    <u>UNITED TEXTILES</u>
    <u>7621 SOUTH BEND ROAD</u>
    <u>POTTERSVILLE, CT 07590</u>

12. **Length of Current Employment**   You   <u>17 YEARS</u>   Spouse _____

13. **College Education for Children** (If Applicable).

	Child's First Name	Date of Birth	Current Grade	Projected Number of Years in College	Monthly Savings for This Child	Current Assets in Child's Name	% Total College Bills You Will Pay	Other Income Available Per Year
1.	Sarah	070970	13	4	$ 0	$ 18,000	100%	$ 0
2.	Chris	110873	10	4	$ 50	$ 14,900	100%	$ 0
3.								
4.								
5.								

14. **College Choice for Children** (If Applicable).
    a. Do you know which college or university each of your children will attend? If yes, please answer questions A,B,and C below.
    b. If you don't know which institution they will attend, would you prefer we assume a more expensive private college, less expensive public college, or an average of the two? (Check either question D,E, or F below)

	Child's First Name	(A) Name of Instit.	(B) City and State	(C) Current Tuition Cost	(D) Private Instit.	(E) Public Instit.	(F) Average
1.	Sarah			$ 6,000		X	
2.	Chris			$ 6,000		X	
3.							
4.							
5.							

Page 2 of 5.

15. Existing Assets of You (and Your Spouse)
(Please do not include assets listed only in children's names.)

Category	Current Value	Current Savings Per Month
Cash		
- Checking Accounts	$ 3,500	$ 0
- Passbook/Credit Unions	$ 0	$ 0
- Certificates of Deposit	$ 67,000	$ 0
- Money Market Accounts (Banks/Credit Unions)	$ 25,000	$ 100
- Money Markets (Mutual Funds)	$ 185,000	$ 100
Stocks (Common, Preferred and Stock Mutual Funds)	$ 175,000	$ 100
Bonds		
- U.S. Savings Bonds	$ 0	$ 0
- Gov't Bonds/Treasury Issues	$ 62,000	$ 0
- Corporate Bonds	$ 0	$ 0
- Bond Mutual Funds	$ 57,000	$ 0
- Tax Free Municipal Bonds and Mutual Funds	$ 0	$ 0
Pension Accounts		
- Employer Contribution (Vested Portion)	$ 108,000	N/A
- Voluntary Contribution	$ 0	$ 0
Profit Sharing Accounts		
- Employer Contribution (Vested Portion)	$ 52,000	N/A
- Voluntary Contribution	$ 0	$ 0
IRAs (Husband & Wife)	$ 16,000	$ 0
Keogh Account(s)	$ 0	$ 0
Other Corporate Plans (401K, Stock Purchase, Thrift, Savings, Etc.)	$ 27,000	$ 100
Home and Personal Possessions (Market Value)	$ 285,000	N/A
Other Privately Owned Real Estate	$ 0	N/A
Real Estate Limited Partnerships	$ 78,000	N/A
All Other Limited Partnerships	$ 0	N/A
Gold, Silver, Rare Coins, or Precious Metal Mutual Funds	$ 0	$ 0
Gems, Jewelry, Art, Antiques, Other Collectibles (Market Value)	$ 0	$ 0
Automobiles	$ 22,000	N/A
Other Assets (list)		
- CASH VALUE LIFE INS.	$ 17,000	$ 0
-	$ 0	$ 0
-	$ 0	$ 0
-	$ 0	$ 0

16. Existing Liabilities of You (and Your Spouse) - Remaining Balances	Estimated Current Balance
- Home Mortgage	$ 108,000
- Other Mortgages	$ 0
- Auto Loan(s)	$ 12,500
- Credit Cards	$ 0
- Bank (Personal) Loans	$ 62,000
- Credit Union Loans	$ 0
- Educational Loan(s)	$ 0
- Other Liabilities (list)	
-	$ 0
-	$ 0
-	$ 0
-	$ 0
-	$ 0

17. What is your **tax filing status?** (Front page of tax return immediately below name).
(Check one)
__ Single _x_ Married, filing jointly __ Married, filing singly __ Head of Household __ Qualifying Widow

18. What is your total **annual earned income** from employment before taxes?
You $100,000   Spouse $ 0

19. What is your **take home pay**? (Round up to the nearest dollar)
a. $ 1,500   Each paycheck _52_ times/year - You
b. $ 0   Each paycheck _0_ times/year - Spouse

20. a. Do you have **sources of income other than salary?**   Yes __ No _x_
If yes, approximately how much per month do you receive? $ 0

b. Does your spouse have **sources of income other than salary?**   Yes __ No _x_
If yes, approximately how much per month does he/she receive? $ 0

21. What is your **taxable income**?
You $ 84,975   Spouse $ 0   Joint $ 0

22. a. Do you expect to receive a substantial **gift, inheritance, or lump sum distribution** from any source ?   Yes __ No _x_

b. If yes, what is the approximate amount? $ 0
In what year will these funds be received? ___   Don't know ___

23. Personal budget-How much do you (and your family) spend monthly or annually on the following?

Type of Expense	Monthly Expenditure	OR	Annual Expenditure
- Housing (Mortgage or Rent Payment)	$ 1,000		$ 12,000
- Food	$ 400		$ 4,800
- Utilities (telephone,gas,electric,oil,water,sewer)	$ 200		$ 2,400
- Auto (maintenance,gas,parking,tolls,public transportation)	$ 250		$ 3,000
- Medical expenses (other than insurance premiums)	$ 0		$ 0
- Clothing	$ 200		$ 2,400
- Club and professional dues	$ 200		$ 2,400
- Yard maintenance, property repairs	$ 100		$ 1,200
- Domestic help (cleaning)	$ 250		$ 3,000
- Property taxes	$ 0		$ 0
- Entertainment and vacations	$ 750		$ 9,000
- Donations - church, charitable	$ 250		$ 3,000
- Child care	$ 0		$ 0
- Alimony/child support	$ 0		$ 0
- Books, magazines, periodicals, newspapers	$ 25		$ 300
- Home furnishings and appliances	$ 100		$ 1,200
- Gifts, birthdays, etc.	$ 250		$ 3,000
- Unreimbursed business expenses	$ 0		$ 0
- Insurance premiums	$ 700		$ 8,400
- Laundry and dry cleaning	$ 25		$ 300
- Pet care	$ 15		$ 180
- Loan payments	$ 400		$ 4,800
- Credit card payments	$ 350		$ 4,200
- Other expenses (explain)			
-	$ 0		$ 0
-	$ 0		$ 0
-	$ 0		$ 0
-	$ 0		$ 0
-	$ 0		$ 0
TOTAL	$ 5,465		$ 65,580

24. At what age would you like the choice of retiring with financial independence?
<u>62</u> You <u>00</u> Spouse

25. Look at your total monthly expenses in Question 23.
How much would you (and your spouse) spend per month in today's dollars to live the lifestyle you expect to live at retirement? <u>$ 8,000</u>

26. a. Approximately how much per month do you expect your employer's retirement plan to pay you when you retire? <u>$ 2,500</u>
At what age is it available to you? <u>62</u>

    b. Approximately how much per month does your spouse expect his/her employer's retirement plan to pay when he/she retires? <u>$ 0</u>
At what age is it available to him/her? <u>0</u>

27. **a.** Are you covered by Social Security? _x_ Yes __ No
    b. Is your Spouse covered by Social Security? _x_ Yes __ No

28. **a.** Do you (and your spouse) have any sources of income other than Social Security and employer retirement benefits at retirement? _ Yes _x_ No

    b. If yes, how much will be available monthly? $____0

29. If you died tomorrow, how much money would your life insurance coverage provide your family? $ 650,000

30. If your spouse died tomorrow, how much money would his/her life insurance coverage provide your family? $____0

31. If you became disabled today, how much money per month would your disability insurance coverage provide your family? $ 5,500

32. If your spouse became disabled today, how much money per month would his/her disability insurance coverage provide your family? $____0

33. How would you describe your financial attitude? (Choose One Letter) _C_

Ultra Conservative	Conservative	Middle of the Road	Moderately Aggressive	Ultra Aggressive
A	**B**	**C**	**D**	**E**

34. What do you think the average inflation rate will be for the next five years? _5.50%_

35. **a.** Do you have a will? _x_ Yes __ No
    b. If yes, in what approximate year did you sign your will? 1980

    c. Does your spouse have a will? _x_ Yes __ No
    d. If yes, in what approximate year did your spouse sign his/her will? 1980

36. Please rank your financial objectives below from 1 (most important) through (the last area of importance to you).

    _4_ minimize income tax liability   _2_ provide income at retirement   _7_ provide additional income now
    _3_ fund my children's education   _1_ maximize my return on investments   _5_ provide wealth growth
    _6_ review my current use of debt   _8_ other N/A

GOALS AND OBJECTIVES INTERVIEW

EXCERPTS FROM GOALS AND OBJECTIVES INTERVIEW WITH LOUIS AND ALICE JOHNSON

Louis and Alice, this afternoon we had a long, fruitful, and interesting discussion on all aspects of your financial life. We discovered that there were questions on the Financial Personality Questionnaire that were not clear to you and sometimes were even interpreted differently than intended. We also found out that some of the data included in your Personal Data Sheet needed to be modified. None of this, of course, should affect the quality of the Plan we will develop for you.

We recall that when you first contacted me, you said everything was "in a mess" and you wanted to have things organized as soon as possible. That was your main objective for starting the planning process and we should keep that in mind as we proceed to develop the Plan.

Today our discussion has centered around six major areas. I will summarize the essential elements of this discussion by using the acronym, R-E-T-I-R-E:

R: Risk Management Planning
E: Essentials of Budgetary, Savings, and Credit Planning
T: Tax Planning
I: Investment Planning
R: Retirement Planning
E: Estate Planning

R-Risk Management Planning

Life insurance.   We started our discussion with life insurance. Louis, currently you have $650,000 of life insurance. At this time we do not know whether or not you need additional life insurance. However, even before examining our life insurance analysis you have argued rather forcefully that you do not wish to purchase additional life insurance. The reason is that you believe buying life insurance is wasteful and it may even discourage Alice from going back to work and keeping her mind occupied in the event of your untimely death. I should mention, however, that Alice is very uncomfortable with your adamant attitude and believes that you should not have such a closed mind toward life insurance. Incidentally, Alice does not carry life insurance and does not care if you refuse to buy life insurance on her life.

Disability insurance.   Louis, currently you carry $5,500 per month worth of disability insurance. Interestingly, you are anxious to find out if you need additional disability insurance and are not opposed to buying additional disability insurance if we recommend it. Alice, you do not have a disability insurance policy because you are not employed.

Liability insurance. Louis and Alice, you were surprised to learn about the umbrella policy and how little it costs relative to the benefits it offers. You are anxious to purchase this policy right away; in fact, you would prefer to purchase this policy even before your Plan is finalized.

E-Essentials of Budgeting, Savings, and Credit Planning

Louis and Alice, both of you have a distaste for maintaining a budget, primarily because you feel that keeping a budget makes you behave like pennypinchers. However, after a long discussion of various aspects of budgetary and savings planning you realized that the purpose of maintaining a budget is to lay the foundation for a systematic growth of net worth. In addition, a sound budgetary plan will help you achieve your education, investment, and retirement goals in a more efficient fashion. As a result of this discussion you are now ready to set up a budget and religiously maintain it on a monthly basis.

T-Tax Planning

We had a most unusual discussion about tax planning. Alice, you said that you loved this country and have no difficulty paying your fair share of taxes. On the other hand, Louis, you believe that you have already paid a lot of taxes in your life and if you can help it you would not want to pay any more taxes. I would have to take these two opposite views into account when developing an appropriate tax strategy for you.

I-Investment Planning

During the course of discussion it became very clear that investment planning is critical for you. There are several reasons for this: (1) you wish to leave a large estate for your children which is possible only if you invest wisely; (2) your educational funds have fallen short of those needed to educate your children; and (3) you have paid very little attention to managing your investable funds.

Our discussion indicates that you are a moderate risk taker. In addition, by your own admission, you are not very knowledgeable about the investment world. Finally, you have already stated that you do not mind taking a risk with a small portion of your funds. We will take all of these facts into account in developing an investment plan for you.

R-Retirement Planning

Louis, you wish to retire at age 62. During the discussion you told me that after retirement you haven't got the faintest idea of how much monthly income you would need at the prices which are likely to prevail at that time. However, you did tell me that, upon retirement, you would like to have at least $8,000 per month in *today's dollars*. You also agreed to tighten your belt if our analysis shows that you would have difficulty reaching your retirement goals.

E-Estate Planning

Louis and Alice, you would like to leave a large estate for your children. To you, a large estate is equal to about $1 million in today's prices. During the course of our discussion it became clear that you have some confusion regarding trusts, estate taxes, gift giving, and the esoteric term "marital deduction." In fact, you were surprised to discover that estate planning is a lot more involved than having a valid will. This is because you were led to believe that you can pass on an unlimited amount of estate to your spouse without paying taxes. However, now that you understand that there is a lot more to estate planning than will drafting, you are anxious to get going in this area.

Summing Up

At the very beginning I asked each of you a simple question: What is your greatest concern at the present time? Alice, you replied that your concern is to invest the funds as wisely and safely as possible. On the other hand, Louis, you said that your major concern is the preservation of capital.

This goals and objectives interview has helped us articulate your short- and long-range goals, your risk tolerance level, and the gaps in your knowledge of various financial planning areas. This interview has also revealed your resolve to get the comprehensive financial plan developed and implement the recommendations as soon as possible. We promise to make sure that your objectives are fulfilled in the most expeditious manner.

OVERALL FINDINGS

Before we begin the analysis of the information you have given us, you might find it helpful to review our overall findings.

1. Louis Johnson, you are currently age 44 and wish to retire at age 62. Your child Sarah entered college in 1988. Your child Chris will enter college in 1991.

2. Your current net worth is $997,000.

3. Your gross income is $100,000. After paying your withholding taxes, monthly expenses, and providing for your savings, you have a monthly surplus of $685.

4. Your projected annual retirement income excess is $30,692. That is, under the assumptions we have made, you will have an annual surplus of this amount during retirement.

5. Sarah's and Chris's educational fund dollar status is $0 and −$6,849, respectively. This means that currently there is a large deficit in Chris's educational fund.

6. Our analysis shows that you are currently in the 33 percent tax bracket and have tax problems which might require aggressive tax strategies.

7. You currently have adequate life insurance coverage. Alice, too, has adequate life insurance coverage.

8. You currently have adequate disability insurance coverage.

9. Our analysis shows that currently both you and your spouse have wills. However, we also notice that both of these wills need to be updated to take advantage of the unlimited marital deduction. We suggest that you contact a competent attorney immediately to update both documents.

10. Lastly, your estate is above the $600,000 exemption equivalent which requires sophisticated estate planning techniques.

Throughout our analysis we have used an after-tax return of 10.1 percent when we needed to see how much you could expect to earn on your money. Let us explain here the reason for our using the 10.1 percent rate in our analysis. Each of your current investments has an individual percentage return figure which we monitor. We calculate a different rate of return for each investment category. Each rate of return is based on a five-year average for that particular asset. For example, if you currently have a money market account, we would compound this account at 6.8 percent because that is what money market accounts have returned over the last five years. We would do the same kind of calculation if you owned stocks, bonds, gold bullion, real estate, and so on. From all of these individual calculations we figure a weighted average return from all investments. That figure, which in your case is 10.1 percent, is used in calculating your retirement, insurance, and children's educational needs. However, we should add here that past performance is no guarantee for future results.

We have provided next a checklist of those areas in which you are satisfactory, and those in which you need help. Our recommendations will cover those areas which fall in the Attention Needed column.

	Satisfactory	Attention Needed
Children's education		X
Retirement	X	
Emergency funds	X	
Income taxes (taxable income)		X
Wills and estate plan		X
Life insurance	X	
Disability insurance	X	
INVESTMENTS		
Liquidity	X	
Diversification		X
Debt/equity asset mix		X
Savings	X	

THE PLAN

NET WORTH

The Basis of Our Analysis

You have probably heard of the terms balance sheet, assets, liabilities, and net worth. In its simplest form, your balance sheet lists what you own (your assets), subtracts what you owe (your liabilities), and calls the balance your net worth.

Your personal balance sheet is presented in Table 1. Please take a look at your net worth dollar amount of $997,000 which we have displayed at the bottom of Table 1. While there is no "ideal" net worth figure, it is certainly better to have a large positive net worth implying that you own significantly more than you owe. Next to establishing personal financial objectives, an evaluation of what you own and what you owe is probably the most important ingredient in securing your financial future. Only by taking stock of where you stand financially today can you look towards a better future.

From the information contained in the balance sheet, we can determine the impact of federal estate taxes on your estate, the nature of diversification

TABLE 1   Net Worth: Louis and Alice Johnson, May 8, 1989

Assets

Asset type	This year's balance May 8, 1989	This year's percent of assets
Checking accounts/cash	$ 3,500	0.3%
Passbooks/money markets/CDs	$ 277,000	23.5%
IRAs/Keoghs*	$ 16,000	1.4%
Bonds	$ 119,000	10.1%
Pension/profit sharing*	$ 160,000	13.6%
Other corporation plans*	$ 27,000	2.3%
Stocks	$ 175,000	14.8%
Home/possessions	$ 307,000	26.0%
Other real estate	$ 0	0.0%
Real estate partnerships	$ 78,000	6.6%
Other partnerships	$ 0	0.0%
Gold/silver/metals	$ 0	0.0%
Other assets	$ 17,000	1.4%
Total assets	$1,179,500	100.0%

Liability type	This year's balance May 8, 1989
Remaining home mortgage	$ 108,000
Other mortgages	$ 0
Auto loan(s)	$ 12,500
Credit cards	$ 0
Bank (personal) loans	$ 62,000
Credit union loans	$ 0
Educational loans	$ 0
Other liabilities	$ 0
Total liabilities	$ 182,500
Total assets:	$1,179,500
Total liabilities:	− 182,500
	$ 997,000

Your total net worth
   $ 997,000

* For purposes of computing your debt/equity asset ratio, we have assumed these assets are invested in debt securities.

of your investments, your liquidity, and your debt/equity asset ratio. Your net worth figure is also used in your retirement status calculation, and in evaluating your insurance needs. In other words, much of what we will be discussing in your plan will relate to your net worth, which is derived from your balance sheet.

One of our major challenges is to help you increase each year your net worth. We look forward to working with you in accomplishing this and other important financial goals. You will notice that the asset section of your balance sheet includes a column marked "This Year's Percentage of Assets." This data relates to diversification of your assets and will be discussed in the section entitled "Investment Analysis."

We have just presented a detailed analysis of your net worth. As you can see, you have a net worth of slightly less than $1 million. With proper planning, discipline, and careful monitoring, over time this net worth is likely to significantly appreciate in value.

We will now undertake a detailed analysis of each of the six key areas of financial planning articulated by the acronym, R-E-T-I-R-E.

YOUR WORKSHEET

Net Worth Analysis

Do you have questions? Jot them down here.

Questions.
1.
2.
3.
4.
5.

Make a note of the steps you feel you need to take in order to accelerate the growth of net worth.

Action needed.
1.
2.
3.
4.
5.

R-RISK MANAGEMENT PLANNING

Life Insurance

When you buy insurance, you are protecting yourself against the unexpected risk. Of course, you do not expect to lose your home to a fire, or to become seriously ill. Protecting yourself against such tragedies is a vital link in your overall financial game plan.

First, let us discuss your needs for life insurance which performs two major functions: (1) it replaces the earning power of the primary breadwinner; and (2) it provides your estate with sufficient money to meet your family's cash needs and the legal costs of settling your estate in the event of your untimely death.

We begin by calculating the amount of life insurance you should carry to satisfy your family's financial goals. Our analysis of your life insurance needs is presented in Table 2. According to this analysis, your life insurance needs are being sufficiently met by your current policies. We congratulate you for protecting the future of your loved ones. Should there be any changes, however, such as a substantial increase in income, or an addition to your family that would affect your monthly expenses, we would appreciate your letting us review your insurance needs at that time.

TABLE 2   Life Insurance

Louis Johnson			Alice Johnson		
Amount of insurance	$650,000		Amount of insurance	$	0
At Louis's death:			*At Alice's death:*		
Alice's cash flow per month available	$	0	Louis's cash flow per month available	$	6,500
Income per month if insurance proceeds invested at 10.17%	+$	5,507	Income per month if insurance proceeds invested at 10.17%	+$	0
Total dollars per month available to Alice	$	5,507	Total dollars per month available to Louis	$	6,500
Current expenses per month	−$	5,465	Current expenses per month	−$	5,465
Monthly surplus for Alice	+$	42	Monthly surplus for Louis	+$	1,035

Disability Insurance

Disability insurance has a mission similar to life insurance. Total and permanent disability is a tragedy we do not expect to occur. Yet, statistics show that for every ten persons between the ages of 25 and 40, before retirement nearly five will be disabled for at least 90 consecutive days. In many cases, Social Security and employer group disability plans are insufficient to meet the family's needs in the event of the breadwinner's long-term disability.

The results of our analysis of your disability insurance are presented in Table 3. This analysis shows that currently your spouse is not working outside the home and is therefore not eligible for disability insurance. Consequently, our analysis, which concentrates on your disability insurance needs, shows that the policy you now have will provide for your current living expenses should you become disabled.

Homeowner's Insurance

There are three basic components to your homeowner's insurance: the building, its contents, and liability. If you do not keep your home insurance attuned to inflation, you may find that the policy premium you have been faithfully paying all these years will leave you painfully short if you need to submit a claim. For example, if your garage is damaged due to your negligence, the claim will reflect the soaring cost of construction when repair work is done. It is your responsibility, and not that of your insurance company, to keep the amount of insurance you carry up to the level of the current value of the property. We recommend that you insure your dwelling for 100 percent of its current replacement cost at today's prices, or the "actual cash value" which reflects the age and wear and tear on the possession less the value of the lot. For instance, the actual cash value coverage is generally less costly but it does not give you a new television to replace your five-year-old model in the event of a claim. Instead, you would only receive payment for the value of a five-year-old television. If you have valuable jewelry, stereo equipment, art, cameras, and sporting equipment, they should be listed separately on your policy

TABLE 3   Disability Insurance Analysis

Louis Johnson	
Amount of Insurance per Month	$ 5,500
If Louis Is Disabled:	
Income per Month Available from Your Disability Insurance	$ 5,500
Current Expenses per Month	− $ 5,465
Monthly Surplus for the Johnson Family	+ $ 35

and insured for the current appraised value. Also, under a personal property floater, you should insure for glass breakage.

The last topic with regard to homeowner's insurance is liability. Today, liability awards of $1 million are commonplace. While your standard homeowner's policy includes liability coverage, we suggest that you carry an umbrella liability policy providing additional coverage. This policy would supplement your existing coverage on auto and home liability exposures. We have found that monthly cost for this type of coverage is only $10 to $20 per month, which in our view is quite affordable. Contact your current homeowner's insurance agent for a quote on an umbrella liability policy.

Automobile Insurance

Automobile insurance covers both you and your car and is intended to prevent serious financial loss. We suggest that you take several steps to keep your auto insurance costs to a minimum: (1) increase your deductible if your accident history is favorable; (2) drive defensively; (3) do not let others drive your car; and (4) always place your valuables out of sight in your trunk.

Before buying your dream car, ask your insurance advisor about the cost of insuring the vehicle—you might find that the cost is beyond your budget. Expensive and superpowered cars cost more to insure. Also, if you own more than one car, insure all of them with the same company. You will more than likely get a discount on all cars and will avoid administrative hassles if you have a claim. Have your cars insured by the same company which insures your home; this will save on your total premiums. Be sure to keep receipts for the improvements or extraordinary repair bills on your car. They will help you get a better settlement for damage claims. Finally, ask your insurance advisor about all the discounts a particular company offers. Companies vary greatly in what credits (such as a "good driver" credit) they will grant you and the value of those credits in your overall insurance plan.

Medical Insurance

Medical insurance is a costly but necessary family expense. We notice that your employer pays your health care premiums. However, be aware of what the policy does not cover. We asked your employer for a description of what is deductible and in the event of sickness how much you will be left to pay. We discovered that benefits such as maternity coverage are not included; also, certain exclusion periods apply in your medical coverages. Lastly, if you leave your employer and must shop for your own health insurance, of which there is a distinct possibility, here are seven simple guidelines to follow: (1) Compare policies—standard coverage in one policy may be a costly supplement in another. (2) Don't overinsure yourself; duplicate benefit payments for the same claim are disallowed. (3) Check the policy on preexisting conditions, which refer to an illness you have at the time of purchasing the policy. You do not want to eliminate yourself from coverage you may need. (4) Know your maximum benefits; that is, know how long you will receive the benefits and in what amounts. (5) Check on the out-of-pocket expenses; namely, in each case how much are you left to pay? (6) Find out about the premium adjustment privileges; that is, how often and by how much can they raise the cost? (7) Take advantage of the trial review period. Review the policy for ten days and receive a total refund of your premium if you decide to cancel the policy.

All family members should be covered by health insurance. Do not neglect to notify your insurer immediately should there be any changes in the size of your family.

YOUR WORKSHEET

Insurance Analysis

Do you have questions? Jot them down here.

Questions.
1.
2.
3.
4.
5.

Make a note of the steps you need to take in order to improve your insurance coverage.

Action needed.
1.
2.
3.
4.
5.

E-ESSENTIALS OF BUDGETING, SAVINGS, AND CREDIT PLANNING

An Overview

Your budget is presented in Table 4. You may find it interesting to compare how you spend your money each month relative to the national average for your age group and income level. While there are no right or wrong dollar

TABLE 4   Family Budget

Type of expense	Monthly amount	Percentage of your spending	Average percentage of spending*
Housing	1,000	22.35%	12.50%
Food	400	8.94%	16.60%
Utilities	200	4.47%	6.00%
Auto maintenance	250	5.59%	19.40%
Medical expenses	0	0.00%	2.80%
Clothing	200	4.47%	6.90%
Club/professional dues	200	**	N/A
Property maintenance	100	2.23%	2.40%
Domestic help	250	5.59%	1.50%
Property taxes	0	0.00%	2.10%
Entertainment/vacations	750	16.76%	7.40%
Donations	250	5.59%	3.10%
Child care	0	**	N/A
Alimony/child support	0	**	N/A
Books, periodicals, etc.	25	0.56%	0.70%
Home furnishings	100	2.23%	5.00%
Gifts, birthdays, etc.	250	5.59%	2.60%
Unreimbursed business expenses	0	**	N/A
Insurance premiums	700	15.64%	11.00%
Laundry/dry cleaning	25	**	N/A
Pet care	15	**	N/A
Loan payments	400	**	N/A
Credit card payments	350	**	N/A
Other expenses	0	**	N/A
	5,465	100.00%	100.00%

* *Source:* "Consumer Expenditure Survey," U.S. Department of Labor, Bureau of Labor Statistics, 1988.
** At the present time, there are no comparative figures available for these spending categories and so we have not included these monthly expense amounts in our calculations of "Percentage of Your Spending."

amounts for each type of expense, this comparison might show you those areas where you are spending significantly more than the average. Of course, your situation is unique and your expenditures could be justifiable even if they are much higher than the average. However, these disproportionate spending decisions might deserve your attention.

Cash Flow Analysis

You may wish to learn about the nature of your monthly expenses. Your expenses by general categories are presented in Table 5 so that you can see

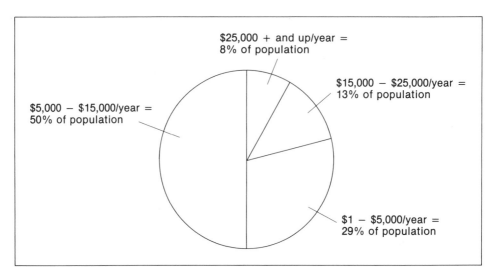

FIGURE 1   Current income for Americans at age 65

how much goes toward personal expenses, savings, taxes, and so on. You might find this information useful as you analyze the ways in which your spending patterns might be modified to help you reach your financial goals.

Savings Goals

As we all know, saving money is more than just a function of dollars and cents; it requires discipline and perseverance. In the end, however, those who

TABLE 5   Expense Analysis

Spending category	Amount spent per month	Percentage of total spending
Personal savings	400	5%
Education savings	50	1%
Monthly spending	5,465	66%
Tax liability (Fed only)	1,689	20%
Monthly surplus/deficit, payroll deductions, FICA, state & local tax	729	8%
Total	$8,333	100%

$8,333 = Your Gross Income ($100,000 divided by 12)

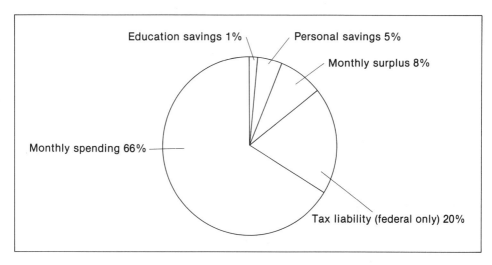

FIGURE 2 Expense-analysis for Mr. and Mrs. Louis Johnson

have mastered this discipline win because they succeed in accumulating the wealth necessary to meet their financial objectives.

You may find it helpful to develop the habit of "paying yourself first" and then living each month on the balance. Unfortunately, most of us do just the reverse and find a way to spend all that is earned without ever saving any money for the future. Once you are used to living on what remains "after" you have put something away for a rainy day, you will find that developing good savings habits is really a painless process and its benefits far outweigh the cost.

YOUR WORKSHEET

Budget Analysis

Do you have questions? Jot them down here.

Questions.
1.
2.
3.
4.
5.

Make a note of the steps you need to take in order to improve your budgetary situation.

Action needed.
1.
2.
3.
4.
5.

T-TAX PLANNING

Currently, you are in the 33 percent marginal tax bracket. This tax bracket is the rate at which your last income dollar is taxed. This year, for every extra dollar you earn the federal government takes $.33, while you take home only $.67 of that dollar. And that is in addition to your Social Security, state, and local income taxes.

Knowing your tax bracket is helpful in inspiring you to keep good records for Uncle Sam. The reason is that if you are able to itemize deductions, your tax bracket determines how much your tax deductions are worth. For each dollar of deduction you claim, your federal income tax is reduced by $.33. Be sure to keep all receipts which justify deductions. If you are unsure of what is deductible, contact our office for details. While less than two percent of all individual tax returns are audited, proper records will ensure that you are among the one out of every five taxpayers who emerge from an audit owing no additional tax. Incidentally, the IRS can audit a return up to 36 months after it has been filed. You should therefore keep copies of your tax returns forever and the supporting receipts for at least five years.

Many people believe that "tax planning" is only for the very rich. Yet, research released by the Tax Foundation shows that most Americans spend an average of one-third of an eight-hour working day earning money to pay federal and state taxes. It is true that the higher your tax bracket, the more you stand to gain by sheltering your income, but everyone can gain from some simple strategies. The real question is: What is an appropriate strategy for you?

We believe that tax shelters, such as limited partnerships, are appropriate for individuals or families in the 33 percent tax bracket. In 1989 this bracket referred to $44,900 in taxable income for a single taxpayer and $74,850 for married taxpayers filing jointly. Below that level, several tax saving strategies may be employed, but public or private tax-sheltered investments are generally not needed. Use of tax-deferred or tax-free investments (where no current taxes are paid on the investment's earnings) should be considered in tax/investment planning. Some examples of these strategies include municipal bonds (including unit trusts and municipal bond funds), single premium life (both whole life and variable life) insurance, and annuities. Of course, each investment has its own advantages and disadvantages, and careful consideration should be given to your personal needs and circumstances. Money placed in these types of investments will generally not be tax-deductible. However, not having to report the yearly earnings of these investments will certainly help lower your tax bill and increase the growth potential of these tax-deferred and tax-free investments.

The Tax Reform Act of 1986 requires that all of us take another look at our personal tax strategies. A summary of the key changes that will impact you personally was given to you during the goals and objectives interview. We hope that this summary is useful to you as you reevaluate your own unique situation.

We begin our tax analysis by presenting your *taxable income limit* in Table 6.

What do we mean by taxable income limit? This figure is the current qualifying income level for the 33 percent federal income tax bracket, given your "married filing jointly" tax status. We do not recommend aggressive tax sheltering techniques for individuals and families whose taxable income level places them below the 33 percent bracket. Your taxable income limit figure will remain the same as long as the IRS does not change the tax brackets. Our analysis indicates that your current taxable income places you at the 33 percent tax bracket in earnings, and therefore you should consider aggressive tax planning strategies.

TABLE 6 Income Tax Analysis

Tax Filing Status: Married filing jointly

	May 8, 1989 current year	*Taxable income limit*	*± Variance from current year limit**
Gross earned income			
Louis	$100,000		
Alice	$ 0		
Total gross earned income	$100,000		
Total taxable income (after all deductions)	$ 84,975	$ 74,850	− $ 10,125

* The difference between your taxable income and your taxable income limit. A *positive number* means that you *do not* have significant problems with tax management. A *negative number* means that you should consider strategies to *lower your current taxable income* by the amount of this variance.

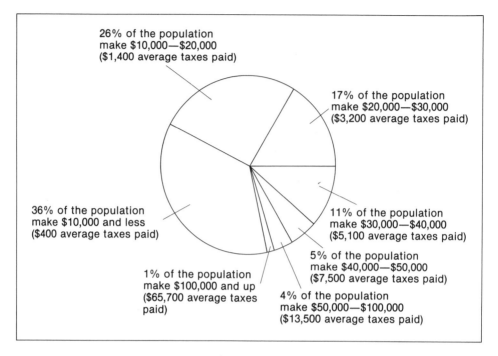

26% of the population
make $10,000—$20,000
($1,400 average taxes paid)

17% of the population
make $20,000—$30,000
($3,200 average taxes paid)

36% of the population
make $10,000 and less
($400 average taxes paid)

11% of the population
make $30,000—$40,000
($5,100 average taxes paid)

5% of the population
make $40,000—$50,000
($7,500 average taxes paid)

1% of the population
make $100,000 and up
($65,700 average taxes
paid)

4% of the population
make $50,000—$100,000
($13,500 average taxes paid)

FIGURE 3   Current income and taxes paid—all Americans today

Some years ago, Congress decided to offer tax incentives in certain investments to stimulate private investment rather than offering direct government assistance to these investments. A broad variety of products is now available. Among the most popular are: real estate, equipment leasing, low-income housing, agricultural products, municipal bonds, and tax-deferred annuities. However, be aware that a dollar's worth of tax deduction means tax savings of only $.33 for you.

There are two types of tax-sheltered investments: public shelters that are registered with, and come under the scrutiny of, the Securities and Exchange Commission (SEC), and private offerings. A public program may be offered in many states other than the home state of the general partner who is the promoter and manager of the program. The sales representatives in a public offering must be licensed in each state in which they do business. These programs are exempt from registration with the SEC, there is no public advertising, and the investor must meet high suitability requirements. We recommend that you stay clear of private offerings.

Before you decide on any public tax shelter program, follow these sensible rules: (1) avoid a questionable general partner. If the business record is less than sterling, the chances of your losing the entire investment are high; (2) do your tax planning early in the year. As December draws closer, less reputable shelters are heavily promoted; (3) look for programs with a solid economic reason for existing. Programs based on a questionable idea are called "an audit looking for a place to happen;" (4) be reasonable in what you expect the program to do. Generally, a modest write-off and good projected return on your money are reasonable; and (5) seek professional, unbiased advice on the attractiveness of a public tax shelter program.

YOUR WORKSHEET

Tax Analysis

Do you have questions? Jot them down here.

Questions.
1.
2.
3.
4.
5.

Make a note of the steps you need to take in order to improve your tax status.

Action needed.
1.
2.
3.
4.
5.

I-INVESTMENT PLANNING

Over the years you have been on the receiving end of a vast amount of investment advice and information. Some of it may have proven effective, but much of it has either lost your money or you never carried through the suggestions due to a lack of time or confusion. You should learn how to be a smart investor in order to: (1) increase your income; (2) make your money grow; (3) put inflation to work for you; and (4) lower your tax liability.

Wealth maximization need not be a hopeless pursuit. To get you started, let us review three useful concepts for successful investment management.

Liquidity

The first concept is liquidity, which is a term used by professionals to mean how quickly you can get your hands on your money. For example, if you had $1,000 in a passbook account at your local bank, you would simply withdraw the money at your convenience. Dollars invested in passbook accounts are highly liquid. However, if your only source of $1,000 was the equity in your home, you would have a much more difficult time converting the equity into liquid cash. You would then have to take out another mortgage or find a buyer, all of which takes precious time. Real estate is a relatively illiquid investment.

It is a simple enough concept, but what impact does it have on you? You should monitor how much of your assets are relatively liquid, since it is not wise to have most of your dollars invested in illiquid investments. Our lives are full of emergencies which require quick and easy access to some cash. On the other hand, during most periods in our history, relatively illiquid investments have provided a higher return to patient investors. Because of their potential, it is useful to tie up a portion of your assets in illiquid investments. Naturally, individual liquidity needs vary according to age, income level, and special situations.

Placed next is a partial list of liquid and illiquid investments. We have divided the liquid investments into two categories: those that are riskless and those which are exposed to capital risk. All illiquid assets have capital risk associated with them.

Liquid	*Illiquid*
Riskless funds	Home
Liquid cash	Personal possessions
Checking accounts	Other real estate
Money market accounts	Raw land
Certificates of deposit	Limited partnerships
Capital risk assets	Rare coins, stamps, art gems,
Stocks	antiques, and other collectibles
Mutual funds	
Bonds—corporate, U.S. Savings	
Bonds and treasury notes	
Treasury bills	

Diversification

Let us now ask what the word "risk" means to you. If you are like most people, you will think of Las Vegas or the lottery. In investment planning, risk is often thought of as the chance that your investment will be worth less now than it was when you bought it. Would it not be great to find a riskless

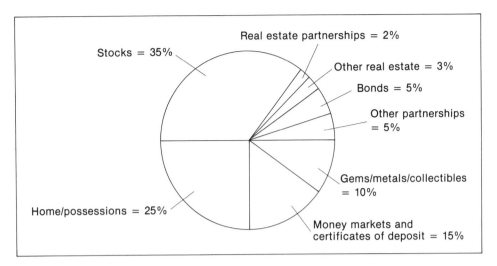

FIGURE 4   Typical diversification—moderate investor?

investment which returned, say, 25 percent? Unfortunately, even average risk investments rarely produce such a high return over the long term. Those that have the potential for sky-high returns, such as commodities, are extremely risky. Therefore, you should be aware of the classic investment trade-off: the higher the potential return, the higher the risk.

Fortunately, there is a way to reduce your risks. Asset diversification is an important element of any financial plan. Think of this concept as the "don't put all your eggs in one basket" idea. In ancient times, shipping moguls recognized that they could lower the risk of losing their cargo to a freak storm if they split the goods among many ships which departed on different days. If a storm arose and one ship was destroyed, they had lost only a portion of their cargo and their profits. You can apply this principle to your own assets and hedge your bet against a loss in any one asset.

Incidentally, for any given family, goals, needs, investable funds, and opportunities affecting investment decisions are always changing. For example, a change in your income, net worth, tax status, or family responsibilities should alert you to the need to reexamine your investment portfolio and financial goals. Factors beyond your control, such as changes in economic conditions and tax and estate planning laws, may affect how well your current portfolio is meeting your needs, even if your individual goals have not changed. During these times, a review and reallocation of your assets is essential.

There are a number of reasons for repositioning your assets: (1) the rate of return on certain investments may have changed; (2) proper asset allocation may reduce portfolio losses; (3) a reduction in diversification may make it possible for you to manage your own portfolio; (4) current income level may have changed; (5) tax laws may have changed; and (6) the need for providing financial protection for your family may have increased or decreased.

How well have you diversified your assets? Our analysis shows that you need work in this area. Take a moment to look at the assets section of your balance sheet, presented in Table 1. We have given you the percentage that each of your assets represents of your total asset base. By carefully analyzing the percentage distribution of each category of asset you should have a fairly good idea of how well you have achieved your diversification goal. For instance, currently you have 23.5 percent in passbook savings/money market category, whereas only 14.8 percent is invested in stocks and 10.1 percent in bonds. Clearly, your total diversification needs work.

Debt/Equity Asset Ratio

The debt/equity asset ratio is calculated by dividing your total debt assets by the total equity assets. Incidentally, we define "debt" assets as those based on lending your money, not on your debts like mortgage or car loans.

But why is your debt/equity asset ratio so important? No one has to tell you what inflation has done to the value of your dollars. In 1940, you could buy ten loaves of bread for $1.00. By 1950, you could only buy six loaves. By 1960, your dollar would buy only four and by 1970, three. Today, we are able to buy one loaf for that same dollar. Between 1900 and 1980, your dollar lost over 90 percent of its value. The average American family must earn twice what it earned in 1970 to maintain the same standard of living today.

In inflationary times, equity investments generally preserve the purchasing power of your dollar, while debt investments may not. This is because when you own investments like stocks or real estate, because of inflation you may receive more for your investment than you paid for it when you sell. However, a debt investment such as a bond pays a fixed amount of return no matter what inflation is doing. Of course, the advantage of a debt investment is that your cash flow from the investment is assured. An XYZ utility company bond purchased for $1,000 at eight percent interest will pay you $80 a year for the life of the bond. In addition, since you are lending your money to XYZ, upon maturity it is obligated to return your principal. Therefore, for those who need the security of a steady income flow, debt investments have a place in the total investment mix.

Our calculation of your debt/equity asset ratio indicates that you need help in this area. Your current ratio of debt to equity investments is 53 to 47 percent. After a detailed analysis of your investment portfolio relative to your risk tolerance level and your short- and long-range goals, we have concluded that your assets should be invested approximately 20 percent in debt investments and 80 percent in equity investments.

Since your debt/equity asset ratio is more than 15 percent off our sug-

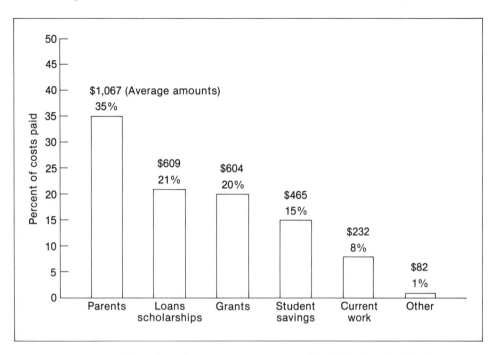

FIGURE 5 Where do students get money to go to college? The American Freshman National Norms.

gested level, you should consider changing your diversification under careful supervision.

Educational Planning

We will now turn to a discussion of educational planning which is an integral part of investment planning.

The cost of educating your children is skyrocketing. A college education already costs more than most families are able to pay. During the past three years, tuitions have risen an average of 15 percent, while median family income has slipped about three percent. In the same period, total aid per student dropped 14 percent, and 28 percent fewer students received outright grants. Currently the government-subsidized student loan program has limits on loans for students of families with incomes in excess of $30,000. Congress is considering proposals to limit these loans even further.

Since it is likely that the price tag for a college education will continue to rise, the time for planning your child's education fund is NOW, as this may well be one of the largest and most important investments your family will make. A four-year degree at a private college will cost $73,000 in ten years, and $116,000 in 18 years (assuming a modest six percent per year increase in educational costs). College costs are not tax-deductible. They must be paid with expensive "after-tax" dollars.

Child's name	Projected years in college	Existing assets in child's name	Savings per month	Total dollars needed for education	May 8, 1989 projected surplus/deficit
Sarah	4	$18,000	$ 0	$18,000*	$ 0
Chris	4	$14,900	$50	$27,073**	$ – 6,849

* Since Sarah is about to enter college, inflationary adjustment to the educational fund is not necessary.

** This amount is calculated as follows: existing assets in child's name plus growth of existing assets for three years at a "weighted average" annual rate plus additional savings set aside for college plus growth of additional savings at a "weighted average" annual rate.

We are pleased to note that Sarah has an adequate fund for college. Your diligent planning and savings habits have paid off for Sarah.

Unfortunately, the deficit in Chris's educational fund is $6,849. To wipe out this deficit, either you must save an additional $227 per month or increase the percentage return on his educational assets to 26.5 percent. However, note that a return of 16 percent or above is an unrealistic investment assumption, and you must increase your savings for this child to make up the deficit.

YOUR WORKSHEET

Investment Analysis

Do you have questions? Jot them down here.

Questions.
1.
2.
3.
4.
5.

Make a note of the steps you need to take in order to improve your investment portfolio.

Action needed.
1.
2.
3.

4.

5.

R-RETIREMENT PLANNING

Planning for your retirement is vital. Today, out of every 100 Americans who reach the age of 65, 75 are dependent on children, friends, or charity. What a tragedy! Three-quarters of us would like to retire earlier than age 65, but less than one-quarter expect to be able to do so. Social Security is not the answer. On an average, only one-third of what retirees receive from Social Security is the money they contributed while working, and the remaining two-thirds is government aid. You should not count on Social Security as your sole support during retirement. Planning for retirement now is therefore essential.

   Unfortunately, most of us spend more time planning for our next vacation than we do planning for our retirement. However, if you have a workable plan for your financial future, retirement can be an enjoyable and carefree time in your life. Your retirement status is presented in Table 7. This table shows that

TABLE 7   Retirement Analysis

Louis Johnson		Alice Johnson	
Current age:	44	Current age:	44
Retirement age goal:	62	Retirement age goal:	N/A
Life expectancy:	74	Life expectancy:	80
Current			
Net worth			$997,000
Savings per month			$ 400
Expenses per month			$ 5,465
Estimated monthly expenses			
Expenses at retirement in today's dollars			$ 8,000
Expenses at retirement in 2007, given 5.5% inflation			$ 20,785
Projected monthly income available at retirement			
Employer's monthly benefit			$ 2,500
Social Security benefits			$ 1,321
Income from current assets & projected future savings			$ 47,656
Total monthly retirement income			$ 51,477

Retirement income status per month

Projected income at retirement	$ 51,477
Estimated expenses at retirement	−$ 20,785
May 8, 1989	
YOUR MONTHLY RETIREMENT INCOME STATUS	+$ 30,692

your retirement income status is currently in good shape. In other words, since the expected income over expenses at the retirement age is a positive number, you are on a financial course to retire when you have chosen. Keep up the good work! However, do not be tempted to stray from a sound retirement plan merely because you are now positively funded. We want to be sure that you enjoy those retirement years you have planned so well.

Since you have a positive retirement status, you will be able to retire by the age 62 and live the lifestyle you expect. However, you also have the pleasant option of retiring earlier at age 52.

Our retirement analysis has revealed two important facts which should be of interest. First, currently you do not have enough assets set aside in Chris's name for funding her college education. Second, you have a monthly budget surplus which can be utilized to fund Chris's education. This use of savings for funding Chris's education will, obviously, decrease your retirement savings. However, we believe that in this case a slightly later retirement age is more desirable than carrying a large deficit in the educational fund.

YOUR WORKSHEET

Retirement Analysis

Do you have questions? Jot them down here.

Questions.
1.
2.
3.
4.
5.

Make a note of the steps you need to take in order to achieve financial independence.

Action needed.
1.
2.
3.
4.
5.

E-ESTATE PLANNING

Estate planning should not be a frightening or depressing subject. To many people, an "estate" is something reserved for the very wealthy and it is activated only upon death. The fact is that if you carry cash in your pocket, you have an estate. Spending a little time now can save thousands of dollars and give you the peace of mind of knowing that your financial affairs are in order. Also, since you have dependent children, we cannot stress strongly enough how important it is for you to be certain that your estate has adequately provided for them in the most efficient manner.

Let us begin our discussion of estate planning by reviewing some important legislation. Through the use of what is called the unified gift and estate tax credit (also known as the exemption equivalent) you may leave the first $600,000 of your estate to anyone without incurring federal estate taxes. This law also allows for unlimited tax-free transfers of assets between spouses through the marital deduction.

The value of your estate gives us important information and helps us: (1) structure your will; (2) decrease your federal estate taxes; (3) determine the best property ownership plan; and (4) evaluate the need for creating trusts. The current status of your estate is presented next:

Current Value of Estate	
Net worth	$ 997,000
Total life insurance proceeds	$ 650,000
Total estate	$1,647,000

Our calculations indicate that your estate is above $600,000. Since this is a significant figure, you need to consider certain steps to hold down your potential estate taxes. While we are going to provide you with several areas to consider, you must seek assistance from a qualified attorney to make sure that your estate plan takes maximum advantage of the applicable law.

Let us begin by considering property ownership. The way you own your property affects you and your survivors in three ways: (1) while you are alive, it affects what you can do with your property and the taxes you pay; (2) after your death, it affects whether your property is subject to probate and how it is distributed to your survivors; and (3) ownership also affects how much of your property is subjected to estate taxes.

Any asset owned individually, including life insurance, is included in the owner's estate for estate tax purposes. Also, the entire value of jointly owned property is included in the owner's estate. Therefore, property ownership questions are crucial for persons like you with substantial estates. Careful ownership strategies can lead you to have certain assets eliminated from probate. If a property is held in a trust, estate tax treatment depends on the kind of trust. If the trust is revocable, the property in it usually becomes part of a taxable estate of the person who has the right to revoke the trust. However, property in an irrevocable trust is usually removed from the taxable estate.

Our discussion of property ownership and your estate plan must remain general in nature. While a careful strategy for asset ownership is vital, it is equally important that you and your spouse feel comfortable with your ownership arrangements. We urge you to contact your attorney who will review your current property ownership schedule and make adjustments as needed.

Your will has several specific functions: (1) it lists how your personal property is to be disposed of after your death; (2) it allows you to choose the administrators of your estate; (3) it permits the naming of substitute parents for your children; (4) it may influence how your estate will be taxed; and (5) it enables your heirs to save money by avoiding legal problems with your estate after your death. After your death, but prior to the time when your heirs receive the assets you have left to them, your estate undergoes a legal process called probate. The probate process can cause long delays in settling an estate. It can also lead to unwanted publicity, since an estate is open to "public eye" as a matter in the courthouse records.

Probate can also be an expensive process, since the costs can be up to nine percent of the probatable assets. Probate essentially involves an administrative procedure. Your will's legality and authenticity is tested, your personal representative pays your debts and taxes due, and finally distributes your assets according to your desires. Frequently, all or part of the probate process can be avoided by using estate planning devices available to you.

Through planning, financial demands on your estate's assets, such as living expenses for your family, estate settlement costs, and taxes, can be minimized at the time of death. Another way to reduce estate tax liability at both deaths is through the effective use of trusts. By establishing trusts you have the flexibility in the distribution of your estate and, at the same time, reduce the aggregate estate taxes at both deaths. By setting up a trust you can arrange for the distribution of a portion of the estate equal to the unified credit to pass ultimately to heirs at the spouse's subsequent death with no estate tax consequences at either death. The assets within the trust can be managed on behalf of the beneficiaries, in the event the beneficiaries are minors.

Our discussion of estate taxes has included only federal estate taxes. Individual states also levy taxes on an estate which represent an additional burden for your heirs. We suggest that you review your state's current laws with your attorney.

Our analysis shows that currently both you and your spouse have wills. However, we also notice that both of these wills need to be updated. We suggest that you contact a competent attorney immediately to update both documents.

There have been significant changes in the federal estate tax laws within the last five years. In addition, your wishes and net worth have probably changed in the past five years and we feel that attention should be given to your will in order to insure that it is current. As you know, the costs of administering your estate (called probate) and federal and state estate taxes are significant. Recent changes in the estate laws have raised the tax percentage that the federal government may place on any of your assets that are exposed to estate taxes. Due to these factors, we strongly suggest that you have your will reviewed with regard to your current assets, lifestyle, wishes, and current state and federal laws that would affect your estate.

YOUR WORKSHEET

Estate Analysis

Do you have questions? Jot them down here.

Questions.
1.
2.
3.
4.
5.

Make a note of the steps you need to take in order to improve your estate plan.

Action needed.
1.
2.
3.
4.
5.

CONCLUSION

You are probably feeling a little overwhelmed with information right now. We suggest that you put this analysis down and put your feet up.

After you feel rested, take another look at this document. We hope that the information included in your comprehensive financial plan will be useful to you. And we don't just mean as a bunch of good ideas. You have to ACT on our suggestions to get anywhere. Financial success, like anything worthwhile, takes patience, persistence, and action in a timely fashion.

So, grab yourself a pencil. Use the worksheets we have provided to make a list of those things you must accomplish to get yourself on a healthy financial course. Below each item, note how you are going to go about performing each task and where to get the help you need. Now there is only one more step. Give yourself a deadline so you won't put it off.

We look forward to working with you in the years to come. Nothing will give us more satisfaction than to watch your financial status improve over the years. Next year you will receive a summary of this year's questionnaire answers and we will ask you for an update. We will send you back a *new* analysis which hopefully will show you that all of your hard work this year is starting to pay off.

Thank you for the opportunity to be of service.

THE ANNUAL REVIEW

On May 9, 1989, Wyn Webb developed a comprehensive financial plan for Louis and Alice Johnson. The plan contained a detailed analysis of the Johnsons' financial situation and a set of recommendations for implementation.

In April of 1990, financial planner Wyn Webb sent the Johnsons a new questionnaire as a first step towards completing the first annual review. The following is the annual review plan compiled by Mr. Webb on May 8, 1990.

WYN WEBB FINANCIAL PLANNERS, INC.

May 8, 1990

Mr. and Mrs. Louis Johnson
1565 Main Street
Pikesville, CT 07589

Dear Alice and Louis,

Most successful Americans realize that any important task in life usually requires some planning on their part. Your financial success certainly falls into this category. You are to be commended for the efforts you have made to date toward reaching your financial goals. Since financial decisions are influenced by ever-changing circumstances as well as the many investment opportunities available, regular check-ups are necessary to insure progress towards your financial goals. In addition, changes in inflation rates, interest rates, tax laws, and economic conditions require that you continue the ongoing financial review process to optimize your financial decisions.

We are consistently shown that the task of reaching our financial goals is not easy in today's ever-changing world. In this financial "check-up" we have analyzed your financial facts and assumptions and have indicated what progress you have made with your various financial goals during the past year. Of course, your stated goals, inflation assumptions, changes in your investment diversification, assumed return, and savings rates—all have greatly contributed to the state of your financial health.

We are pleased to present the details of your financial progress and look forward to serving you for a long time.

Cordially,

Wyn Webb
Financial Planner

LOUIS AND ALICE JOHNSON

Summary of your financial conditions and their changes since your last review.

May 8, 1989 through May 8, 1990

	Improving	Declining
Retirement Status		
Possible income available in comparison to projected expenses, at your retirement goal	X	
Higher Education Status		
Sarah		X
Chris	X	

Your retirement status and your higher education planning are calculated using your personal estimates of your income needs at retirement and assets needed to pay higher education bills. We have used historical investment returns to determine whether your retirement and education planning are showing improvement since the development of your financial plan. More details concerning changes in these important areas will be found later in this report. We encourage you to watch closely the direction in which your retirement and education planning efforts are going and to take the necessary steps to reach these important goals.

	Improving	Declining
Weighted Average Return		
Changes in various investments as well as changes in your personal investment diversification	X	

Your weighted return is based upon the five-year moving average from various investment categories in which you have placed your investable funds. It is important to base your investment plans and subsequent changes on longer-term strategies and not react to short-term investment fluctuations. Like most investors, you will find that a well-thought-out, long-term, diversified approach, and a serious savings plan will serve your needs for gaining ground towards your various financial goals.

	You're OK	Attention Needed
Life Insurance		
Louis	X	
Alice	X	
Disability Insurance		
Louis	X	
Alice	Not applicable	

As you know, your life and disability insurance needs are calculated in a very conservative manner. In the event of your untimely death, life insurance proceeds that will be used to produce income should generally be invested more conservatively than funds that are invested for growth.

Disability coverage is one of the most necessary components of a sound financial plan. Currently, your disability insurance coverage is satisfactory.

STATUS REPORT

Our evaluation indicates that your retirement income status has stayed nearly the same since your last financial review. Continued efforts to maintain a satisfactory retirement status should, however, be maintained.

Our analysis indicates that you are making progress toward one of your children's higher education goals and, at the same time, you are falling behind with the other education goal. Please take the necessary steps to adjust your planning toward the educational goal that is currently being ignored.

Our analysis of your investment strategies indicates that your weighted average return has remained fairly stable since your last financial review. It is important to maximize the return on your investment in a manner commensurate with the risk you are willing to accept. As we discussed earlier, an increasing return on your investments should provide you with more cash flow as you approach your various financial goals. It is important to watch for, and act upon, opportunities that can be exploited to your advantage.

We notice that, given your needs at this time, your life insurance coverage appears to be sufficient. Congratulations! However, the various innovative life insurance solutions being offered to you by the marketplace are changing every day. We encourage you to review this important financial area on a regular basis so you may determine if you can improve the use of your premium dollar.

One of the most common mistakes individuals make in their financial plan is to not protect their stream of ongoing earned income. We congratulate you for buying the necessary disability coverage. Since this area is so important for your financial well being, we encourage you to review your coverage on a regular basis.

GENERAL INFORMATION

Important Dates of Your Financial Check-ups	Original 5-8-89	5-8-90
Your ages	44/43	45/44
Total actual inflation	5.00%	5.00%
		Estimate
Looking forward at inflation: Your five-year projection	5.5%	5.5%

Your concern over inflation is shared by many consumers. The government's monetary policies and congressional spending habits appear to have insured that inflation will be with us for many years to come. The question is, "How much inflation?"

The inflation rate, as measured by the Consumer Price Index (CPI), has slowed from the large increases of the 1970s. It is important to maintain a close watch on this important component of your personal financial plan. Please keep in mind that an inflation rate of six percent will find prices doubling every 12 years. Since your life expectancy is approximately 75 years, it is important to closely monitor this financial nemesis. Even a small change in your inflation projection can significantly increase your projected income needs or lump sum requirements.

	Original 5-8-89	5-8-90
Age goal	62	62
Your weighted average return	10.2%	10.2%
Your marginal federal tax bracket	33.0%	33.0%

RETIREMENT STATUS

Your retirement status is presented in Table 8.

You will notice that your current retirement surplus condition has remained virtually unchanged since we first developed your comprehensive fi-

TABLE 8 Retirement Status

Important dates of your financial check-ups	Original 05/08/89	05/08/90	Change since last review
Your ages	44/43	45/45	1 year
Retirement goal (age)	62	62	
Possible income at retirement— per month	$51,477	$50,573	−$904 or −1.8%
− Possible budget at retirement—per month	$20,785	$19,701	−$1,084 or −5.2%
= Possible status at retirement—per month	$30,692	$30,872	+$180 or +0.6%
Additional savings needed per month—for retirement	$0	$0	+$0
Percentage needed on investments—to reach retirement goal	0.0%	10.2%	+10.2%
Alternate retirement age	52	52	0 years

TABLE 9 Education Status

Important dates of your financial check-ups	Original 05/08/89	05/08/90	Change since last review
Children			
Sarah	18	19	1 year
Chris	15	16	1 year
Total projected college costs			
Sarah	$18,000	$12,000	− $6,000
Chris	$27,073	$25,661	− $1,412
Total projected surplus or deficit			
Sarah	$0	$0	+ $0
Chris	− $6,849	− $5,865	+ $984
Additional savings needed per month			
Sarah	$0	$0	+ $0
Chris	$227	$368	+ $141

nancial plan. We encourage you to constantly monitor your progress in the area.

EDUCATION STATUS

Your current education status is presented in Table 9.

As you know, the cost of one year of higher education today is more than what an entire college education cost in the not-too-distant past. While some progress has been made toward your education planning, it appears that additional work needs to be done. Please take the necessary steps so that all of your education goals are met.

NET WORTH

Your net worth analysis is presented in Table 10.

Your net worth has increased 10.8 percent since the development of your

TABLE 10 Net Worth Analysis

Important dates of your financial check-ups	Original 05/08/89	05/08/90	Change since last review
Total assets	$1,179,500	$1,271,916	+ $92,416 or + 7.8%
− Total liabilities	$ 182,500	$ 167,000	− $15,500 or − 8.5%
= Net worth	$ 997,000	$1,104,916	+ $107,916 or + 10.8%
Liquid investments	$ 607,500	$ 667,916	$60,416

TABLE 11   Cash Flow Analysis

Important dates of your financial check-ups	Original 05/08/89	05/08/90	Change since last review
Monthly cash flow	$6,500	$6,717	+$217
− Stated monthly spending	$5,465	$5,540	+$75
− Personal monthly savings	$ 300	$ 300	+$0
− Higher education savings	$ 50	$ 100	+$50
= Your monthly surplus or deficit	$ 685	$ 777	+$92

comprehensive plan. Inflation has increased 5.6 percent. Generally, increasing wealth can be attributed to proper investment strategies, converting income into assets (saving on a regular basis), or inheritance. It is important to choose the proper investment strategies that are needed to accomplish your specific goals. As always, these strategies should be commensurate with the risk you are willing to take. A regular savings plan is an important aspect of any financial plan. You should closely monitor your amount of liquid assets for investment and emergency fund needs.

CASH FLOW

Your cash flow analysis is presented in Table 11.

Take a look at the changes and direction of your take-home pay, monthly spending, and savings habits. It is important to have a regular savings plan towards your short-, intermediate-, and long-term financial goals. You can see the direction you are taking in accumulating wealth on a regular basis by converting your income and cash flow into assets.

YOUR WORKSHEET

Annual Review and Update

Do you have questions? Jot them down here.

Questions.
1.
2.
3.
4.
5.

Make a note of the steps you need to take in order to improve your financial situation.

Action needed.
1.
2.
3.
4.
5.

CONCLUSION

As we have indicated, regular, objective, and comprehensive financial evaluations and check-ups can determine whether or not you are making progress toward your specific personal financial goals. Many factors will influence your progress over your lifetime. We encourage you to make a conscientious effort to monitor your progress each year in the important areas we have discussed in this annual progress report. As mentioned, you should seek specific solutions to your current problems and act upon them as speedily as possible to optimize all components of your financial plan.

Financial awareness is necessary in today's complex world. The traditional belief that there is no "free lunch" generally holds true in the world of financial and investment choices. Professional assistance is often needed in planning and making financial decisions for your successful future.

We have prepared a series of informational materials which we believe you will find of interest and value. These materials are presented in the appendix to this plan.

Once again, thank you for taking the time to review this progress report. We look forward to serving you for a long time.

APPENDIX

GLOSSARY OF INVESTMENT TERMS

ANNUITY A contract, usually issued by an insurance company, that provides an income for a specified period of time, such as a number of years or for life.

ASSET Anything of value owned by a person or a company.

BALANCE SHEET A financial statement showing a person's or a company's assets (what is owned), their liabilities (what is owed), and the difference, called "net worth."

BEAR MARKET A declining trend in stock prices usually occurring in a time period of months or years.

BENEFICIARY The person, company, or organization you mention in your will or other documents which will receive the payments from your life insurance policy or annuity. Also, the person who is to receive the benefits of a trust.

BLUE CHIP The common stock of a large, well-known company with a stable record of earnings and dividend payments.

BOND A certificate of indebtedness extending for more than one year. A bond is an obligation that must be repaid at a certain time. The borrower (the company) pays interest to the lender (you) for the use of the money. Bonds are also called debt or fixed income securities.

BROKER A person in the business of making transactions in securities for the account of others. The broker receives a commission for the sale and purchase of securities on your behalf.

BULL MARKET A rising trend in stock prices generally occurring within a time period of months or years.

CAPITAL GAINS The amount of money over the purchase price (the "gain") through the sale or exchange of assets.

CERTIFICATE OF DEPOSIT A certificate for a time deposit at a commercial bank which earns a specified rate of interest over a specified time. Also called a "CD."

COMMON STOCK A security representing ownership of a corporation's assets. Common stockholders have the right to vote on certain corporate policies.

COUPON The interest rate a bond promises to pay the investor. Also, a coupon may be the slip attached to a bond which is detached and submitted for payment on the due date.

CUSTODIAN The bank or trust company which holds the securities and does the bookkeeping for a mutual fund, a trust, or an individual.

DIVIDEND A payment to stockholders, usually in the form of a quarterly check. The dividend will vary depending on the company's profit for that quarter.

DOLLAR COST AVERAGING An automatic method of investing money that requires average purchases of equal dollar amounts of a security and results in a lower *average* cost per share over time.

EARNINGS For a company, the earnings is the income left after all expenses and charges are paid.

EMERGENCY FUNDS As a rule of thumb, these are usually liquid assets (savings) equivalent to three to six times your total monthly budget.

ESTATE The property owned by an individual, trust, or company.

ESTATE TAXES Taxes imposed by the federal government on the value of all the property owned at the time of your death.

EQUITY The value (in dollars) of your ownership in stocks or real estate.

GROWTH STOCK A stock of a company that has shown better-than-average growth in earnings and is expected to continue to do so.

INFLATION The state of our economy when the prices of goods and services rise. In inflation, your dollar buys less and there are more dollar bills in circulation.

INHERITANCE TAXES Taxes imposed by some states on the passing of your property at your death to your heirs.

INTEREST The money a borrower pays a lender for the use of the money borrowed.

LEVERAGE The effect of the use of borrowed money in investing.

LIABILITY Anything an individual or company owes. An individual may owe a mortgage company; a company may owe a creditor. These are liabilities for the person or the firm.

LIMITED PARTNERSHIP INVESTMENT A form of business in which a general partner supplies expertise and the ability to operate in a certain industry and a group of individual investors called limited partners supply the working capital. The partners report their share of the partnership's profits, losses, and deductions on their individual tax returns.

LOAD/NO LOAD When a mutual fund investor must pay a fee to invest in the fund's shares, the fund is said to be a "load" fund. If there is no fee charged for investing, the fund is "no load."

MONEY MARKET FUND A mutual fund whose investments are primarily short-term (less than one year) debt securities.

MORTGATE A lien on property created by your pledge of that property as security for repayment of your loan.

MUNICIPAL BONDS The debt obligation of states, cities, towns, school districts, and other public authorities. Interest paid on municipal bonds is not subject to federal taxes.

MUTUAL FUNDS An investment company which pools the monies from several investors and invests in a group of securities with a specific philosophy in mind. The investors gain the benefits of diversification and professional management of their money.

PORTFOLIO A group of securities and/or properties owned by an individual or an investment company. The performance of each element is watched and sales or purchases are made when necessary to increase the total return of the entire investment.

PROBATE OF A WILL The legal process of proving that your will is valid, after you are deceased.

PROSPECTUS The official document which describes a new security issue or a mutual fund and must be supplied to each investor prior to purchase.

SEC The Securities and Exchange Commission. An independent agency of the U.S. Government which administers the various securities laws.

SHAREHOLDER The individual who owns shares of stock in a company or a mutual fund.

TRUST A legal arrangement by which title to your property is given to one party who manages the property on behalf of another, who is called the beneficiary.

TRUSTEE An individual or corporation appointed by law to administer, manage, or execute a trust.

VARIABLE ANNUITY An annuity contract under which the dollar payments received over time fluctuate with the performance of the underlying investments.

WILL A statement of your wishes concerning the distribution of your property after your death, the guardianship of your children, and the administration of your property.

ASSUMPTIONS

We have made the following assumptions which are important for you to keep in mind as you read your analysis:

1. College Costs:

Private College	$9,650
Public College	$6,000
Average of Both	$7,825

(This cost includes tuition only. Room and board vary with institution.)

2. Inflation: The five-year trailing average of the Consumer Price Index of 4.0% is assumed throughout your analysis if you did not give us an in-

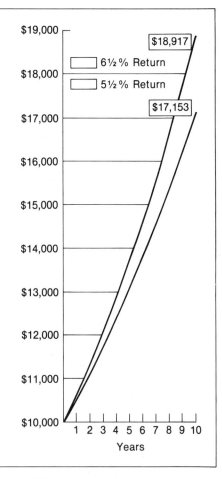

Almost everybody likes to keep a portion of their money in a place where it's easy to get to, and where there's no worry about principal fluctuation. But, when looking for an investment that offers these features some fail to consider the importance of the investment's yield.

While the differences may appear to be small, the spread between, for example, a 5½% and a 6½% yield can be significant over time. That's why so many people invest in money market funds. Money market funds constantly adjust their rates of return to money market rates, assuring investors that the yield on their investment will reflect those available to large institutional investors.

To see how small differences can add up, look at the graph to the right. It shows how $10,000 would grow, earning an annual return of 5½% versus an annual return of 6½%, over a 10 year period. The end result is that the $10,000 earning 6 ½% would be worth $18,917 — $1,764 more than the investment earning 5½%.

Money market funds seek to maintain a constant $1.00 per share net asset value and it offers free unlimited checkwriting for checks of $100 or more. Most money market funds begin with an investment of as little as $500.

FIGURE 6   The one-percent difference

TABLE A1   Investment Results: Average Returns

Inflation:	2.6%	3.2%	6.0% (A)
		Total returns	
Investment type	3 Years	5 Years	10 Years
Banks/money markets			
Passbook savings account	5.3%	5.3%	5.3% (D)
Money market account	6.3%	7.8%	9.5% (I)
(Mutual funds)			
Bonds			
Tax-free municipal bonds*	10.8%	10.0%	5.3% (F)
Long-term government bonds	16.5%	12.9%	9.4% (G)
High quality corporation bonds	10.8%	10.5%	9.0% (F)
Stocks			
Dow-Jones industrials average	21.4%	18.0%	14.6% (A)
S&P 500 stock index	17.7%	15.9%	14.8% (F)
Income mutual fund average	13.1%	12.3%	12.5% (A)
Balanced mutual fund average	16.4%	14.3%	13.6% (A)
Growth and income fund average	15.2%	13.9%	15.2% (A)
Growth fund average	13.7%	10.8%	15.2% (F)
Aggressive growth fund average	8.9%	8.0%	15.5% (F)
International stock funds	33.4%	24.3%	18.6% (F)
Metals (hedge investments)			
Gold bullion prices	16.0%	.6%	8.8% (B)
Numismatic (rare coins)	N/A	11.4%	16.3% (B)
Real estate (USA)			
Residential housing prices			
N.E. (Median resale = $105,100)	13.3%	8.8%	8.9% (E)
South (Median resale = $78,200)	4.2%	4.0%	7.9% (E)
Midwest (Median resale = $63,600)	4.0%	3.2%	6.4% (E)
West (Median resale = $100,500)	1.9%	.9%	8.1% (E)
National average	5.7%	8.5%	12.1% (H)
All property index (includes commercial)	5.0%	4.4%	6.5% (E)

public real estate partnerships − average total return = 13.5%/year [1978–1986] (C)

Sources: (A) Johnson's Charts (thru 12-31-87); (B) Handy & Harmon Troy Ounce Associates/ Salomon Brothers (thru 12-31-87); (C) Stanger Report (1986); (D) FDIC (thru 12-31-85); (E) National Association of Realtors (thru 2-1-87); (F) Lipper Analytical Services (as of 12-31-87); (G) Shearson Lehman Index; (H) Frank Russell Company; (I) The Donoghue Organization.

The returns noted above are generic in nature and should not be taken as indicative of future results. Each investment type has its own features which reflect its advantages and disadvantages and risks and rewards. Past performance cannot guarantee future results. All total return information is noted without any tax consequences. (Returns are rounded).

* These returns are generally free from federal income taxation.

flation estimate on the questionnaire. We used your inflation figure unless the figure was greater than 7.0% or less than 1.0%. If this was the case we "capped" your estimate and used 7.0% if you thought inflation will be high, or 4.0% if you thought inflation will be low.

3. Social Security: If you are covered by Social Security, we assume that you will receive the maximum benefits for purposes of your retirement analysis. We have used the Social Security Administration estimate of a 4.2% annual increase in benefits over the years.

4. For purposes of this analysis, we have assumed that you will liquidate all assets—excluding your home and personal possessions—at retirement to produce income. This included such things as partnerships, other real estate, collectibles, and so on.

5. Projected Retirement Income from Employer: If you provided a monthly income projection from your employer's retirement plan and did *not* indicate at what age this income will be available, we have assumed age 65.

Your analysis provides you with your current financial status and a guide to meet your goals. However, this analysis is meant to give you guidance and should not be used to replace consultation with your financial consultant.

SUPPLEMENTS

How to Get Information on College Financial Aid

We hope you will find the following books and pamphlets useful in planning your child's college education.

Applying for Financial Aid; Financial Aid Services, American College Testing Program, P.O. Box 168, Iowa City, Iowa 52243; annual; free.

Chronicle Student Aid Annual; Chronicle Guidance Publications, Aurora Street, Moravia, New York 13118; $17.49 prepaid.

The College Financial Aid Emergency Kit; Sun Features, Inc., Box 368, Cardiff, California 92007; $3.50.

College Money Book: How to Get a High-Quality Education at the Lowest Possible Cost, by David M. Brownstone & Gene R. Hawes; Bobbs & Merrill Co., Inc., P.O. 7083, Indianapolis, Indiana 46206; 1984; $12.95 prepaid.

College Scope (scholarships; study fields, college cost, size of student body for 1,300 colleges); annual; $1.00 if you include a self-addressed, long white envelope stamped with postage to cover 2 oz. of first-class mail; available from: College Student Financial Aid Services, Inc., Suite 208, Shady Grove Professional Building, 16220 S. Frederick Road, Gaithersburg, Maryland 20877.

Financial Aid for Self-Supporting Students: Defining Independence, by Alan P. Wagner & Nancy Carlson; College Board, 1717 Massachusetts Avenue N.W., Washington, D.C. 20036; 1983; $4.00 prepaid.

Financial Aid for Higher Education, by Oreon Keeslar; Wm. C. Brown Co., 2460 Kerper Blvd., Dubuque, Iowa 52001; annual; $28.95 prepaid.

Guide to Undergraduate External Degree Programs in the United States, second edition; American Council on Education, One Dupont Circle, Washington, D.C.; 1983; $16.95.

1985 Internships, edited by Lisa S. Hulse; Writer's Digest Books, 9933 Alliance Road, Cincinnati, Ohio 45242, annual; $14.45 prepaid.

The Student Guide: Five Federal Financial Aid Programs; The Student Guide, Department DEA-86, Public Documents Distribution Center, Pueblo, Colorado 81009; free.

Winning Money for College: This High School Student's Guide to Scholarship Contests, by Alan Deutschman; Peterson's Guides, P.O. Box 2123, Princeton, New Jersey 08540; 1984; $9.20 prepaid.

Information on Tax Preparation and Tax-Sheltered Investments

Your Federal Income Tax; Washington, D.C.: Department of the Treasury, Internal Revenue Service; annual.

United States Master Tax Guide; Chicago: Commerce Clearing House; annual.

Julian Block's Guide to Year-Round Tax Savings; Julian Block; Homewood, Illinois: Dow Jones-Irwin; 1985.

The Tax-Shelter Answer Book; Jonathan W. Skiba and Joseph P. Sullivan; Greenvale, New York; Panel Publishers, Inc. 1984.

Where to Send Your Request for Information, Free Publications, and Forms

You can write to the following address in your state to request free publications and forms from the IRS. The Internal Revenue Service has a number of publications which will help you to better understand our tax laws and how they affect you as a taxpayer.

Alabama—Caller No. 848, Atlanta, GA 30370

Alaska—P.O. Box 12626, Fresno, CA 93778

Arizona—P.O. Box 12626, Fresno, CA 93778

Arkansas—P.O. Box 2924, Austin, TX 78769

California—P.O. Box 12626, Fresno, CA 93778

Colorado—P.O. Box 2924, Austin, TX 78769

Connecticut—P.O. Box 1040, Methuen, MA 01844

Delaware—P.O. Box 25866, Richmond, VA 23260

Dist. of Columbia—P.O. Box 25866, Richmond, VA 23260

Florida—Caller No. 848, Atlanta, GA 30370

Georgia—Caller No. 848, Atlanta, GA 30370

Hawaii—P.O. Box 12626, Fresno, CA 93778

Idaho—P.O. Box 12626, Fresno, CA 93778

Illinois—P.O. Box 338, Kansas City, MO 64141

Indiana—P.O. Box 6900, Florence, KY 41042

Iowa—P.O. Box 338, Kansas City, MO 64141

Kansas—P.O. Box 2924, Austin, TX 78769

Kentucky—P.O. Box 6900, Florence, KY 41042

Louisiana—P.O. Box 2924, Austin, TX 78769

Maine—P.O. Box 1040, Methuen, MA 01844

Maryland—P.O. Box 25866, Richmond, VA 23260

Massachusetts—P.O. Box 1040, Methuen, MA 01844

Michigan—P.O. Box 6900, Florence, KY 41042

Minnesota—P.O. Box 338, Kansas City, MO 64141

Mississippi—Caller No. 848, Atlanta, GA 30370

Missouri—P.O. Box 338, Kansas City, MO 64141

Montana—P.O. Box 12626, Fresno, CA 93778

Nebraska—P.O. Box 338, Kansas City, MO 64141

Nevada—P.O. Box 12626, Fresno, CA 93778

New Hampshire—P.O. Box 1040, Methuen, MA 01844

New Jersey—P.O. Box 25866, Richmond, VA 23260

New Mexico—P.O. Box 2924, Austin, TX 78769

New York

   Eastern New York: P.O. Box 1040, Methuen, MA 01844

   Western New York: P.O. Box 260, Buffalo, NY 14201

   New York City: P.O. Box 1040, Methuen, MA 01844

North Carolina—Caller No. 848, Atlanta, GA 30370

North Dakota—P.O. Box 338, Kansas City, MO 64141

Ohio—P.O. Box 6900, Florence, KY 41042

Oklahoma—P.O. Box 2924, Austin, TX 78769

Oregon—P.O. Box 12626, Fresno, CA 93778

Pennsylvania—P.O. Box 25866, Richmond, VA 23260

Rhode Island—P.O. Box 1040, Methuen, MA 01844

South Carolina—Caller No. 848, Atlanta, GA 30370

South Dakota—P.O. Box 338, Kansas City, MO 64141

Tennessee—Caller No. 848, Atlanta, GA 30370

Texas—P.O. Box 2924, Austin, TX 78769

Utah—P.O. Box 12626, Fresno, CA 93778

Vermont—P.O. Box 1040, Methuen, MA 01844

Virginia—P.O. Box 25866, Richmond, VA 23260

Washington—P.O. Box 12626, Fresno, CA 93778

West Virginia—P.O. Box 6900, Florence, KY 41042

Wisconsin—P.O. Box 338, Kansas City, MO 64141

Wyoming—P.O. Box 2924, Austin, TX 78769

Foreign Addresses—Taxpayers with mailing addresses in foreign countries should send this order blank to either: Forms Distribution Center, Caller No. 848, Atlanta, GA 30370 or Forms Distribution Center, P.O. Box 12626, Fresno, CA 93778, whichever is closer. Send letter requests for other forms and publications to: Richmond Distribution Center, P.O. Box 25866, Richmond, VA 23260.

Puerto Rico—Director's Representative, U.S. Internal Revenue Service, Federal Office Building, Chardon Street, Hato Rey, PR 00918

Virgin Islands—Bureau of Internal Revenue, Charlotte Amalie, St. Thomas, VI 00801.

CHECKLIST: WHAT TO DO AFTER THE DEATH OR DISABILITY OF A SPOUSE*

The death or serious disability of your spouse is a traumatic event. Dealing with the event, your own feelings, and those of your family can result in overlooked details and additional confusion.

The following checklist is designed to help you get through the details as easily as possible. The suggestions are general, and should be adapted to your particular situation through conferences with your family and legal and financial advisors.

1. If you are alone, telephone a friend who can spend the next few hours with you. Shock and trauma can take unexpected forms.

2. Locate the family's important papers. Gather as many as possible, and continue to do so for the next few weeks.

3. Be aware that certain jointly held assets, such as safe deposit boxes and joint checking or savings accounts, may be frozen as soon as the institution involved becomes aware that one of the joint owners has died. Although such assets are intended to pass to the surviving spouse outside the normal probate process, actual possession may be delayed pending a court order releasing them. The order may depend on proving to inheritance or estate tax officials that the estate owns other assets adequate to pay potential estate or inheritance tax.

---

* Reprinted from *Tax Management's Financial Planning Series* with the permission of Tax Management, Inc., a subsidiary of The Bureau of National Affairs, Washington, D.C. 20037.

4. Notify a funeral director, and make an appointment to discuss funeral arrangements. Request several copies of your spouse's death certificate, which you'll need for your spouse's employer, life insurance companies, and legal procedures.

5. Notify your attorney. Make an appointment to review your spouse's will and to discuss state and federal death taxes that are payable.

6. Notify your state office for inheritance tax, which will be listed in the phone book under the state if you live in an urban area. If you do not, your funeral director can provide the proper address. Ask for the required forms. In many states you must have a release from the state inheritance tax office before company or insurance benefits can be paid.

7. Telephone your spouse's employee benefits office with the following information: your spouse's name, Social Security number, date of death; whether the death was due to accident or illness; and your name and address. The company can begin to process benefits immediately.

8. If your spouse was eligible for Medicare, notify your program office and provide the same information as in number 7.

9. Notify life or accident insurers of your spouse's death. Give them the same information as in number 7, and ask what further information is needed to begin processing your claim. Ask which payment option your spouse had elected, and select another option if you would so prefer. If there is no payment option, you will be paid in a lump sum.

10. Notify your Social Security office of the death. Claims may be expedited if you go in person to the nearest office to sign a claim for survivors benefits. Look for the address under U.S. Government in the phone book.

11. If you need emergency cash before insurance claims are paid, a cash advance may be made from any life insurance benefits to which you are entitled.

12. If your spouse was ever in the service, notify the Veterans' Administration. You may be eligible for death or disability benefits.

13. Record in a small ledger all money you spend. These figures will be needed for tax returns.

14. Remember that you are in a highly emotional state. Avoid contracting for anything, and avoid spending or lending large sums of money.

15. Make an appointment with your financial planner to discuss tax planning.

After a Few Weeks

After a few weeks, the paperwork will begin to diminish. Make any changes in ownership registration that may be necessary, focusing on the following items: autos; stocks, bonds, investments; residences; boats; savings and checking accounts (you may wish to have a joint account with another member

TABLE A2 Location of Papers and Records

	Safe deposit box	Office	Residence		
Wills					
Trust agreements					
Powers of attorney					
Burial instructions					
Cemetery deed					
Safe combination					
Employment benefits					
Employment contracts					
Stock plans					
Stock options					
Pension records					
Social Security records					
Life insurance					
Property insurance					
Casualty insurance					
Birth certificate					
Passport					
Naturalization papers					
Military discharge					
Marriage certificate					
Family personal papers					
Partnership agreements					
Checking account records					
Savings account passbook					
Credit card records					
Certificates of deposit					
Record of investment portfolio					
Stock certificates					
Bonds					
Mutual fund shares					
Tax returns					
Real estate titles and deeds					
Title insurance					

Source: Reprinted from *Tax Management's Financial Planning Series* with the permission of Tax Management, Inc., a subsidiary of The Bureau of National Affairs, Washington, D.C. 20037.

of your family); charge accounts; and safe deposit boxes. You may wish to make a new will.

Papers, Records, and Advisors

Table A2 is a checklist on location of important papers and records. Store documents that would be difficult or impossible to replace in a location where the danger of destruction by fire or other accidental means is minimal. A fireproof safe might be a worthwhile investment. Bear in mind that there might be a delay in gaining access to a safe deposit box.

SUPPLEMENTS

Tips on Estate Planning*

There are 13 key estate planning questions which should be answered *before* a family seeks assistance of an estate planning professional. These questions are listed below.

1. Is your net estate: (1) more than $600,000?; (2) more than $1.2 million?
2. If you die before your spouse, are you willing to leave your entire estate to your spouse?
3. If both of you die, would you like to have your entire estate held in one trust?
4. At what age or ages should your children be entitled to receive their inheritance outright?
5. Who do you want to serve as trustee for the trusts established for your children?
6. Who would you like to serve as the guardian for your children?
7. If the entire family dies in a common disaster, to whom should the estate pass?
8. What specific items of property would you like to leave to specific individuals or charity?
9. Do you want any portion of your estate to go to a religious organization?
10. Are there special instructions you would wish to leave for the personal representative?
11. Do you desire that your organs be available for research or transplantation following your death?

12. If you were terminally ill and could die momentarily unless you were given support procedures, would you like to have your family members empowered with the right to have those life support procedures withheld?

13. Are there special wishes you wish to have fulfilled with the help of the estate plan?

BEEN PUTTING OFF MAKING A WILL? CONSIDER THE CONSEQUENCES OF DYING WITHOUT ONE

YOUR MONEY MATTERS

Some attorneys and financial planners have a simple but effective strategy for prodding clients to write wills: They give them a copy of the "will" dictated by the laws of their state for a person who dies without one.

"It makes people squirm," says Karen W. Spero, a financial planner in Cleveland.

While state formulas for distributing a person's assets favor close relatives, the particulars are often quite different from what people want.

For instance, a man with a wife and two adult children may be surprised to learn that most states would give his spouse only one-third to one-half of his estate. Married people without children may be taken aback by the fact that many states give parents or siblings as much as half of a person's estate. In both cases, people who write wills often leave the bulk of their money to the spouse.

Nothing for Friends

State laws also make no provision for favorite charities, for friends or for long-standing relationships outside the marriage laws when a person dies intestate (without a will). And the states themselves get the money in the absence of family.

There are other drawbacks, as well. Heirs may face cumbersome proceedings and added legal expenses. People with large estates forgo opportunities to reduce the tax burden. Perhaps most tragic, parents give up their say in who will bring up minor children if they both die.

"If you fail to have a will, you give up the right to make sure your loved ones are adequately provided for," says C. Wyn Bowman, a tax partner in the Salt Lake City office of Ernst & Whinney.

The hardest part of drawing up a will may be psychological—accepting that one will die and then planning for that eventuality. "It's easy to put off—and lawyers are the worst in doing wills for themselves," says James R. Ledwith, chairman of the estates department at the Philadelphia law firm of Pepper, Hamilton & Scheetz.

Once a person decides to proceed, however, "It's very simple," Mr. Ledwith says. A pair of relatively uncomplicated wills for a husband and wife may require only one consultation with an attorney and cost a total of $200 to $400—a small price considering what can happen if one dies without a will.

Attorneys and other advisers say the biggest problems occur when there are young children. Most significant, in the event the parents die simultaneously, the courts could designate someone to bring up the children whom the parents wouldn't have selected. The courts might, for instance, have the children live with relatives in a distant state, while the parents would prefer that their children be reared by friends in their community.

"Even if you have nothing, you should still have a will to select who would be guardian of the minor children," says Theodore E. Hughes, an assistant attorney general in Michigan.

An intestate death can cause a number of problems even when there is a surviving spouse to look after the children. For example, if a man with a wife and three young children died leaving a $200,000 estate, more than $130,000 might go to the children. Because of their youth, however, the surviving parent or another adult would be appointed guardian by the courts to watch over the children's share.

A guardianship "is a very expensive and cumbersome proceeding," says Thomas B. Wells, an Atlanta attorney with Shearer & Wells. In at least one state, Pennsylvania, the surviving parent can't be the sole guardian. The guardian may need to pay an attorney to request court approval for every major expenditure. The guardian, even if it's the surviving parent, may face the added expense of posting a performance bond with the court.

'Financially Strapped'

That can be the least of it when a large share of an estate passes to minor children in a guardianship arrangement. "What you potentially do . . . is make the family financially strapped while the children are growing up, and then, at age 18, the children get a big chunk of money," says Ralph Turner, an attorney with Luedtke, Hartweg & Turner in Bloomington, Ill.

The courts' oversight over the children's money can translate into a significant say in how they are brought up. In Illinois, for example, only "necessary" expenditures can be paid out of the children's money. Getting court approval to spend those dollars on, say, private schooling "would be a definite uphill battle," Mr. Turner says.

Dividing a very large estate among the spouse and the children also raises estate-tax problems. "If you have a large estate and die without a will, you really shoot your beneficiaries in the foot," says Shirley D. Peterson, an attorney with Steptoe & Johnson in Washington.

Source: Reprinted by permission of *Wall Street Journal,* © Dow Jones & Company, Inc., 1986. All Rights Reserved Worldwide.

Under current federal law, a person can leave an unlimited sum to a spouse without any tax liability. Estate tax is due when more than $600,000 is left to other people. An attorney might advise a client with an anticipated estate of, say, $2 million to eliminate all estate tax by leaving only that $600,000 to children and other beneficiaries. The remainder would go to the spouse.

If the client died intestate, however, as much as $1.5 million would go directly to the children, generating an immediate estate tax bill.

UNNECESSARY HARDSHIP

Mr. Wells, the Atlanta attorney, recalls the unnecessary hardship created when a man with a wife and adult children died intestate, leaving an estate of $1.5 million. The tax bill was $70,000. The family had to borrow to pay it because much of the estate consisted of the family farm. With a will and a different distribution, Mr. Wells says, "we could have deferred all of that tax to the wife's death."

When a person dies without a spouse or children, the intestacy statutes can provide some particularly odd distributions of property. Mr. Turner, the Illinois attorney, remembers one that turned on the fact that half-blood relatives are treated the same as full-blood kin for purposes of the Illinois intestacy distribution.

A bachelor who died when he was about 55 would presumably have wanted most of his money to go the elderly mother he was supporting, or perhaps to his full-blood sister. He had been estranged from his father, since deceased, because the father left the family for another woman.

Under the state statute, however, his mother got only two-sevenths of his estate and the full-blood sister one-seventh, while the four children of his father's second marriage got one-seventh each. "It was not a pleasant thing to convince the mother the law was going to give over half of her son's wealth to the children of her husband's second marriage," Mr. Turner says.

CHAPTER 17

Business Planning for a Financial Planning Practice

INTRODUCTION

While providing quality service is their primary goal, financial planners also need to focus on establishing and effectively marketing a financial planning business. In order to clarify to potential clients what financial planning really is, to combat competition from the growing number of people—sometimes with questionable credentials—who enter the financial services marketplace, and to establish a credible, professional business, it is necessary to develop and use an effective written business plan.

Financial planning businesses vary greatly in size, from one-person operations to large, well-structured corporations. Between these two extremes are many firms with three to five principals, which frequently lack a written business plan and perform all the planning functions on an ad hoc basis. There are also many small- and medium-sized firms which operate according to well-written, frequently updated business plans.

We firmly believe that, regardless of business size, every financial planning firm should have a written business plan. Operating a business without a written plan is like driving without a road map through an unknown territory: You *may* reach your destination, but only by accident or by taking a series of costly detours.

This chapter is devoted to a discussion of some of the time-tested methods for developing a business plan for a financial planning practice. Clearly, some of what is included will be either too advanced for small businesses or too basic for large ones. However, we have decided that the most practical compromise is to present our approach to developing a *typical* financial planning business plan. We have ensured that the plan presented here is flexible enough to be modified to suit the needs of a financial planning business of any given size.

CREATING A BUSINESS PLAN

Like most other professional service businesses, financial planning is labor intensive. This feature of the planning business causes problems in a profession

---

WILL YOUR BUSINESS MAKE IT?

Answer the following questions to test whether you're using the kinds of management practices that will give your business the best chance of success. If you are in the prebusiness stage, answer the questions on the basis of expectations as well as anything you may already have done. The more yes answers, the better the chance that your management techniques won't cause the downfall of your business.

- Do you have a written plan that sets out the goals you want to achieve in the next five years? Has it been revised recently?
- Can you prove that you've made progress toward the goals with hard numbers?
- Can you generate a cash flow without having to suffer through too many dry spells?
- Does your accountant prepare and thoroughly explain reports other than tax re-

turns, such as monthly profit-and-loss statements and balance sheets?
- Have you consulted an expert recently about financial or marketing strategy?
- Have you talked about your business with your bank's loan officer even though a loan wasn't the object right then?
- Do you know your break-even point and whether you are on target for reaching it?
- Do you know how much it actually costs you to make each sale?
- Do you belong to a trade association for your industry?
- Do you read the same publications that your competitors and your clients read?
- Do you talk regularly about business-related topics with other professionals?
- Do you get regular feedback from your clients and base changes on their suggestions?
- Do you consistently study your competitors' ads and read their promotional literature?
- Do you have training sessions for and regular motivational meetings with your staff?

Source: Reprinted with permission from *Changing Times* Magazine, © Kiplinger Washington Editors, Inc., "7 Mistakes That Can Kill Your Business," August 1988, p. 48. This reprint is not to be altered in any way, except with permission from *Changing Times.*

subject to ever-increasing labor costs, intense price competition, shortage of qualified personnel, and restricted client budgets for professional planning services. In such an environment, efficient management of available resources is especially important. In a financial planning business these are comprised of human (professional and support), physical (equipment, office, furniture), and capital resources. Management of these resources requires the development of a business plan which determines the goals of the business and actions that should be taken to meet these goals.

An overview of a financial planning business plan is presented in Figure 17-1. This figure suggests that at the heart of the business plan are the financial planner's personal goals, which should always be consistent with the goals of the business. The reasoning behind this assertion should be clear. As mentioned, financial planning is a labor intensive business, with the planner often the most valuable resource. In a situation where the goals of business conflict with the planner's personal goals, the long-term failure of that planning business is almost certain.

The cornerstones of a financial planning business plan are organization,

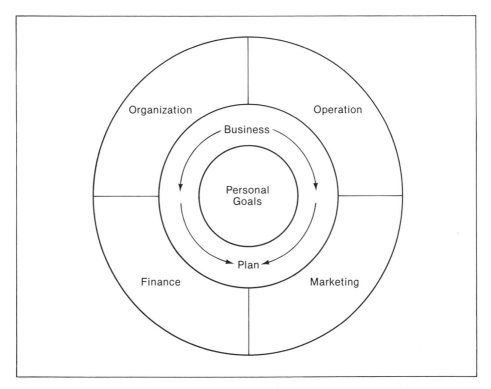

FIGURE 17-1 Financial planning business plan: an overview. From Robert J. Martel, *Strategic Business Planning for Your Financial Planning Practice,* handout material for a seminar on business planning.

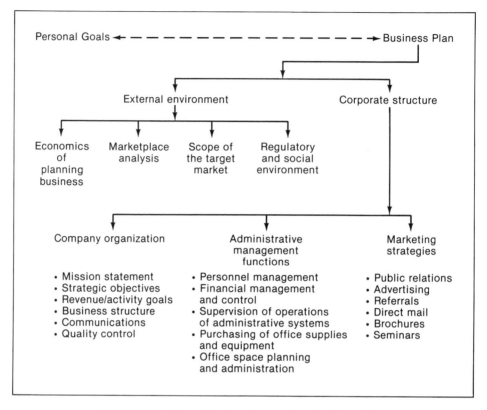

FIGURE 17-2   Financial planning: a written business plan.

operation, finance, and marketing. Each area must be developed fully and coordinated with the rest in order to make the business plan truly functional.

A detailed blueprint of a financial planning written business plan is presented in Figure 17-2. The business plan is divided into two broad segments: The external environment and the corporate structure.

EXTERNAL ENVIRONMENT

The best business plans are developed in the context of a thorough analysis of the external factors which have an impact upon the business, such as the economics of the planning business, the nature of the marketplace, the scope of the target market, and the regulatory and social environment.

Economics of the Planning Business

As mentioned, the financial planning business is labor intensive. That is, the primary factor in production is people, as opposed to capital resources, such as land, factories, and equipment. Since labor—or more specifically labor with high technical competence and marketable skills—is expensive, a financial planning firm is often faced with costs which rise faster than the ability of the firm to increase earnings, resulting in a perennial income squeeze.

The problem of income squeeze often leads to ancillary problems which can best be described as "growing pains." Eventually, many successful financial planning practices are faced with the decision of either to expand the business or let the work suffer in both quality and efficiency. If the former is selected and professional staff is added, support services must simultaneously be increased, thereby reinforcing the increasing labor cost aspect of the business.

There are three key alternatives to expanding the business: (1) the firm can raise fees, but market competition and the existing fee structure set at limits clients are willing to pay often make this alternative unacceptable; (2) the financial planner can work longer hours. This, too, may be unacceptable, for it may interfere with the planner's personal goals in addition to affecting the quality and timeliness of the work the planner produces; and (3) the financial planner can *manage* the practice. Professionals who can successfully manage their practice are able to grow gracefully and economically, ultimately succeeding in building a practice which will support them for life.

In general, practice management is the efficient use of available human, physical, and capital resources to achieve the business goals established by the professional financial planner. More specifically, management requires planning which establishes the organization's goals and the steps which should be taken in the process of meeting those goals; namely: (1) organization, which includes the positioning of resources to enable goals to be achieved; (2) implementation of each of the activities designed to achieve goals; and (3) control which is exercised on a regular basis.[1]

Marketplace Analysis

The state of the competition must be addressed when a financial planning firm is developing a business plan. Questions pertinent to marketplace analysis are: (1) What are other financial planners and advisers doing to market themselves? (2) What services and products are they providing? (3) What are their fee structures? (4) What are their relative sizes that make them competitive in the marketplace? (5) Are bankers, brokers, insurance agents, attorneys, CPAs, and financial consultants approaching clients for financial planning?

Several generalizations can be made about the marketplace analysis. First, the general public may be ignorant about what constitutes a compre-

---

[1] Ward Bower, "Effective Management Helps Planners Realize their Own Financial Goals." *The Financial Planner*, March 1983, p. 97.

TABLE 17-1 Financial Services Market: The Four Tiers

	Products & services	Who will service
LEADERSHIP PLANNING MARKET		
Net worth 1 + MM Income 250 + K Wealthy individuals Chief executives	• Specialized products • Integrated estate, tax, corporate benefit, etc., planning, including tax liability, cash flow, credit lines • Comprehensive planning, cash/asset management	• Individual financial planners • Interdisciplinary planning firm of specialists
SOPHISTICATED PLANNING MARKET		
Net worth 250–500K Income 75–100K Professionals Small business owners Upper management "Corporate" market	• Private placements, direct investments for specialized needs • Some packaged products • Goal setting, implementation • Counseling, professional relationships	• Individual financial planners • Interdisciplinary specialists • Boutiques • Large planning firms • Financial supermarkets (minor importance)
DIRECTED PLANNING MARKET		
Net worth 50 + K Income 50K Lower management White collar Two-income families	• Packaged products (money-market funds, mutual funds, REITs, etc.) • Data gathering; computerized packaged plans (No personal planning services)	• Large planning firms • Financial supermarkets • Banks, insurance cos., national securities firms • Financial services professionals
PRODUCT PLANNING MARKET		
Net worth 0–25K Income 25 + K One-income families Blue collar Marginal savers	• IRAs, life insurance, money-market funds (No personal planning services)	• Financial supermarkets • Banks, insurance cos., securities firms • Individual product vendors

Note: This exhibit is adapted from a seminar promotion item developed by Richard G. Wollack, president of Consolidated Capital Institutional Advisers Inc., Emeryville, California. It has been modified by the author for use here.

hensive financial plan. Many planners and financial products sales organizations may take advantage of this situation by offering products or substandard plans as state-of-the-art comprehensive financial plans. Second, because of their size and financial strength, large brokerage and insurance firms may provide formidable competition, since they can inundate the marketplace with commercials, bulk mailings, seminars, and other large-scale promotional schemes. Third, planning services performed by many competitors may be influenced by commission structures rather than client need. Knowledge of what the competition is doing in each of these areas can help a planner design a better business plan.

Scope of the Target Market

A market can be defined in terms of income, age, sex, education, occupation, religion, and a host of other criteria. While the most commonly used criteria for marketing financial planning services are income and net worth, they are by no means the only criteria which can be used to successfully define a financial planning target market.

An outstanding overview of the financial services market, developed by Richard G. Wollack, is presented in Table 17-1. This table provides a starting point for deciding which segment of the market the professional financial planner wishes to serve. Once decided, the planner can further refine the marketing strategy by superimposing on it other criteria. For instance, having made the decision to serve clients in the top bracket (income of $250,000 or more), a financial planner may decide to deal only with business owners. Another planner selecting the same income and net worth bracket may decide to work exclusively with corporate executives.

Regulatory and Social Environment

An effective business plan must take into account the existing regulatory and social environment. An individual offering comprehensive financial planning services for compensation must be a registered investment adviser under the Investment Advisers Act of 1940. In addition, a planner marketing investment products must be a registered representative of a broker-dealer who is a member of the NASD and SIPC. However, the problems of dealing with the prevailing regulatory environment go far beyond getting properly licensed. In view of numerous abuses by unethical, self-designated financial planners, the SEC, NASD, and individual states are not only establishing tougher standards against unscrupulous practices, but are also raising the regulatory standards. The overall trend toward more regulation and more control continues unabated.

The tougher regulatory environment is not the only challenge financial planners face. There is a widespread negative attitude shown by the media and some of the general public toward the financial services industry. A business plan must include ways of marketing legitimate, comprehensive, respectable financial planning services to a highly suspicious and nervous public.

CORPORATE STRUCTURE

We now focus on that part of a business plan which deals with corporate structure. This topic can be discussed in terms of company organization, administrative management functions, and marketing strategies.

Company Organization[2]

Mission statement. A financial planning firm's mission statement should contain the following points:

1. Definition of the purpose of the business, including identification of the target market.
2. Strategy for organizing the entire business into divisions, the responsibility assigned to each, and the general authority under which each division operates.
3. Definition of relationships between company entities.
4. Specific goals to be achieved for profitability, development of new business, sales, motivation, and management skills.
5. Company principles to be implemented throughout all company entities.
6. Company commitment to human resource development.
7. Statement of how the mission will be regularly reviewed to assure that it is current.

In smaller companies, it is often sufficient for a mission statement to include simply a definition of the general marketplace in which the company operates, a general explanation of the products and services the company provides to this marketplace, and a broad statement of the company philosophy of how it will provide these particular products and services. In addition, some companies like to use the mission statement as an internal device, and are very clear in stating how they intend to treat employees.

Strategic objectives. Strategic objectives are those long-term strategies the company would like to achieve but which are not necessarily measurable or set within specific time frames. For example, a company may desire to

---

[2] This discussion is adapted from John H. Melchinger, *Marketing Your Financial Planning Services.* Handout material distributed at the workshop conducted at the IAFP, Detroit, February 15, 1989.

BLUEPRINT FOR PRACTICE MANAGEMENT SUCCESS: THE BIG NINE ELEMENTS

In "working through" the big nine components that are essential to sound practice management, it is important to also consider each step in light of the following questions: Does this make good business sense? How will this affect the synergy and "personality" of the organization?

Goal identification.
- Know who you are.
- Know what you want to accomplish.
- Know who will have an effect on your decisions.

Strategic Planning.
- Long-term goals—more than one year.
- Short-term goals—less than one year.
- Business planning.
- Budgeting.

Associate Staff.
- How involved will other planners be in the running of the business?
- How many now—and in the future?
- What are their special talents?
- What is the psychological profile of the associate staff?

Client Administration.
- Who works with them and what are the functions performed for them?
- How effectively do you serve their needs?
- What is the division of the client work load?
- Is there continuity of attitude toward clients?

Structure of the Business.
- In deciding on a company name, consider: community identity, avoiding confusion with the competition
- Will the business be a sole proprietorship, partnership, regular corporation, sub-S corporation?

- What are the implications of becoming a Registered Investment Adviser?
- Will there be officers and directors? Consider length of service as a criterion if there are; consider also the advantage you may gain in having a "devil's advocate" viewpoint.
- What type of insurance do you need for the business?
- Where will you locate? Remember, plan for growth.

Support Staff.
- Remember, you *do* get what you pay for.
- Remember also, they are a valuable asset.
- When prospecting and screening for support staff, don't forget: know what you want, interview carefully, have others interview the applicants, prepare written job descriptions, be prepared to train, provide a career path.

The Work Environment.
- Is it stress-free (relatively!) and conducive to everyone's being productive?
- Does it provide for good physical interaction of people?
- What do your employees think about the workplace? Ask them!
- How's the lighting, heating/cooling, phone system, furniture?
- Aim for a first class image—professional, clean, productive.

Administration and Operations.
There's no getting around it. You *must* consider all of the following:
- Staffing.
- Policies and procedures.
- Filing systems.
- Bookkeeping systems.
- Computer needs.
- Stationery/business cards.

- Compliance, compliance, compliance!
- Library development.
- Banking relationships.
- Business meetings.
- Design of forms and contracts, interoffice and for clients.
- Office equipment.
- Incentives and awards.

Image.
- How's your office location? What's the parking like?
- Is the decor warm and inviting?
- Get a good conference table—don't deal with clients across your desk.
- The little things *do* count—have coffee cups and ashtrays on hand.
- Consider translating your image to something tangible—a good, well designed corporate brochure or an audio-visual presentation.

Source: Ruth N. Goldstein, "The Business of a Practice," *Financial Strategies,* Summer 1987, p. 13.

achieve a certain size, but it cannot do this in one workable time frame such as one year. As a result, the strategic objective may be to *ultimately* gross $500,000 a year, but the goal for the *current* year might be to achieve $150,000 of gross revenue.

Revenue/Activity Goals. Revenue goals are very important and need to be considered as measurable within very specific time frames. It is equally important to specify the monitoring and adjustment of activities so the achievement of goals within workable time frames is assured. For example, an annual goal of $240,000 gross revenue for a firm is important, but it is equally important to understand how much progress has been made at any time during the course of the marketing plan's year. Put differently, the revenue goal would be to make $20,000 per month. The planner should know where the firm stands at the end of each month on a pro rata basis against the annual goals.

In addition to revenue goals, activity goals are also critically important in a small organization. To this end, departments with sales producers who also have marketing responsibilities should be monitored for the amount of activity they have in the marketplace in addition to their sales results. The achievement of aggressive revenue goals will certainly come more from aggressive activity levels than from simply focusing on the goals. It is the responsibility of the financial planner with management responsibilities to assure that high activity levels are sustained.

Business Structure. The most effective way to develop an efficient business structure is to chart the organization. Such a chart may be very detailed, or it may take the shape of a pyramid, as shown in Figure 17-3. Furthermore, the basic structure of an organization should clearly indicate the lines of accountability and communication as revealed by Figure 17-4.

Communications. There is a wide variety of ways to experience communications. With the nature and form of most important communications in

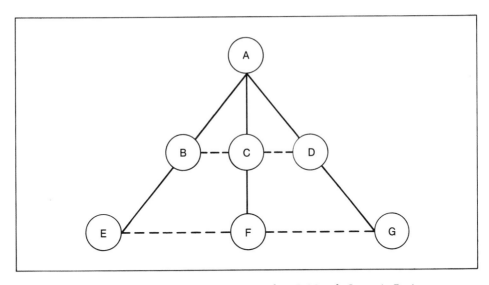

FIGURE 17-3 Business structure. From Robert J. Martel, *Strategic Business Planning for Your Financial Planning Practice*, handout material for a seminar on business planning.

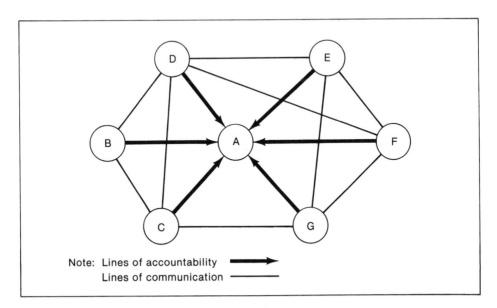

FIGURE 17-4 Lines of communications connecting financial planners in a network organization. Adapted from Robert J. Martel, *Strategic Business Planning for Your Financial Planning Practice*, handout material for a seminar on business planning.

a company—including meetings and forums—the lines of communication and significant styles of communication should be clearly indicated. Also, as lines of communication are developed, special attention should be paid to improve their effectiveness.

Quality control. Finally, the topic of quality control should be briefly discussed. In a financial planning practice it is very easy to become totally absorbed in the production of financial plans at the expense of quality, especially in the case of a booming business. Unfortunately, in a financial planning business long-term success cannot be achieved if the quality of the planning process is compromised. A mechanism for maintaining quality control should therefore be an integral part of the company organization.

Administrative Management Functions[3]

Administrative management functions in a medium- or large-size financial planning office should include the following:

Personnel management. This function includes hiring, disciplining, and discharging staff employees; performance evaluation and review and salary administration of those employees; maintenance of personnel records; and promulgation and enforcement of personnel policies.

Financial management and Control. Financial planning firms should develop: (1) budgets for income, expense, and capital items; (2) control cash flow and disbursements; (3) invest excess cash prudently; (4) supervise bookkeeping personnel; and (5) work with the firm's accountants to ensure timely financial statement preparation and tax return preparation.

Supervision of operation of administrative systems. This function includes the supervision of systems for handling new clients and matters, indexing, reminder systems, timekeeping and/or billing systems, and the like.

Purchasing of office supplies and equipment. Purchasing requires extensive research and establishment of systems for replenishing supplies.

Office space planning and administration. Functions here include landlord relationships, space planning and design, and leasehold improvements.

These functions are necessary, and become increasingly time-consuming with the growth of a professional service firm. Ultimately, retention of a professional business manager can be justified by the incremental income that would

---

[3] Ward Bower, op. cit., p. 100.

be generated by the planner's spending additional time on client-related activities, rather than on internal management administration.

Marketing Strategies[4]

After completing an in-depth analysis and committing to the decisions made regarding the company organization and administrative management functions, an effective marketing plan can be constructed. The basic marketing devices include the following:

1. Public relations.
2. Advertising.
3. Referrals.
4. Direct mail.
5. Brochures.
6. Seminars.

Determining the right combination of all these elements is critical during planning so that the implementation of the marketing plan will be both successful and rewarding.

Public relations. Public relations (PR) activities are among the most cost-effective means of placing and keeping the planner's story in front of the public. Essentially, PR involves: (1) articles written by or about the planning professional; (2) press releases; (3) public speaking; (4) statements made by the planner that appear in consumer-related publications; and (5) television and radio appearances. These activities cost relatively little in hard dollars, but their effective use requires a great deal of time and preparation.

The first step in starting a PR campaign is to determine what contacts and sources are available and which ones are necessary. The list should include television and radio stations and names of key people in magazines, newspapers, civic groups, and professional associations. Also, the organizations within the marketing area that use speakers should be listed.

Press Releases. Steps in using press releases effectively include: (1) getting to know the key editors and writers and having something to offer them; and (2) announcing office relocation, personnel changes, seminars, awards received, civic recognition, or new services offered. In all cases, the format the publication prefers should be used. Planners should be as accessible and cooperative as possible to make it easy for the media to

---

[4] Adapted from John C. Sweet, "Precision Marketing: Choosing and Using the Right Medium." Reprinted with permission from *Personal Financial Planning:* Volume I, Number 1, November/December 1988, pp. 18–22. Copyright Warren, Gorham and Lamont, Inc., 210 South St., Boston, MA, 02111. All rights reserved.

work with them. This strategy can be used primarily to develop and maintain name recognition.

Writing Articles. Articles can be used to position the planner as an authority, in addition to developing and maintaining name recognition. Articles should be submitted to trade journals, consumer magazines, or local newspapers. A recent photograph and a brief biography should be included with the article. If possible, relationships should be developed with

---

finances and you
Sid
Mittra

IRAs are still alive and still worthwhile

First of 2 parts

People don't talk about IRAs anymore as if they are dead. But they are alive, well and a good idea.

The provisions regarding the deductibility of an IRA are summarized in the top table.

If neither spouse is covered by a qualified plan, a tax deduction of $2,000 per worker or $2,250 per one-income-couple is allowed, regardless of income.

Married couples covered by a corporate plan with an adjusted gross income of less than $40,000 keep the full deduction. The deduction vanishes altogether when adjusted gross income exceeds $50,000, but is prorated between $40,000 and $50,000.

The comparable limits for a single person are $25,000 and $35,000, respectively.

Limits for an unmarried person who files separately are not as straightforward. In general, no deduction is allowed if the adjusted gross income is more than $10,000. If the adjusted gross income is less than $10,000, a partial deduction is allowed, and the amount of deduction calculated by using a special formula.

For instance, suppose John Johnson is married, files a separate return, and is an active participant in an employer plan. John's adjusted gross income is $7,500. The maximum deductible IRA contribution is $500:

Step 1: $7,500 ($7,500 — $0)
Step 2: $2,500 ($10,000 — $7,500)
Step 3: $500 ($2,500 x .20)

THE MAGIC OF *compounding and the concept of time value of money make IRAs grow. Two thousand dollars invested at the beginning of every year at 10 percent for 30 years would total $361,887. If the investment earns a 12-percent return, in 30 years the IRA fund would grow to a half million dollars.*

deductibility of IRA

	adjusted gross income	pension plan? yes	no
joint	$40,000 or less	$2,000	$2,000
	$40,000-50,000	$200-2,000	$2,000
	Above $50,000	None	$2,000
single	$25,000 or less	$2,000	$2,000
	$25,000-35,000	$200-2000	$2,000
	Above $35,000	None	$2,000
married filing jointly	$10,000 or less	partial deduction*	$2,000
	Over $10,000		$2,000

*special deductibility rules apply.

long-term accumulation in IRA

investment return	years 5	10	15	20	25	30
7%	$12,307	$29,567	$53,776	$87,730	$135,353	$202,146
8%	12,672	31,291	58,649	98,846	157,909	244,692
9%	13,047	33,121	64,007	111,529	184,648	297,150
10%	13,431	35,062	69,899	126,005	216,364	361,887
11%	13,826	37,123	76,380	142,530	253,998	441,826
12%	14,230	39,309	83,507	161,397	298,668	540,585

Note: Annual contribution of $2,000 is made at the beginning of each year.

Source: "Finances and You," *Observer and Eccentric Newspapers*, November 30, 1989, p. 3C.

the financial editors in each publication. A professional planner who can consistently produce timely and informative copy may even gain the opportunity to become a regular columnist. A sample of a newspaper column by a financial planner is reproduced in the accompanying boxed insert.

Public Speaking. In public speaking, targeting the audience and developing a presentation that is of special interest to the group being addressed are critical. Practicing the speech beforehand is a necessity and may include taping and listening to the written speech and rehearsing the material in front of office staff or family. Being comfortable in front of an audience will make for a more effective presentation. The first moments of the introduction are critical and should be smooth. If handout materials and visual aids are necessary, they should have a professional appearance.

If at all possible, handouts with information about the financial planning firm should be made available at the presentation. Also, the planner should keep in mind that each attendee is a prospective client and should be treated with care.

Broadcast Appearances. If a suitable radio or television forum exists in the geographical marketplace, the planner should contact the program director to discuss his or her qualifications for an appearance on a financial program. If the director is amenable to the idea, the topics that may be of interest to the audience and that would fit the station's format should be discussed in detail. Since financial issues and concerns are always of interest to some people and sometimes interesting to everyone, a regular appearance might be possible. This device works to establish a visual image of the planner as an authority on financial planning within a geographical area. It should be noted, however, that broadcast appearances are very time intensive, and if poorly produced, the planner's image could suffer.

Advertising. Advertising the practice and its activities should help create a demand for the firm's services and differentiate it and the planner from other firms in the marketplace. Unlike PR, advertising is time intensive *and* costs hard dollars. Therefore, before embarking on an advertising campaign and committing money to advertising, the planner must be very knowledgeable about the media that will influence the target clients and prospects. What do they read? What do they listen to? What sources of advice do they generally pay attention to? These questions must be answered in order to receive the greatest return on the investment of advertising dollars.

Radio and Television Ads. Radio can be effective if used selectively. The message should point out one or more consumer needs and suggest that the advertiser is the one who can meet those needs. Radio ads are generally wasteful if used only to create awareness. When using this medium the planner should:

- Select a station that reaches the target audience.
- Use repetition: ten 30-second ads work better than five 60-second ads.
- Buy a "block of time" that will be heard before an interesting program.
- Always use a professional voice.
- Always use a professional script.

The use of television advertising for the vast majority of financial planners is questionable due to production and air time costs. It is therefore rarely recommended unless the planner has deep pockets, is in a smaller marketplace, and can place the ads before or after a popular stock market or business program.

Publications. As with any advertising, knowing the target market is critical when selecting the proper print media. The planner's and the firm's image should be matched to the publication's image and target market for both magazines and newspapers.

The ad's design, copy, size, and location, both on the page and in the publication, all contribute to the creation and development of the planner's image. From a design standpoint, the ad should command attention, be pleasant and easy to read, and generously use white space and margins. Copy should attract attention, help create a need in the reader's mind, show how the planner can meet that need, and project the difference between the planner and other planning professionals. A provocative headline can help to attract attention and spark interest.

The size of the ad will depend on the planner's budget. The cost and the required budget allotment depend, of course, on the publication's circulation, the day or days the ad will run, the cost of the design, and the section of the publication that will work best to fulfill the planner's purpose. In a newspaper, the ad should be placed near the sports section, business section, or lifestyle pages to attract different targeted audiences. Even the best designed and most costly ads will fail if improperly placed.

Yellow Pages. Another advertising option is to buy a yellow pages ad that provides more information than the standard listing. What follows are some basic yellow page guidelines:

- Design a display ad that describes the planner's credentials, and use "sell" copy.
- Use a headline that shows some specialization, such as "Small Business Tax Adviser" or "Preretirement Specialist."
- Place the display ad in the financial planning or adviser section.

Referrals. Referrals are a cost-effective means of identifying prospective clients. Many people are willing to help planners by suggesting names if the referral process is made easy for them, they are not embarrassed by what is done with the referral, and they are kept informed on how things are going. Referrals can come from a variety of sources, including current clients and local allied professionals.

To use referrals effectively, the planner should create a story about the business. This task should not be too difficult, considering the amount of time that was spent and the information that was summarized in the formal business planning process. The planner should then tell the story to individual clients, small groups of clients, accountants, and attorneys, and ask if they will endorse the planner either directly or indirectly in a presentation of their referral. They might be willing to write a letter or recommendation on their letterhead, or they might allow the planner to write it for them. They also might be willing personally to introduce the planner to the interested individual.

Most accountants and attorneys are concerned about client control. This concern should be addressed up front, and the planner should indicate how he or she will attempt to make them the "hero" throughout the relationship. From a cost/return standpoint, this referral device can be the most effective tool in finding new clients.

Direct mail. As with other strategies, direct marketing will only be effective if meaningful targets have been chosen. General mailings with general information will only produce a smaller bottom line profit. The purpose of client segmenting is to attract the best potential clients while spending as little as possible.

Developing the mailing list is the first step. This list may be bought, rented, or created by the planner. In renting, the planner should be selective in terms of demographics, and take the time to find the most appropriate list broker. The list can include as many or as few names as the planner chooses, and mailing activity can begin in only a few weeks' time.

Creating a list is time-consuming but worth the effort because it can be used repeatedly. To build the list, the planner can refer to reverse telephone directories and member rosters of important clubs, civic groups, churches or synagogues, chambers of commerce, trade associations, or professional organizations.

Cost control is important. The budget must provide for the list purchase, postage (first class or bulk rate), artwork (unless the mailing is a simple letter), typesetting and printing or copying, and the cost of folding the enclosures and stuffing the envelopes.

For best results, the mailing should not coincide with a holiday or prime vacation times. To determine the effectiveness of the mailing, the results should be analyzed. Great care should be taken to compare the resultant income against expenses to determine the project's profitability.

Brochures. Although considered only a part of direct marketing activities, brochures are actually appropriate for the firm's use in other ways. For example, brochures can be used in handouts at seminars, speaking engagements, and small group presentations as well as for clients, prospects, and allied professionals.

An attractive, well-written brochure can be a valuable marketing tool. It can be a great waste of money, however, if it is developed without specific attention to the target audience, brochure content and copy, or the piece's general purpose. The company brochure should include:

- An introduction to the benefits of a financial plan.
- The planner's background, credentials, and philosophy.
- The planning process according to the planner.
- An explanation of how people can engage and pay for the planner's services.

Professionals can be hired to complete the design, copy, and production phases. The design should be simple, the copy direct and informative, and the paper stock somewhat heavy. The brochure's size should allow for easy mailing and storage in a standard file folder.

Not every financial planning organization needs an expensive brochure. Any attractive and informative written piece that tells the story and presents the services in a fashion consistent with the desired image should achieve the planner's objective.

Seminars. Seminar presentations can be an excellent source of financial planning engagements. A successful seminar benefits everyone—the planner, the attendees, and the clients. Seminars provide the planner with visibility, an opportunity to demonstrate expertise, and a vehicle with which to build rapport while conveying professionalism to the audience.

Seminars also present an opportunity for the planner to convey his or her message to a group in a nonthreatening, low pressure atmosphere.

The key to conducting a successful seminar is advance planning. The following is a typical advance planning schedule for conducting a financial planning seminar.

Six Weeks Before the Seminar. Six weeks prior to the seminar the following decisions/actions should be completed:

1. Decide on the subject and speaker.
2. Determine the seminar objective and attendee profile.
3. Develop a theme for the presentation and marketing materials.

4. Decide on program style.

5. Contact the speaker.

6. Line up those NASD registered personnel who will staff the seminar.

7. Determine the order of seminar presentation.

8. Select and contract for a location.

9. Determine the seating configuration.

10. Select the marketing plan for the seminar.

11. Prepare and clear through broker/dealer's compliance department all advertising, invitations, and sales materials.

Two to Four Weeks Prior to Seminar. Two to four weeks prior to the seminar, the following actions/decisions should be completed:

1. Write the script and finalize it.

2. Address invitations.

3. Mail seminar invitations.

4. Place advertisements.

5. Make name badges.

Day of the Seminar. If all of the preceding steps have been successfully completed, the seminar will also be a success. The seminar speaker must never forget that the main purpose of conducting a financial planning seminar is to convert a potential client into a long-term client. However, it is also important to remember that the speaker should also educate the audience so the attendees will receive true value from attending the seminar.

Follow-up. Follow-up is extremely important both with attendees and those who registered for the seminar but did not show up. Studies show that less than 25 percent of what is seen and heard is retained after 48 hours without reinforcement and reiteration. For this reason all seminar attendees should be contacted within two days to assure high receptivity. The no-shows should also be contacted because often they are as receptive as the attendees. In the end, the key to any successful seminar is preparation and follow-up.

CONCLUSION

In this chapter we have discussed various issues involved with the drawing up of a business plan for a financial planning firm. Clearly, the task of developing a comprehensive and effective financial planning business plan is far more complex than what has been presented here. Furthermore, each business plan must reflect the preferences and sophistication of the associated financial planner. Consequently, we have presented in the accompanying boxed insert an outline for a sample business plan which can be used as a guide for developing the desired business plan.

OUTLINE FOR A BUSINESS PLAN

CHARTER

A short statement of the business's purpose including services and products offered, types of clients, and where your business operates.

LONG-TERM OBJECTIVES AND STRATEGIES

Goals for the next three to five years in each functional business area. For example:

- Operations: financial planning process, compliance concerns, fee structure, services, broker-dealer relations.
- Finance: gross income, expenses, net income by product and by service.
- Marketing: direct mail, brochures, video, seminars, public relations, advertising used to reach business owners, professionals, executives, or retirees.
- Personnel: hiring, training policies, promotions.
- Facilities: location, space requirements, decor.
- Equipment: computers, telephone systems, typewriters, copiers.

    Each objective is followed by one or more strategy statements regarding the allocation of personnel, money, and time to achieve the goal.

INDUSTRY ANALYSIS

Statement of issues affecting the business but over which the planner has little or no

Source: John C. Sweet, "Successful Planning for your Business," *The Stanger Register,* March 1987, p. 20.

control. Observe trends in services and products, tax laws, regulatory requirements, and market conditions and interest rates.

MARKET ANALYSIS

Divide current clients in terms of geography, demographics (income, investable assets, net worth, and profession), and attitudes toward investing.

COMPETITIVE ANALYSIS

Competitors' strengths and weaknesses and unfilled market niches.

STRENGTHS AND WEAKNESSES

Four to six strengths and weaknesses of the planner and the business.

CRITICAL ISSUES

Potential problems that may hinder completion of long-term objectives or near term progress.

ONE-YEAR ACTION PLAN

Specific projects and activities required in the next year, including allocation of time and personnel. Each strategic statement will have one or more projects during the next year.

ICFP Code of Ethics and Standards of Practice

INTRODUCTION

Ethical conduct is the hallmark of any profession. The International Board of Standards and Practices for Certified Financial Planners, Inc. ("IBCFP") Code of Ethics (the "Code") recognizes the responsibility of the Certified Financial Planner™ ("CFP") to the public, clients and colleagues. The professional conduct of the CFP has a direct effect upon the reputation of the profession as a whole.

The Code establishes minimum levels of acceptable professional conduct. The IBCFP Standards of Practice (the "Standards") supplement the Code. The Standards, as periodically amended, provide guidance in interpreting the Code.

The Institute of Certified Financial Planners (ICFP) and the International Board of Standards and Practices for Certified Financial Planners (IBCFP) share the same code of ethics.

CFP and Certified Financial Planners are certification marks of the International Board of Standards and Practices for Certified Financial Planners, Inc. (IBCFP).

Adherence to the Code and Standards is mandatory for all Certified Financial Planners. Their provisions will be strictly enforced by the IBCFP. The following sets forth the provisions of the Code and the Standards.

I. INTEGRITY

A. CODE: A CERTIFIED FINANCIAL PLANNER SHALL OFFER AND PERFORM SERVICES IN THE FIELD OF FINANCIAL PLANNING IN AN HONEST AND FORTHRIGHT MANNER. A CERTIFIED FINANCIAL PLANNER SHALL DISCLOSE TO THE CLIENT ALL INFORMATION MATERIAL TO THEIR PROFESSIONAL RELATIONSHIP, INCLUDING, WITHOUT LIMITATION, ALL ACTUAL OR POTENTIAL CONFLICTS OF INTEREST. A CERTIFIED FINANCIAL PLANNER SHALL CONDUCT ALL ACTIVITIES IN A LAWFUL MANNER CONSISTENT WITH THE HIGHEST STANDARDS OF HONESTY, INTEGRITY AND ETHICS.

B. STANDARDS

1. **Guidelines for Professional Conduct.** In all professional activities a CFP shall perform services in accordance with:

   a. Applicable laws and the rules and regulations of governmental agencies.

   b. Generally accepted standards of practice in the field of financial planning.

   c. Applicable rules, regulations or other established policies of the IBCFP.

2. **Acceptance of Clients.** A client relationship should be established only on the basis of disclosure by both parties of material information relevant to the client's financial affairs.

   A CFP shall take reasonable and appropriate initiatives to obtain from clients, and disclose to clients, all material facts relating to the client relationship.

3. **Disclosure by CFP.** Disclosures to clients by and about the CFP should be governed by the nature of the relationship, the scope of the proposed engagement and such other factors as will reasonably respond to the need of a prospective client to become fully informed about the CFP, and the CFP's organization or firm. In all instances, the disclosures shall be made in advance of acceptance of the client. The IBCFP encourages use of a written disclosure format or brochure in advance of the engagement of CFP by a client which includes:

   a. A statement of the basic philosophy of the CFP (or firm) in working with clients. The disclosure should include the philosophy, theory or principles of financial planning which will be utilized by the CFP.

   b. Resumes of principals and employees of a firm who are expected to provide financial planning services to the client and description of those services. Such disclosures should include: (1) educational background; (2) professional/employment history; and (3) areas of competence and specialization.

   c. A statement of fees and commissions which in reasonable detail discloses any contingencies or other aspects material to the fee or commission arrangement. Any estimates made should be clearly identified as such, and should be based on reasonable assumptions. Referral fees or arrangements, if any, should be fully disclosed.

    d. A statement indicating whether the CFP's compensation arrangements involve (1) fee only; (2) fee and commission; or (3) commission only. A CFP shall not be held out as a fee only financial planner if the CFP receives commission or other forms of economic benefit from affiliated companies.

    e. Material agency or employment relationships a CFP (or firm) has with third parties including fees or commissions resulting from any such arrangement with the CFP's employer; and

    f. An explanation of all material actual or potential conflicts of interest. Prior to establishing a client relationship, a CFP should disclose all firm and individual relations which might affect the client relationship. Should a conflict of interest develop subsequent to establishing a client relationship, prompt disclosure of the conflict of interests should be made to the client.

4. **Disclosure by Client.** A CFP should only enter into a client relationship after securing sufficient information to satisfy the CFP that (i) the relationship is warranted by the individual's needs and objectives, and (ii) the CFP has no personal reservations concerning the provision of services to the individual.

5. **Advertising**

    a. **Misleading Advertising.** Use of a CFP's name in connection with false or misleading advertising is prohibited. In particular, it is improper to misrepresent the size, scope or areas of competence of a firm.

    b. **Yellow Pages-Type Advertising.** A CFP may be listed in Yellow Pages-type advertising under the heading Financial Planner. The marks CFP or Certified Financial Planner may be used after a CFP's name, but not in connection with a firm name, since firms are not licensed to use the mark. In Yellow Pages-type advertising under the category "Financial Planner" or similar listings, a firm must not advertise in such a way as to imply that the firm itself is authorized to use the marks CFP or Certified Financial Planner. The heading "Financial Planner-Certified" in Yellow Pages-type advertising is considered an improper use of the mark Certified Financial Planner.

    c. **Promotional Activities.** In promotional activities of any kind a CFP should take special care to avoid deception of the public in matters relating to financial planning or the professional activities and competence of the CFP. Personal opinions should be clearly identified as such, and under no circumstances should a CFP give the impression that a CFP is representing the views of the IBCFP or any other group unless the CFP has been authorized to do so. The term "promotional activities" as used herein includes speeches, interviews, books and/or printed publications, seminars, radio and television shows and video cassette performances.

    d. **Newsletters and Publications Prepared by Others.** A CFP (or a firm with which a CFP is affiliated) may publish a newsletter, tax booklet or similar publication provided the author or publisher is clearly identified if it is someone other than the CFP (or a firm with which a CFP is affiliated).

    e. **Product Endorsements.** In making public statements concerning specific products or services, a CFP should not indicate that the IBCFP endoreses or approves such products or services. A CFP should disclose any possible conflict of interest in relation to personal endorsements.

II. OBJECTIVITY

A. CODE: A CERTIFIED FINANCIAL PLANNER SHALL EXERCISE REASONABLE AND PRUDENT PROFESSIONAL JUDGMENT AND SHALL OTHERWISE ACT IN THE BEST INTERESTS OF THE CLIENT.

B. STANDARDS

1. **Responsibilities to Clients.** A CFP should provide dedicated, competent and responsible service to all financial planning clients.

   a. **Dedication, Due Care and Suitable Advice.** A CFP should always provide services to the best of the CFP's ability and which are in the best interests of the client. Diligence and care should be maintained in all professional activity. Recommendations to a client should be appropriate to the client's needs and circumstances, and the client's instructions in all matters should be followed faithfully.

   b. **Credibility.** A CFP shall not deceive or mislead a client on any matter.

III. COMPETENCE

A. CODE: A CERTIFIED FINANCIAL PLANNER SHALL PERFORM FINANCIAL PLANNING SERVICES IN A COMPETENT, EFFICIENT AND ECONOMICAL MANNER. A CERTIFIED FINANCIAL PLANNER SHALL KEEP ABREAST OF DEVELOPMENTS IN THE FIELD AND STRIVE TO IMPROVE PROFESSIONAL COMPETENCE IN ALL AREAS OF FINANCIAL PLANNING IN WHICH THE CERTIFIED FINANCIAL PLANNER IS ENGAGED. A CERTIFIED FINANCIAL PLANNER SHALL OFFER ADVICE ONLY IN THOSE AREAS IN WHICH THE CERTIFIED FINANCIAL PLANNER HAS COMPETENCE.

B. STANDARDS

1. **Competence and Knowledge.** A CFP should strive constantly to maintain and enhance professional competence. In areas of untested or uncertain ability, a CFP should seek the counsel of qualified individuals and/or refer clients to such parties.

2. **Continuing Education.** A CFP should keep abreast of new developments in the philosophy, technique and application of the principles of financial planning. To this end, a CFP should employ both traditional and non-traditional methods of continuing education throughout the CFP's financial planning career and shall satisfy all minimum continuing education requirements established for CFPs by the IBCFP.

3. **Legal and Accounting Advice.** A CFP should not give the impression that the CFP provides legal or accounting advice unless the CFP is qualified to practice in those fields and is licensed as required by state law.

4. **Reasonable Fees and/or Commissions.** A CFP's fees and/or commissions must be limited to amounts which are fair and reasonable. Actual or potential compensation from agency relationships should be disclosed, in advance, to clients. Compensation or potential economic benefit in the nature of prizes, trips and other gratuities accruing to a CFP and relating to a transaction recommended to a client by a CFP should be disclosed to the client at or prior to the time of the transactions. When a CFP is reimbursed for reasonable and actual travel expenses associated with a due diligence

trip to a vendor's area of business activity, such reimbursement will not be considered compensation for purposes of this Standard.

5. **Reasonable Diligence.** A CFP should be satisfied that a reasonable investigation has been made regarding the financial products recommended to clients. Such an investigation may be made by the CFP or by others provided the CFP acts reasonably in relying upon such investigation in accordance with customary and accepted practices among financial planners.

6. **Objectivity and Independence.** A CFP should strive to develop judgments and recommendations on an objective and independent basis without consideration of personal gain. A CFP should avoid relationships which compromise the CFP's objectivity or independence.

IV. **FAIRNESS**

A. CODE: ALL TRANSACTIONS BETWEEN THE CERTIFIED FINANCIAL PLANNER AND THE CLIENT SHALL BE FAIR AND REASONABLE TO THE CLIENT. A CERTIFIED FINANCIAL PLANNER SHALL PERFORM SERVICES IN A LAWFUL AND ETHICAL MANNER IN THE CLIENT'S BEST INTERESTS. A CERTIFIED FINANCIAL PLANNER WHO HOLDS A CLIENT'S PROPERTY, SHALL DO SO WITH THE CARE REQUIRED OF A FIDUCIARY.

B. STANDARDS

1. Fairness in Client Relationships.

   a. **Presentation of Credentials.** Prior to establishing client relationship, a CFP may provide references to a prospective client which may include recommendations from present and former clients. Client presentation should be made in the light of the client's level of experience, education and financial expertise.

   b. **Client Engagement Letter.** In many instances a CFP should provide to the client a written engagement letter which describes the terms and conditions of the financial planning arrangement which should be signed by both the client and the CFP. In most instances, such an agreement should include the material terms of all fee arrangements and an estimate of fees to be charged for the financial planning services to be provided by the CFP.

   c. **Follow Up.** After a financial plan or individual recommendation has been presented to the client, if the scope of the engagement requires the CFP to do so, the CFP should:

      (i) Monitor the implementation of the plan and/or recommendation on an ongoing basis;

      (ii) Keep the client apprised of any developments which might warrant review of the actions taken and planned; and

      (iii) Report on the overall status of the implementation of the plan/recommendation on a regular basis.

      If a CFP is not engaged to carry out these supervisory functions, the CFP should make sure the client understands any limitations relating to the CFP's engagement.

   d. **Stewardship.** A CFP shall keep strict account of all funds and/or other property of a client over which the CFP has been given authority or custody. Commingling of client funds with a CFP's personal funds or the funds of a CFP's firm is prohibited. Commingling one or more clients' funds together is permitted, subject to compliance with applicable legal requirements and provided accurate records are maintained.

 e. **Disclosure of Changes.** A CFP should disclose to clients, on a timely basis, any material changes in the CFP's address, telephone number, credentials, qualifications, licenses, fees or commission structure, or affiliations.

 f. **Advance Disclosure.** A CFP should enter an employment or agency relationship on the basis of mutual disclosure. A CFP employed as a financial planner should withdraw from any relationship which may place client assets or finances at unreasonable and extraordinary risk.

2. **Fairness in Agency Relationships.**

 a. **Scope of Agency Relationships.** Before conducting business for a principal, a CFP should make sure that the scope of his/her authority as an agent is clearly defined and properly documented. A CFP serving as an agent should faithfully follow all legitimate instructions given by the principal. A CFP should advise clients of the existence of the agency relationship and the scope of the CFP's authority in that capacity.

 b. **General Responsibilities to Employers and Principals.** A CFP who is employed by a financial planning firm or an investment institution, or who serves as an agent for such an organization should adhere to the same standards of disclosure and of dedicated service as those governing a CFP's client relationships.

 c. **Accounting for Funds.** A CFP serving as agent should periodically account for all funds or other properties entrusted to the CFP's custody.

3. **Fairness in Employment Relationships.**

 a. **Dedication and Faithful Service to Employers.** A CFP who is an employee should perform professional services with dedication to the legitimate objectives of the employer and in accordance with the IBCFP Code of Ethics and Standards of Practice.

 b. **Loyalty to Employer.** A CFP should (i) advise the CFP's employer of outside affiliations which could compromise service to an employer, (ii) maintain the same standards of confidentiality to employers as to clients, and (iii) provide timely notice to the employer and clients in the event of resignation.

 c. **Employee Agent.** A CFP who deals with outside parties as an agent of an employer firm has the same obligations to such outside parties as are owed by an independent agent to a principal.

4. **Fairness in Partnership Relationships.**

 a. **Responsibilities to Partners or Other Co-Owners.** A CFP doing business as a member of a partnership, or otherwise as a co-owner of a firm, bears to the CFP's partners or co-owners a responsibility of the highest order.

 b. **Advance Disclosure.** A CFP should join a partnership only on the basis of full and mutual disclosure regarding credentials, competence, experience and finances of the individual partners and partnership.

     c. **Good Faith.** A CFP owes to the CFP's partners the highest duty of good faith and full disclosure in all business matters. This includes (but is not limited to) full disclosure of all relevant financial information concerning the firm and adherence, both while in partnership and thereafter, to legitimate expectations of confidentiality.

     d. **Transaction of Business.** In transacting partnership business, a CFP should exercise the same degree of care and skill as is used in services for clients, and should not exceed the authority granted the CFP in the partnership agreement.

     e. **Reasonable Record.** A CFP in partnership should keep and provide to the firm a reasonable record of all business transacted for the firm.

     f. **Full-Time Commitment.** Unless there is a clear agreement to the contrary, a CFP in partnership should make a full-time commitment of services exclusively for the benefit of the firm and its client.

     g. **Withdrawal from Partnership.** A CFP in partnership who elects to withdraw from the partnership should do so in compliance with the partnership agreement, and deal with the CFP's partnership interests in a fair and equitable manner.

5. **Disclosure of Suspected Wrongdoing.** A CFP who has reason to suspect illegal conduct within the CFP's organization should make timely disclosure of the available evidence to the CFP's immediate supervisor and/or partners. If the CFP is convinced that illegal conduct exists within the CFP's organization and that appropriate measures are not taken to remedy the situation, the CFP should, where appropriate, alert regulatory authorities.

V. CONFIDENTIALITY

A. CODE: WITHOUT THE PRIOR CONSENT OF THE CLIENT, A CERTIFIED FINANCIAL PLANNER SHALL NOT DISCLOSE ANY CONFIDENTIAL INFORMATION OBTAINED AS A RESULT OF THE CLIENT RELATIONSHIP NOR SHALL THE CERTIFIED FINANCIAL PLANNER USE ANY SUCH INFORMATION EITHER TO THE DETRIMENT OF THE CLIENT OR THE BENEFIT OF THE CERTIFIED FINANCIAL PLANNER, UNLESS SUCH DISCLOSURE OR USE IS NECESSARY (I) TO COMPLY WITH LEGAL REQUIREMENTS OR LEGAL PROCESS, (II) TO DEFEND THE CERTIFIED FINANCIAL PLANNER AGAINST CHARGES OF WRONGDOING OR (III) IN CONNECTION WITH A CIVIL DISPUTE BETWEEN THE CERTIFIED FINANCIAL PLANNER AND THE CLIENT.

B. STANDARDS

1. **Confidentiality.** A CFP shall not disclose the identity of the client or any confidential client information to third parties without obtaining the express consent of the client or in response to proper legal process or to the extent reasonably required to defend against charges of wrongdoing or in connection with a civil dispute.

2. **Use of Information.** A CFP shall not, without the client's consent, use confidential client information even though such use does not cause harm to the client. In particular, without the client's consent, a CFP shall not use confidential client information in any fashion which materially benefits the CFP or others.

VI. PROFESSIONALISM

A. CODE: A CERTIFIED FINANCIAL PLANNER'S CONDUCT IN ALL MATTERS SHALL REFLECT CREDIT UPON THE PROFESSION. A CERTIFIED FINANCIAL PLANNER SHALL USE THE MARKS "CFP" AND "CERTIFIED FINANCIAL PLANNER" IN COMPLIANCE WITH THE RULES AND REGULATIONS OF THE IBCFP, AS ESTABLISHED AND AMENDED FROM TIME TO TIME.

B. STANDARDS

1. **Responsibilities to Subordinates, Competitors, Other Professional Financial Planners and Practitioners in Related Fields.** A CFP has a special responsibility to subordinates, including promotion of ethical conduct. A CFP should show respect for other financial planning professionals, and related occupational groups, by engaging in fair and honorable competitive practices. Collegiality among Certified Financial Planners should not, however, impede enforcement of the Code and Standards. Professionalism extends beyond a CFP's personal professional conduct and includes the following:

   a. **Supervision.** A CFP should exercise careful and supportive supervision of immediate subordinates. A CFP should take responsibility for the conduct of subordinates, and refuse to accept or condone conduct in violation of the Code or Standards.

   b. **Respect for Competitors in Related Fields.** In the course of professional activity, a CFP should avoid misleading, derogatory or other inappropriate references to the quality of service available from other financial planners, or from practitioners in fields which relate to or overlap with financial planning.

   c. **Complaint of Adverse Testimony.** A CFP who has information, which is not required hereunder to be kept confidential, relating to a possible violation of the Code or Standards by another CFP should bring such information to the attention of the IBCFP Board of Ethics and Standards within a reasonable period of time after obtaining such information. A CFP called to testify in judicial proceedings before a governmental agency or before the IBCFP shall testify candidly and openly without regard to personal or professional bias.

   d. **Extra-Professional Conduct.** A CFP shall obey the law and act in a socially responsible manner outside the realm of the CFP's business or professional activity. A CFP should avoid conduct or associations which might discredit the CFP's professional standing in the community.

   e. If a CFP has information, which is not required hereunder to be kept confidential, of unprofessional conduct, illegal activity, or any other similar information relative to a CFP or other financial professionals, the CFP shall inform the appropriate regulatory and/or professional disciplinary body of such misconduct.

2. **Use of CFP Mark, Degrees and Other Professional Marks.**

   a. **Use of CFP Mark.** All applicable guidelines and regulations of the IBCFP regarding the use of the marks "CFP" and "Certified Financial Planner" shall be strictly followed.

b. **Use of Designations.** A CFP who has attained a CLU, CPA, JD or MBA degree or other designations, may list them after a CFP's name in order of personal preference in advertising, letter head stationery and business cards. The Investment Advisers Act of 1940 requires registration of investment advisers with the Securities and Exchange Commission. CFPs may disclose their status as registered investment advisers to clients. Under present standards of acceptable business conduct, it is proper to use Registered Investment Adviser if the CFP is registered individually; however, RIA or R.I.A. following a CFP's name in advertising, letterhead stationery and business cards may be misleading and is not permitted.

APPENDIX 2

International Association for Financial Planning Code of Professional Ethics*

The reliance of the public and the business community on sound financial planning and advice imposes on financial planning professionals an obligation to maintain high standards of technical competence, morality, and integrity. To this end, the following Code of Professional Ethics serves as the guiding document.

CANON 1

Members should endeavor as professionals to place the public interest above their own.

Rules Of Professional Conduct:

R1.1 A member has a duty to understand and abide by all Rules of Professional Conduct which are prescribed in the Code of Professional Ethics of the Association.

Source: Reprinted with permission of The International Association for Financial Planning.

R1.2 A member shall not directly or indirectly condone any act which the member is prohibited from performing by the Rules of this Code.

CANON 2

Members should seek continually to maintain and improve their professional knowledge, skills, and competence.
Rules Of Professional Conduct:

R2.1 A member shall keep informed on all matters that are essential to the maintenance of the member's professional competence in the area in which he/she specializes and/or claims expertise.

CANON 3

Members should obey all laws and regulations, and should avoid any conduct or activity which would cause unjust harm to others.
Rules Of Professional Conduct:

R3.1 A member will be subject to disciplinary action for the violation of any law or regulation, to the extent that such violation suggests the likelihood of professional misconduct.

R3.2 A member shall not allow the pursuit of financial gain or other personal benefit to interfere with the exercise of sound professional judgment and skills.

R3.3 In the conduct of business or professional activities, a member shall not engage in an act or omission of a dishonest, deceitful, or fraudulent nature.

CANON 4

Members should be diligent in the performance of the occupational duties.
Rules Of Professional Conduct:

R4.1 A member shall competently and consistently discharge the member's occupational duties to every employer, client,* purchaser or user of the member's services, so long as those duties are consistent with what is in the client's best interests.

---

* As used throughout this Code, the term "client" refers broadly to any individual, business firm, governmental body, educational institution or other entity that engages the professional advice or services of a member, as an independent profession and not as common law employee of the client.

CANON 5

Members should establish and maintain honorable relationships with other professionals, with those whom the members serve in a professional capacity, and with all those who rely upon the members' professional judgments and skills.

Rules Of Professional Conduct:

R5.1 A member has a duty to know and abide by the legal limitations imposed upon the scope of the member's professional activities.

R5.2 In rendering or proposing to render a professional service for another individual of an organization, a member shall not knowingly misrepresent or conceal any material limitation on the member's ability to provide the quantity or quality of service that will adequately meet the financial planning needs of the individual or organization in question.

R5.3 In marketing or attempting to market a product to another individual or an organization, a member shall not knowingly misrepresent or conceal any material limitations on the product's ability to meet the financial planning needs of the individual or organization in question.

R5.4 A member shall not disclose to another person any confidential information entrusted to or obtained by the member in the course of the member's business or professional activities, unless a disclosure of such information is required by law or is made to a person who necessarily must have the information in order to discharge legitimate occupational or professional duties.

R5.5 In the making of oral or written recommendations to clients, a member shall (a) distinguish clearly between fact and opinion, (b) base the recommendations on sound professional evaluations of the client's present and future needs, (c) place the needs and best interests of the client above the interests of the member or the member's employer or business associates, (d) support the recommendations with appropriate research and adequate documentation of facts, and (e) scrupulously avoid any statements which are likely to mislead the client regarding the projected future results of any recommendation.

R5.6 Before rendering any professional service, a member has a duty to disclose, to a prospective client, any actual or potential conflict of interest that is or should be known by the member and is likely to impair the member's objectivity as an advisor or provider of professional services to the prospective client in question.

R5.7 In the rendering of a professional service to a client, a member has the duty to maintain the type and degree of professional independence that (a) is required of practitioners in the member's occupation or (b) is otherwise in the public interest, given the specific nature of the service being rendered.

CANON 6

Members should assist in improving the public understanding of financial planning.
Rules Of Professional Conduct:

R6.1 A member shall support efforts to provide laypersons with objective information concerning their financial planning needs, as well as the resources which are available to meet their needs.

R6.2 A member shall not misrepresent the benefits, costs or limitations of any financial planning service or product, whether the product or service is offered by the member or by another individual or firm.

CANON 7

Members should use the fact of membership in a manner consistent with the Association's Rules of Professional Conduct.
Rules Of Professional Conduct:

R7.1 A member shall not misrepresent the criteria for admission to Association membership, which criteria are: (1) a professional interest in financial planning; and (2) a written commitment to abide by the Bylaws and the Code of Professional Ethics of the Association.

R7.2 A member shall not misstate his/her authority to represent the Association. Specifically, a member shall not write, speak, or act in such a way as to lead another to believe that the member is officially representing the Association, unless the member has been duly authorized to do so by the officers, directors or Bylaws of the national Association.

R7.3 A member shall not use the fact of membership in the Association for commercial purposes but may use the fact of membership for the following non-commercial purposes: in resumes, prospectuses, and in introductions if the speaker clearly states that the opinions and ideas presented are his/her own and not necessarily those of the IAFP.

R7.4 A member or prospective member applying for Association membership shall not misrepresent any credentials or affiliations with other organizations.

CANON 8

Members should assist in maintaining the integrity of the Code of Professional Ethics of the Association.

Rules Of Professional Conduct:

R8.1 A member shall not sponsor as a candidate for Association membership any person who is known by the member to engage in business or professional practices which violate the Rules of this Code.

R8.2 A member possessing unprivileged information concerning an alleged violation of the Code shall, upon request, reveal such information to the body or other authority empowered by the Association to investigate or act upon the alleged violation.

APPENDIX 3

Future Value
and Present
Value Tables*

_____

* *Source:* Adapted from Sid Mittra and Chris Gassen, *Investment Analysis and Portfolio Management,* Harcourt Brace Jovanovich, 1981, pp. 841–47.

TABLE A3-1 Future Value Fixed Sum Factor: FVFF

Period	1%	2%	3%	4%	5%	6%	7%	8%	9%	10%	12%	14%	15%	16%	18%	20%	24%	28%	32%	36%
1	1.0100	1.0200	1.0300	1.0400	1.0500	1.0600	1.0700	1.0800	1.0900	1.1000	1.1200	1.1400	1.1500	1.1600	1.1800	1.2000	1.2400	1.2800	1.3200	1.3600
2	1.0201	1.0404	1.0609	1.0816	1.1025	1.1236	1.1449	1.1664	1.1881	1.2100	1.2544	1.2996	1.3225	1.3456	1.3924	1.4400	1.5376	1.6384	1.7424	1.8496
3	1.0303	1.0612	1.0927	1.1249	1.1576	1.1910	1.2250	1.2597	1.2950	1.3310	1.4049	1.4815	1.5209	1.5609	1.6430	1.7280	1.9066	2.0972	2.3000	2.5155
4	1.0406	1.0824	1.1255	1.1699	1.2155	1.2625	1.3108	1.3605	1.4116	1.4641	1.5735	1.6890	1.7490	1.8106	1.9388	2.0736	2.3642	2.6844	3.0360	3.4210
5	1.0510	1.1041	1.1593	1.2167	1.2763	1.3382	1.4026	1.4693	1.5386	1.6105	1.7623	1.9254	2.0114	2.1003	2.2878	2.4883	2.9316	3.4360	4.0075	4.6526
6	1.0615	1.1262	1.1941	1.2653	1.3401	1.4185	1.5007	1.5869	1.6771	1.7716	1.9738	2.1950	2.3131	2.4364	2.6996	2.9860	3.6352	4.3980	5.2899	6.3275
7	1.0721	1.1487	1.2299	1.3159	1.4071	1.5036	1.6058	1.7138	1.8280	1.9487	2.2107	2.5023	2.6600	2.8262	3.1855	3.5832	4.5077	5.6295	6.9826	8.6054
8	1.0829	1.1717	1.2668	1.3686	1.4775	1.5938	1.7182	1.8509	1.9926	2.1436	2.4760	2.8526	3.0590	3.2784	3.7589	4.2998	5.5895	7.2058	9.2170	11.703
9	1.0937	1.1951	1.3048	1.4233	1.5513	1.6895	1.8385	1.9990	2.1719	2.3579	2.7731	3.2519	3.5179	3.8030	4.4355	5.1598	6.9310	9.2234	12.166	15.916
10	1.1046	1.2190	1.3439	1.4802	1.6289	1.7908	1.9672	2.1589	2.3674	2.5937	3.1058	3.7072	4.0456	4.4114	5.2338	6.1917	8.5944	11.805	16.059	21.646
11	1.1157	1.2434	1.3842	1.5395	1.7103	1.8983	2.1049	2.3316	2.5804	2.8531	3.4785	4.2262	4.6524	5.1173	6.1759	7.4301	10.657	15.111	21.198	29.439
12	1.1268	1.2682	1.4258	1.6010	1.7959	2.0122	2.2522	2.5182	2.8127	3.1384	3.8960	4.8179	5.3502	5.9360	7.2876	8.9161	13.214	19.342	27.982	40.037
13	1.1381	1.2936	1.4685	1.6651	1.8856	2.1329	2.4098	2.7196	3.0658	3.4523	4.3635	5.4924	6.1528	6.8858	8.5994	10.699	16.386	24.758	36.937	54.451
14	1.1495	1.3195	1.5126	1.7317	1.9799	2.2609	2.5785	2.9372	3.3417	3.7975	4.8871	6.2613	7.0757	7.9875	10.147	12.839	20.319	31.691	48.756	74.053
15	1.1610	1.3459	1.5580	1.8009	2.0789	2.3966	2.7590	3.1722	3.6425	4.1772	5.4736	7.1379	8.1371	9.2655	11.973	15.407	25.195	40.564	64.358	100.71
16	1.1726	1.3728	1.6047	1.8730	2.1829	2.5404	2.9522	3.4259	3.9703	4.5950	6.1304	8.1372	9.3576	10.748	14.129	18.488	31.242	51.923	84.953	136.96
17	1.1843	1.4002	1.6528	1.9479	2.2920	2.6928	3.1588	3.7000	4.3276	5.0545	6.8660	9.2765	10.761	12.467	16.672	22.186	38.740	66.461	112.13	186.27
18	1.1961	1.4282	1.7024	2.0258	2.4066	2.8543	3.3799	3.9960	4.7171	5.5599	7.6900	10.575	12.375	14.462	19.673	26.623	48.038	85.070	148.02	253.33
19	1.2081	1.4568	1.7535	2.1068	2.5270	3.0256	3.6165	4.3157	5.1417	6.1159	8.6128	12.055	14.231	16.776	23.214	31.948	59.567	108.89	195.39	344.53
20	1.2202	1.4859	1.8061	2.1911	2.6533	3.2071	3.8697	4.6610	5.6044	6.7275	9.6463	13.743	16.366	19.460	27.393	38.337	73.864	139.37	257.91	468.57
21	1.2324	1.5157	1.8603	2.2788	2.7860	3.3996	4.1406	5.0338	6.1088	7.4002	10.803	15.667	18.821	22.574	32.323	46.005	91.591	178.40	340.44	637.26
22	1.2447	1.5460	1.9161	2.3699	2.9253	3.6035	4.4304	5.4365	6.6586	8.1403	12.100	17.861	21.644	26.186	38.142	55.206	113.57	228.35	449.39	866.67
23	1.2572	1.5769	1.9736	2.4647	3.0715	3.8197	4.7405	5.8715	7.2579	8.9543	13.552	20.361	24.891	30.376	45.007	66.247	140.83	292.30	593.19	1178.6
24	1.2697	1.6084	2.0328	2.5633	3.2251	4.0489	5.0724	6.3412	7.9111	9.8497	15.178	23.212	28.625	35.236	53.108	79.496	174.63	374.14	783.02	1602.9
25	1.2824	1.6406	2.0938	2.6658	3.3864	4.2919	5.4274	6.8485	8.6231	10.834	17.000	26.461	32.918	40.874	62.668	95.396	216.54	478.90	1033.5	2180.0
26	1.2953	1.6734	2.1566	2.7725	3.5557	4.5494	5.8074	7.3964	9.3992	11.918	19.040	30.166	37.856	47.414	73.948	114.47	268.51	612.99	1364.3	2964.9
27	1.3082	1.7069	2.2213	2.8834	3.7335	4.8223	6.2139	7.9881	10.245	13.110	21.324	34.389	43.535	55.000	87.259	137.37	332.95	784.63	1800.9	4032.2
28	1.3213	1.7410	2.2879	2.9987	3.9201	5.1117	6.6488	8.6271	11.167	14.421	23.883	39.204	50.065	63.800	102.96	164.84	412.86	1004.3	2377.2	5483.8
29	1.3345	1.7758	2.3566	3.1187	4.1161	5.4184	7.1143	9.3173	12.172	15.863	26.749	44.693	57.575	74.008	121.50	197.81	511.95	1285.5	3137.9	7458.0
30	1.3478	1.8114	2.4273	3.2434	4.3219	5.7435	7.6123	10.062	13.267	17.449	29.959	50.950	66.211	85.849	143.37	237.37	634.81	1645.5	4142.0	10143.
40	1.4889	2.2080	3.2620	4.8010	7.0400	10.285	14.974	21.724	31.409	45.259	93.050	188.88	267.86	378.72	750.37	1469.7	5455.9	19426.	66520.	*
50	1.6446	2.6916	4.3839	7.1067	11.467	18.420	29.457	46.901	74.357	117.39	289.00	700.23	1083.6	1670.7	3927.3	9100.4	46890.	*	*	*
60	1.8167	3.2810	5.8916	10.519	18.679	32.987	57.946	101.25	176.03	304.48	897.59	2595.9	4383.9	7370.1	20555.	56347.	*	*	*	*

*FVIF > 99,999

TABLE A3-2 Present Value: Fixed Sum Factor: PVFF

Period	1%	2%	3%	4%	5%	6%	7%	8%	9%	10%	12%	14%	15%	16%	18%	20%	24%	28%	32%	36%
1	.9901	.9804	.9709	.9615	.9524	.9434	.9346	.9259	.9174	.9091	.8929	.8772	.8696	.8621	.8475	.8333	.8065	.7813	.7576	.7353
2	.9803	.9612	.9426	.9246	.9070	.8900	.8734	.8573	.8417	.8264	.7972	.7695	.7561	.7432	.7182	.6944	.6504	.6104	.5739	.5407
3	.9706	.9423	.9151	.8890	.8638	.8396	.8163	.7938	.7722	.7513	.7118	.6750	.6575	.6407	.6086	.5787	.5245	.4768	.4348	.3975
4	.9610	.9238	.8885	.8548	.8227	.7921	.7629	.7350	.7084	.6830	.6355	.5921	.5718	.5523	.5158	.4823	.4230	.3725	.3294	.2923
5	.9515	.9057	.8626	.8219	.7835	.7473	.7130	.6806	.6499	.6209	.5674	.5194	.4972	.4761	.4371	.4019	.3411	.2910	.2495	.2149
6	.9420	.8880	.8375	.7903	.7462	.7050	.6663	.6302	.5963	.5645	.5066	.4556	.4323	.4104	.3704	.3349	.2751	.2274	.1890	.1580
7	.9327	.8706	.8131	.7599	.7107	.6651	.6227	.5835	.5470	.5132	.4523	.3996	.3759	.3538	.3139	.2791	.2218	.1776	.1432	.1162
8	.9235	.8535	.7894	.7307	.6768	.6274	.5820	.5403	.5019	.4665	.4039	.3506	.3269	.3050	.2660	.2326	.1789	.1388	.1085	.0854
9	.9143	.8368	.7664	.7026	.6446	.5919	.5439	.5002	.4604	.4241	.3606	.3075	.2843	.2630	.2255	.1938	.1443	.1084	.0822	.0628
10	.9053	.8203	.7441	.6756	.6139	.5584	.5083	.4632	.4224	.3855	.3220	.2697	.2472	.2267	.1911	.1615	.1164	.0847	.0623	.0462
11	.8963	.8043	.7224	.6496	.5847	.5268	.4751	.4289	.3875	.3505	.2875	.2366	.2149	.1954	.1619	.1346	.0938	.0662	.0472	.0340
12	.8874	.7885	.7014	.6246	.5568	.4970	.4440	.3971	.3555	.3186	.2567	.2076	.1869	.1685	.1372	.1122	.0757	.0517	.0357	.0250
13	.8787	.7730	.6810	.6006	.5303	.4688	.4150	.3677	.3262	.2897	.2292	.1821	.1625	.1452	.1163	.0935	.0610	.0404	.0271	.0184
14	.8700	.7579	.6611	.5775	.5051	.4423	.3878	.3405	.2992	.2633	.2046	.1597	.1413	.1252	.0985	.0779	.0492	.0316	.0205	.0135
15	.8613	.7430	.6419	.5553	.4810	.4173	.3624	.3152	.2745	.2394	.1827	.1401	.1229	.1079	.0835	.0649	.0397	.0247	.0155	.0099
16	.8528	.7284	.6232	.5339	.4581	.3936	.3387	.2919	.2519	.2176	.1631	.1229	.1069	.0930	.0708	.0541	.0320	.0193	.0118	.0073
17	.8444	.7142	.6050	.5134	.4363	.3714	.3166	.2703	.2311	.1978	.1456	.1078	.0929	.0802	.0600	.0451	.0258	.0150	.0089	.0054
18	.8360	.7002	.5874	.4936	.4155	.3503	.2959	.2502	.2120	.1799	.1300	.0946	.0808	.0691	.0508	.0376	.0208	.0118	.0068	.0039
19	.8277	.6864	.5703	.4746	.3957	.3305	.2765	.2317	.1945	.1635	.1161	.0829	.0703	.0596	.0431	.0313	.0168	.0092	.0051	.0029
20	.8195	.6730	.5537	.4564	.3769	.3118	.2584	.2145	.1784	.1486	.1037	.0728	.0611	.0514	.0365	.0261	.0135	.0072	.0039	.0021
21	.8114	.6598	.5375	.4388	.3589	.2942	.2415	.1987	.1637	.1351	.0926	.0638	.0531	.0443	.0309	.0217	.0109	.0056	.0029	.0016
22	.8034	.6468	.5219	.4220	.3418	.2775	.2257	.1839	.1502	.1228	.0826	.0560	.0462	.0382	.0262	.0181	.0088	.0044	.0022	.0012
23	.7954	.6342	.5067	.4057	.3256	.2618	.2109	.1703	.1378	.1117	.0738	.0491	.0402	.0329	.0222	.0151	.0071	.0034	.0017	.0008
24	.7876	.6217	.4919	.3901	.3101	.2470	.1971	.1577	.1264	.1015	.0659	.0431	.0349	.0284	.0188	.0126	.0057	.0027	.0013	.0006
25	.7798	.6095	.4776	.3751	.2953	.2330	.1842	.1460	.1160	.0923	.0588	.0378	.0304	.0245	.0160	.0105	.0046	.0021	.0010	.0005
26	.7720	.5976	.4637	.3607	.2812	.2198	.1722	.1352	.1064	.0839	.0525	.0331	.0264	.0211	.0135	.0087	.0037	.0016	.0007	.0003
27	.7644	.5859	.4502	.3468	.2678	.2074	.1609	.1252	.0976	.0763	.0469	.0291	.0230	.0182	.0115	.0073	.0030	.0013	.0006	.0002
28	.7568	.5744	.4371	.3335	.2551	.1956	.1504	.1159	.0895	.0693	.0419	.0255	.0200	.0157	.0097	.0061	.0024	.0010	.0004	.0002
29	.7493	.5631	.4243	.3207	.2429	.1846	.1406	.1073	.0822	.0630	.0374	.0224	.0174	.0135	.0082	.0051	.0020	.0008	.0003	.0001
30	.7419	.5521	.4120	.3083	.2314	.1741	.1314	.0994	.0754	.0573	.0334	.0196	.0151	.0116	.0070	.0042	.0016	.0006	.0002	.0001
35	.7059	.5000	.3554	.2534	.1813	.1301	.0937	.0676	.0490	.0356	.0189	.0102	.0075	.0055	.0030	.0017	.0005	.0002	.0001	*
40	.6717	.4529	.3066	.2083	.1420	.0972	.0668	.0460	.0318	.0221	.0107	.0053	.0037	.0026	.0013	.0007	.0002	.0001	*	*
45	.6391	.4102	.2644	.1712	.1113	.0727	.0476	.0313	.0207	.0137	.0061	.0027	.0019	.0013	.0006	.0003	.0001	*	*	*
50	.6080	.3715	.2281	.1407	.0872	.0543	.0339	.0213	.0134	.0085	.0035	.0014	.0009	.0006	.0003	.0001	*	*	*	*
55	.5785	.3365	.1968	.1157	.0683	.0406	.0242	.0145	.0087	.0053	.0020	.0007	.0005	.0003	.0001	*	*	*	*	*

*The factor is zero to four decimal places.

TABLE A3-3 Future Value Annuity Factor: FVAF

Periods	1%	2%	3%	4%	5%	6%	7%	8%	9%	10%	12%	14%	15%	16%	18%	20%	24%	28%	32%	36%
1	1.0000	1.0000	1.0000	1.0000	1.0000	1.0000	1.0000	1.0000	1.0000	1.0000	1.0000	1.0000	1.0000	1.0000	1.0000	1.0000	1.0000	1.0000	1.0000	1.0000
2	2.0100	2.0200	2.0300	2.0400	2.0500	2.0600	2.0700	2.0800	2.0900	2.1000	2.1200	2.1400	2.1500	2.1600	2.1800	2.2000	2.2400	2.2800	2.3200	2.3600
3	3.0301	3.0604	3.0909	3.1216	3.1525	3.1836	3.2149	3.2464	3.2781	3.3100	3.3744	3.4396	3.4725	3.5056	3.5724	3.6400	3.7776	3.9184	4.0624	4.2096
4	4.0604	4.1216	4.1836	4.2465	4.3101	4.3746	4.4399	4.5061	4.5731	4.6410	4.7793	4.9211	4.9934	5.0665	5.2154	5.3680	5.6842	6.0156	6.3624	6.7251
5	5.1010	5.2040	5.3091	5.4163	5.5256	5.6371	5.7507	5.8666	5.9847	6.1051	6.3528	6.6101	6.7424	6.8771	7.1542	7.4416	8.0484	8.6999	9.3983	10.146
6	6.1520	6.3081	6.4684	6.6330	6.8019	6.9753	7.1533	7.3359	7.5233	7.7156	8.1152	8.5355	8.7537	8.9775	9.4420	9.9299	10.980	12.135	13.405	14.798
7	7.2135	7.4343	7.6625	7.8983	8.1420	8.3938	8.6540	8.9228	9.2004	9.4872	10.089	10.730	11.066	11.413	12.141	12.915	14.615	16.533	18.695	21.126
8	8.2857	8.5830	8.8923	9.2142	9.5491	9.8975	10.259	10.636	11.028	11.435	12.299	13.232	13.726	14.240	15.327	16.499	19.122	22.163	25.678	29.731
9	9.3685	9.7546	10.159	10.582	11.026	11.491	11.978	12.487	13.021	13.579	14.775	16.085	16.785	17.518	19.085	20.798	24.712	29.369	34.895	41.435
10	10.462	10.949	11.463	12.006	12.577	13.180	13.816	14.486	15.192	15.937	17.548	19.337	20.303	21.321	23.521	25.958	31.643	38.592	47.061	57.351
11	11.566	12.168	12.807	13.486	14.206	14.971	15.783	16.645	17.560	18.531	20.654	23.044	24.349	25.732	28.755	32.150	40.237	50.398	63.121	78.998
12	12.682	13.412	14.192	15.025	15.917	16.869	17.888	18.977	20.140	21.384	24.133	27.270	29.001	30.850	34.931	39.580	50.894	65.510	84.320	108.43
13	13.809	14.680	15.617	16.626	17.713	18.882	20.140	21.495	22.953	24.522	28.029	32.088	34.351	36.786	42.218	48.496	64.109	84.852	112.30	148.47
14	14.947	15.973	17.086	18.291	19.598	21.015	22.550	24.214	26.019	27.975	32.392	37.581	40.504	43.672	50.818	59.195	80.496	109.61	149.23	202.92
15	16.096	17.293	18.598	20.023	21.578	23.276	25.129	27.152	29.360	31.772	37.279	43.842	47.580	51.659	60.965	72.035	100.81	141.30	197.99	276.97
16	17.257	18.639	20.156	21.824	23.657	25.672	27.888	30.324	33.003	35.949	42.753	50.980	55.717	60.925	72.939	87.442	126.01	181.86	262.35	377.69
17	18.430	20.012	21.761	23.697	25.840	28.212	30.840	33.750	36.973	40.544	48.883	59.117	65.075	71.673	87.068	105.93	157.25	233.79	347.30	514.66
18	19.614	21.412	23.414	25.645	28.132	30.905	33.999	37.450	41.301	45.599	55.749	68.394	75.836	84.140	103.74	128.11	195.99	300.25	459.44	700.93
19	20.810	22.840	25.116	27.671	30.539	33.760	37.379	41.446	46.018	51.159	63.439	78.969	88.211	98.603	123.41	154.74	244.03	385.32	607.47	954.27
20	22.019	24.297	26.870	29.778	33.066	36.785	40.995	45.762	51.160	57.275	72.052	91.024	102.44	115.37	146.62	186.68	303.60	494.21	802.86	1298.8
21	23.239	25.783	28.676	31.969	35.719	39.992	44.865	50.422	56.764	64.002	81.698	104.76	118.81	134.84	174.02	225.02	377.46	633.59	1060.7	1767.3
22	24.471	27.299	30.536	34.248	38.505	43.392	49.005	55.456	62.873	71.402	92.502	120.43	137.63	157.41	206.34	271.03	469.05	811.99	1401.2	2404.6
23	25.716	28.845	32.452	36.617	41.430	46.995	53.436	60.893	69.531	79.543	104.60	138.29	159.27	183.60	244.48	326.23	582.62	1040.3	1850.6	3271.3
24	26.973	30.421	34.426	39.082	44.502	50.815	58.176	66.764	76.789	88.497	118.15	158.65	184.16	213.97	289.49	392.48	723.46	1332.6	2443.8	4449.9
25	28.243	32.030	36.459	41.645	47.727	54.864	63.249	73.105	84.700	98.347	133.33	181.87	212.79	249.21	342.60	471.98	898.09	1706.8	3226.8	6052.9
26	29.525	33.670	38.553	44.311	51.113	59.156	68.676	79.954	93.323	109.18	150.33	208.33	245.71	290.08	405.27	567.37	1114.6	2185.7	4260.4	8233.0
27	30.820	35.344	40.709	47.084	54.669	63.705	74.483	87.350	102.72	121.09	169.37	238.49	283.56	337.50	479.22	681.85	1383.1	2798.7	5624.7	11197.9
28	32.129	37.051	42.930	49.967	58.402	68.528	80.697	95.338	112.96	134.20	190.69	272.88	327.10	392.50	566.48	819.22	1716.0	3583.3	7425.6	15230.2
29	33.450	38.792	45.218	52.966	62.322	73.639	87.346	103.96	124.13	148.63	214.58	312.09	377.16	456.30	669.44	984.06	2128.9	4587.6	9802.9	20714.1
30	34.784	40.568	47.575	56.084	66.438	79.058	94.460	113.28	136.30	164.49	241.33	356.78	434.74	530.31	790.94	1181.8	2640.9	5873.2	12940.	28172.2
40	48.886	60.402	75.401	95.025	120.79	154.76	199.63	259.05	337.88	442.59	767.09	1342.0	1779.0	2360.7	4163.2	7343.8	22728.	69377.	*	*
50	64.463	84.579	112.79	152.66	209.34	290.33	406.52	573.76	815.08	1163.9	2400.0	4994.5	7217.7	10435.	21813.	45497.	*	*	*	*
60	81.669	114.05	163.05	237.99	353.58	533.12	813.52	1253.2	1944.7	3034.8	7471.6	18535.	29219.	46057.	*	*	*	*	*	*

TABLE A3-4 Present Value Annuity Factor: PVAF

Number of Payments	1%	2%	3%	4%	5%	6%	7%	8%	9%	10%	12%	14%	15%	16%	18%	20%	24%	28%	32%
1	0.9901	0.9804	0.9709	0.9615	0.9524	0.9434	0.9346	0.9259	0.9174	0.9091	0.8929	0.8772	0.8696	0.8621	0.8475	0.8333	0.8065	0.7813	0.7576
2	1.9704	1.9416	1.9135	1.8861	1.8594	1.8334	1.8080	1.7833	1.7591	1.7355	1.6901	1.6467	1.6257	1.6052	1.5656	1.5278	1.4568	1.3916	1.3315
3	2.9410	2.8839	2.8286	2.7751	2.7232	2.6730	2.6243	2.5771	2.5313	2.4869	2.4018	2.3216	2.2832	2.2459	2.1743	2.1065	1.9813	1.8684	1.7663
4	3.9020	3.8077	3.7171	3.6299	3.5460	3.4651	3.3872	3.3121	3.2397	3.1699	3.0373	2.9137	2.8550	2.7982	2.6901	2.5887	2.4043	2.2410	2.0957
5	4.8534	4.7135	4.5797	4.4518	4.3295	4.2124	4.1002	3.9927	3.8897	3.7908	3.6048	3.4331	3.3522	3.2743	3.1272	2.9906	2.7454	2.5320	2.3452
6	5.7955	5.6014	5.4172	5.2421	5.0757	4.9173	4.7665	4.6229	4.4859	4.3553	4.1114	3.8887	3.7845	3.6847	3.4976	3.3255	3.0205	2.7594	2.5342
7	6.7282	6.4720	6.2303	6.0021	5.7864	5.5824	5.3893	5.2064	5.0330	4.8684	4.5638	4.2883	4.1604	4.0386	3.8115	3.6046	3.2423	2.9370	2.6775
8	7.6517	7.3255	7.0197	6.7327	6.4632	6.2098	5.9713	5.7466	5.5348	5.3349	4.9676	4.6389	4.4873	4.3436	4.0776	3.8372	3.4212	3.0758	2.7860
9	8.5660	8.1622	7.7861	7.4353	7.1078	6.8017	6.5152	6.2469	5.9952	5.7590	5.3282	4.9464	4.7716	4.6065	4.3030	4.0310	3.5655	3.1842	2.8681
10	9.4713	8.9826	8.5302	8.1109	7.7217	7.3601	7.0236	6.7101	6.4177	6.1446	5.6502	5.2161	5.0188	4.8332	4.4941	4.1925	3.6819	3.2689	2.9304
11	10.3676	9.7868	9.2526	8.7605	8.3064	7.8869	7.4987	7.1390	6.8052	6.4951	5.9377	5.4527	5.2337	5.0286	4.6560	4.3271	3.7757	3.3351	2.9776
12	11.2551	10.5753	9.9540	9.3851	8.8633	8.3838	7.9427	7.5361	7.1607	6.8137	6.1944	5.6603	5.4206	5.1971	4.7932	4.4392	3.8514	3.3868	3.0133
13	12.1337	11.3484	10.6350	9.9856	9.3936	8.8527	8.3577	7.9038	7.4869	7.1034	6.4235	5.8424	5.5831	5.3423	4.9095	4.5327	3.9124	3.4272	3.0404
14	13.0037	12.1062	11.2961	10.5631	9.8986	9.2950	8.7455	8.2442	7.7862	7.3667	6.6282	6.0021	5.7245	5.4675	5.0081	4.6106	3.9616	3.4587	3.0609
15	13.8651	12.8493	11.9379	11.1184	10.3797	9.7122	9.1079	8.5595	8.0607	7.6061	6.8109	6.1422	5.8474	5.5755	5.0916	4.6755	4.0013	3.4834	3.0764
16	14.7179	13.5777	12.5611	11.6523	10.8378	10.1059	9.4466	8.8514	8.3126	7.8237	6.9740	6.2651	5.9542	5.6685	5.1624	4.7296	4.0333	3.5026	3.0882
17	15.5623	14.2919	13.1661	12.1657	11.2741	10.4773	9.7632	9.1216	8.5436	8.0216	7.1196	6.3729	6.0472	5.7487	5.2223	4.7746	4.0591	3.5177	3.0971
18	16.3983	14.9920	13.7535	12.6593	11.6896	10.8276	10.0591	9.3719	8.7556	8.2014	7.2497	6.4674	6.1280	5.8178	5.2732	4.8122	4.0799	3.5294	3.1039
19	17.2260	15.6785	14.3238	13.1339	12.0853	11.1581	10.3356	9.6036	8.9501	8.3649	7.3658	6.5504	6.1982	5.8775	5.3162	4.8435	4.0967	3.5386	3.1090
20	18.0456	16.3514	14.8775	13.5903	12.4622	11.4699	10.5940	9.8181	9.1285	8.5136	7.4694	6.6231	6.2593	5.9288	5.3527	4.8696	4.1103	3.5458	3.1129
21	18.8570	17.0112	15.4150	14.0292	12.8212	11.7641	10.8355	10.0168	9.2922	8.6487	7.5620	6.6870	6.3125	5.9731	5.3837	4.8913	4.1212	3.5514	3.1158
22	19.6604	17.6580	15.9369	14.4511	13.1630	12.0416	11.0612	10.2007	9.4424	8.7715	7.6446	6.7429	6.3587	6.0113	5.4099	4.9094	4.1300	3.5558	3.1180
23	20.4558	18.2922	16.4436	14.8568	13.4886	12.3034	11.2722	10.3711	9.5802	8.8832	7.7184	6.7921	6.3988	6.0442	5.4321	4.9245	4.1371	3.5592	3.1197
24	21.2434	18.9139	16.9355	15.2470	13.7986	12.5504	11.4693	10.5288	9.7066	8.9847	7.7843	6.8351	6.4338	6.0726	5.4510	4.9371	4.1428	3.5619	3.1210
25	22.0232	19.5235	17.4131	15.6221	14.0939	12.7834	11.6536	10.6748	9.8226	9.0770	7.8431	6.8729	6.4642	6.0971	5.4669	4.9476	4.1474	3.5640	3.1220
26	22.7952	20.1210	17.8768	15.9828	14.3752	13.0032	11.8258	10.8100	9.9290	9.1609	7.8957	6.9061	6.4906	6.1182	5.4804	4.9563	4.1511	3.5656	3.1227
27	23.5596	20.7069	18.3270	16.3296	14.6430	13.2105	11.9867	10.9352	10.0266	9.2372	7.9426	6.9352	6.5135	6.1364	5.4919	4.9636	4.1542	3.5669	3.1233
28	24.3164	21.2813	18.7641	16.6631	14.8981	13.4062	12.1371	11.0511	10.1161	9.3066	7.9844	6.9607	6.5335	6.1520	5.5016	4.9697	4.1566	3.5679	3.1237
29	25.0658	21.8444	19.1885	16.9837	15.1411	13.5907	12.2777	11.1584	10.1983	9.3696	8.0218	6.9830	6.5509	6.1656	5.5098	4.9747	4.1585	3.5687	3.1240
30	25.8077	22.3965	19.6004	17.2920	15.3725	13.7648	12.4090	11.2578	10.2737	9.4269	8.0552	7.0027	6.5660	6.1772	5.5168	4.9789	4.1601	3.5693	3.1242
35	29.4086	24.9986	21.4872	18.6646	16.3742	14.4982	12.9477	11.6546	10.5668	9.6442	8.1755	7.0700	6.6166	6.2153	5.5386	4.9915	4.1644	3.5708	3.1248
40	32.8347	27.3555	23.1148	19.7928	17.1591	15.0463	13.3317	11.9246	10.7574	9.7791	8.2438	7.1050	6.6418	6.2335	5.5482	4.9966	4.1659	3.5712	3.1250
45	36.0945	29.4902	24.5187	20.7200	17.7741	15.4558	13.6055	12.1084	10.8812	9.8628	8.2825	7.1232	6.6543	6.2421	5.5523	4.9986	4.1664	3.5714	3.1250
50	39.1961	31.4236	25.7298	21.4822	18.2559	15.7619	13.8007	12.2335	10.9617	9.9148	8.3045	7.1327	6.6605	6.2463	5.5541	4.9995	4.1666	3.5714	3.1250
55	42.1472	33.1748	26.7744	22.1086	18.6335	15.9905	13.9399	12.3186	11.0140	9.9471	8.3170	7.1376	6.6636	6.2482	5.5549	4.9998	4.1666	3.5714	3.1250

Index

S